# CONFERENCE PROCEEDINGS

## object technology, naturally

Conference on Object-Oriented Programming, Systems, Languages, and Applications

October 5-9, 1997 - 12th Annual Conference

**The Association for Computing Machinery, Inc.**
1515 Broadway
New York, NY 10036



...In proceedings of the OOPSLA '97, 1997 (Atlanta, GA, USA, October 5-9, 1997) ACM, New York, 1997 pp. 23-35.

**Ordering Information**

**Nonmembers**
Nonmember orders placed within the U.S. should be directed to:

Addison-Wesley Publishing Company
Order Department
Jacob Way
Reading, MA 01867
Tel: +1 800 447 2226

Addison-Wesley will pay postage and handling on orders accompanied by check. Credit card orders may be placed by mail or by calling the Addison-Wesley Order Department at the number above. Follow-up inquiries should be directed to the Customer Service Department at the same number. Please include the Addison-Wesley ISBN number with your order:

ISBN 0-201-32231-5

Nonmember orders from outside the U.S. should be addressed as noted below:

**Europe/Middle East**

Addison-Wesley Publishing Group
Concertgebouwplein 25
1071 LM Amsterdam
The Netherlands
Tel: +31 20 6717296
Fax: +31 20 6645334

**Germany/Austria/Switzerland**

Addison-Wesley Verlag Deutschland GmbH
Hildachstrasse 15d
Wachsbleiche 7-12
53111 Bonn
Germany
Tel: +49 228 98 515 0
Fax: +49 228 98 515 99

**UK/Ireland/Africa**

Addison Wesley Longman Ltd.
Edinburgh Gate
Harlow, Essex CM20 2JE
United Kingdom
Tel: +44 1279 623623
Fax: +44 1279 431059

**Asia**

Addison-Wesley Singapore Pte. Ltd.
No. 11 Cantonment Road
Singapore 089736
Tel: +65 223 8155
Fax: +65 223 7155

**Japan**

Addison-Wesley Publishers Japan Ltd.
Nichibo Building
1-2-2 Sarugakucho
Chiyoda-ku, Tokyo 101
Japan
Tel: +81 33 291 4581
Fax: +81 33 291 4592

**Australia**

Addison Wesley Longman Australia Pty. Ltd.
95 Coventry Street
South Melbourne, VIC 3205
Australia
Tel: +61 3 9697 0666
Fax: +61 3 9699 2041

**New Zealand**

Additon Wesley Longman
New Zealand Ltd.
46 Hillside Road
Glenfield
Auckland 10
New Zealand
Tel: +64 9 444 4069
Fax: +64 9 444 4957

**Latin America**

Addison-Wesley Iberoamericana S.A.
Boulevard de las Cataratas #3
Colonia Jardines del Pedregal
Delegacion Alvaro Obregon
01900 Mexico D. F.
Tel: +52 5 660 2695
Fax: +52 5 660 4930

**Canada**

Addison-Wesley Publishing (Canada) Ltd.
26 Prince Andrew Place
Don Mills, Ontario M3C 2T8
Canada
Tel: +416 447 5101
Fax: +416 443 0948

**ACM Members**
A limited number of copies are available at the ACM member discount. Send order with payment in US dollars to:

ACM Order Department
P.O. Box 12114
Church Street Station
New York, N.Y. 10257

**OR**

ACM European Service Center
108 Cowley Rd. Oxford
OX4/JF, UK
Tel: +44 1865 382338
Fax: +44 1865 381338
email:acm_europe@acm.org

Credit card orders from U.S.A. and Canada:
+1 800 342 6626

New York Metropolitan Area and outside of the U.S.:
+1 212 626 0500
Fax +1 212 944 1318
Email:orders@acm.org

Please include your ACM member number and the ACM Order number with your order.

ACM Order Number: 548971
ACM ISBN: 0-89791-908-4

# welcome

Welcome to OOPSLA '97! We are glad you are here. Over two-hundred people (mostly volunteers) have devoted their time, energy and ideas to organize this conference, with the objective of making OOPSLA '97 an outstanding experience for you.

OOPSLA is well-known as the premier conference for object technology. The technical program has much to offer you, whether you're an object technology expert, a novice, or somewhere in between. There's a large variety of sessions to choose from: highly interactive workshops, an outstanding offering of tutorials and invited speakers on a broad range of thought-provoking topics, panels intended to stir up controversy, technical papers capturing the latest in research advances and experiences, a first-rate product exhibition, demonstrations of new technologies, practitioners' reports of real-life experiences and lessons learned, posters displaying brand new ideas and summarizing workshop results, special programs for Ph.D. students (the Doctoral Symposium) and for academic and industrial educators (the Educators' Symposium), and our ever-popular DesignFest. We're also introducing sessions on technology directions, a reprise of our new mid-year workshops (Long Island, NY in June '97), and a meeting area designed to enable you to mingle and talk privately with speakers and other leaders in the object technology field. And of course, we have a full plate of social events for you. The networking opportunities are unparalleled!

There's something special for nearly everyone here. For example, educators may want to couple our new Educators' Tutorials with the Educators' Symposium. Designers and implementers will find many relevant workshops, tutorials and technical presentations, and won't want to miss the DesignFest, If you're introducing object technology into your organization, look for the practitioners' reports, experience papers, demonstrations and the exhibits. Don't miss the invited speakers and the panels! Welcome and enjoy the conference.

Mary Loomis
Conference Chair, OOPSLA '97

# program committee

**OOPSLA Steering Committee**

John Pugh
*The Object People*

Mehmet Aksit
*University of Twente*

Lougie Anderson
*Sequent Computer Systems*

Toby Bloom, 1997 Program Chair
*Engage Technologies, Inc.*

Craig Chambers
*University of Washington*

Alistair Cockburn
*Humans and Technology*

Derek Coleman
*King's College London*

Jim Coplien, 1996 Program Chair
*Bell Labs*

Ward Cunningham
*Cunningham & Cunningham, Inc.*

Mark Day
*Lotus*

Amer Diwan
*Stanford University*

Kathleen Fisher
*AT&T Research*

Yossi Gil
*Technion, Israel Institute of Technology*

Adele Goldberg
*Neometron, Inc.*

Rachid Guerranoui
*Swiss Federal Institute of Technology*

Laura Hill
*Robertson, Stephens & Co.*

Mamdouh Ibrahim
*Electronic Data Systems*

Gregor Kiczales
*Xerox PARC*

Gary Leavens
*Iowa State University*

Barbara Staudt Lerner
*University of Massachusetts, Amherst*

Boris Magnusson
*Land Institute of Technology*

Satoshi Matsuoka
*Tokyo Institute of Technology*

Ron Morrison
*University of St. Andrews*

Gail C. Murphy
*University of British Columbia*

Linda M. Northrop
*Software Engineering Institute*

Atsushi Ohori
*Kyoto University*

Mary Beth Rosson
*Virginia Tech*

Guy Steele
*Sun Microsystems Laboratories*

Jacob Stein
*Sybase*

Joe Sventek
*Hewlett Packard Laboratories*

Lizette Velazquez
*Lucent Technologies*

John Vlissides
*IBM*

# technical program

On behalf of the OOPSLA '97 Program committee, I would like to welcome you to OOPSLA '97. The technical program provides presentations and panels on a wide variety of topics. Those topics range from the latest technical advances and research in the field to perspectives from those putting object technology to use in real-world settings.

We have a number of invited talks this year, some focused specifically on object technology and others on technical areas of general interest. In response to the results of last year's survey, we have included a number talks on distributed applications and the web. We have four sessions devoted to "Practitioners' Reports" - first hand accounts of experiences using object technology. There are six panels at which you can hear experts in various aspects of object technology debate some controversial issues facing object technology practitioners and researchers. And we have eight sessions devoted to the technical papers selected by the program committee for presentation and for publication in the OOPSLA proceedings. There were 127 papers submitted this year, from which the program committee selected 22. These papers include experience papers, which provide insight into the successes and failures of object technology in practice, as well as research papers that describe the latest advances in the technology.

We have added a new item to this year's program: a Forum on New Research Directions. This forum should provide you with a perspective on what's coming next. We will be presenting some exciting new ideas, and following with a discussion about the direction to proceed. look for some exciting debate here!

As in previous years, we'll have a DesignFest going on through the early part of the week, culminating with a panel and report on the last day of the conference. The Educators' Symposium will also report back on Thursday afternoon, as will participants from the Mid-year Workshops .

I hope you find the OOPSLA '97 technical program as interesting and thought-provoking to attend as it has been for us to prepare! We welcome you to OOPSLA'97.

Toby Bloom
Program Chair, OOPSLA '97

# conference committee

**Conference Chair**
Mary Loomis
*Hewlett-Packard Laboratories*

**Program Chair**
Toby Bloom
*Engage Technologies, Inc.*

**Operations**
Sandi Coe
*Sequent Computer Systems*

**Treasurer**
Moira Mallison
*Cold Springs Harbor Laboratory*

**Computers/Audio Visual**
Rod Olafson
*Object Technology International, Inc.*

**Demonstrations**
Gus Lopez
*North WestNet*

**DesignFest**
Peter Kriens
*aQute*

**Doctoral Symposium**
John D. McGregor
*Clemson University*

**Educators' Symposium**
Mahesh Dodani
*IBM Object Technology University*

**Exhibits**
Jim Johnson
*Meetings & More, Inc.*

**Experience Reports**
Jay Almarode
*Gemstone Systems, Inc.*

**Meeting Planning**
Nancy Wilson
*NJW Meetings*

**Mid Year Workshops**
Bob Marcus
*American Management Systems*

**Panels**
Mary Beth Rosson
*Virginia Tech*

**Posters**
Jim Haungs
*TeamTools, Inc.*

**Proceedings**
Deb Ayers
*Zephyr Technologies, Inc.*

**Addendum to Proceedings**
Deb Ayers
*Zephyr Technologies, Inc.*

**Publicity/WWW**
Brent Hailpern
*IBM* T J. *Watson Research Center*

**Registration**
Carole Mann
*Registration Systems Lab*

**Student Volunteers**
Ken Bauer
*Object Technology International, Inc.*

**Tutorials**
Mamdouh Ibrahim
*Electronic Data Systems*

**Workshops**
Shall Arora
*IBM Object Technology Services*

**ACM Director, Office of SIG Services**
Donna Baglio
*Association for Computing Machinery*

**1998 Conference Chair**
Bjorn Freeman-Benson
*Object Technology International, Inc*

# papers and panels

## tuesday, 7 october 1997

# papers and panels

## wednesday, 8 october 1997

## thursday, 9 october 1997

**8:30 am** **General Session - Invited Speaker**

*Cryptopolitics*
Whitfield Diffie (Sun Microsystems)

**10:30 am** **Session 8: Compilers and Tools**



**Practitioner Reports: Architecture and Implementation**
Reports are published in the Addendum, after the conference

**Panel 6: Beyond the Hype: Do Patterns and Frameworks Reduce Discovery Costs?**



**1:30 pm** **Invited Speaker:**

*Securing the Networked Future: Can Objects Help?*
Edward W. Felten (Dept of Computer Science, Princeton University)

**Panel : Mid-Year Workshops Report**

**Moderator:** Bob Marcus (American Management Systems)
Conference Reports will appear in the Addendum

**1:30 pm** **Panel : Educators' Symposium Report**

**Moderator:** Mahesh Dodani (IBM Object Technology University)
Conference Reports will appear in the Addendum

**Panel : DesignFest Report**

**Moderator:** Peter Kriens (aQute)
Conference Reports will appear in the Addendum

# Maintaining the Consistency of Class Libraries During Their Evolution

Mira Mezini
Department of Electrical Engineering and Computer Science (FB 12)
University of Siegen, Hölderlin 3, D-57068 Siegen, Germany
E-mail: mira@informatik.uni-siegen.de

## Abstract

Two important problems of object-oriented reuse are the propagation of design and implementation specifics of the base software to the inheritors, and the protection of the inheritors against changes in the base software. In this paper, we argue that the simple inheritance rules of existing object-oriented languages are not sufficient for properly dealing with these problems. In the proposal presented in this paper, programmers are enabled to make metalevel declarations of the internal protocols and dependencies of their classes. Additionally, changes of the base module are automatically monitored to filter out information about the alterations that may invalidate already existing inheritors. Based on these informations, the subclassing semantics is adjusted such that the maintenance of the base module properties and the protection of the inheritor is ensured during their integration. In this way, language support is provided for keeping the behavior of reusable software consistent during its evolution.

## 1 Introduction

Class libraries are (re)used in a substantially different way than their procedural counterparts. Besides using the library functionality by means of message calling, clients can also add new functionality, or redefine parts of the base functionality by means of subclassing. More importantly, in the extended functionality, inheritor's redefinitions can be called from within the library instead of the library code they redefine. Although subclassing enables incremental programming [5], the simple inheritance rules of existing object-oriented languages are insufficient for providing reuse in a fully satisfactory manner. This is partly due to the fact that subclassing implies non-encapsulated reuse, resulting in two categories of problems accompanying the evolution of class libraries. The term evolution is used here to uniformly describe both the extension of the base module by the inheritor (which we call *vertical evolution*) and changing the base module after inheritor modules have been already developed (which we call *horizontal evolution*).

In order to redefine parts of the base module, the inheritor should have knowledge about the implementation of the base module: the redefinitions of the inheritor are based on assumptions made with respect to the calling structure of the base. If the base module is later changed by its designer, these assumptions may not hold anymore, and the inheritor's behavior could therefore get invalidated. Steyaert et al. [24] provide a comprehensive analysis of these problems, motivating the need for mechanisms to manage the changes a base module may undergo in order to be improved. The absence of such mechanisms has also been recognized by other authors [8] as a major obstacle to successful reuse. In the remainder of the paper, this category of problems will be referred to as *horizontal evolution issues*.

The problems of the second category, called *vertical evolution issues*, occur during the extension of the base module, and are due to the fact that in the extended module the base definitions may get substituted by the inheritor's redefinitions in a way that could not be anticipated by the base module designer. First, it is possible that the base module has certain design properties which must be propagated in order to avoid inconsistencies in the composition of base and inheritor modules [13, 20]. Second, the base module designer is impeded to supply efficient implementations. Since no assumptions can be made about the redefinition patterns of future applications, the implementation should remain generic. Otherwise inconsistencies may occur, if the properties on which the efficient implementation of the base module is based are not maintained by the inheritor. This trade-off between easy reuse and efficient implementations has been discussed by Kiczales and Lamping in [11].

The problems outlined above have recently attracted the attention of several authors [9, 11, 13, 14, 24]. However, the existing approaches deal only with one category of problems and ignore the other. The approach proposed in [11] is based on informal descriptions of complex protocols which should be considered by the inheritor. Other proposals [9, 23, 24] approach the problems by means of formal descriptions of the internal protocols of the base module, aimed at improving the documentation of class libraries and providing a better methodology for reuse. As argued by Minsky [20], because of their global nature, manual implementations of implicit protocols are not only hard to be realized by the inheritor, but also unreliable, unstable and difficult to verify and to change. Other proposals [13, 14] make use of type-systems, or tools built on top of design languages, in order to support the detection of some problematic cases of the first category.

The first contribution of this paper is the uniform treatment of both problem categories, based on the observation that the composition mechanisms currently used to integrate the base with the inheritor functionality are strongly responsible for the presence of the problems. The main point is that the substantial difference in (re)use between class and procedural libraries is not accompanied by a similar difference in the nature of the composition. The composition is *trivial* in the sense that it does not take into account any properties of the modules to be composed. The trivial composition works fine for procedural libraries, since none of the modules to be composed has insight into the internals of the other. However, this does not hold for class libraries, where the modules to be composed are strongly coupled. To deal with this situation, the composition semantics should be enhanced to make the integration process a function of the properties of the modules to be composed. Supporting this enhanced form of composition, which we call *smart composition*, is the main motivation of the work presented in this paper. Thus, in contrast to existing approaches, we intend to support managing problems in the evolution of class libraries at the language level.

The second contribution of the paper is the proposal of a smart composition model which is based on the *open implementation* principle of software engineering [12]. There are two main features of this model. First, the properties of the base module to be maintained by the inheritors are made explicit by enabling the designer to formulate them as expressions of a simple language. As the result of evaluating these declarations, the semantics of the composition is automatically customized at the inheritor site, such that the propagation of the base module properties is ensured during the composition with the inheritor. Second, information about the calling structure exposed to inheritors is automatically filtered out of the base module definitions. By monitoring changes in the recorded calling structure during future exchanges of the base module, possible invalidations of inheritors are detected. Based on this information the composition behavior is again automatically customized at the inheritor site, such that the protection of the inheritor during its composition with the exchanged base is ensured. Both the propagation of base module properties and the protection of the inheritor may lead to a transformation of the application code.

The design of the constructs involved in the composition allows the automatic customization of subclassing semantics in a flexible and modular way. Another important feature of the model is that the set of declarations it can deal with can be extended incrementally. Besides the support for managing problems in the evolution of class libraries at the class level, demonstrating the effectiveness of a metalevel approach to this support and the proposal of a proper design of the metalevel that enables the management in a modular, flexible and extensible way are two important points made by this paper. The feasibility of the proposed approach is demonstrated by presenting a prototype implementation as an extension of Smalltalk-80 [7].

The paper is organized as follows. Section 2 provides illustrative examples for the problems arising during the evolution of class libraries. In section 3, the open implementation approach to smart composition is presented. Section 4 discusses the issues associated with designing the metalevel. The implementation is described in section 5, and related work is discussed in section 6. Section 7 concludes the paper and outlines areas of future work.

## 2 Issues During the Evolution of Class Libraries

In this section, the issues that may arise during the evolution of a class library when the modules are composed trivially will be illustrated by a hypothetical software system that naively models daily activities in a bank. For example, consider the class Account which implements the behavior of account objects, as shown in Fig. 1. Account defines three attributes: amount for storing the amount of money available in the account, debitLimit for storing the amount of money the account is allowed to be overdrawn, and logObject for recording all deposit and withdrawal operations performed on this account. It defines methods for depositing and withdrawing money into/from the account, as well as for printing relevant information about the account.

```
Account
instance variables: amount debitLimit logObject
  credit: cr
    amount := amount + cr.
    logObject update: #credit value: cr
  debit: db
    (amount - db > self debitLimit)  ifTrue:[amount:=amount-db].
    logObject update: #debit value: db
  debitLimit
    ^debitLimit
  printInfo
    logObject printInfo.
    self printAmount
  printAmount
    amount printString
```

Figure 1: A base class

## 2.1 Vertical Evolution Issues

To illustrate vertical evolution problems, consider the hypothetical extension of Account by the class SpecialATMAccount in Fig 2. SpecialATMAccount specializes Account in two ways. First, it models accounts that can be operated on via an automatic teller machine (ATM). For this purpose, the implementation of debitLimit has been changed to calculate the overdrawing limit by taking into account an additional limit specific for transactions performed via an ATM. This limit is calculated by self ATMLimit, e.g. by simply returning the value of a global attribute shared by all ATM-accounts (class variable in Smalltalk-80). Additionally, SpecialATMAccount reimplements debit to check whether the account should be locked for any transactions from an ATM after a withdrawal has taken place. This happens if the amount of money remaining after the standing orders for the current day are paid would be less than the overdrawing limit. This check is performed by toBeLocked, and the account gets locked by calling getLocked.

Second, besides of being operated on via an ATM, checking accounts modeled by SpecialATMAccount also have an associated deposit account, referred to by depositAcc. If the amount of money that would remain after paying current standing orders (returned by self standOrder) is larger than a certain limit (stored in saveLimit), a small percent of the money to be deposited into the checking account (0.1 * cr) is moved to the corresponding deposit account. For this purpose, credit: is reimplemented to call the new method validate: before actually increasing amount. Additionally, printAmount is extended to print not only the amount of money in the checking account, but also the amount in the associated deposit account (by invoking depositAcc printAmount)[1].

```
SpecialATMAccount   subclass: Account
instance variables: saveLimit depositAcc
credit: cr
  (self validate: cr) ifFalse: [amount := amount+cr]
                     ifTrue: [depositAcc credit: (cr*0.1).         ?
                              amount := amount+(0.9*cr)]
debit: db
  super debit:db.
  self toBeLocked ifTrue: [self getLocked]                         ?
validate: cr
  (amount - self standOrder > saveLimit)
debitLimit
  ^(self ATMLimit min: debitLimit)                                 ?
toBeLocked
  ^((amount - self standOrder) < self debitLimit)                  ?
printAmount
  super printAmount.
  depositAcc printAmount
```

Figure 2: An inheritor class

A simple design property of Account is that each method that changes amount (debit and credit in this case) should require an update of logObject (the update:value: method call in debit and credit). This dependency between Account and the class of logObject is essential for the design and should be maintained by all extensions of the base module. The issue to be dealt with during the extension of Account with SpecialATMAccount is how to ensure that the reimplementations of debit and credit in SpecialATMAccount will send the update request to the corresponding logObject. This issue is illustrated by the question mark aside the implementation of debit and credit in SpecialATMAccount in Fig 2. Otherwise, the design property of the base module gets lost, when the methods for debit and credit in SpecialATMAccount substitute those in the base class Account. A class whose design has the property illustrated above will be referred to as having the *dependent* property in the remainder of this paper. In the example above, the inheritor does actually violate the dependent property of the base: credit in SpecialATMAccount overrides its counterpart in Account and does not invoke itself the update message on logObject.

While the above example has been kept simple, since it will be used for illustration throughout the paper, real application frameworks incorporate a diversity of more complex, general purpose, or application domain specific properties that should propagated to the inheritors. In [20], Minsky presents several examples of general purpose properties to be propagated to the inheritor, such as:

[1] Some methods in SpecialATMAccount such as ATMLimit, getLocked, and standOrder, are omitted in Fig. 2 for the sake of brevity.

(a) the declaration that certain methods, a whole class, or a set of classes, should not be overridden, henceforth called the *non-override* property,

(b) the declaration that certain methods are abstract in the base module and should be implemented by any inheritor class that gets instantiated, henceforth called *required* property,

(c) the declaration that certain classes build a *cluster*, which means that while classes belonging to the cluster are allowed to invoke any of each other methods, they provide a common interface to the rest of the system, i.e. classes outside the cluster can invoke only methods present in this interface.

(d) the declaration that a cluster of classes build a *kernel*, in the sense that their implementations should be independent of the rest of the system and have exclusive access to some lower-level functionality, etc.

Other interesting assertions refer to the layered structure of the design of particular classes in the base module and/or the base software as a whole. Stata and Guttag [23] propose to divide the calling structure of a class into *method groups*. Each method group encapsulates a subset of the attributes defined by the class. A method in one group cannot directly access attributes encapsulated by another group. By establishing internal abstraction barriers within a class definition, method groups facilitate modularity in the presence of subclassing [23], since individual groups can be reasoned about, implemented and specialized independently of each other. However, for this to work, the inheritors should respect the internal encapsulation boundaries of the base (henceforth referred to as the *partition* property) and are allowed to change them only according to well-defined rules. While Stata and Guttag propose the specialization interface partition at the specification level, it is interesting to state and enforce it at the language level.

In a similar vein, Minsky [20] investigates the benefits of establishing abstraction barriers of a reusable software as a whole. In this case, classes that constitute the software system are divided into layers and the message exchange between different layers should obey well-defined rules. Minsky argues that this kind of design, which he calls *layered design*, cannot be established in the base software unless it is enforced to the inheritors as well. Except for the general purpose properties outlined so far, particular application domains may have their own specific design properties. For example, Klarlund et al. [13] present several examples of properties that are specific for telecommunication applications.

After this survey of a set of design properties of base modules to be propagated to inheritors, let us now illustrate properties that should be propagated to the inheritor to enable more efficient implementations of the base module. For this purpose, let us consider *functional protocols*, as presented by Kiczales and Lamping [11, 14]. A message is said to follow a *functional protocol*, if its result does not depend on the internal state of the receiver, but only on the class of the object and on the parameters of the methods [14]. In this paper, we adopt a weaker definition of the term "functional" to also include messages that are "quasi-functional" in the sense that their result may depend on some values (possibly being part of the internal state of the object) which, however, remain (most of the time) constant after having been initialized.

To be more concrete, consider again the implementation of Account in Fig. 1. In this implementation, debit invokes debitLimit via the self-reference instead of directly accessing the attribute debitLimit. This implementation facilitates reuse; in order to implement a special debit behavior for ATM-accounts, only the lower-level method debitLimit needs to be reimplemented in SpecialATMAccount in Fig. 2. However, by being more "polymorphic" than an implementation that would directly access the debitLimit attribute, the implementation of debit in Fig. 1 is less efficient.

This additional overhead could be avoided: knowing that the value of debitLimit does not change after being initialized, the base module designer can exploit inline caching techniques to avoid the self call of debitLimit in debit. Even if in a more realistic situation the overdrawing limit may get changed from time to time (increasing it because the account owner's income gets higher or decreasing it in the opposite case), this does not happen very often, and therefore using inline caching is still worthwhile. In this case, the method(s) that change the value of debitLimit should be monitored such that the inlined result of debitLimit gets recalculated as soon as its value changes.

However, the base module designer cannot make use of the more efficient implementation as long as there is no guarantee that inheritors will maintain this property of debitLimit. Suppose that a certain inheritor redefines debitLimit or other methods that access the attribute debitLimit in a non-functional way, i.e. by making it dependent on a frequently changing internal state. Since the redefined debitLimit method is called from within the base code, it substitutes the original definition in the composition. Consequently, the caller (debit in Account) becomes inconsistent: it will use a stored result for a non-functional message! Even under the optimistic assumption that this will not happen, it would be desirable to ensure that the inheritor also exploits caching techniques instead of calling a quasi-functional method. In the implementation of ATM-accounts shown in Fig. 2, propagating the functional property of debitLimit would imply that ATMLimit also is (quasi-)functional. Provided that ATMLimit is actually functional, the next question is whether the implementation of toBeLocked also exploits inline caching for debitLimit.

The (quasi)functional property may be specified at the level of: (a) a single method, (b) a method group encapsulating an immutable subpart of a class structure, or (c) at the level of a whole class. In the remainder of this paper, the functional property will refer to the quasi functional flavor specified at the level of a single method as illustrated by the example above. The other flavors are treated in a similar way and are therefore not considered in this paper.

Recapitulating the discussion on the vertical evolution issues, the problem is that the base module entails a kind of implicit contract, including important design and implementation properties, as well as the calling structure. The inheritors that extend the library should "agree" to this contract, in the sense that they should maintain the properties contained in it. However, with a trivial composition the properties of the base module remain implicit, and hence there is no possibility for negotiation and agreement during the vertical evolution. In order to avoid conflicts, the designer of the base module has to give up efficiency improvements, and the inheritor must carefully analyze and manually maintain complex protocols.

## 2.2 Horizontal Evolution Issues

When an horizontal evolution takes place, the base module has already been extended, i.e. there are inheritors which have accepted its implicit contract in the sense that their implementation makes use of the knowledge about the calling structure of the base. Exchanging the base implementation by an improved one may change the method calling structure and violate the contract. The trivial composition does not provide any means for detecting such violations and possibly making the inheritor compatible with the updated contract. Horizontal evolution conflicts, as illustrated below, may happen. A detailed discussion of the issues related to base module exchange is provided in [24]. In the context of this work, these problems fall into the same category and can be solved in a similar way. Therefore, only two of them, the issues of *captured methods* and *inconsistent methods*, will be considered in the remainder of this paper.

A method that is implemented by an inheritor and which was not implemented in the original definition of the base module is said to get *accidentally captured* after a change of the base module, if it is implemented in the improved version of the base module and is also invoked by a method that did exist in the original implementation [24]. In contrast to method captures which may occur when method calls are added, a method may get *inconsistent* [11, 24] during the integration with previously existing inheritors, if some of the self-invocations within it are omitted during an exchange, as frequently done for efficiency reasons. To illustrate these two invalidations of the inheritor, consider the implementation of the base class Account and its extension SpecialATMAccount shown on the left side of Fig. 3.

Now, suppose that the base designer exchanges the implementation of Account with the one in Account', shown on the right side of Fig. 3. The exchanged base, Account', differs from the original implementation in two ways. First, the overdraw limit check which in the original implementation is inlined within debit:, is implemented as a separate method, called validate:, that gets invoked within debit:. Second, calling printAmount has been omitted, after having inlined its functionality within printInfo. Putting together Account' with the existing inheritor class SpecialATMAccount would cause two invalidations of the inheritor's code (this inconsistent situation is illustrated by the zig-zag line connecting the "non-compatible" classes Account' and SpecialATMAccount on the right side of Fig. 3).

First, due to the combination of super and self calls within the respective implementations of debit: in SpecialATMAccount and Account', validate: in SpecialATMAccount gets invoked within debit: in Account' (instead of the corresponding implementation of validate: in Account') in a way that was not anticipated by the inheritor. Thus, SpecialATMAccount's validate: gets accidentally captured, which results in an erroneous behavior. The second invalidation concerns printInfo whose behavior becomes inconsistent after the exchange. Based on the calling structure of the original definition of Account, the inheritor redefines only printAmount in SpecialATMAccount, in order to implement special printing functionality for ATM-accounts with an associated deposit account, being sure that this will result in the desired behavior of the more general method printInfo. However, in the exchanged version Account', printInfo does not invoke printAmount anymore, resulting in an erroneous behavior when sent to an instance of SpecialATMAccount.

The discussion in this section motivates the need for a *smart composition* in which the contract implied by the base module is made explicit. An explicit contract would allow to predict and avoid conflicting situations.

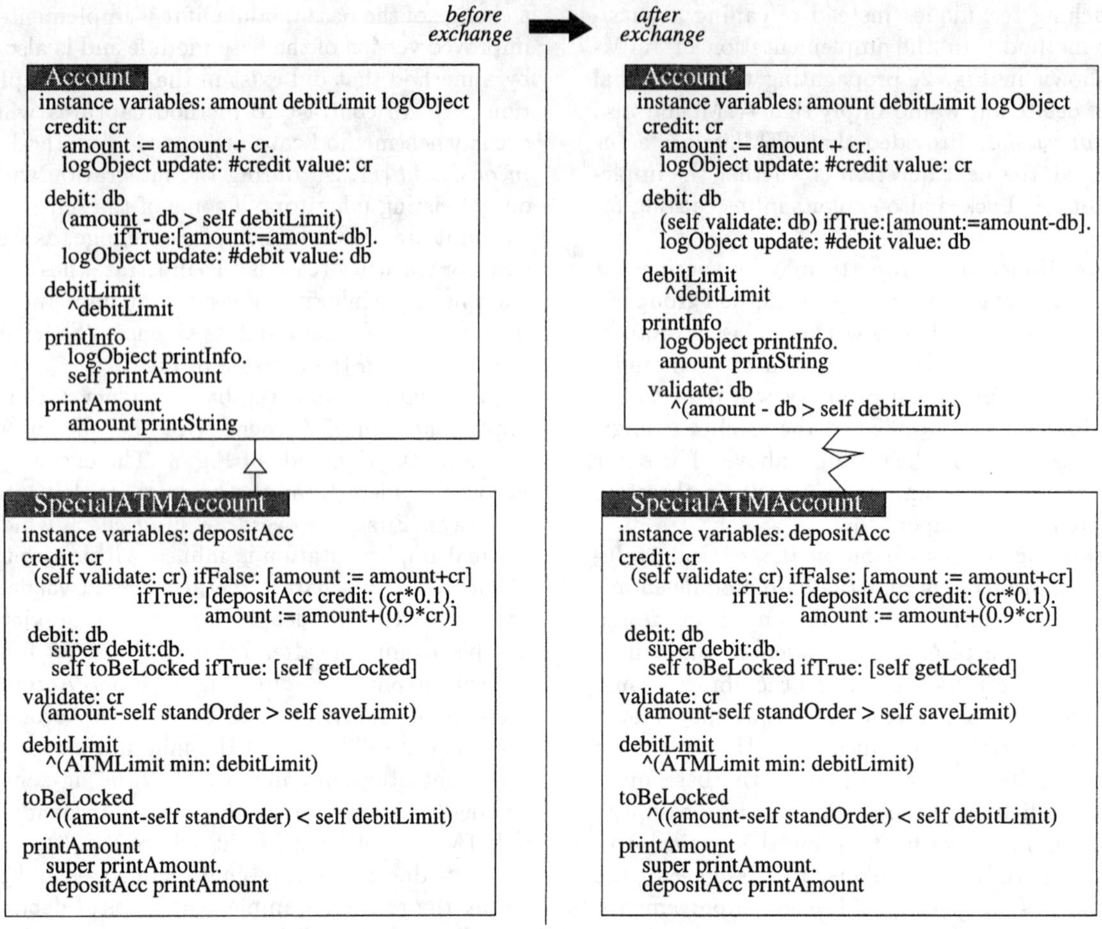


Figure 3: Horizontal evolution issues

## 3 A Smart Composition Model

The term *open implementation* [12] stands for a software engineering approach for constructing computational systems that can be customized to satisfy particular application requirements. All computational systems are about a domain, i.e. they provide a model of the domain. This model, also called *base-level functionality*, is made available by means of the base interface. Underneath the base level, there is a *metalevel* which implements the base level. Open implementations are computational systems that supply controlled access to their metalevel, which is "programmable" to a certain extent via an additional interface, called *meta-interface*, allowing metalevel declarations to flow into the system and influence its semantics.

An object-oriented language is used to define and reuse application-level functionality. It provides constructs such as classes and method definitions for defining application-level functionality, and subclassing for extending existing functionality. The metalevel consists of the internal model of these constructs. In an object-oriented language with a "closed" computational model properties of the application-level functionality cannot influence the metalevel. Subclassing works always the same way, independently of the particular application-level definitions to be composed at the base system. Since we do want the composition process to take into account properties of the application-level definitions, "opening" the implementation of the constructs involved in the composition seems to be a natural approach to the problems discussed in the previous section.

In our approach, application-level definitions are associated with explicit specifications of their properties which constitute the so-called *cooperation contract*. The contract's specifications penetrate into the metalevel as directives on how the composition should be performed, resulting in a "switch" to a customized implementation of the constructs involved in the composition process. Before performing the composition during an exten-

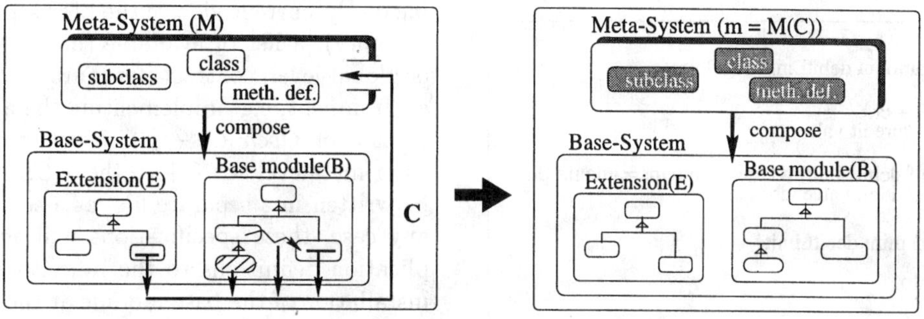


Figure 4: A class library with an open implementation for smart composition

sion, or after an exchange, the customized metalevel first starts an interaction process with the inheritor, also called *cooperation process*, which ensures that the inheritor's definition fulfills the assertions declared by the base module designer, or that it is protected against possible invalidations, respectively. In both cases this may lead to a transformation of the application code.

The intuitive idea behind our model is illustrated in Fig. 4, where the computational system before the customization is presented on the left side of the figure. The meta-system M is a generic template parameterized by a set of specifications C. The specifications constituting C are illustrated by special symbols annotating the graphical representation of the modules in the base-system. For a certain cooperation contract C, the generic meta-system template returns a particular meta-system instance (M(C)) adjusted to the content of C, as illustrated by changing the color of the metalevel components in the resulting system represented on the right side of Fig. 4.

## 3.1 Cooperation During an Extension

Specifications about properties of the base module to be propagated to inheritors are explicitly formulated by the base module designer in a mini-language, called *CCL* (*cooperation contract language*). CCL expressions are generally composed of a property name and a clause specifying the subpart of application definitions that has this property: CCL-expr = property def-clause, where def-clause = {appl-def-expr+}. A set of properties currently supported in CCL, along with a brief description of each is given in Fig. 5. As it will be discussed later, this set can be incrementally extended to support other general purpose properties or properties specific for particular application domains.

The simplest form of an appl-def-expr is a symbol being the name of a method/class in the application definition. In the general case, appl-def-expr may be an expression that given an application definition returns

| Property | States that: |
|---|---|
| functional | the implementation of the definition in def-clause follows a functional protocol |
| dependent | the implementation of the methods in def-clause should invoke certain messages |
| required | any concrete subclass should implement the methods in def-clause |
| partitition | methods in def-clause constitue a group with an associated encapsulated substate |
| non-override | the definitions in def-clause are not allowed to be overridden |
| abstract | classes in def-clause cannot be instantiated |

Figure 5: CCL-Properties

the elements of the definition that satisfy a certain condition. For instance, the expression writes(instVar) returns all methods of a class where instVar appears on the left side of an assignment. For illustration, the class Account and its contract are given in Fig. 6. The contract states that (a) the implementation of debitLimit is "quasi-functional", (b) any inheritor redefinition of those methods in Account that access amount in write modus (debit and credit in this case) should invoke update:value: on logObject as the last method in the flow of control (indicated by the arrow preceding the method call), and (c) there are two method groups: {debit, credit, printAmount} and {debitLimit}, encapsulating the amount and logObject, respectively the debitLimit instance variables[1], which implies that redefinitions from one group are not allowed to directly access the substate encapsulated by the other group and that changing the group structure may happen only in accordance to predefined rules.

There are two categories of properties. The first category includes properties that must be maintained by the inheritor. Examples for this category are the non-

[1]The affiliation of state to method groups is omitted in the contract for the sake of simplicity.

```
Account
instance variables: amount debitLimit logObject
credit: cr
   amount := amount + cr.
   logObject update: #credit value: cr
debit: db
   (amount - db > self debitLimit) ifTrue: [amount:=amount-db].
   logObject update: #debit value: db
debitLimit
   ^(self ATMLimit) min: debitLimit
printInfo
   logObject printInfo.
   self printAmount
printAmount
   amount printString

                                              Account contract
   functional {debitLimit}
   dependent {write(amount), -> logObject>>update:value:}
   partition {credit, debit, printAmount} {debitLimit}
```

Figure 6: Account with explicit contract

override, dependent, or required properties. The second category includes properties that are negotiable in the sense that they may be accepted or rejected by the inheritor. A representative for this category is the functional property. At the inheritor site, the base module becomes subpart of the inheritor's functionality. Hence, the inheritor should be responsible for deciding to continue, or break the contract concerning the quasi-functional methods if he/she decides to reimplement the method or the corresponding class in a way that makes inlining useless. The ability of being negotiable or not is an integral part of a property's definition.

Additionally, properties may be inheritable or not. There are properties which once satisfied by an inheritor's class do not need to be inherited to the subclasses of this class. For instance, consider the required property. Once an inheritor class, Cl, does actually implement the operations that are declared as required by the base class designer, the property should not be propagated further to subclasses of Cl. On the contrary, the non-override, or functional properties should be propagated further along the inheritance chain, even if they get satisfied by a certain inheritor class. Again, being inheritable or not is an integral part of a property's definition.

The exact mode of programmer's operation for specifying the contract depends on the concrete environment supporting smart composition. In the prototype implementation as an extension of Smalltalk-80, which will be discussed in Sect. 5, the definition of the contract happens in a similar way as the definition of the application – interactively via the graphical user interface. The user interface of the standard Smalltalk environment is modified such that the designer may choose an item of the cooperation contract from the browser menu. Depending on the current view of the browser (method, class, or category), a list of available (method-level, class-level, or global-level) contract items are displayed. In another environment, e.g. implementing the approach as an extension of *Open C++* [3], which provides an explicit class metalevel for C++, the *CCL* expressions would be written in a separate file, as a separate program. In any case, these specifications will accompany the application definitions to the inheritor site. During the installation of the base module at the inheritor site, the contract is first evaluated resulting in a switch to a customized implementation of the metalevel.

The influence of the cooperation contract on the metalevel semantics is reflected in the simplified formal specification given by the abstract data type in Fig. 7. In this specification, B denotes the base module, E the inheritor module[1]. According to the specification, there is a particular metalevel instance, called the *default metalevel* ($\mathsf{m}_{def}$), corresponding to the situation where no explicit contract has been specified ($\mathsf{m}_{def} = \mathsf{negotiate}(\epsilon)$). The default metalevel entails the trivial composition, specified by trivialCompose: smartly composing B and E when C is empty is equivalent to trivially composing them. With a customized metalevel ($\mathsf{m}_C = \mathsf{negotiate(C)}$), the result module M of extending the base B with the extension E by means of extend is gained by applying the trivial composition to an appropriate transformation of the modules rather than to the original modules.

The applied transformation $\mathcal{T}_{CPT}$ aims to preserve the consistency of E and B with regard to the contract C. The exact specification of $\mathcal{T}_{CPT}$ is missing in Fig. 7, since it requires a formal description of the semantics for each CCL-expression, which is beyond the scope of this paper. For this reason, an informal description is given instead. The $\mathcal{T}_{CPT}$ transformation happens as an interaction (negotiation) process between the metalevel and the inheritor. For each inheritor definition which is included in one of the clauses associated with a property in the contract, the following happens.

(1) The property is not negotiable. A check of the inheritor's definition is first performed. If the property is violated, the inheritor is notified about that and depending on the given property:

  (a) The redefinition is simply rejected. For instance, if the property is non-override, rejecting the inheritor's redefinition is the only meaningful action.

  (b) An automatic modification of the inheritor's code that would satisfy the property is per-

[1] The specification is merely aimed at expressing more concisely the behavior of the meta-system template and does not claim to be a strict formal specification.

**Meta**

**Operations:**

negotiate: Contract $\rightarrow$ Meta

trivialCompose: Module $\times$ Module $\rightarrow$ Module

smartCompose: Contract $\rightarrow$ [Module $\times$ Module $\rightarrow$ Module $\times$ Contract]

extend:, exchange Meta $\rightarrow$ [Module $\times$ Module $\rightarrow$ Module $\times$ Meta]

**Axioms:**

trivialCompose(B, E) = B $\boxed{\triangleright}$ E

The inheritance operator, $\boxed{\triangleright}$ is defined in [5] as an operator on classes. We use the same symbol to denote a generalized version, applying the inheritance operator to all pairs of classes related by a subclass relationship in two modules.

smartCompose(C, B, E) = (trivialCompose(B', E'), accepted(C)) where:

$$(B', E') = \begin{cases} (B,E) & C = \epsilon \\ \mathcal{T}_{CPT}(E,B,C) & \text{otherwise} \end{cases}$$

accepted(C) is the set of contract items being confirmed by the inheritor (accepted($\epsilon$) = $\epsilon$).

extend(negotiate(C), B, E) = (M, negotiate(C')), where:

(M, $C_a$) = smartCompose(C, B, E), and C' = $C_a$ ∪ Inheritable($C_a$) ∪ newC

exchange(negotiate(C), B', B $\boxed{\triangleright}$ E) = (M, negotiate(C)), where:

(M, -) = smartCompose(detectContract(B, B'), B', E)

Figure 7: The specification of a meta-system behavior

formed and the inheritor is requested to accept it. Consider, for example, the depend property. If the position where to put the dependent call in the control flow of the inheritor's definition being processed is exactly specified in the contract, as it is the case in Fig. 6, than the transformation can be performed automatically.

(c) If no automatic modification can be performed, or none is accepted by the inheritor, he/she should fix the problem him/herself. For instance, in the case of a dependent property, if the position where to put the dependent call in the control flow is not uniquely specified in the contract, generally no automatic modification of the code can be provided.

(2) The property is negotiable. The inheritor is notified about the property and is required to accept or reject it. Depending on the inheritor's response, the base, respectively inheritor code may be automatically transformed. Consider the functional property, and suppose that the inheritor accepts it. In this case, the process of inline caching wherever the method gets invoked, as well as monitoring of those values the method depends on is performed automatically. The transformations are however, visible to the inheritor. On the contrary, if the inheritor decides to reject the functional property, the base code is modified to normally invoke the previously inlined method.

As pointed out in the formal specification in Fig. 7, a non-trivial extension may result in a changed contract as well. First, in the case of a negotiable property, if the property is rejected, the contract is changed to remove the property. In Fig. 7, the contract returned by smartCompose, $C_a$, contains only the accepted properties. The new contract C' returned by the extend operation is gained from the accepted part of the original contract, $C_a$, by adding the specifications in $C_a$ that are inheritable (Inheritable($C_a$)), as well as new ones that might be declared by the inheritor (newC), or that might be automatically added by the system. A property is added automatically, when it is implied by the satisfaction of another property, as it will be illustrated below.

For illustration, let us consider the cooperation process during the extension of the Account class, defined in Fig. 6, with the implementation of ATM-accounts given in Fig. 2. This process is illustrated in Fig. 8. In order to satisfy the Account's contract, the inheritor's code is transformed as follows (the modified parts of the code are put within dark boxes on the right side of Fig. 8). First, the update:value: message call is added into the reimplementation of credit, since credit is one of the Account's methods that write in amount. In this case, an automatic modification can be performed, since the position where to add update:value: in the control flow of credit is defined in the contract. Concerning the parameters, the same setting as in the corresponding method in the base is chosen per default. Notice that update:value is not added into the reimplementation of debit although debit also belongs to the write(amount) set. This is because in contrast to credit, the reimplementation of debit does a super call, whereby the update:value: gets invoked.

The second transformation concerns toBeLocked. Its implementation now makes use of the cache instead of performing a message call. Note that the system keeps track of all information related to inline caching, such that it can be consistently undone, if necessary. Also, if inlining requires monitoring of other methods, this is done automatically. In the example above, for the sake of simplicity, the assumption is made that both debitLimit and ATMLimit remain constant after being initialized, and thus no monitoring is needed. Further details about automatic inlining and the monitoring related to it are beyond the scope of this paper. Both modifications in Fig. 8 are actually done only after the inheritor has accepted them, as illustrated by the arrow placed over the accept item of the menu displayed on the right side of Fig. 8.

The third item in the contract is satisfied by the definition of SpecialATMAccount in Fig. 8. The reimplementations of the methods that belong to different groups (debit, credit, and printAmount, respectively debitLimit) do not directly access attributes encapsulated by the other group. In Fig. 8, the inheritor class has its own contract after the extension. In this case, it inherits all items of the base module contract. If the inheritor had disagreed to keeping the functional property of debitLimit, the corresponding item would have been removed from the Account contract in Fig. 8. In addition to the inherited items, a property specifying that ATMLimit should also remain functional is automatically added into the contract of SpecialATMAccount. The fact that the inheritor accepts the functional property of debitLimit implies that ATMLimit should follow a functional protocol as well.

### 3.2 Cooperation During an Exchange

In contrast to the cooperation during an extension, which is based on the explicit specifications of the base module designer, the information needed for the cooperation process during an exchange is collected automatically by the metalevel. The first step in collecting this information consists of automatically recording the specialization interface of the base class before any extension takes place. The specialization interface provides important information to be used for detecting possible conflicts during a horizontal evolution. Steyaert et al. [24] define a set of operations for expressing the relationship between two specialization interfaces[1]. Based on an investigation of the interaction between these operations, possible horizontal conflicts can be detected.

In contrast to extending, the exchange process is usually not achieved by language constructs, but rather by file systems or version control mechanisms external to the language. However, for the purpose of this discussion, we assume that exchange is provided as a language construct, reflected by the operation exchange in the specification in Fig. 7. According to this specification, performing a non-trivial exchange is equivalent to performing a non-trivial extend of the modified base B' with the existing inheritor E, directed by a contract that results from comparing the original base, B with the exchanged base, B' by means of the auxiliary operation detectContract. This detects changes in the specialization interfaces that might invalidate the inheritor.

Two possible invalidations, *accidental method capture* and *inconsistent methods*, which were defined in Sec. 2.2, will be discussed in the following in the context of an example. Thus, the contract that is "automatically formulated" by detectContract would contain expressions like captured $\{$appl-def-expr$^+\}$, or inconsistent $\{$appl-def-expr$^+\}$. This conceptual description suggests that the metalevel "writes" a CCL-program. In fact, what happens is that the detection of risky changes in the specialization interface directly triggers a change of the metalevel semantics, which will start an interaction process with the inheritor during its composition with the exchanged base. For each inheritor's definition that is noted as risky, the cooperation process happens as follows.

(a) First, the metalevel makes sure that the definition is actually invalidated, since not every detected risky definition is indeed an invalidation.

(b) If this is the case, the inheritor is informed about the invalidation and is requested to accept or reject automatic protective transformations, if any available, or to fix the problem him/herself if no automatic solution can be proposed, or none of the existing ones is accepted by the inheritor.

For illustration, consider the exchange of Account from Fig. 8 with Account' put on top of it in Fig. 9. As described in Sec. 2.2, Account' implements a new method validate: which is called from within the changed implementation of debit:. Since debit: is a method that

[1] In fact, Steyaert et al. operate on what they call a *reuse contract* which is an explicit description of the subpart of a class specialization interface relevant for the design.

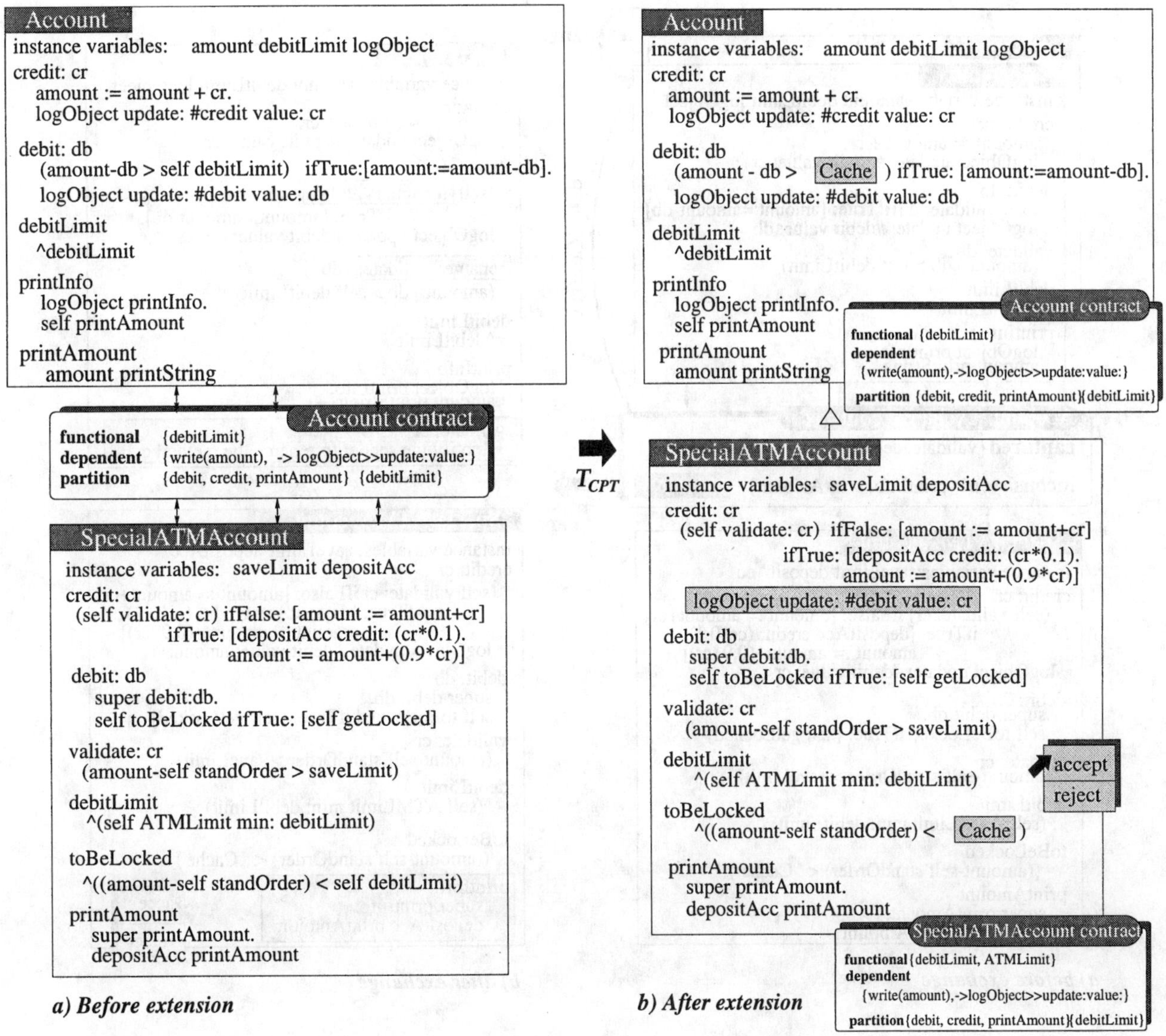


Figure 8: Cooperation process during extension

did exist in the original version of Account, this definition is detected as risky to cause an accidental capture, by the detectContract operation. Checking the implementation of SpecialATMAccount shows that the introduction of validate: in Account' causes indeed a method capture that invalidates the inheritor's definition. Due to the super call within debit: in SpecialATMAccount, the implementation of the method validate: in SpecialATMAccount will get accidentally invoked by debit: in Account', resulting in an erroneous behavior. However, if the reimplementation of debit: in SpecialATMAccount did not invoke the super-method, the definition noted as risky would cause no accidental method capture.

Besides the introduction of validate:, also the implementation of printInfo is changed in Account'. The new implementation is coarser than the previous one, since a method call has been removed. Coarsening the implementation of a class may cause a method to get inconsistent on the integration with existing inheritors [11, 24]. By checking the implementation of SpecialATMAccount during the non-trivial composition with the exchanged base, the metalevel detects that printInfo gets indeed inconsistent: for SpecialATMAccount instances it will not behave the same as before the exchange.

As illustrated by the contract in Fig. 9, the inheritor is informed about both invalidations, and automatic transformations to avoid the inconsistencies are

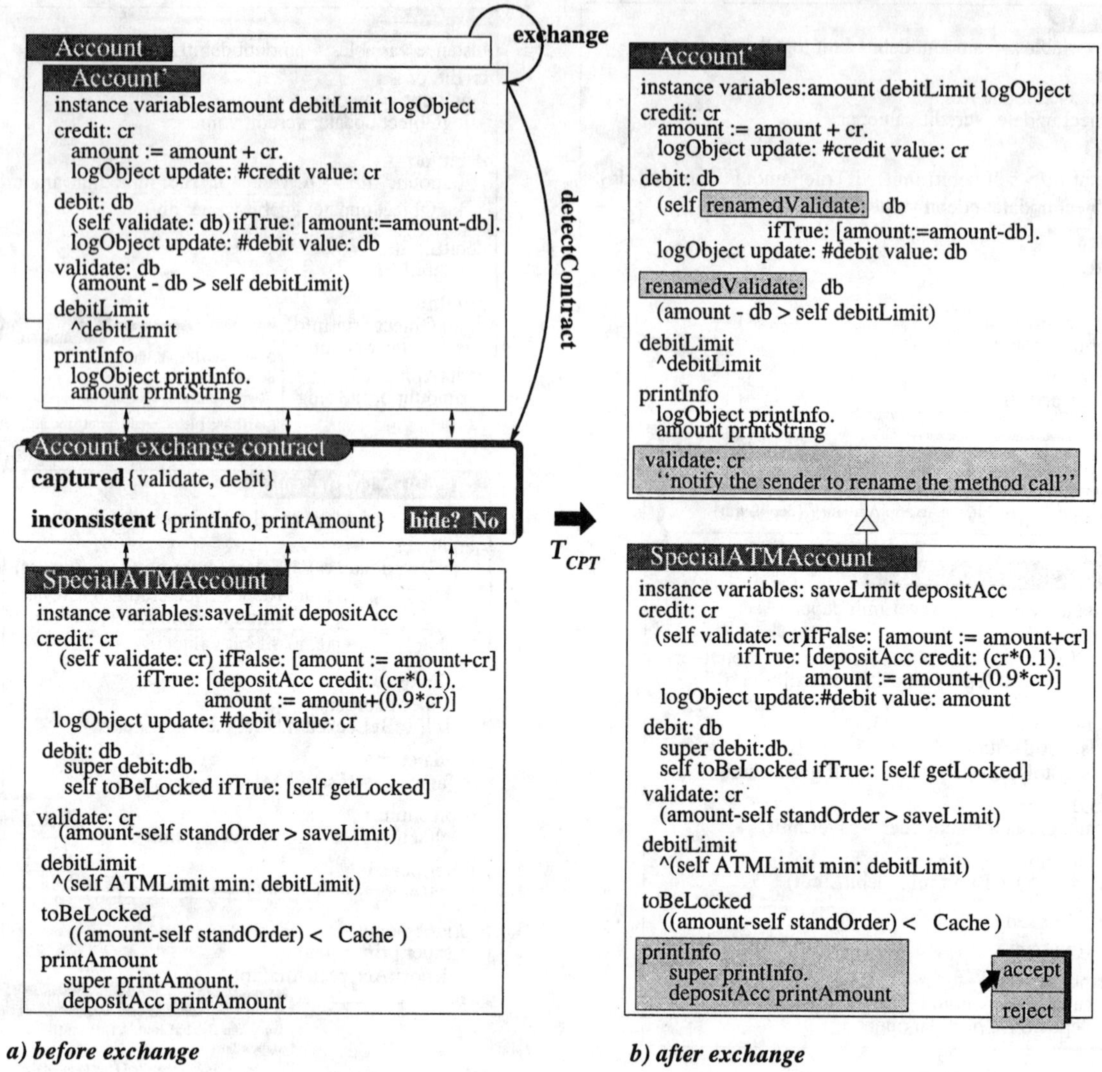


Figure 9: Cooperation process during exchange

proposed. The transformation proposed for avoiding capturing is to rename the captured method in Account', thus protecting the inheritor without losing the improvement. As shown on the right side of Fig. 9, validate: is renamed to renamedValidate: within Account'. However, in order for the renaming to be consistent, all invocations of validate: on an instance of Account' should be renamed throughout the base module. For this purpose, as illustrated in the figure, the renamed method (validate: in this case) gets automatically reimplemented in Account' to propagate renaming to the caller site[1].

[1] In a typeless language like Smalltalk it is generally not possible at compile time to find out where a method gets invoked on an instance of a class. For this purpose, renaming will be fully performed only at run-time.

The situation is not as favorable concerning inconsistent methods. A straightforward automatic protection is to create a "dummy" class between the exchanged base and the inheritor and copy the old versions of the methods becoming inconsistent – printInfo and printAmount in this case – down the inheritance hierarchy in the dummy class. In this way the situation before the exchange is reestablished: the improvement intended by the designer gets lost for the class SpecialATMAccount. In Fig. 9, the assumption is made that the programmer ignores this possibility (illustrated by the negative response to the question "hide?") and fix the problem him/herself by redefining printInfo in SpecialATMAccount as shown in Fig. 9.

## 4 Designing the Metalevel

In this section, our model for designing the metalevel will be presented. In order to motivate the design considerations of the model, the main approaches to the metalevel design of existing object-oriented languages regarding their suitability of supporting smart composition will be briefly discussed first.

### 4.1 Design Issues

With respect to their metalevel, object-oriented languages can be classified into two categories. The first category contains languages which are designed according to the black-box principle: their metalevel is hidden behind the functionality interface, and there is no possibility to influence it. Examples of such languages are C++ [25] and Eiffel [16].

Languages of the second category such as CLOS [10], Smalltalk-80 [7], SOM [6], ObjVlisp [4], or Open C++ [3], follow a *metaobject protocol* [10] approach to the design of the metalevel. Along the decomposition of the application into class definitions there is a decomposition of the metalevel into class-objects, each encapsulating "the local metalevel" of the corresponding class definition in the application. In general, class-objects are instances of a particular predefined class, e.g. Class in Smalltalk-80.

The question is how suitable the metalevel design of the languages of the second category is for supporting the requirements posed by a smart composition model. As indicated by the discussion in the previous section, a first requirement is that in addition to the default metaclass – the predefined class of class-objects – a variety of customized metaclasses should be available: in the worse case, one for each contract property supported in the system, plus one for any setting of properties that may appear in a contract. Second, the design should allow the type of a class-object to change after the class has been created, for two reasons. First, the base designer declares the contract after the application-level functionality is defined, i.e. after the corresponding class-objects are created. Second, at the inheritor site the type of a class may change after it has been inherited along the inheritance hierarchy of the application.

To illustrate the second case, suppose that the designer has declared a method M of a certain base class C to be required, i.e. any concrete subclass of C should implement M. This should cause the type of the class-object for C at the inheritor site to be one that takes care of imposing this property. This type should be further inherited by any subclass of C. Suppose that an inheritor subclass C' does actually implement M. After that, the required property is definitively imposed and does not need to be propagated to subclasses of C': the C' class-object should cancel that part of its behavior which was responsible for imposing the required property.

The approach taken by most languages, including ObjVLisp, CLOS, SOM, and Open C++, to support special class semantics is to create subclasses of the predefined class of class-objects. For example, consider the SOM model in Fig. 10, where solid lines are used to represent inheritance relationships, and dashed lines to represent the "instance of" relationship. There is a predefined class, SOMObject, modeling the behavior common to all objects, and the predefined metaclass SOMClass, modeling the standard behavior of class-objects. Assume that two user-defined subclasses of SOMClass, FunctionalClass and DependClass, implement special semantics of classes that have functional or dependent definitions, respectively. SOM uses multiple inheritance to compose special class semantics, as illustrated by the metaclass DependFuncClass. Thus, in this model the class Account in Fig. 6 whose contract contains the functional and dependent properties would be created as an instance of the metaclass DependFuncClass[1].

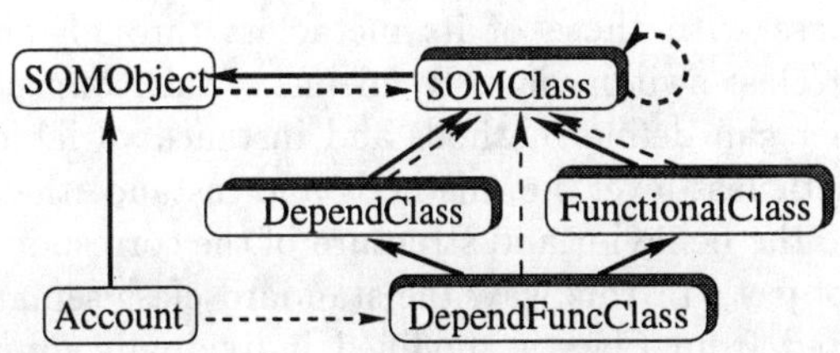


Figure 10: SOM Model

Modeling the different metalevel semantics required by the smart composition approach by means of static inheritance hierarchies of metaclasses would result in complex multiple classification hierarchies, with all the well-known problems such as *combinatorial explosion of sparse metaclasses*, and *name collisions*. For any class in the base module, the programmer should know which specialized metaclass corresponds to the particular property setting in the contract of the class. Furthermore, extending the system to support new kinds of properties is not easy in such tangled hierarchies. Finally, as argued in [18, 19, 21], dynamic behavior alterations of an existing (meta)object are difficult to handle when static inheritance is used as the mechanism for behavior variation.

Smalltalk-80 takes a different approach to support classes with special semantics, as presented in Fig. 11 (for the sake of simplicity, only a part of the Smalltalk-

[1] The third property of the contract in Fig. 6 has been ignored for the sake of simplicity

80 hierarchy is presented). The default class semantics are implemented in the metaclass Class. However, class-objects are not created as direct instances of this metaclass. For each new class-object to be created, the system first creates an instance of another predefined metaclass, called Metaclass. Metaclass instances are "class-like" constructs: they can be instantiated – however, only once – and serve as behavior definition repositories of their particular instance. Instead of Class, the newly created Metaclass instance is instantiated to create the new class-object. The created metaclass is anonymous in the sense that it is reachable only by sending the message class to its instance. In Fig. 11, the implicit metaclass of Account is called Account class. The implicit metaclasses created in this way are put in the same inheritance relationship as their instances, with the metaclass of the root class, Object class, being a subclass of the main metaclass Class.

This ensures that any class-object in the system supports the default semantics. But due to the implicit metaclasses situated between a class-object and Class, it is possible to specialize the default behavior of the class-object. Although the implicit metaclasses are anonymous, the system browser connects the definitions of any class with those of its metaclass through an instance/class switch view. By means of this connection, the user can define methods and instance variables at the metaclass level, i.e. methods and instance that belong to the behavior and structure of the corresponding class-object. In this way, the standard class semantics inherited from Class is modified individually for each class.

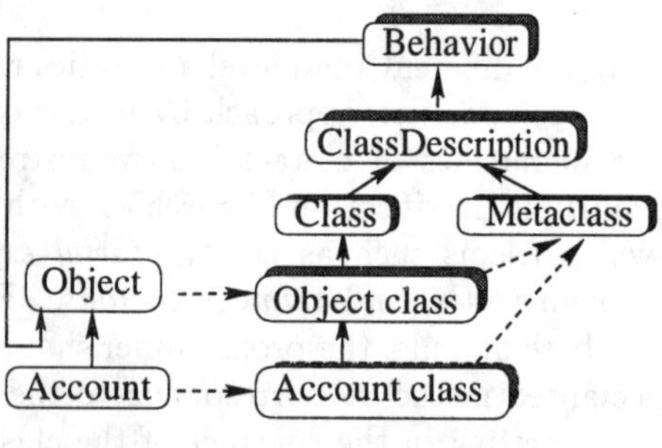


Figure 11: The metalevel approach of Smalltalk-80

This implicit approach avoids the problems related to multiple classification hierarchies. However, while appropriate for supporting specific instantiation or initialization behavior for a hierarchy of classes, which is the main motivation for introducing metaclasses in Smalltalk-80, the approach is too limited to support smart composition. As argued in [2], it provides too a rigid coupling between a class and its metaclass, leading to limitations of the expressiveness. Since it is impossible to assign an explicit customized metaclass to a class, the programmer of the base class Account should implement the special semantics corresponding to the functional and dependent properties manually by inserting methods and instance definitions in Account class. Additionally, once the default behavior of a class is modified, this is inherited by all subclasses, and cannot be canceled.

Our design of the metalevel avoids the problems exhibited by both approaches presented above. A survey of this design being integrated into Smalltalk-80, called *SmartTalk*, will be presented in the following. A more detailed discussion of SmartTalk, from the viewpoint of metalevel engineering issues, is provided in [17].

## 4.2 The SmartTalk Model

In order to enable the customization of the subclassing semantics at the level of individual classes, SmartTalk, the model of which is presented in Fig. 12, adopts the fine-grained decomposition of the metaobject-protocol approaches described above. However, SmartTalk differs in two ways from the previous approaches. First, it is based on a more fine-grained modularization. As in the other approaches there is a predefined metaclass, called Class, which implements the default semantics of the class functionality. Class behavior which deviates from the default semantics is provided by other modules, called *adjustments*. An adjustment is a mixin-like [1] construct which implements a particular choice in the design of class-objects, by providing a set of method and attribute definitions indicating only how a class-object differs from the default behavior, without being bound to any particular superclass.

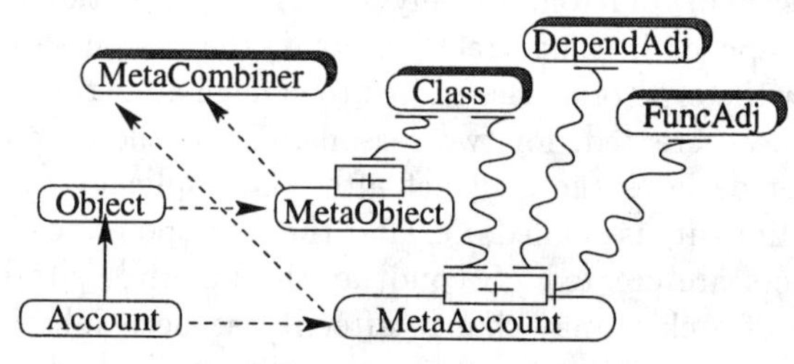


Figure 12: The metalevel approach of SmartTalk

In general, the behavior of a class-object at a certain point in time is given by Class and a (probably empty) set of adjustments, e.g. the behavior of Account in Fig. 12 is dispersed among Class, FuncAdj and DependAdj, while the behavior of Object is given by Class. In Fig. 12, the adjustment FuncAdj implements the same deviation from the default semantics as FunctionalClass does in Fig. 10. However, there is no statically established inheritance relationship between FuncAdj and Class, as between SOMClass and FunctionalClass in Fig. 10. It is at this point that the second difference between SmartTalk and the other models comes into play: in SmartTalk, managing the diversity of the class semantics is not based on static inheritance, but on the *MetaCombiner* approach to behavior modification presented in [18]. *Metacombiners* are instances of the predefined class MetaCombiner[1], and play two roles.

In their first role, metacombiners resemble metaclasses of Smalltalk-80: they are class-like constructs that are implicitly created and made the class of any new class-object. The second role played by metacombiners which distinguishes them from Smalltalk metaclasses is that they provide functionality for (dynamically) connecting and/or disconnecting definitions from Class and adjustments, in order to yield or customize a complete class behavior. In other words, a metacombiner is not simply an empty, implicit class of a class-object which can be manually filled in with behavior via the browser. It is instead a kind of connector that can arrange together definitions from Class and different predefined adjustments. For this purpose, a metacombiner encapsulates information about the set of adjustments involved in the behavior definition of its instance and the relationship among these different definitions. The latter includes information about the visibility relationships, the order in which implementations from different adjustments and Class that refine each other should be executed, etc. Additionally, it encapsulates instantiations of the attributes defined by the involved adjustments. This information controls the dispatching of messages sent to the class that is the sole instance of the metacombiner.

Thus, it is the metacombiner that establishes a kind of "virtual" inheritance relationship between Class and adjustments involved in the implementation of a class, which are otherwise not related by any globally valid inheritance. There is only one set of modules that implements class functionality, which is shared among all class-objects in the system. But there may be as many different virtual "inheritance" orderings between these modules as there are classes in the system. In Fig. 12, the virtual "inheritance" relation among Class, FuncAdj, and DependAdj as established by MetaAccount is presented by the wave-like lines connecting these modules with MetaAccount. Since only the local "inheritance" information managed by the metacombiner needs to be properly updated, changing the semantics of a class-object can be achieved in a flexible manner. For this purpose, a metacombiner provides two operations for including, respectively excluding an adjustment into/from its internal behavioral organization structures. This update will be automatically reflected in the behavior of the class being the instance of the metacombiner.

The set of adjustments existing in the system determines the diversity of the class semantics supported, and is administered by another component of the system called ClassManager, which has been omitted in Fig. 12 for the sake of simplicity. The latter represents a kind of class semantics repository: for each adjustment it records the event that causes its activation, i.e. when it should be part of the behavior definition of a class. The relationship between an adjustment and (de)activating events is established when the adjustment is defined. The system can be enriched with new flavors of class semantics at any time. In order do so, a new adjustment is created and a request is sent to the ClassManager to add it into the set of currently managed adjustments. After that, the new adjustment can be used as part of the behavior of new and existing class-objects.

To summarize, SmartTalk combines the advantages of the SOM-like and Smalltalk-80 approaches. Like in SOM, there are explicit modules implementing special class semantics. However, by creating implicit metacombiners like in Smalltalk-80, the problems related to static inheritance hierarchies are avoided. Due to its two main features – fine-grained modularization and explicit constructs for managing dynamic behavior modification – SmartTalk satisfies the requirements outlined in the previous section.

### 4.3 Smart Composition in SmartTalk

Let us now outline how smart composition is supported in SmartTalk. There is an adjustment for each contract property supported by the system: it implements how the semantics of a class differs from the default one in order to ensure the propagation of the property. Despite their differences, the implementations of special semantics in different adjustments exhibit similarities, which are pointed out in the abstract template shown in Fig. 13. The subprotocol attribute serves to store the information about the part of the application-level definitions that should be affected by the property the adjustment stands for. As it can be noticed in their abstract definition in the Subprotocol template in Fig. 13, subprotocol objects encapsulate a container data structure and provide interface operations for checking whether a certain application-level definition (method) is included in the container (includes), as well as for adding elements to and removing elements from the container.

The special class semantics implemented by an adjustment are represented by three operations in the

[1] Lower-case lettering is used for MetaCombiner instances to distinguish them from their class

adjustment template. Among these operations, redefine: symbolically represents operations from the standard class functionality that should reimplemented to reflect the special semantics. The reimplementation of redefine: tests whether a certain application definition (applDef) is included into the subprotocol structure. If this is the case, it calls the enforceMyConstraint method which is responsible for "enforcing" the property the adjustment stands for. Otherwise, the next reimplementation of the redefine: method will be called. This may be the standard implementation of redefine: in Class or another reimplementation from another adjustment. In abstract terms, the property "enforcement" consists of (a) a test whether the property is actually maintained by the definition, and (b) the application of the corresponding transformation if this is not the case.

```
Adjustment Templatte
instance variables: subprotocol
redefine: applDef
  "Suppose this is the part of class functionality
   that should have special semantics"
  (self subprotocol includes: applDef)
     ifTrue: [self enforceMyConstraint: applDef].
  execute next definition
enforceMyConstraint: applDef
  test whether applDef maintains the property
  If not call transform: applDef
transform: applDef
  the implementation of the elementary
  transformation corresponding to the property
```

```
Subprotocol Templatte
instance variables: containerStructure
includes: applDef
  tests whether applDef is
  stored in data structure
add: applDef
  • • •
remove: applDef
  • • •
initialize: applDefContainer
  • • •
```

Figure 13: Adjustment template

Any concrete adjustment specifies the concrete data structure type and concrete tests and transformation operations. For example, in the adjustment that implements the special semantics a class should adopt when a method capture is detected in it, the data structure would be a list associating the names of the captured methods to the names and the original definitions of the messages whose reimplementation is the source of the capturing. The test in the enforcement part would make sure that there actually is a method capture in the definition of a concrete inheritor definition, and the transformation would be as already discussed in Fig. 9.

The functionality of ClassManager is extended to allow the reading of the cooperation contract. For each item (CCL expression) in the contract, the ClassManager (a) selects the adjustment corresponding to the item's property, (b) initializes the subprotocol attribute of the chosen adjustment with the information about the part of the application definition to be affected by the property (described in item's def-clause), and (a) sends an insert message to the metacombiner of the class(es) for which the property being read has been declared (also contained in def-clause), with the chosen adjustment and the initialized subprotocol object as parameters.

In response to the received insert message, a metacombiner updates its internal structures such that the definitions of the adjustment passed as a parameter are integrated into the behavior of the underlying class. In this way, the metalevel of the underlying class is adjusted to satisfy the requirements posed by the contract. Since the internal structures of any new metacombiner are initialized with the information contained in the metacombiner of the superclass of its instance, the functionality of all subclasses will automatically have the semantics required by the contract, as well. However, the behavioral structures of the metacombiners can be changed independently of the inheritance relationship of their instances. This is important to support changes in the contract during the evolution of the class library, as the result of either an explicit change request by the library designer/inheritor, e.g. for undoing a contract item, or an automatic change following e.g. the definitive satisfaction of a property. For illustration, the process of reading the contract of the class Account in Fig. 6 is schematically presented in Fig. 14, where the operations are labeled with numbers to reflect the chronological order in which they are called. The result of the reading process presented in Fig. 14 is the behavior definition for Account presented in Fig. 12.

Besides its flexibility and modularity, another important feature of SmartTalk is its openness in the sense that it can be incrementally extended to support new contract properties. In order to support new items, the type of the subobject, the test and transformation operations need to be implemented first. These are then integrated into a special metalevel behavior by introducing a new adjustment together with the CCL-expression corresponding to it. The question is, however, who is responsible for the extension. While it is the application designer who can formulate new properties, he or she should not be involved in implementing the related special metalevel semantics. For this reason, it is desirable to support the application designer with a kind of formal declarative language in which the semantics related

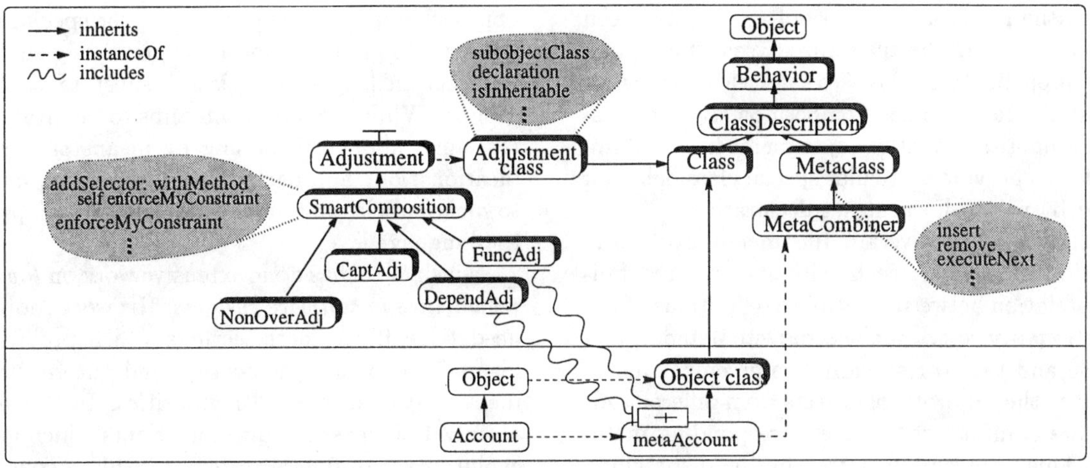


Figure 15: Integrating SmartTalk into Smalltalk-80

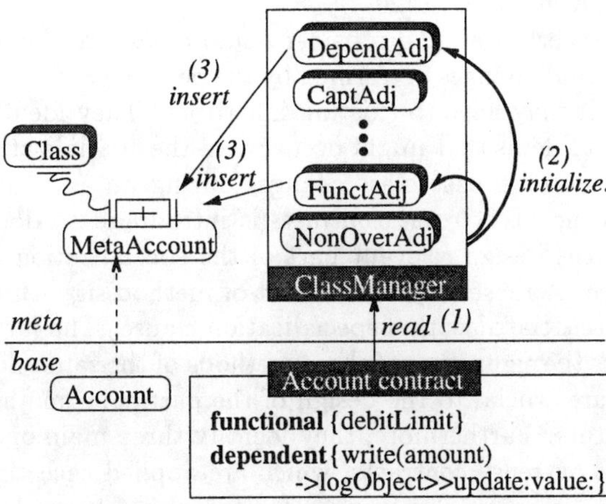


Figure 14: Reading the Contract

to new properties can be expressed in abstract terms, and let the system generate the test operations of the corresponding adjustment out of the declarative expression. Logics on parse trees and attribute grammars, or logic programming can be used for this purpose. In this way, the application designer is allowed to extend the architecture in a declarative way. If this is not sufficient, the metalevel designer is required to perform procedural extensions. While the metalevel model discussed here does not currently provide such higher level constructs, it can be orthogonally enhanced to support them.

## 5 Implementation

SmartTalk has been implemented as an extension of Smalltalk-80 ParcPlace VisualWorks 2.5., and fully integrated into the Smalltalk image. The user can create classes that support customized functionality by using a class definition template which is slightly different from the standard one – the keyword adaptableSubclass is used instead of subclass. This causes an instance of MetaCombiner to be used as the metaclass of the class to be created instead of the standard Metaclass. MetaCombiner is implemented as a subclass of Metaclass (see Fig. 15). The implicitly created metacombiner is made a subclass of Class (in fact of the metaclass of the first non-adaptable superclass in the inheritance hierarchy of the corresponding class, as illustrated by metaAccount being a subclass of Object class in Fig. 15). A subclass of an adaptable class is also adaptable, however their metacombiners are not put in the same inheritance relationship. This allows the metalevel of a subclass to be customized independently of its superclass.

The implementation of adjustments as linguistic constructs is provided by the metaclass Adjustment class. Since the latter is a subclass of Class, any adjustment has the attributes of a class. Additionally, an adjustment encapsulates the property it corresponds to, the class of its subobject part, if any, etc. All adjustments are subclasses of the empty class Adjustment. The adjustment SmartComposition implements the generic redefinition template discussed in the previous section (Fig. 13). It reimplements that part of Class the semantics of which need to be customized in the presence of an explicit contract. In Fig. 15, the method addSelector withMethod:, which is called each time a new (or a modified) method definition is compiled and needs to be stored in the method dictionary of a class, has been chosen for illustrating the customized Class functionality. The reimplementation invokes enforceMyConstraint, which is left abstract in SmartComposition. By subclassing SmartComposition, a set of adjustments has been implemented that provide particular special class behavior as required by particular contract declarations.

Generally, there are several adjustments involved in the definition of a class, each with its own redefinitions. The relation between multiple redefinitions of the same functionality, e.g. addSelector:withMethod:, between those and the corresponding enforcement methods, as well as the subprotocol objects from different adjustments are administered by the corresponding metacombiner. This information is used by the dispatching functionality, illustrated in Fig. 15 by the method executeNext. The prototype implementation of the dispatching functionality of MetaCombiner makes use of the reflective facilities of Smalltalk-80 that allow access to the execution stack, in order to keep the expected overhead related to the additional indirection level introduced by metacombiners minimal, as discussed in detail in [18].

The standard user interface has been modified to allow introducing adjustment modules into the system, together with information such as the property declaration that should cause their insertion, and the class of the corresponding subobject. After that, the contract item related to the newly introduced adjustment appears in the list of items that can be chosen to annotate application level code.

## 6 Related Work and Discussion

### 6.1 Overview of Related Work

In [11], Kiczales and Lamping discuss the issues involved in the design of class libraries and emphasize the importance of documenting and maintaining internal dependencies. In [14], Lamping proposes to extend type systems in order to formalize not only information valuable for the client interface, but also indications about the part of resources of the class each method utilizes during its execution. In this way, the advantages of type systems are made available to the specialization interface, since checks can be performed to see whether a subclass is a coherent extension of a superclass. However, the expressiveness of type systems is limited.

In contrast to [14], Stata and Guttag [23], propose a methodology for specialization interfaces that is specification oriented instead of type-system oriented. Their approach extends the *object-type specifications* by Liskow and Wing [15] to support specialization interface specifications besides client interface specifications. Their approach improves the partition of the specialization interface into groups of methods previously suggested by Lamping in [14] by associating substate with method groups. While this approach aims to facilitate modular reasoning about subclassing by means of formal specifications, our approach can be viewed as an attempt to make subclassing more modular and encapsulated at the language level.

Minsky [20] has done extensive work on *law-governed regularities in software systems*. His work motivates the need for software architectures which provide mechanisms for explicit specification and automatic enforcement of system internal regularities. In this approach, a central law base supplies invariants which govern the evolution of a software system, just like a constitutional system governs the life of a civil society. The applicability of the general approach in the domain of object-oriented systems has been investigated in [20]. Our proposal provides a metalevel approach for realizing the issues formalized in [20].

Steyaert et al. [24] consider issues related to the impacts that changes performed by the developer of a base module may have to existing inheritors. They identify four problems that might occur when the specialization interface of a base class changes during an exchange. The concept of *reuse contracts* is introduced to document the design relevant part of the specialization interface. A reuse contract is a set of method signatures, each associated with a specialization clause. The latter names the signatures of those methods of the same class that are crucial to the design of the particular method signature. Furthermore, they identify three main operations on reuse contracts, which are applied each time a class is reused by being inherited or is changed by its developer. An examination of the interaction between the operations applied to a base reuse contract in order to gain the inheritor reuse contract, or the changed reuse contract, respectively, provides useful information for detecting possible problems during the horizontal evolution. In contrast, our work deals with both horizontal and vertical evolution problems. More importantly, whereas the reuse contracts approach only indicates problematic situations at the design level, we provide a metalevel infrastructure to automatically deal with them at the language level. Thus, both approaches are complementary and could be combined with each other.

In [13], Klarlund et al. consider the propagation of design constraints of a base telecommunication platform to the applications by means of a general purpose design language. In this approach, design constraints are formally described and named in a design constraint language, called *DCL*. The statements of DCL specify logics on parse trees, which a decision procedure translates into attribute grammars. The system architect defines a set of constraints, grouped into DCL-categories. The application developer selects the appropriate categories to annotate the design being proposed and requires the decision procedure to check whether the proposed design satisfies all categories. Our approach differs from the DCL approach as follows. The DCL approach enables design constraints which are specific for a particular platform to be expressed in a general purpose design language, by building a decision procedure on top of the black-box design of the language. In contrast, we propose an open implementation design such that the programming language, while remaining general, is able to customize itself to enforce special constraints of particular base applications. The DCL approach deals only with issues in the vertical evolution axis. Furthermore, the application designer is responsible for annotating the design with the appropriate set of DCL categories. This implies that the application developer knows exactly what constraints its design should satisfy. As also pointed out by Minsky [20], understanding the internal characteristics of the base platform is actually the most subtle part of the problem. On the contrary, in our approach it is the base module that is annotated by its designer.

### 6.2 Why Metaprogramming?

While it might be easy to motivate that language support is needed for managing the evolution of object-oriented reusable software, justifying the use of metaprogramming for this purpose might be not as obvious. One can argue that these mechanisms could be built-in elements of a compiler. They obviously could, and actually there are examples of properties that are built into some object-oriented languages, such as the non-override property which is available as the annotation finalize in Java, or frozen in Eiffel. However, besides the pragmatic argument that making use of reflective facilities allows to provide a prototype realization of the smart composition without designing a new language from scratch or modifying the compiler or virtual machines of existing languages, there are several objections against this choice:

1. Only few general purpose properties can be built into any given language. Moreover, a property that is built into the implementation of a language tends to be rigid, and not easily adaptable to a particular application.

2. There are application domain specific properties which should not be built into a general purpose language. A related issue is that the set of properties to be propagated should be extensible.

3. Another argument against building properties into the language semantics is separation of concerns. Having properties as part of the language, their specification becomes part of the application code, making it harder to read and understand.

4. Programming languages generally adopt the decomposition of software systems into functional modules and provide no means for making explicit statements about the system as a whole. Consequently, global properties such as imposing a layered structure cannot supported in an easy manner.

5. Finally, as demonstrated by the automatic renaming of a captured method, accomplishing the consistency preserving transformation may requires a global view of the software structure to be available even during the run-time of the system, which cannot be provided by compilers.

The arguments outlined above apply also to the use of the type-system as the basis for managing evolution of class libraries, as well as to approaches based on tools built on top of a language, such as the DCL approach. However, they do not apply to the law governed approach. A comprehensive comparison of both approaches is unrealistic by the time this paper is written, since the model presented here is currently reporting its first achievements, while the LGA-approach has by now profited from several years of experience. However, we are confident that the metalevel approach presented here is at least as powerful as the LGA approach. To support our confidence we quote Minsky in his recent work presented in [20]:

> "... The metaobject protocol [of CLOS and Open C++] is somewhat analogous to our law, and is, *in many ways, more powerful than it* since it harnesses the whole power of the underlying programming language. However, the metaobject protocol does not provide a truly global view of a system, which is central to LGA. This is because the code of the MOP is distributed among individual classes, and cannot formulate rules concerning the interaction between arbitrary sets of classes. ..."

Our model inherits the power of its predecessor MOP-models, but avoids the problems of these MOPs by extending the metalevel with the ClassManager component that has a global view of the class-architecture.

## 7 Conclusions

In this paper, we have argued that the composition mechanisms based on the simple inheritance rules of existing object-oriented languages are not sufficient to deal with consistency issues during the evolution of class libraries.

A smart composition model has been proposed which makes the integration process a function of the characteristics of the modules to be composed. In this model, library designers are enabled to declare properties of their module to be propagated to inheritors and changes of the base module are monitored to detect risky alterations that may invalidate existing inheritors. In response to the designer declarations or detected risky alterations, the behavior of the linguistic constructs involved in the composition gets adjusted such that before performing the composition of the modules, it is first ensured that the consistency of the library is preserved. Furthermore, a proposal for designing the metalevel has been presented which allows a flexible and modular customization of the metalevel and which is incrementally extensible to support new application designer declarations. Finally, the feasibility of the proposed approach has been demonstrated by presenting its implementation as an extension of the Smalltalk-80 standard environment.

There are several interesting areas for future work. First, the model is still in progress. As such, it needs to be extended in order to deal with more properties as well as to provide more sophisticated means to deal with conflicting situations. Applying the model to several large class libraries in order to assess its merits and to gather experience about typical general purpose and application domain specific properties and the transformations associated with them is very important. A second area concerns the development of tools that allow the designer to formulate new constraints in a declarative way. Finally, a challenging area is to investigate the applicability of the model proposed here (or adequate extensions of it) in the context of the emerging work on *software architectures* [22].

## Acknowledgements

The author is grateful to Wolfgang Merzenich for promoting this work and to Bernd Freisleben for comments on interim drafts of this paper. I would like to thank members of the reuse contracts group, Patrick Steyaert, Tom Mens, and Kim Mens, for the constructive discussions on the topic and for their comments on the paper. Many thanks to Barbara Staudt Lerner for her assistance in preparing the final version of this paper and to the anonymous referees for their helpful comments.

## References

[1] Bracha G. and Cook W. Mixin-Based Inheritance. In *Proceedings OOPSLA/ECOOP '90*, ACM SIGPLAN Notices, pp. 303–311, Vol. 25, No. 10, 1990.

[2] Briot J.-P., Cointe P. Programming with Explicit Metaclasses in Smalltalk-80. In *Proceedings of OOPSLA '89*, ACM SIGPLAN Notices, Vol. 23 No. 10, pp. 419–431, 1989.

[3] Chiba S. A Metaobject Protocol for C++. In *Proceedings of OOPSLA '95*, ACM SIGPLAN Notices, Vol. 29 No. 10, pp. 285–299, 1995.

[4] Cointe P. Metaclasses are First Class: the ObjVlisp Model. In *Proceedings of OOPSLA '87*, ACM SIGPLAN Notices, Vol. 21 No. 10, pp. 156–167, 1987.

[5] Cook W. and Palsberg J. A Denotational Semantics of Inheritance and its Correctness. In *Proceedings OOPSLA '89, ACM SIGPLAN Notices*, Vol. 24, No. 10, pp. 433–443, 1989.

[6] Danforth S. and Forman I. Reflections on Metaclass Programming in SOM. In *Proceedings OOPSLA '94, ACM SIGPLAN Notices*, Vol. 29, No. 10, p. 440–452, 1994.

[7] Goldberg A. and Robson D. Smalltalk 80: The Language and its Implementation. Addison-Wesley, 1983.

[8] Goldberg A. and Rubin K. Succeeding with Objects: Decision Frameworks for Project Management. Addison-Westley, 1995.

[9] Helm R., Holland I. M., and Gangopadhyay D. Contracts: Specifying behavioral compositions in object-oriented systems. In *Proceedings OOPSLA/ECOOP '90*, ACM SIGPLAN Notices, pp. 169–180, Vol. 25, No. 10, 1990.

[10] Kiczales G. and des Rivières J. and Bobrow D. G. The Art of the Metaobject Protocol. MIT Press 1991.

[11] Kiczales G. and Lamping J. Issues in the Design and Documentation of Class Libraries. In *Proceedings of OOPSLA '92*, ACM SIGPLAN Notices, Vol. 27 No. 10, pp. 435–451, 1992.

[12] Kiczales G. Towards a New Model of Abstraction for the Engineering o f Software. Invited Talk in OOPSLA '94, 1994 (http://www.xerox.com/PARC/spl/eca/oi.html).

[13] Klarlund N., Koistinen J. and Schwartzbach M. Formal Design Constraints In *Proceedings OOPSLA '96*, ACM SIGPLAN Notices, Vol. 31, No. 10, pp. 370–384, 1996.

[14] Lamping J. Typing the Specialization Interface. In *Proceedings of OOPSLA '93*, ACM SIGPLAN Notices, Vol. 28, No. 10, pp. 201–214, 1993.

[15] Liskow B. and Wing J. A Behavioral Notation of Subtyping. In *Proceedings of OOPSLA '94*, ACM SIGPLAN Notices, Vol. 16, No. 16, 1994.

[16] Meyer B. *Object-Oriented Software Construction.* Prentice Hall, 1988.

[17] Mezini M. Dynamic Metaclass Construction for an Explicit Specialization Interface. In *Proceedings of Reflection '96*, pp. 203–219, 1996.

[18] Mezini M. Dynamic Object Modification without Name Collisions. In *Proceedings of ECOOP '97*, LNCS 1241, pp. 190–219, 1997.

[19] Mezini M. Ph.D. Thesis, University of Siegen, 1997 (in preparation).

[20] Minsky N. Law-Governed Regularities in Object Systems. In *Theory and Practice of Object Systems (TAPOS)*, Vol. 2, No. 4, John Wiley, 1996.

[21] Seiter L., Palsberg J., and Lieberherr K. Evolution of Object Behavior using Context Relations. In Garlan D., (ed.), *Proceedings of the 4th ACM SIGSOFT Symposium on the Foundations of Software Engineering*, Software Engineering Notes, Vol.21, No. 6, pp.46–56, ACM Press, Nov. 1996.

[22] Shaw M and Garlan D. *Software Architecture. Perspectives on an Emerging Discipline.* Prentice Hall, 1996.

[23] Stata R. and Guttag J. Modular Reasoning in the Presence of Inheritance. In *Proceedings of OOPSLA '95*, ACM SIGPLAN Notices, Vol. 21 No. 10, pp. 200–214, 1995.

[24] Steyaert P., Lucas C., Mens K., and D'Hondt T. Reuse Contracts: Managing the Evolution of Reusable Assets. In *Proceedings of OOPSLA '96*, ACM SIGPLAN Notices, Vol. 31 No. 10, pp. 268–286, 1996.

[25] Stroustrup B. *The C++ Programming Language.* Addison-Wesley, 1986.

# Analyzing and Measuring Reusability in Object-Oriented Designs

Margaretha W. Price
MountainNet, Inc.
2816 Cranberry Square
Morgantown, WV 26505-9289 USA
+1 304 594 9075 ext. 28
mprice@rbse.mountain.net

Steven A. Demurjian, Sr.
The University of Connecticut
Computer Science & Engrg. Dept.
191 Auditorium Rd., U-155
Storrs, CT 06269-3155 USA
+1 860 486 4818
steve@eng2.uconn.edu

## ABSTRACT

In this paper, we present a technique to analyze and measure the reusability of object-oriented (OO) designs. The metrics can be incorporated into a design/development environment, so that reusability measurements, analysis, and improvements can be part of "business as usual" for an organization. Design reusability measurements also enable early identification of poor reuse potential, when it is still possible to modify/refine the design. The essential components of our approach are two reuse-specific characterizations of classes and hierarchies, and a set of metrics which objectively measures the dependencies among design components based on those reuse-specific characterizations.

## 1 INTRODUCTION

Software components that are reused most often tend to be small components, since they are normally less specific (i.e., string functions, abstract data types (ADT), or utility routines), and thus, more likely needed by other systems. However, small code reuse produces minimal savings representing only a small percentage of the final product [2]. Poulin argues that there are three classes of software that make up a typical software application [20]:

- **Domain-independent** (20% of the whole application): This includes ADTs, utility routines, math libraries and other components which are useful in a wide range of problem areas.
- **Domain-specific** (65% of the whole application): This is for software which is only useful within the specific domain. The examples given include high-speed communications device drivers, navigational aids for aircraft, and financial services libraries.
- **Application-specific** (15% of the whole application): This includes software which implements the unique details of an application.


OOPSLA '97 10/97 GA, USA


From the above breakdown, we can expect the most savings if we reuse the domain-specific software. Software companies do not have to make their software be reusable in all systems, but they only have to make their software reusable in anticipated future systems in their organizations. Our approach to reusability measurement facilitates domain-specific reuse, particularly, domain-and-organization-specific reuse. This more restrictive goal of reusability makes domain analysis more manageable, thereby minimizing the impact of the actual domain on the potential reuse.

The design of a program is normally described in terms of the program's components and the interactions among them [16]. Our reusability metrics measure the level of interactions of software design components which are expected to be reused together to the components that comprise the rest of the system. Most of the implementation details are not specified in software designs, thus the software designer has a significant amount of flexibility in modifying portions of an existing design to accommodate future systems, thereby attaining design reuse.

Figure 1 illustrates an OO design/development process which incorporates design reusability measurements. A software engineer starts the process by designing a system. After the major components of the system (and the interactions between them) have been determined, our metrics can be used to identify, measure, and provide feedback on the reusability of the OO design. The software designers then have the opportunity to modify their OO design and reevaluate the reusability of their system. The two arrows (1) can be repeated as many times as necessary, in an iterative process that is intended to make the OO design more complete. After the reusable portions have been clearly identified and it has been determined that there exists no interactions which inhibit reuse, we can store the design and document the system architecture (2). Step (3) leads to the implementation process (object coding, testing, and debugging) and the storing of the completed implementation (4). Future software projects will then have the choice to reuse a previous OO design (5) and its corresponding implementation (6) or just reuse the design and write a new implementation. In some cases, it may be necessary to revisit earlier stages of this process after the implementation has commenced.

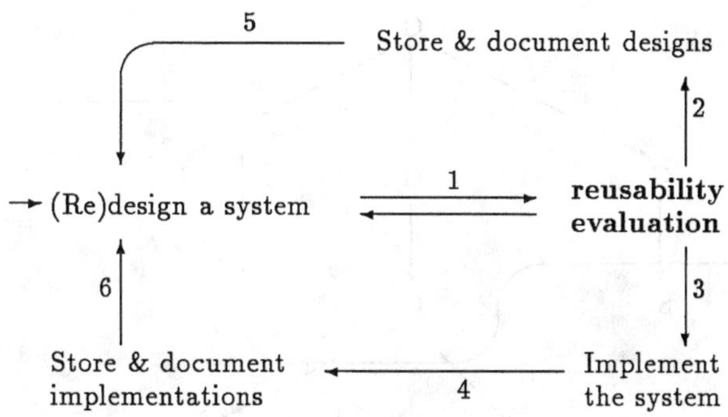


Figure 1. Design and Implementation Process

Design reusability measurements are important for two reasons. First of all, measurements can be automated and they can quickly provide feedback to the software designers. The metrics can also be incorporated into a design and development environment, so that reusability measurements, analysis, and design improvements can be part of "business as usual" for an organization. The second reason for design reusability measurements is to enable early identification of poor reuse potential, when it is still possible to modify/refine the design.

The remainder of this paper is organized into six sections. In Section 2, we present the background concepts for our conceptual model that supports OO design-level reuse. In Section 3, we detail the framework of the OO design-level measurements. Section 4 contains an empirical study that demonstrates our approach via a design reusability evaluations tool that we have developed. In Section 5, we review ongoing research in metrics theory against our approach as presented in Sections 2 and 3. Section 6 examines related work in the areas of reusable, hierarchical, OO models and in reusability measurements. Finally, Section 7 contains the conclusions and a note on our effort to incorporate these measurements into a design/development environment.

## 2 BACKGROUND CONCEPTS

The major components of our design reuse metrics are two subjective (designer-defined) characterizations of classes and hierarchies. Because of the intellectual nature of the software design process, important components of it must be measured subjectively, while the tangible representation of the design product can be measured objectively for many purposes [4]. Our two characterizations of classes and hierarchies, which are presented in Sections 2.2 and 2.3, are the important reusability properties of a software design, hence they are to be defined subjectively by the software designers. After the characterizations have been defined, we provide a framework in Section 3 which objectively measures the dependencies among design components. These dependencies are the tangible representation of the design product, thus they are measured objectively. This section starts by identifying the unit of abstraction that is used in our reusability measurements.

### 2.1 Unit of Abstraction

Research efforts in OO metrics [3, 5] are mostly concerned with 'good-design' criteria at the class level. For reusability evaluations, we believe it is more appropriate to evaluate the criteria at the class hierarchy level of abstraction and to study the reusability of a class hierarchy as a whole, portions of a class hierarchy, or a set of related class hierarchies. This has also been argued in another context, namely that the unit of abstraction for OO applications should not only be at the class/object type level, but also at the class hierarchy level [7].

A class hierarchy is the result of an OO mechanism referred to as *inheritance* or *class derivation*. Class inheritance allows members (functions and data) of one class (parent) to be used as if they were members of another class (child or subclass). During system design, class hierarchies are used to group similar classes so that they can have one parent class containing the common operations and/or data. The subclasses will then only need to define operations/data specific to each subclass. Thus, a class is only made to be a child of another class if it needs some members of the parent class. Consequently, it is the nature of OO design with inheritance to migrate more general information and operations up the hierarchy where they can be reused by all descendants while simultaneously pushing domain-specific information and operations down the hierarchy where their potential reuse is limited.

From a reuse perspective, since a child class needs members of its parent, if we want to reuse a child class we have to also reuse the parent class. However, if we want to reuse the parent class, we are not required to reuse its subclasses, since the parent class does not use members of its subclasses. As a result, new systems can reuse the top portion of a hierarchy or the whole hierarchy, but they cannot reuse just a lower part of a hierarchy. Reusing just the top portion of a hierarchy is desirable in many cases, since the lower level classes are more specific classes, so with respect to their parents, they are less likely to be needed in other applications.

### 2.2 General versus Specific Classes

From our discussion in Section 2.1, it is clear that the individual classes in any inheritance hierarchy can be characterized based on their overall position. In our approach, we require the software designer to identify individual classes to be either General or Specific with respect to its purpose in the overall design. A *General* class is one that is expected to be reused in other applications. A *Specific* class is a class that is only applicable in this application. Abstract classes, which are a design technique used to define templates for specifying subclasses, are examples of classes which would normally be defined as General classes. However, not all General classes have to be defined as abstract classes; rather, a class is General if it is recognized by the software designer as being able to solve problems in addition to the context (inheritance hierarchy and underlying application) that it is defined within.

To further explain this characterization, we use a simple software design of a Health Care Application (HCA) system [13]. Figure 2 presents the class hierarchies of HCA. The Person hierarchy is used to represent and process information common to all people in a hospital application. The Record hierarchy is used for various record processing, the Item hierarchy is used to represent general physical items used in a hospital, and the Organization hierarchy is used to represent the various entities in a hospital.

This Health Care Application system however, is not only applicable in hospitals. Portions of this system might

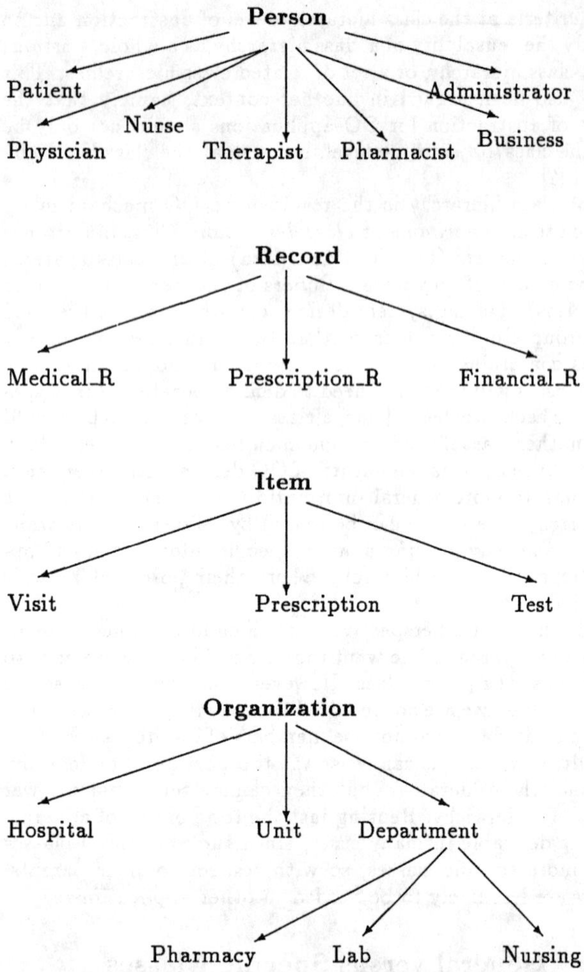


Figure 2. Health Care Application (HCA) Classes

be reusable in other facets of health care, both in large and small scales (e.g., dental office, eye care center, etc.). If our organization's future projects are expected to target those smaller health care establishments, we can define the following classes as General classes: Person, Patient, Physician, Business, Record, Medical_R, Prescription_R, and Financial_R. The other classes can be defined as Specific classes, since it is likely that they will not be needed in our future systems.

As stated previously, we cannot reuse just a lower part of a hierarchy. Thus, as illustrated in Figure 3, the General classes must be towards the top and the Specific classes must be towards the bottom of the hierarchy. A General class cannot be a descendant of a Specific class, since to reuse a class, we also have to reuse its parents. A design tool can be used to enforce this: when creating a root class, this class is first defined as a General class. If at some point of a hierarchy, a class is defined as a Specific class by the software designer, descendants of that Specific class, will also have to be Specific. Thus, every class hierarchy has a line that divides all of the General classes from all of the Specific classes.

It has been known that the generalization of classes is an important software development activity, and should be in-

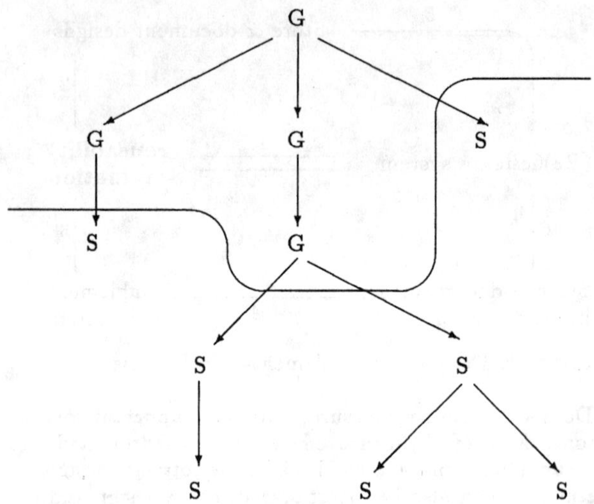


Figure 3. General(G)/Specific(S) Classes of a Hierarchy

cluded as an integral part of a software development process. Generalizations arise in systems in two ways, during the initial design phase and during the maintenance phase. Work in program restructuring [9, 10, 15] discusses generalizations in terms of structural modifications during the maintenance of completed applications. On the other hand, our metrics bring up the issue of generalizations during the initial design process in an effort to maximize the reusable portions of applications..

## 2.3 Related Class Hierarchies

While General and Specific classes provide a characterization mode within an inheritance hierarchy, from a design-reuse perspective, it is also important to identify the interactions between the hierarchies that comprise an OO application. These interactions provide the important first step in discerning the couplings between classes when viewed from the perspective of entire hierarchies. Thus, to augment the General/Specific classes, the software designer is asked to define the class hierarchies that are related to one another in an OO application. A hierarchy is defined as *related* to another hierarchy if they are related in concept and are expected to be reused together in future systems. Relating class hierarchies encourages the designers to group their components into reusable portions at the earliest stages in the design process.

OO frameworks [17] is a similar technique in codifying design knowledge to produce a generic design. Like OO frameworks, related hierarchies also provide a means to describe the interactions between objects of a program. OO frameworks are domain specific, hence they require the software designer to have a solid understanding about the application domain. In determining related hierarchies, it is also important for software designers to understand the application domain, but more importantly, they need to have some ideas on the kinds of systems they expect to build in the future. Thus, the determination of related hierarchies is not only domain specific, but also organization specific.

In the HCA design given in Figure 2, a software designer may decide that the hierarchies with root classes 'Person' and 'Record' will always be needed together in future projects. The reason can be that in any health care system, we will always need to represent the people involved and to process patients' records. Moreover, current or future subclasses of Person will be the ones that manipulate records. In this case, the software designer knows that there are (will be) many couplings between these two hierarchies, but these couplings will not affect the reusability of HCA, or portions of HCA, in this organization's future projects. In our metrics, these two hierarchies can be defined as related to each other.

A dependency to a related hierarchy is not a hindrance to reuse, because the related hierarchy will also be reused together; thus, the dependency will always be satisfied. On the other hand, a *dependency to an unrelated* hierarchy is a hindrance to reuse and can arise later in design or implementation phase. This characterization of related hierarchies, if done during the initial design phase, can prevent the occurrence of unrelated dependency. Requiring software designers to define related hierarchies provides a way to differentiate between couplings that do affect reuse and those that do not.

## 3 A Design Reusability Measurement Framework

This section discusses the objective dependency measurements which are based on the subjective characterizations of classes and hierarchies described in Section 2. Unlike the characterizations of General/Specific classes and related hierarchies, the measurements presented here are domain-independent. The first subsection details the types of couplings between General and Specific classes, which are foundational in identifying those portions of the design that have the greatest reuse potential. The next subsection discusses couplings between hierarchies and provides suggestions on either eliminating them (if they are a hindrance to reuse) or moving them to locations where they can add value to the reusable design. The final subsection presents the design-reusability metrics which are based on subjective characterizations of Sections 2.2 and 2.3 and the objective concepts of Sections 3.1 and 3.2.

### 3.1 Coupling between General and Specific Classes

The first aspect of our design-reusability measurements involves an understanding of the different types of couplings that can exist between General and Specific classes, and their positive or negative impact on reuse. Figure 4 illustrates the four types of coupling between General (G) and Specific (S) classes of two hierarchies: a General class can depend on another General class (1), a General class can depend on a Specific class (2), a Specific class can depend on a General class (3), and a Specific class can depend on another Specific class (4). According to [5], inter-class coupling occurs when methods of one class use methods or instance variables of another class. Since the unit of abstraction used here is at the hierarchy level, we define coupling as inter-hierarchy coupling for when methods of one hierarchy use methods or instance variables of another hierarchy. There are actually eight types of couplings. The four couplings illustrated in Figure 4 can be either directed to a related hierarchy or to an unrelated hierarchy. Our metrics measure these eight types of dependencies separately, as we will justify in Section 5.

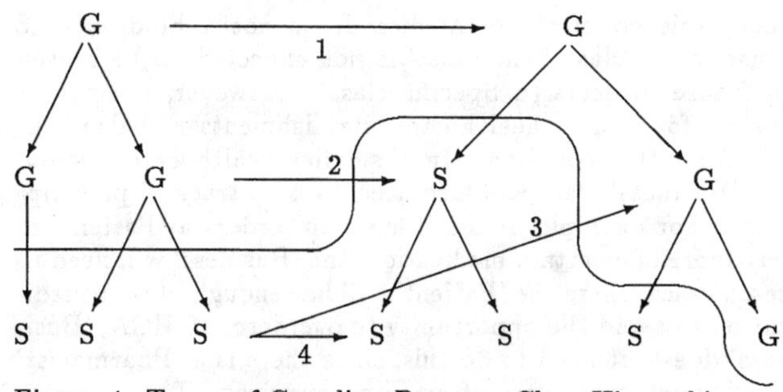
Figure 4. Types of Coupling Between Class Hierarchies

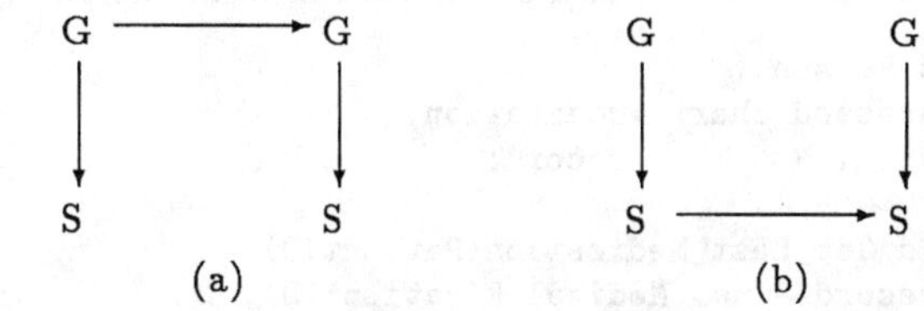
Figure 5. Favorable Couplings between: (a) Related Hierarchies and (b) Unrelated Hierarchies.

Not all dependencies are bad for reuse. Dependencies between classes which are expected to be reused together (i.e., related hierarchies) are not a hindrance to reuse. In fact, they add more value to the design, because a larger portion of the design is reused. Our metrics separate the measurements for couplings which are good for reuse, bad for reuse, and those which are neither but might be able to increase the value of the reusable classes. As illustrated in Figure 5, our goal is to have a design where:

- there exists many couplings between the related General classes (a), and
- the couplings among unrelated hierarchies are only between their Specific classes (b).

Using our previous assumptions of classes in Figure 2, the hierarchy with root class 'Person' is related to the one with root class 'Record.' Moreover, all classes of 'Record' are General, while only 'Person,' 'Patient,' 'Physician,' and 'Business' are General in the other hierarchy. If the Specific class 'Therapist' has a method 'Give_Therapy' which calls a method of 'Medical_R' named 'Get_Last_Medications' as shown in the code segment below:

```
class Therapist {
  ...
  void    *Give_Therapy(PatientID){
    char       *medication;
    Medical_R  *record;
    ...
    record = new Medical_R(PatientID);
    medication = (char *)
       record->Get_Last_Medication();
    if (strcmp(medication, "abc")==0){...}
    ...
  }
  ...
}
```

then, this coupling to 'Medical_R' is not a hindrance to reuse, since class 'Therapist' is not expected to be reused in future projects (a Specific class). However, our future system for smaller health care establishments will also benefit from this coupling. In a smaller health care system, the 'Business' class will also need to keep track of prescriptions. For example, if the 'Physician' orders a 'Patient' to buy more of a certain medication, the 'Business' will need to catch cases where the 'Patient' still has enough of that medication to avoid the opportunity to overdose. In HCA, 'Business' does not need to do this, since there is a 'Pharmacist' class which takes care of avoiding overdose. To accommodate reuse, we can move the coupling from 'Therapist' (for Get_Last_Medication) to 'Person,' such as in the following:

```
class Person {
  protected char  *medication;
  Medical_R       *record;
  ...
  void Get_Last_Medication(PatientID){
    record = new Medical_R(PatientID);
    medication =
      (char *) record->Get_Last_Medication();
  }
}

class Therapist : public Person {
  ...
  void    *Give_Therapy(PatientID){

    // using Person's method
    Get_Last_Medication(PatientID);

    // using Person's protected variable
    if (strcmp(medication, "abc")==0){ ... }

  }
  ...
}
```

The above allows the coupling to 'Medical_R' to be reused in our next project and leaves only those methods and operations specific to a 'Therapist,' such as 'Give_Therapy' and all other detailed operations, in the 'Therapist' class.

## 3.2 Understanding Coupling between Hierarchies

The second aspect of our design-reusability measurements involves an understanding of the couplings that exist between General/Specific classes when the hierarchies that they are in are related and unrelated. The four coupling types of Figure 4, when combined with related/unrelated hierarchies, yields eight types of reusability couplings. Each of these coupling types is discussed in turn with the intent to provide suggestions on eliminating non-desirable couplings and/or moving couplings to add value to the design whenever possible. The changes in the characterization of a class from General to Specific (or vice versa) and of hierarchies from related to unrelated (or vice versa) are not included in the suggested actions. These types of changes can greatly affect the overall design and the resulting reusable design components. Thus, these subjective characterizations should only be modified after a thorough review of the design, and not done just to eliminate an undesirable coupling.

1. **G—>G among related hierarchies.**
A dependency from a General class to another General class in a related hierarchy is not a hindrance to reuse. Metrics to count this kind of coupling may denote the value of reuse. Increasing these couplings in a design yields a potential for more reuse.
**Action:** None.

2. **G—>G among unrelated hierarchies.**
A dependency from a General class to another General class in an unrelated hierarchy is undesirable because the source and destination are not expected to be reused together.
**Action:** Attempt to move the dependency to their Specific descendant classes that are most relevant. Create new classes if necessary.

3. **G—>S among related hierarchies.**
A dependency from a General class to a Specific class, even if they are among related hierarchies, is undesirable. This is because the General class, which is expected to be reused, depends on a class which is not expected to be reused. There are two possible movements: either move the source to a Specific descendant class or move the destination to an appropriate General ancestor. Since this coupling is between related hierarchies, the second option is better since it will become type #1.
**Action:** Attempt to move the destination to an appropriate General ancestor class.

4. **G—>S among unrelated hierarchies.**
A dependency from a General class to a Specific class is undesirable because the source is expected to be reused but the destination is not expected to be reused. There are two possible ways to eliminate this coupling: move the source to its Specific descendant class or move the destination to its General ancestor class. Since this is between unrelated hierarchies, the first option is better since if the second option is chosen, it would introduce another kind of undesirable coupling (type #2).
**Action:** Attempt to move the source to an appropriate Specific descendant class.

5. **S—>G among related hierarchies.**
A dependency from a Specific class is not a hindrance to reuse, since the source is not expected to be reused. However, we might be able to increase the value of reuse. The two options in moving this coupling are either to move the source to a General ancestor or to move the destination to a Specific descendant. The first option is better since the coupling will then be between two classes which are expected to be reused together (type #1). Hence, this type of move increases the value of the reusable design components.
**Action:** Attempt to move the source to an appropriate General ancestor.

6. **S—>G among unrelated hierarchies.**
This is not a hindrance to reuse because the source of the coupling is not expected to be reused. In this case, there is nothing we can do to increase the value of the reusable design components, because the dependency is between two hierarchies which are not expected to be reused together. Moving the source to its General ancestor would create another undesirable

coupling (type #2) and moving the destination to a Specific descendant does not add value to the reusable design components (type #8).
**Action:** None.

7. **S—>S among related hierarchies.**
This is also not a hindrance to reuse because the source of coupling is not expected to be reused. However, we might be able to increase the value of the reusable design components if both the source and destination are moved to their General ancestors. The dependency would then be between two classes which are expected to be reused together (type #1).
**Action:** Attempt to move both the source and destination to appropriate General ancestors.

8. **S—>S among unrelated hierarchies.**
This is not a hindrance to reuse, rather, it represents the desired situation for couplings between unrelated classes: they need to be among the Specific classes.
**Action:** None.

Overall, our goal is to direct the software designer to strive for maximum reuse by organizing all couplings into G—>G, if they are in related hierarchies, or S—>S, if they are in unrelated hierarchies.

Before we define the metrics in Section 3.3, it is important that we formalize the idea of related hierarchies. One hierarchy (H1) is defined as related to another hierarchy (H2) if they are expected to be reused together in one or more future systems. Let us use the operator '$\triangleright$' to define this binary relation. We can now express the relation between H1 and H2 as H1 $\triangleright$ H2. This relation is transitive but not commutative:

- if H1 $\triangleright$ H2 and H2 $\triangleright$ H3, then H1 $\triangleright$ H3
- H1 $\triangleright$ H2 does not imply H2 $\triangleright$ H1

This means that if we only have the following relations H1 $\triangleright$ H2 and H2 $\triangleright$ H3, we only expect to reuse one of the following sets of hierarchies: {H1,H2,H3}, {H2,H3} or {H3}. In this case, neither {H1} nor {H2} nor {H1,H2} can be reused in isolation.

## 3.3 Software Design Reusability Metrics

The metrics are defined in eight summations that correspond to the eight types of couplings given in Section 3.2. Coupling is defined as an inter-hierarchy dependency that results when methods of one hierarchy use methods or instance variables of another hierarchy. We use the term Coupling Counts, CC, to represent these interactions between hierarchies. These reusability measurements for a class hierarchy are then defined as:

$$CC_1 = \sum_{i=1}^{m} \sum_{j=1}^{x} G_j G_i \qquad CC_5 = \sum_{i=1}^{m} \sum_{j=1}^{y} S_j G_i$$
$$CC_2 = \sum_{i=1}^{n} \sum_{j=1}^{x} G_j G_i \qquad CC_6 = \sum_{i=1}^{n} \sum_{j=1}^{y} S_j G_i$$
$$CC_3 = \sum_{i=1}^{m} \sum_{j=1}^{x} G_j S_i \qquad CC_7 = \sum_{i=1}^{m} \sum_{j=1}^{y} S_j S_i$$
$$CC_4 = \sum_{i=1}^{n} \sum_{j=1}^{x} G_j S_i \qquad CC_8 = \sum_{i=1}^{n} \sum_{j=1}^{y} S_j S_i$$

where

*m: # of hierarchies which are related to this one*
*n: # of hierarchies which are not related to this one*
*x: # of General classes in this hierarchy*
*y: # of Specific classes in this hierarchy*

$G_jG_i$: *# of couplings from the j-th General class to all General classes in the i-th hierarchy*
$G_jS_i$: *# of couplings from the j-th General class to all Specific classes in the i-th hierarchy*
$S_jG_i$: *# of couplings from the j-th Specific class to all General classes in the i-th hierarchy*
$S_jS_i$: *# of couplings from the j-th Specific class to all Specific classes in the i-th hierarchy*

To understand these counts, we provide a plausible scenario of the way that they can be utilized in practice.

Suppose that a software designer has characterized all of his/her classes as either General or Specific classes (see Section 2.2 again), and the related classes have also been defined (see Section 2.3 again). $CC_1$ through $CC_8$ can initially be calculated. High $CC_1$ values indicate that there are many couplings between classes which are expected to be reused together. This is very good in terms of reuse since we will be reusing many design components. Low $CC_1$ values denote that there are not many couplings to reuse, which may indicate that the software designer needs to review couplings for possible changes. If any of $CC_2, CC_3$, or $CC_4$ have values greater than 0, the software designer will need to either remove or move these dependencies. This is because these coupling sources are expected to be reused, but the coupling destinations are either not expected to be reused or belong to unrelated hierarchies. To accomplish this, the actions defined in Section 3.2 need to be consulted. The couplings in $CC_3$ can actually be used to create more couplings of type # 1 in Section 3.2, which increases the value of $CC_1$, the desirable kind of coupling.

Any value in $CC_5$ and $CC_7$ does not indicate a hindrance to reuse, since they are counting dependencies where the source is not expected to be reused. However, the designer might want to look into these couplings more closely, since they can be utilized to create more desirable couplings and thereby increase $CC_1$. Any value in $CC_6$ and $CC_8$ are also not indicating a hindrance to reuse because the coupling source is not expected to be reused. These values denote the dependencies which are specific to this application. There is no action needed for any value of $CC_6$ and $CC_8$; rather they are provided for the next time the software designer does an overall design review. At this time, the software designer can only move or remove dependencies, and when the couplings are changed, $CC_1$ to $CC_8$ can be automatically recalculated to provide a current view of the reuse potential of the OO design. However, during an overall design review, the characterizations of classes (General/Specific) and hierarchies (related/unrelated) can be reviewed and modified to increase the reusability of the design.

# 4 EMPIRICAL STUDY

We have conducted an experiment to study the effectiveness of our reusability measurement framework. This was done as part of a joint graduate/undergraduate project. The graduate student, M. Price, has been conducting work to verify the framework presented in Sections 2 and 3 as part of her dissertation efforts, by developing a tool that can be utilized to analyze C++ code when given information on the General and Specific classes, and the Related hi-

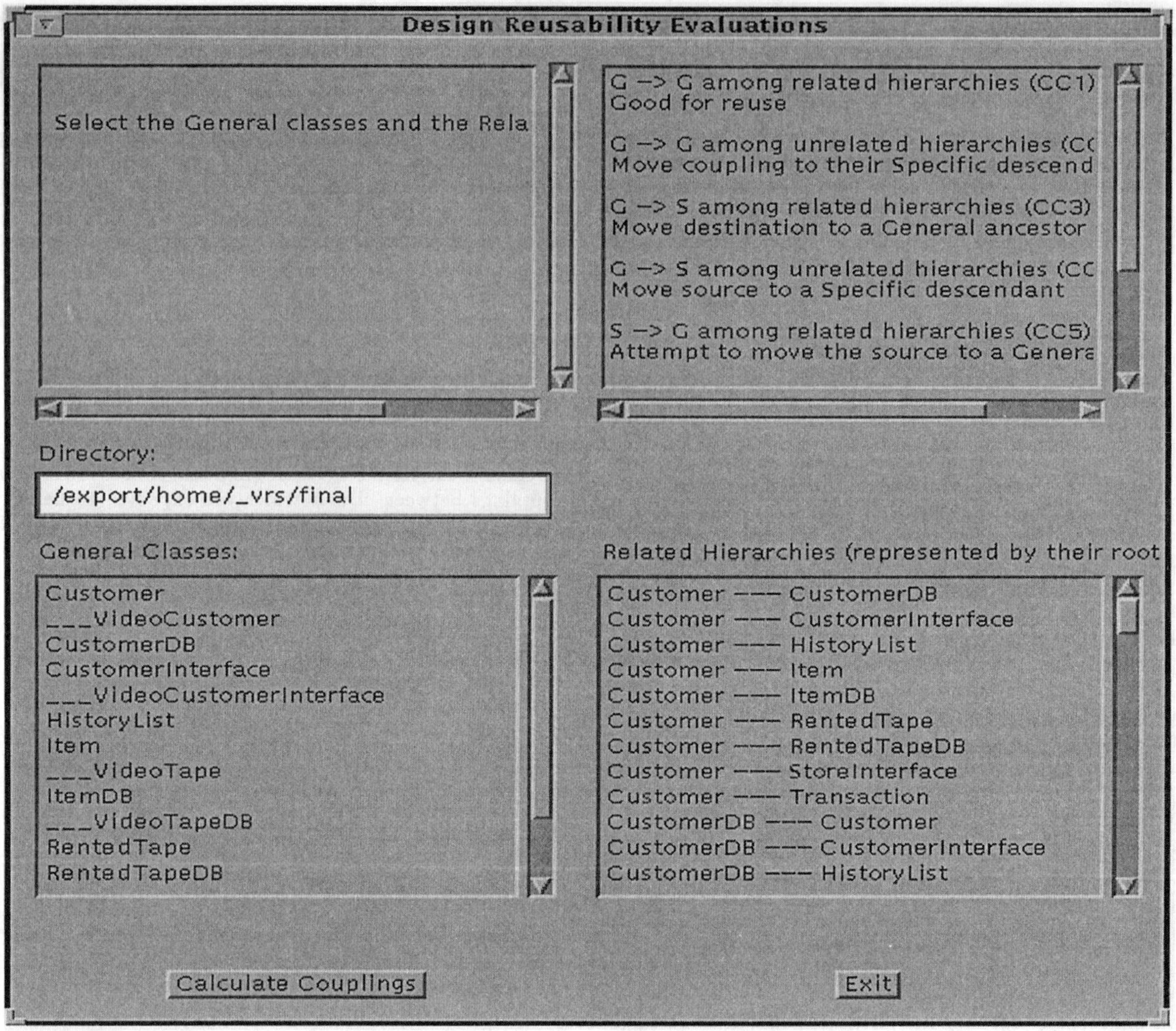


Figure 6. Design Reusability Evaluations (DRE).

erarchies. The undergraduate student, Kevin Jin, a senior, was responsible for designing and developing two applications that have significant overlap in spite of their domain differences. Each of these efforts contributes to the overall goal of providing empirical results and an automated framework to support the analyses of C++ code, which has been derived from object-oriented designs according to our reuse approach.

Specifically, we have developed the first prototype of a tool to calculate C++ couplings using our measurement framework, which we call Design Reusability Evaluations (DRE). DRE takes a directory containing C++ classes as input that is parsed to return the hierarchical list of classes and the list of all combinations of root classes as shown in Figure 6. Users can then select the classes which are to be characterized as General classes (all classes not chosen are assumed to be specific) and those hierarchies which are supposed to be Related. After the choices have been made and the "Calculate Coupling" button is clicked, the resulting metrics (CC1 through CC8) are displayed in the upper left window as shown in Figure 7. The upper right window identifies the actions for the various dependencies as specified in Section 3.2. The software engineer can then utilize the measurements to identify those portions of the code that need to be changed, or to rethink which classes should be General/Specific and which hierarchies should be Related. DRE can be used to analyze the reusability of completed C++ code, and is intended to be incorporated into either design or development environments. Its key purpose is to promote an iterative process that evolves design/code to a more reusable state.

Given this tool, it was then necessary to provide input for at least two applications, that while different, have the potential to share significant portions of both design and code. This was the responsibility of the undergraduate student, who was asked to design and develop a video rental system (VRS) and an auto service center system (ASCS). VRS maintains customer and video databases, keeps track of each transaction (borrow/return), and logs the tapes that have been rented. There are two interfaces to VRS: a Customer Interface, which lets customers browse and search the video tapes; and a Store Interface, which lets store atten-

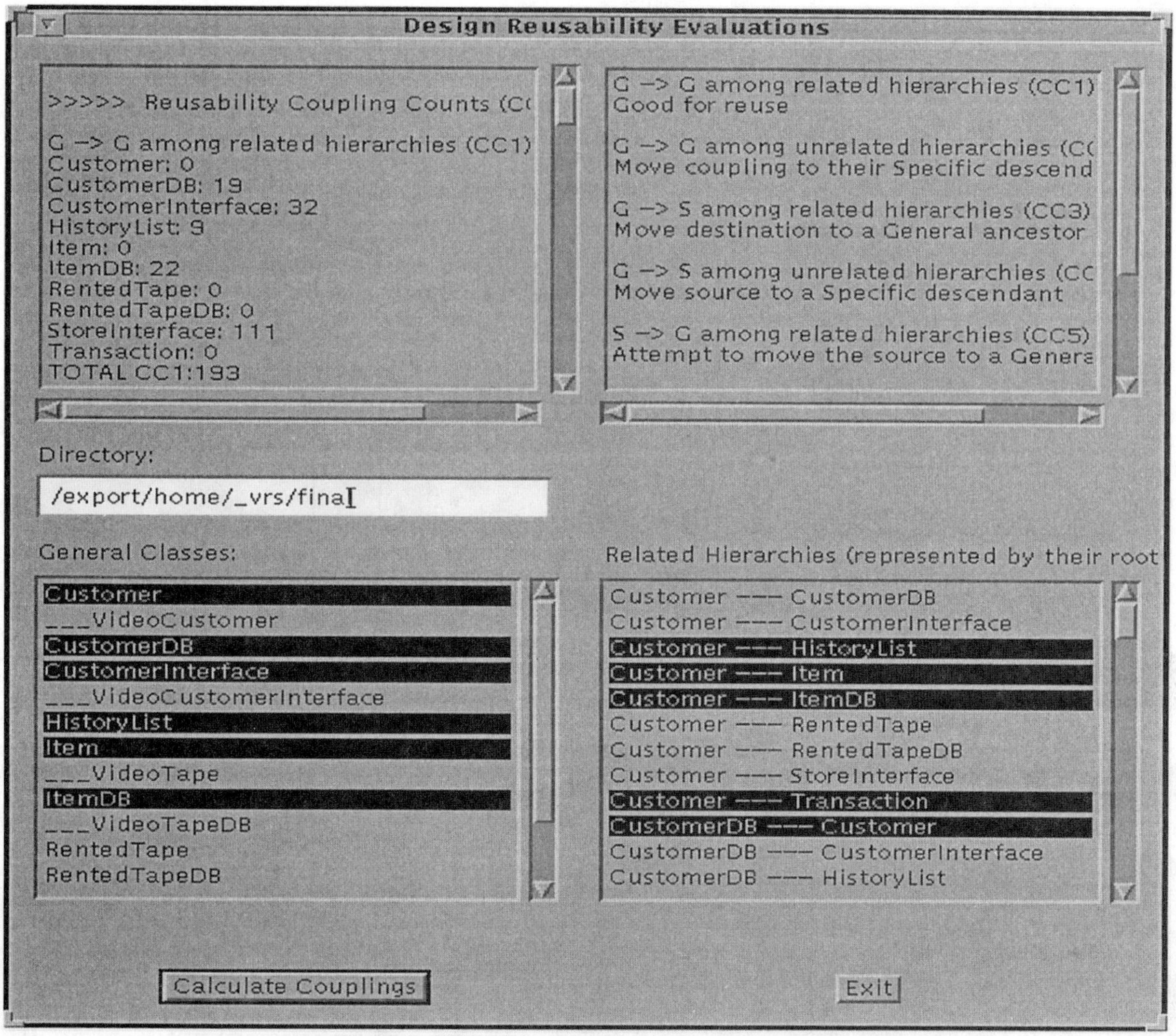


Figure 7. DRE: After the Couplings are Calculated.

dants manipulate tapes, manipulate customers' information, and process the borrowing/returning of tapes.

The undergrad was advised that we also had to build another application at a later time in the semester, ASCS, which is to be used to keep track of an auto parts inventory, customer information, and the services that are performed on the cars. While VRS and ASCS have many similarities, they also have some interesting differences. They both need a database of items, which can be either tapes or auto parts. Both types of items have names, categories, descriptions, number of available items, and suppliers. Video tapes have specific information such as running time and rating. Auto parts have specific information, such as the minimum number of items (before they need to reorder) and the price of each item. Similarities and differences also exist in the customer database. The auto service customer database needs to keep information on the car owned by each customer, such as the year and model. Both systems need to keep track of customers' account balances and the history of transactions. But the transaction history is very different. In ASCS, a customer who needs a certain part installed on their car, buys the item without needing to return it. Thus, when a customer buys an item, we need to increase his/her balance and log the transaction. In VRS, the customers borrow the tapes, so that in addition to increasing the balance and logging the transaction, we also need to keep track of the tapes being borrowed.

These applications were chosen because they are easily understood. The undergrad was able to define and interpret the requirements. This allowed us to concentrate on the concepts, since the contexts are well understood. Moreover, there are many similarities, so we can expect many reusable dependencies. During the design of VRS, the object-oriented CRC based approach was utilized. The characterizations of the General/Specific classes and the Related hierarchies were incorporated into the CRC approach. The design process of the undergrad was closely monitored and discussed in several walkthroughs.

During the design stage, the student first identified the major classes and determined their General/Specific char-

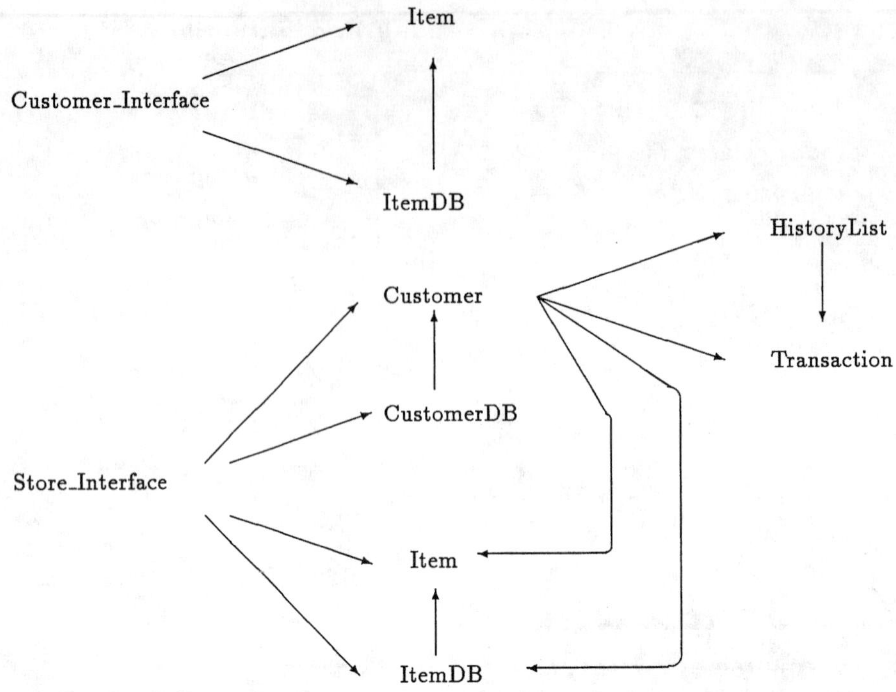


Figure 8. General Root Classes and Related Hierarchy Relationships of the Video Rental System.

| Type | Metric | I | II | III | IV | V | VI | VII |
|---|---|---|---|---|---|---|---|---|
| **Good** for Reuse | CC1 | 8 | 54 | 79 | 109 | 166 | 167 | 193 |
| **Bad** for Reuse | CC2 | 0 | 0 | 0 | 0 | 0 | 0 | 0 |
| | CC3 | 6 | 0 | 0 | 0 | 4 | 4 | 0 |
| | CC4 | 0 | 0 | 1 | 1 | 0 | 0 | 0 |
| Can Improve | CC5 | 0 | 19 | 28 | 39 | 94 | 92 | 75 |
| Reuse (if moved) | CC7 | 0 | 6 | 6 | 18 | 28 | 30 | 25 |
| No Impact | CC6 | 0 | 0 | 0 | 0 | 0 | 5 | 0 |
| on Reuse | CC8 | 0 | 0 | 11 | 11 | 21 | 22 | 26 |
| | # of lines | 410 | 1386 | 2088 | 2695 | 3784 | 3824 | 3867 |

Table 1. Reusability Measurements of VRS.

acterizations. He first identified all of the classes as General classes, except for those used to keep track of the rented tapes. These General classes are shown in Figure 8. This is reasonable, since these classes are needed by the auto service center. However, when he started to define the attributes, he realized that he could not include some of the attributes in the General classes, such as the running time and rating of video tapes. This resulted in the creation of subclasses of Item, ItemDB, Customer, CustomerInterface, and StoreInterface to support VRS initially, and ASCS subsequently.

After all of the attributes and classes were identified, the undergrad defined not only the methods, but also, for each method, the other methods that are required to realize the needed functionality. By defining these dependencies, the Related hierarchies could be identified. Even though this process is subjective, the student was able to define the classes which need to be reused together. We asked him to define hierarchy A to be related to hierarchy B if he expected the methods in A to use many methods in B and if both A and B will be needed in ASCS. The General root classes and the Related hierarchy relationships (the arrows) are also shown in Figure 8.

Couplings between the methods in the design were examined carefully and changed according to actions specified in Section 3.2. Even though we have clearly defined the General classes and the Related hierarchies and their purpose, many undesirable couplings occurred during both the design and the coding stages. In this paper, it is more interesting to show the results of the coding phase, because the design is relatively small. More complicated systems have many more dependencies which can be identified during the design phase and they can expect the same benefit in automating the measurements.

During our seven code walkthroughs, we utilized the DRE tool and discussed its results. We have included the results in Table 1 to illustrate the improvements gained by

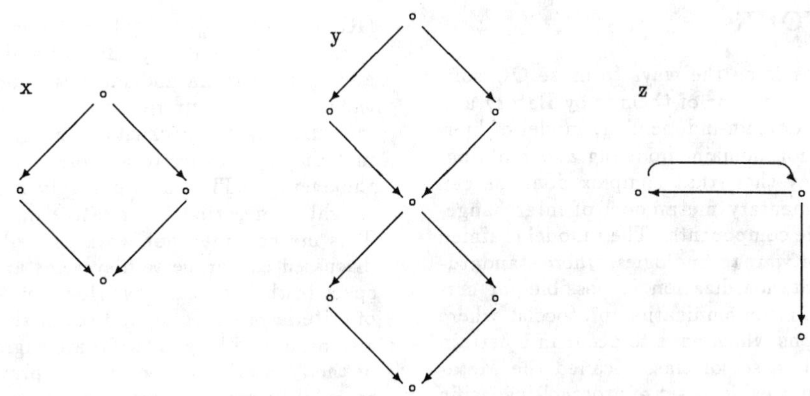


Figure 9. Incomparable Program Complexity [11]

using an automated framework. The reusable portion of the VRS system was then used in ASCS. The VRS code contains a total of 3867 lines, among which 2485 of them are reusable as is for ASCS. The number of lines are relatively small, because we use web browsers as our interface. VRS is written as Common Graphics Interface (CGI) code which responds to requests from any web browser. The number of lines reused are only provided for completeness; we believe that the value of reuse relies more on the number of good dependencies that are reused, as reflected in the CC1 count.

Because of the subjectivity aspect of this approach, it is necessary for the software engineers/designers to have a good understanding about:

- the application domain, and
- the types of systems that they expect to build in the future.

If software engineers continue to design in a vacuum, they will continue to produce code with minimal or no reuse. Our General/Specific classes and Related hierarchies are intended to provide a framework for software engineers to think about reuse at early and all stages of the design and development process. The resulting metrics of this framework can be used to provide automatic guidance during those time periods in between walkthroughs. Whenever a design walkthrough is conducted, the subjective characterizations of classes and hierarchies can then be reviewed and modified if necessary. These characterizations are very critical in the success of this approach, thus they should only be changed after a careful analysis of the overall system.

## 5 CONSIDERING METRICS THEORY

There is not yet an agreement on the set of properties which make some software more reusable than others. Poulin states that in general, most sets of reusability guidelines reflect the same properties as those promoted by good software engineering principles [20]. These good software engineering principles include low coupling. However, as we have seen in Sections 3.2 and 3.3, not all couplings are bad for reuse. Software designs are composed of the system's components and the interactions between those components. These interactions (or couplings) are valuable to the design, and many of them tie those reusable classes together to create a meaningful design.

In the context of software complexity, Fenton showed that the search for a general-purpose real-valued complexity measure is doomed to failure [11]. In dozens of proposed complexity measures, there is a minimum assumption that the empirical relation system for complexity of programs leads to at least an ordinal scale. An ordinal scale involves a ranking, from best to worst. But there is a problem with this, because some programs are "incomparable." In his paper, Fenton provides the example given in Figure 9 (which is Figure 1 in [11]). Most would agree that x is less complex than y. However, when people are asked which is more complex between x and z or y and z, they end up asking questions like "what is meant by complexity" before attempting to answer. From the measurement theory perspective, it is good enough if most programmers agree on the complexity order of x, y and z; but there is no such agreement in the order of their complexity.

Software reusability metrics have the same problems. We cannot try to put an empirical value on a poorly understood attribute [20]. Software engineers working on different domains will have different opinions on the reusability of a component. Some components are more reusable in one domain and less reusable in others, so they are incomparable with respect to reusability. This means that we should stop searching for a general reusability metric, and instead look for the specific properties or aspects of reuse. This is one goal of our work as presented in this paper.

In his recent book, Fenton states that measurements of internal software attributes can be useful when restricted to locally specified, commonly accepted definitions of the underlying terms [12]. We believe that the metrics defined in this paper are restricted to specific properties of object-oriented software. They are not only specific to couplings, but they are also separated by the kinds of couplings with respect to the reusability of a set of related hierarchies. It is not correct to combine the measurements of those couplings which are good for reuse and those which are bad for reuse. We also believe that they are based on a commonly accepted understanding of reusability: a set of related components in a system is more reusable if it has less dependencies to other parts of the system.

## 6 RELATED WORK

There are several proposals on the ways to make OO software systems more reusable. One of them is by Batory and O'Malley [1] which is a domain-independent model of hierarchical systems, based on domain modeling and building-block technologies. They show that complex domains can be expressed by an elementary metamodel of interchangeable and plug-compatible components. Their model is aimed specifically at mature software technologies, where standardization makes sense. Standardization is possible for certain domains, such as in communication protocols, where there is a set of operations which have to occur in a certain order. Strayer has built a set of classes called the Meta-Transport Library which provides a set of protocol-inspecific base classes for transport layer protocols [22]. Specific transport layer protocols can be built through derivations from these classes.

On the other hand, our techniques can assist the design and development process of reusable systems which do not yet have a standard set of operations. Extensive domain analysis tends to be expensive and not always possible. Moreover, our measurement techniques are aimed at organizations which have some ideas on what kinds of systems they would like to build in the future. Software companies do not have to make their software reusable for any system in the domain, but they only have to make their software designs be reusable in anticipated future systems in their organizations.

Once there is a reusable design, we create other specific systems by extending the base classes. Our form for extending these classes is by inheritance. Another way to extend the behavior of a class hierarchy is by combining the base hierarchy with one or more extension hierarchies [19]. The extension hierarchies can extend or overwrite the behavior of the existing classes, so that the existing classes do not have to be changed. However, overwriting the behavior of existing classes has the same impact as changing those existing classes, since it is possible that the behaviors of the combined hierarchies are incompatible. The combined hierarchies will need to be thoroughly re-tested. They define conditions that the hierarchies have to be non-conflicting, non-interfering, and semantically compatible. The definition of semantic compatibility is still an area of research. We are in full agreement with the authors that in large systems, extending classes by inheritance becomes unmanageable. However, if the original classes are designed to support reusability, extension by subclassing has the potential to be very manageable.

In the area of reusability measurements, there are various empirical and qualitative methods which have been proposed [20]. Prieto-Diaz and Freeman identify five reusability metrics: size (favors small module size), structure (favors simple structure, low coupling, and low complexity), good documentation (subjective rating), programming language (favors same language), and reuse experience (in the domain and the programming language) [21]. We agree with the last three. The first two are arguable. Smaller size and less complex code are easier to understand, which makes them easier to reuse. But they do not produce high savings. The best way to approach this comprehensibility problem is by making the large components more understandable by having well-defined interfaces and good documentation.

Another technique, which is also reviewed in [20], is developed by the Reuse Based on Object-Oriented Techniques (REBOOT) project. They define four reusability factors (portability, flexibility, understandability and confidence) and many criteria and metrics under each factor. Some of the metrics are empirical and some are qualitative which are measured using checklists. They define reusability by normalizing all metrics to a value between 0 and 1 and taking the average. They also multiply each metric value with its weight to describe the relative importance of each metric. This method may not work as well for reusability since as discussed earlier, certain systems are incomparable with respect to their reusability. However, their comprehensive list of criteria provides a good set of those properties which are also promoted by good software engineering principles. Each of their criteria can be used to provide an idea of software reusability with respect to that specific property, but they probably should not be combined into a general reusability metric.

## 7 CONCLUSIONS & AN ONGOING EFFORT

We have presented a framework for reusability measurements which facilitates large-scale OO design reuse. The following summarizes the contributions of this measurement framework:

1. It provides an effective and subjective method to distinguish between what is expected to be reused and what is not. This is accomplished by the differentiation between General and Specific classes as presented in Section 2.2.

2. It provides an effective and subjective method to group related components into reusable portions. This is accomplished by the differentiation between related and unrelated class hierarchies as presented in Section 2.3.

3. It presents specific metrics based on the above concepts, which can work at any level of design detail. This is achieved by the mathematical formulas for $CC_i$ in Section 3.3, which are based on the types of couplings and refinement actions presented in Sections 3.1 and 3.2. This is demonstrated in Section 4 in our empirical study via the design reusability evaluations tool.

The first two items listed above are the important components of a software design, and they are to be determined subjectively by the software designer. The last item is the metrics that objectively measure the couplings of design components; couplings are the tangible representation of a design product, thus they can be measured objectively. The last item includes a set of suggestive actions to automatically advise software designers/developers on the ways to improve their products' reusability, and follows through with an actual tool that evaluates reuse potential in C++ code according to our framework.

Our approach relies heavily on subjective decisions and it requires the software designers to have a good understanding about the application domain and the types of systems that they expect to build in the future. When changes are made to the subjective characteristics of an OO design, the objective measures are recalculated to provide the software designer with an evolving and incremental perspective on those portions of the OO design that have the most potential to be reused. This was illustrated in Section 4 with our experimental work on the reuse between video rental and auto service center systems (see Figures 6 and 7 and Table 1 again). Our coupling measurements also conform with the results and recommendations of research in metrics theory, which is described in Section 5.

We are working on integrating this reusability evaluation framework in the Active Design and Analysis Modeling (ADAM) environment [6, 8, 14, 18]. ADAM supports a language-independent design process, where software designs can be entered and code can be generated in various languages (Ada 83, Ada 95, C++, Ontos C++ and Eiffel). We are inserting this reusability evaluation technique into ADAM to support the subjective aspects of our framework that can then be utilized to automatically warn the software designer whenever a non-reusable coupling is introduced and provide suggestions on the way to eliminate the coupling and/or move it to add value to the reusable design.

## References


[1] D. Batory and S. O'Malley, "The Design and Implementation of Hierarchical Software Systems with Reusable Components," *ACM Transactions on Software Engineering and Methodology*, Vol. 1, No. 4, October 1992, pp.355-398.

[2] T. Biggerstaff and A. Perlis, editors, *Software Reusability*, ACM Press, New York, NY, 1989, volume I, pp. xv-xxv.

[3] L. Briand, S. Morasca, and V. Basili, "Defining and Validating High-Level Design Metrics," University of Maryland, Technical Report number CS-TR-3301.

[4] D. Card and R. Glass, *Measuring Software Design Quality*, Prentice-Hall, Englewood Cliffs, NJ, 1990.

[5] S. Chidamber and C. Kemerer, "A Metrics Suite for Object Oriented Design," *IEEE Transactions on Software Engineering*, June 1994, pp. 476-493.

[6] S. Demurjian, T. Daggett, T.C. Ting, and M.-Y. Hu, "URBS Enforcement Mechanisms for Object-Oriented Systems and Applications," in *Database Security, IX: Status and Prospects*, D. Spooner, S. Demurjian, and J. Dobson (eds.), Chapman Hall, 1995.

[7] S. Demurjian and T.C. Ting, "The Factors that Influence Apropos Security Approaches for the Object-Oriented Paradigm," *Workshops in Computing*, Springer-Verlag, 1994.

[8] H. Ellis and S. Demurjian, "Object-Oriented Design and Analyses for Advanced Application Development - Progress Towards a New Frontier," *Proceedings of the 21st Annual ACM Computer Science Conference*, February 1993.

[9] W. Griswold, "Program Restructuring as an Aid to Software Maintenance," Department of Computer Science and Engineering, University of Washington, Technical Report number 91-08-04, August 1991.

[10] W. Griswold and D. Notkin, "Automated Assistance for Program Restructuring," Department of Computer Science and Engineering, University of Washington, Technical Report number 90-08-05, August 1990.

[11] N. Fenton, "Software Measurement: A Necessary Scientific Basis," *IEEE Transaction on Software Engineering*, Vol. 20, No.3, March 1994, pp. 199-206.

[12] N. Fenton and S. Pfleeger, *Software Metrics - A Rigorous & Practical Approach*, PWS Publishing Company, 1997.

[13] M.-Y. Hu, S. Demurjian, and T.C. Ting, "User-Role Based Security Profiles for an Object-Oriented Design Model," in *Database Security, VI: Status and Prospects*, C. Landwehr and B. Thuraisingham (eds.), North-Holland, 1993.

[14] M.-Y. Hu, S. Demurjian, and T.C. Ting, "Unifying Structural and Security Modeling and Analyses in the ADAM Object-Oriented Design Environment," in *Database Security, VIII: Status and Prospects*, J. Biskup, C. Landwehr, and M. Morgenstern (eds.), Elsevier Science, 1994.

[15] R. Johnson and W. Opdyke, "Refactoring and Aggregation," *Object Technologies for Advanced Software*, November 1993, volume 742, pp. 264-278.

[16] R. Johnson and B. Foote, "Designing Reusable Classes," *Journal of Object-Oriented Programming*, June/July 1988.

[17] R. Johnson and V. Russo, "Reusing Object-Oriented Designs," University of Illinois, Technical Report number UIUCDCS 91-1696, May 1991.

[18] D. Needham, S. Demurjian, K. El Guemhioui, T. Peters, P. Zemani, M. McMahon, and H. Ellis, "ADAM: A Language-Independent, Object-Oriented, Design Environment for Modeling Inheritance and Relationship Variants in Ada 95, C++, and Eiffel," *Proceedings of 1996 TriAda Conference*, Philadelphia, PA, December 1996.

[19] H. Ossher and W. Harrison, "Combination of Inheritance Hierarchies," *OOPSLA 1992 Conference Proceedings*, pp. 25-40.

[20] J. Poulin, *Measuring Software Reuse - Principles, Practices and Economic Models*, Addison-Wesley, 1997.

[21] R. Prieto-Diaz and P. Freeman, "Classifying Software for Reusability," *IEEE Software*, Vol. 4, No. 1, January 1987, pp. 6-16.

[22] T. Strayer, "A Class-Chest for Deriving Transport Protocols," *Proceedings of the 21st Local Computer Networks Conference*, Minneapolis, MN, October 13-16, 1996.

# Reuse of Algorithms:
# Still a Challenge to Object-Oriented Programming

Karsten Weihe
Universität Konstanz, Fak. Mathematik und Informatik
Fach D188, D-78457 Konstanz, Germany
karsten.weihe@uni-konstanz.de

## Abstract

This paper is about reusable, efficient implementations of complex algorithms and their integration into software packages. It seems that this problem is not yet well understood, and that it is not at all clear how object-oriented and other approaches may contribute to a solution. We analyze the problem and try to reduce it to a few key design goals. Moreover, we discuss various existing approaches in light of these goals, and we briefly report experiences with experimental case studies, in which these goals were rigorously addressed.

## 1 Introduction

Many sophisticated algorithms for solving various problems have been proposed in the literature. These include, for example, algorithms for numerical computations, for graph and network problems, for computer graphics, and for symbolic computations.

Implementing such an algorithm is time consuming and prone to error and requires expert knowledge in algorithmics. Since algorithmic problems appear quite frequently, libraries of algorithms for solving various problems might be useful. However, to be widely usable, the components of such a library must meet two requirements: efficiency and flexible adaptability.

Efficiency must in no way be disregarded, because algorithmic software is often time-critical. For example, efficient algorithms are indispensable for real-time programming. In the other extreme, algorithmic software is often applied to large-scale problems, where a single run of an algorithm may take hours, days, or weeks (even when executed massively in parallel). In engineering and operations research, the run time of the algorithmic software is sometimes crucial for the time of the whole developmental or decision process. Many algorithmic problems cannot be solved exactly, for example, numerical and geometric problems on real numbers and $\mathcal{NP}$-hard discrete problems. If such an algorithm is critical for a development or decision process, which is usually subject to strict deadlines, a loss of efficiency results inevitably in a loss of accuracy. Lack of algorithmic efficiency also has an impact on user interfaces: often the response time is dominated by complex graphical algorithms. Hence, efficiency of algorithms is necessary to overcome the "temporal usability problem [16]."

On the other hand, flexible adaptability is necessary to customize the implementation of an algorithm to various specific applications. It is the author's subjective impression that this problem is not yet well understood and often underestimated. The following design goals are an attempt to summarize the properties that make implementations of algorithms truly reusable.


OOPSLA '97 10/97 GA, USA


## Key design goals:

1. An algorithm should be implemented such that it can be easily adapted to existing and application-specific realizations of the underlying abstract data types without sacrificing efficiency.

2. The interfaces of data structures to algorithms should be designed such that a small set of generic or polymorphic classes makes the implementation of such interfaces easy, convenient, and straightforward.

3. An algorithm should be implemented such that its *algorithmic functionality* is flexibly adaptable.

4. An algorithm should be implemented such that it is possible to inspect all potentially relevant details during its execution.

### 1.1 Overview

Each of the following sections is devoted to one of these goals. All goals are explained and discussed in detail. This includes a discussion of various existing design methodologies that may be relevant for the respective goal. In that, the focus is on object-oriented methodologies. Each section is concluded by a discussion of the experiences that we gained from practical case studies in C++. Ref. [23] and the technical reports [21, 22, 30] describe selected details of the implementations.

We focus on a specific area, graph algorithms, because a discussion that covers various algorithmic domains and is still sufficiently concrete would exceed the limits of this paper. However, analogous arguments apply to other algorithmic areas as well.

A few concrete examples presented in the following sections are taken from projects in which the author of this paper has been involved during the last years [13, 20, 29, 31]. A certain number of further examples are taken from the *L*ibrary of *E*fficient *D*ata types and *A*lgorithms (*LEDA* [25, 27]), which is written in C++. Additional examples are taken from the *S*tandard *T*emplate *L*ibrary (*STL* [28]), which greatly influenced the prospective definition of the C++ standard library and the design of many other libraries. We also refer the reader to the libraries CGAL [6], ffGraph [9], Karla [18], and the AAI base class library [1].

We focus on LEDA to some extent, because LEDA matches the topic of this paper quite well: it is especially devoted to graph algorithms, and maximum efficiency and ease of use were the primary design goals (and have essentially been achieved). The design of LEDA uses various object-oriented and generic features of C++ and might be representative for many other packages. LEDA is mature and used by many groups both in academics and in the software industry. It is applied in various domains, and in some areas it has become a de-facto standard.

## 1.2 Further Reading

Several books (*e.g.* [5, 14, 33]) present implementations of basic and advanced algorithms in object-oriented and hybrid programming languages, most of them in C++. However, only a few publications address the specific design problems inherent in algorithmic software. Barton and Nackman [3] demonstrate how the object-oriented and generic features of C++ may be used to achieve a better structure for algorithmic code in scientific and engineering computing. Flamig [10] implements algorithms as classes to let them act like input streams (which he calls *algorithmic generators*). Soukop [35] incorporates a few advanced algorithmic examples in his general design discussions (notably section 2.6).

In a concrete case study in Object Pascal (*maximum-flow problem* [2]), Gallo and Scutella [11] apply the *strategy* pattern [12] to keep subalgorithms interchangeable.

Holland [15] implements algorithms as frameworks, which can be adapted to a specific application by subclassing. VanHilst and Notkin [37] re-implement this design using C++ templates.

Several articles discuss extensions to existing mainstream languages, which are intended to support design and implementation of efficient, reusable library components. For example, Biggerstaff [4] discusses the problem to design efficient, reusable libraries such that the number of components remains manageable. He argues that the features of "conventional, mainstream programming languages" are not sufficient for that, and he surveys and discusses software development systems which add extra-linguistic expressibility to the language.

Yu and Zhuang [39] concentrate on efficient, reusable algorithms and propose an extension to C++ (named *kinds*). In Yu and Zhuang's own words, this extension is intended to "realize algorithmic abstraction" and to close the "abstraction gap between algorithms and procedures."

Further publications are concerned with implementations of graph algorithms in functional languages [8, 19, 24].

We will discuss selected approaches from the literature in greater detail in the relevant sections. Moreover, we will discuss the relevance of various design patterns [12] to the individual goals. Here we are interested in the general ideas of these patterns, not in the concrete realization of the interplay between the collaborators. For example, this realization may be based on inheritance as in [12], but also on generic features.

# 2 Adaptation to Data Structures

**Goal 1**

An algorithm should be implemented such that it can be easily adapted to existing and application-specific realizations of the underlying abstract data types without sacrificing efficiency.

The discussion will be grouped into two variations of this goal: *different implementations and variations of one abstract type* and *different implementations of the item parameters.*

In the following, the term *abstract type* refers to general concepts such as *directed* or *undirected* graphs. For instance, figures 1(a) and 1(d)–(e) are examples of the abstract type *undirected graph,* and figures 1(b)–(c) of the abstract type *directed graph.* More specifically, figures 1(c)–(e) show examples of specializations of these abstract types: symmetric directed graph, plane graph (a graph is *plane* if it can be drawn such that no two edges cross each other), and grid graph. In turn, grid graphs are a specialization of the specialized abstract type *plane graph.*

## 2.1 Different Implementations and Variations of One Abstract Type

### Different implementations

Typically, an abstract data type such as a directed graph may be implemented in many different ways. Goal 1 means that an implementation of an algorithm should be independent of this concrete implementation.

On one hand, it is crucial for time-critical applications that an algorithm can be adapted to data structures which are tuned for efficiency. This tuning usually varies from application to application, and thus requires a high degree of flexibility. On the other hand, an implementation of an algorithm can be integrated into existing software only if it can be adapted to the data structures on which this software is built. These data structures might have been developed a long time ago and designed to meet absolutely different, non-algorithmic, needs. Clearly, in such a case, the algorithm cannot achieve its best possible run time, because the data structures have not been designed for that. However, the algorithm's interface should be flexible enough so that—within the bounds of possibility—a reasonable degree of efficiency can be achieved.

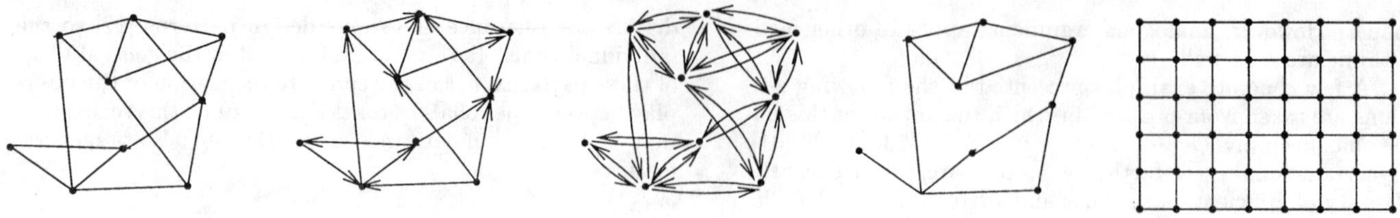

(a) (b) (c) (d) (e)

Figure 1: (a) an undirected graph, that is, edges are not oriented; (b) a directed graph constructed from (a) by assigning arbitrary orientations; (c) the directed graph constructed from (a) by substituting a pair of mutually opposing directed edges for each undirected edge; (d) a plane undirected graph, embedded without crossings; (e) a grid graph.

### Different abstract types

Moreover, many graph algorithms apply to a broad range of abstract graph types. For example, for many algorithms, it does not matter whether the graph is directed or undirected. Likewise, the same algorithm may apply to *hypergraphs* (*i.e.* an edge may connect more than two nodes) and other, similar variations. Goal 1 also means that an implementation of such an algorithm should work with every abstract graph type to which the algorithm applies "in theory."

### Alternatives

There are two alternatives to goal 1: either each algorithm is implemented on its own, specific interface, and the data is converted back and forth for each call of an algorithm; or a standard is defined on which the implementations of all algorithms are based.

*Alternative* I (*conversions*): very often, the first alternative is simply infeasible in algorithmic software design, because the amount of data to be converted is too large. This problem is aggravated by the fact that algorithms are usually not (and should not be) implemented monolithically, but composed of other, more basic algorithms, which are, in turn, composed of even more basic algorithms, and so on. Such a decomposition would result in a large number of expensive conversions. Quite often, the run times of the most basic algorithms are sublinear in the size of the data structures (at least in an empirical sense). In this case, the run time is not even proportional to the theoretical efficiency.[1]

*Alternative* II (*standardized abstractions*): Many existing libraries for graph algorithms (incl. LEDA) adopt the second alternative, which is to define a class for graphs and to implement all algorithms on top of this interface. However, experience suggests that the following undesired consequence might inevitably occur when a library is actually used in real applications in different fields: from release to release, the class is equipped with more and more functionality to fulfill the users' demands; the implementation thus becomes less and less efficient, but without the ideal state ever being reached.

It is essential to note that this missing functionality is not only a problem of "exotic" applications, which means that all "mainstream" applications would be satisfied by a well-chosen subset. In fact, even the requirements imposed by mainstream applications differ in many details.

For example, many algorithms require an access method that gets two nodes as arguments and returns the edge connecting these nodes. In principle, this access can be realized efficiently in two ways: either as a matrix whose columns and rows are nodes and whose entries are edges, or as an associative array with pairs of nodes as keys and edges as the associated units of information. However, the overhead in space or run time caused by such a solution may not be acceptable for an algorithm that does *not* require this particular functionality.

The potential present and future variations might not be predictable. Hence, a common generalization of all variations is not possible (even if it were possible, it might not be efficient). In summary, all of these variations should be realized by different classes with different interfaces.

**Experience 1**

The alternatives to goal 1 do not suffice to achieve a high degree of flexibility without sacrificing efficiency.

## 2.2 Different Implementations of the Item Parameters

A graph may be viewed as a composition of containers. For example, a directed graph class that is intended for various purposes often consists of a container of nodes, a container of edges, and for each node, a container of references to the edges leaving this node. Further containers may be included, for instance, for each node, a container of references to all edges entering this node.

The items of a container may be assigned *item parameters*. For example, the nodes of a graph are usually assigned parameters such as names, flags, and coordinates, and likewise, the edges are assigned parameters such as lengths, costs, and capacities. Goal 1 states that the concrete organization of these item parameters shall be hidden from each algorithm.

[1] For example, effects like these occurred in a project in which the author of this paper was involved a few years ago and which used conversions to a common format to integrate various algorithms for scheduling problems into one package [20].

From an abstract viewpoint, the values of all item parameters for all items form a table: there is a row for each item and a column for each parameter, and the value of a parameter for an item is the entry at the table slot specified by this row and this column. Many algorithms insert and remove items, which means that the set of rows is usually dynamic.

## Dynamic column set

It is essential to note that the set of columns should also be dynamic to some extent. For example, many algorithms rely on auxiliary parameters, which are meaningless for all other parts of the program. A concrete example is the "*seen*" label of nodes inside an algorithm that constructs a path from some node $s$ to some node $t$ using a depth-first or breadth-first search: $s$ and $t$ are the input, the path is the output, and the label is internally used to ensure that no subgraph is searched more than once.

In some cases, it may be preferable to instantiate such an auxiliary parameter only temporarily, immediately before invoking the algorithm, and to drop the parameter after termination of the algorithm. For the sake of argument, suppose that a program applies algorithms $A_1, \ldots, A_k$ one after another to the same graph and each algorithm $A_i$ requires a different set of auxiliary parameters. If the set of node and edge parameters is organized statically (*i.e.* fixed once and for all at compile time), we have to maintain the union of these parameter sets throughout the program, which causes a waste of space and additional run-time overhead. The same effect occurs when $A_1, \ldots, A_k$ are not called after each other, but are made exchangeable using the *strategy* pattern [12]: here only one of $A_1, \ldots, A_k$ is invoked, and the algorithm $A_i$ to be invoked is chosen only at run time. Hence, if all node and edge parameters are static, all parameters of all algorithms must be unnecessarily maintained.

## Non-materialized parameters

Even more, in some applications, it might not even be reasonable to store certain node and edge parameters in any way. For example, consider the case that the nodes of a graph are points in the plane and the length of an edge is the normal (*i.e. Euclidean*) distance of its nodes. The number of edges is potentially quadratic. Hence, it may be preferable not to store the lengths of the edges explicitly, but to compute the length of an edge from the node coordinates when needed.

## Data organization

The abstract view of item parameters as a table suggests two ways of organizing all data: row-wise and column-wise.

**Row-wise organization.** in principle, this means that every item is attached a tuple which comprises all item parameters. This organization is supported by many graph libraries.

For example, in LEDA [25] and in the AAI base class library [1], certain node and edge types are generic.[2] Hence, a static set of node and edge parameters can be realized by instantiating the node and the edge type with records which comprise all item parameters.

In contrast, the graph class in the ffGraph library [9] provides a means of adding and removing node and edge parameters (called *labels*) at run time. Each parameter gets a unique ID. Roughly speaking, each node (resp. edge) maintains an associative array of parameters, and the set of IDs in this associative array is the same for all nodes. To allow parameters of different types, each parameter must be a subclass of a prescribed base class for node (edge) labels. This row-wise approach is fully dynamic, however, at the cost of efficiency and type safety.

In addition to the generic features mentioned above, the AAI graph also supports user-defined extensions of the node and edge types: the node and the edge type are designed to serve as base classes, and the graph class only handles pointers and references to nodes and edges. Thus, it is possible to create graphs which handle extended node and edge classes. In particular, this allows the integration of a user-defined row-wise implementation of node and edge parameters.

**Column-wise organization.** For each item parameter, an associative array is instantiated, which contains the values of this parameter for all items. Each item has a unique ID, which can be used to access its value in this array. Instantiating a new item parameter at run time amounts to instantiating a new array. In contrast to the row-wise case, this concept is dynamic *and* fully type-safe.

For example, the LEDA graph class comes with so-called *node* and *edge arrays*. A node or edge array is an associative array with a static index set, which is the set of nodes or edges at the moment when the array is instantiated. Thus, LEDA allows an arbitrary mixture of a row-wise and a column-wise organization.

However, a normal array or an associative array with a static index set becomes invalid once items are inserted or removed. Hence, such an array is of limited use. On the other hand, an associative array with a dynamic index set might increase the run time significantly, even by more than a constant factor. Moreover, when items are inserted or removed, the corresponding associative arrays should be updated automatically, which requires an expensive solution based on the *observer* pattern [12].

## Discussion

In summary, neither a row-wise nor a column-wise organization (nor any other puristic organization) is sufficient for all applications. Hence, to achieve goal 1, an implementation of an algorithm must be able to cope with different ways of organizing the item parameters in the underlying containers.

Very often, a mixed solution may be suitable, in which the records attached to items hold the permanent data, and for temporary data, additional arrays are instantiated when needed. However, whether a certain parameter is permanent or temporary depends on the context, and hence an algorithm cannot assume a specific constellation. Moreover, even when such a mixed solution is applied, the question of non-materialized data remains open.

It seems that the problem of organizing the item parameters in a container is often underestimated or even overlooked. For example, the design of the STL does not address this problem at all [28]. The items of an STL-style container are accessed through *iterators* [12]. However, the

[2] To be precise, certain graph classes in LEDA are generic, and the generic type parameters are the information types of nodes and edges.

syntactic requirements for iterator classes in STL contain only one method for accessing an item's data (the C++ dereferencing operator, `operator*`).

Obviously, the design of the STL only considers containers such that each item is the (only) item parameter itself. In fact, all algorithms in STL assume this scenario. Hence, if there is more than one item parameter, the STL algorithms are not easily applicable (see the example below; STL-function `replace`).

As mentioned above, a typical graph algorithm accesses several node and edge parameters, which may be permanent or temporary. Hence, the problem of organizing the item parameters is addressed by designers of graph libraries. We have analyzed some of the solutions in the above discussion of row-wise and column-wise schemes.

The solutions adopted for LEDA are certainly the most efficient implementations of row-wise and column-wise data organization. This allows one to choose the most efficient intermixed solution for a specific application. Hence, to achieve goal 1, an implementation of an algorithm must be able to cope with both approaches and with mixed solutions.

However, all graph algorithms in LEDA assume that the node and edge parameters are organized column-wise, although this is often not the method of choice. The fact that the organization of node and edge parameters is hard-wired in these algorithms shows that data abstraction has still not been achieved. However, it is not surprising that a column-wise organization is preferred over a row-wise one: C++ does not provide any feature for renaming the members of a record. Therefore, in each algorithm, the names of all accessed parameters had to be hard-wired, when a row-wise organization was adopted. This is impractical because of potential name conflicts.

### Experience 2

The concrete organization of the item parameters may be completely hidden from the algorithm by *data accessors* without significant loss of efficiency.

We introduced the concept of *data accessors* in [23]. Roughly speaking, a data accessor is a class that is responsible for the access to a single item parameter. The type of the item parameter is a type tag `vtype` of the data accessor.

A data accessor class provides one or more methods named `get`, which gets a handle or iterator type for items as an argument and returns the parameter value for the item identified by the argument. The method `get` is overloaded for every relevant handle and iterator type. More specifically, if `It_1`...`It_n` are the relevant iterator classes, the data accessor class must conform[3] to the following C++ class definition:

```
class AnyDataAccessor
  {
  public:
    typedef ... vtype;
    vtype get (It_1) const;
    ...
    vtype get (It_n) const;
  };
```

Since `get` is overloaded, an algorithm only needs one data accessor for each item parameter, no matter how complicated the underlying graph data structure is. The concrete examples below will demonstrate that `get` is usually not overloaded "by hand," but by genericity.

We distinguish between *read* and *read/write* accessors. A *read/write* accessor provides an additional method `set` for each relevant handle and iterator type `It`:

```
void set (It, vtype);
```

This method overwrites the current parameter value by the value of the second argument.

## Example

This is a simplified version of the running example in [23]. Consider the STL-function `replace` [28]. This function runs over a linear sequence of items of the template type `T` and replaces all occurrences of the value `old_value` by `new_value`. The linear sequence is given by two iterators, `first` and `sentinel`. Iterator `first` identifies the beginning of the sequence, and `sentinel` is a past-the-end marker (*e.g.* the Null value if the sequence is a linked list and the iterator is a mere pointer).

```
template <class It, class T>
void replace
       (It first, It sentinel,
        T old_value, T new_value)

  {
    for (It it=first; it!=sentinel; ++it)
       if ( *it==old_value )
          *it = new_value;
  }
```

For instance, this function `replace` is applicable if we have a sequence `salaries` of STL-type `list<int>`, which contains the salaries of all employees, and we want to replace every occurrence of a $1,000 salary by $2,000:

```
replace (salaries.first(),
         salaries.last(),
         1000, 2000);
```

[3] For conformance, we make no distinction as to whether the arguments and the return value of a method are values or constant references. In the following code fragments, we will generally disregard this difference.

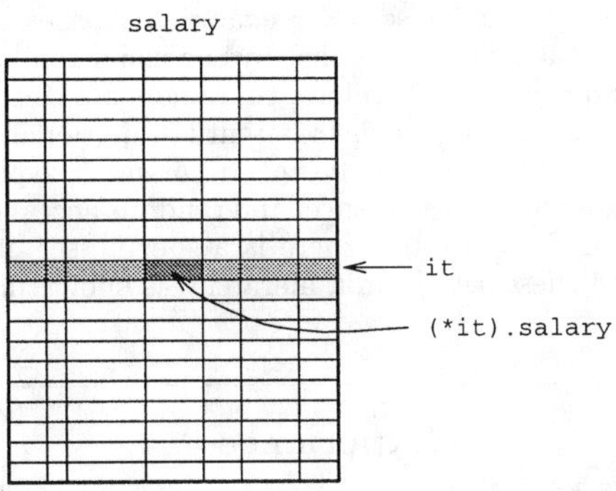


Figure 2: the scenario in the STL version of replace. A reference to the grey row is returned by the method operator* of the iterator. The row must exist as a materialized object of a record type.

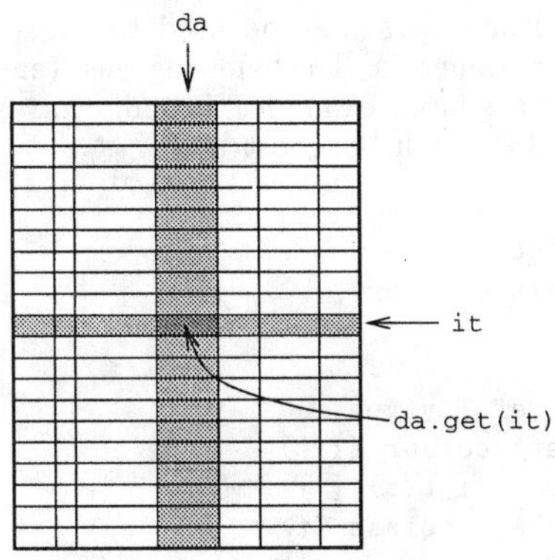


Figure 3: the modified scenario when data accessors are used. The iterator accesses the grey row, and the data accessor, the grey column. The individual columns may be organized arbitrarily (not necessarily materialized).

However, now assume that we have a struct type `Employee`, which contains an employee's salary as a member `salary`, and we want to perform the same update of salaries on a `list<Employee>`. The `operator*` of a list iterator returns the whole struct (see figure 2). To apply the above implementation of `replace`, `It` must be an adapter [12] for iterators, which overwrites `operator*` to drop all parameters but one. However, this is inconvenient when implementing algorithms which access more than one item parameter, because usually, what one wants is to access *all* parameters of an item through *one* iterator. If this is not possible, an algorithm must handle one iterator for each item parameter, which induces consistency problems.

A revised version of `replace`, which relies on a data accessor `DA` for accessing the salary, is flexible enough. We use the type tag `vtype` to drop the template parameter `T`.

```
template <class It, class Da>
void replace
      (It first, It sentinel, DA da,
       typename DA::vtype old_value,
       typename DA::vtype new_value)
  {
    for (It it=first; it!=sentinel; ++it)
      if ( da.get(it)==old_value )
         da.set (it, new_value);
  }
```

Figures 2 and 3 illustrate the difference.

The following class template `MemberAccessor` solves our exemplary problem. The type of the member `salary` appears as template argument `T`, the struct type `Employee` as template argument `Str`, and the concrete member `salary` as an argument of the constructor (namely as a pointer-to-member). Hence, this template covers all scenarios in which all relevant iterator types are STL-compliant, `operator*` returns a (reference to a) struct type, and the item parameter is a member of this struct type.

```
template <class Str, class T>
class MemberAccessor
  {
  public:
    typedef T vtype;
    MemberAccessor (T Str::*ptr)
      : i_ptr(ptr) { }
    template <class It>
      vtype get (It it) const
        { return (*it).*i_ptr; }
    template <class It>
      void set (It it, vtype value)
        { (*it).*i_ptr = value; }
  private:
    T Str::*i_ptr;
  };
```

Using this class template, we can update all salaries as follows:

```
MemberAccessor<Employees,int>
          acc (&Employees::salary);

replace (our_employees.first(),
         our_employees.last(),
         acc, 1000, 2000);
```

This concludes the example.

Pure read accessors may be used to encapsulate non-materialized parameters. The following class template, `ConstAccessor`, is a simple example: it uniformly returns the value received through the constructor.

```
template <class T>
class ConstAccessor
  {
  public:
     typedef T vtype;
     ConstAccessor (T t)
           : i_t(t) { }
     template <class It>
        T get (It) const
           { return i_it; }
  private:
     T i_t;
  };
```

## 3 Toolboxes for Interfaces

> **Goal 2**
>
> The interfaces of data structures to algorithms should be designed such that a small set of generic or polymorphic classes makes the implementation of such interfaces easy, convenient, and straightforward.

For a simple exposition, assume that there are $n$ graph algorithms and $m$ data structures for graphs, and each algorithm shall work on each data structure. This requires $n \cdot m$ customizations of algorithms to data structures. Hence, it might be useful to have a toolbox of generic or polymorphic classes from which these adapters may be constructed with a relatively modest programming effort. In the ideal case, tailoring an algorithm to a data structure would then amount to instantiating these polymorphic or generic types with the appropriate parameters.

However, this introduces a tradeoff: on one hand, the toolbox should be small and coherent, which significantly restricts the freedom in designing interfaces. On the other hand, a large degree of freedom is necessary to adapt an algorithm to various applications without sacrificing efficiency.

### STL viewed as a toolbox

Goal 2 is one of the main design goals of the STL. The most important sort of generic classes in the STL are iterators: each container class comes with a couple of specific iterator classes, and each algorithm accesses the underlying containers solely through these iterators. Containers and algorithms can be easily combined, because the iterator classes are template parameters of the algorithms, the interfaces of all iterator classes conform to a set of *requirements*, and the algorithms access iterators only according to these requirements.

Of course, not every combination of an algorithm and a container makes sense. For example, it does not make sense to sort a singly-linked list by the usual random-access variant of quicksort. Therefore, containers are classified into five groups according to their potential functionality: input stream, output stream, singly-linked (forward) sequence, doubly-linked (bidirectional) sequence, and random-access container. For each of these groups, there is a specific set of requirements, and these sets form a hierarchy as shown in figure 4.

> **Experience 3**
>
> At least in C++, it is possible to implement toolboxes which realize goal 2 and do not sacrifice efficiency. As a prerequisite, the interface of a complex data structure to algorithms is not realized by a single, large class, but by a couple of *light-weight classes.*

We have implemented an experimental toolbox for graph algorithms. This toolbox is written in C++. [23] and the technical reports [21, 22] address the basic ideas and crucial details of the implementation. A restricted version, which is less flexible but specifically adapted to the LEDA data types, is described in [30]. This version will be integrated into LEDA.

Our toolbox consists solely of small, light-weight types. Each of these types is responsible for a specific aspect of the data structure. The most important types in our toolbox are iterators and data accessors.

### Handle/iterator hierarchy

Iterators are provided for all relevant ways of iterating over a graph: over the whole set of nodes, the whole set of edges, and the set of edges incident to a single node. The essential details are summarized in [21]. In principle, we follow the guidelines for iterators in STL [28]. However, for reasons discussed in [21], our iterators deviate from the STL conventions in several technical details, which are beyond the scope of this paper.

As a result of our practical case studies, the toolbox offers each of these iterator types in a *normal* and a *reduced* version,[4] and in addition node and edge *handle* types (figure 5). The main difference between normal and reduced iterators is that a normal iterator must provide certain methods which require that the iterator object has some "global knowledge" about the underlying graph. In contrast, an object of a reduced iterator type is only assumed to have knowledge about its specific type of iteration. Finally, a node or edge handle type refers to a single, fixed node or edge and is not assumed to "know" anything about the underlying graph or about any way of iteration.

Often, the reduced version of an iterator class is smaller than the normal version, and the corresponding handler class is even smaller. Hence, if an algorithm manages large containers of iterators, using the reduced version or even

[4] Called the *heavy* and the *light* version in [21].

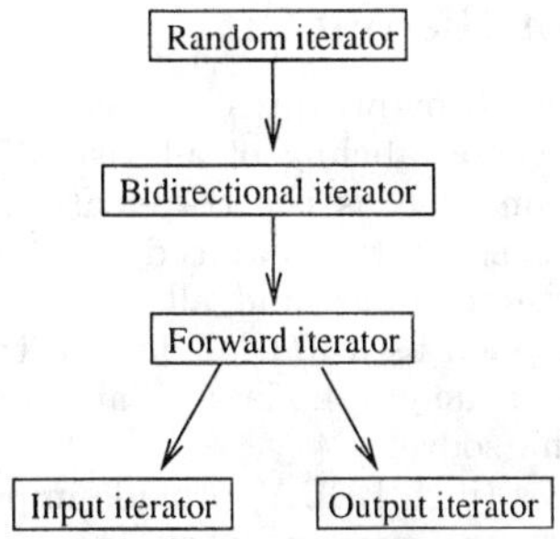


Figure 4: The STL hierarchy of iterator requirements. An arrow indicates that the requirements on the tail side are a superset of the requirements on the head side.

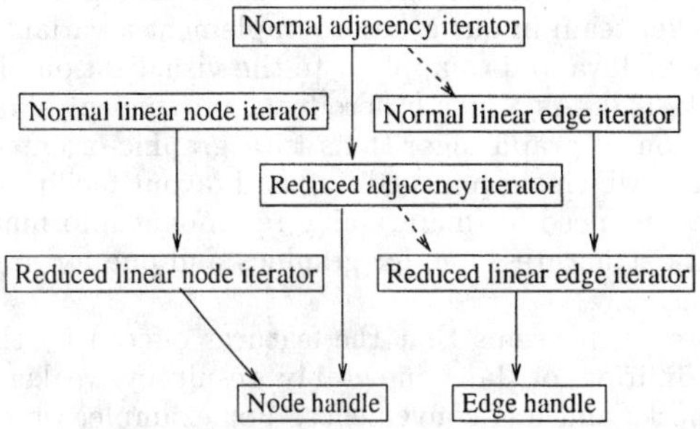


Figure 5: The hierarchy of requirements for iterators on graphs in our toolbox. A dashed line indicates that the relation between the requirements on the head and the tail side are *only syntactical* in nature, but the semantics may be different (to be concrete: iterating over all edges of the graph vs. over all edges leaving a single node).

the handle class may save space and decrease the run-time overhead induced by copy operations.[5]

On the other hand, the reduced version often gets the global knowledge required for the normal version "for free" from the underlying graph data structure. For example, each node and edge in the graph data structure in LEDA and AAI holds a pointer to the graph to which it belongs. Hence, a mere pointer to the node or edge type suffices as a normal iterator, and the normal and the reduced versions collapse into one class. Nonetheless, an algorithm may distinguish between the normal and the reduced version of an iterator class. If the algorithm is generic with these two classes being type parameters, both type parameters are then instantiated with the same type.

## Proxies

Moreover, the toolbox provides several generic proxies [12] for iterators, data accessors, and other types.

**Example.** the following class template, named `Filter`, is a simple, small proxy for iterators.[6] It constructs a *filter iterator* from an object `it` of iterator type `It` and from an object `pred` of predicate type `Pred`. This iterator skips all items which do not fulfill the predicate. As in STL, the predicate is evaluated in function notation (`operator()`). For notational convenience, we do not follow the STL guidelines for iterators: the sentinel is dropped, and instead the Boolean method `valid` returns `false` if and only if the end of the sequence has been passed. Moreover, `advance` performs one forward step, and `get_data` returns the data associated with the current item.

```
template <class It, class Pred>
class Filter
  {
  public:
     typedef typename It::vtype vtype;
     Filter (It it, Pred pred)
        : i_it(it), i_pred(pred)
        { advance_if_false(); }
     bool valid () const
        { return i_it.valid(); }
     vtype& get_data ()
        { return i_it.get_data(); }
     void advance ()
        {
          i_it.advance();
          advance_if_false();
        }
  private:
     It    i_it;
     Pred  i_pred;
     void advance_if_false ()
        {
          while (i_it.valid() &&
                 !i_pred(i_it) )
             i_it.advance();
        }
  };
```

## Programming languages

We apply many advanced features of C++ to achieve this degree of flexibility and convenience. For example, we use many features of the template mechanism in C++, which is much more flexible than the generic mechanisms in many other languages. Moreover, pointer-to-members [36] are used in our toolbox; see the example `MemberAccessor` in section 2.2.

Of course, the design of our toolbox can be realized in other programming languages, because a flexible generic mechanism and pointer-to-members may be simulated by

[5]To our surprise, it has turned out that simple copy operations may cause a significant overhead. Applying reference semantics to reduce this effect is often problematic in a language such as C++, because there is no built-in garbage collector, and techniques such as reference counting may cancel out the savings.

[6]Recently, we have successfully applied generic iterator proxies like this to the internal design of a database query engine [13].

inheritance. In fact, an effort is currently being undertaken by another team in our group to implement a variant of our toolbox in Java and to apply it to the visualization of social networks [38]. As a nice by-product, our concept allows the adaptation of graph algorithms to a graphic-oriented data structure, which supports editing and layout facilities. This removes the need for maintaining redundant information in *two* data structures: one for graphics and one for graph algorithms.

However, it seems that the features offered by the current definition of Java inevitably result in weaker static type checks and less convenience. For example, we did not find a surrogate for the class template `MemberAccessor` (section 2.2) which is equally general and type-safe (not to mention efficient).

## 4 Algorithmic Functionality

> **Goal 3**
>
> An algorithm should be implemented such that its *algorithmic functionality* is flexibly adaptable.

Goal 3 addresses many aspects of the design of algorithms. First we will briefly illustrate two aspects: *exchangeable subalgorithms* and *variations of the output.* Afterwards, we will start a more detailed discussion of yet another aspect: *heuristic speed-up techniques.*

### Exchangeable subalgorithms

To give a concrete example, many graph algorithms rely on a subalgorithm which determines a path from some specified node $s$ to some other node $t$. This subalgorithm might start one of various kinds of graph searches at $s$, for instance, a depth-first search or breadth-first search, or a shortest-path algorithm, which determines the cheapest path with respect to an arbitrary definition of edge costs. Goal 3 states that the concrete strategy for determining this path should be left open in the implementation of the main algorithm. This is necessary to achieve both overall goals—efficiency and reusability—simultaneously, because none of these path algorithms is efficient in all possible applications. Furthermore, some applications even rely on specific properties of the path, which are only guaranteed by specific subalgorithms.

The *strategy* pattern [12, 11] seems to be appropriate to meet this goal. However, the situation is even more complex, and it does not suffice to base the design solely on the *strategy* pattern. The problem is that the usual algorithms for depth-first search, breadth-first search, and shortest paths determine spanning trees, not paths. For reasons of efficiency, it does not suffice to run one of these algorithms up to its regular termination and to extract the path afterwards from the tree. Rather, the algorithm should terminate once the path from $s$ to $t$ is determined. Therefore, these algorithms must be adapted to the problem of finding a single path.

### Variations of the output

A depth-first search or breadth-first search algorithm may either return a mere labeling of all visited nodes or additional information such as the traversal order. Moreover, it may also return the tree induced by the search, which comprises all visited nodes and all traversed edges. This tree may be encoded as a 0/1-labeling of the edges, as an (acyclic) object of the graph class, as an object of a specific tree class, or whatsoever.

Many libraries (incl. LEDA) provide implementations of depth-first search and similar algorithms which only return node labelings or the traversal order of all nodes. Constructing a depth-first tree from this information amounts to performing another complete depth-first search. This simple example demonstrates that the concrete variation of the output cannot always be delegated to postprocessing routines. Consequently, this flexibility should be inherent in the implementation of the algorithm itself.

### Speed-up techniques

As mentioned above, we discuss this aspect in greater detail. We illustrate this task by means of an example: we are given a traffic network, that is, the nodes are cities and towns, and the edges are traffic connections. The system receives a potentially infinite number of pairs $(s, t)$ of nodes as runtime events. For each pair, it has to compute a shortest path from $s$ to $t$ in the network (see figure 6). This is a special case within the wide range of algorithmic problems that are best solved by Dijkstra's famous algorithm ([7], sect. 25). Our concrete scenario offers a wealth of algorithmic speed-up techniques. If $t$ is often in the vicinity of $s$, the speed-up factor gained from these techniques may be in the order of 1,000 to 10,000. Unless stated otherwise, $s$ is the node from which the search starts.

**Early termination.** The first, most basic speed-up technique is to let the algorithm terminate immediately when the shortest path from $s$ to $t$ is found. Actually, Dijkstra's algorithm computes shortest paths from $s$ to *all* other nodes. Unfortunately, the typical implementations of Dijkstra's algorithm in libraries [25] and in the literature [10] do not even allow this simple speed-up technique.

**Version stamps.** In combination with the technique *early termination*, the following trick can be applied to achieve expected sublinear run time for a single shortest-path computation: the node distances are not initialized with a value representing $+\infty$ in every shortest path computation. Instead, a version stamp is maintained for every node, which is the number of the last shortest path computation in which the distance of this node was updated. If the version stamp of a node is not up to date, this node is regarded as having infinite distance (clearly, to avoid an integer overflow, all version stamps must be reset to the initial value after a—huge—number of steps).

**Goal-directed search.** The length $\ell(v, w)$ of an edge $(v, w) \in E$ is replaced by the reduced length $\ell'(v, w) := \ell(v, w) - \Delta(v, t) + \Delta(w, t)$, where $\Delta(x, y)$ is a lower bound on the shortest path from $x$ to $y$: for example, the normal distance of $x$ and $y$ ([26], sect. 3.8.5.1). There is empirical evidence that this modification may direct the search towards $t$.

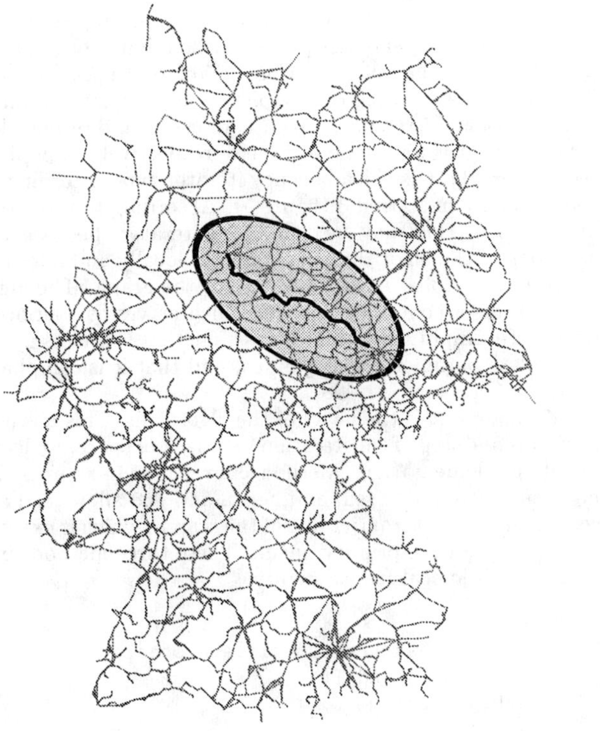

Figure 6: a shortest path from $s = Hannover$ to $t = Leipzig$ in the German rail network. Whenever $s$ and $t$ are relatively close, restricting the search horizon to a small ellipsis reduces the run time dramatically.[7]

**Bidirectional search.** The shortest $(s,t)$-path is computed from two nodes, $s$ and $t$, simultaneously, from $s$ in a forward direction and from $t$ in a backward direction ([26], sect. 3.8.5.2). That is, two slightly different executions of Dijkstra's algorithm are "merged" into one loop, in each step one of these two algorithms is chosen to scan one single node, and this choice is made by an on-line heuristic. The algorithm terminates once a node $u$ has been reached by both searches (the concatenation of the shortest paths from $s$ and from $t$ to $u$ is the solution).

**Restricted search horizon.** Often it may be safely assumed (though not provable) that the real shortest path does not deviate too much from the straight line segment connecting $s$ with $t$. In this case, the search may be restricted to, say, an ellipsis around $s$ and $t$ (see figure 6). This ellipsis may even be changed dynamically during the algorithm, depending on intermediate results. In other words, two algorithms—the shortest path routine and a routine that extends the search horizon on-line—are "merged" into one loop and affect each other.[8]

[7] This figure stems from a joint project with the *Deutsche Bahn AG* [34]; permission to visualize the railway data is granted by the TLC/Deutsche Bahn AG.

[8] For example, heuristical strategies of this kind have been implemented in the on-line information system of the *Deutsche Bahn AG*, the central German train and railway company.

**Variations of the $A^*$ algorithm.** This sort of algorithm for shortest $(s,t)$-paths in the plane also fits into this general scheme [17]. In general, the effective length of an edge is a combination of its nominal length and an additional cost function, which penalizes large angles between this edge and the direction towards $t$. The effective cost of an edge must not be initialized in advance, but computed when needed, because otherwise, the initialization destroys the advantage of the $A^*$ heuristic: that the amortized run time is highly sublinear in the size of the graph.

## Concept

Our concept to achieve goal 3 consists of two principles: *loop kernels* and *full logical inspectability.*

**Loop kernels.** We introduced this principle in [22]. The crucial observation is that probably every non-trivial algorithm essentially consists of one or more loops (or nested loops), plus some pre- and postprocessing operations for each loop. We call these loops the *core loops* of the algorithm. For example, Dijkstra's algorithm for shortest paths, which we discussed above, has one core loop. In each iteration of this loop, the current distance estimation of exactly one node is decreased, provided that the currently available information allows that.

More systematically, implementing an algorithm as a loop kernel means the following:

1. The core loops of an algorithm are the basic units of reuse, not the algorithm as a whole.
2. A core loop is implemented as a class (the *loop-kernel class*), not as a subroutine.
3. Subalgorithms are polymorphic members of the class (design pattern *strategy* [12]).
4. The loop-kernel class provides a method which executes exactly one iteration of the core loop.[9]
5. Pre- and postprocessing operations are regarded as customizations of the core loop and left to the user of the class.
6. In particular, the algorithm does not initialize the data on which it works; it expects that this data has been initialized before the first iteration (not necessarily before instantiating the loop-kernel object).
7. Only the basic functionality of the algorithm, which is common to all applications, is provided by the loop-kernel class. Extensions are regarded as customizations of the core loop and left to the user of the class.

The fourth and fifth items enable the user to extend the basic functionality: the core loop is implemented by the user "around the loop kernel," and the user can freely insert additional stuff in the loop:

[9] For some algorithms, it may even be reasonable to divide ta single iteration into several steps. In other words, a couple of methods is provided such that one iteration is performed when all of these methods are called once in a specific order.

```
Algorithm A (...);  // Loop-kernel object
do_some_stuff_1 ();
while ( ! break_condition_fulfilled(A) )
  {
    do_some_stuff_2 ();
    A.next ();   // one iteration
    do_some_stuff_3 ();
  }
  do_some_stuff_4 ();
```

We are aware of the problem that algorithms which are implemented as classes and leave all pre- and postprocessing to the client are much harder to understand and to apply than algorithms which are implemented as subroutines. Hence, it might be useful to additionally implement a couple of subroutines, which are mere partial or complete customizations of the algorithm class to typical scenarios (incl. pre- and postprocessing). Clearly, these subroutines are much more convenient to use than the loop kernel itself.

Typically, the implementation of such a customizing subroutine is very short. Thus, if the sources of these subroutines are freely distributed as a part of the documentation, they may also serve as tutorials for using the full power of the underlying loop kernel. Moreover, it might be reasonable to implement various speed-up techniques in advance and to describe their potential applications and their usage in the documentation. All of these tasks form an integral part of [30].

**Full logical inspectability.** We call a class *fully logically inspectable*, if it provides methods to read all details of the current logical state of an object. In that, the *logical state* of an object of some class at some stage is defined as the bunch of information about its state which is necessary to predict the results of all possible sequences of calls to methods to this object after this stage.

For example, many libraries provide stack classes which offer access to the topmost element only (by methods *push*, *pop*, and *top*). However, the logical state of a stack object is not fully determined by the topmost element. Rather, it is described by the ordered sequence of items in the stack object. The principle of full logical inspectability requires methods which allow one to iterate over this sequence and to read the values of all items in this order.

Note that full logical inspectability does not contradict the encapsulation of implementation details, because no details of the implementation are exhibited and the access is read-only.[10] However, a stack class that is fully logically inspectable contradicts the abstract idea of a stack being a sequence that is only accessible at its front. In the discussion below, we will argue that for algorithm classes, the advantages of inspectability outweigh the resulting violation of abstraction.

### Experience 4

If an algorithm is implemented as a fully logically inspectable loop kernel class, its algorithmic functionality is flexibly and efficiently adaptable.

[10] In some cases, it might even be reasonable to offer a disciplined *write* access to selected details.

## Example

We continue with our example of speed-up techniques: Dijkstra's algorithm for shortest paths. Although it is only a simplified version, the following class template, `Dijkstra`, may illustrate our two design principles. The template parameters `Length` and `Distance` are data accessors and responsible for edge lengths and node distances, respectively. Template parameter `AdjIt` is the adjacency iterator type according to the hierarchy in section 3 (figure 5). According to the terms of section 3, this may be a reduced iterator, because the core loop of the algorithm works purely locally and does not require any "global knowledge" about the graph. The algorithm needs a container `PriorQ`, which serves as a priority queue. To simplify notation, we assume that this class is not a template parameter of `Dijkstra`, and that it is compliant to the list class in STL [28].

Method `next` is the heart of the algorithm. This method performs one step of the iteration. For lack of space, we leave out its implementation. Method `current_node` returns the node currently processed, and `begin` and `end` allow read access to the current frontier line of the search, which is exactly the contents of the priority queue. These three methods implement full logical inspectability.

```
template <class Length, class Distance,
          class AdjIt>
class Dijkstra
  {
  public:
     Dijkstra (Length len, Distance dist)
        : i_len(len), i_dist(dist) { }
     void make_root (AdjIt it)
        { i_pq.push_back(it); }
     void next ();
     bool finished () const
        { return i_pq.empty(); }
     AdjIt current_node () const
        { return i_pq.front(); }
     PriorQ::const_iterator begin ()
        { return i_pq.begin(); }
     PriorQ::const_iterator end ()
        { return i_pq.end(); }
  private:
     PriorQ     i_pq;
     Length     i_len;
     Distance   i_dist;
     // ...
  };
```

The "classical" variant of Dijkstra's algorithm, in which we want to compute shortest paths from root $s$ to every other node, can be realized as follows:

```
AdjIt s;
/* init. s */
/* init. length accessor 'len' */
/* init. distance accessor 'dist' */
Dijkstra<Length,Distance,AdjIt>
   dijk (len, dist);
dijk.make_root (s);
while (!dijk.finished())
   dijk.next();
```

In the following variant, we assume that the function wait_for_request waits until a user wants to know the shortest connection from node s to t, which are specified in the call to wait_for_request. The speed-up technique "*early termination*" in our traffic network example can simply be realized as follows:

```
while (true)
 {
    AdjIt s, t;
    wait_for_request (s, t);
    /* init. length accessor 'len' */
    /* init. distance accessor 'dist' */
    Dijkstra<Length,Distance,AdjIt>
       dijk (len, dist);
    dijk.make_root (s);
    while (dijk.current_node() != t)
       dijk.next();
 }
```

Recall the speed-up technique "*version stamps*" defined above. To realize this variant, we write a data accessor class VersionAccessor, whose get methods return $+\infty$ if the version stamp of the node does not equal the global version number. The access to the node distance and to the version number are delegated to further data accessor classes: DA and VA. Hence, it is an example of proxies for data accessors. Since DA and VA are template arguments, VersionAccessor is broadly applicable. To simplify notation, we assume that all version numbers are of type int, and that INT_MAX represents $+\infty$.

```
template <class DA, class VA>
class VersionAccessor
  {
  public:
    typedef typename DA::vtype vtype;
    VersionAccessor
       (DA da, VA va, int global)
       : i_da(da), i_va(va),
         i_global(global) { }
    template <class It>
       vtype get (It it) const
          {
            return i_va.get(it)==i_global
                   ? i_da.get(it) : INT_MAX;
          }
    template <class It>
       vtype set (It it, vtype const& value)
          {
            i_va.set (it, i_global);
            i_da.set (it, value);
          }
  private:
    DA   i_da;
    VA   i_va;
    int  i_global;
  }
```

Here is the code to incorporate the speed-up technique "*version stamps*:"

```
int global_version = 0;
/* init. all node stamps to 0 */
while (true)
 {
    AdjIt s, t;
    wait_for_request (s, t);
    global_version++;
    /* init. length accessor 'len' */
    /* init. distance accessor 'dist' */
    /* init. data accessor 'stamp' for node
       version stamps */
    typedef
          VersionAccessor</*...*/,/*...*/> VA;
    VA stamped_dist
          (dist, stamp, global_version);
    Dijkstra<Length,VA,AdjIt>
          dijk (len, stamped_dist);
    dijk.make_root (s);
    while (dijk.current_node() != t)
       dijk.next();
 }
```

This adaptation is only possible because Dijkstra is a loop kernel. Full logical inspectability is not required for this speed-up technique. However, it is required for the speed-up technique *bidirectional search.* We only give a high-level description of the adaptation:

1. Reserve or establish two distance labels for each node and inititialize them.
2. Inititialize shortest-path loop kernel $A$ with the first distance label and make $s$ the (unique) root of $A$.
3. Inititialize shortest-path loop kernel $B$ with the second distance label and make $t$ the (unique) root of $B$.
4. WHILE no node is seen by both $A$ and $B$:
   (a) let $C$ be either $A$ or $B$, depending on a heuristic on-line choice;
   (b) apply C.next().

The full logical inspectability is necessary in step 4(a): a sophisticated on-line choice must access the logical states of both loop kernels.

The speed-up techniques "*goal-directed search*" and "*variations of the* $A^*$ *algorithm*" can be easily realized through specific data accessor classes (cf. section 2.2 and 3). Finally, the restriction of the search horizon to an ellipsis can be realized by a filter iterator as defined in section 3. This iterator must be instantiated with a predicate that returns true for a node if and only if this node is inside the search horizon. To increase the search horizon on-line, the heuristic which computes the new search horizon must be invoked in every iteration of the core loop. Because of the loop kernel concept, this loop is "inside-out," and hence this is easily done. Because of full logical inspectability, this heuristic is well informed.

## Comparison to algorithmic generators

Loop kernels are a generalization of the *algorithmic generators* introduced by Flamig [10], which are similar to graph search iterators [1] and to built-in concepts for streams and iterations in various object-oriented programming languages (notably the *iterator* concept in Sather [32]). Like a loop kernel, an algorithmic generator encapsulates an algorithm in a class and offers a method to perform exactly one iteration of the core loop. The main differences between loop kernels and algorithmic generators are the following:

- Algorithmic generators are only intended to implement algorithms which consist of one core loop, and in each iteration of the core loop, a single piece of the algorithm's output is constructed. For example, a generator for a sequence of prime numbers falls into this category. However, Dijkstra's algorithm does not, and many other algorithms do not either. Consequently, Dijkstra's and many other algorithms are not formulated as algorithmic generators in [10], but in a conventional style as subroutines.

- An algorithmic generator does all pre- and postprocessing itself, namely in its constructors and destructor, whereas a loop kernel delegates this to the client. Hence, a speed-up technique such as "*version stamps*" cannot be incorporated afterwards in an existing algorithmic generator, unless this technique was antipicated by the designer of the algorithmic generator.

- After an iteration of the core loop, an algorithmic generator provides a means of accessing the piece of the output generated in this iteration. This is far from full logical inspectability. Consequently, a speed-up technique such as "*bidirectional search*" cannot be incorporated either.

### Comparison to algorithm frameworks

Goal 3 can alternatively be approached through a framework-like design (see Holland [15] for a concrete example). In such an algorithm framework, the algorithm is designed as a base class, and this base class provides a method which executes the algorithm as a whole. The crucial design task is to identify the "skeleton" of the algorithm, which is common to all applications, and to determine all points in the algorithm where a possibility to change or extend the behavior is necessary to achieve flexible adaptability. Each of these points is realized as a method of the base class. Derived classes may overwrite these methods to customize the algorithm to concrete applications.

As demonstrated above, variations of the break condition, extensions of the algorithmic functionality, and intermixed algorithms (*e.g.* bidirectional search) are straightforward if the loop-kernel concept is applied. In contrast, in an algorithm framework, any of these modifications requires implementing a derived class. Moreover, these derived classes might often be tricky to implement. For instance, intermixed algorithms can indeed be realized in an algorithmic framework, but the task is not at all trivial, and the design of the whole algorithmic package might suffer. To give another example: suspending an algorithm temporarily to perform other, unrelated tasks is trivial in the loop-kernel concept, but might cause severe design problems in an algorithm framework.

## 5 Inspectability

> **Goal 4**
>
> An algorithm should be implemented such that it is possible to inspect all potentially relevant details during its execution.

> **Experience 5**
>
> Goal 4 may also be achieved through fully logically inspectable loop kernels.

Goal 4 addresses various tasks. We discuss two different tasks to illustrate experience 5.

- **Animation:** To give a concrete example, a possible visualization of Dijkstra's algorithm in slow motion would be to distinguish unseen nodes, nodes in the current frontier line of the search, and finished nodes from each other by color. It is not hard to write iterator adapters which deliver all necessary information to the graphical display (using the *observer* pattern [12]).

  Sometimes it might be necessary to refresh the whole display. This requires information about the current logical state of the algorithm. Because of the principle of full logical inspectability, no redundant bookkeeping outside the algorithm is necessary.

- **Snapshots:** Another point, which might not be interesting for Dijkstra's algorithm, but may be important for algorithms which take significant more time per run: if the loop kernel concept is applied, the algorithm may be "snapshot" at frequent occasions to recover after a crash.

## 6 Conclusion

We have implemented several algorithms based on the toolbox in section 3 and on the loop kernel concept and the principle of full logical inspectability.[11]

In particular, we compared the shortest-path algorithm in LEDA with our adaptable implementation. To achieve a realistic comparison, we customized our implementation exactly to the same algorithmic problem and the same data structures.

> **Experience 6**
>
> The overhead of the techniques discussed in this paper compared to traditional implementations of algorithms might be acceptable for most applications.

[11] Using the GNU C++ compiler, version 2.7.2, on Sparc Stations.

Figures 7-9 show the results of computational studies in which we compared the performance of LEDA's implementation of Dijkstra's algorithm (labeled "Direct") with the performance of our implementation ("Adaptable"). Figures 7 and 9 show the results of two studies in which the "classical" variant of Dijkstra's algorithm was applied to determine the shortest paths from a designated root $s$ to all other nodes. On the other hand, to obtain figure 8, we computed the shortest paths for all pairs of nodes: the classical variant is called once for every node as the root node. Figure 8 shows the accumulated times.

This computational study is based on random graphs. In figures 7 and 8, each graph was constructed such that it is highly connected and highly cyclic. Figure 9 is based on random triangulated graphs: a triangulated graph is a plane graph (cf. figure 1) such that each internal area is a triangle. In addition, we studied all-pairs shortest-path computations on several national and international train networks such as the one shown in figure 6:

| Train network | Overhead factor |
|---|---|
| Austria | 1.48 |
| Europe | 1.53 |
| France | 1.68 |
| Germany | 1.60 |
| Germany (local trains only) | 1.62 |
| Switzerland | 1.57 |

This overhead is certainly acceptable for the overwhelming majority of all applications. "In theory," the overhead may be even smaller in all situations in which the run-time flexibility of dynamic binding is not required, because all function calls could be inlined and optimized as if they were hand-coded. Hence, there is hope that progress in compiler technology will reduce the overhead even further.[12]

## Acknowledgements

I would like to thank Ulrik Brandes, Dieter Gluche, Dietmar Kühl, Kurt Mehlhorn, Stefan Näher, Marco Nissen, Wolfgang Pree, and Christian Uhrig for fruitful discussions. Special thanks to Dietmar Kühl and Marco Nissen for their strong engagement in the project and to Dorothea Wagner for her overall support and encouragement. Moreover, I would like to thank the anonymous reviewers for their valuable comments and for their hard, constructive criticism. In particular, I am very grateful to my "shepherdess," Lougie Anderson. Finally, I would like to thank Tina Deveny for proof-reading.

## References

[1] AAI base class library home page. http://www.aai.com/AAI/IUE/spec/base/base-classes.html.

[2] Ravindra K. Ahuja, Thomas L. Magnanti, and James B. Orlin. *Network flows.* Prentice Hall, 1993.

[3] Robert Barton and Lee R. Nackman. *Scientific and Engineering C++.* Addison-Wesley Publish. Comp., 1994.

[4] Ted J. Biggerstaff. The library scaling problem and the limits of concrete component reuse. In *Proceedings 3rd International Conference on Software Reuse*, 1994. http://www.research.microsoft.com/research/ip/tedb/limits/limits.htm.

[5] T. Budd. *Classic Data Structures in C++.* Addison–Wesley Publishing Company, 1994.

[6] CGAL home page. http://www.cs.ruu.nl/CGAL/.

[7] Thomas H. Cormen, Charles E. Leiserson, and Ronald L. Rivest. *Introduction to Algorithms.* MIT Press and McGraw–Hill, 1994.

[8] Martin Erwig. Graph algorithms = iteration + data structures? In *Proceedings 18th International Workshop on Graph-Theoretic Concepts in Computer Science, WG'92, Wiesbaden-Naurod, Germany, June 18-20, 1992*, pages 277–292. Springer-Verlag, Lecture Notes in Computer Science, vol. 657, 1992.

[9] ffGraph home page. http://www.fmi.uni-passau.de/~friedric/ffgraph/main.shtml.

[10] Bryan Flamig. *Practical algorithms in C++.* Coriolis Group Book, 1995.

[11] Giorgio Gallo and Maria G. Scutella. Toward a programming environment for combinatorial optimization: a case study oriented to max–flow computations. *ORSA J. Computing*, 5:120–133, 1993.

[12] Erich Gamma, Richard Helm, Ralph Johnson, and John Vlissides. *Design patterns, elements of reusable object-oriented software.* Addison–Wesley Publishing Company, 1994.

[13] Dieter Gluche, Dietmar Kühl, and Karsten Weihe. Evaluation of database queries through iterator proxies, 1997.[13]

[14] Mark R. Headington and David D. Riley. *Data abstractions and structures using C++.* D.C. Heath and Company, 1994.

[15] Ian M. Holland. Specifying reusable components using contracts. In *Proceedings Europoean Conference on Object-Oriented Programming (ECOOP)*, pages 287–308, 1992.

[16] Chris Johnson and Philip Gray. Assessing the impact of time on user interface design. *SIGCHI Bulletin*, 28(2):33–35, 1996.

[17] Laveen Kanal and Vipin Kumar. *Search in Artificial Intelligence.* Springer, 1988.

[18] Karla home page. http://i44www.info.uni-karlsruhe.de/~zimmer/karla/index.html.

[19] Yugo Kashiwagi and David S. Wise. Graph algorithms in a lazy functional programming language. In *Proceedings 4th International Symposium on Lucid and Intensional Programming*, pages 35–46, 1991.

[12] The overhead was essentially caused by failure of method inlining. In principle, zero overhead is possible. In fact, in additional experiments, we found that at least one commercial compiler already comes close to this ideal. We could not use this compiler for the above studies, because LEDA has not been ported to it.

[13] http://www.informatik.uni-konstanz.de/Preprints

[20] Dietmar Kühl, Arfst Ludwig, Rolf H. Möhring, Rudolf Müller, Jörn Schulze, and Karsten Weihe. ADLIPS user manual, 1993.[13]

[21] Dietmar Kühl and Karsten Weihe. Iterators and handles for nodes and edges in graphs.[13]

[22] Dietmar Kühl and Karsten Weihe. Using design patterns for reusable, efficient implementations of graph algorithms - working paper.[13]

[23] Dietmar Kühl and Karsten Weihe. Data access templates. *C++ Report*, 9(July/August), 1997.

[24] John Launchbury. Graph algorithms with a functional flavour. In *First International Spring School on Advanced Functional Programming Techniques*, pages 308–331. Springer-Verlag, Lecture Notes in Computer Science, vol. 925, 1995.

[25] LEDA home page. http://www.mpi-sb.mpg.de/LEDA/leda.html.

[26] Thomas Lengauer. *Combinatorial algorithms for integrated circuit layout.* Wiley, 1990.

[27] Kurt Mehlhorn and Stefan Näher. LEDA: a library of efficient data structures and algorithms. *Communications of the ACM*, 38:96–102, 1995.

[28] David R. Musser and Atul Saini. *STL Tutorial and Reference Guide.* Addison–Wesley Publishing Company, 1995.

[29] Gabriele Neyer, Wolfram Schlickenrieder, Dorothea Wagner, and Karsten Weihe. PlaNet — a demonstration package for algorithms on planar networks.[13]

[30] Marco Nissen and Karsten Weihe. Combining LEDA with customizable implementations of graph algorithms.[13]

[31] PlaNet home page. http://www.informatik.uni-konstanz.de/Forschung/Projekte/PlaNet/.

[32] Sather home page. http://www.icsi.berkeley.edu/~sather.

[33] Robert Sedgewick. *Algorithms in C++.* Addison–Wesley Publishing Company, 1992.

[34] SIMI home page. http://www.informatik.uni-konstanz.de/Research/projects_algo.html#projekt7.

[35] Jiri Soukop. *Taming C++.* Addison–Wesley Publishing Company, 1994.

[36] Bjarne Stroustrup. *The C++ programming language (2nd edition).* Addison–Wesley Publishing Company, 1991.

[37] Michael VanHilst and David Notkin. Using C++ templates to implement role-based design. http://www.cs.washington.edu/homes/vanhilst/research.html.

[38] visone home page. http://www.informatik.uni-konstanz.de/Research/projects_algo.html#projekt8.

[39] Sheng Yu and Qingyu Zhuang. Software reuse via algorithmic abstraction. In *Conference Series Technology of Object-Oriented Languages and Systems (Tools USA '95)*, pages 277-292, 1995.

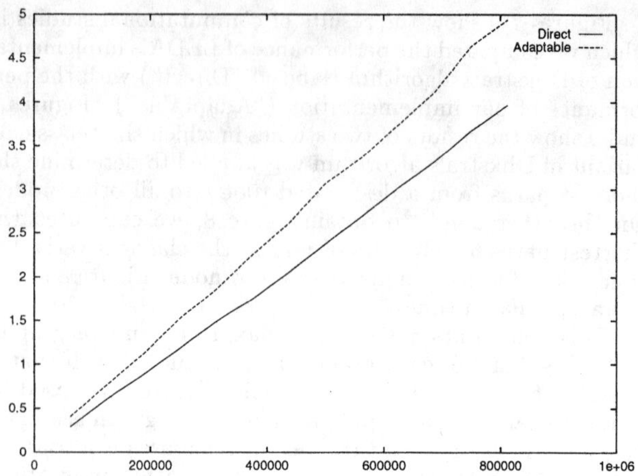


Figure 7: single–source shortest paths on random graphs with 1000 nodes ($x$: number of edges, $y$: run time in seconds).

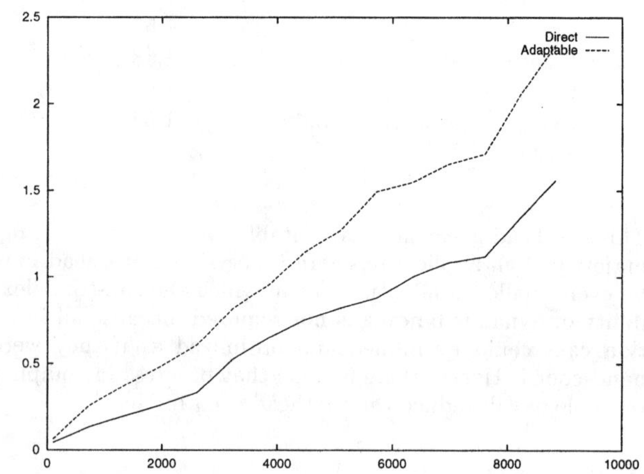


Figure 8: all–pairs shortest paths on random graphs with 100 nodes ($x$: number of edges, $y$: run time in seconds).

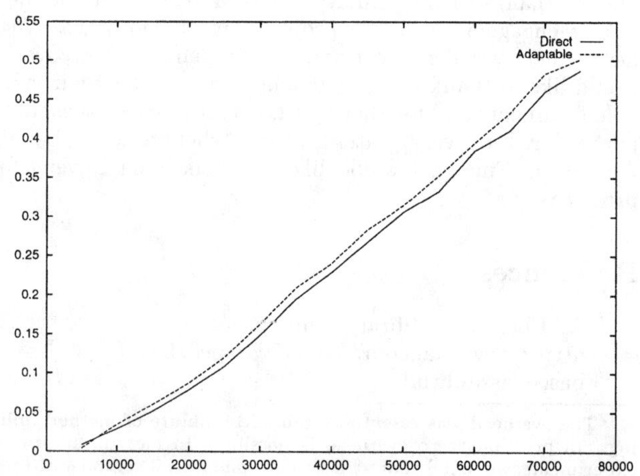


Figure 9: single–source shortest paths on random triangulated planar graphs ($x$: number of nodes, $y$: run time in seconds).

# Adding Type Parameterization to the Java™ Language

Ole Agesen
Sun Microsystems Laboratories
2 Elizabeth Drive
Chelmsford, MA 01824
ole.agesen@Sun.COM

Stephen N. Freund* John C. Mitchell*
Department of Computer Science
Stanford University
Stanford, CA 94305-9045
{freunds, mitchell}@cs.stanford.edu

## Abstract

Although the Java programming language has achieved widespread acceptance, one feature that seems sorely missed is the ability to use type parameters (as in Ada generics, C++ templates, and ML polymorphic functions or data types) to allow a general concept to be instantiated to one or more specific types. In this paper, we propose parameterized classes and interfaces in which the type parameter may be constrained to either implement a given interface or extend a given class. This design allows the body of a parameterized class to refer to methods on objects of the parameter type, without introducing any new type relations into the language. We show that these Java extensions may be implemented by expanding parameterized classes at class load time, without any extension or modification to existing Java bytecode, verifier or bytecode interpreter.

## 1 Introduction

In Ada generics [US 80], C++ templates [ES90], and ML polymorphic functions and data types [Mil85, Ull94], type parameterization is used to allow a general concept to be instantiated to one or more specific types. For example, we may define a package or class implementing a generic `List` datatype, and instantiate it to produce lists of integers, lists of database records, or lists of other types of objects. As borne out by experience with these and other languages, the ability to define and instantiate a general concept is particularly useful in the design and construction of reusable libraries. To cite a specific example, the C++ Standard Template Library (STL) [MS95, PSLM96] uses C++ templates extensively.

While the current Java language does not provide any form of type parameterization, it does include a supertype `Object` of all object types. This allows some classes that could be written in other languages using parametric polymorphism to be expressed using `Object` in place of a parameter type. However, there are several disadvantages of this substitute for type parameterization. First, the programmer must insert type casts to change an expression with static type `Object` to a more specific type. This can be an annoyance and, since Java type casts are checked at run time, it also leads to some decrease in execution speed. The use of superclass `Object` becomes more cumbersome when binary operations (such as an ordering) are needed on objects of the parameter type, since typing considerations become more complex. Finally, use of a fixed type `Object` does not allow us to capture certain generic concepts that could be expressed as parameterized classes or interfaces. For all of these reasons, we believe that it is important to add type parameterization to the Java language.

This paper proposes a language design and implementation. Although we considered the language design problem from first principles, the result of our deliberation and programming experiments coincides substantially with other proposals [MBL97, OW97a, OW97b]. Our implementation approach, based on instantiation of generic classes and interfaces at class load time, differs significantly from other approaches that have been explored in any detail. This implementation technique allows us to support a more expressive form of parameterized classes than competing implementation techniques. It may also be considered an alternative implementation mechanism for related language design proposals.

The Java language extensions that we consider allow classes and interfaces to be defined using type parameters that may be instantiated with classes, interfaces, or primitive types. To enable classes to refer to the meth-

*Funded in part by NSF Grants CCR-9303099 and CCR-9629754. Stephen Freund received additional support through an NSF Graduate Research Fellowship.


**OOPSLA '97 10/97 GA, USA**
**© 1997 ACM 0-89791-908-4/97/0010...$3.50**

ods of objects from a parameter type, each type parameter may be assumed to implement a given interface or extend a given class. This reuse of existing Java type relations **extends** and **implements** to constrain type parameters reduces the number of new concepts added to the language. This is essentially similar to the design used in [OW97b], also based on so-called F-bounded quantification [CCH+89, Mit96].

Our implementation technique adds a preprocess phase to the Java Virtual Machine loader. The preprocessor instantiates parameterized classes at class load time to achieve a balance between pre-run-time expansion (for expressive power and run-time efficiency) and minimization of compiled (or transmitted) code size. We have implemented a prototype version of the loader preprocessor using approximately 500 lines of Java code. While it was necessary to make one small change to the Java Virtual Machine loader in order to invoke our preprocessor at the correct time, this small change could be incorporated into future versions of the Java Virtual Machine without affecting backwards compatibility. More importantly, it is not necessary to change the verifier or bytecode interpreter. This is significant since many of the security and portability properties of Java are tied to the design of these parts of the virtual machine.

To summarize, our goals in adding type parameters to the Java language are:

- Allow common parameterized classes to be programmed easily. We are more interested in making it easy to handle common, useful cases than in maximizing absolute language expressiveness.
- Avoid introduction of extraneous concepts into the Java language, where possible.
- Support separate compilation. In keeping with the Java emphasis on security, it should be possible to check each compilation unit separately for consistency and type correctness.
- Implement the extended language with as few changes to the virtual machine as possible. In particular, avoid any changes in the Java bytecode, Java verifier, or bytecode interpreter.
- Maintain static type checking insofar as possible. In particular, eliminate the need for programmers to write casts, minimize associated run-time costs, and avoid introduction of additional constructs that would increase the use of run-time tests to preserve type safety.

We review type parameterization in other languages in Section 2 and describe four representative and increasingly difficult "benchmark" program examples. In Section 3 we summarize relevant features of the existing Java language and outline how the lack of type parameterization requires work-arounds for each of the four program examples. Then, in Section 4, we present our language extension. Section 5 presents our preprocessor-based implementation technique and describes a prototype that we have built to validate our ideas. Section 6 compares our design and implementation with related proposals, while Sections 7 and 8 outline directions for future work and conclude.

## 2 Parameterized Classes

Many programmers are familiar with generic program units, as supported by Ada generics [US 80], C++ templates [ES90], and ML functors, polymorphic functions, and data types [Mil85, Ull94]. In brief, each of these constructs provides some mechanism for treating a program unit as a "generic abstraction" that can be instantiated for specific choices of actual type parameters and function parameters. To give a familiar example, a generic C++ `Vector` class may be defined as follows [ES90]:

```
template <class T> class Vector {
    T* v;
    int size;
public:
    Vector(int);
    T& operator[](int);
    T& elem (int i){return v[i];}
    // ...
}
```

For any class `C`, the class `Vector<C>` is a class of vectors of `C` objects, determined by instantiating the class `Vector` with actual class `C` in place of the formal parameter `T` in the definition above. Parametric polymorphism seems to have originated with the design of CLU [L+81], which allows procedures and clusters (approximately analogous to Ada packages or ML structures) to be parameterized by types. The prevalence of type parameterization across a wide variety of programming languages provides some evidence for the general applicability and power of this concept.

### 2.1 Compiling Parameterized Classes

Any type parameterization mechanism will involve both a technique for compiling parameterized constructs and a mechanism or set of conventions for using specific instances of a generic construct. We discuss the general issues that arise in any language using parameterized classes as an example. However, the main points apply to parameterized interfaces or other parameterized entities as well.

In many cases, it is necessary for a parameterized class to invoke methods on objects of the parameter type. This does not occur with certain "container" classes, such as `List` or `Vector`, but arises in the implementation of priority queues, for example, since it is necessary to have an ordering on the elements inserted into a priority queue. Such method invocations raise the question of how to ensure type safety. More specifically, we must be able to ensure that methods invoked on objects whose types are parameters are actually defined on the types with which the parameters are instantiated.

Four representative examples may be used to illustrate some of the challenges involved in designing an expressive type parameterization mechanism. In order of increasing complexity, these are:

`Stack` class: Like vectors, lists, and other simple container classes, stacks of `T` objects may be implemented without invoking any methods on objects of type `T`.

`Hashtable` class: In implementing a hash table, it is necessary to obtain a hash code for each object inserted in the table. For the purposes of illustration, we assume that objects have a `hashCode` method returning an integer.

`PriorityQueue` class: This is similar to `Hashtable`, since a priority queue of `T` objects requires a method on `T` objects. However, the type of the method is more complicated, since the method must provide a binary relation that would be assumed to be a linear order.

"mix-in," a term we use for a parameterized class that uses a type parameter as a base class. An example is a generic construct that adds methods `notEqual`, `greaterThan`, `lessEqual`, and `greaterEqual` to any class with `equal` and `lessThan` methods. In a parameterized class of this form, it may be necessary to assume that certain binary methods are provided by the actual parameter class.

The increasing complexity of these examples is really a measure of the complexity of the way in which the parameterized classes use the type parameters. The `Stack` class performs no operations on instances of the parameter class and does not need to make any assumptions about the type parameter. The `Hashtable` and `PriorityQueue` classes invoke methods on instances of a type parameter class and therefore must ensure that these methods are defined and have the appropriate types. Finally, mix-ins, the most complex example, use the type parameter as a superclass. This will generally require information about the methods and constructors associated with the type parameter.

All of these examples may be programmed in our extension of the Java language. However, the last one is not possible in some of the competing proposals described in Section 6. There are also differences regarding the use of constructors and static variables, as discussed in Section 2.2 below and in more detail in Section 6.

## 2.2 Instances of Generic Classes

Once we have defined a generic construct, such as a parameterized `List` class, we may wish to write a program with several specific types of lists, such as lists of integers and lists of employee record objects. We refer to each class name, such as `List<int>`, `List<Emp>`, or `List<Color>`, obtained by specifying an actual type parameter, as a *syntactic instance* of the parameterized class `List`. In any implementation of generic classes, it will be necessary to decide how to represent objects of type `List<int>`, `List<Emp>`, and `List<Color>`, and whether to generate separate code for methods associated with objects of these types.

In some languages, it may be possible to use the same implementation (code and static variables) for all syntactic instances. For example, if list cells are represented appropriately, with pointers to data (instead of the data itself) in each cell, then it may be possible to use the same representation and compiled operations for all types of lists. This is done in ML, for example. We refer to the situation where all instances of a parameterized construct share the same implementation as a *homogeneous* approach, following the terminology of [OW97b].

Alternatively, parameterized classes could be implemented *heterogeneously*, with different syntactic instances resulting in different run-time representations or different compiled code for methods. This is generally the case for C++, for example. In a heterogeneous implementation, we refer to the data structure and compiled code associated with a specific syntactic instance of a generic class as a *semantic instance*, or *instantiation*, of the class. In general, semantic instances might be *instantiated* at compile time, link time, or run time. While a heterogeneous implementation may result in larger code size, a heterogeneous strategy makes it possible to support type parameterization in a language where it is not feasible to represent or refer to values of all types in a uniform way.

Since it is related to some of the subsidiary design decisions we discuss in this paper, we note that there are some interactions between compilation of generic classes and the eventual creation of semantic instances. For example, C++ templates are compiled without statically checking the use of member functions, in part because

```java
class Stack {
  void push(Object o)  { ... }
  Object pop() { ... }
  ...
}

String s = "Hello";
Stack st = new Stack();
st.push(s);
...
s = (String)st.pop();
```

```java
class Stack<A> {
  void push(A a) { ... }
  A pop() { ... }
  ...
}

String s = "Hello";
Stack<String> st = new Stack<String>();
st.push(s);
...
s = st.pop();
```

Figure 1: Java code for a generic Stack class: versions without and with parameterized classes.

of the complexity of determining in advance how a reference to a function might be eventually resolved. Instead, type checks are made later, at link time, when the actual type parameter is determined and a semantic instance is created.

The choice between homogeneous and heterogeneous implementation strategies is often determined by language semantics. For example, consider a parameterized class that defines a static variable. If the semantics specify that each instance of the parametric class gets its own location for the static variable, it may be more straightforward to use a heterogeneous implementation strategy. On the other hand, if the semantics specify that all instances should share a single location for the static variable, a homogeneous implementation strategy may be a better choice (with respect to this particular aspect of parameterized classes).

## 3 The Java Programming Language

Since the Java language has received considerable attention, we assume that most readers have at least a passing acquaintance with it. The main features of the Java language that are relevant to our proposal are: the presence of interfaces and classes, the absence of type parameterization, the fact that type casts are checked at run time (to ensure type security), and, for our implementation, the architecture of the Java Virtual Machine. These features are documented in standard Java language reference books such as [AG96]. We also review the architecture of the Java Virtual Machine briefly in Section 5 and summarize other features in passing as needed.

In the following subsections, we discuss alternative programming techniques that may be used to work around the lack of type parameterization when solving the four representative problems from Section 2.1. The purpose of this discussion is to motivate our specific combination of language extension and implementation technique, as well as to provide a basis for comparison with various alternatives. In particular, the first three examples may be written in the other extensions described in Section 6. However, the last example, which is expressible in our extenstion, cannot be written and implemented properly by some of the other proposals. The main difference here is not the form of the language extension, but our heterogeneous implementation technique.

### 3.1 Stack

Without type parameterization, it is possible to write a Java `Stack` class using the fact that all classes are subclasses of `Object`. A typical approach is shown on the left in Figure 1.

This `Stack` class defines two essential operations: `push` places an object on the stack, and `pop` removes and returns the top object. The type `Object` occurs in two places: for the argument of the `push` method and for the result of the `pop` method. While the type of `push` is very generous, allowing any type of object to be added to a stack, a price is paid when the object is removed. Specifically, since the return type of the `pop` method is just `Object`, it is only possible to invoke methods from class `Object` on an object removed from a stack, even though the object may have additional methods. It is possible to cast an object removed from a stack to a more specific type, but this action requires either that the type be known to the programmer or that some test be performed to determine the type. In addition, to ensure type safety, the Java compiler inserts a run-time test with such a cast, causing some performance penalty.

In the best-case scenario for the current Java language, a programmer really wants heterogeneous stacks containing many types of objects and, before invoking certain methods, must cast objects removed from stacks to more specific types.

In the worst-case scenario, however, a programmer defines a stack class as above, and builds stacks with every element drawn from some specific type, such as `String`. Then, in spite of the fact that the program only builds homogeneous stacks, it must contain casts and run-time type tests to verify something already known to the programmer. These casts can be avoided by using a parameterized class, as shown on the right of Figure 1.

### 3.2 Hashtable

To define a general Java `Hashtable` class without type parameterization, we define an interface `Hashable` which asserts that objects with this interface have a `hashCode` method. Then, to use objects of some type as keys for a hash table, the class of these objects must explicitly be declared to implement the `Hashable` interface. Moreover, the cast issues described above for stacks remain for `Hashtable`. This approach can be compared with the parameterized hash table class described in Section 4 and given in Figure 2.

### 3.3 Priority Queue

A priority queue is a data structure that allows insertion and removal of objects of some type `T`. The objects must come from a linearly ordered set so that removal may return the minimum of all the elements stored in the data structure. The ordering, which we assume is provided by a `lessThan` method, poses certain problems in writing a generic priority queue class. A specific complication is that the `lessThan` method on objects of type `T` takes another object of type `T` as an argument. However, this type dependence cannot be expressed in Java without type parameterization. It is possible to work around the problem by assuming that each object to be inserted into the queue has a `lessThan` method that accepts any object as a parameter. However, the work-around sacrifices compile-time type checking and is cumbersome: the `lessThan` method must perform a run-time type check to make sure that the argument actually has the correct type. (See [BCC+96] for further discussion.) We demonstrate how a priority queue may be written with our language extension after we present the required syntax in Section 4.

### 3.4 Mix-in

For examples such as a generic "mix-in" class that adds operations to a class provided as a parameter, there does not appear to be any reasonable approach short of parameterized classes. Figure 4 in Section 4 demonstrates a generic mix-in class.

## 4 Language Design

### 4.1 Java Language Extensions

In our extension to the language, parameterized classes have the following general form:

```
class C< parameters > {
    ...
}
```

where *parameters* is a list of type variables, each of which may be constrained or unconstrained. Interfaces can be parameterized in the same way. The type variables, which represent unknown classes, interfaces, or primitive types, may be used inside the declaration of `C` wherever a type name is allowed to appear.

Constraints on type variables have two forms, **`implements`** and **`extends`** clauses. These concepts, already familiar to Java programmers, have the following intended meanings:

- **`A implements I`**: The parameter `A` is either a class which implements `I` or an interface which has `I` as a superinterface.
- **`A extends B`**: The parameter `A` is a class which is derived from `B` in the implementation hierarchy.

A similar syntax is used in [OW97b], where a BNF grammar, formal typing rules, and other syntactic issues are considered. The main difference between our proposed language extension and Pizza lies the way that our heterogeneous implementation may be used to support certain uses of type variables that Pizza disallows. These differences are discussed in Section 6.

Figure 2 demonstrates the use of constraints to specify that the `Key` parameter for `Hashtable` must implement a certain interface. The `Key` argument is constrained to only those classes that implement the `Hashable` interface, ensuring that the `Hashtable` code can invoke the `hashCode` operation on the keys. In contrast, no specific operations are required on the values inserted in the hash table, so the `Value` parameter is unconstrained, and any type will suffice.

In general, a parameterized class may be statically type checked by the compiler using the constraint information about the parameters. However, there are several situations in which the constraints do not express enough information to guarantee that all possible instantiations will conform to all the existing

```
interface Hashable {
  int hashCode();
}

class Hashtable<Key implements Hashable, Value> {
  void insert(Key k, Value v) {
    int bucket = k.hashCode();
    insertAt(bucket, k, v);
  }
  void insertAt(int bucket, Key k, Value v) { ... }
  ...
}

class Name implements Hashable {
  int hashCode() { ... }
  ...
}

Hashtable<Name, Integer> h1 = new Hashtable<Name, Integer>();
Hashtable<Name, Point> h2 = new Hashtable<Name, Point>();
Name n = new Name("Hello");
h1.insert(n, new Integer(2));
h2.insert(n, new Point(0));
```

Figure 2: A parameterized `Hashtable` class and instantiations.

rules of the Java language. For example, when a type variable is constrained to extend a class, the actual parameter must be a class since Java interfaces cannot extend classes. In the following code example,

```
class C<A> extends A {
  void f() {
    A a = new A();
  }
}
```

the actual parameter `A` must be a class because it is used as a base class. In this case, `A` must also be a class because the method `f` creates an object of type `A`. Similarly, since the extension of an interface must be an interface, the following code,

```
interface I<B implements J> extends B {
  ...
}
```

implies that `B` is an interface with superinterface `J`.

The Java typing rule for method overloading creates another similar restriction. Consider the following class declaration:

```
class L<A> {
  void m(A s)      { ... }
  void m(String s) { ... }
}
```

The class overloads the method name `m` to operate either on a string or an instance of the formal type parameter `A`. In this situation, the instantiation `L<String>` must be rejected because it leads to a class defining two methods with the same signature `m(String)`.

In practice, situations that impose such additional restrictions on actual type parameters occur rarely. They can be statically determined and checked for each instantiation by the compiler. We do not expect them to be difficult for programmers to understand because they all arise from the unsurprising rule that "an instantiation of a parameterized class must conform to all the rules for regular (non-parameterized) classes."

### 4.2 Discussion

This type parameterization mechanism meets our primary language design goals. As previously mentioned, the **extends** and **implements** constraints are based on concepts already present in the Java language. This should make these constraints readily understandable and easy to use by any Java programmer.

```
interface Comparable<I> {
  boolean lessThan(I);
}

class PriorityQueue<T implements Comparable<T>> {
  T queue[];
  void insert(T t) {
    ...
    if (t.lessThan(queue[i])) ...
    ...
  }
  T remove() { ... }
  ...
}
```

Figure 3: A parameterized `PriorityQueue` demonstrating the declaration and use of a contravariant method.

```
interface LessAndEqual<I> {
  boolean lessThan(I);
  boolean equal(I);
}

class Relations<C implements LessAndEqual<C>> extends C {
  boolean greaterThan(Relations<C> a) {
    return a.lessThan(this);
  }
  boolean greaterEqual(Relations<C> a) {
    return greaterThan(a) || equal(a);
  }
  boolean notEqual(Relations<C> a) { ... }
  boolean lessEqual(Relations<C> a) { ... }
  ...
}
```

Figure 4: A mix-in class to add additional relations to any class defining `lessThan` and `equal` relations.

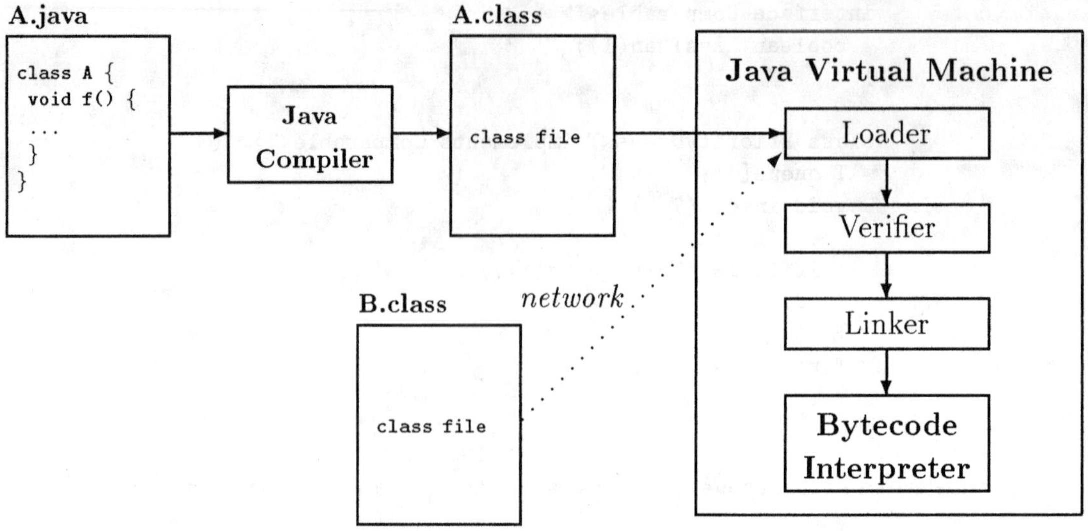


Figure 5: The Java Virtual Machine

The parameterization mechanism is also quite expressive. In addition to the examples already discussed, contravariant method constraints can be described. (A contravariant method is one which takes an argument of the same type as the class in which the method is defined; see [Cas95] for a detailed discussion.) The binary `lessThan` method of the priority queue described in Section 3.3 is a contravariant method. Figure 3 shows how this type of relation may be expressed in our language extension. An even more complex example is shown in Figure 4. The mix-in class defined in the figure not only specifies the existence of contravariant methods for its parameter type, but it also inherits from the parameter.

Parameterized classes and interfaces can be statically type checked using the constraints associated with the parameters. This kind of static checking has been implemented in the Pizza compiler [OW97b] and also the Rapide compiler [KLM94], now in use for several years.

### 4.3 Primitive Types

Our design is sufficiently flexible to allow instantiation with primitive types such as `int` and `float`. However, since primitive types do not implement or extend any classes or interfaces, they can only be used for unconstrained parameters. Also, the resulting instantiations must adhere to all Java type rules relating to primitive types. For example, the class `Stack<int>` is valid, but `Hashtable<int, float>` is not since the primitive type `int` does not implement the `Hashable` interface. While allowing instantiation with primitive types enhances expressiveness, it, comes at a cost in implementation complexity, as discussed in Section 5.3.

To allow basic types to be used where class types are required, the Java class library defines "wrapper" classes for primitive types [AG96, §13.3]. These wrappers can also allow primitive types to be used as actual parameters to classes that only allow instantiation with class or interface types.

### 4.4 Extended Constraints

While the syntax used in this paper allows only one constraint per type parameter, it is essentially straightforward to allow combinations of constraints. For example, we could use the form

```
class C<A implements I extends B>
```

to require `A` to both implement interface `I` and extend class `B`. For longer constraints, it seems more convenient to write constraints after the parameter list, as is customary with `where` clauses [LSAS77].

## 5 Implementation

To set the context for a discussion of our implementation technique, Figure 5 shows a schematic diagram of the Java Virtual Machine. When a running program refers to a class that has not been loaded, compiled bytecode passes through three largely independent components of the virtual machine. The *loader* obtains the bytecode for the class from either a local file or a remote site. The *verifier* validates the bytecode by checking that operation codes are valid, branches are to legitimate locations, methods have structurally correct signatures, and that every instruction obeys the Java type discipline. Finally, the *linker* initializes static fields of the new class and may load related classes. Further information may be found in [LY96].

It is possible for Java programs to modify the behavior of the loader on certain classes by extending the Java **ClassLoader** class. For example, while the default loading mechanism searches the local file system for classes, an alternate **ClassLoader** could obtain classes over the network.

Parameterized classes can be implemented without changing the Java Virtual Machine. Homogeneous implementations, such as those described in [OW97b, Tho97], represent a type variable as a general type, such as **Object**, and use run-time casts to provide the appropriate functionality for different instantiations. Some limitations of this strategy are discussed in more detail in Section 6.

In order to overcome these limitations, we propose a heterogeneous implementation based on *load*-time expansion. This choice is attractive for Java systems for the following reasons:

- Expanding parameterized classes to a form used by non-parameterized classes allows current Java Virtual Machine verifiers, interpreters, and just-in-time compilers to remain unchanged. In addition to retaining compatibility, we also avoid security and other issues that would arise if we changed the Java execution model.
- Postponing expansion from compile time to load time reduces the size of compiled code. This could be significant when compiled code is transmitted over a network.

The general strategy is to compile a parameterized class into an extended form of the class file. In addition to all the information usually found in a class file, the extended file includes information about parameters and constraints. When the virtual machine attempts to load an instantiation of a parameterized class or interface, a loader preprocess phase transforms the parameterized class file into the desired instantiation and then declares it as if it were a normal class. In other words, one "template" class file is used to generate regular, non-parameterized **Class** objects for each instantiation of a parameterized class. For example, the contents of the **Hashtable.class** file is used by the loader to generate both the **Hashtable<Name, Integer>** and **Hashtable<Name, Point>** classes.

The rest of this section describes our implementation technique in more detail. Section 5.1 outlines the Java class file format. Section 5.2 describes our preprocessor, focusing on the transformation used to instantiate a parameterized class with a class or an interface. Then, Section 5.3 sketches instantiation with primitive types. Section 5.4 discusses advantages and disadvantages of this implementation technique, and Section 5.5 describes a prototype implementation and our experience with it.

### 5.1 Java Class Files

A class file is a binary representation for a compiled class that can be loaded by any Java Virtual Machine. The major pieces of the class file are a header, starting with a distinguishing magic number, a constant pool, and a description of the fields and methods in the class. This format is summarized in Figure 6 and discussed in detail in [LY96].

The constant pool contains strings representing all names mentioned in the class file, including class names, field and method names, type names, and so on. The index of an entry in the constant pool is used wherever that constant is needed in the class file. The Java Virtual Machine uses these strings for many operations including type checking, dynamic linking, and run-time resolution of field and method names. For example, Figure 7 shows some Java bytecodes and the corresponding program text. The **#4**, **#5**, and **#6** in the bytecodes refer to entries in the constant pool, and the text printed after these numbers are the strings stored in the constant pool.

### 5.2 Load-Time Expansion

One very convenient aspect of the class file format is that most type information generated when a class is compiled is stored in its constant pool as strings. The only exception is type information about primitive types, such as integers, which is embedded directly into the bytecode instructions (see Section 5.3).

To support load-time instantiation of parameterized class files, we propose an extended class file format, as shown in Figure 6. The file begins with a unique identifying number different from the standard class file magic number. Following this are the argument constraints, whose form is also shown. The format of the constraints is straightforward. The one constraint generated by our **Hashtable** example is:

| 1 |
|---|
| implements |
| "Hashable" |

If we were to allow multiple constraints on each type parameter, the constraint format could be adapted straightforwardly.

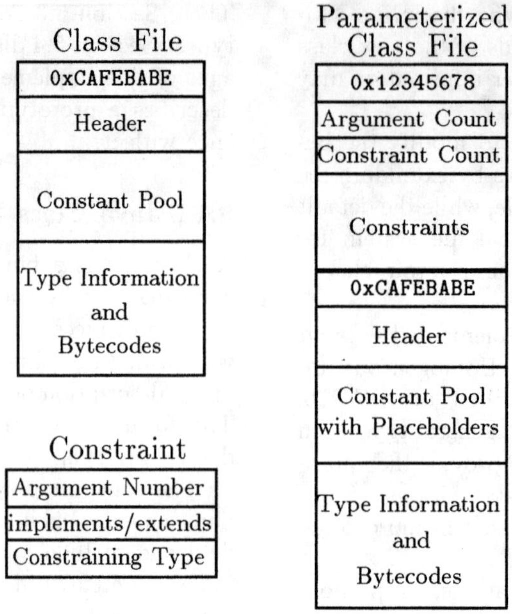


Figure 6: The original class file format, extensions for parameterized classes, and the format of a constraint.

```
class A {
   int i;
   void increment() {
     set(i + 1);
   }



   void set(int value) {
     i = value;
   }
}


 A a;
 a.increment();
```

```
Method void increment()
  aload_0
  aload_0
  getfield #5 <Field A.i I>
  iconst_1
  iadd
  invokevirtual #6 <Method A.set(I)V>
  return

Method void set(int)
  ...



  aload_0    /* push a onto stack */
  invokevirtual #4 <Method A.increment()V>
```

Figure 7: Sample Java class and bytecodes

The entire binary representation for the parameterized class follows after the constraints. The only difference between this section and a standard class file is that special placeholders take the place of type names wherever parameters are used in the constant pool. In this paper, we will use `$1`, `$2`, etc. for these placeholders, but they can be any strings not appearing in the constant pool entries containing type information in a standard class file.

As discussed earlier, the Java Virtual Machine loads and links classes dynamically. The operations performed when a `ClassLoader` loads a class (or an interface) are:

- Fetch the bytes in the binary representation of the required class, perhaps from a file or over the network.
- Pass the bytes into the virtual machine to have them verified and turned into the virtual machine's internal representation of classes. This step produces a `Class` object.

All loaded classes are stored in a table so that they can be used again without reloading.

The design of the loader provides a great deal of flexibility in the way the binary representation of a class is located. We take advantage of this flexibility by augmenting the existing Java loader to create instantiations of parameterized classes. The steps involved in this process are listed below. Note that non-parameterized classes continue to be loaded in the usual manner. The steps to load an instantiation are:

- Convert the name of the class into a parameterized class name and argument names.
- Translate the argument names to class and interface types. This may involve loading other class files.
- Find the file containing the binary representation of the parameterized class and read it into memory.
- Check the parameter constraints against the arguments. If a constraint is violated, raise an exception.
- If the instantiation is valid, generate the binary representation of the instantiation from the parameterized class file and arguments; proceed in the usual manner to create a `Class` object for it. The bytecode verification process will ensure that the few remaining type checks described in Section 4.1 are performed.

Since the Java Virtual Machine specification does not allow class names of the syntactic form `Hashtable<Name, Integer>`, the compiler and `ClassLoader` must rewrite parameterized class names into a valid form. (This is similar to the way that inner class names are mapped onto the flat name-space of the virtual machine [Jav96]).

The heart of the implementation, when instantiating a parameterized class with a class or interface type, is the algorithm for transforming a parameterized class file into binary representations for different instantiations. For each parameter, we replace each occurrence of its placeholder with the actual argument's name in the constant pool. Figure 8 shows an example of this replacement method.

Once the replacements are made, the binary representation for the instantiation can be treated by the loader, verifier, and interpreter just as if it were an unparameterized class.

### 5.3 Instantiation with Primitive Types

The implementation technique described above does not work for instantiating classes with primitive types since different bytecodes are used for different primitive types. For example, the bytecode instruction for integer addition is different from the instruction for real addition. A load-time preprocessor can support instantiation with primitive types by modifying the bytecode instructions for parameterized classes. However, this is clearly a more complex transformation than required for class or interface arguments.

### 5.4 Discussion

By delaying instantiation until load time, we are able to achieve many of the stated design goals. Since the bytecode verifier and interpreter remain unaffected, type correctness and other properties of Java program execution are not compromised.

Our class file format for parameterized classes allows for separate compilation of a parameterized class and programs which create instances of it. Once the parameterized class file has been generated, a check against the constraints stored in that file guarantees type correctness of an instantiation, except for a few situations in which there is insufficient information in the constraints to guarantee this. As mentioned in Section 4.1, these cases can be checked by the compiler, but they must also be checked at load time since the Java Virtual Machine cannot assume all programs originate from a trusted compiler. We rely on the existing run-time bytecode verification process to catch these instantiations that conform to the declared constraints but are not valid classes.

*Hashtable<$1,$2>*.`insert` method:

```
Method void insert($1,$2)
 aload_1
 invokevirtual #6 <Method $1.hashCode()I>
 istore_3
 aload_0
 iload_3
 aload_1
 aload_2
 invokevirtual #7 <Method Hashtable<$1,$2>.insertAt(IL$1;L$2;)V>
 return
```

*Hashtable<Name,Integer>*.`insert` method:

```
Method void insert(Name,Integer)
 aload_1
 invokevirtual #6 <Method Name.hashCode()I>
 istore_3
 aload_0
 iload_3
 aload_1
 aload_2
 invokevirtual #7 <Method Hashtable<Name,Integer>.insertAt(ILName;LInteger;)V>
 return
```

Figure 8: Java bytecodes for the `insert` method as it appears in the `Hashtable` parameterized class file, and the same method instantiated as `Hashtable<Name, Integer>.insert`. The italicized names would be replaced by "mangled" names conforming to the rules for Java class names.

Load-time instantiation provides size and speed tradeoffs that are consistent with the rest of the Java system. The existence of only a single compiled class file for all instantiations of a parameterized class makes binary representations compact on disk and furthermore allow efficient distribution of Java classes over a network. At run time, there is some memory consumption increase, compared with a homogeneous implementation, because a new class is generated for each instantiation. Most Java Virtual Machines in use today do not share data structures between similar classes (such as the classes resulting from multiple instantiations of a parameterized class), leading to a memory demand increase proportional to the number of instantiations of the parameterized class. We have no absolute numbers yet, and cannot obtain such numbers until we have a better understanding of the extent to which parameterized types will be used in typical Java applications, but we expect that the memory increase will be small relative to the memory requirements for the system as a whole. This expectation seems to be confirmed by other systems, such as C++ and Ada, that use heterogeneous implementations of parameterization mechanisms.

Compared with a homogeneous implementation, load-time instantiation of parameterized classes increases the time spent loading classes during program execution, but in exchange enables faster execution because the resulting classes often contain fewer run-time type checks. Based on our preliminary tests and analysis of Java programs, we expect both the slow-down and the speed-up effects to be relatively small and have little impact on overall performance. Most Java applications today spend little time loading classes and performing run-time type checks.

It is important that the bytecodes produced for a parameterized class instantiation match the intended semantics of that language feature. For example, one would expect that adding an `Integer` object to the `Stack<String>` object in Figure 1 would be a type error, meaning that the bytecode verifier and interpreter should not allow that operation at run time. If it were allowed, a potential security problem would exist. Since parameterized class files are instantiated with the actual type parameters, our implementation prevents incorrect operations like this. However, implementations in which type variables are represented by a more general type than specified by the instantiation declaration may in fact compromise the language semantics in this way. This is true of some of the homogeneous implementations discussed in Section 6.

The idea of using a load-time preprocessor to expand parameterized classes is a general implementation tech-

| Proposal | Language Extension | | | | Implementation | | | |
|---|---|---|---|---|---|---|---|---|
| | Type Parameters | | | Inheritance | Instantiations use Shared Code | | Instantiations use Separate Code | |
| | Constraints | | No Constraints | | | | | |
| | implements/ extends | new type relation | | | Shared type info | Separate type info | Compile-time | Load-time |
| Pizza | X | | | | X | | | |
| where Clauses | | X | | | | X | | |
| C++ | | | X | | | | X | |
| Virtual Types | | | | X | | | X | |
| This Paper | X | | | | | | | X |

Figure 9: A summary of the language extensions and implementation techniques described in the different proposals. C++ is included as a reference point.

nique. It can be used to implement other proposals for type parameterization, as long as their semantics can be realized by a heterogeneous implementation. The preprocessor could also be used to experiment with other language features in the context of Java systems.

We have found the Java bytecode format to be an attractive representation when developing systems that use load-time expansion. The Java bytecode format offers architecture independence and a much higher abstraction level compared to more traditional systems, such as the C++ compile-time or link-time template instantiation that operates on machine code. The level of abstraction is particularly important when it may be necessary to report errors at instantiation time. Without high-level format and type information, it can be difficult to detect and report errors in a meaningful way (i.e., relate them to the source code).

### 5.5 A Prototype Implementation

A prototype of the virtual machine extension described in Section 5.2 has been implemented and tested using Sun's JDK 1.0.2 source release. While a full compiler for parameterized classes has not been implemented, this prototype is sufficient to test the effectiveness of load-time instantiation. The implementation consists of approximately 500 lines of Java code and a ten line change to the default loader in the Java Virtual Machine. A successful prototype was built as a subclass of the `ClassLoader` class, but we found that this was too restrictive for general use since we could not install that `ClassLoader` as the default for the Java Virtual Machine. Therefore, we made one minor change to the underlying default loader to make it recognize parameterized classes. Although this prototype makes several minor assumptions (such as "_" not appearing in any class name and that all classes are loaded by the same `ClassLoader`), it is clear that the changes to Java's runtime environment are very straightforward and isolated to one small section of the virtual machine. In a later implementation, we plan to remove the limitations on the existing version and to add primitive type arguments, which were also left out of the original prototype.

In addition to creating parameterized class files for all examples in this paper, we have taken several classes from the `java.util` package, such as `java.util.Hashtable`, and transformed them into parameterized classes. Making these new classes required virtually no change to the existing code other than replacing `Object` with the parameter identifiers, `$1`, `$2`, etc., and inserting constraint information at the top of the class files. The run-time speed of the parameterized versions of these classes improved slightly. To cite one specific example, a program which populated a `java.util.Hashtable` and then performed one million lookup operations increased in speed by 2–3% when the hash table was replaced by our parameterized version of it.

## 6 Related Work

There have been several other proposals for adding parameterized types or generic classes to Java. Although it may appear that the language extensions from these proposals are equally expressive and that the different implementation strategies are more or less equal in power, fundamental differences do exist between them. This section discusses the other proposed designs, touching on the distinguishing features, as well as potential advantages and disadvantages, of each. The language and implementation choices of all proposals described below are summarized in Figure 9.

### 6.1 `where` Clauses

One proposal, described in [MBL97], presents a Java extension similar to `where` clauses in CLU [LSAS77]. There are several semantic differences between that constraint mechanism and the ones used in both Pizza (discussed below) and this paper. On the positive side,

```
class BroadcastList<C extends Channel> {
  C channels[];
  void add(C c) { ... }
  void broadcast(String s)  {
    int i;
    for (i = 0; i < channels.length(); i++)
      channels[i].send(s);
  }
  ...
}

class EncryptedChannel extends Channel;
class UnencryptedChannel extends Channel;

BroadcastList<EncryptedChannel> list = ...;
list.add(new EncryptedChannel());
(*)
list.broadcast("Hello");
```

Figure 10: A list of `EncryptedChannels` that could be attacked by handwritten bytecodes to add an `UnencryptedChannel` if `C` does not contain the exact type of the argument for each instantiation.

**where** clauses allow the programmer to state that a class conforms to a certain constraint without explicitly declaring the relationship when the class is defined. In our `Hashtable` example, **where** clauses would allow the programmer to use any class that has a `hashCode` method as the `Key` instead of just those declared to implement the `Hashable` interface. If only existing Java constructs for subtype relations are used, namely **implements** and **extends**, this type of constraint cannot be expressed. However, since this problem in Java arises in situations outside of parameterized classes, it seems more reasonable to solve this problem for Java as a whole instead of introducing a new type relation only in the context of parameterized class constraints. Section 7 describes two possible Java extensions that allow subtyping relations to be declared without changing class declarations.

The main implementation described in [MBL97] for **where** clauses changes the bytecodes and virtual machine significantly in order to allow shared code, but separate constant pool information, among instantiations of a parameterized class. This makes the implementation more costly and the virtual machine more complicated than our method. Any change to the bytecodes and bytecode verifier will require all safety and security aspects of the system to be reevaluated. Clearly, this could be an undesirable and daunting task. An implementation based on load-time instantiation would be possible for **where** clauses by adding more forms of constraints to those described in Section 5.

## 6.2 Pizza

Pizza [OW97b] is another parametric class extension using a constraint mechanism based on F-bounded quantification [CCH+89] and the **extends** and **implements** type relations. However, the type parameters in Pizza are prevented from appearing in certain places were class names may appear. For example, two errors occur in the following program when compiled in Pizza [OW97a]:

```
class List<A> {
  static A a;     // not allowed in Pizza
  void newA() {
    A a;
    a = new A();  // not allowed in Pizza
  }
}
```

Both statements would be allowed in our implementation and the **where** clause approach of [MBL97]. Another restriction is that a class cannot inherit from a parameter, making mix-ins impossible to express.

Although these limitations may result from a different model of parametric types, the homogeneous implementation used by the Pizza compiler makes these features difficult, if not impossible, to implement. Pizza creates a single class file for each parameterized class. This class represents each type argument as the most general possible type for that argument. The compiler then inserts casts into the bytecodes that use instances of a parameterized class to ensure type correctness. These casts are similar to those discussed in the context of the `Stack` class and other examples in Section 3, but are added by the compiler instead of by the programmer. This strategy does allow the Java Virtual Machine to remain unchanged, but it clearly limits how type variables can be used and also still requires run-time casts. Our implementation does not have these limitations since the instantiation of a parameterized class replaces type variables with the actual type of an implemented class, allowing type variables to appear wherever a class name may appear.

It is also worth keeping the security implications of each implementation technique in mind. If the type used in the place of a parameter is more general than the actual argument type in an instantiation, as it is in Pizza, there is the possibility that hand-coded bytecode could take advantage of this discrepancy. Specifically, compiler type checking and the compiler-inserted run-time checks guaranteeing type safety when parameterized types are used could be circumvented by using bytecodes not generated by the Pizza compiler.

For example, someone may be able to insert an unencrypted channel into a list of encrypted channels used by a library for secure communication, as shown in Figure 10. In Pizza, the `EncryptedChannel` instantiation of `BroadcastList` would use bytecodes based on `C` having the type `Channel`, meaning `BroadcastList<EncryptedChannel>.add` would take an argument of type `Channel`. If we manually inserted bytecodes to add an `UnencryptedChannel` object to `list` at position `(*)`, there would be no way to catch this error in the bytecode verifier or at run time since an `UnencryptedChannel` is a subtype of `Channel`. The only way to prevent this is to give `BroadcastList<EncryptedChannel>.add` a type where the parameter can only be an `EncryptedChannel`.

As discussed in [DFW96], it is very important that the semantics of the Java language matches the semantics of the generated bytecode instructions. In that paper, the authors discuss a situation where valid bytecodes are able to perform an action prohibited by the language. A similar situation occurs in Figure 10. Bytecodes that are seemingly valid to the Java Virtual Machine do in fact perform an operation which the language restricts. In order to maintain the desired security properties, such situations must be prevented. An alternative heterogeneous implementation based on C++ -style macro expansion, also discussed in the Pizza paper, does eliminate this problem, but it is unclear whether that implementation would be able to support separate compilation of parameterized classes without changing the class file in a way similar to our method.

### 6.3 Virtual Types

Virtual types have also been suggested as a way to implement parametric types [Tho97]. The main idea is to allow type members of classes that are "virtual" in the sense of C++ virtual members, with derived classes allowed to redefine a virtual type member to any of its subtypes. This idea can be used in a manner similar to parameterized types, since in each subclass, the virtual type could be given the same value as the argument to the corresponding parameterized class. In general, redefining a type member in a subclass does not create a subtype due to contravariance. To ensure that a subtype is created, the virtual types proposal forces covariance through run-time casts and type checks. This is similar to the checking required to ensure type safety of Java's covariant arrays. In addition to the loss of static typing for parameterized classes due to these required casts, tying genericity to inheritance also limits expressiveness. For example, mix-ins can not be expressed.

In the implementation described in [Tho97], compiler generated virtual methods and casts perform run-time type checks and typecasts needed to ensure type correctness of all contravariant uses of virtual types. Due to this reliance on compiler generated code, the system is potentially susceptible to the same type of security loopholes as described above.

### 6.4 Run-time Efficiency

One final point of comparison between these methods is that inserted type casts add run-time overhead. The cost of casts used for type correctness of instantiations have been measured to be anywhere from 1% to 5% [Tho97] of the run time, with degenerate cases costing up to 17% [MBL97]. Our own measurements are within the range cited in [Tho97]. Considering Java's design goals, this penalty is not overly restrictive, but it should still be considered in the tradeoffs between different proposals. This overhead may become more or less significant as better optimized bytecode and native compilers are used for Java programs.

## 7 Additional Language Issues

There are two main avenues for future work. The first is to examine some remaining language issues. A second, more tentative, future direction involves studying aspects of the Java language that have been more problematic for us and suggesting language modifications.

Two language design issues that require further examination are the exact format of **extends** and **implements** clauses and interactions between overloaded methods and parameterized classes. Overloaded

```
class B extends A { ... }

class Printer {
  void print(A a) { ... }
  void print(B b) { ... }
}

class C<T extends A> {
  void callPrint(Printer p) {
    T temp;
    ...
    p.print(temp);
  }
}

C<B> c = new C<B>();
Printer printer = new Printer();
c.callPrint(printer);
```

Figure 11: An example of overloaded methods and parameterized classes.

methods could either be resolved on a per-instantiation basis, or once for all instantiations. Figure 11 shows a situation where the two resolution strategies result in different method invocations.

We also believe it will be useful to examine some of the Java type restrictions and determine whether they can be made more lenient. Two specific items of interest are specification of constructors and post-facto declaration of subtype relationships.

Constructors are not inherited by subclasses and cannot be specified in an interface. As a consequence, there is no way to specify that a type variable will always be instantiated with a class that has a certain constructor available. Thus, requiring the presence of a constructor falls into the category of type rules which must be checked on each instantiation individually. However, it may be beneficial to be able to express the presence of constructors in parameter constraints. The `where` clause proposal described in Section 6.1 allows explicit constraints on the presence of constructors, and that aspect of `where` clauses could be adapted to our method. A more suitable solution may be to allow constructors to be specified in an interface, but it remains to be seen if this is a feasible addition to the Java language.

The inability to specify a subtype relationship for an existing class limits not only the expressive power of our constraint mechanism but the expressive power of the Java language as a whole. One way to alleviate this limitation would be through an `implementedBy` declaration. An example is shown in Figure 12. Structural conformance has also been proposed as a solution to this problem [LBR96]. Any class implementing all the methods listed in an interface could be used as a value of that interface type, regardless of whether the class was declared to implement it or not. There are many issues and tradeoffs involved with structural conformance, such as accidental conformance, and it is unclear whether or not it is a good match for the Java language.

## 8 Conclusions

This paper describes a parameterized type mechanism for the Java programming language and an implementation based on inserting a preprocess step into the load phase of the Java Virtual Machine. The language extension, based in part on an analysis of parameterization in object-oriented languages reported in [CCH+89] and essentially similar to the extension considered in [OW97b], appears adequate for most common situations. It uses only type relations `implements` and `extends`, which are familiar to Java programmers.

In comparison with competing proposals described in Section 6, our implementation is relatively simple and supports more flexible language extensions than others. By delaying instantiation until load time, we are able to achieve what we believe is an appropriate balance between language expressiveness, run-time efficiency and compiled code size. Since the changes to the Java virtual machine are restricted to the loader, we expect that our implementation can be easily added to most Java virtual machines. Moreover, use of the standard verifier and bytecode interpreter means that our Java language extensions do not compromise any security properties. We believe that this language extension will be easy for Java programmers to adopt and use effectively, and interfere minimally with any current

```
class Name {
  int hashCode() { ... }
  ...
}

interface Hashable implementedBy Name {
  int hashCode();
}

class Hashtable<Key implements Hashable, Value> { ... }

Hashtable<Name, Integer> table = new Hashtable<Name, Integer>();
```

Figure 12: Specifying an `implements` relationship after a class has been declared.

or future developments in Java implementation.

Our prototype implementation of an extended Java Virtual Machine demonstrates that load-time instantiation is an effective mechanism with many clear benefits. Although we believe that language extensions should be considered slowly and conservatively, it is possible that our implementation strategy using the Java loader may be a useful starting point for other potential extensions to the Java language.

*Acknowledgments:* We would like to thank Guy Steele for his comments and suggestions, including the `implementedBy` construct shown in Figure 12. We also thank Gilad Bracha, David Detlefs, and Kathleen Fisher for their many useful discussions and comments.

## References

[AG96] Ken Arnold and James Gosling. *The Java Programming Language.* Addison-Wesley, 1996.

[BCC+96] Kim B. Bruce, Luca Cardelli, Giuseppe Castagna, the Hopkins Objects Group, Gary T. Leavens, and Benjamin Pierce. On binary methods. *Theory and Practice of Object Systems*, 1(3):221–242, 1996.

[Cas95] Giuseppe Castagna. Covariance and contravariance: Conflict without a cause. *ACM Transactions on Programming Languages and Systems*, 17(3):431–447, May 1995.

[CCH+89] P. Canning, W. Cook, W. Hill, J. Mitchell, and W. Olthoff. F-bounded quantification for object-oriented programming. In *Functional Prog. and Computer Architecture*, pages 273–280, 1989.

[DFW96] Drew Dean, Edward W. Felten, and Dan S. Wallach. Java security: from HotJava to netscape and beyond. In *Proceedings of the IEEE Computer Society Symposium on Research in Security and Privacy*, pages 190–200, 1996.

[ES90] M. Ellis and B. Stroustrup. *The Annotated C++ Reference Manual.* Addison-Wesley, 1990.

[Jav96] JavaSoft. Innerclasses in Java 1.1. available from http://java.sun.com, 1996.

[KLM94] D. Katiyar, D. Luckham, and J.C. Mitchell. A type system for prototyping languages. In *Proc. 21-st ACM Symp. on Principles of Programming Languages*, 1994.

[L+81] B. Liskov et al. *CLU Reference Manual.* Springer LNCS 114, Berlin, 1981.

[LBR96] Konstantin Läufer, Gerald Baumgartner, and Vincent F. Russo. Safe structural conformance in java. Technical Report CSD-TR-96-077, Purdue University, December 1996.

[LSAS77] Barbara Liskov, Alan Snyder, Russell Atkinson, and Craig Schaffert. Abstraction mechanisms in CLU. *Communications of the ACM*, 20(8):564–576, August 1977.

[LY96] Tim Lindholm and Frank Yellin. *The Java Virtual Machine Specification.* Addison-Wesley, 1996.

[MBL97] Andrew C. Myers, Joseph A. Bank, and Barbara Liskov. Parameterized types for Java. In *Proc. 24th ACM Symposium on Principles of Programming Languages*, pages 132–145, January 1997.

[Mil85] R. Milner. The Standard ML core language. *Polymorphism*, 2(2), 1985. 28 pages. An earlier version appeared in Proc. 1984 ACM Symp. on Lisp and Functional Programming.

[Mit96] J.C. Mitchell. *Foundations for Programming Languages.* MIT Press, 1996.

[MS95] D. R. Musser and A. Saini. *STL Tutorial and Reference Guide.* Addison-Wesley, 1995.

[OW97a] Martin Odersky and Philip Wadler. The Pizza compiler. available from http://www.math.luc.edu/pizza, February 1997.

[OW97b] Martin Odersky and Philip Wadler. Pizza into Java: Translating theory into practice. In *Proc. 24th ACM Symposium on Principles of Programming Languages*, January 1997.

[PSLM96] P. J. Plauger, A. A. Stepanov, M. Lee, and D. R. Musser. *The Standard Template Library.* Prentice-Hall, 1996.

[Tho97] Kresten Krab Thorup. Genericity in Java with virtual types. In *European Conference On Object Oriented Programming*, 1997.

[Ull94] J.D. Ullman. *Elements of ML programming.* Prentice Hall, 1994.

[US 80] US Dept. of Defense. *Reference Manual for the Ada Programming Language.* GPO 008-000-00354-8, 1980.

# Parasitic Methods: An Implementation of Multi-Methods for Java

John Boyland*
Computer Science Department,
Carnegie Mellon University,
5000 Forbes Avenue,
Pittsburgh, PA 15213-3891, USA
E-mail: john.boyland@acm.org

Giuseppe Castagna
CNRS, LIENS,
École Normale Supérieure,
45 rue d'Ulm,
75005 Paris, France.
E-mail: castagna@dmi.ens.fr

## Abstract

In an object-oriented programming language, method selection is (usually) done at run-time using the class of the receiver. Some object-oriented languages (such as CLOS) have *multi-methods* which comprise several methods selected on the basis of the run-time classes of all the parameters, not just the receiver. Multi-methods permit intuitive and type-safe definition of binary methods such as structural equality, set inclusion and matrix multiplication, just to name a few. Java as currently defined does not support multi-methods. This paper defines a simple extension to Java that enables the writing of "encapsulated" multi-methods through the use of *parasitic* methods, methods that "attach" themselves to other methods. Encapsulated multi-methods avoid some of the modularity problems that arise with fully general multi-methods. Furthermore, this extension yields for free both covariant and contravariant specialization of methods (besides Java's current invariant specialization).

Programs using this extension can be translated automatically at the source level into programs that do not; they are modular, type-safe, and allow separate compilation.

## 1 Introduction

In an object-oriented language, method selection is (usually) done at run-time using the class of the receiver. Some object-oriented languages (such as CLOS [DG87, Ste90]) have *multi-methods* (also known as *generic functions*) which comprise several methods selected on the basis of the run-time classes of all the parameters, not just the receiver. Unfortunately Java, like its predecessor C++, does not provide multi-methods. Stroustrup, the designer of C++, regrets that he was unable to consider providing multi-methods in his language, essentially because, as he admits, he was not able to find how to do it (see Section 13.8 of [Str94]). With this work, we demonstrate that this situation can be avoided for Java.

In this paper, we show how one can implement the special case of "encapsulated" multi-methods for Java. While specific to Java, our ideas can be applied with little change to other languages. Our solution does not implement multi-methods in their most general form, since we want to preserve two of the most important properties of Java: modularity and separate compilation. Another goal is that our extension should be *conservative*, that is, have no effect on existing Java programs. To these ends, we adapt the well-established technique of *encapsulated* multi-methods (one of the solutions proposed by Bruce *et al.* [BCC+96] for typing binary methods). We call the enabling technical feature *parasitic* methods.

A *parasitic* method is a Java method in its own right which, *additionally*, extends the functionality of other methods (the *host* methods) for certain argument cases. If a host method is called with arguments that fit the parasitic method's parameter types, the parasitic method body is called instead of the host method body. A parasitic method usually *covariantly specializes* host methods, that is, handles some subset of the cases handled by the hosts. In earlier work [BC96], we have shown that covariant specialization is type safe, if, as with the parasitic methods described here, the new method only *partially overrides* the original method, that is, it overrides the method only for those arguments it can handle. A parasitic method may also *contravariantly specialize* a host method, that is, handle any possible set of arguments passed to the host, and handle other cases as well. In this case, the host method body will never be executed. Analogous to a mistletoe plant that draws nourishment from its host oak tree, a parasitic method draws from its host methods calls that the parasite can handle (according to the dynamic types of the arguments). Parasitic methods reconcile covariant and contravariant specialization in a single simple framework, while standard Java allows only invariant specialization (that is, a method can be overridden only by a method defined for the same parameter types), without sacrificing type safety or separate compilation.

Extending Java with parasitic methods is conservative; the extension does not affect the typing or the semantics (or even the performance) of Java programs that do not contain parasitic methods. Indeed, we show later that parasitic methods can be considered as a sort of syntactic sugar since they can be directly translated into standard Java.

*Effort sponsored by the Defense Advanced Research Projects Agency, and Rome Laboratory, Air Force Materiel Command, USAF, under agreement number F30602-97-2-0241. The views and conclusions contained herein are those of the authors and should not be interpreted as necessarily representing the official policies or endorsements, either expressed or implied, of the Defense Advanced Research Projects Agency, Rome Laboratory or the U.S. Government.


**OOPSLA '97 10/97 GA, USA**

The paper is organized as follows. In Section 2, we introduce parasitic methods using several examples. We then describe how they are inherited and overridden, and informally describe type-checking and run-time selection. The latter two topics are detailed precisely in Section 3. In Section 4, we demonstrate a translation of parasitic methods into standard Java. Some of the design issues we engaged are exposed in Section 5. We discuss practical implications in Section 6, review related work in Section 7, and present issues for further work in Section 8. A conclusion ends the body of the paper.

```
class IntList {
  public IntList union(IntList l)
          { body for unioning two lists  }
}

class IntSortedList extends IntList {
  public parasitic IntSortedList union(IntSortedList l)
          { body for merging two ordered lists  }
}
```

Figure 1: Parasite of an inherited host method

## 2 Parasitic Methods

In this section we describe parasitic methods informally. First we give several examples. Then we describe what hosts a parasite "attaches" to, what additional static checking rules parasitic methods entail, and which parasite is selected dynamically when a host with multiple parasites is called. We end the section with a discussion of how our proposal preserves modularity.

### 2.1 Examples

In this section, we show several different ways to use parasitic methods. We start by showing what we consider their "standard" use, namely the covariant specialization of another method. Next, we show how parasites can be used to express contravariant method overriding. Lastly, we show some static parasites.

Despite their different uses, all parasitic methods obey the same selection discipline: at compile-time the standard Java overloading resolution[1] is performed for every method invocation (ignoring whether methods are declared as parasites or not); at run time if a method is selected and has a parasite, it passes the control to it when the parasite is applicable to the run-time types of the method's arguments.

#### 2.1.1 Covariant parasites

A method is declared *parasitic* using the method modifier `parasitic`. For a simple example of parasitic methods, consider a class `IntList` with a method `union` that takes as argument another instance of `IntList` and produces a list that contains all the elements of `this` (Java's identifier for message receiver), as well as all elements from the argument that do not already occur in `this`. The method might be implemented using a naive $O(mn)$ algorithm (where $m$ and $n$ are the lengths of the two lists), or perhaps by a more sophisticated $O(m \lg m + n \lg n)$ algorithm that sorted them first.

Later, we define a subclass `IntSortedList`, in which methods are overridden so that the instances of this class are always ordered. The method `union` can be inherited from `IntList`. However it is clear that computing the union of two ordered lists can be done more efficiently using a simple $O(m+n)$ merge. The merge is implemented in a parasitic method in the definition of `IntSortedList` as shown in Figure 1. In Figure 1, the class `IntSortedList` inherits a method `union` that works on general `IntList`'s and also defines a new more specific method that handles the case of unioning two sorted lists. Java uses compile-time overloading to select methods, and so if the static type of two lists is `IntSortedList`, the more efficient method will be selected. However, if one of the two lists being unioned has static type of `IntList`, the Java compiler will select the general, less efficient method. By making the more efficient method a *parasitic* method, the general method yields to the efficient method *at run-time*. Indeed when a method is declared parasitic it automatically parasitizes every method *less specific* than it (a method is less specific than a second method if it has the same name and number of parameters, and the type of each parameter is a supertype of the type of the corresponding parameter in the second method; informally, a method is less specific than a parasite if it handles every argument the parasite could handle). In the example then the method declared in `IntList` parasitizes the method inherited from `IntSortedList`. Technically, the parasite does not *override* the host (the inherited method). It "attaches" itself to the host and diverts calls away that the parasite can handle. In essence, before executing its body, the general method checks the run-time type of the argument and calls the specific method if it is applicable. (As with static method selection, `null` is assumed to be an instance of every class.)

In Figure 1, the method in the subclass parasitizes a method inherited from the superclass. Of course, it is also possible to parasitize a method that is defined in the same class. For instance, in our example, even if only one of the two lists to union is ordered, it is possible to execute more efficiently (if $m$ is the length of the ordered list, we have an $O(n \lg n + m)$ algorithm). Thus an even more efficient solution would be to override the method inherited from `IntList` as well, as shown in Figure 2. In this case, when the argument of the method is an instance of `IntList`, the overriding version of `union` is executed.[2]

[1] The static class of the receiver and its superclasses are examined for accessible definitions of the method. The most specific method applicable to the static types of the arguments, if one exists, is chosen at compile time. Otherwise, the call is flagged as either being ambiguous or having no applicable method. In standard Java, the actual method to be invoked will be determined at run time, using dynamic method lookup (i.e., using the dynamic type of the receiver to select among the methods that override the statically selected method).

[2] In the example in Figure 2, the return type of overriding method `union(IntList l)` in class `IntSortedList` is a subclass of the return type of the method it overrides. This discipline of overriding was implemented in an early version of the Java compiler and Drossopoulou and Eisenbach have shown it to be type safe [DE97]. Thus, although the actual Java specification requires the result type of an overriding method to be the same as the result type of the method it overrides, we have chosen to adopt the less strict discipline.

```
class Union {
  public static parasitic IntList union(IntList l1, IntList l2)
      { return union(IntSortedList.sort(l1),IntSortedList.sort(l2)); }
  public static parasitic IntList union(IntList l1, IntSortedList l2)
      { return union(IntSortedList.sort(l1),l2); }
  public static parasitic IntList union(IntSortedList l1, IntList l2)
      { return union(l1,IntSortedList.sort(l2)); }
  public static parasitic IntSortedList union(IntSortedList l1, IntSortedList l2)
      { body for merging two ordered lists }
}
```

Figure 4: Static parasitic method example

```
class IntList {
  public IntList  union(IntList l)
            { body for unioning two lists }
}

class IntSortedList extends IntList {
  public IntSortedList  union(IntList l)
            { body for efficiently unioning two
              lists when the first is ordered }

  public parasitic IntSortedList  union(IntSortedList l)
            { body for merging two ordered lists }
}
```

Figure 2: Parasite of a local host method

```
interface IntBag {
      :       // various method signatures
}

class IntList implements IntBag {
  public IntList union(IntList l) { ... }
      :       // implementation of interface's signatures
}

class IntSortedList extends IntList {
  public parasitic IntSortedList union(IntBag b)
        { super general version }
  public parasitic IntSortedList union(IntSortedList l)
        { efficient specific version }
}
```

Figure 3: Contravariant Parasite

### 2.1.2 Contravariant parasites

In the examples above, all the parasites covariantly specialize their host, that is, they handle fewer arguments than their host. Our proposal gives the programmer the power of *contravariant specialization*, in which a new method handles *more* cases than the method it takes the place of. A parasite not only attaches to all less specific methods defined in the class (that is, declared or inherited), but also to any more specific inherited method. In the latter case, the host yields *all* control to the parasite, as if it had been overridden. For example, suppose in `IntSortedList` we decided to implement `union` for any `IntBag` object, where `IntBag` is declared as an interface and that `IntList` implements it (see Figure 3). By declaring the general version of the method parasitic, we completely shadow the union method in `IntList`. When an instance of `IntSortedList` receives a union message, it executes the second method declared in its class if the argument is an `IntSortedList`, the first one otherwise.

### 2.1.3 Parasites for static methods

It is also possible to attach parasites to static methods, as long as the parasites are also static. In this case, all the methods must be declared in a single class, since static methods are not overridden in subclasses, only shadowed. Figure 4 shows how one could write a multi-method of four methods for unioning lists. Here, for uniformity, all methods are declared `parasitic`, although the first has no hosts. The static method `IntSortedList.sort` is used to sort a list and return an `IntSortedList` instance. The most specific method will be chosen at run-time.

## 2.2 Inheritance

When one class extends another class with parasitic methods, the parasite-host relation is inherited.

As with regular methods, a parasitic method is *overridden* whenever a method with the same name and the same parameter types is defined in the subclass. Otherwise, assuming the method is accessible, it is *inherited*.

When a parasitic method is overridden by a non-parasitic method, the new method remains implicitly parasitic, with exactly the hosts (and the parasites) it had before, except that if any of these methods is overridden by a method declared parasitic, the connection is broken.

For the sake of an example, we define in Figure 5 the class `IntSortedList`, a subclass of `IntList` from Figure 1, with three `union` methods for arguments of type `IntList`,

```
class IntSortedList extends IntList {
  public IntSortedList  union(IntList l)
            { body for efficiently unioning two
              lists when the first is ordered }

  public parasitic IntSortedList  union(IntSortedList l)
            { body for merging two ordered lists }

  public parasitic IntSortedList  union(IntSet l)
            { specialized body for IntSet }
}


class IntSet extends IntSortedList {
  public IntSortedList  union(IntSortedList l)
            { some specialized body }
}
```

Figure 5: Overridden parasite

IntSortedList, and IntSet respectively, together with a new subclass IntSet where the "middle" parasite of signature IntSortedList union(IntSortedList) is overridden. The parasite for IntSortedList has been overridden with a normal method, and thus it keeps the host it had before, that is the method union(IntList l). Furthermore the inherited method union(IntSet l) becomes a parasite of the method declared in IntSet. For example the command,

```
(new IntSet()).union((IntList)new IntSortedList())
```

executes the "some specialized body" while

```
(new IntSet()).union((IntSortedList)new IntSet())
```

executes the "specialized body for IntSet."

### 2.3 Intuitive hosts

As shown by the preceding examples, a method declared parasitic attaches itself to every less specific method declared in the class or inherited. It also parasitizes every *inherited* method that is more specific. Furthermore, a method not declared parasitic is nonetheless parasitic if it overrides a parasitic method. It has the hosts that this method had, with the exception of any methods that have subsequently been overridden by methods declared parasitic. In other words, the parasite-host relation is only changed when one of the two methods at issue is overridden by a method declared parasitic. This rule permits the body of the parasite to be changed without changing the parasite-host relation.

The inheritance of the parasite-host relation was one of the most difficult design issues of our work (see Section 5 later on). The actual machinery may seem overly complicated but, actually, it obeys a few simple principles. The reader/programmer must consider that all the parasitic methods with the same name and number of arguments together form a multi-method. These methods interact so that whenever one of them is called, the most specific (more precisely, a maximally specific) among those that can handle the arguments is executed. Now if we have a class with a multi-method and we want to define a subclass of it, we may wish either to inherit the multi-method as it is or to modify it. In the latter case, three possible modifications can be envisaged: (1) To replace (override) one or more methods of the multi-method; (2) to replace the whole multi-method by a brand new (multi-)method; (3) to add new methods to the multi-method.

The first case is obtained by the standard Java overriding; so if we want to override a particular method of the multi-method it suffices to declare in the subclass a new method with the same signature (with possibly smaller return type) but not declared parasitic.

The second case, defining a new multi-method, is obtained when a subclass declares one or more parasitic methods that are either more or less specific than some method of the old multi-method. The newly defined parasitic methods form a new multi-method that, in a sense, "partially overrides" the old multi-method. Roughly speaking, the methods of the old multi-method are called when no method of the new multi-method applies. In other words, a method is first looked for locally among the methods declared in the class and if none applies, the search continues in the old multi-method.

The addition of new methods (the third case) is straightforward when the methods to add are more specific than all the methods of the multi-method (which should be the most frequent case). As we have seen in many examples in this section, it suffices to declare the new methods parasitic. However, our system is less flexible when the method to add is less specific than some method of the multi-method, since this addition can be obtained only by overriding all the methods more specific than the new method with methods that perform super calls.

In conclusion, the programmer needs to remember that plain overriding causes the replacement of the method in the multi-method, while parasitic overriding (or declaration) entails a new multi-method partially overriding the old multi-method, if it exists.

### 2.4 Static type-checking and other rules

We add a single type rule to handle parasitic methods:

> *The result type of a parasite must be assignment compatible with the result type of its hosts.*

A parasite is called from the host if the run-time types of the arguments fit the parasite. The condition says it is a compile-time error if the return value of the parasite could not be returned by the host.

Further restrictions apply. The parasite cannot name an exception in its throws clause not mentioned in the host's throws clause. The parasitic method must be static if and only if the host method is static. An inherited host cannot be final (because we change its meaning in the subclass). For simplicity, we require the parasite to have the same accessibility as the host. For ease of implementation, we disallow parasites from being abstract, and hosts from being native.

### 2.5 Intuitive selection

When multiple parasites are attached to the same host, there is the issue of *priority*: which parasite is checked for applicability first. The priority closest to the semantics of most multi-method systems would be to use the most-specific parasite. However, requiring that such a parasite always exist poses many problems (see Section 2.6 for a detailed explanation). Thus we decided to use textual order as a tie-breaker: the textually last parasite that applies is chosen.

However, since parasites themselves can have other parasites, the most specific parasite (if it exists) will always be called, no matter what priority is used. If a less specific parasite is selected, then this parasite will be a host to more specific parasites which then have another "chance."

The semantics of parasites can be informally stated as follows:

> *When a host method with attached parasites is selected, the system searches for a parasite that is applicable to the run-time types of the method arguments.*
> *The search starts from the class of the method receiver and follows an ascending order. Namely, the parasites are checked within a class from the last defined to the first defined and every class is searched before its superclasses.*
> *The first parasite found to be applicable is executed in the place of the method. If no parasite applies, then the body of the method is executed.*

Thus textual order is a simple solution to the problem of how to choose the "most-specific" method, which must be addressed by any multi-method system.[3]

## 2.6 Modularity

As we said in the introduction we do not implement multi-methods in their most general form since we want to preserve two of the most important properties of Java: modularity and separate (type-checking and) compilation.

Textual order is one important ingredient. For example, if `I1` and `I2` are two unrelated interfaces, there is no harm in defining

```
class A {
   void m(Object x) { ... }
   parasitic void m(I1 x)  { ... }
   parasitic void m(I2 x)  { ... }
}
```

Indeed, if later a new class `B` that implements both `I1` and `I2` is added to the system, it is not necessary to modify the definition of `A`, since the conflict caused by an expression such as `(new A()).m((Object)new B())` is handled by the textual order.[4]

Consider what would happen if we had adopted the semantics that the most specific parasite were chosen, instead of using textual ordering. If there were such a class `B` in the final program that implemented both interfaces, then no most specific parasite would exist. Thus a "most specific parasite" rule would break modularity. Extending the type system with an explicit null type and new types of the form $T_1 \& T_2$, representing the greatest lower bound of the two types, would permit a set of parasites to be checked separately. For instance, by adding a parasite

```
parasitic void m(I1&I2 x)
```

to the example, one could ensure the existence of a most specific parasite in all situations. But this solution would not only entail a significant change to the type system, but also require the writing of many parasites that may never be called.

The other ingredient for modularity is maintaining Java's restriction that all methods must be declared in the class of the receiver (`this` in Java). The price to pay is less flexibility in the use of multi-methods; parasitic methods achieve the full generality of multi-methods only if the writer of a class anticipates what subclasses will be derived from it, as explained by Bruce *et al.* [BCC+96]. For example in order to define all the possible cases of `union` in Figure 2, the class `IntList` should be defined as

```
class IntList {
   public IntList union(IntList l)
       { body for unioning two lists }
   public parasitic IntSortedList union(IntSortedList l)
       { body for efficiently unioning two lists
         when the second is ordered }
}
```

But then either the programmer writing the class `IntList` must already know that the class `IntSortedList` will be defined, or else the second method must be added to the class `IntList`, which then must be recompiled. In more general systems such as CLOS and Cecil, there is no such restriction on where multi-methods may be declared.[5]

It would be possible to define an extension of Java with general multi-methods, on the lines of the work [Cas97], but at the expenses of modularity. In languages that permit methods to be added to existing classes, parasitic methods would be equivalent to general multi-methods. Such a feature is compatible with separate compilation (as in $O_2$ [BDK92] where method addition and separate compilation coexist), but breaks modular type-checking.

# 3 Type-Checking and Selection

In this section, we define hosts, type rules, and parasite selection precisely. We begin with some definitions and then proceed to consider hosts, types and selection individually.

## 3.1 Formal definitions

We define two relations on types: *subtyping*, and a broader relation, *assignment subtyping*. A type $T$ is a subtype of type $T'$ (written $T \leq T'$) if $T = T'$ or if $T$ is a descendant of class or interface $T'$ (in case of array types, recursively apply this definition to the element types). We say $T$ is a *strict subtype* of $T'$ (written $T < T'$) if only the second condition holds. Additionally the *null type* is a strict subtype of all *reference types*.[6] A type $T$ is an *assignment subtype* of type $T'$ (written $T \leq_A T'$) if $T$ is a subtype of $T'$ or there is a primitive widening conversion (§5.1.2 in [GJS96]) from $T$ to $T'$. For example, int is an assignment subtype of `float`, but not a subtype. Method invocation conversion (§5.3) is legal precisely from a type to an assignment supertype.

[3] Textual order thus plays somewhat the same role as class precedence lists in CLOS.

[4] Without the cast, the expression would be an *ambiguous method invocation* and would be rejected by the Java compiler.

[5] A similar observation can be made for general multi-method management. In languages such as CLOS and Cecil, new method definitions can be added to existing multi-methods at any time and anywhere in the source code. This can be simulated in our extension by adding new parasites in some particular classes, with a certain amount of recompilation.

[6] *Reference types* (§4.3 of [GJS96]) are class types, interface types, and array types. Together with the null type and *primitive types* (`boolean`, `byte`, `short`, `int`, `long`, `char`, `float`, and `double`) they comprise the types of Java.

Subtyping is extended to method signatures. Consider the following method definition:

$$T\ m(S_1\ x_1, \ldots,\ S_n\ x_n)\ \{\ \ldots\ \}$$

This method has *signature* $(S_1, \ldots, S_n) \rightarrow T$ or, in short, $\vec{S} \rightarrow T$. A type vector $\vec{S}$ is a subtype of $\vec{S}'$ if they have the same number of components and respective components are subtypes ($S_i \leq S_i'$). If at least one component is a strict subtype as well, the vector $\vec{S}$ is a strict subtype of $\vec{S}'$ (written $\vec{S} < \vec{S}'$).

A method signature $\vec{S} \rightarrow T$ is *more specific* than another method signature $\vec{S}' \rightarrow T'$ if and only if $\vec{S} < \vec{S}'$ (the return types are ignored).[7] Analogously, a signature $\vec{S} \rightarrow T$ is *less specific* than another method signature $\vec{S}' \rightarrow T'$ if and only if $\vec{S} > \vec{S}'$.

We say a method named $m$ with signature $\vec{S} \rightarrow T$ is *defined* in a class $C$ if it is declared in $C$ or is inherited from a superclass or a superinterface. The existing Java type system ensures that for two different methods with the same name defined in a class $C$ with signatures $\vec{S} \rightarrow T$ and $\vec{S}' \rightarrow T'$, we have $\vec{S} \neq \vec{S}'$.

### 3.2 Hosts

A *parasitic* method is one declared using the `parasitic` method modifier, or one overriding a parasitic method. A parasitic method $m$ with signature $\vec{S} \rightarrow T$ defined in a class may have *hosts*, which are drawn from the set of methods defined in the class with the same name and number of parameters. If this parasite has a host with signature $\vec{S}' \rightarrow T'$ in the class $C$, we write the following:

$$m(\vec{S}) \rightarrow T \hookleftarrow_C m(\vec{S}') \rightarrow T'$$

**Definition 1** *Let $C$ be a class, possibly extending a class $B$. $m(\vec{S}) \rightarrow T \hookleftarrow_C m(\vec{S}') \rightarrow T'$ if and only if both methods are defined in $C$ and one of the following conditions is satisfied:*

1. *A method $m$ with signature $\vec{S} \rightarrow T$ is declared parasitic in class $C$ and $\vec{S} < \vec{S}'$.*
2. *A method $m$ with signature $\vec{S} \rightarrow T$ is declared parasitic in class $C$, a method $m$ with signature $\vec{S}' \rightarrow T'$ is inherited from $B$ and $\vec{S} > \vec{S}'$.*
3. *No method $m$ with signature either $\vec{S} \rightarrow T$ or $\vec{S}' \rightarrow T'$ is declared parasitic in class $C$, and $m(\vec{S}) \rightarrow U \hookleftarrow_B m(\vec{S}') \rightarrow U'$ for some types $U$ and $U'$.*[8]

An important property of this definition is that there can never be a cycle in the parasite-host relation within any class. New edges are only added between method signatures when one is declared parasitic, and the definition does not inherit *any* edge impacting such method signatures.

According to the definition above, a parasite is either more specific or less specific than its host. This means that the signatures of the two methods differ over some parameters with reference types but must be the same over parameters with primitive types (see Footnote 7). This restriction can be harmlessly weakened to permit parasites with primitive type parameters to have hosts where the corresponding parameters' types are assignment subtypes, but we preferred not to do so since it might have confused the programmer without bringing any significant enhancement.

It is possible to *declare* a method with a contravariant parasite:

```
class A {
  public void m(B x) { ... }
}

class B extends A {
  public parasitic void m(A x) { ... }
}

class C extends B {
  public void m(B x) { ... }
}
```

The method in `C` will never be executed since it is shadowed by the (inherited parasitic) method declared in `B`. The compiler issues warnings for such cases.

### 3.3 Typing

From the typing point of view, a method with signature $\vec{S} \rightarrow T$ having a host with signature $\vec{S}' \rightarrow T'$ must return an assignment subtype ($T \leq_A T'$). If the condition is not satisfied, the compiler generates an error message. If the involved parasite is inherited, then the compiler signals that the host's return type must be an assignment supertype of any parasite's return type. If the involved parasite is not inherited, then the compiler signals that the parasite's return type must be assignment compatible with the return type of its host.

### 3.4 Selection

Let us define more formally the discipline of selection of parasitic methods. For a class $C$ let $\Sigma_m^C$ be the set of signatures of the (possibly inherited) parasites of a method $m(\vec{S}) \rightarrow T$ in the class $C$:

$$\Sigma_m^C = \{\vec{S}' \rightarrow T' \mid m(\vec{S}') \rightarrow T' \hookleftarrow_C m(\vec{S}) \rightarrow T\}$$

On $\Sigma_m^C$ we define a total order $\prec_m^C$ as follows.

**Definition 2** *Let $C$ be a class, possibly extending a class $B$ and consider $\vec{S_i} \rightarrow T_i, \vec{S_j} \rightarrow T_j \in \Sigma_m^C$. $\vec{S_i} \rightarrow T_i \prec_m^C \vec{S_j} \rightarrow T_j$, if and only if one of these conditions is satisfied.*

1. *the method for $m$ with signature $\vec{S_i} \rightarrow T_i$ appears in class $C$ after the definition of the method with signature $\vec{S_j} \rightarrow T_j$;*
2. *the methods for $m$ with signature $\vec{S_i} \rightarrow T_i$ is declared in $C$ while the method with signature $\vec{S_j} \rightarrow T_j$ is inherited from $B$;*
3. *the method for $m$ with signature $\vec{S_i} \rightarrow T_i$ and the one with signature $\vec{S_j} \rightarrow T_j$ are both inherited from $B$, and $\vec{S_i} \rightarrow T_i \prec_m^B \vec{S_j} \rightarrow T_j$*

[7]The Java language specification uses the broader relation $\vec{S} <_A \vec{S}'$ for compile-time overloading resolution. Note that our choice implies that whenever one signature is more specific than another then the two signatures may differ for parameters with reference types but are the same for the parameters with primitive types.

[8]The types $U$ and $U'$ may be different from $T$ and $T'$ respectively because of covariant return types in overriding methods.

The order relation $\prec^C_m$ on $\Sigma^C_m$ is a total order, since it is a subrelation of the total order obtained by listing the ancestors of $C$ in the (single) inheritance order and listing the methods within each class in order of declaration.

Then the selection discipline for parasites has the following definition:

**Definition 3 (Selection)** *When m in class C is applied to a tuple of arguments of type $\vec{S}$ then the method whose signature is* min *w.r.t.* $\prec^C_m$ *of* $\{\vec{S}_i \to T_i \in \Sigma^C_m \mid \vec{S} \leq \vec{S}_i\}$, *is then applied to the arguments. If this set is empty, the body of the host method is executed.*

This definition entails an iteration if the selected parasite itself has parasites. Since the definition of hosts ensures that the parasite-host relation never has cycles, this iteration must terminate.

## 4 Translation

Parasitic methods are easily translated to standard Java using that language's type testing primitives (see Figures 6 and 7), by adding conditional calls to the parasites at the beginning of the body of each non-abstract host method. First, the body of each parasite is packaged in a `final` (non-overrideable) method so that it can be called by the hosts. The name of this new method is formed by concatenating the class name, a dollarsign and the original method name. Next, if the host method is inherited (as in Figure 1), it is rewritten as an overriding method that simply calls super.[9] Then, a host's body is preceded by conditions that check applicability for each parasite in the inverse order they are declared in the class (tests for inherited parasites come last, as seen in Figure 8). As with standard Java, the null type is considered a subtype of every reference type. Only if none of the parasites is applicable, does control fall through to the original method body.

Some tests for applicability can be omitted. More precisely, in order to test that a parasitic method is applicable, the system need not consider a host's arguments when their types are assignment subtypes of the type of the corresponding parasitic method parameter. This situation occurs for contravariant parasites, as seen in Figure 9.

The generated argument checks are always legal since they are only needed to go down the inheritance hierarchy. The return statements type-check as long as the type condition described in Section 3.3 is satisfied.

Our modified compiler generates legal Java class files that can be verified and executed by a standard Java runtime system. It is even possible to use a standard Java compiler to compile clients or subclasses of classes using parasitic methods, but in this case of course, the parasite-host relation is not preserved in subclasses.

[9] Because of the definition of *more specific* used for static overloading resolution in standard Java, this step may introduce (or eliminate) ambiguous method resolution in the resulting program. Our implementation avoids this problem by translating directly to Java byte code. Even when compiling a client class using a class with parasitic methods, our implementation hides the generated methods from static dispatching, but if a standard Java compiler is used to compile the client, they become visible.

```
class IntList { ... } // unchanged

class IntSortedList extends IntList {
  public IntList union(IntList l) {
    if (l == null ||
        l instanceof IntSortedList) {
      return IntSortedList$union((IntSortedList)l);
    }
    else return super.union(l);
  }

  public IntSortedList union(IntSortedList l) {
    return IntSortedList$union(l);
  }

  public final IntSortedList
      IntSortedList$union(IntSortedList l)
    { body for merging two ordered lists }
}
```

Figure 6: Translation of Figure 1 (the host is inherited).

```
class IntList { ... } // unchanged

class IntSortedList extends IntList {
  public IntSortedList union(IntList l) {
    if (l == null ||
        l instanceof IntSortedList) {
      return IntSortedList$union((IntSortedList)l);
    }
    else { body for efficiently unioning two
           lists when the first is ordered }
  }

  public IntSortedList union(IntSortedList l) {
    return IntSortedList$union(l);
  }

  public final IntSortedList
      IntSortedList$union(IntSortedList l)
  { body for merging two ordered lists }
}
```

Figure 7: Translation of Figure 2 (the host is local).

```
class IntSet extends IntSortedList {
  public IntSortedList union(IntList l) {
    if (l == null || l instanceof IntSortedList) {
      return IntSet$union((IntSortedList)l);
    } else if (l == null || l instanceof IntSet) {
      // this branch will never be taken but it is checked
      // last since it corresponds to an inherited parasite
      return IntSortedList$union((IntSet)l);
    } else {
      return super.union(l);
    }
  }

  public IntSortedList union(IntSortedList l) {
    return IntSet$union(l);
  }

  public final IntSortedList
      IntSet$union(IntSortedList l) {
    if (l == null || l instanceof IntSet) {
      return IntSortedList$union((IntSet)l);
    } else { some specialized body }
  }
}
```

Figure 8: Translation of `IntSet` from Figure 5 (the parasite is overridden)

```
interface IntBag { ... } // unchanged

class IntList implements IntBag { ... } // unchanged

class IntSortedList extends IntList {
  public IntList union(IntList l) {
    if (l == null ||
        l instanceof IntSortedList) {
      return IntSortedList$union((IntSortedList)l);
    } else {
      return IntSortedList$union((IntBag)l);
    }
  }

  public IntSortedList union(IntBag b)
  { return IntSortedList$union(b); }
  public final IntSortedList
      IntSortedList$union(IntBag b)
  { super general version }

  public IntSortedList union(IntSortedList l)
  { return IntSortedList$union(l); }
  public final IntSortedList
      IntSortedList$union(IntSortedList l)
  { efficient specific version }
}
```

Figure 9: Translation of Figure 3 (contravariant parasite).

# 5 Design issues

The Java extension defined in this work is the result of a series of decisions. We summarize here the main design options, showing for each the pros (⊕) and, above all, the cons (⊖) that made us to reject them.

### Multi-methods

**1.** Multi-methods could be added to Java by extending the language with CLOS's generic functions.

⊕ This would be the most powerful extension of Java with multi-methods and it subsumes all the others.

⊖ We excluded it from the very beginning since it would have broken modularity and separate compilation. In any case their power can be obtained from parasites by breaking modularity. So we preferred to make their use an exception rather than the standard.

**2.** We could have considered all methods as parasitic methods by default. This is what it is done in KOOL [Cas97] and what we proposed [BC96] for the database programming language $O_2$ (the goal being to make $O_2$'s covariant specialization statically safe).

⊕ This solution is very clean and easy to understand. Practically speaking this solution consists of having dynamic (rather than static) resolution for Java overloaded methods.

⊖ It changes the semantics of existing programs that use overloading (but in our opinion it would be the best solution for a brand new language).

### Parasites

**3.** Replace the use of the textual priority for the choice of parasites by a condition ensuring the existence of a best matching parasites. In other words, instead of performing parasite selection with an upward search for the the first parasite that can handle the arguments, select the parasite whose parameters best match the actual arguments.

⊕ This option was attentively considered since it is very intuitive and clean, and the conditions to ensure static type-safety are well-known (see [ADL91] or [Cas97]). Furthermore, by a clever compilation the average selection time can be logarithmic in the number of parasites (while with textual ordering it is linear).

⊖ A plain implementation of this discipline would break modularity as we have shown in Section 2.6. We considered a way to recover modularity in this case that consists of requiring the set of parasite signatures to always contain a least type. Such a requirement could not be met in many situations without also extending the type systems with an explicit null type and new types of the form $T_1\&T_2$, in which one of $T_1$ and $T_2$ is an interface type, representing the greatest lower bound of the two types. A parasite defined for the type $T_1\&T_2$ would then be executed when there is a selection conflict between $T_1$ and $T_2$. But besides the fact that we disliked the introduction of new types, this would have sometimes required the programmer to define a large number of parasites that would be never selected (typically, parasites defined for $T_1\&T_2$ where the $T_i$'s are unrelated interfaces that will never have a common subtype) and could be very cumbersome.

**4.** Permit downward casts in primitive types for parasites

⊕ This solution treats primitive types in the same way as reference types.

⊖ It does not fit the semantics of Java very well (there is no corresponding `instanceof` operator for primitive types). However it is a possible choice for future extensions.

### Overriding and inheritance

**5.** Use invariant result type overriding.

⊕ It is standard Java.

⊖ It is a useless and unjustified restriction and limits the power of parasitic methods (and of standard Java's methods in general).

**6.** Inherit parasitic methods as if declared locally. (Part of an earlier draft of this proposal.)

⊕ This solution has the advantage of the simplicity. It differs from the one we presented here in that a parasitic method does not parasitize more specific inherited methods but, on the contrary, if these methods are also parasitic it is parasitized by them.

⊖ This solution is less expressive; it is possible to add new parasites in a subclass and to override the existing ones, but the structure of the parasite-host relation is inherited as it is and it cannot be modified. In particular, one cannot define contravariant parasites such as ones that cover a whole set of inherited parasites. This is a flagrant violation of object-oriented principles.

7. Adopt a more powerful typing discipline for contravariant parasites: the host is redeclared with the return type of the parasite (possibly a strict subtype).

   ⊕ More precise typing discipline that (slightly) enhances the language's expressiveness.

   ⊖ This extension would have complicated the typing discipline for parasites by requiring additional type rules such as "if a method with a contravariant parasite is overridden, the return type must be a subtype of the contravariant parasite."

8. Parasitic method definitions are not inherited in subclasses.

   ⊕ It fits the concept of "parasite" according to which a parasite attaches to a particular host.

   ⊖ It does not fit Java's and, more generally, object-oriented inheritance philosophy according to which a method definition is valid in all subclasses as long as a new definition with the same signature is not given.

### Implementation

9. Rewrite runtime system.

   ⊕ Potentially more efficient.

   ⊖ This solution may slow down programs *not* using parasitic methods.

   ⊖ Implementation becomes harder to optimize.

   ⊖ Makes adoption of multi-methods much less likely.

10. Call parasitic method signature directly, rather than create new `final` methods.

    ⊕ Potentially more efficient since fewer dispatches are required.

    ⊕ If a parasite is overridden, then the translation would not need to override the host as well.

    ⊖ Overridable parasitic bodies make analysis and thus optimization harder.

    ⊖ Overridable methods are potentially more expensive to call than `final` methods.

    ⊖ In certain situations, `super` calls leads to surprising infinite recursion.

## 6 Practice

The practical benefit of parasitic methods is manifest. The simplest example is given by the method `Object.equal` that is used and overridden in a large number of Java programs. Even in the simple built-in class `java.lang.Boolean`, we have:

```
public boolean equals(Object obj) {
   if ((obj != null) && (obj instanceof Boolean)) {
      return value == ((Boolean)obj).booleanValue();
   }
   return false;
}
```

With parasitic methods this can be equivalently (and more naturally) written as

```
public parasitic boolean equals(Boolean obj) {
  return (obj != null) && (value == obj.booleanValue());
}
```

A much larger example of code in which parasitic methods would be useful is the method `sameStructure` defined in class `UpdatableImpl` of Doug Lea's `collections` package version 0.96.[10]

Moreover, the systematic use of the `parasitic` keyword in every overloaded method definition transforms the overloaded method selection from static into dynamic. In other words, the method to execute is selected according to the dynamic type of its arguments rather than the static ones. Of course the price for this is run-time overhead, but the resulting behavior is, in our opinion, much more intuitive and predictable. For instance, the following program (due to Doug Lea)

```
class Classifier {
  String identify(Object x)  { return "object"; }
  String identify(Integer x) { return "integer"; }
}

class Relay {
  String relay(Object obj)
      { return (new Classifier()).identify(obj); }
}

public class App {
  public static void main(String[] args) {
    Relay relayer = new Relay();
    Integer i = new Integer(17);
    System.out.println(relayer.relay(i));
  }
}
```

prints "`object`" as result, while a definition of `Classifier` such as

```
class Classifier {
  String identify(Object x)  { return "object"; }
  parasitic String identify(Integer x)
  { return "integer"; }
}
```

prints "`integer`".

## 7 Related Work

Agrawal *et al* [ADL91] describe the basic problem of type-checking systems of multi-methods and forming precedences between applicable method branches. Checking types has two parts: the set of method branches comprising a multi-method must be mutually *consistent*, and the static call sites must type-check. The first part consists of applying the rule that if one method branch is more specific than another, the former's return type must be included in the latter's. In our context, this rule is the one that a parasite's return type must be an assignment subtype of the host's return type. The second part consists of checking the call using the static types of the arguments to compute the static type of the result. In our context, this check is already performed by the Java compiler.

The same condition as consistency was found in the more type-theoretic approach of [CGL92, Cas97], where it was

[10] See `http://gee.cs.oswego.edu/dl/classes/collections` for code and documentation of this package.

called *covariance condition*. There a second condition on the formation of multi-methods was required, namely the existence of a most specialized branch. Such a condition is not necessary (in a sense, it is trivially satisfied) in our approach since the use of textual order makes the search order be total.

Mugridge, *et al.* [MHH91] define the language Kea, where multi-methods and encapsulation are obtained thanks to a mechanism similar to the *partial overriding* of [BC96]. However, the self parameter is considered a parameter like the others (thus this approach is not strictly comparable to ours), and programs may not be modular since the addition of a class can invalidate previously acceptable multi-methods. Furthermore, the approach seems incompatible with Java's overloading and thus not applicable to our specific problem.

Chambers and Leavens [CL95] show that type-checking uses of multi-methods in a powerful language with modules (Cecil) can be done in the context of separate compilation. They also describe an algorithm for statically checking whether a set of multi-method implementations is complete and consistent. However, the test must be performed at link-time, as it requires a list of all concrete classes. Our proposal permits checking to be done separately for each Java class.

## 8 Future work

Our proposal here is not meant to be the final word on parasitic methods. We have several extensions that we are considering:

1. The set of hosts of a parasitic method is currently determined by the rules of Definition 1. We want to allow the programmer to explicitly define the set of hosts of a parasites by specifying their signatures in an `extends` clause that precedes the body of the parasite. This possibility, besides giving a total control over the parasite-host relation, would also allow every kind of specialization (covariant, contravariant, invariant), at the granularity of parameters. Thus for example

```
class A {
    void m(A x, B y)
          { ... }
}

class B extends A {
    parasitic void m(B x, A y) extends  m(A x, B y)
          { ... }
}
```

   the parasite in `B` specializes the method in `A` covariantly on the first parameter and contravariantly on the second.

2. The implementation of the prototype we propose is based on the translation we described in Section 4. Such an implementation is far from being the most efficient one. Many optimizations are possible. For example when a multi-method is called, the most specific method (if it exists) is selected among those that handle the arguments. However this process of selection may involve several dispatchings. For instance, if a programmer declared the methods of a class so that a more specific parasite always precedes the less specific ones, then in the worst case, the message can be dispatched successively to all the parasitic methods; the first dispatches to the second that dispatches to the third and so on. A clever compiler could drastically reduce this cost by calculating the method to be executed and by dispatching directly to it. Other examples of possible optimizations include inlining the final $-methods into the hosts, and redirecting dispatches to methods with contravariant parasites to go directly to the parasite.

3. We may consider dispatching also on primitive types. A difficulty here is that there is no analog to "instanceof" to determine, for instance, if a `double` value can be represented as an `int`.

## 9 Conclusion

Multi-methods are selected dynamically based on the type of arguments, and provide a type-safe solution to the problem of binary methods with inheritance. Our implementation of them in Java, parasitic methods, unifies covariant and contravariant specialization in a single feature. Parasitic methods give the programmer run-time multi-method dispatch in the same spirit as Java's current (static) method selection. They permit the programmer to write more elegant and readable code than the equivalent (but error prone) use of `instanceof` and type casts.

The extension preserves Java's type-safety, modularity and separate compilability, and has a cost only when it is used. In fact, inasmuch as the existence of multi-methods encourages programmers to write specialized efficient versions of methods, programs using parasitic methods may be *faster* than ones without. Furthermore, we have learned that some instructors recommend students never use type overloading in Java methods (at least when they have related parameter types), because static resolution yields unexpected behavior. Parasitic methods would make type overloading acceptable again.

Parasitic methods are straightforward to implement; we currently have an implementation on top of the Java Development Kit (version 1.0.2).

Parasitic methods would work nicely in Java extended with parametric polymorphism as proposed by Odersky and Wadler [OW97] and by Banks *et al* [BLM97]. Both encapsulated multi-methods and parametric classes are features originally proposed in the type theory community. We are pleased to see that they are starting to take root in more practical settings.

Finally most design trade-offs in our work derive from the fact that we wanted to define a conservative extension of Java. Most of the difficulties in particular were due to keeping the semantics of Java's static overloading unchanged. Indeed a cleaner, but non-conservative, extension would be to consider all methods as parasitic methods (this is what it is done in KOOL [Cas97] and what we proposed [BC96] for the database programming language $O_2$). Practically speaking, this solution consists precisely in having dynamic (rather than static) resolution for Java overloaded methods. In any case, we are certain this would be the best solution for a brand new language.

## Acknowledgments

The authors are grateful to Manuel Fähndrich, Edwin Chan, and Doug Lea for their valuable information and suggestions. We are sincerely obliged to the OOPSLA's referees whose pertinent remarks stimulated us to deeply modify and, we hope, decisively improve the work we had submitted. Special thanks to Gary Leavens for his constructive remarks on several drafts.

## References

[ADL91] Rakesh Agrawal, Linda G. DeMichiel, and Bruce G. Lindsay. Static type checking of multimethods. In *Conference Proceedings of OOPSLA '91 — Object Oriented Programming Systems, Languages and Applications*, pages 113–128, New York, October 1991. ACM Press. Appeared as *ACM SIGPLAN Notices 26* (11), November 1991.

[BC96] John Tang Boyland and Giuseppe Castagna. Type-safe compilation of covariant specialization: A practical case. In *ECOOP '96 — Object-Oriented Programming (10th European Conference)*, volume 1098 of *Lecture Notes in Computer Science*, pages 3–25. Springer-Verlag, Berlin, Heidelberg, New York, July 1996.

[BCC+96] K. Bruce, L. Cardelli, G. Castagna, The Hopkins Object Group, G. Leavens, and B. Pierce. On binary methods. *Theory and Practice of Object Systems*, 1(3):221–242, 1996.

[BDK92] F. Bancilhon, C. Delobel, and P. Kanellakis, editors. *Implementing an Object-Oriented Database System: The Story of $O_2$.* Morgan Kaufmann, 1992.

[BLM97] Joseph A. Banks, Barbara Liskov, and Andrew C. Meyers. Parameterized types and Java. In *Conference Record of the Twenty-fourth Annual ACM SIGACT/SIGPLAN Symposium on Principles of Programming Languages*, pages 132–145, New York, January 1997. ACM Press.

[Cas97] G. Castagna. *Object-Oriented Programming: A Unified Foundation.* Progress in Theoretical Computer Science series. Birkäuser, Boston, 1997.

[CGL92] G. Castagna, G. Ghelli, and G. Longo. A calculus for overloaded functions with subtyping. In *ACM Conference on LISP and Functional Programming*, pages 182–192, 1992. Extended and revised version in *Information and Computation* 117(1):115-135, 1995.

[CL95] C. Chambers and G. T. Leavens. Type-checking and modules for multi-methods. *ACM Transactions on Programming Languages and Systems*, 17(6):805–843, November 1995.

[DE97] Sophia Drossopoulou and Susan Eisenbach. Java is type safe - probably. In *ECOOP '97 — Object-Oriented Programming (11th European Conference)*, volume 1241 of *Lecture Notes in Computer Science*, pages 389–418. Springer Verlag, Berlin, July 1997.

[DG87] L. G. DeMichiel and R. P. Gabriel. Common Lisp Object System overview. In Bézivin, Hullot, Cointe, and Lieberman, editors, *Proc. of ECOOP '87 European Conference on Object-Oriented Programming*, number 276 in Lecture Notes in Computer Science, pages 151–170, Paris, France, June 1987. Springer.

[GJS96] James Gosling, Bill Joy, and Guy Steele. *The Java Language Specification.* Addison-Wesley, Reading, Massachusetts, 1996.

[MHH91] W. B. Mugridge, J. Hamer, and J. G. Hosking. Multi-methods in a statically-typed programming language. In Pierre America, editor, *Proceedings of ECOOP '91 Conference, Geneva, Switzerland*, volume 512 of *Lecture Notes in Computer Science.* Springer, 1991.

[OW97] Martin Odersky and Philip Wadler. Pizza into Java: Translating theory into practice. In *Conference Record of the Twenty-fourth Annual ACM SIGACT/SIGPLAN Symposium on Principles of Programming Languages*, pages 146–159, New York, January 1997. ACM Press.

[Ste90] Guy Steele. *Common Lisp the Language.* Digital Press, 2nd edition, 1990.

[Str94] Bjarne Stroustrup. *The design and evolution of* C++. Addison-Wesley, Reading, Massachusetts, 1994.

# Modeling Dynamic Collections of Interdependent Objects Using Path-Based Rules

**Diane Litman**
**Peter F. Patel-Schneider**
AT&T Labs—Research
180 Park Avenue
Florham Park, NJ 07932
{diane,pfps}@research.att.com

**Anil Mishra**
AT&T Network and Computing Services
480 Red Hill Road
Middletown, NJ 07748
anilm@research.att.com

## Abstract

Standard object-oriented languages do not provide language support for modeling changing collections of interdependent objects. We propose that R++, an integration of the rule and object-oriented paradigms, provides a mechanism for easily implementing such models. R++ extends C++ by adding a new programming construct called the *path-based* rule. Such data-driven rules are restricted to follow pointers between objects, and are like "automatic methods" that are triggered by changes to monitored objects. Path-based rules encourage a more abstract level of programming, and unlike previous rule integrations, are not at odds with the object-oriented paradigm and offer performance advantages for natural applications.

## 1 Introduction

Object-oriented languages have simplified the design and implementation of sophisticated applications. However, as application domains have become increasingly dynamic and complex, it has become necessary to model such domains using changing collections of interdependent objects. Such models are difficult to implement in standard object-oriented languages due to a lack of programming constructs at the right level of abstraction.

Consider the creation and maintenance of a model containing a multiple-object invariant, e.g., a model where a manager must always make as much as each employee reporting to a manager that reports to him or her, enforced by raising the manager's salary whenever necessary.[1] To implement such a model using standard object-oriented languages, a significant amount of low-level code must be written. Code to enforce the invariant must be added in multiple classes, each time slightly different. In other words, code must be written to simulate a multiple-object method. Code to trigger the code to enforce the invariant must also be added, in exactly all the appropriate places. Bookkeeping code such as maintaining backpointers between the interdependent objects must be provided.

Although the inherent difficulty of specifying and implementing models with changing inter-object dependencies is well known, and a number of proposals to solve this problem have recently emerged [19, 21], there is a notable lack of language support for such proposals in the context of commercial object-oriented languages. Thus, most object-oriented programmers must still model changing inter-object dependencies by designing and implementing their own low-level solutions using standard object-oriented techniques.

We propose that the problem of modeling dynamic collections of interdependent objects can be given a systemic solution, by providing explicit language support in terms of data-driven computation. Our solution, called R++ [9], extends the C++ language[2] [27] with a single new programming construct—*the rule.* Informally, a rule is a statement composed of a condition and an action specifying what to do when the condition becomes true. Whenever some program data changes, the rules whose conditions involve that data are examined, and if a rule's condition succeeds its action is executed. The action may of course modify data and therefore trigger other rules. Returning to the example above, our solution allows a C++ programmer to directly specify the multiple-object invariant using the R++ rule construct. The R++ translator then automatically generates low-level C++ code to implement the invariant (e.g., to do the bookkeeping, to associate the invariant with the multiple objects, and to trigger the code enforcing the invariant).

While there have been previous attempts to integrate standard (OPS5-style [5]) production rules into the object-oriented paradigm [20, 22, 1, 14, 18], R++ is notable in its use of a new kind of a rule—the *path-based* rule. Path-based rules allow R++ to be in conformance with, rather than at odds with, the object-oriented paradigm. Path-based rules are a new kind of class member, conceptually like an "automatic method". Path-based rules have syntax and semantics similar to C++ member functions. Unlike member functions, however, path-based rules are triggered automatically rather than explicitly called. Path-based rules are so named because they strictly follow a path of inter-object pointers from the '`this`' object to related objects. Because they have no more access capabilities than member functions, path-based rules cannot bypass the relationships designed into an object-oriented domain model. In contrast, OPS5-style

[1] The usual statement of this example is that a manager must make more than his or her direct reports. When we were working at Bell Labs we found that this was not realistic, so we have modified the problem to fit reality more closely, as well as to be a better example.

[2] Little of R++ actually depends on C++, which was chosen as the base language for R++ largely because of its popularity.


**OOPSLA '97 10/97 GA, USA**
**© 1997 ACM 0-89791-908-4/97/0010...$3.50**

rules can perform arbitrary joins between unrelated objects, thus violating the locality of reference designed into domain models. In addition, path-based rules yield a performance advantage over OPS5-style production rules, as the algorithm that processes path-based rules is simpler and typically faster than the algorithm that process production rules.

In this paper we discuss the design and implementation of R++ and analyze the costs and benefits of its use. Our experience suggests that path-based rules are an effective way to model changing collections of interdependent objects [8]. With respect to C++, the major cost of using R++ is less efficiency. R++ programs have longer compilation and execution times, and higher memory needs. The corresponding benefit, however, is increased programmer productivity. R++ programs are shorter, contain fewer similar-but-not-identical pieces of code, and are more modular. These conclusions should not be particularly surprising, as they are typical of higher-level programming paradigms. What is perhaps more surprising is that R++ has several benefits when compared to the standard high-level rule-based approach. Most notably, R++ programs typically run faster, and are more cleanly integrated with the object-oriented paradigm.

## 2 R++

### 2.1 Overview

R++ rules are *path-based* in that their conditions must start with some root object and can reach other objects only by following paths of pointers (*access paths*).[3] The conditions of path-based rules are evaluated in response to certain activities in the rest of the system. If the condition succeeds, then the action of the rule is executed. The action of a path-based rule has access to the object bindings from its condition.

R++ rules are associated with classes, just as data and functions are associated with classes, and not directly on the objects that are instances of the class. In effect, R++ views rules as "member rules" of classes. To further this resemblance, rules are given class-specific names, as are the data and functions associated with the class. Rules also follow the same access limitations as member functions.

The association of rules with classes provides a type for the root object of a rule, namely that class with which the rule is associated. Further, the association provides a specification for when objects are brought to the attention of rules, namely that the *creation* of an instance of a class brings the object to the attention of the member rules of the class. The only way to remove an object from consideration by the rules of its classes is to destroy it. Therefore a rule associated with a class is active on all objects that belong to the class.

Rules are "inherited" by sub-classes, just as member functions are. Rules can be overridden in sub-classes, just as member functions can. A sub-class can have a rule with the same name as a rule in a super-class. Such a rule will override the rule in the super-class for instances of the sub-class.

R++ rules work directly on all instances of a class so there is no need for a separate working memory nor even a

```
<rule declaration> ::= rule <identifier> ;
<rule definition> ::=
      rule <class name>::<identifier> {
         <condition> => <action>
      }
<action> ::= <statement>+
<condition> ::= <binding> |
                <boolean expression> |
                <binding> && <condition> |
                <boolean expression> && <condition>
<binding> ::=
      <class name> * <identifier> = <expression> |
      <class name> * <identifier> @ <data member> |
      <class name> * <identifier> @
                              <variable>-><data member>
```

Figure 1: Simplified R++ Rule Syntax

mechanism to keep track of which objects are active in the rule system. The object-oriented paradigm provides all the control required, obviating any need for control of rules via explicit activation or deactivation of rules or via grouping of rules.

The conditions of R++ rules monitor data in various objects. Changes to this data may cause the condition of the rule to succeed, or succeed in a different manner than before. Therefore, the conditions of rules are re-evaluated whenever the data they inspect changes or when a new object of the appropriate type is constructed. We call these changes *relevant changes*, and *relevant constructions* for the creation of relevant objects, when construction needs to be distinguished from other kinds of relevant change. There is no need for any other mechanism for causing the conditions of rules to be evaluated—changes to object data is the only mechanism required or allowed. The only priority mechanism for R++ rules is that rules on sub-classes are executed before rules on super-classes.

Because R++ rules are data-driven, they have to access the actual data members in objects, not just the values returned from member functions.[4] This may seem to violate the encapsulation principles of the object-oriented paradigm, except that R++ rules should be considered to form part of the implementation of collections of objects, where the underlying data is available. In fact, one major use of R++ rules is to maintain invariants on the data structures themselves.

### 2.2 Rule Syntax and Semantics

R++ rules look and act as much like the rest of C++ as possible. Externally, R++ rules are declared and defined in a manner similar to C++ class members, as shown in the simplified rule syntax given in Figure 1. An example R++ rule, illustrating the multiple-object invariant discussed in Section 1, is shown in Figure 2.

The condition (left-hand side) of an R++ rule is a sequence of C++ boolean expressions[5] interspersed with vari-

[3] Such *path-based rules* are not new, having appeared explicitly as "access-limited rules" in the Algernon implementation of access-limited logic [10, 7].

[4] It would be possible to determine which data member functions depend on, but this would require analysis by the underlying programming language.

[5] C++ does not have boolean expressions per se. The intent here is to allow anything that can be interpreted as a boolean expression, such as pointers or integers.

```
class Employee {
protected:
  monitored set<Employee *> directReports;
  monitored int salary;
}

class Manager : public Employee {
  Employee * delegate;

  rule maintainSalary;
}


rule Manager::maintainSalary {
  Employee* drctRpt @ this->directReports &&
  Employee* scndLvlRpt @
                   drctRpt->directReports &&
  this->salary < scndLvlRpt->salary
 =>
  this->set_salary(scndLvlRpt->salary);
}
```

Figure 2: An Example Use of R++

able bindings. The boolean expressions, and the expressions in the bindings can, of course, use the variables bound earlier, just as in C++.

The bindings in a condition look very much like C++ variable definitions. The first kind of binding, such as `Employee * dlg = this->delegate`, looks just like a C++ variable definition, and simply sets a variable to the value of an expression, succeeding if that value is non-null. The example binding declares a variable of type pointer to `Employee` and sets it to the value of `this->delegate`, succeeding only if the value is non-null. The other kinds of bindings, for example, `Employee * drctRpt @ this->directReports` in Figure 2, are similar to C++ variable definitions but use "`@`" instead of "=". These are branch bindings, where the "`@`" should be read as "at" or "in", and they bind a variable to elements of a set or list of values.[6] The example branch binding says to iterate over all values in the `directReports` data member, which is declared to be a set of pointers to employees, succeeding for each element of the set.

A condition is evaluated in the obvious way. It succeeds for those successful bindings that make its boolean expressions all evaluate to "true", or non-zero.

The action (right-hand side) of an R++ rule is just a sequence of C++ statements. In the action of a rule, the variables bound in its condition can be used as expected.

To make the connection between data members and rules explicit, R++ requires that the `monitored` keyword be given for any data member used in a rule. It is a syntax error for R++ rules to access non-monitored data members. R++ generates accessor functions for monitored data members, such as the function `set_salary` used in the rule in Figure 2.

### 2.3 Rule Execution

There are three parts to rule execution:

1. triggering of rules by relevant change (including relevant construction),

2. subsequent evaluation of the rule condition, possibly delayed if other rules have been triggered by the same change, and

3. execution of the rule action for each way the rule condition succeeded.

The conditions of R++ rules are evaluated only in response to relevant change. However, the portion of the condition that is evaluated in response to a relevant change is unspecified, as is the order of evaluation. Because of this, any side-effect in a rule condition is not particularly useful, and thus rule conditions should be side-effect free. The actions of R++ rules are executed only when their conditions succeed, and only on the data that caused the condition to succeed.

There is no programmer control over the order of R++ rule execution. The order of rule execution is guaranteed only as follows:

- Rules respond to relevant change in a last-in, first-out fashion. That is, if the action of a rule makes a relevant change for some other rules, these other rules are triggered, evaluated, and potentially executed, before any other rules that may have been waiting to be evaluated.

- In response to a particular relevant change, rules on sub-classes are evaluated before rules on superclasses.

The order of rule evaluation is otherwise unspecified.

R++ rules do not execute on "old" data, nor execute more than once on the same data. For example, suppose a relevant change triggers two rules in a way that would cause both rule conditions to succeed, but the first rule to be evaluated and executed changes the original triggering data, thus retriggering both rules. Suppose that the first rule's condition does not succeed on this new data. Then there would be two triggerings of the second rule waiting to be evaluated. Only the most recent of these triggering can possibly cause the rule's action to be executed, as the older triggering is the result of data that has since been modified.

The actions of R++ rules are executed whenever possible under the above criteria. Thus, no rules are waiting to execute if and only if there is no current collection of data that causes a rule's condition to succeed for which the rule's action has not been executed.

## 3 R++ Implementation

R++ does not have a "rule interpreter" per se. Instead R++ rule execution is handled by a collection of data members and member functions, most of which are placed on the root class of a rule, the class in which the rule is declared. The R++ translator inserts declarations of these data members and member functions into the appropriate classes and adds definitions of the member functions.

There are three aspects to executing R++ rules:

1. determining when and how to trigger rules;

2. determining when and how the condition of a rule succeeds; and

[6] C++ does not have sets or lists. R++ thus requires some minimal set and list implementation, currently that from the Standard Template Library [24] or the Standard Components [28].

3. executing the action of a rule.

To handle the problem of stale data, R++ keeps track of its notion of the current time and timestamps all monitored data by means of extra data members in the class. Any change to a monitored data element or construction of an object in a class with rules increments R++'s current time. A change to a data element then sets the timestamp for that data element to the current time.

## 3.1 Triggering Rules

R++ has a strong notion of relevance, and only responds to relevant change (including relevant construction). To handle relevant construction, the constructors of classes that have rules are modified to trigger each rule defined in or inherited by the class on the new object, the root object, with current time set to when the object was created. Thus when a manager is created, the rule `Manager::maintainSalary` is triggered on the new object.

To handle other relevant change, the modifiers for monitored data members are constructed to trigger each rule that mentions that data member in its condition. This is done on each root object that could possibly result in the action of the rule being executed. The current time used for these triggerings is the time when the relevant change happened. These triggerings are also provided with the object that had its data member changed, the causative object, to further restrict the search for potential rule actions to execute.

The collection of root objects to use is determined by the root pointers for the rule and rule variable in the object being modified. For each rule and variable in the rule condition, R++ sets up a data member, called the root pointers, in the class of the variable.[7] Root pointers are maintained as rule conditions are evaluated, as detailed below. The basic idea is that every time the evaluation of a condition of a rule binds a new variable, a root pointer for that variable is added from the variable's value back to the current root object.

In the above example, a data member with the type `set<Manager *>` (and with a name constructed from the name of the rule `Manager::maintainSalary` and the variable `scndLvlRpt`) will be added to `Employee` to hold root pointers for the variable `scndLvlRpt` of rule `Manager::maintainSalary`. When a change is made to the salary of an employee, this is a relevant change for the `secondLevelReport` variable of the rule `Manager::maintainSalary` and the root pointers for this variable will be used to trigger the rule.[8] The employee where the change was made is also given to the rule execution process as the causative object.

Additions to data members used in branch bindings are handled in a special manner. In this case, both the object whose data member is being modified and the object being added are passed to the rule execution, so that only paths that involve the new link being added are used.

Because R++ controls the root pointers, R++ must arrange to remove the pointers when the root object is destroyed. R++ does this by keeping, in root objects, reverse root pointers for all root pointers pointing to the object.

[7]For the implicit this variable the root pointer would just point back to the object itself. Rule triggering for relevant changes involving this are handled in an optimized fashion.

[8]Note that if the employee is also a manager this is also a relevant change for the this variable of the rule, and would trigger the rule using that variable also.

When a root object is destroyed, these reverse root pointers are traversed to find and remove the root pointers to the object being destroyed. Similarly, when any object with root pointers is destroyed, its root pointers are traversed to find and remove the reverse root pointers to it.

R++ also has to be very careful to not follow pointers to objects that have been deleted. For this purpose R++ registers each of the pointers that it uses in the object being pointed to. These registered pointers are each set to null when the object is deleted, and R++ checks any pointer it uses to ensure that the pointer has not been set to null.

## 3.2 Evaluating Rule Conditions

Rule conditions are evaluated by means of member functions that are added to the root class of the rule. This means that the rule condition has exactly the access rights of a member function of the root class.

The simplest case of evaluating a rule condition is for relevant construction. The member function responsible for relevant construction evaluation for the rule is called with the root object and a current time. Each element of the condition is evaluated in turn until one fails or they all succeed. If one fails, then there is nothing left to do. If they all succeed, then the action of the rule is executed.

Evaluating a boolean expression in the condition is simply a matter of evaluating the expression and checking to see whether a value of "true" (non-zero) results. If so, the expression succeeds and evaluation continues; if not, the expression fails and this (branch of the) evaluation is abandoned. However, before the expression is evaluated, there is a check to see if the data it uses is still current. For each data member used in the expression, the timestamp for that data member is checked. If this timestamp is more recent than the time passed into the rule evaluation, the expression is considered to have failed, because the data it uses has been modified after the rule was triggered.

Evaluating a branch binding starts by checking the timestamp on the data member, just as for boolean expressions. Then, the rule variable for this binding is bound to one object in the set, if there is one, and rule evaluation continues in a branch evaluation, otherwise the binding fails. When this branch fails or succeeds, the rule variable for this binding is bound to another object in the set and a new branch is started, until all objects in the set have been considered, and the binding fails. In this way a branch binding iterates through all object in the set, potentially causing the execution of the rule's action on each of them.

Just after the rule variable is bound to a value, a pointer from the object back to the current root object is added to the root pointers for this variable, recording this path so that relevant changes to this object correctly trigger rules. Thus, evaluation of the above example rule will add root pointers for `drctRpt` from all `directReports` of all instances of `Manager` back to their supervisor and root pointers for `scndLvlRpt` from all `directReports` of `directReports` of instances of `Manager` back to their second-level supervisor.

Evaluating a non-branch binding is just like evaluating a branch binding with one element in the set, if the value of the expression is non-null, or a branch binding with an empty set, if the value of the expression is null.

As an example, when a new manager, `Bill`, with salary 90000 and no `directReports`, is created, R++ will execute the rule in Figure 2, starting from `Bill`. The evaluation of the rule's condition will not get very far, as Bill will not have any directReports, and this branch binding will immediately fail.

The evaluation of rule conditions in response to a relevant change is slightly more complex, but follows the same general path. The extra complexity is required to ensure that the rule is evaluated only on the object being changed, and not on other objects reachable from the root object. When the binding for the variable whose root pointer was used to trigger the rule is reached, any value bound to the variable is checked against the causative object passed into the evaluation. Any value different from the causative object results in the evaluation branch failing. Further, if no branch reaches the causative object, then there is no valid path from the root object back to the causative object. In this case the root pointer is no longer valid and is removed from the root pointers.

In the above example, rule evaluations resulting from changes to the salary of an employee passing through root pointers for scndLvlRpt will be passed a pointer to an employee as a causative object. When a value is bound to scndLvlRpt, it will be checked against the causative object, and values different from the causative pointer will cause that branch to fail, and the next element of the set to be checked.[9] If the causative object is never reached in some evaluation, the root object for this evaluation is removed from the root pointers for scndLvlRpt on the causative object.

In cases involving additions to data members used in branch bindings, both variables involved must match the values passed in to the rule execution. In the above example, when a new pointer is added to the directReports of some employee, the rule is triggered on the values of the root pointer for the drctRpt variable with both the employee who received a new direct report and the reportee as parameters.[10] Only branches that result in the causative pointer as a value for drctRpt and the new reportee as a value for scndLvlRpt will succeed for *these* triggerings.

For example, if a manager, say Dan, who has no directReports, is added to the directReports of Bill, the rule in Figure 2 will be triggered on Bill. This triggering only allows Dan as a value for drctRpt, and puts a root pointer for drctRpt from Dan back to Bill. As Dan has no directReports, the evaluation will not progress past the second assignment. If an employee, Harry, with salary 100000, is then added to the directReports of Dan, the rule of Figure 2 will be again triggered, starting with root object Bill, because Bill is in the root objects of Dan for variable drctRpt on the rule. This triggering will proceed to Dan (and to no other of the directReports of Bill), and thence to Harry, finally succeeding and resulting in execution of the action of the rule.

A further complication is that if some change is relevant for another, later variable of the rule, bindings for this later variable have to be different from the causative object. This complication is required so that rules will not be executed more than once for the same collection of variable bindings. (The same collection *will* be considered during triggering on the root objects for the later variable!) If the data member is used in a branch binding later branch bindings must be checked to ensure that they do not follow the same link. It is not sufficient to just check just the value of the branch variable or just the value of the variable of the data member in this case, both must be checked.

For example, when the salary of an Employee, say Bill, is changed, Manager::maintainSalary is triggered in two different manners. First, Bill is considered the root of the rule. In this triggering, Bill cannot be bound to the variable scndLvlRpt. Second, Bill is considered as a binding for scndLvlRpt and the root pointers for this variable are used to find root objects to trigger from. If the exclusion on binding Bill was not in the first triggering, and Bill was his own scndLvlRpt, then the rule's condition would be evaluated twice on the same data, possibly causing the rule's action to be executed twice using the same data.

### 3.3 Executing Rule Actions

The action of a rule is executed in the same member function as the evaluation of its condition. Therefore the code in a rule action has exactly the same access rights as a member function of the root class of the rule. The evaluation of the condition results in the correct variable bindings for the action, so the action is simply spliced into this member function. In the example just above, the execution of the rule would set the salary of Bill to 100000.

However, to ensure that the data examined by the rule are still current, the timestamps for all the data are checked just before the action is executed, and if any are newer than the time passed into the evaluation, the action is not executed.

## 4 Analysis

As with any new tool, R++ has both benefits that accrue from its use, and costs that it imposes, compared with C++. Most of the costs of R++ have to do with increased resource consumption. Other than these costs, the main cost with R++ is the time required to learn it, which is partially alleviated by its close integration with C++.

R++ adds a number of data members to classes. These extra data members increase the size of affected classes by a constant amount. For each variable of each rule, a data member is added to the class of the variable (the root pointers) and to the root class of the rule (the reverse root pointers). For each data member mentioned in a rule, a data member is added to the class (the timestamp).

As rule conditions are evaluated, elements are added to root and reverse root pointer sets. Each path investigated by a rule adds elements to two of these sets, provided that this element was not already there. These elements are deleted when they are discovered to be no longer valid.

When an instance of a root class is created or a relevant change is performed, R++ triggers rules. The resulting evaluation can take an arbitrary amount of time, so these operations cannot be considered to take negligible time.

Rule evaluation after relevant change proceeds by going back to the root object and following paths attempting to get back to the object where the change occurred. If R++ kept more data, then this rule evaluation would be faster. In the current implementation of R++, such evaluation can process a number of useless paths, but storage costs are reduced

[9] Actually, the set is not iterated over in this case. Instead a optimized version is used where a check is made to see if the causative pointer is in the set. If so, it is bound to the variable. If not, the binding fails.

[10] There is also triggering using the this root pointer.

from an amount potentially exponential in the number of objects to an amount potentially quadratic in the number of objects.

One other cost that R++ imposes is incurred not at execution time, but at compile time. The methods the R++ translator inserts into user code increase compilation time, sometimes dramatically. One reason for this is that much of this additional code shows up in "`.H`" files, which are compiled multiple times in one recompilation, and involve templates, which are expensive to compile.

R++ provides a number of important benefits to weigh against its costs. These benefits have been determined by the use of R++, including its use in a major project to analyze and diagnose the 4ESS® telephone switching system, the major switch in AT&T's domestic long-distance telephone network [23].

In this project, the use of R++ allowed a fifty-percent reduction in the amount of code required to model and monitor the 4ESS switch over the amount required in a straight C++ implementation. Along with this reduction came a corresponding reduction in the amount of time and resources required to implement this portion of the system.

A related benefit is that the use of R++ eliminates the low-level, hard-to-understand portion of the code, resulting in a more-declarative implementation with clearer semantics. This makes for fewer errors in coding, a clearer and cleaner system, and easier modification and extension of the system. The rules in the 4ESS monitoring system were deemed to be much easier to understand than any C++ system developed to solve the same task. As well, the object-model was cleaner, at least in part because there was less need for the many low-level methods that would have been required to implement the rules in C++.

These benefits, while hard to quantify in many cases, are significant. In particular, the dominant software cost in many large software systems is not the initial development, but the subsequent modification and extension. Any tool that can ease these important tasks can be of great benefit.

R++ should be effective whenever there is a need for computation to be performed whenever a condition involving data of path-related objects becomes true, except in situations where time and space costs must be aggressively minimized.

## 5 Comparisons

### 5.1 Comparison with Rule Systems

There are other rule systems besides R++ that can be used to represent dynamic collections of interdependent objects. These systems generally belong to the OPS5 paradigm [5] of general pattern-matching rules. There are a number of modern systems that attempt to marry OPS5-style rules and object-oriented programming, including ART-IM [20], CERS [22], ILOG rules [1], RAL/C++ [14], and Rete++ [18].

The rules of OPS5 are more general[11] than the rules of R++, but, as they can form arbitrary "joins" between unrelated objects, violating the locality assumptions implicit in the object-oriented paradigm, there is a basic mismatch between this sort of rule and the object-oriented paradigm. OPS5-style rules also have a different semantics than R++ rules, involving a conflict resolution scheme with rule priorities, which is outside the object-oriented paradigm and which has to be kept in mind when programming with this sort of rules. The rules of R++, in contrast, exist completely within the object-oriented paradigm.

In fact, a number of the modern OPS5 systems use their own object system, called working memory, and not the object system of their base programming language. Applications using these rule systems thus need to move information between the working memory and object storage. Other systems (such as CERS [22]) require special calls to bring objects of the language to the attention of the rule system. Although this means that information does not need to be moved, it does require facilities outside of the object-oriented paradigm to control rules. In contrast, R++ directly uses the objects of its underlying object-oriented language, C++.

OPS5-style rules also sit outside the class hierarchy, unlike R++ rules, and thus are not organized in the same way as classes and objects, eliminating a beneficial interaction between R++ rules and the object-oriented paradigm.

[11] However, the arbitrary joins of OPS5-style rules can be simulated by adding new paths to the object model.

| *path length* | *branching factor* | *# of leaves* | *R++ rate (for sets)* | *C5 rate* |
|---|---|---|---|---|
| 0 | NA | 1 | 120000 | 2083 |
| 1 | 1 | 1 | 25575 | 1428 |
| 1 | 2 | 2 | 23831 | 1428 |
| 1 | 4 | 4 | 23301 | 1333 |
| 1 | 8 | 8 | 22310 | 1391 |
| 1 | 16 | 16 | 21399 | 1391 |
| 1 | 32 | 32 | 20164 | 1411 |
| 1 | 64 | 64 | 19418 | 1383 |
| 1 | 128 | 128 | 18078 | 1383 |
| 2 | 1 | 1 | 13797 | 1363 |
| 2 | 2 | 4 | 8065 | 1333 |
| 2 | 4 | 16 | 4854 | 1317 |
| 2 | 8 | 64 | 2849 | 1280 |
| 2 | 16 | 256 | 1524 | 1024 |
| 2 | 32 | 1024 | 682 | 640 |
| 2 | 64 | 4096 | 309 | 244 |
| 2 | 128 | 16384 | 138 | 42 |
| 3 | 1 | 1 | 9362 | 1200 |
| 3 | 2 | 8 | 3196 | 1142 |
| 3 | 4 | 64 | 1024 | 1200 |
| 3 | 8 | 512 | 264 | 682 |
| 3 | 16 | 4096 | 57 | 107 |
| 3 | 32 | 32768 | 13 | 13 |

Table 1: Rule-firing rates for R++ and C5

### 5.2 Resource Consumption

Because R++ rules are simpler than OPS5-style rules, R++ admits a simpler, and more efficient, rule evaluation mechanism. First, R++ requires less data than a full algorithm for evaluating OPS5-style rules. Given $n$ objects, $r$ rules, and $v$ variables in the largest rule condition, the worst-case heap-storage requirements for R++ are $O(rn^2)$, mostly for root pointers, whereas the RETE algorithm [13] and its variants use space $O(rn^v)$.

The speed comparison of R++ and OPS5-style rules is more complicated. Both R++ and the RETE algorithm and its variants use their stored data to reduce computa-

| input size | C5 | | R++ | | | | C++ | | | |
|---|---|---|---|---|---|---|---|---|---|---|
| | | | Standard Sets | | Hash Sets | | Standard Sets | | Hash Sets | |
| | secs | MB | secs | MB | secs | MB | secs | MB | secs | MB |
| 12 | 166 | 1.0 | 5 | 1.3 | 1.0 | 0.7 | 3.4 | 0.7 | 0.6 | 0.5 |
| 25 | 737 | 1.7 | 15 | 2.1 | 2.5 | 1.1 | 13.1 | 0.9 | 1.6 | 0.7 |
| 37 | 1839 | 2.3 | 30 | 2.8 | 4.2 | 1.4 | 27.4 | 1.2 | 3.1 | 0.8 |
| 50 | 3752 | 2.9 | 53 | 3.6 | 6.4 | 1.6 | 49.1 | 1.5 | 4.9 | 0.9 |

Table 2: Waltz resource consumption for C5, R++, and C++

tion time. The speed of RETE is generally dominated by the recomputation of its stored data. In the worst case, it is possible to have to recompute all the stored data. The speed of R++ is generally dominated by finding the appropriate path from the root object back to where the change occured, which can take time $O(rn^v)$, the same as RETE.

Table 1 gives an empirical comparison between R++ and C5, a C-based superset of OPS5 using a RETE algorithm, on a single rule. Rates are given in rule firings per second on a Sun SPARCstation 10. In each performance measurement a tree[12] of objects of a specified depth (path length) and breadth (branching factor) was created; a path-length of $n$ means that $n+1$ objects are in the path. The tree is monitored by a single rule that follows a path from the root object to a leaf object.

To test the worst-case for R++, all triggering changes were made in leaf objects. R++ outperforms C5, especially with small path lengths and low branching factors, where it is much faster.[13] This is largely due to the elimination of the bookkeeping that is required for the RETE algorithm.

Table 2 compares R++, C5, and C++ implementations of Waltz's line labeling algorithm [31], a standard benchmark for OPS5 performance. The interesting sections of the programs are contained in Appendix A. (All measurements are from a Sun SPARCstation 20.) The two sets of figures for R++ and C++ are for the Standard Components version of sets, and for an already-existing hash-set implementation optimized for good storage consumption with very small sets. The sets in this application are almost all of size 2 or 3.

Because C5 and R++ have different rule languages, the algorithm had to be recoded between C5 and R++. The C5 version is a slightly-modified version of an OPS program obtained from Daniel P. Miranker, used in a comparison study of various rule engines [3]. The R++ version was derived from the OPS program by first creating C++ data structures for the OPS working memory elements, modifying as appropriate to fit within the C++ object model. Then R++ rules were written to mimic the OPS rules that naturally fit within the R++ model. The other OPS rules were implemented in C++ code. This resulted in R++ code that was a close match to the original OPS code, and not in particularly efficient R++ rules.

[12]Trees can be implemented in C++ with either lists or sets, depending on whether order is important or not. Table 1 shows only the R++ rate for sets because trees in C5 are inherently unordered since they arise from joins among working memory elements. If order *is* important, it is easy to obtain in R++ simply by using lists instead of sets, though there is a performance penalty to be paid. In C5 and other OPS5 derivatives it is much more difficult and time-consuming to process a tree in an ordered way.

[13]Where R++ is slow, performance can be improved by tuning a model, for example, by connecting distant objects with shorter paths.

The initial OPS program had 33 rules, 18 of which were directly related to the core of the line labeling algorithm, 7 of which were control rules, and 8 of which were printing and setup rules. The 18 labeling rules had a total of 92 conditions and 34 actions. They were turned into 9 R++ rules with a total of 42 conditions and 22 action lines of code. Usually, OPS rules that translate into R++ rules translate on a one-for-one basis, but because OPS has no sets, the OPS code represents sets as sequences, and rules that act on any member (or subset) of the set have to be duplicated in OPS but not in R++. The reason that there are slightly more lines of action code per rule in the R++ example is that iterating over a set takes about three lines of code in R++ whereas the OPS rules, because they are duplicated, can directly access the appropriate element.

The C++ implementation is a recoding of the R++ implementation. The R++ rules were turned into C++ methods, and the classes were augmented to incorporate extra data member pointers to allow these methods to run as appropriate. The C++ implementation incorporates quite a number of optimizations over the R++ implementation, taking into account the following analysis of the entire program:

- All rules have the same triggering conditions, so
  - only one version of each rule needs to be written,
  - all rules can be triggered from a single virtual method, and
  - only one set of "root pointers" need be created.
- All rules can safely be run on stale data, so data timestamps are not necessary.
- All rules can be run more than once on the same data, so rule timestamps are not necessary.
- Some variables are only set once, so there is no need for a check to see if the value actually changes.
- Neither objects nor pointers between objects are removed, so there is no need for any pointer management.

The C++ code for rule definitions and the definitions of functions that trigger the rules is over twice as long as the R++ rule definitions (224 lines to 111 lines), even though the C++ code does not perform many of the functions that the R++ code has to.

The R++ implementation is much faster than the C5 implementation on this example, largely due to the fact that the rules are small-branching-factor rules with a path length of 1. R++ consumes somewhat more storage than C5 when a set implementation with a large overhead is used; with a better set implementation R++ consumes somewhat less storage. Further, as the input size increases, R++'s speed advantage becomes even bigger.

The R++ implementation is slower than the C++ implementation, as expected. However, even though this example admits quite a number of optimizations over the rule control mechanism used by R++, the C++ implementation still consumes roughly 60% to 70% of the resources of the R++ implementation. Most of this difference has to do with the fewer pointers used in the C++ implementation; examples that need more of the R++ features, such as rules with differing data used in their conditions or management of pointers, would show a much smaller differential.

The above measurements are insufficient to confidently generalize. Nevertheless, the results here provide evidence that R++ is much faster on certain kinds of applications than OPS-style rules and that R++ rules are similar in size and number to OPS-style rules. R++ is somewhat slower than C++ code for the same task, but the C++ code is considerably larger, even when global conditions are used to optimize the C++ code and reduce the amount of bookkeeping it needs to do.

### 5.3 Comparison with Database Rule Systems

The work on rules in active object-oriented databases has some similarities to R++. Many active databases (e.g., Sentinel [2], Ode [16, 17], ADAM [12], REACH [4], SAMOS [15]) have rules that follow an event-condition-action paradigm [11]. Events are monitored and trigger rules; rule conditions are evaluated when rules are triggered; and rule actions are executed when rule conditions are satisfied. Much of the work in active databases thus focuses on the specification and detection of events. Although the details of particular systems vary, primitive event sets typically include method invocation, and sometimes also internal database events and time events. Primitive events can be generated by objects before or after they invoke methods, and in some systems also at any user-specified point in the method. All member functions can be assumed to be potential events, or users can specify which member functions generate events. Most systems allow complex events to be composed from primitive events using operators such as sequence, conjunction, disjunction, and negation. Different coupling modes between events, conditions, and actions address the composition of events relative to transaction boundaries, and specify when rules should be executed relative to their triggering.

R++, in contrast, reflects its roots in the condition-action paradigm of standard OPS5-style production systems, in that R++ rules do not explicitly specify events. Instead, as discussed above, R++ rules are implicitly triggered in response to relevant change, including relevant construction. Events are thus implicitly specified in rule conditions, and event detection is implicitly performed by C++ code that is automatically output by the R++ translator. Thus, compared to many active databases, R++ does more of the work involving event specification and detection. However, some active database systems also transparently detect primitive events, e.g., SAMOS modifies method bodies so that primitive events can be detected without user intervention. In addition, since R++ primitive events are at a finer level of granularity than typical database events, we believe that R++ helps guard against unexpected rule firings. On the other hand, R++ rules are less expressive than most database rules with respect to events. R++ event composition is restricted to conjunction, and R++ does not allow users to specify rule execution preferences via coupling modes. The path-based restriction of R++ also makes its rules less expressive. As discussed above, we view this as a positive restriction, as global OPS5-style production rules are less object-oriented than R++ rules.

Independently of the rule paradigm, there are many other ways for systems to vary, based on how rules are incorporated into the object-oriented environment. For example, rules can have intra-object or inter-object scope, can be declared in classes or as first-class objects, and can be compiled into the host language and/or processed at runtime. In fact, many of the R++ design choices and implementation techniques have already been used in the active object-oriented database community. What is particularly novel about R++ is that it *simultaneously* allows inter-object rules to be declared in classes and pre-processed into the host language.

To elaborate, R++, inspired by the constraints and triggers of Ode, allows rules to be specified only at class definition time, which allows them to be pre-processed into host-language code. This approach has runtime efficiency advantages, and also naturally supports rule inheritance. REACH similarly requires rules to be specified at compile time, although in REACH rules are first class objects; a rule is mapped into a rule object and two C functions (for condition evaluation and action execution). SAMOS defines rules and events using a high-level specification language, then translates them into first-class objects.

In all of these approaches, rule modification requires system recompilation. Although compiler-based approaches often work well when rule bases do not change with high frequency, in our major application, namely ANSWER-4ESS, the most frequent user complaint was in fact that R++ increased compilation time. Although not a concern for R++, the compilation approach is also problematic for interpretive object-oriented environments. Finally, the compilation approach limits the extensibility of the system when there are pre-existing objects in a database, a situation which is somewhat similar to when there are legacy classes in an object-oriented system. These concerns have led to runtime rule specifications in ADAM, and to both class definition and runtime rule specifications in Sentinel. Other reasons for supporting run-time rule specifications, as well as for treating rules and events as first class objects rather than as "member rules", are based on database concerns such as transaction semantics and persistence. Again, since R++ is not an active *database* system, concerns arising from the need to provide full database capabilities are not applicable to R++, and have led to different design choices.

Unlike many active database systems (e.g., Ode, ADAM, REACH), both R++ and Sentinel support rules that can be triggered by changes to multiple instances of objects, even from different classes. For example, while the triggers of Ode allow for the execution of C++ code when a condition is satisfied on an object, an Ode trigger on an object is executed only when a method is run on that object—there is no mechanism for deferring the execution of the trigger action until a condition involving other objects is satisfied. In contrast, the rules of R++, like the rules of Sentinel, allow objects to react to their own changes as well as to the changes of other objects. R++ achieves this functionality while allowing rules to be declared only in classes. The designers of Sentinel mistakenly believed that rules must be treated as objects in order to allow rules to be shared across objects. They felt that if rules were declared only inside classes, then "...a rule that ensures an employer's salary is always less than his/her manager's salary needs to be declared twice—once within the employee class and once within the manager class" [2]. As shown by the R++ coding of the example in Figure 2, rules can both be declared inside classes and shared.

Other active database work is less similar to R++. The event-condition-action rules in POSTGRES [25] and Starburst [29], trigger on specific events in the database, such as adding a tuple to a relation, and not on a boolean condition involving the data members of various objects (but then allow a condition to filter the rule action). VenusDB [6] extends a C++ traditional rule-based language to allow rule-based applications to execute against standard relational databases.

Rules have also been added to deductive databases, including object-oriented deductive databases such as `Coral ++` [26]. Rules in deductive databases are run to satisfy queries and so have a very different purpose than do the rules in R++.

## 6 Conclusion

The R++ integration of rules into the object-oriented programming paradigm provides a mechanism for easily implementing changes to interdependent collections of objects. R++ extends C++ with a single programming construct—the *path-based* rule—as a new kind of class member, subservient to the object-oriented paradigm. Path-based rules strictly follow the inter-object paths in a domain model. Such member rules define the automatic behavior of a class, by monitoring data members for changes that could cause a rule's condition to succeed, then executing the rule's action. A rule monitors all instances of its class and, by inheritance, all instances of derived classes. By adding the path-based rules to the object-oriented programmer's repertoire, R++ expands the kinds and complexity of tractable applications, and can result in considerable savings of both code and expense. Our discussion of R++ has highlighted both the design choices behind the notion of path-based rules, and the algorithmic details needed to implement such data-driven computation.

Our analysis and comparisons of R++ have highlighted both its costs and benefits. The main cost of R++ compared to C++ is that R++ programs require more memory and take longer to compile and execute than equivalent C++ programs. In addition, there is a cost to learning R++, although with syntax similar to C++ member functions and semantics like "automatic" member functions, R++ rules are relatively easy to learn and apply.

The main benefit of R++ compared to C++ is that the addition of rules provides a useful level of abstraction, allowing C++ programmers to avoid focusing on low-level implementation details when modeling dynamic collections of objects. Rules can make programs clearer and more robust because a single rule to express a "multiple-object method" can replace several variants of the same logic scattered throughout standard object-oriented code. Also, rules relieve the programmer of the burden of explicit procedural control since rules are triggered automatically by relevant construction and relevant change.

The main benefit of R++ compared to previous integrations of rules and objects is that R++ uses path-based rather than OPS5-style pattern-matching rules. Because path-based rules must follow pointers already in a domain model, and because such rules have no more access capabilities than member functions, path-based rules are in conformance with the object-oriented paradigm. In contrast, there are many ways in which OPS5-style rules can violate the locality of reference designed into object-oriented domain models. In addition, because path-based rules are simpler than OPS5-style rules, R++ admits a simpler, and more efficient, rule evaluation mechanism. R++ thus offers performance advantages for many natural applications.

The ideas and implementation underlying R++ do not depend on the details of C++. We believe that it would be quite easy to produce a path-based-rule extension to any class-based object-oriented language that supports method inheritance and overriding and a notion of sets. The only change required to R++ would be to change the syntax of R++ rules to conform to the syntax of the underlying object-oriented language. For most such languages, the R++ implementation would also need only minor changes. We have been contemplating a JAVA version of R++, and have done some of the design work for it.

R++ is available free to research institutions. For further information, including the *R++ User Manual*, see the R++ home page on the world-wide web at

`http://www.research.att.com/sw/tools/r++`

or send e-mail to

`r++@orbit.hr.att.com`.

## Acknowledgments

Jimi Crawford and Dan Dvorak were part of the original team of developers for R++. Much of the work reported here derives from their efforts in the team. The support of Ron Brachman, Raj Dube, Henry Kautz, Dick Machol, Brian Minnihan, Jennifer Thien, and Pramod Warty was instrumental to the research and development effort behind R++. We would also like to thank Amal Ahmed, Steve Correl, Johannes Ros, Walid Saba, Anoop Singhal, and Gary Weiss, for being some of the first users of R++ and Amal Ahmed for adding Standard Template Library functionality to R++. Dan Miranker provided the Waltz line-labeling OPS implementation.

## References

[1] Patrick Albert. ILog Rules, embedding rules in C++: Results and limits. In *Position Papers for the OOPSLA'94 Embedded Object-Oriented Production Systems Workshop (EOOPS)*, October 1994.

[2] E. Anwar, L. Maugis, and S. Chakravarthy. A new perspective on rule support for object-oriented databases. In *Proceedings of the 1993 ACM SIGMOD International Conference on Mangement of Data*, pages 99–108, 1993.

[3] David A. Brant, Timothy Grose, Bernie Lofaso, and Daniel P. Miranker. Effects of database size on rule system performance: Five case studies. In *Proceedings of the Seventeenth International Conference on Very Large Data Bases*, pages 287–296, 1991.

[4] A. P. Buchmann, J. Zimmermann, J. A. Blakeley, and D. L. Wells. Building an integrated active oodbms: Requirements, architecture, and design decisions. In *Proceedings of the 11th International Conference on Data Engineering*, 1995.

[5] Thomas A. Cooper and Nancy Wogrin. *Rule-Based Programming with OPS5*. Morgan Kaufmann, San Mateo, California, 1988.

[6] Stephen Correl and Daniel P. Miranker. On isolation, concurrency, and the venus rule language. In *Proceedings of the 4th International Conference on Information and Knowledge Management (CIKM'95)*, 1995.

[7] J. M. Crawford. *Access-Limited Logic—A language for knowledge representation*. PhD thesis, Department of Computer Sciences, The University of Texas at Austin, 1990. Also published as Technical Report AI 90-141, Artificial Intelligence Laboratory, The University of Texas at Austin.

[8] James Crawford, Daniel Dvorak, Diane Litman, Anil Mishra, and Peter F. Patel-Schneider. Device representation and reasoning with affective relations. In *Proceedings of the Fourteenth International Joint Conference on Artificial Intelligence*, pages 1814–1820. International Joint Committee on Artificial Intelligence, August 1995.

[9] James Crawford, Daniel Dvorak, Diane Litman, Anil Mishra, and Peter F. Patel-Schneider. Path-based rules in object-oriented programming. In *Proceedings of the Thirteenth National Conference on Artificial Intelligence*, Portland, Oregon, August 1996. American Association for Artificial Intelligence.

[10] James M. Crawford and Benjamin Kuipers. Negation and proof by contradiction in access-limited logic. In *Proceedings of the Ninth National Conference on Artificial Intelligence*, pages 897–903. American Association for Artificial Intelligence, July 1991.

[11] U. Dayal, B. Blaustein, A. Buchmann, S. Chakravarthy, D. Goldhirsch, M. Hsu, R. Ladin, D. McCarthy, and A. Rosenthal. The hipac project: Combining active databases and timing constraints. *ACM Sigmod Record*, 17(1), 1988.

[12] O. Diaz, N. Paton, and P. Gray. Rule management in object-oriented databases: A unified approach. In *Proceedings of VLDB*, 1991.

[13] Charles L. Forgy. RETE: A fast algorithm for the many pattern/many object pattern matching problem. *Artificial Intelligence*, 19:17–37, 1982.

[14] Charles L. Forgy. RAL/C and RAL/C++: Rule-based extensions to C and C++. In *Position Papers for the OOPSLA'94 Embedded Object-Oriented Production Systems Workshop (EOOPS)*, October 1994.

[15] Stella Gatziu and Klaus R. Dittrich. Events in an active object-oriented database system. In *Proceedings of the 1st International Workshop on Rules in Database Systems*, 1993.

[16] Narain H. Gehani and H. V. Jagadish. Active database facilities in Ode. In *Proceedings of the Seventeenth International Conference on Very Large Data Bases*, pages 327–336, 1991.

[17] Narain H. Gehani and H. V. Jagadish. Ode as an active database: Constraints and triggers. In Widom and Ceri [30], pages 207–232.

[18] The Haley Enterprise. *Rete++: Seamless Integration of Rules and Objects Using the Rete Algorithm and C++*, 1993.

[19] Richard Helm, Ian M. Holland, and Dipayan Gangopadhyay. Contracts: Specifying behavioral compositions in object-oriented systems. In *Proceedings OOPSLA'90*, 1990.

[20] Inference Corporation. *Art Reference Manual*, 1987.

[21] Haim Kilov and V. J. Harvey, editors. *Fifth Workshop on Specification of Behavioral Semantics, OOPSLA'96*, San Jose, California, 1996.

[22] Daniel P. Miranker, Frederic H. Burke, Jeri J. Steele, David R. Haug, and John Kolts. The C++ embeddable rule system. *International Journal on Artificial Intelligence Tools*, 2(1):33–46, 1993.

[23] Anil Mishra, Johannes P. Ros, Anoop Singhal, Gary Weiss, Diane Litman, Peter F. Patel-Schneider, Daniel Dvorak, and James Crawford. R++: Using rules in object-oriented designs. In *Addendum to Object Oriented Programming Systems, Languages, and Applications*. Association for Computing Machinery, 1996.

[24] ObjectSpace. *STL Toolkit, Version 2.0*, 1996.

[25] Spyros Potamianos and Michael Stonebraker. The POSTGRES rule system. In Widom and Ceri [30], pages 43–61.

[26] Divesh Srivastava, Raghu Ramakrishnan, S. Sudarshan, and Praveen Seshadri. Coral++: Adding object-orientation to a logic database language. In *Proceedings of the Nineteenth International Conference on Very Large Databases*, 1993.

[27] Bjarne Stroustrup. *The C++ Programming Language*. Addison Wesley, Reading, Massachusetts, second edition, 1991.

[28] USL. *C++ Standard Components Release 3.0 Documentation*, 1992.

[29] Jennifer Widom. The Starburst rule system. In Widom and Ceri [30], pages 87–109.

[30] Jennifer Widom and Stefano Ceri, editors. *Active Database Systems: Triggers and Rules for Advanced Database Processing*. Morgan Kaufmann, San Francisco, California, 1996.

[31] Patrick Henry Winston, editor. *Artificial Intelligence*. Addison-Wesley, Reading, Massachusetts, 2nd edition, 1984.

# A Waltz Line Labeling Example

The Waltz line labeling algorithm takes a collection of edges that represent a 3-dimensional solid, joined at vertices, and assigns labels to these edges showing whether the edge is a boundary (B in the C5 rules), a front edge (+, or a back edge (-). Full details of the algorithm are available in [31].

## A.1 C5 rules

The following rules implement the Waltz line-labeling algorithm. There are other rules in the C5 implementation, but they are used to set up the data structures and print the results, not to do the basic algorithm. The C5 rules are a minor modification of an OPS implementation of the algorithm written by Dan Miranker. This implementation can be obtained at
`ftp://ftp.cs.utexas.edu/pub/ops5-benchmark-suite/`

```
(literalize stage value)
(literalize edge p1 p2 joined label plotted)
(literalize junction p1 p2 p3 base_point type)

(p label_L
  (stage ^value labeling)
  (junction ^type L ^base_point <p1>)
  (edge ^p1 <p1> ^p2 <p2> ^label << + - >>)
  (edge ^p1 <p1> ^p2 <> <p2> ^label nil)
--> (modify 4 ^label B))

(p label_tee_A
  (stage ^value labeling)
  (junction ^type tee ^base_point <bp>
        ^p1 <p1> ^p2 <p2> ^p3 <p3>)
  (edge ^p1 <bp> ^p2 <p1> ^label nil)
  (edge ^p1 <bp> ^p2 <p3>)
--> (modify 3 ^label B)
    (modify 4 ^label B))

(p label_tee_B
  (stage ^value labeling)
  (junction ^type tee ^base_point <bp>
        ^p1 <p1> ^p2 <p2> ^p3 <p3>)
  (edge ^p1 <bp> ^p2 <p1>)
  (edge ^p1 <bp> ^p2 <p3> ^label nil)
--> (modify 3 ^label B)
    (modify 4 ^label B))

(p label_fork-1
  (stage ^value labeling)
  (junction ^type fork ^base_point <bp>)
  (edge ^p1 <bp> ^p2 <p1> ^label +)
  (edge ^p1 <bp> ^p2 {<p2> <> <p1>} ^label nil)
  (edge ^p1 <bp> ^p2 {<> <p2> <> <p1>})
--> (modify 4 ^label +)
    (modify 5 ^label +))

(p label_fork-2
  (stage ^value labeling)
  (junction ^type fork ^base_point <bp>)
  (edge ^p1 <bp> ^p2 <p1> ^label B)
  (edge ^p1 <bp> ^p2 {<p2> <> <p1>} ^label -)
  (edge ^p1 <bp> ^p2 {<> <p2> <> <p1>} ^label nil)
--> (modify 5 ^label B))

(p label_fork-3
  (stage ^value labeling)
  (junction ^type fork ^base_point <bp>)
  (edge ^p1 <bp> ^p2 <p1> ^label B)
  (edge ^p1 <bp> ^p2 {<p2> <> <p1>} ^label B)
  (edge ^p1 <bp> ^p2 {<> <p2> <> <p1>} ^label nil)
--> (modify 5 ^label -))

(p label_fork-4
  (stage ^value labeling)
  (junction ^type fork ^base_point <bp>)
  (edge ^p1 <bp> ^p2 <p1> ^label -)
  (edge ^p1 <bp> ^p2 {<p2> <> <p1>} ^label -)
  (edge ^p1 <bp> ^p2 {<> <p2> <> <p1>} ^label nil)
--> (modify 5 ^label -))

(p label_arrow-1A
  (stage ^value labeling)
  (junction ^type arrow ^base_point <bp>
        ^p1 <p1> ^p2 <p2> ^p3 <p3>)
  (edge ^p1 <bp> ^p2 <p1>
               ^label {<label> << B - >>})
  (edge ^p1 <bp> ^p2 <p2> ^label nil)
  (edge ^p1 <bp> ^p2 <p3>)
--> (modify 4 ^label +)
    (modify 5 ^label <label>))

(p label_arrow-1B
  (stage ^value labeling)
  (junction ^type arrow ^base_point <bp>
        ^p1 <p1> ^p2 <p2> ^p3 <p3>)
  (edge ^p1 <bp> ^p2 <p1>
               ^label {<label> << B - >>})
  (edge ^p1 <bp> ^p2 <p2>)
  (edge ^p1 <bp> ^p2 <p3> ^label nil)
--> (modify 4 ^label +)
    (modify 5 ^label <label>))

(p label_arrow-2A
  (stage ^value labeling)
  (junction ^type arrow ^base_point <bp>
        ^p1 <p1> ^p2 <p2> ^p3 <p3>)
  (edge ^p1 <bp> ^p2 <p3>
               ^label {<label> << B - >>})
  (edge ^p1 <bp> ^p2 <p2> ^label nil)
  (edge ^p1 <bp> ^p2 <p1>)
--> (modify 4 ^label +)
    (modify 5 ^label <label>))

(p label_arrow-2B
  (stage ^value labeling)
  (junction ^type arrow ^base_point <bp>
        ^p1 <p1> ^p2 <p2> ^p3 <p3>)
  (edge ^p1 <bp> ^p2 <p3>
               ^label {<label> << B - >>})
  (edge ^p1 <bp> ^p2 <p2>)
  (edge ^p1 <bp> ^p2 <p1> ^label nil)
--> (modify 4 ^label +)
    (modify 5 ^label <label>))

(p label_arrow-3A
  (stage ^value labeling)
  (junction ^type arrow ^base_point <bp>
        ^p1 <p1> ^p2 <p2> ^p3 <p3>)
  (edge ^p1 <bp> ^p2 <p1> ^label +)
```

```
  (edge ^p1 <bp> ^p2 <p2> ^label nil)
  (edge ^p1 <bp> ^p2 <p3>)
--> (modify 4 ^label -)
    (modify 5 ^label +))

(p label_arrow-3B
  (stage ^value labeling)
  (junction ^type arrow ^base_point <bp>
        ^p1 <p1> ^p2 <p2> ^p3 <p3>)
  (edge ^p1 <bp> ^p2 <p1> ^label +)
  (edge ^p1 <bp> ^p2 <p2>)
  (edge ^p1 <bp> ^p2 <p3> ^label nil)
--> (modify 4 ^label -)
    (modify 5 ^label +))

(p label_arrow-4A
  (stage ^value labeling)
  (junction ^type arrow ^base_point <bp>
        ^p1 <p1> ^p2 <p2> ^p3 <p3>)
  (edge ^p1 <bp> ^p2 <p3> ^label +)
  (edge ^p1 <bp> ^p2 <p2> ^label nil)
  (edge ^p1 <bp> ^p2 <p1>)
--> (modify 4 ^label -)
    (modify 5 ^label +))

(p label_arrow-4B
  (stage ^value labeling)
  (junction ^type arrow ^base_point <bp>
        ^p1 <p1> ^p2 <p2> ^p3 <p3>)
  (edge ^p1 <bp> ^p2 <p3> ^label +)
  (edge ^p1 <bp> ^p2 <p2>)
  (edge ^p1 <bp> ^p2 <p1> ^label nil)
--> (modify 4 ^label -)
    (modify 5 ^label +))

(p label_arrow-5A
  (stage ^value labeling)
  (junction ^type arrow ^base_point <bp>
        ^p1 <p1> ^p2 <p2> ^p3 <p3>)
  (edge ^p1 <bp> ^p2 <p2> ^label -)
  (edge ^p1 <bp> ^p2 <p1>)
  (edge ^p1 <bp> ^p2 <p3> ^label nil)
--> (modify 4 ^label +)
    (modify 5 ^label +))

(p label_arrow-5B
  (stage ^value labeling)
  (junction ^type arrow ^base_point <bp>
        ^p1 <p1> ^p2 <p2> ^p3 <p3>)
  (edge ^p1 <bp> ^p2 <p2> ^label -)
  (edge ^p1 <bp> ^p2 <p1> ^label nil)
  (edge ^p1 <bp> ^p2 <p3>)
--> (modify 4 ^label +)
    (modify 5 ^label +))
```

## A.2 Common Code for R++ and C++

The following file is common to both the R++ and C++ implementation. It defines the class Point that is used during the set-up for the line labeling algorithm.

### A.2.1 waltz.H

```
#include <Set.h>

enum EdgeLabel { nil , plus, minus, boundary };

class Vertex;
class Edge;

class Point {
public:
  Point(int loc) : location(loc), edges(), v(0) {}
  int operator==(const Point &o)
        { return this->location==o.location; }
  operator int() const { return location; }
  void addEdge(Point * pt1,Point * pt2) const;
  Vertex * makeVertex();
private:
  int location;
  Set_of_p<Edge> edges;
  Vertex * v;
};
```

## A.3 R++ Rule Code

The following two files implement the R++ rules for the algorithm. The R++ rules have been given names analogous to the names of the C5 rules that they mirror.

The file `waltz.rh` is processed by R++ and turned into a `.h` file that defines the classes that have rules defined on them, including the declarations of the methods used for the rules. The file `waltz.rC` is also processed by R++, but is turned into a `.C` file that has the definitions of the rule methods.

### A.3.1 waltz.rh

```
#include "waltz.H"

class Edge {
public:
  Edge(Point * pt1, Point * pt2) : points(pt1,pt2)
              { set_label(nil); }
  const Point* otherPoint(const Point* point)const;
  EdgeLabel get_label() const { return label; }
  monitored EdgeLabel label;
private:
  Set_of_p<Point> points;
};

class Vertex {
protected:
  Vertex() { }
public:
  virtual void cornerLabel();
};

class Ell : public Vertex {
public:
  Ell(Set_of_p<Edge> edgs) {
    Set_of_piter<Edge> iter_edge =
        Set_of_piter<Edge>(edgs);
    for (Edge *edge1 = iter_edge.next();
         edge1; edge1 = iter_edge.next()) {
      insert_edges(edge1);
```

```
    }
  }
  virtual void cornerLabel();
private:
  monitored Set_of_p<Edge> edges;
rule label;
};

class Tee : public Vertex {
public:
  Tee(Edge * barb1, Edge * shaft, Edge * barb2)
  {
      set_upright(shaft);
      set_side1(barb1);
      set_side2(barb2);
  }
private:
  monitored Edge * upright;
  monitored Edge * side1;
  monitored Edge * side2;
rule label;
};

class Fork : public Vertex {
public:
  Fork(Edge * barb1, Edge * shaft, Edge * barb2) {
      insert_sides(shaft);
      insert_sides(barb1);
      insert_sides(barb2);
  }
private:
  monitored Set_of_p<Edge> sides;
rule label_1;
rule label_2;
rule label_3;
rule label_4;
};

class Arrow : public Vertex {
public:
  Arrow(Edge * barb1, Edge * shaft, Edge * barb2)
  {
      set_center(shaft);
      insert_sides(barb1);
      insert_sides(barb2);
  }
  virtual void cornerLabel();
private:
  monitored Edge * center;
  monitored Set_of_p<Edge> sides;
rule label_12;
rule label_34;
rule label_5;
};
```

### A.3.2 waltz.rC

```
$include "waltz.rh"

Vertex * Point::makeVertex() {
  if ( this->v ) {
    return this->v;
  } else if ( this->edges.size()==3 ) {
    return this->v =
        make_3_junction(this,this->edges);
  } else {
    return this->v = new Ell(this->edges);
  }
}

rule Ell::label {
  Edge * edg1 @ this->edges &&
  ( edg1->label==plus || edg1->label==minus ) &&
  Edge * edg2 @ this->edges &&
  ( edg2->label==nil )
=> edg2->set_label(boundary);
}

rule Tee::label {
  Edge * sde1 = this->side1 &&
  Edge * sde2 = this->side2 &&
  ( sde1->label==nil  || sde2->label==nil )
=> sde1->set_label(boundary);
  sde2->set_label(boundary);
}

rule Fork::label_1 {
  Edge * sde1 @ this->sides &&
  sde1->label==plus
=> Set_of_piter<Edge> sdes = this->sides;
  for ( Edge * sde = sdes.next();
        sde; sde = sdes.next() ) {
    sde->set_label(plus);
  };
}

rule Fork::label_2 {
  Edge * sde1 @ this->sides &&
  sde1->label==boundary &&
  Edge * sde2 @ this->sides &&
  sde2 != sde1 &&
  sde2->label==minus
=> Set_of_piter<Edge> sdes = this->sides;
  for ( Edge * sde = sdes.next();
        sde; sde = sdes.next() ) {
    if (sde->label==nil) sde->set_label(boundary);
  }
}

rule Fork::label_3 {
  Edge * sde1 @ this->sides &&
  sde1->label==boundary &&
  Edge * sde2 @ this->sides &&
  sde2 != sde1 &&
  sde2->label==boundary
=> Set_of_piter<Edge> sdes = this->sides;
  for ( Edge * sde = sdes.next();
        sde; sde = sdes.next() ) {
    if (sde->label==nil) sde->set_label(minus);
  }
}

rule Fork::label_4 {
  Edge * sde1 @ this->sides &&
  sde1->label==minus &&
  Edge * sde2 @ this->sides &&
  sde2 != sde1 &&
  sde2->label==minus
=> Set_of_piter<Edge> sdes = this->sides;
```

```
    for ( Edge * sde = sdes.next();
          sde; sde = sdes.next() ) {
      if (sde->label==nil) sde->set_label(minus);
    }
}

rule Arrow::label_12 {
  Edge * sde @ this->sides &&
  (sde->label==boundary || sde->label==minus) &&
  Edge * osde @ this->sides &&
  osde != sde &&
  Edge * centr = this->center &&
  (osde->label==nil || centr->label==nil)
=> centr->set_label(plus);
   osde->set_label( sde->label );
}

rule Arrow::label_34 {
  Edge * sde @ this->sides &&
  (sde->label==plus) &&
  Edge * osde @ this->sides &&
  osde != sde &&
  Edge * centr = this->center &&
  (osde->label==nil || centr->label==nil)
=> centr->set_label(minus);
   osde->set_label(plus);
}

rule Arrow::label_5 {
  Edge * centr = this->center &&
  centr->label==minus &&
  Edge * sde @ this->sides &&
  (sde->label==nil )
=> Set_of_piter<Edge> sdes = this->sides;
   for ( Edge * sde = sdes.next();
         sde; sde = sdes.next() ) {
     sde->set_label(plus);
   }
}
```

## A.4 C++ "Rule" Code

The following two files correspond closely to the two R++ files above.

### A.4.1 waltzC.H

```
#include "waltz.H"

class Edge {
public:
  Edge(Point * pt1, Point * pt2)
                : points(pt1,pt2), vertices()
        { set_label(nil); }
  const Point* otherPoint(const Point* point)const;
  void addVertex(Vertex * v) {vertices.insert(v);}
  void set_label(EdgeLabel l);
  EdgeLabel get_label() const { return label; }
private:
  EdgeLabel label;
  Set_of_p<Point> points;
  Set_of_p<Vertex> vertices;
};

class Vertex {
protected:
  Vertex() { }
public:
  virtual void cornerLabel();
  virtual void labelEdges() = 0;
};

class Ell : public Vertex {
public:
  Ell(Set_of_p<Edge> edgs) : edges() {
    Set_of_piter<Edge> iter_edge =
                Set_of_piter<Edge>(edgs);
    for (Edge *edge1 = iter_edge.next();
         edge1; edge1 = iter_edge.next()) {
      insert_edges(edge1);
    }
  }
  virtual void cornerLabel();
  virtual void labelEdges();
  void insert_edges(Edge *);
private:
  Set_of_p<Edge> edges;
};

class Tee : public Vertex {
public:
  Tee(Edge * barb1, Edge * shaft, Edge * barb2) {
      upright = shaft;
      side1 = barb1;
      side2 = barb2;
      this->labelEdges();
  }
  virtual void labelEdges();
  void set_upright(Edge *);
  void set_side1(Edge *);
  void set_side2(Edge *);
private:
  Edge * upright;
  Edge * side1;
  Edge * side2;
};

class Fork : public Vertex {
public:
  Fork(Edge * barb1, Edge * shaft, Edge * barb2) {
      insert_sides(shaft);
      insert_sides(barb1);
      insert_sides(barb2);
  }
  virtual void labelEdges();
  void insert_sides(Edge *);
private:
  Set_of_p<Edge> sides;
};

class Arrow : public Vertex {
public:
  Arrow(Edge * barb1, Edge * shaft, Edge * barb2)
                                  : sides() {
    set_center(shaft);  // must be first
    insert_sides(barb1);
    insert_sides(barb2);
  }
  virtual void cornerLabel();
```

```
  virtual void labelEdges();
  void set_center(Edge *);
  void insert_sides(Edge *);
private:
  Edge * center;
  Set_of_p<Edge> sides;
};
```

### A.4.2 waltzC.rules.C

This file implements the effects of the R++ rules in C++, under the following assumptions:

- All rules have the same triggering constraints, so rule triggering can be very simple.
- All rules are additive, so it doesn't matter if rules run on old data.
- All rules are idempotent, so it doesn't matter if rules run more than once on the same data.
- Some variables are only set once, so there is no need to check for actual changes.
- No links are deleted, so there is no need for maintainance of backpointers.
- No objects are deleted, so there is no need to check to see if objects still exist nor is there any need to remove backpointers.

```
#include "waltzC.H"

void Edge::set_label(EdgeLabel l) {
  if ( label != l ) {
    label = l;
    Set_of_piter<Vertex> iter = this->vertices;
    for ( Vertex * v = iter.next();
          v; v = iter.next() ) {
      v->labelEdges();
    }
  }
}

Vertex * Point::makeVertex() {
  if ( this->v ) {
    return this->v;
  } else if ( this->edges.size()==3 ) {
    Vertex * vertex =
        make_3_junction(this,this->edges);
    Set_of_piter<Edge> edgs = this->edges;
    for ( Edge * edge = edgs.next();
          edge; edge = edgs.next() ) {
      edge->addVertex(vertex);
    }
    return this->v = vertex;
  } else {
    Vertex * vertex = new Ell(this->edges);
    Set_of_piter<Edge> edgs = this->edges;
    for ( Edge * edge = edgs.next();
          edge; edge = edgs.next() ) {
      edge->addVertex(vertex);
    }
    return this->v = vertex;
  }
}

void Ell::insert_edges(Edge * e) {
  if ( ! this->edges.contains(e) ) {
    this->edges.insert(e);
    this->labelEdges();
  }
}

void Ell::labelEdges() {
  if ( this->edges.size()==2 ) {
    Set_of_piter<Edge> iter = this->edges;
    Edge * edg1 = iter.next();
    Edge * edg2 = iter.next();
    if ( ( edg1->get_label()==plus ||
           edg1->get_label()==minus ) &&
         ( edg2->get_label()==nil ) ) {
      edg2->set_label(boundary);
    }
    if ( ( edg2->get_label()==plus ||
           edg2->get_label()==minus ) &&
         ( edg1->get_label()==nil ) ) {
      edg1->set_label(boundary);
    }
  }
}

void Tee::set_upright(Edge * e) {
  this->upright = e;
  this->labelEdges();
}
void Tee::set_side1(Edge * e) {
  this->side1 = e;
  this->labelEdges();
}
void Tee::set_side2(Edge * e) {
  this->side2 = e;
  this->labelEdges();
}

void Tee::labelEdges() {
  if ( this->side1 && this->side2 &&
       ( this->side1->get_label()==nil ||
         this->side2->get_label()==nil ) ) {
    this->side1->set_label(boundary);
    this->side2->set_label(boundary);
  }
}

void Fork::insert_sides(Edge * e) {
  if ( ! this->sides.contains(e) ) {
    this->sides.insert(e);
    this->labelEdges();
  }
}

void Fork::labelEdges() {
  // label_1
  Set_of_piter<Edge> iter1 = this->sides;
  for ( Edge * sde1 = iter1.next();
        sde1; sde1 = iter1.next() ) {
    if ( sde1->get_label()==plus ) {
      Set_of_piter<Edge> sdes = this->sides;
      for ( Edge * sde = sdes.next();
            sde; sde = sdes.next() ) {
```

```
        sde->set_label(plus);
      }
    }
  }
  // label_2
  Set_of_piter<Edge> iter2 = this->sides;
  for ( Edge * sdeb = iter2.next();
        sdeb; sdeb = iter2.next() ) {
    if ( sdeb->get_label()==boundary ) {
      Set_of_piter<Edge> iter = this->sides;
      for ( Edge * sdeo = iter.next();
            sdeo; sdeo = iter.next() ) {
        if ( sdeo->get_label()==minus ) {
          Set_of_piter<Edge> sdes = this->sides;
          for ( Edge * sde = sdes.next();
                sde; sde = sdes.next() ) {
            if ( sde->get_label()==nil) {
              sde->set_label(boundary);
            }
          }
        }
      }
    }
  }
  // label_3
  Set_of_piter<Edge> iter3 = this->sides;
  for ( Edge * sdec = iter3.next();
        sdec; sdec = iter3.next() ) {
    if ( sdec->get_label()==boundary ) {
      Set_of_piter<Edge> iter = this->sides;
      for ( Edge * sdeo = iter.next();
            sdeo; sdeo = iter.next() ) {
        if ( sdeo != sdec &&
             sdeo->get_label()==minus ) {
          Set_of_piter<Edge> sdes = this->sides;
          for ( Edge * sde = sdes.next();
                sde; sde = sdes.next() ) {
            if ( sde->get_label()==nil) {
              sde->set_label(minus);
            }
          }
        }
      }
    }
  }
  // label 4
  Set_of_piter<Edge> iter4 = this->sides;
  for ( Edge * sde4 = iter4.next();
        sde4; sde4 = iter4.next() ) {
    if ( sde4->get_label()==minus ) {
      Set_of_piter<Edge> iter = this->sides;
      for ( Edge * sde5 = iter.next();
            sde5; sde5 = iter.next() ) {
        if ( sde5->get_label()==minus ) {
          Set_of_piter<Edge> sdes = this->sides;
          for ( Edge * sde = sdes.next();
                sde; sde = sdes.next() ) {
            if ( sde->get_label()==nil) {
              sde->set_label(minus);
            }
          }
        }
      }
    }
  }
}

void Arrow::set_center(Edge * e) {
  this->center = e;
  this->labelEdges();
}
void Arrow::insert_sides(Edge * e) {
  if ( ! this->sides.contains(e) ) {
    this->sides.insert(e);
    this->labelEdges();
  }
}

void Arrow::labelEdges() {
  if ( this->sides.size()==2 && this->center) {
    Set_of_piter<Edge> iter = this->sides;
    Edge * side1 = iter.next();
    Edge * side2 = iter.next();
    // label_12
    if ( ( side1->get_label()==boundary ||
           side1->get_label()==minus ) &&
         ( side2->get_label()==nil ||
           this->center->get_label()==nil ) ) {
      this->center->set_label(plus);
      side2->set_label(side1->get_label());
    }
    if ( ( side2->get_label()==boundary ||
           side2->get_label()==minus ) &&
         ( side1->get_label()==nil ||
           this->center->get_label()==nil ) ) {
      this->center->set_label(plus);
      side1->set_label(side2->get_label());
    }
    // label_34
    if ( ( side1->get_label()==plus ) &&
         ( side2->get_label()==nil ||
           this->center->get_label()==nil ) ) {
      this->center->set_label(minus);
      side2->set_label(plus);
    }
    if ( ( side2->get_label()==plus ) &&
         ( side1->get_label()==nil ||
           this->center->get_label()==nil ) ) {
      this->center->set_label(minus);
      side1->set_label(plus);
    }
  }
  // label_5
  if ( this->center &&
       this->center->get_label()==minus ) {
    Set_of_piter<Edge> iter = this->sides;
    for ( Edge * side = iter.next();
          side; side = iter.next() ) {
      if ( side->get_label()==nil ) {
        side->set_label(plus);
      }
    }
  }
}
```

# Looking for the Objects in Object-Relational DBMSs

## Panel Session

Moderator: Lougie Anderson

Panelists: Mike Carey, Ken Jacobs, Erin Kinikin, David Maier

**Abstract:** The Relational Model first came into vogue in the early 1980's. It was based on the simplifying idea that all data could be modeled as mathematical relations (tables in "normal form"). Permissible operations on this table data structure were specified by the relation algebra and calculus. The Relational Model led to years of research in areas such as query languages, query optimization, transaction models, and database design methodologies. This research has dominated DBMS conferences for the last fifteen years and has also lead to major products offerings in wide-spread use in the computer industry today.

While the Relational revolution was happening in the DBMS community there was a minority opinion emerging from the object community. This minority opinion surfaced in heated debates and panels at DBMS conferences where it was often pitted against "relational purists." The object proponents wanted to discuss storing and retrieving complex objects and relationships in databases while the relational purists insisted on maintaining "mathematical purity and simplicity". These panels were often some of the most acrimonious (and entertaining) at these conferences and many thought there was no way to bridge the chasm between the two schools of thought.

However times changes and so do the realities of the commercial world. Object languages such as C++, Smalltalk, and Java have become *de facto* standards. The Internet and the PC have increased the demand for complex data types. And the relational model is evolving to accommodate these realities.

All of the major RDBMS vendors have announced plans for, or are already shipping, Object-Relational DBMS (ORDBMS) products. A natural question for the object community is how well these new products will address the well-known "impedance mismatch" between a pure object model and the relational model. For example, how does one make Java, Smalltalk, or C++ objects persist using an ORDBMS? Can one search for these objects in the database using their methods?

The vendors for ORDBMS are claiming well-known OO features in their implementations, such as extensible data types, inheritance, object identity, and object language bindings. This panel will allow the major vendors to explain how those features match up with the kinds of object models that OO developers are accustomed to. The panel will consist of representatives from three of the major ORDBMS vendors as well as a representative of "pure object think". The vendor representatives will each present a brief overview of the object-related features of their products and will explain why OO programmers are going to have an easier time with these ORDBMSs. This will be followed by counterpoint discussion from the pure object thinker.

*Lougie Anderson is employed by Sequent Computer Systems.*

*Mike Carey is a Research Staff Member at the IBM Almaden Research Center.*

*Ken Jacobs is Vice President of Product Strategy at Oracle.*

*Erin Kinikin is Executive Director of Product Management at Informix.*

*David Maier is a Professor at the Oregon Graduate Institute.*

# A Framework for Scalable Dissemination-Based Systems*

*Michael Franklin*
University of Maryland
franklin@cs.umd.edu

*Stanley Zdonik*
Brown University
sbz@cs.brown.edu

## Abstract

The dramatic improvements in global interconnectivity due to intranets, extranets, and the Internet has led to an explosion in the number and variety of new data-intensive applications. Along with the proliferation of these new applications have come increased problems of scale. This is demonstrated by frequent delays and service disruptions when accessing networked data sources. Recently, push-based techniques have been proposed as a solution to scalability problems for distributed applications. This paper argues that push indeed has its place, but that it is just one aspect of a much larger design space for distributed information systems. We propose the notion of a Dissemination-Based Information System (DBIS) which integrates a variety of data delivery mechanisms and information broker hierarchies. We discuss the properties of such systems and provide some insight into the architectural imperatives that will influence their design. The DBIS framework can serve as the basis for development of a toolkit for constructing distributed information systems that better match the technology they employ to the characteristics of the applications they are intended to support.

## 1 Introduction

### 1.1 The World-Wide Wait

The scenario is all too familiar — a major event, such as a national election, is underway and the latest, up-to-the minute results are being posted on the Web. You want to monitor the results for the important national races and for the races in your state, so you fire up your trusty web browser, point it at the election result web site and wait, and wait, and wait.... What's the problem? It could be any number of technical glitches: a congested network, an overloaded server, or even a crashed server. In a larger sense, however, the problem is one of scalability; the system cannot keep up with the heavy load caused by the (transient) surge in activity that occurs in such situations.

We argue that such scalability problems are the result of a mismatch between the data access characteristics of the application and the technology (in this case, HTTP) used to implement the application. An election result server, such as that of the preceding scenario, is an example of a *data dissemination*-oriented application. Data dissemination involves the delivery of data from one or more *sources* to a large set of *consumers*. Many dissemination-oriented applications have data access characteristics that differ significantly from the traditional notion of client-server applications as embodied in navigational web browsing technology. For example, the election result server has the following characteristics: 1) There is a huge population of users (potentially many millions) who want to access the data; 2) There is a tremendous degree of overlap among the interests of the user population; 3) Users who are following the event closely are interested only in new data and changes to the existing data; and, 4) The amount of data that must be sent to most users is fairly small. When looking at these characteristics, it becomes clear that the request-response (i.e., RPC), unicast (i.e., point-to-point) method of data delivery used by HTTP is the wrong approach for this application.

Using request-response, each user sends requests for data to the server. The large audience for a popular event can generate huge spikes in the load at servers, resulting in long delays and server crashes. Compounding the situation is

*This work has been partially supported by the NSF under grant IRI-9501353, by Rome Labs Agreement Number F30602-97-2-0241 under ARPA order number F078, by an IBM Cooperative Graduate Fellowship, and by research funding and equipment from Intel Corporation.

that users must continually *poll* the server to obtain the most current data, resulting in multiple requests for the same data items from each user. In this example application, where the desires of a large part of the population are known *a priori*, most of these requests are unnecessary.

The use of unicast data delivery likewise causes problems in the opposite direction (from servers to clients). With unicast the server is required to respond individually to each request, often transmitting identical data. For an application with many users, the costs of this repetition in terms of network bandwidth and server cycles can be devastating.

## 1.2 Is "Push" the Answer?

The above scenario is well-known to web users and, not surprisingly, an increasing number of products are being introduced to address it. A number of these products have received tremendous media attention lately because they are based on a technology called data *Push*. Using data push, the transmission of data to users is initiated without requiring the users to explicitly request it. Examples of systems that employ some form of push technology include Pointcast, Marimba, BackWeb, and AirMedia. Push has also been added to recent versions of the major Web browsers, and the battle for data push standards is well underway.

Systems that are truly implemented with data push can indeed solve some of the scalability problems attributed above to request-response. Since users do not have to poll servers for new and updated data, the number of client requests that must be handled by a server can be reduced dramatically. Simply changing from a client "Pull" model to a push model, however, does not solve all the problems for an application such as the election result server. In particular, performing push to millions of clients using a unicast communication protocol does little to address network bandwidth problems and still requires the server to perform substantial work for each client it is serving. Compounding the confusion is the fact that many systems that provide a "push" interface to users are actually implemented using a programmed polling mechanism. These systems simply save the user from having to click, but do nothing to solve the scalability problems caused by the request-response approach.

The election result server is an example of just one type of dissemination-oriented application. Other examples include news and entertainment delivery, software distribution, traffic information systems, and navigational web browsing. These applications differ widely in the characteristics of the data involved (e.g., size, consistency constraints, etc.), access patterns, and communication channel properties (e.g., symmetric vs. asymmetric, continuously or intermittently connected, etc.). No one data delivery mechanism can provide adequate support for the wide variety of such applications.

To address this need, we are developing a general framework for describing and ultimately constructing Dissemination-Based Information Systems (DBIS). In this framework, push vs. pull is a choice along just one of several dimensions of the design space for data delivery mechanisms. In this paper, we outline a number of data delivery mechanisms and investigate the tradeoffs among them. The goal is to develop a flexible architecture that is capable of supporting a wide range of applications across many varied environments, such as mobile networks, satellite-based systems, and wide-area networks. By combining the various data delivery techniques in a way that matches the characteristics of the application and achieves the most efficient use of the available server and communication resources, the scalability and performance of dissemination-oriented applications can be greatly enhanced.

## 1.3 Overview of the Approach

We view an integrated DBIS as a distributed system in which the links between the computing elements vary in character: from standard pull-based unicast connections to periodic push over a broadcast channel. A key point is that the character of a link should be of concern only to the nodes on either end. For example, the fact that an information provider receives its data from a broadcast link as opposed to a request-response protocol should make no difference to clients of that provider.

In our approach, we distinguish between three types of nodes: (1) *data sources* provide the base data for the application; (2) *clients* consume this information; and (3) *information brokers* add value to information and redistribute it. By creating hierarchies of these nodes connected by various data delivery mechanisms, the information flow can be tailored to the needs of many different applications.

We aim to provide a *toolkit* of architectural components that can be used to construct a DBIS. A builder of an information resource would make use of these components to construct the interfaces to their service. Example components include a broadcast generator, a set of dissemination services, a client cache manager, a client prefetcher, a backchannel monitor, etc.

In the remainder of the paper we outline our current ideas on the development of such a toolkit. Section 2 describes several options for data delivery mechanisms (i.e., the "links") and discussesthe tradeoffs among them. Section 3 addresses the various types of nodes in a DBIS. Section 4 uses the DBIS model to describe several existing dissemination-oriented systems. Section 5 outlines issues in the development of a DBIS toolkit. Section 6 lists related work. Finally, Section 7 presents our conclusions.

## 2 Options for Data Delivery

As stated in the Introduction, a key aspect of the DBIS framework is that it supports a wide variety of links for data delivery between sources and clients. Support for different styles of data delivery allows a DBIS to be optimized for various server, client, network, data, and application properties.

### 2.1 Three Characteristics

We identify three main characteristics that can be used to compare data delivery mechanisms: (1) push vs. pull; (2) periodic vs. aperiodic; and (3) unicast vs. 1-to-N. Figure 1 shows these characteristics and how several common mechanisms relate to them.

#### 2.1.1 Client Pull vs. Server Push

The first distinction we make among data delivery styles is that of "push vs. pull". Current database servers and object repositories manage data for clients that explicitly request data when they require it. When a request is received at a server, the server locates the information of interest and returns it to the client. This *request-response* style of operation is *pull-based*— the transfer of information from servers to clients is initiated by a client pull. In contrast, push-based data delivery involves sending information to a client population in advance of any specific request. With push-based delivery, the server initiates the transfer.

#### 2.1.2 Aperiodic vs. Periodic

Both push and pull can be performed in either an aperiodic or periodic fashion. Aperiodic delivery is *event-driven* — a data request (for pull) or transmission (for push) is triggered by an event such as a user action (for pull) or data update (for push). In contrast, periodic delivery is performed according to some pre-arranged schedule. This schedule may be fixed, or may be generated with some degree of randomness.[1] An application that sends out stock prices on a regular basis is an example of periodic push, whereas one that sends out stock prices only when they change is an example of aperiodic push.

#### 2.1.3 Unicast vs. 1-to-N

The third characteristic of data delivery mechanisms we identify is whether they are based on unicast or 1-to-N communication. With unicast communication, data items are sent from a data source (e.g., a single server) to one other machine, while 1-to-N communication allows multiple machines to receive the data sent by a data source. Two types of 1-to-N data delivery can be distinguished: multicast and broadcast. With multicast, data is sent to a specific subset of clients. In some systems multicast is implemented by sending a message to a router that maintains the list of recipients. The router reroutes the message to each member of the list. Since the list of recipients is known, it is possible to make multicast reliable; that is, network protocols can be developed that guarantee the eventual delivery of the message to all clients that should receive it. In contrast, broadcasting sends information over a medium on which an unidentified and unbounded set of clients can listen. This differs from multicast in that the clients who may receive the data are not known *a priori.*

### 2.2 Classification of Delivery Mechanisms

It is possible to classify some existing data delivery mechanisms using the characteristics described above. Such a classification is shown in Figure 1. We discuss several of the leaves in this diagram below.

[1] For the purposes of this discussion, we do not distinguish between fixed and randomized schedules. Such a distinction is important in certain applications. For example, algorithms for conserving energy in mobile environments proposed by Imielinski et al. [Imie94b] depend on a strict schedule to allow mobile clients to "doze" during periods when no data of interest to them will be broadcast.

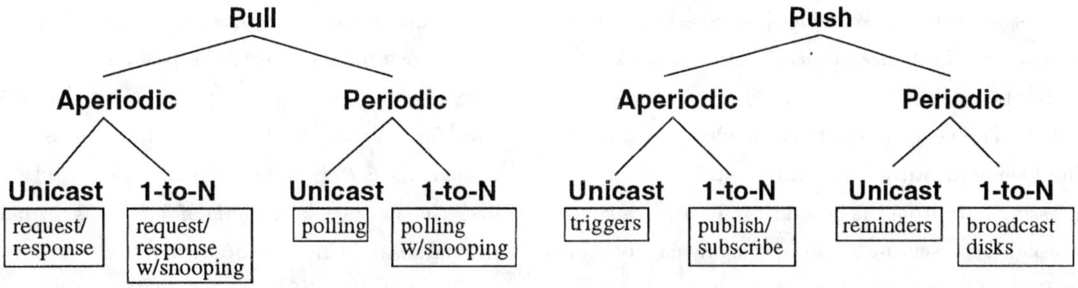


Figure 1: Data Delivery Options

**Request/Response** - Traditional request/response mechanisms use aperiodic pull over a unicast connection. If instead, a 1-to-N connection is used, then clients can "snoop" on the requests made by other clients, and obtain data that they haven't explicitly asked for.

**Polling** - In some applications, such as remote sensing, a system may periodically send requests to other sites to obtain status information or to detect changed values. If the information is returned over a 1-to-N link, then as with request/response, other clients can snoop to obtain data items as they go by.

**Publish/Subscribe** - Publish/subscribe protocols are becoming a popular way to disseminate information in a network [Oki93, Yan95, Glan96]. Publish/subscribe is push-based; data flow is initiated by the data sources, and is aperiodic, as there is no predefined schedule for sending data. Such protocols are typically performed in a 1-to-N fashion, but a similar protocol can be used over a unicast channel, as is done for triggers in active database systems.

**Broadcast Disks** - Periodic push has been used for data dissemination in many systems such as TeleText [Amma85, Wong88], DataCycle [Herm87, Bowe92], Broadcast Disks [Acha95a, Acha95b] and mobile databases [Imie94a]. Clients needing access to a data item that is pushed periodically can wait until the item appears. As with aperiodic push, periodic push can also be used with both unicast and 1-to-N channels, but we believe that 1-to-N is likely to be much more prevalent.

## 2.3 Some Example Tradeoffs

As can be seen from the preceding discussion, the design space for data delivery mechanisms is quite large. Choosing the proper mechanism (or combination of them) to use for a given link requires an understanding of the tradeoffs among them. In a recent paper, we studied one such set of tradeoffs; namely, those between broadcasting data using periodic push (Broadcast Disks) and aperiodic pull (request-response with snooping) [Acha97]. Here, we briefly discuss some observations from that study.

The tradeoffs between push and pull in general revolve around the costs of initiating the transfer of data. A pull-based approach requires the use of a backchannel for each request. Furthermore, as described in the Introduction, the server must be interrupted continuously to deal with such requests and has limited flexibility in scheduling the order of data delivery. Also, the information that clients can obtain from a server is limited to that which the clients know to ask for. Thus, new data items or updates to existing data items may go unnoticed at clients unless they periodically poll the server.

Push-based approaches, in contrast, avoid the issues identified for client-pull, but have the problem of deciding which data to send to clients in the absence of specific requests. Clearly, sending irrelevant data to clients is a waste of resources. A more serious problem, however, is that in the absence of requests it is possible that the servers will not deliver the specific data needed by clients in a timely fashion (if ever). Thus, the usefulness of server push is dependent on the ability of a server to accurately predict the needs of clients. One solution to this problem is to allow the clients to provide a *profile* of their interests to the servers. As mentioned above, *Publish/subscribe* protocols are one popular mechanism for providing such profiles.

In [Acha97] we studied a hybrid push/pull broadcast system. In this system, a broadcast server is responsible for allocating a fixed broadcast bandwidth between data items (pages) that are broadcast according to a fixed schedule (i.e., periodic push) and pages that are broadcast in response to client requests sent over a backchannel (i.e., aperiodic pull). The fundamental performance tradeoff between these two approaches can be seen in in Figure 2, which shows results from [Acha97][2]. The x-axis in the figure models the number of clients (all having identical access rates and distributions) that are accessing data from the broadcast. Thus, at a value of 250, the broadcast is serving 25 times as many clients than at a value of 10. The y-axis indicates the average number of items that a client must watch go by on the broadcast before the item it wants appears.

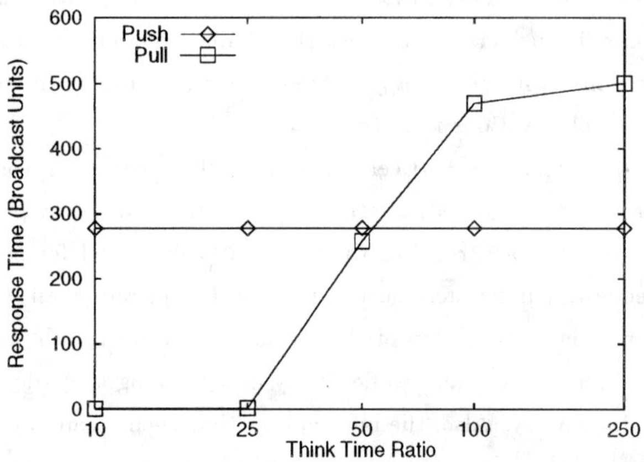


Figure 2: Push vs. Pull for Broadcast

The flat line in the figure (marked by diamonds) indicates the performance of a pure push approach, in which all data is broadcast repeatedly with no requests sent by the clients. This figure was generated using a skewed (Zipfian) access pattern over 1000 items. The broadcast schedule used by the push approach was tailored to support a skewed access pattern through the use of Broadcast Disks which allow the frequency of broadcast for an item to be based on that item's popularity [Acha95a, Acha95b]. As can be seen in the figure, the performance of pure push is *independent* of the number of clients listening to the broadcast here. This is a fundamental property of data broadcast using periodic push — if there is a large overlap in the interests of clients, it provides tremendous scalability in terms of client population.

The other curve in the figure (marked by boxes) shows the performance of a pull-based approach, in which clients submit requests to the server via the backchannel, and the server broadcasts the requested pages in FIFO order.[3] As can be seen in the figure, the pull-based approach exhibits an S-shaped behavior — it provides extremely fast response time for a lightly loaded server, but as the server becomes loaded, its performance degrades, until it ultimately stabilizes (in this case, at a value of 500 items, or half the size of the database being broadcast here).

The behavior of aperiodic pull in this case can be explained as follows. With a lightly loaded system, the server is typically idle so it can respond immediately when a request is received. As the load increases, however, the server saturates and becomes less responsive. Compared to periodic push, it is clear that aperiodic pull demonstrates less scalability in this case. It is, however, important to note that aperiodic pull over a *unicast* channel would be far less scalable — wait time would increase in an unbounded fashion as the server approached saturation. In contrast using broadcast, the performance of aperiodic pull eventually flattens out in this case, because of the overlap in the interests of the client population. Once the server reaches the state where all data items are in the FIFO queue, additional clients receive all of their data by simply "snooping" on the broadcast. In this case the performance of aperiodic pull at saturation is worse than that of periodic push, because the broadcast schedule generated by the FIFO discipline is less well suited to the access pattern than the pre-computed schedule used by periodic push. As discussed in [Acha97], the problems of pull can be exacerbated if the server drops client requests when it becomes overloaded.

The tradeoffs described above give an indication of the kinds of concerns that must be balanced when choosing the proper data delivery mechanism for a given situation. Another set of options arises in the organization of the nodes for a DBIS, as described in the following section.

## 3 Design Options for Nodes

While the discussion so far has focused on the ways in which data is communicated between computing devices, the nodes in a Dissemination-Based Information System play a crucial role as well: the nodes provide the glue that pastes various data distribution schemes together. A DBIS toolkit should contain classes that model some of the basic features

[2] We briefly summarize these results here, interested readers are referred to [Acha97]for more details

[3] Because a single broadcast of an item satisfies all clients waiting for that item, we do not enqueue a request for an item that is already in the FIFO queue.

of nodes. This section outlines some of those features.

### 3.1 Classification

In an integrated DBIS, there will be three types of nodes: (1) *data sources*, which provide the base data that is to be disseminated; (2) *clients*, which are net consumers of information; and (3) *information brokers*, that acquire information from other sources, add value to that information (e.g., some additional computation or organizational structure) and then distribute this information to other consumers. By creating hierarchies of brokers, information delivery can be tailored to the needs of many different users.

Information brokers perform many important functions in our architecture. While the previous discussion focused primarily on different modes of data delivery, the brokers provide the glue that binds these modes together. It is typically the expected usage patterns of the brokers that will drive the selection of which mode of delivery to use. For example, a broker that typically is very heavily loaded with requests could be an excellent candidate for a push-based delivery mechanism to its clients.

As we move upstream in the data delivery chain, brokers look like data sources to their clients. Receivers of information cannot detect the details of interconnections any further upstream than their immediate predecessor. This principle of *network transparency* allows data delivery mechanisms to change without having global impact. Suppose that node $B$ is pulling data values from node $A$ on demand. Further, suppose that node $C$ is listening to a cyclic broadcast from node $B$ which includes values that $B$ has pulled from $A$. Node $C$ will not have to change its data gathering strategy if $A$ begins to push values to $B$; changes in links are negotiated purely between the two nodes involved.

Of course, nothing is ever simple. In some cases, brokers can also be sources by maintaining their own databases. In this case, the *hybrid* broker can add data of its own to what it receives from its upstream counterparts. The principle of network transparency also protects clients from having to depend on this situation. A data source, be it a pure source, a broker, or a hybrid source, only guarantees that it can provide specific data — independently of where it comes from.

### 3.2 Caching

While nodes can perform many functions, the most ubiquitous data management facility is caching. Unlike caching in client-server systems, the path from data sources to a client can be of length greater than two. Thus, items might be cached at any of many points along the data path in the network. Thus, caching in this context resembles the kind of proxy caching that one might find in a wide-area network (e.g., the Internet).

While the problems here are very similar to those of any proxy caching scheme, the broad view of data movement available in a DBIS makes the potential solutions much richer. For example, if there are copies of a particular data item in multiple caches, there will always be an issue of how those copies are refreshed when the primary copy is updated. One solution is to send invalidations to each client cache manager. An invalidation message results in the purge of the item from the cache. Alternatively, the new value could be propagated to the client cache managers. For typical client/server systems, invalidation is usually preferable. However, in our broadcast disk studies [Acha96b] we showed that for periodic broadcast, performance can often be improved using propagation.

The decision about how current to keep the cached copies is the same as in other caching mechanisms. Once that has been decided, the means by which it is achieved can vary. In a DBIS, we could propagate (i.e., push) the changes to the clients or wait for the client to request the item again (i.e., pull). In the latter case, if a cache manager cares about keeping items very current, it will have to poll the state of the object often. It is interesting to note that if the data delivery mechanism in a DBIS changes, the means by which updates are propagated (or not) may also need to change.

Deciding which object to evict from the cache when a new candidate arrives is another issue that must be addressed by any cache manager. Many systems use some form of LRU for this purpose. We have shown in previous work [Acha95a] that for some styles of data delivery (e.g., broadcast disks), LRU is not the most effective choice. For cyclic data delivery, in which different items can have different arrival frequencies, a cost-based caching scheme performs significantly better.

In a DBIS, the modes of data delivery might change. In such an environment, the caching policy could change to match the prevailing conditions. We will need heuristics for deciding the appropriate caching policies for a particular configuration of distributed components. As an example, if node $B$ initially pulls data from node $A$, $B$ might reasonably use LRU as its caching policy. When $A$ creates a broadcast disk which is read by $B$, $B$ might then change its caching policy to a cost based scheme similar to the one that we propose in [Acha95a].

### 3.3 Value-Added Nodes

Some nodes may also add value to data as it passes through, by performing specific computations on that data. The computations can be simple or complex, or they can act on single values or sets of values. Other nodes may simply pass values on to other nodes.

As an example, suppose node $A$ pushes stock prices for Fortune 500 companies that are picked up by node $B$. Node $B$ keeps a database of previous stock prices and when a new price for the day is picked up from node $A$, it calculates the difference between the most current price and yesterday's close, and pushes this value out to yet another community. Node $B$ is a push-based, value-added server. Of course, it need not be based on push. Other clients could pull stock deviations from $B$ as well.

Another kind of value-added service that a node can perform is *merging* of values from multiple sources. Merging can occur in several ways. The first involves multiple sources that maintain similar information. The merge node can make the most reliable or most current version of a value available. Alternatively, multiple sources may maintain a set of values which the merge node combines to a single value. An example of this might involve nodes that maintain demographic information for towns including their current population. Another node may read these values and consolidate them into a single population figure for the state.

Nodes can also perform the service of *filtering*. A filtering node will receive a large volume of data from another node, only some fraction of which it makes available to its clients. For example, a node could receive all stock prices from the NYSE and provide information about only the Fortune 500 stocks to its clients.

### 3.4 Recoverable Nodes

Often it will be useful to make guarantees about the reliability of some node. Thus, nodes that implement some degree of recoverability will be a useful component in a DBIS. Consider a node that must guarantee the delivery of the latest version of IBM's stock price. Such a node must not lose its information in the event of a failure. That is, if the information was received, then the node must be able to guarantee that it will eventually be made available to its clients.

Of course, having recoverable brokers is not enough on its own to guarantee that nodes will not miss disseminated information while they are down. In order to address this issue, a scheme like reliable multicasting would have to be used. Reliable multicasting will eventually deliver all messages, but it cannot make real-time guarantees about when an object will arrive.

### 3.5 The Burden of Push

As mentioned in Section 2.3, any node that provides a push service must do so on the basis of some knowledge of the access patterns of its client base. If the node pushes data that few clients care about, then bandwidth is wasted. The trick is to broadcast items that are of interest to a large segment of the user community. This, of course, is only possible if there is high commonality of interest for at least some data items.

In order to optimize its push schedule, the server must rely on profiles of user needs. Profiles could be learned by servers if clients provide feedback about the effectiveness of the push schedule. Alternatively, a client could communicate a profile to the server at appropriate times, such as when it begins to listen to the push, at regularly scheduled intervals, or whenever the client notices that the current schedule deviates significantly from what it would like to see.

What would such a profile look like? A profile is very much like a continuously executing query [Terr92]. In other words, it is a predicate that indicates the items that the client would like to see. It is continuously executing because the server will push items as long as there are currently valid profiles that match the items.

Profiles can be interpreted to mean that whenever a new item is added to the database that matches a profile, the owner of that profile will receive the new data. On the other hand, the profile could be treated more as a hint to the server indicating interest with no requirement on the server's part to send matching items. In this case, the server may choose to conserve bandwidth and not send a matching item in order to best serve the client community as a whole.

## 4 Systems Viewed as DBIS

In this section, we describe some existing systems using the concepts of our DBIS framework.

### 4.1 Pointcast

Pointcast is a dissemination service that has attracted a large population of users. It obtains profiles from users that describe their interests, and then uses these profiles to assemble and update customized "newspapers" from a database of current stories.

The Pointcast system has been touted as one of the first push-based systems. This is not exactly true. Other systems such as Teletex [Amma85], BCS at MIT [Giff90], and Datacycle [Herm87] used push long before Pointcast. However, Pointcast was one of the first push-based systems to achieve wide-spread use. It is instructive, therefore, to see exactly how push is used in Pointcast 1.0 [4].

From the point of view of a DBIS, the use of push within Pointcast is extremely limited. In fact, in terms of the network architecture, push is non-existent; that is, the flow of requests and responses within the global architecture is pull-based. The Pointcast client on a user's workstation generates requests for news stories that match the user's profile. For example, if the user indicates an interest in the computer industry, the Pointcast client polls the Pointcast server for news stories with the keyword "computer industry" whenever the Pointcast screen saver is enabled. All of these requests can generate lots of network traffic.

So, where's the push? If we look at Figure 3, we see that there are essentially two processes in the client machine. One of these processes is responsible for *pulling* the latest news stories down to the user's machine, and the other is responsible for displaying these stories on the user's screen. The push really occurs between these two components. When the pull-based story acquisition module gets a new story, it pushes it to the screen manager. From the user's point of view, this *is* push because things are happening to the screen without any intervention. The use of push as a technique for managing heavy network loads, however, is not part of the design.

[4] Hereafter, referred to as Pointcast.

### 4.2 Broadcast Disks

Our own work on broadcast disks is based on a model of data delivery that is virtually the direct opposite of that described above for Pointcast (see Figure 4).

In our model, an application process on the client workstation behaves exactly as it would in a traditional pull-based environment. It generates pull requests as it needs data and blocks until that data is received.

The server, however, proactively sends data to the client community in advance of any request (i.e., push). A process on the client listens to the broadcast stream and picks up data items for which the application might be waiting. Thus, the places where pushes and pulls happen have been inverted over the Pointcast case.

It should be noted that in the broadcast disk case, the push is periodic and is scheduled by the server. In the Pointcast case, the pull is also periodic, but the interval is set by the user.

### 4.3 SIFT

The SIFT [Yan95] system was developed at Stanford University as a way to disseminate documents to a user community. SIFT combines data management ideas from information retrieval with a *publish/subscribe* model for dissemination. We describe the way the publish/subscribe model works in terms of our DBIS architecture.

Looking at Figure 5, we see three active components: the document source, the SIFT server, and a SIFT client (one of potentially many). The connection between the document source and the SIFT server (on the left side of the figure) is push-based, unicast, and aperiodic. The document source could alternatively deliver new documents through a 1-to-n broadcast medium, such as a satellite feed, if there were multiple interested recipients (SIFT servers or otherwise). A backchannel (not shown in the figure), is used only to set up the initial connection. Thereafter, the document source forwards all new documents to the SIFT server. There is no filtering that happens on this link. We could think of the profile held at the document source for the SIFT server as

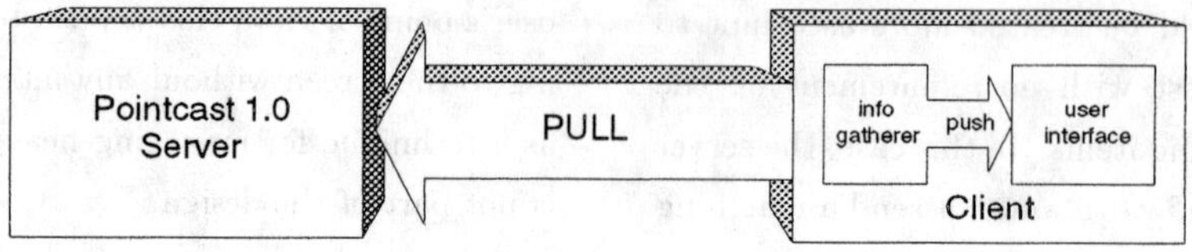


Figure 3: Pointcast 1.0

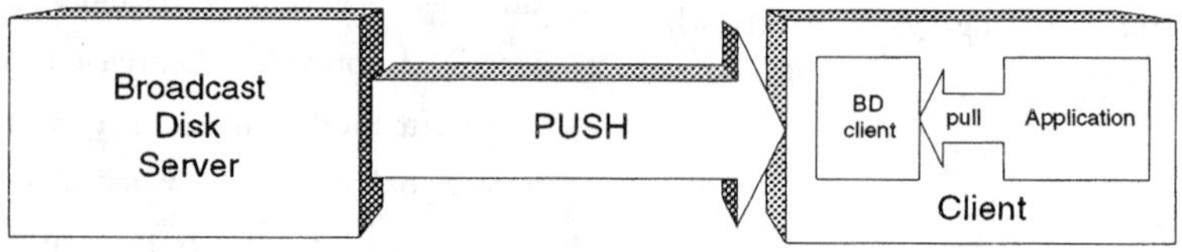


Figure 4: Broadcast Disks

being *send everything.*

The connection between the SIFT server and a given SIFT client (shown on the right side of the figure) is also push-based, unicast, and aperiodic. In this case, though, the client profile that is held at the SIFT server is customized for each client. It consists of a series of keywords and weights that describe documents of interest to that client. The SIFT server provides novel technology for indexing client profiles. Such an index is used for matching profiles against newly arriving documents. This indexing technique allows the server to accommodate a large client population with reasonable performance. The original SIFT prototype disseminated entire articles to clients. With the existence of the web, it becomes possible to send short article descriptions plus the corresponding URLs to conserve bandwidth.

It should be noted that clients get exactly what their profiles specify and nothing more. This is in contrast to a 1-to-n (broadcast) style of delivery in which all clients see the same information stream. It is the server's responsibility to optimize this stream to suit the needs of the largest number of users. It is unlikely that such a stream will be optimal for any one user.

## 5 Putting it All Together

In the preceding discussion, we described a vision of how distributed information systems should be built in the future. Our framework focused on techniques for delivering data in wide-area network settings in which nodes and links reflect extreme variation in their operating parameters. By adjusting the delivery mechanism to match these characteristics, we believe that we can achieve high performance and scalability without the need to invest in additional hardware. In this section, we briefly discuss our approach to this problem and outline some of the open research questions.

### 5.1 Toolkit Approach

We intend to realize our solutions to the problems of designing a DBIS through a toolkit that provides the proper components from which any DBIS could be built. This toolkit can be thought of as a set of object classes that support concepts such as *network connections* and *local caches.*

A key part of the toolkit will be a set of classes to allow distributed nodes to negotiate in order to establish a proper connection. This is required at several levels. At the highest level, the nodes must agree on how data is to be transferred. A client node that is relying on data from some server must know whether that server will be using push or accepting requests. There are also handshaking protocols that must occur at lower levels. For example, if a push-based broadcast connection is to be established in an Ethernet, the nodes must agree on which Ethernet address will be used for that broadcast. The parties must also agree on the parameters that will be used to configure that broadcast. For example, if it is a broadcast disk, the frequency of broadcast of each item is of interest to the clients.

The usefulness of a toolkit will rely on the precise definition of the DBIS classes. These classes must be of general utility. Also, as indicated in Section 2.3, the definition of

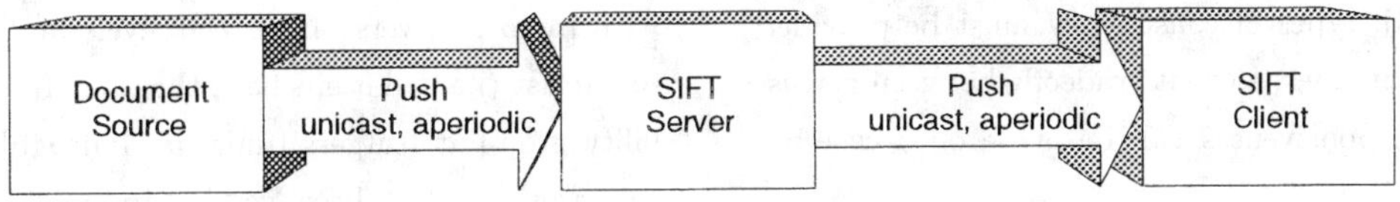


Figure 5: High-Level SIFT Architecture

these classes must be based on a substantial body of experimental results that help to delineate the sometimes subtle tradeoffs.

### 5.2 Dynamic Reconfiguration

A network can be characterized by prevailing loads on the nodes and the connections. This characterization changes rapidly, and a responsive DBIS must be able to adapt to these changes. Thus, our vision of a fully functional DBIS includes facilities to support the dynamic reconfiguration of the data delivery mechanisms.

A key element of a reconfiguration facility is a statistics gathering component that collects the right performance numbers and that can intelligently select among the available delivery options. This is not a simple matter. Our previous experiments in the area of broadcast disks has shown that the design space here is very complex with many places in which intuitions from more traditional distributed system design often produces poor results.

### 5.3 Some Design Issues

In addition to the plumbing issues that we have discussed so far, there are some higher-level issues that must be addressed in developing an integrated DBIS. In the following, we briefly outline some of these issues:

- *Bandwidth Allocation* - For a given link, policies are needed for allocating bandwidth among the various data delivery mechanisms.
- *Push Scheduling* - For the push-based approaches, intelligent scheduling is necessary in order to obtain the maximal benefit from the available bandwidth. Scheduling must also take into account the likelihood and distribution of transmission errors. Also, for periodic push, the broadcast should include index and/or schedule information that describes the objects that are to appear in the upcoming broadcast. Such information allows clients to minimize the amount of time and/or processing they devote to monitoring the broadcast and can aid in storage management decisions.
- *Client Storage Management* - Clients must allocate their storage resources among the data obtained through the various delivery mechanisms. Furthermore, as stated earlier, different methods of data delivery impose differing demands on the policies for client caching and prefetching. Furthermore, in some cases (e.g., mobility), storage management must also take into account the likelihood of disconnection and of data becoming stale due to updates or expiration.
- *User Profiles and Feedback* - Profiles of client needs are key for making allocation, scheduling and other policy decisions at both clients and servers. The form of the profiles will be important to achieve the most effective use of the medium. For example, access probabilities are one specific representation of the client needs. The server must also have effective models for combining client profiles. The integration of a *backchannel* from clients to servers is needed to allow for updating profiles and making additional requests.
- *Security Issues* - Another set of important issues that must be addressed revolves around the security and privacy concerns that arise in any distributed information system. The emphasis on one-to-N communication in a DBIS, however, increases the significance of such issues.
- *Consistency Issues* - The final issue we list here is the maintenance of data consistency, particularly in the face of possibly intermittent connection. Two types of consistency must be considered. First, guarantees on the timeliness of individual data items must be provided if required by the clients. Second, *mutual consistency* across multiple items will be required in some

instances. All types of consistency must be provided in a flexible manner, so that tradeoffs between consistency and responsiveness can be made on a case-by-case basis.

## 6 Related Work

Work on distributed object computing has generated many important standards and systems. CORBA [OMG91] and DCE [OSF94], for example, are two important approaches to system interoperability. This work is not incompatible with the notion of a DBIS. A DBIS can be thought of as infrastructure for such object-oriented middleware.

There is much previous work that relates to the architectural issues of a DBIS. The brief discussion that follows samples some of the work that is most related to the issues presented in this paper.

The management of data in distributed settings has a long history. The preponderance of previous work assumes that data is requested when needed (i.e., pull) and that servers respond to these requests in an orderly fashion. Some of this work has occurred in a client/server database setting [Fran96a] while other work has been done in the distributed file system context [Levy90]. There has been a lot of work on caching in these environments, much of which has focused on the maintenance of cache consistency in the face of updates.

More recently, there has been work on data management issues for wireless environments [Katz94]. Some of work in this area has focused on satellite-based systems [Dao96, Dire96] in which the downstream bandwidth is quite high.

The idea of the publish/subscribe model as a dissemination mechanism has been used in many contexts including SIFT [Yan95] and the Information Bus[Oki93].

There has also been work on broadcasting in Teletex systems [Amma85, Wong88]. [Wong88] presents an overview of some of the analytical studies on one-way, two-way and hybrid broadcast in this framework.

The Datacycle Project [Bowe92, Herm87] at Bellcore investigated the notion of using a repetitive broadcast medium for database storage and query processing. An early effort in information broadcasting, the Boston Community Information System (BCIS) is described in [Giff90]. BCIS broadcast news articles and information over an FM channel to clients with personal computers specially equipped with radio receivers. Both Datacycle and BCIS used a flat broadcast (i.e., all items have the same frequency). The mobility group at Rutgers [Imie94a, Imie94b] has done significant work on data broadcasting in mobile environments. A main focus of their work has been to investigate novel ways of indexing in order to reduce power consumption at the mobile clients. Some recent applications of dissemination-based systems include information dissemination on the Internet [Yan95, Best96], and Advanced Traveler Information Systems [Shek96].

Our work on Broadcast Disks differs from these in that we consider multi-level disks and their relationship to cache management. In [Acha95a], we proposed an algorithm to generate Broadcast Disk programs and demonstrated the need for cost-based caching in this environment. Recently, [Baru96] gave an algorithm to determine the parameters controlling a broadcast program. In [Acha96a], we showed how opportunistic prefetching by the client can significantly improve performance over demand-driven caching. More recently, in [Acha96b], we studied the influence of volatile data on client performance and showed that the Broadcast Disk environment can be made very robust in the presence of updates. In [Acha97], we explored the tradeoff between cyclic broadcast and pull.

## 7 Conclusions

The increasing ability to interconnect computers through internetworking, mobile and wireless networks, and high-bandwidth content delivery to the home, has resulted in a proliferation of dissemination-oriented applications. A key attribute of many such applications is their huge scale. These applications present new challenges for data management throughout all components of a distributed information system. We have proposed the notion of a dissemination-based information system that integrates many different data delivery mechanisms and types of information brokers. We described some of the unique aspects of such systems and discussed how several existing dissemination-based architectures fit in to the DBIS model.

The ideas presented in this paper have grown out of our previous work on the Broadcast Disks paradigm for data delivery. A key lesson from that work was the importance of applying a data management perspective to distributed systems architecture issues. We are currently completing a prototype that combines the push-based Broadcast Disks with a pull-based broadcast model. We view that prototype as the first step in the development of a generic DBIS toolkit that will support the creation of a variety of large-scale dissemination-based applications across several different communication media.


## Acknowledgments

We would like to thank Swarup Acharya for his contributions to these ideas through the development of the Broadcast Disks paradigm and Demet Aksoy who has provided us with important insights into the properties of broadcast scheduling.


## References


[Acha95a] S. Acharya, R. Alonso, M. Franklin, S. Zdonik, "Broadcast Disks: Data Management for Asymmetric Communication Environments", *Proc. ACM SIGMOD Conf.*, San Jose, CA, May, 1995.

[Acha95b] S. Acharya, M. Franklin, S. Zdonik, "Dissemination-based Data Delivery Using Broadcast Disks", *IEEE Personal Communications*, 2(6), December, 1995.

[Acha96a] S. Acharya, M. Franklin, S. Zdonik, "Prefetching from a Broadcast Disk", *12th International Conference on Data Engineering*, New Orleans, LA, February, 1996.

[Acha96b] S. Acharya, M. Franklin, S. Zdonik, "Disseminating Updates on Broadcast Disks", *Proc. $22^{nd}$ VLDB Conf.*, Bombay, India, September, 1996.

[Acha97] S. Acharya, M. Franklin, S. Zdonik, "Balancing Push and Pull for Data Broadcast", *Proc. ACM SIGMOD Conf.*, Tucson, AZ, May, 1997.

[Amma85] M. Ammar, J. Wong, "The Design of Teletext Broadcast Cycles", *Perf. Evaluation*, 5 (1985).

[Baru96] S. Baruah and A. Bestavros, "Pinwheel Scheduling for Fault-tolerant Broadcast Disks in Real-time Database Systems", Technical Report TR-96-023, Boston University, August, 1996.

[Best96] A. Bestavros, C. Cunha, "Server-initiated Document Dissemination for the WWW", *IEEE Data Engineering Bulletin*, 19(3), September, 1996.

[Bowe92] T. Bowen, G. Gopal, G. Herman, T. Hickey, K. Lee, W. Mansfield, J. Raitz, A. Weinrib, "The Datacycle Architecture", *CACM*, 35(12), December, 1992.

[Care91] M. Carey, M. Franklin, M. Livny, E. Shekita, "Data Caching Tradeoffs in Client-Server DBMS Architectures", *Proc. ACM SIGMOD Conf.*, Denver, June, 1991.

[Dao96] S. Dao, B. Perry, "Information Dissemination in Hybrid Satellite/Terrestrial Networks", *IEEE Data Engineering Bulletin*, 19(3), September, 1996.

[Dire96] Hughes Network Systems, DirecPC Home Page, `http://www.direcpc.com/`, Oct, 1996.

[Erik94] H. Erikson,"MBONE: The Multicast Backbone", *CACM*, 37(8), August, 1994.

[Fran96a] M. Franklin, *Client Data Caching: A Foundation for High Performance Object Database Systems*, Kluwer Academic Publishers, Boston, MA, February, 1996.

[Fran96b] M. Franklin, S. Zdonik, "Dissemination-Based Information Systems", *IEEE Data Engineering Bulletin*, 19(3), September, 1996.

[Giff90] D. Gifford, "Polychannel Systems for Mass Digital Communication", *CACM*, 33(2), February, 1990.

[Glan96] D. Glance, "Multicast Support for Data Dissemination in OrbixTalk", *IEEE Data Engineering Bulletin*, 19(3), September, 1996.

[Herm87] G. Herman, G. Gopal, K. Lee, A. Weinrib, "The Datacycle Architecture for Very High Throughput Database Systems", *Proc. ACM SIGMOD Conf.*, San Francisco, CA, May, 1987.

[Imie94a] T. Imielinski, B. Badrinath, "Mobile Wireless Computing: Challenges in Data Management", *CACM*, 37(10), October, 1994.

[Imie94b] T. Imielinski, S. Viswanathan, B. Badrinath, "Energy Efficient Indexing on Air", *Proc. ACM SIGMOD Conf.*, Minneapolis, MN, May, 1994.

[Katz94] R. Katz, "Adaption and Mobility in Wireless Information Systems", *IEEE Personnal Comm.*, 1st Quarter, 1994.

[Levy90] Levy, E., Silbershatz, A., "Distributed File Systems: Concepts and Examples", *ACM Computing Surveys*, 22(4), December, 1990.

[OMG91] Object Management Group and X/Open, "Common Object Request Broker: Architecture and Specification", *Reference OMG 91.12.1*, 1991.

[Oki93] B. Oki, M. Pfluegl, A. Siegel, D. Skeen, "The Information Bus - An Architecture for Extensible Distributed Systems", *Proc. 14th SOSP*, Ashville, NC, December, 1993.

[OSF94] Open Software Foundation, "Introduction to OSF DCE", *Prentice Hall*, Englewood Cliffs, NJ, 1994.

[Shek96] S. Shekhar, A. Fetterer, D. Liu, "Genesis: An Approach to Data Dissemination in Advanced Traveller Information Systems", *IEEE Data Engineering Bulletin*, 19(3), September, 1996.

[Terr92] D. Terry, D. Goldberg, D. Nichols, "Continuous Queries Over Append-Only Databases", *Proc. ACM SIGMOD Conf.*, San Diego, CA, June, 1992.

[Wong88] J. Wong, "Broadcast Delivery", *Proceedings of the IEEE*, 76(12), December, 1988.

[Yan95] T. Yan, H. Garcia-Molina, "SIFT – A Tool for Wide-area Information Dissemination", *Proc. 1995 USENIX Technical Conference*, 1995.

# Exploring Largeness, Complexity and Scalability from the OOT Perspective

## Panel Session

Moderator: Bindu Rama Rao

Panelists: Chad Edwards, Ted Linden, Reagan Moore, Mark Seager

**Abstract:** This panel will lay the foundation for understanding the needs of Large Systems so that OO practitioners can:

- appreciate the problems faced;
- understand the issues involved; and
- re-orient their approaches to provide a viable solution when participating in similar efforts.

Specifically, this panel will establish the foundation for discussions on Large Systems by establishing concepts, exposing terminology, and highlighting the state-of-the art.

Large applications are usually complex and display one or more of the following dimensions of largeness:

- *Processing power*: requiring tens to hundreds of gigabytes of memory and hundreds of gigaflops performance
- *High connectivity*: highly-connected systems can show aggregate behavior with complex characteristics: they can become chaotic.
- *Online access*: Archival of terabytes of information, with the need to provide online access to information.
- *Archival and online retrieval*: The two technologies (database and archival storage), however, currently do not interoperate. There is a need to develop interfaces to integrate these two technologies.
- *Data-intensive scientific applications*: These involve constructing a data handling infrastructure that simplifies the effort required to maintain petabyte archives, identify relevant data sets within the archive, move the data to processing platforms, and distribute the data sets across multiple nodes.
- *Internet access*: Large applications often require simultaneous access of information by millions of users worldwide;they must provide acceptable response times.
- *Scaleable architecture*: The systems must be prepared to support exponential growth of application load.

Is OOT up to the task? OO practitioners will be encountering some of these application domains in the near future. Some may have already gained some experience in trying to solve these problems. However, the literature in OO does not provide sufficient evidence to believe that OO is ready for such large systems today. Part of the problem is the cross-disciplinary nature of these problems requires a steep learning curve for OO practitioners to be effective. The modeling of these problems with an OO approach is also a challenge. Current OO methods do not do a good job of supporting multiple views of a domain, and multiple layers of a complex application domain.

**Format:** The panel provides a plurality of experts, each expert experienced in designing a solution to a "large" problem in his domain, and an opportunity to express the problems of designing solutions. Each expert will summarize the problems faced in developing large, complex and scaleable applications in his particular vertical market. This will be followed by a general session in which the experts collectively attempt to "characterize large system development", and the potential of OOT for addressing their specific and shared difficulties. The panel will close with questions and comments from audience members.

*Bindu Rama Rao is Technical Consultant at Stanford & Bennett, L.L.P.*

### Chad Edwards

*The Deep Space Network Project:* The NASA Deep Space Network is an international network of antennas that supports interplanetary spacecraft missions and radio and radar astronomy observations for the exploraton of the solar system and the universe. The network also supports some Earth-orbiting missions, including emergency support of the Shuttle Space Transportation System.

NASA's scientific investigation of the Solar System is being accomplished mainly through the use of unmanned automated spacecraft. The DSN provides the vital two-way communications link that guides and controls these planetary explorers, and brings back the images and new scientific information they collect. All DSN antennas are steerable, high-gain, parabolic reflector antennas.

*Chad Edwards is Manager of Telecommunications and Mission Operations Technology Office at NASA, JPL. The mission of the TMO Technology Office is to identify, develop, and demonstrate new technologies and innovative approaches to meet the telecommunications, mission operations, and science needs of present and future TMOD customers at minimum end-to-end cost to NASA.*

*The Telecommunications and Mission Operations Directorate has the responsibility to provide telecommunications for successful execution of a broad spectrum of space exploration missions; to provide mission operations that add significant value to the conduct of space exploration missions; to conduct ground-based radio astronomy, solar system radar, and radio science observations; and to manage and operate flight projects assigned to the Directorate.*

### Ted Linden

*Object Infrastructure for Incrementally Extending Large, Distributed Systems*: Complex systems grow incrementally. Some systems that are simply large can be specified in advance and then built to original specifications. For complex systems, however, there is no hope of understanding all the requirements in advance. Today, most software developers work on complex systems; however, they still use processes and tools that have not yet come to terms with the fundamental problem of software complexity: how to build systems that can interact with independently developed subsystems and can be readily extended and scaled up to meet unanticipated future requirements.

This paper is about extending object technology to support incremental extension and scaling of distributed applications. Object technology has been successful largely because it makes software easier to modify, extend, and reuse. However, large, complex, scalable systems are distributed, and choices made among alternative distribution standards often become pervasive and irrevocable commitments of the system. Programmers using current object distribution models often mix application logic with object communication logic in ways that hinder future extension, interactions, and growth.

MCC's Object Infrastructure Project is developing prototype frameworks that make it easier to separate application logic from underlying distributed communication and service functionality. The framework complements and builds on OMG, DCOM, or other distributed system architectures. It isolates the application logic from underlying service functionality, and it provides a prototype set of plug-and-play services to support availability, replication, reliability, consistency, manageability, security, real time, and other common problems within complex distributed applications.

Complexity is the fundamental problem in software systems, and adding a requirment that the system be distributed initially only adds to complexity. However, distribution is the only way to overcome the fundamental problems of developing systems that can easily interact with independently-developed systems and can scale up to meet unanticipated future requirements. By developing a framework that handles the complexity associated with object distribution and isolates that complexity away from the rest of the software, it becomes practical to exploit the advantages of distributed objects for handling complexity and scalability.

*Ted Linden is an MCC Technical Director for Distributed Systems working at the MCC West Coast Labs. He manages MCC's Object Infrastructure Project, leads a study on Federated Systems Security, and pursues development of additional research opportunities in the area of distributed systems. The Object Infrastructure Project (OIP) aims to improve delivery of products and services in global, networked environments sby developing and demonstrating an integrated set of services required to support advanced, distributed, object-oriented applications. This resulting object infrastructure will be based on a combination of object standards, commercially available technology, emerging research results, and targeted research performed within the project.*

*Linden came to MCC from Lockheed Martin's Palo Alto Advanced Technology Center where he worked on resource allocation problems and security for federated systems. Linden was also the founder Myriad Software (Palo Alto, Calif.), where he developed agent technology for distributed training simulations under contracts from the National Science Foundation and Stanford University. Previously, while with Advanced Decision Systems in Mountain View, CA, Linden applied artificial intelligence planning techniques in applications that included air operations and logistics planning. While at Xerox in Palo Alto, Linden helped commercialize early Ethernet-based products and documented early application-level network protocols. Linden holds a Ph.D. in Mathematics from the Belfer Graduate School of Science, Yeshiva University.*

## Reagan Moore

*Synopsis of MDAS Research*: Our research effort involves defining and prototyping an architecture for accessing very large data archives. The proposed architecture will support data-intensive applications that manipulate very large data sets by building upon object-relational database technology and archival storage technology. The two technologies (database and archival storage), however, currently do not interoperate. We will develop interfaces to integrate these two technologies. Another goal is to research the software intrastructure needed to replace the UNIX file system paradigm with a data analysis and API system capable of accessing terabyte data sets.

*Reagan Moore is Associate Director of the Enabling Technologies Group at the San Diego Supercomputer Center. At present he is Principle Investigator of the Massive Data Analysis Project (MDAS).*

## Mark Seager

*The ASCI Blue Pacific Teraflop Platform*: LLNL has recently taken delivery of a 512-node SP2 parallel processor, as a first step in the eventual delivery of a very large 3-Tflop SMP computer platform, called ASCI Blue Pacific. A sequence of refresh steps in 1997, 1998, and 1999 will move the system from single processor nodes, to 4-way, then to 8-way SMP nodes.

By 1999, the system will consist of a 512-node, 8-way SMP configuration with 2.5 TB of memory, 75 TB of disk, and a peak speed of 3.2 Tflops. Most nodes will realize 3 GB of memory, but 64 nodes will feature 16 GB of memory. This creates a very flexible architecture for the execution of midscale to extremely large 3D applications. This resource will be able to securely shift from classified to unclassified use in a matter of hours, allowing scientists the benefit of collaborative research with workers in industry and academia.

*The Facility for Advanced Scalable Computing Technology*: The Facility for Advanced Scalable Computing Technology (FAST) opens up new, unclassified opportunities for research in fields such as energy, stockpile stewardship, and biosciences at Lawrence Livermore National Laboratory (LLNL). FAST gives researchers computing cycles along with an archival storage system interconnected by state-of-the-art, standards-based network technology. FAST is also accessible via the information superhighway, which is important to successful collaboration. FAST development goals include:

- A world-class, high-performance computing environment.
- Scalability to efficiently serve a variety of users and applications.
- Support for work with other Department of Energy (DOE) laboratories and industry.

FAST will also support the Accelerated Strategic Computing Initiative (ASCI) program, a three-lab, one-program collaboration between LLNL, Sandia, and Los Alamos national laboratories. The result will be a dramatically increased computing capability to support the need for advanced modeling techniques to allow the U.S. to maintain a viable nuclear stockpile without underground nuclear tests.

*Mark Seager is a system architect at the Lawrence Livermore National Labs.*

# Call Graph Construction in Object-Oriented Languages

David Grove, Greg DeFouw, Jeffrey Dean*, and Craig Chambers

Department of Computer Science and Engineering
University of Washington
Box 352350, Seattle, Washington 98195-2350 USA
{grove, gdefouw, jdean, chambers}@cs.washington.edu

## Abstract

Interprocedural analyses enable optimizing compilers to more precisely model the effects of non-inlined procedure calls, potentially resulting in substantial increases in application performance. Applying interprocedural analysis to programs written in object-oriented or functional languages is complicated by the difficulty of constructing an accurate program call graph. This paper presents a parameterized algorithmic framework for call graph construction in the presence of message sends and/or first-class functions. We use this framework to describe and to implement a number of well-known and new algorithms. We then empirically assess these algorithms by applying them to a suite of medium-sized programs written in Cecil and Java, reporting on the relative cost of the analyses, the relative precision of the constructed call graphs, and the impact of this precision on the effectiveness of a number of interprocedural optimizations.

## 1 Introduction

Interprocedural analysis can enable substantial improvements in application performance by allowing optimizing compilers to make less conservative assumptions across procedure call boundaries. Given a program call graph representing the possible callees at each call site in each procedure, interprocedural analyses typically produce summaries of the effect of callees at each call site and/or summaries of the effect of callers at each procedure entry. These summaries are then consulted when compiling and optimizing individual procedures. Unfortunately, in the presence of dynamically dispatched messages or invocations of computed functions, the set of possible callees at each call site is difficult to compute precisely, necessitating interprocedural analysis to compute the possible classes of message receivers or the possible function values invoked. In effect, interprocedural dataflow and control flow analysis is needed to build the data structure over which interprocedural analysis operates. A number of algorithms have been proposed to solve this dilemma, typically by computing the program call graph simultaneously with performing interprocedural dataflow analysis. The algorithms make different trade-offs between the precision of the resulting call graph and any associated dataflow information, and the cost of computing the call graph. An algorithm's cost and the precision of its result are also impacted by application programming style: the depth and breadth of class hierarchies, the relative frequency of message sends versus direct procedure calls, and the prevalence of applications of computed function values should all be considered when selecting a call graph construction algorithm.

Our main contributions are developing a common framework for describing a wide range of existing call graph construction algorithms and assessing the precision and cost of the algorithms on programs of substantial size.

- In section 2 we present a lattice-theoretic model of context-sensitive call graphs. Each element of the lattice corresponds to a possible call graph for a program, and call graphs in the lattice are ordered in terms of relative precision. In section 3 we use this model along with a generalized call graph construction algorithm to describe many different families of call graph construction algorithms. By formalizing the model of call graphs, we can highlight important similarities and differences between the algorithms and make our descriptions and comparisons more precise than previous work. We also can specify the properties required of any safe solution, and, in some cases, compare the precision of call graphs constructed by different algorithms. Our model leads to a natural parameterized implementation framework, and we have implemented this framework and a number of call graph construction algorithms in the Vortex optimizing compiler system [Dean et al. 96]. Finally, the call graph model and algorithmic framework helped us to identify several new and interesting points in the design space of call graph construction algorithms.
- In section 4, we empirically assess the precision and cost of the implemented algorithms, applying them to a suite of Cecil [Chambers 93] and Java [Gosling et al. 96] programs. Our benchmark applications are an order of magnitude larger than those used to evaluate previous work, enabling us to assess how well each algorithm scales to larger programs. By studying two quite different object-oriented languages, one of which uses dynamically dispatched messages and first-class functions extensively while the other mixes dynamically dispatched messages with traditional non-object-oriented operations, we can investigate the impact of programming style on algorithm effectiveness.

  The additional precision produced by some call graph algorithms is only of value if it can be exploited effectively by client optimizations. We assess the bottom-line impact of call graph precision by using the constructed call graphs to drive several interprocedural analyses and optimizations, reporting on both final execution speed and executable size.

Section 5 discusses some additional related work and section 6 offers our conclusions.

---

* Dean's current address: Digital Equipment Corporation, Western Research Lab, 250 University Avenue, Palo Alto, CA 94301; jdean@pa.dec.com


**OOPSLA '97 10/97 GA, USA**
**© 1997 ACM 0-89791-908-4/97/0010...$3.50**

```
procedure main() {
  return A() + B() + C();
}

procedure A() {
  return max(4, 7);
}
procedure B() {
  return max(4.5, 2.5);
}
procedure C() {
  return max(3, 1);
}
```

(a) Example Program

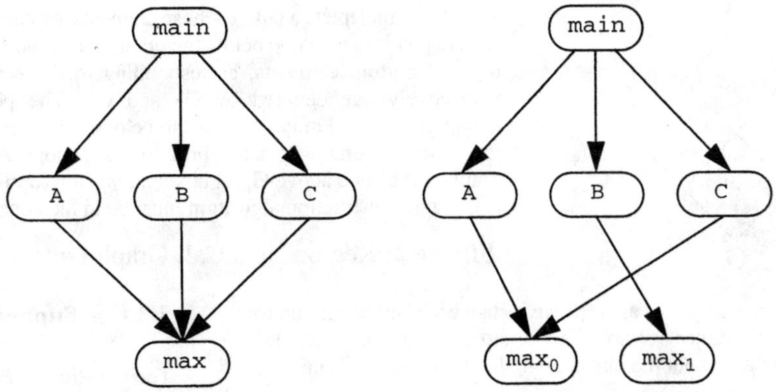


(b) Context-Insensitive (c) Context-Sensitive

**Figure 1:** Example Program and Call Graphs

## 2 Modelling Call Graphs

In the next subsection we present our general model of program call graphs in informal terms. We then formalize this model in lattice-theoretic terms.

### 2.1 Informal Model of Call Graphs

The program call graph is a directed graph that represents the calling relationships between the program's procedures.* In a context-insensitive call graph, each procedure is represented by a single node in the graph. Each node has an indexed set of call sites, and each call site is the source of zero or more edges to other nodes, representing possible callees of that site; multiple callees at a single site are possible for a dynamically dispatched message send or an application of a computed function. Figure 1(b) shows the context-insensitive call graph corresponding to the example program in figure 1(a). In a context-sensitive analysis, a procedure may be analyzed separately for different calling contexts; each of these context-sensitive versions of a procedure is called a *contour* [Shivers 91b]. We model context-sensitive analyses in our call graph by having nodes in the call graph correspond to contours; thus, a call edge from a call site in one contour connects to the appropriate contour(s) of the callee procedure(s). The different context-sensitive analyses differ in how they determine what set of contours to create for a given procedure and which contours to select as targets of a given call. Figure 1(c) depicts one possible context-sensitive call graph for the same example program which distinguishes between calls to `max` with integer and floating point parameters. A context-insensitive analysis can be modeled by restricting the call graph to have only a single contour for each source-level procedure. We abstract these algorithm-specific decisions into a *contour selection function* which, given information about the call site's calling contour and the possible classes of the actual parameters of the call, selects the set of callee contours to create (if not already present in the call graph) and link the call site to.

In addition to the set of callees at each call site, each contour in our call graph also records a set of classes for each formal parameter, local variable, and result of the procedure represented by the contour. These sets of classes represent the possible classes of values stored in the corresponding variables at run-time. To record the class sets for global variables, we introduce a special root contour whose "local variables" correspond to the global variables of the program. Module scopes can be modeled similarly.

Contours also represent lexical nesting relationships in the presence of lexically nested procedures. Each contour has a pointer to its lexically enclosing contour (which may be the global contour), except for the global contour which has no lexically enclosing contour.† In this fashion, we avoid losing precision during context-sensitive analysis of lexically nested procedures that access free variables.

In languages with first-class function values or function pointers, we treat each such source-level occurrence of a function definition (or function whose address is taken) as creating a new class with a single method named `apply` whose body is the body of the function.‡ If the function was lexically nested within another function, then the class and its `apply` method are considered lexically nested in that same function. Evaluating the function definition or taking the address of a function are treated as instantiation sites of the new class, and invoking a function value is treated as sending the `apply` message to the object representing the function value. This encoding lets us focus solely on analyzing the flow of class instances through the program.

We also need to record sets of possible classes for each instance variable, in a manner similar to class sets for local variables. To support array classes, we introduce a single instance variable per array class to model the elements of the array. To support both context-insensitive and -sensitive analyses of instance variable contents, each instance variable declaration is modeled by one or more instance variable contours. An instance variable contour maintains a single set of classes, representing the possible classes of values stored in that instance variable contour at run-time. Most analyses are context-insensitive with respect to instance variables, in that there is a single instance variable contour for each source-level instance variable declaration. More precise analyses could maintain separate instance variable contours for each inheriting subclass, enabling the analysis to track the possible classes in each instance variable separately. We abstract these algorithm-specific decisions into an *instance variable contour selection function*

* We will use the terms procedure, function, and method interchangeably. Our system treats them uniformly.

† Our model could be extend to support a lexically enclosing contour selection function that maps each contour to a set of lexically enclosing contours. This extension would allow us to model the flexible analysis of lexical environments supported by infinitary control flow analysis [Nielson & Nielson 97].

‡ A similar strategy is used by the Pizza implementation to translate closures into Java [Odersky & Wadler 97].

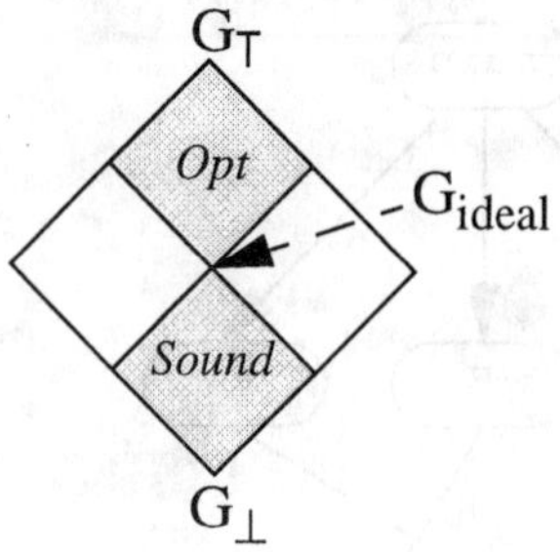


This diagram depicts a lattice whose elements are call graphs. We order one call graph below another (and depict it in the cone below the other) if it is more conservative (less precise) than the other. The top and bottom elements, corresponding to the empty call graph and the complete call graph, respectively, are denoted by $G_\top$ and $G_\bot$. The point $G_{ideal}$ identifies the "real" but usually uncomputable call graph, which can be described precisely as the greatest lower bound over all call graphs corresponding to actual program executions. Any particular program execution induces a call graph in the cone above $G_{ideal}$ labeled *Opt* (for "optimistic"). Any call graph produced by a correct call graph construction algorithm must be in the cone below $G_{ideal}$ labeled *Sound.*

**Figure 2:** Regions in a Call Graph Lattice Domain

which returns the set of appropriate instance variable contours for a particular instance variable load or store operation, given class set information about the object being loaded or stored from.

Some analyses are even more precise in their analysis of classes and instance variable contents. By treating different instantiation sites of a class as leading to distinct (analysis-time) classes with distinct instance variable contours, they can simulate the effect of templates or parameterized types without relying on explicit parameterization in the source program. We model these analyses by associating each source-level class with multiple class contours. A *class contour selection function* is applied at class instantiation sites to select the set of appropriate class contours to model the result of the instantiation. All previously described class information is generalized to be class contour information, including the sets associated with variables in each (procedure) contour, the actual parameter sets used by the (procedure) contour selection function and the instance variable contour selection function, and the information computed during the intraprocedural analysis of individual contours.

To summarize, we use a single general model of the procedure call graph that can encode both context-sensitive and context-insensitive call graphs. A wide range of context-sensitive call graphs can be represented by choosing different values for the three parameterizing functions: the contour selection function, the instance variable contour selection function, and the class contour selection function.

## 2.2 Lattice-Theoretic Model of Call Graphs

This subsection formalizes the intuitive notions of the previous subsection using lattice-theoretic ideas.* This formalization ensures that we have a well-grounded understanding of contour-based call graphs and provides a vocabulary for discussing when a particular call graph is a safe (sound) approximation of the "real" call graph and when one call graph is more precise than another. We formalize the possible outputs of the contour selection functions, giving some formal structure to them that will help in comparing algorithms.

Figure 2 shows some of the interesting elements and regions in a call graph lattice. As is traditional in dataflow analysis [Kildall 73, Kam & Ullman 76] (but opposite to the conventions used in abstract interpretation [Cousot & Cousot 77]), the top lattice element represents the best possible (most optimistic) call graph, while the bottom element represents the worst possible (most conservative) call graph.

* A lattice $D = \langle S_D, \le_D \rangle$ is a set of elements $S_D$ and an associated partial ordering $\le_{DPS}$ of those elements such that for every pair of elements the set contains both a unique least-upper-bound element and a unique greatest-lower-bound element. A downward semilattice is like a lattice but only greatest-lower-bounds are required. The set of possible call graphs for a particular model of context-sensitivity form a downward semilattice; we will use the term domain to refer to a downward semilattice.

### 2.2.1 Supporting Lattice Constructors

The constructor *Pow* maps an input partial order $D = \langle S_D, \le_D \rangle$ to a lattice $DPS = \langle S_{DPS}, \le_{DPS} \rangle$ where $S_{DPS}$ is a subset of the powerset of $S_D$ defined as:

$$S_{DPS} = \bigcup_{S \in PowerSet(S_D)} Bottoms(S)$$

where $Bottoms(S) = \{ d \in S \mid \neg(\exists d' \in S, d' \le_D d) \}$. The partial order $\le_{DPS}$ is defined in terms of $\le_D$ as follows:

$$dps_1 \le_{DPS} dps_2 \equiv \forall d_2 \in dps_2,\ \exists d_1 \in dps_1 \text{ such that } d_1 \le_D d_2$$

If $S_1$ and $S_2$ are both elements of $S_{DPS}$, then their greatest lower bound is $Bottoms(S_1 \cup S_2)$.

Each member of the family of constructors *kTuple,* $\forall k \ge 0$, is the standard *k*-tuple constructor which takes *k* input partial orders $D_i = \langle S_i, \le_i \rangle$, $\forall i \in [1..k]$, and generates a new partial order $T = \langle S_T, \le_T \rangle$ where $S_T$ is the cross product of the $S_i$ and $\le_T$ is defined in terms of the $\le_i$ pointwise, as follows:

$$\langle d_{11}, \dots, d_{k1} \rangle \le_T \langle d_{12}, \dots, d_{k2} \rangle \equiv \forall i \in [1..k],\ d_{i1} \le_i d_{i2}$$

If the input partial orders are downward semilattices, then *T* is also a downward semilattice, where the greatest lower bound of two tuples is the tuple of the pointwise greatest lower bounds of their elements.

The constructor *Map* is a function constructor which takes as input an unordered set *X* and a partial order *Y* and generates a new partial order $M = \langle S_M, \le_M \rangle$ where

$$S_M = \{ f \subseteq X \times Y \mid (x, y_1) \in f \wedge (x, y_2) \in f \Rightarrow y_1 = y_2 \}$$

and the partial order $\le_M$ is defined in terms of $\le_Y$ as follows:

$$m_1 \le_M m_2 \equiv \forall (x, y_2) \in m_2,\ \exists (x, y_1) \in m_1 \text{ such that } y_1 \le_Y y_2$$

If the partial order *Y* is a downward semilattice, then *M* is also a downward semilattice, where if $m_1$ and $m_2$ are both elements of $S_M$, then their greatest lower bound is $GLB_1 \cup GLB_2 \cup GLB_3$ where:

$$GLB_1 = \{ (x, y) \mid (x, y_1) \in m_1,\ (x, y_2) \in m_2,\ y = glb(y_1, y_2) \}$$

$$GLB_2 = \{ (x, y) \mid (x, y) \in m_1,\ x \notin dom(m_2) \}$$

$$GLB_3 = \{ (x, y) \mid (x, y) \in m_2,\ x \notin dom(m_1) \}$$

Finally, the constructor *AllTuples* takes an input partial order $D = \langle S_D, \le_D \rangle$ and generates a downward semilattice $V = \langle S_V, \le_V \rangle$ by lifting the union of the *k*-tuple domains of *D*. Thus, the elements of $S_V$ are $\bot$, all elements of $1Tuple(D)$, $2Tuple(D, D)$, $3Tuple(D, D, D)$, etc., and the partial order $\le_V$ is the union of the individual *k*-tuple partial orders with the partial order $\{ (\bot, e) \mid e \in S_V \}$.

| | |
|---|---|
| *ClassContour* | = *2Tuple(Class, ClassKey)* |
| *ClassContourSet* | = *Pow(ClassContour)* |
| *InstVarContour* | = *3Tuple(InstVariable, InstVarKey, ClassContourSet)* |
| *InstVarContourSet* | = *Pow(InstVarContour)* |
| *ProcContour* | = *7Tuple(Procedure, ProcKey, ProcContour, Map(Variable, ClassContourSet), Map(CallSite, ProcContourSet), Map(LoadSite, InstVarContourSet), Map(StoreSite, InstVarContourSet))* |
| *ProcContourSet* | = *Pow(ProcContour)* |
| *CallGraph* | = *2Tuple(ProcContourSet, InstVarContourSet)* |

**Figure 3:** Definition of Call Graph Domain

### 2.2.2 Call Graph Domain

We define call graphs in terms of three algorithm-specific parameter partial orders: *ProcKey*, *InstVarKey*, and *ClassKey*. The *ProcKey* parameter defines the space of possible contexts for context-sensitive analysis of functions, i.e., the output domain of the algorithm's (procedure) contour selection function. The *InstVarKey* parameter defines the space of possible contexts for separately tracking the contents of instance variables, i.e., the output of the instance variable contour selection function. The *ClassKey* parameter defines the space of possible contexts for context-sensitive analysis of classes, i.e., the output of the algorithm's class contour selection function. The ordering relation on these partial orders (and all derived domains) indicates the relative precision of the elements: one element is less than another if and only if it is less precise (more conservative) than the other. In addition to the three parameterizing partial orders, call graphs rely on several unordered sets that abstract various program features: *Class* is the set of source-level class declarations, *InstVariable* is the set of source-level instance variable declarations, *Procedure* is the set of source-level procedure declarations, *Variable* is the set of all program variable names, *CallSite* is the set of all program call sites, *LoadSite* is the set of source-level loads of instance variables, and *StoreSite* is the set of source-level stores to instance variables.

Given the input parameter domains for a particular call graph construction algorithm and the sets abstracting program features, we construct the domain of call graphs, $CG = \langle S_{cg}, \leq_{cg} \rangle$, produced by that algorithm as shown in figure 3. The *ProcContour* and *ProcContourSet* definitions are mutually recursive; we intend these definitions to correspond to the smallest solution to these equations. Some of the context-sensitive algorithms introduce additional mutually recursive definitions that cause their *CallGraph* domains to be infinitely tall. To guarantee termination, at least one of their contour selection functions must incorporate a *widening* operation [Cousot & Cousot 77]. For example, Agesen's Cartesian Product Algorithm uses elements of the *ClassContour* domain as a component of its *ProcKey* domain elements. In the presence of closures, this can lead to an infinitely tall call graph lattice; Agesen terms this problem *recursive customization* and describes several methods for detecting it and applying a widening operation [Agesen 96].

The two components of a call graph are instance variable contours and procedure contours. Instance variable contours enable the analysis of dataflow through instance variable loads and stores. The first component, *InstVariable*, encodes the source level declaration that the contour is representing; the second component, *InstVarKey*, refines the first component by restricting the contexts in which the contour applies. The final component, *ClassContourSet*, represents the set of class contours stored in the instance variable contour. Similarly, the first two components of a procedure contour encode the source-level procedure declaration and the context to which this contour applies. The third component of the tuple, *ProcContour*, represents the lexically enclosing contour (if any) that should be used to analyze references to free variables. The fourth component maps each of the local variables and formal parameters of the contour's procedure to a set of class contours representing the classes of values that may be stored in that variable. The variable mapping also contains an entry for the special token `return` which represents the set of class contours returned from the contour. The final three components of a procedure contour encode the inter-contour flow of data and control caused by procedure calls and instance variable loads and instance variable stores respectively.

### 2.2.3 Soundness

A call graph is sound (i.e., safely approximates all possible program executions) if it is at least as conservative as each of the call graphs corresponding to possible program executions. Since the call graph domain is a downward semilattice, the greatest lower bound of all these program execution call graphs exists, and we notate it $G_{\text{ideal}}$. Hence, a call graph $G$ is sound iff it is equal to or more conservative than $G_{\text{ideal}}$, i.e., $G \leq_{cg} G_{\text{ideal}}$. Unfortunately, in general it is impossible to compute $G_{\text{ideal}}$ directly, as there are in general an infinite number of possible program executions, so this observation does not make a constructive test for soundness of $G$.

More constructively, a call graph is sound if,

- for each procedure contour:
    - the (language-specific) intraprocedural dataflow constraints that relate the class contour sets of the contour's variables (formals, locals, and the special `result` token) are satisfied, taking into account the `result` tokens of the callee contours at each call site and the contents of the accessed instance variable contours at each instance variable load site,
    - for each formal parameter of each callee contour at each call site, the formal's class contour set is at least as conservative as the class contour set of the corresponding actual parameter at that call site,
    - for each instance variable contour accessed at each instance variable store site, the contents of the instance variable contour is at least as conservative as the class contour set of the value being stored at that store site,

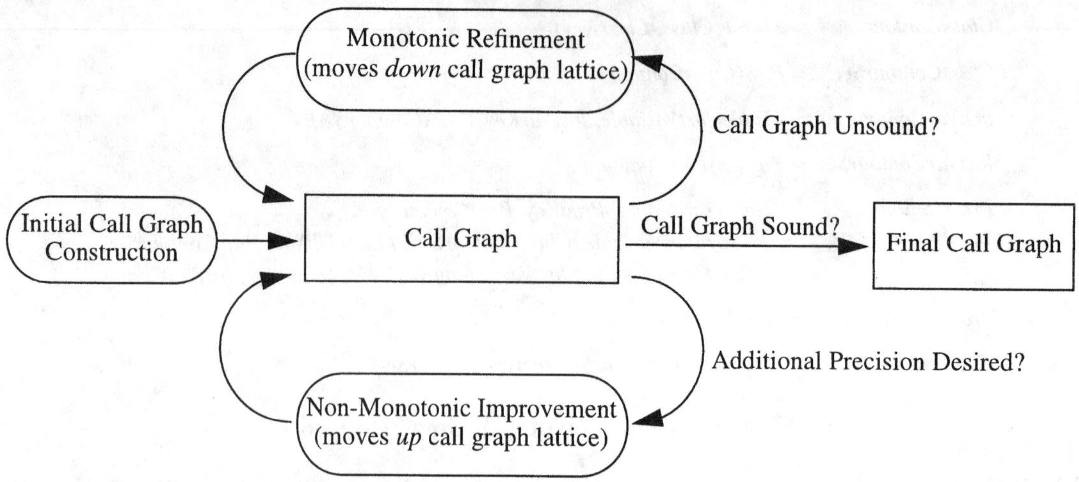


**Figure 4:** Generalized Call Graph Construction Algorithm

- and for each instance variable contour, the contents of the contour are at least as conservative as the contents of any instance variable contour with a less conservative key.

The last constraint on instance variable contents ensures that different degrees of context-sensitivity for instance variables can coexist, while still ensuring that if a class contour is stored in an instance variable at one level of context-sensitivity, then it (or some more conservative class contour) appears in the contents of all more conservative views of that instance variable.

## 3 Algorithmic Design Space

In this section, we present a generalized algorithm for call graph construction. The generalized algorithm is parameterized in several dimensions, and by selecting different values for the parameters it can express many previously described call graph construction algorithms. Figure 4 shows a schematic view of the generalized algorithm. The algorithm maintains a worklist of contours that are potentially unsound, initialized by the initial call graph construction process. The inner loop of the algorithm consists of evaluating the current call graph and selecting one of three possible actions:

- If the current call graph is considered too imprecise (too far below $G_{ideal}$ in the lattice), the algorithm may apply Non-Monotonic Improvement to improve the precision of the current call graph.
- Otherwise, if the worklist is empty, the current call graph is sound and the algorithm terminates.
- Otherwise, the algorithm applies Monotonic Refinement, removing a contour from the worklist and processing it to make it sound, thereby moving the resulting call graph one step closer to soundness and termination.

The key parameters of the generalized algorithm are the choice of domains for *ProcKey*, *InstVarKey*, and *ClassKey* and the associated contour selection functions (section 3.1), the method used to construct the initial call graph (section 3.2), and the available non-monotonic improvement operations, if any (section 3.4). Section 3.3 discusses monotonic refinement, which is the same in all algorithm instances. Section 3.5 contains a comparison of the relative precision of the call graphs produced by the various algorithms described in this section, and section 3.6 describes several aspects of our implementation of the generalized algorithm.

### 3.1 Contour Discrimination

As described in section 2.2.2, the call graph lattice is parameterized over three domains, *ProcKey*, *InstVarKey*, and *ClassKey*, which together define algorithm-specific context-sensitivity. *ProcKey* is used as part of the algorithm's procedure contour selection function: at each call site, for each applicable method, the selection function computes one or more elements of *ProcKey* that model the information about the call site that is relevant to the invoked method. For each procedure, the generalized algorithm maintains a table mapping *ProcKey* elements to their associated contours. By appropriately selecting *ProcKey* values, an algorithm indicates which call sites of a procedure should share contours and which should be given separate contours. When desired, the contour selection function may replace some existing contours with other contours, redirecting callers of the old contours appropriately. This may be done either to avoid producing too many contours for the method (by adding more general contours), or to increase the context-sensitivity in a portion of the analysis (by adding more specific contours). Similarly, *InstVarKey* models the possible outputs of the instance variable contour selection function, applied at each instance variable load and store site to model the relevant information at that site, and represents the ability of an algorithm to track the contents of a single source-level instance variable in multiple ways. Finally, *ClassKey* models some algorithms' ability to distinguish different instances of a single class, primarily to track the contents of instance variables of the different class contours of a single class separately. At an instantiation site for *class*, an algorithm's class contour selection function computes an element *key* of *ClassKey* to model the context of creation and downstream use, and the general framework uses the pair (*class*, *key*) as the class contour of the result of the instantiation. These various parameterizing domains are often interrelated, for example with different *ClassKey* elements giving rise to different *ProcKey* and *InstVarKey* elements to support specializing analysis of procedures and instance variables for different class contours.

Typical values for these domains fall into several general categories:

- **single-point lattice**: Selecting the single-point lattice (the lattice with only a $\perp$ value) for *ProcKey*, *InstVarKey*, and *ClassKey* results in the degenerate case of a context-insensitive analysis. Algorithms such as 0-CFA [Shivers 88, Shivers 91a], Palsberg and Schwartzbach's basic algorithm [Palsberg & Schwartzbach 91], Hall and Kennedy's

**Table 1: Selected Algorithm Descriptions**

| Algorithm | *ProcKey* | *InstVarKey* | *ClassKey* |
|---|---|---|---|
| 0-CFA | single-point lattice | single-point lattice | single-point lattice |
| SCS | *AllTuples(ClassContourSet)* | single-point lattice | single-point lattice |
| b-CPA | *AllTuples(ClassContour)* | single-point lattice | single-point lattice |
| *k-0*-CFA where *k*>0 | *AllTuples(ProcContour)* | single-point lattice | single-point lattice |
| *k-l*-CFA where *k l* > 0 | *AllTuples(ProcContour)* | *ClassContour* | *AllTuples(ProcContour)* |

call graph construction algorithm for Fortran [Hall & Kennedy 92], and Lakhotia's algorithm for building a call graph in languages with higher-order functions [Lakhotia 93] are all examples of this instantiation of the framework. Algorithms that do not perform context-sensitive analysis of instance variables or classes use the single-point lattice for the *InstVarKey* or *ClassKey* domains, independently of their choice for the *ProcKey* domain.

- ***k* levels of dynamic call chain**: One of the most commonly used mechanisms for distinguishing contours is to use a vector of the *k* enclosing calling contours at each call site to select the target contour. If $k = 0$, then this degenerates to the single-point lattice and a context-insensitive algorithm; $k = 1$ for *ProcKey* corresponds to analyzing a callee contour separately for each call site, and for *ClassKey* corresponds to treating each distinct instantiation site of a class as a separate class contour. An algorithm may use a fixed value of *k* throughout the program, as in Shivers's *k*-CFA family of algorithms [Shivers 88, Shivers 91a] or Oxhøj's 1-CFA extension to Palsberg and Schwartzbach's algorithm [Oxhøj et al. 92]. Adaptive algorithms may use different levels of *k* in different regions of the call graph to more flexibly manage the trade-off between analysis time and precision. Finally, a number of algorithms based on unbounded but finite values for *k* have been proposed: Ryder's call graph construction algorithm for Fortran 77 [Ryder 79], Callahan's extension to Ryder's work to support recursion [Callahan et al. 90], and Emami's alias analysis algorithm for C [Emami et al. 94] all treat each non-recursive path through the call graph as creating a new context. Alt and Martin have developed an even more aggressive call graph construction algorithm, used in their PAG system, that first "unrolls" *k* levels of recursion [Alt & Martin 95]. Steensgaard developed an unbounded-call-chain algorithm that handles nested lexical environments by applying a widening operation to class sets of formal parameters at entries to recursive cycles in the call graph [Steensgaard 94]. For object-oriented programs, we define the *k-l*-CFA family of algorithms where *k* denotes the degree of context-sensitivity in the *ProcKey* domain and *l* denotes the degree of context-sensitivity in the *ClassKey* domain.

- **parameter class sets**: Another commonly used mechanism for distinguishing contours is to use some abstraction of the call site's actual parameters. For example, some abstraction of the alias relationships among actual parameters has been used as the basis for context-sensitivity in algorithms for interprocedural alias analysis [Landi et al. 93, Wilson & Lam 95]. Similarly, several algorithms for interprocedural class analysis use information about the classes of actual parameters to drive their contour selection functions:

  - Contour keys in Agesen's Cartesian Product Algorithm (CPA) [Agesen 95] are drawn from the domain *AllTuples(ClassContour)*, i.e., each key is a tuple of single class contours, one per formal parameter. At a call site, its contour selection function computes the cartesian product of the actual parameter class sets; a contour is selected/created for each element of the cartesian product. The "eager splitting" used as a component of each phase of Plevyak's iterative refinement algorithm [Plevyak 96] is equivalent to this straightforward form of CPA.

  - In the worst case, CPA may require $O(N^a)$ contours to analyze a call site, where *a* is the number of arguments at the call site. To avoid requiring an unreasonably large number of contours, Agesen actually implements a variant of CPA that we term bounded-CPA (or b-CPA) that uses a single context-insensitive contour to analyze any call site at which the number of terms in the cartesian product of the actual class sets exceeds a threshold value. Our experiments suggest that only the bounded version of CPA scales beyond the realm of small benchmark programs. For example, on the instr sched benchmark (a 2,400 line Cecil program) b-CPA analysis completed in 146 seconds, while CPA analysis required 3,537 seconds. We observed similar slowdowns in the larger Java benchmarks (those over 10,000 lines).

  - A new algorithm, which we dub Simple Class Sets (SCS), draws its contour keys from the domain *AllTuples(ClassContourSet)*, i.e., each key is a tuple of sets of class contours, one per formal parameter. At a call site, its contour selection function simply selects a contour (possibly creating a new contour) whose key exactly matches the tuple of class sets that appear as actual parameters. If during re-analysis of a contour actual class sets at a call site change from their previous values, new contours are selected/created to exactly match the new actual parameters of the call. A bounded variant, b-SCS, could be defined to limit the number of contours created per procedure by falling back on a context-insensitive summary when the procedure's contour creation budget is exceeded.

  - In languages like Cecil [Chambers 93] and Strongtalk [Bracha & Griswold 93] which have expressive, but optional, parameterized static type declarations, using some abstraction of the static types of the actual type parameters to provide hints to the contour selection function may be very effective.

  - Finally, Pande's algorithm for interprocedural class analysis in C++ [Pande & Ryder 94] is built upon

Landi's alias analysis for C [Landi et al. 93] and uses an extension of Landi's conditional points-to information as a basis for context-sensitivity.

The CPA or SCS-style domains are also useful as *InstVarKey* domains, using the possible class(es) of the object whose instance variable is being accessed to select the right instance variable contour, tracking the contents of instance variables for different inheriting subclasses separately.

- **arbitrary**: Plevyak's "invokes graph" encodes an arbitrary mapping from each contour's call sites to its callee contours [Plevyak 96]. It is clearly the most flexible of the mechanisms, but its lack of structure makes it difficult to easily explain or understand algorithms that rely upon it.

Table 1 itemizes the domains chosen for *ProcKey*, *InstVarKey*, and *ClassKey* by the flow-sensitive algorithms that are experimentally assessed in section 4.

### 3.2 Possible Initial Call Graphs

Although it is possible to use any element of the call graph lattice domain as an initial call graph, all the algorithms of which we are aware start with one of two opposite extremes:

- $G_{\top}$: the top element of the call graph lattice. In practice, algorithms really begin with the call graph with only the global scope's contour and the initial contour for the main function, with all variables in these contours mapped to empty class sets. This is the starting point used by the majority of the algorithms, including 0-CFA and *k*-CFA [Shivers 88, Shivers 91a], the Cartesian Product Algorithm (CPA) [Agesen 95], Plevyak's iterative algorithm [Plevyak & Chien 94], and many others. $G_{\top}$ is a good initial call graph for algorithms that apply Monotonic Refinement since it ensures reaching the best possible fixed-point solution for that algorithm.
- $G_{\bot}$: the bottom element of the call graph lattice, i.e., the complete call graph with all call sites calling all contours and all variables holding all possible classes. In practice, a filtered version of $G_{\bot}$ is used that has had some unnecessary call arcs and classes removed using statically available information or simple analysis:
  - $G_{selector}$: removes those call edges in $G_{\bot}$ between call sites and contours with incompatible names or numbers of arguments.
  - $G_{static}$: uses the static types of variables and the type signatures of procedures to improve on $G_{selector}$ by removing call arcs that are not statically type correct and removing elements from each variable's class set that do not conform to the variable's static type.
  - $G_{intra}$: improves on either $G_{selector}$ or $G_{static}$ (depending on whether or not the language is statically typed) by performing intraprocedural analysis of each procedure to compute more precise approximations to the class sets of local variables and outgoing call arcs, as in Diwan's Modula-3 optimizer [Diwan et al. 96].
  - $G_{RTA}$: improves on $G_{static}$ by performing Bacon and Sweeney's Rapid Type Analysis (RTA), a linear-time optimistic reachability analysis, to eliminate classes that cannot be created and methods that cannot be invoked [Bacon & Sweeney 96]. RTA can be applied to dynamically typed languages as well to build a version of $G_{RTA}$ from $G_{selector}$
  - $G_{unif}$: improves on $G_{RTA}$ by performing a near-linear-time unification-based algorithm to identify disjoint components of the program's dataflow graph and associate a set of reachable classes and methods with each disjoint component [DeFouw et al. 97] (RTA pessimistically assumes that the dataflow graph only contains a single disjoint component, and thus computes a single set of reachable classes and methods for the entire program). Our algorithm for constructing $G_{unif}$ is an adaptation of Steensgaard's algorithm for near-linear-time points-to analysis of C programs [Steensgaard 96].

  Since each of these flavors of $G_{\bot}$ is sound and hence a legal solution, any of them would be a good initial call graph for algorithms that either do not wish to incur the expense of Monotonic Refinement to produce a sound call graph (which is true for all the algorithms listed above that start with some flavor of $G_{\bot}$), or apply Non-Monotonic Improvement to improve the precision of the initially imprecise $G_{\bot}$. The presence of first-class functions, however, may make call graphs close to $G_{\bot}$ very imprecise, since each call site of such a function must be assumed to invoke any first-class function in the program with a matching number of arguments and static type signature. Of the above call graphs, only $G_{unif}$ may reduce this problem.

A potentially interesting new place to start call graph construction algorithms is $G_{prof}$, an optimistic call graph constructed from profile data from one or more runs of the program. Seeding the call graph with (context-insensitive) profile-derived call arcs and sets of classes can enable context-insensitive algorithms to reach the final sound solution more rapidly than if starting with $G_{\top}$, but without sacrificing precision. Profile data with call chain context [Grove et al. 95] can be used to seed some context-sensitive algorithms without degrading the final solution.

### 3.3 Monotonic Refinement

Monotonic Refinement removes an unsound contour from the worklist and processes it, monotonically extending it (moving it lower in the contour domain) to make it locally sound. This involves performing intraprocedural class analysis of the contour beginning with the class sets of its formals, potentially adding to the class sets of local variables and adding new contours to call sites, load sites, and store sites. The centerpiece of this intraprocedural analysis is the analysis of message sends, which consists of the following steps:

1) The set of potentially invoked methods is computed by using the current class contour sets of the arguments to perform compile-time method lookup.
2) For each potentially invoked method, the algorithm-specific contour selection function selects and/or creates a set of contours for that method, called from this call site with these actual argument class contour sets, and these contours are bound to the call site in the calling contour. Any new contours created as part of contour selection are added to the worklist.
3) The class contour sets of the actual parameters are added to the class contour sets of the corresponding formal parameters in each callee contour (using the *ClassContourSet* greatest-lower-bound operation to merge class contour sets). If any formal class contour set changes as a result, that callee contour is added to the worklist, since it may have become locally unsound and in need of reanalysis.
4) Finally, the set of class contours returned from the message send is the greatest lower bound of the class contour sets bound to the `return` token in each callee contour.

Analysis of instance variable loads and stores is similar:

1) An algorithm-specific instance variable contour selection function selects and/or creates a set of instance variable contours for the instance variable being accessed (subject to the soundness restrictions discussed in section 2.2.3), typically based on the instance variable access site and the class contour set of the object being accessed. These contours are bound to the load or store site in the accessing contour.

2) For an instance variable store, the class contours for the value being stored are added to the contents class contour set of the accessed instance variable contours.

3) For an instance variable load, the set of class contours returned by the load is the greatest lower bound of the contents class contour sets of the accessed instance variable contours.

At class instantiation sites the class contour selection function generates a set of class contours, typically based on the source-level class being instantiated and information from the current procedure contour.

Analysis of variable references and assignments traverses the lexical contour links to locate the set of class contours associated with the accessed variable. For an assignment, the assigned class contour set is added to the variable's associated class contour set, while for a reference the associated class contour set is returned as the result of the reference.

Intraprocedural analysis of other kinds of statements and expressions in the method is language-specific but usually straightforward.

Whenever a non-local set of class contours is read during intraprocedural analysis, including the result set of a callee contour, the contents set of an instance variable contour, or the set associated with a global or lexically enclosing variable, the generalized algorithm records a dependency link from the set to the reading contour. If the set later grows, the dependent reading contours are placed on the worklist, since the set of class contours upon which their intraprocedural analysis depended has changed.

### 3.4 Non-Monotonic Improvement

Each phase of Monotonic Refinement results in an output call graph that is lower in the lattice (more conservative) than its input call graph. In contrast, the output of each phase of Non-Monotonic Improvement is a call graph that is higher in the lattice than its input call graph. Algorithms for Non-Monotonic Improvement can be further classified informally as either Local or Global:

- Local Non-Monotonic Improvement is characterized by a series of small, incremental steps up the call graph lattice. For example, the single intraprocedural "clean-up" pass performed to compute $G_{intra}$ from $G_{selector}$ or $G_{static}$ can be viewed as one local non-monotonic improvement step per procedure. A further example of local non-monotonic improvement is based on the notion of *exact unions*. In a sound call graph, each variable's class set must contain the class sets associated with all inflowing data flow arcs. However, algorithms starting from $G_\perp$ often lead to class sets that are proper supersets of the union of their inflowing class sets. Such a call graph can be improved without making it unsound by replacing each variable's class set with the exact union of its inflowing class sets. This narrowing may enable further downstream narrowings and removals of unreachable call arcs. This process continues until a fixed-point is reached. In the face of recursion, the call graph produced by starting from $G_\perp$ and applying local non-monotonic improvement using exact unions to completion can be less precise than the call graph produced by starting from $G_T$ and applying monotonic refinement to completion. But the bottom-up strategy may produce acceptable results more quickly than the top-down strategy, can be interrupted at any time while still resulting in a sound solution, and may be a useful component in a program development environment where a sound but not necessarily optimal call graph is recomputed incrementally after each programming change.

- Global Non-Monotonic Improvement is derived from Shivers's proposal for *reflow analysis* [Shivers 91a]. Unlike local non-monotonic improvement it may examine large regions of the call graph during a single improvement step and may introduce new contours to the call graph. It occurs when an undesirable property of the current call graph is detected that cannot be corrected without making a jump from the current call graph to a (potentially unsound) call graph higher in the lattice. If this undesirable property is considered to be worth resolving, then the source of the imprecision is identified and additional contours are introduced at strategic points, in hopes of causing subsequent phases of Monotonic Refinement to rebuild the call graph without re-introducing the undesired imprecision.

  The only implemented algorithm of which we are aware that includes global non-monotonic improvement is Plevyak's iterative algorithm [Plevyak & Chien 94]. The algorithm considers any message send with more than one possibly invoked method an undesirable property of the call graph and attempts to resolve it via non-monotonic improvement. Its control strategy computes a candidate sound call graph by running Monotonic Refinement to completion, followed by a check for Global Non-Monotonic Improvement. If refinement is desired, new contours are created and recorded in the "invokes graph" data structure for future reference in the contour selection functions. Then the algorithm iterates by resetting the call graph back to $G_T$ and reapplying Monotonic Refinement to completion to reach another candidate sound call graph. This overall process repeats until no more imprecisions can be resolved by introducing new contours, or too many iterations have been performed. One weakness of this coarse-grained control strategy is that large amounts of Monotonic Refinement analysis time may be spent reaching undesirable fixed-points. Our generalized algorithmic framework offers the possibility of intermingling Monotonic Refinement and Non-Monotonic Improvement on a much finer grain, perhaps reaching high-quality solutions faster.

### 3.5 Relative Algorithmic Precision

Figure 5 depicts the relative precision of the final products of the various call graph construction algorithms described in sections 3.1 and 3.2 assuming that no procedure specialization is performed during compilation to preserve the contour-level view of the program (this matches the compilation configurations used during the experiments described in section 4). Algorithm *A* is depicted as being higher in the lattice than algorithm *B* if for all input programs $G_A$ is at least as precise as $G_B$ and there exists some program such that $G_A$ is more precise than $G_B$.

The *k*-*l*-CFA family of algorithms form an infinitely tall and infinitely wide sublattice. The *k* in the *k*-0-CFA, *k*-1-CFA, etc. sub-family of algorithms stands for an arbitrary, but finite value of *k*; infinite values for *k* are represented by the ∞-*l*-CFA family of algorithms (only ∞-0-CFA is shown).

Under the no-specialization assumption, ∞-0-CFA, SCS, and CPA all produce call graphs with identical effective precision. Although the contours created by each of the three algorithms may be

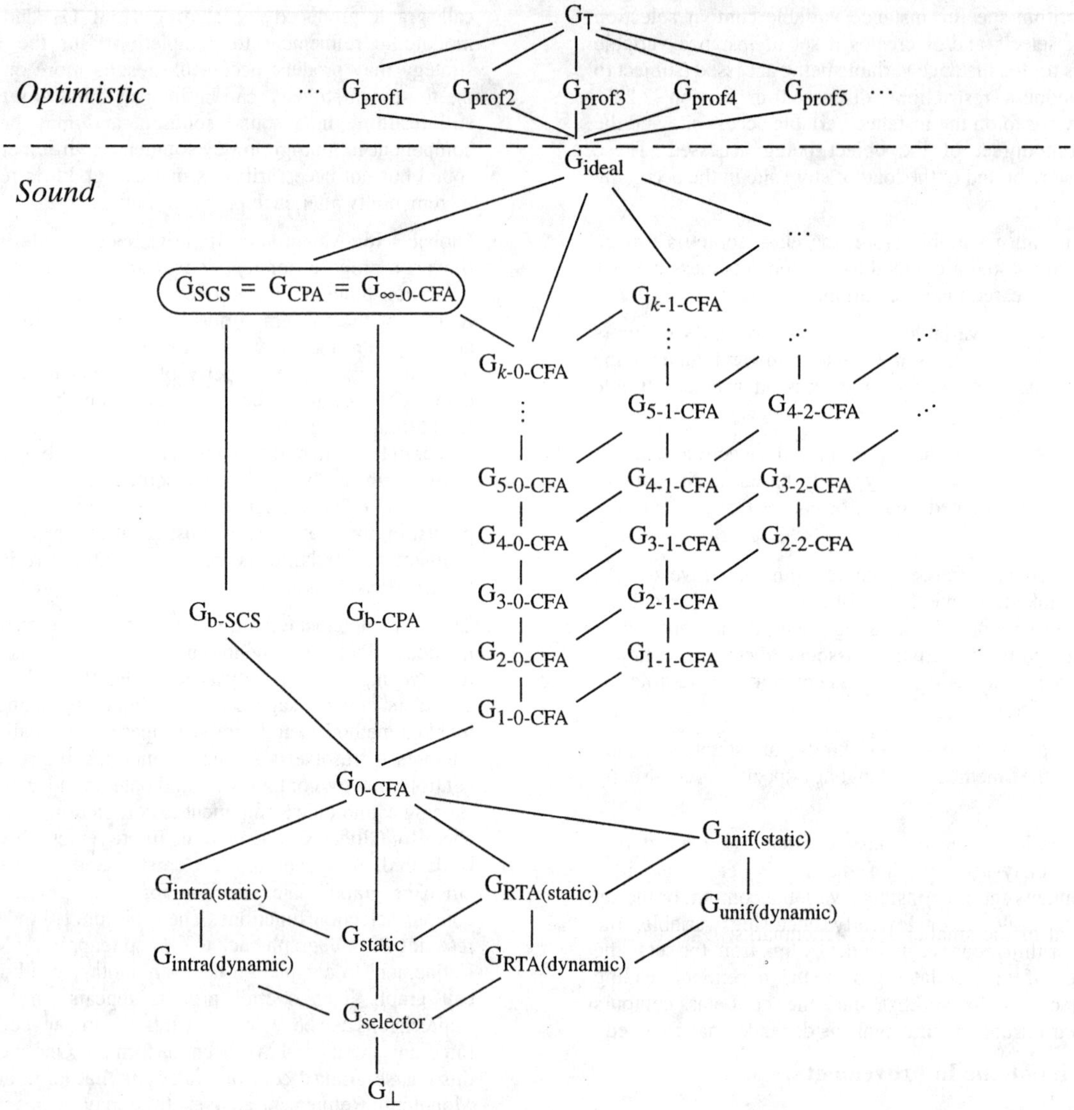


**Figure 5:** Relative Precision of Computed Call Graphs

superficially quite different, if they are collapsed to reflect the lack of procedure specialization then all three call graphs will contain exactly the same call edges and class sets. However, the costs of computing each of the three call graphs are not the same. In the worst case, building the ∞-0-CFA call graph requires creating an infinite number of contours, building the SCS call graph requires creating an exponential number of contours, and building the CPA call graph requires creating a polynomial number of contours.* Despite its poor worst case behavior, the experimental results reported in section suggest that SCS may be the most efficient of the three algorithms.

### 3.6 Implementation

The generalized algorithmic framework is not only a useful tool for exploring the algorithmic design space and understanding previously described algorithms, but also leads to a flexible implementation framework. Our implementation of interprocedural analysis in the Vortex optimizing compiler infrastructure [Dean et al. 96] includes `contour` and `contour_key` abstract classes and related data structures, and a body of centralized code for executing the generalized algorithm and monotonic refinement. We are currently working on adding support for non-monotonic improvement. Instantiating the framework consists of implementing a concrete subclass of the `ipca_algorithm` class that implements the three contour selection functions. Abstract mix-in classes are provided that implement several of the common policies for managing procedure, instance variable, and class contours. The framework itself consists of approximately 4,000 lines of Cecil code and each of the instantiations measured in section 4 is implemented with 100-300 additional lines of code.

One of the most important considerations in the implementation of the framework was managing time/space tradeoffs. Most previous systems explicitly construct the entire interprocedural data and control flow graphs. Although this approach is viable for small programs, the memory requirements quickly become unreasonable during context-sensitive analysis of large programs. In our

* We assume that the number of arguments to a procedure call is bounded by a constant, rather than being a function of program size.

implementation, we only explicitly store those sets of classes that are visible across contour boundaries (those corresponding to formal parameters, local variables, procedure return values, and instance variables). All derived class sets and all intra- and interprocedural data and control flow edges are (re)computed on demand. This greatly reduces the space requirements of the analysis, but increases computation time since dataflow relationships must be continually recalculated.

We also found that the analysis time for the interprocedurally flow-sensitive algorithms on the larger programs could be greatly reduced without a significant loss in precision by eagerly approximating class sets during set union operations. If the number of elements in the union exceeds a threshold value, then a compaction phase examines the elements to see if any classes already in the union share a common parent class. The candidate common parent that has the fewest number of subclasses not already included in the union is selected, and it and all of its subclasses are added to the union. This approximation reduces the size of the union (Vortex supports a compact "cone" representation for the class set corresponding to a class and all of its subclasses [Dean et al. 95]) and may reduce the number of times its contents change (by eagerly performing several subsequent class add operations). For example, for the three largest Cecil programs eager approximation reduced 0-CFA analysis time by a factor of 15 while only resulting in slowdowns of the resulting optimized executables of 2% to 8%.

Currently, the intraprocedural phase of interprocedural class analysis analyzes the entire procedure. We have recently implemented a sparse procedure representation that performs slicing to remove details of non-object data and control flow. Our initial experience has been that the sparse representation has little impact on Cecil programs (since virtually all dataflow is object-related), but that it reduced analysis time and memory usage by 50% for several of the smaller Java benchmarks. Unfortunately, our implementation is not yet complete and all the experiments in the section 4 utilize the old representation.

## 4 Experimental Assessment

To determine how well different interprocedural analysis algorithms perform in practice, we implemented a half-dozen algorithm families using our framework and assessed them according to the following criteria:

- What are the relative precisions of the call graphs produced by the various algorithms?
- What are the relative costs of the various algorithms, measured in terms of analysis time and memory space?
- How do the differences in call graph precision translate into differences in effectiveness of client interprocedural analyses, in terms of program execution speed and executable size?

The remainder of this section presents experimental results answering these questions for nine specific call graph construction algorithms: $G_{simple}$ ($G_{selector}$ for Cecil, $G_{static}$ for Java), RTA (extended to support first-class functions and multi-method dispatching), 0-CFA, b-CPA, SCS, and four instantiations of the *k*-*l*-CFA family of algorithms. Section  addresses the first two questions by presenting data on analysis time and space and call graph precision. Sections 4.2 and 4.3 address the remaining question: section 4.2 reports on the overall impact of interprocedural optimization and section 4.3 focuses on the individual contributions made by each of the interprocedural optimizations.

We performed our experiments on the suite of medium-sized Cecil and Java programs shown in Table 2. All experiments were performed on a Sun Ultra 1 model 170 with 256MB of memory.

**Table 2: Benchmark Applications**

| | Program | Lines[a] | Description |
|---|---|---|---|
| Cecil Programs | richards | 400 | Operating systems simulation |
| | deltablue | 650 | Incremental constraint solver |
| | instr sched | 2,400 | Global instruction scheduler |
| | typechecker | 20,000[b] | Typechecker for *old* Cecil type system |
| | new-tc | 23,500[b] | Typechecker for *new* Cecil type system |
| | compiler | 50,000 | Old version of the Vortex optimizing compiler |
| Java Programs | toba | 3,900 | Java bytecode to C code translator |
| | java-cup | 7,800 | Parser generator |
| | espresso | 13,800 | Java source to bytecode translator[c] |
| | javac | 25,550 | Java source to bytecode translator[c] |
| | javadoc | 28,950 | Documentation generator for Java |

a. Excluding standard libraries. All Cecil programs are compiled with an 11,000-line standard library. All Java programs include a 16,000-line standard library.
b. The two Cecil typecheckers share approximately 15,000 lines of common support code, but the type checking algorithms themselves are completely separate and were written by different people.
c. The two Java translators have no common code and were developed by different people.

### 4.1 Cost and Precision of Call Graph Construction Algorithms

An abstract comparison of the effectiveness of the algorithms can be made based on analysis time and space costs, and the precision of the resulting call graph. Table 3 reports, for each algorithm/program pair, the analysis time in seconds, the growth in process size during analysis in MB*, the average number of contours per procedure, and the average number of times each procedure was analyzed. The difference of these last two numbers represents the average number of times per procedure that one of its contours was reanalyzed. For example, analysis of the instr sched program with the SCS algorithm took 83 seconds and the process size grew by 9.6 MB during analysis. On average, 6.5 contours were created for each procedure, each procedure was analyzed 8.5 times, and thus 2.0 contours per procedure were reanalyzed (and since analysis and re-analysis take roughly the same amount of time, approximately 25% of analysis time was spent reanalyzing contours)

We see several trends in the data:

* This number only roughly approximates the actual maximum heap size during, and is sensitive to the heuristics used by the garbage collector to decide whether to launch a full collection or expand virtual memory.

**Table 3: Analysis Time (secs), Heap Space (MB), Contours per Procedure, Analyses per Procedure[a]**

| | $G_{simple}$ | RTA | 0-CFA[b] | SCS | b-CPA | 1-0-CFA | 1-1-CFA | 2-2-CFA | 3-3-CFA |
|---|---|---|---|---|---|---|---|---|---|
| richards | 2 sec<br>1.6 MB<br>1.0 / 1.0 | 2 sec<br>1.6 MB<br>1.0 / 1.0 | 3 sec<br>1.6 MB<br>1.2 / 2.2 | 3 sec<br>1.6 MB<br>1.8/ 2.0 | 4 sec<br>1.6 MB<br>2.4 / 2.9 | 4 sec<br>1.6 MB<br>1.9 / 3.0 | 5 sec<br>1.6 MB<br>1.9 / 3.7 | 5 sec<br>1.6 MB<br>2.4/ 3.8 | 4 sec<br>1.6 MB<br>2.8 / 4.0 |
| deltablue | 2 sec<br>1.6 MB<br>1.0/ 1.0 | 2 sec<br>1.6 MB<br>1.0 / 1.0 | 5 sec<br>1.6 MB<br>1.4 / 2.4 | 7 sec<br>1.6 MB<br>3.75 / 4.25 | 8 sec<br>1.6 MB<br>4.8 / 5.7 | 6 sec<br>1.6 MB<br>2.5 / 4.0 | 6 sec<br>1.6 MB<br>2.5 / 4.0 | 8 sec<br>1.6 MB<br>3.6 / 6.1 | 10 sec<br>1.6 MB<br>5.0 / 8.2 |
| instr sched | 6 sec<br>2.5 MB<br>1.0 / 1.0 | 4 sec<br>2.5 MB<br>1.0 / 1.0 | 67 sec<br>5.7 MB<br>1.4 / 4.8 | 83 sec<br>9.6 MB<br>6.5 / 8.5 | 146 sec<br>14.8 MB<br>11.8 / 17.0 | 99 sec<br>9.6 MB<br>3.5 / 10.3 | 109 sec<br>9.6 MB<br>3.5 / 10.6 | 334 sec<br>9.6 MB<br>6.7 / 24.9 | 1,795 sec<br>21.0 MB<br>13.3 / 48.3 |
| typechecker | 26 sec<br>12.0 MB<br>1.0 / 1.0 | 25 sec<br>5.5 MB<br>1.0 / 1.0 | 947 sec<br>45.1 MB<br>1.2 / 4.6 | | | 13,254 sec<br>97.4 MB<br>8.7 / 31.4 | | | |
| new-tc | 28 sec<br>6.9 MB<br>1.0 / 1.0 | 29 sec<br>6.9 MB<br>1.0 / 1.0 | 1,193 sec<br>62.1 MB<br>1.2 / 4.9 | | | 9,942 sec<br>115.4 MB<br>8.4 / 27.0 | | | |
| compiler | 87 sec<br>0.2 MB<br>1.0 / 1.0 | 93 sec<br>22.4 MB<br>1.0 / 1.0 | 11,941 sec<br>202.1 MB<br>1.3 / 8.8 | | | | | | |
| toba | 35 sec<br>9.4 MB<br>1.0 / 1.0 | 18 sec<br>7.7 MB<br>1.0 / 1.0 | 79 sec<br>19.8 MB<br>1.0 / 1.0 | 67 sec<br>23.9 MB<br>1.1 /1.3 | 75 sec<br>19.8 MB<br>1.3 / 1.4 | 116 sec<br>20.3 MB<br>2.0 / 2.6 | 1,174 sec<br>19.8 MB<br>1.9 / 3.7 | 8,636 sec<br>19.8 MB<br>3.8 / 6.1 | |
| java-cup | 80 sec<br>76.1 MB<br>1.0 / 1.0 | 89 sec<br>82.4 MB<br>1.0 / 1.0 | 116 sec<br>76.6 MB<br>1.0 / 1.2 | 112 sec<br>76.1 MB<br>1.2 / 1.5 | 124 sec<br>76.2 MB<br>1.4 / 1.6 | 145 sec<br>87.8 MB<br>2.2/ 3.1 | 2,086 sec<br>76.0 MB<br>2.1 / 5.7 | | |
| espresso | 49 sec<br>5.0 MB<br>1.0 / 1.0 | 74 sec<br>5.0 MB<br>1.0 / 1.0 | 136 sec<br>11.4 MB<br>1.0 / 1.4 | 307 sec<br>20.0 MB<br>1.8 / 2.5 | 305 sec<br>19.2 MB<br>2.0 / 2.9 | 1,183 sec<br>30.6 MB<br>3.7 / 7.3 | 51,646 sec<br>28.8 MB<br>3.6 / 16.3 | | |
| javac | 74 sec<br>27.6 MB<br>1.0 / 1.0 | 35 sec<br>27.4 MB<br>1.0 / 1.0 | 289 sec<br>27.4 MB<br>1.0 / 1.7 | 442 sec<br>27.8 MB<br>2.2 / 3.2 | 562 sec<br>27.5 MB<br>2.3 / 3.4 | 2,068 sec<br>60.1 MB<br>4.5 / 10.4 | | | |
| javadoc | 66 sec<br>19.4 MB<br>1.0 / 1.0 | 38 sec<br>19.7 MB<br>1.0 / 1.0 | 169 sec<br>27.4 MB<br>1.0 / 1.3 | 165 sec<br>20.1 MB<br>1.6 / 1.9 | 208 sec<br>19.7 MB<br>1.6 / 2.0 | 295 sec<br>20.4 MB<br>2.6 / 3.6 | 27,991 sec<br>19.9 MB<br>2.1 / 5.9 | | |

a. Shaded cells correspond to configurations that either did not complete in 24 hours or exhausted available virtual memory (450MB).

b. The average number of contours per procedure during 0-CFA analysis of Cecil programs is greater than 1.0 because procedures such as 'if' and 'loop' are analyzed with SCS contours. This limited context-sensitivity partially compensates for Cecil's use of user-defined control structures.

- Analysis time for the flow-insensitive algorithms ($G_{simple}$ and RTA) appears to be roughly linear in the size of the program in practice (as well as asymptotically in the worst case); this suggests that they will scale gracefully to larger programs. In fact, running RTA in combination with the treeshaking optimization described in the next section usually results in a net reduction in compile time due to the removal of unreachable procedures.

- Increasing the value of *k* in the *k*-*l*-CFA algorithms for the two small Cecil programs does not result in a large increase of analysis time because most routines are only called from a small number of call sites (often only one). We start to see the expected exponential blow-up in analysis time in the slightly more realistic instr sched benchmark, which includes abstractions such as sets and hash tables that are used by a number of clients. For the three larger Cecil programs 1-1-CFA is infeasible, and for the compiler even 1-0-CFA fails to complete in under 24 hours.

- The SCS and b-CPA algorithms use different contour discrimination strategies to achieve approximately the same level of context-sensitivity. Although b-CPA has an asymptotically better worst case running time, for the programs in our benchmark suite SCS was uniformly faster.

- There is a much larger relative increase in analysis time between 1-0-CFA and 1-1-CFA for Java than there is for Cecil. This is due to a difference in the idioms used in the two languages. In Cecil, there is almost always just one textual occurrence of the object constructor for a class, within a user-

**Table 4: Average Static/Dynamic Callee Procedures for call site[a]**

| | $G_{simple}$ | RTA | 0-CFA | SCS | b-CPA | 1-0-CFA | 1-1-CFA | 2-2-CFA | 3-3-CFA |
|---|---|---|---|---|---|---|---|---|---|
| richards | 7.4 / 3.4 | 6.7 / 3.3 | 1.2 / 1.9 | 1.2 / 1.9 | 1.2 / 1.9 | 1.2 / 1.9 | 1.2 / 1.9 | 1.2 / 1.9 | 1.2 / 1.9 |
| deltablue | 10.2 / 8.1 | 9.4 / 7.3 | 1.4 / 2.2 | 1.4 / 2.2 | 1.4 / 2.2 | 1.4 / 2.2 | 1.4 / 2.2 | 1.4 / 2.2 | 1.4 / 2.1 |
| instr sched | 22.4 / 24.7 | 16.0 / 15.8 | 1.7 / 3.4 | 1.5 / 3.0 | 1.5 / 3.0 | 1.6 / 3.4 | 1.6 / 3.4 | 1.5 / 3.1 | 1.5 / 3.0 |
| typechecker | 46.7 / 59.3 | 42.9 / 53.4 | 4.4 / 13.9 | | | 4.0 / 11.9 | | | |
| new-tc | 56.4 / 60.2 | 52.8 / 55.6 | 4.0 / 10.5 | | | 3.8 / 10.3 | | | |
| compiler | 71.3 / 23.2 | 68.1 / 17.6 | 10.0 / 7.0 | | | | | | |
| toba | 2.4 / 9.8 | 1.3 / 5.9 | 1.1 / 2.6 | 1.1 / 2.6 | 1.1 / 2.6 | 1.1 / 2.6 | 1.0 / 1.8 | 1.0 / 1.7 | |
| java-cup | 3.2 / 10.9 | 2.2 / 6.9 | 1.1 / 2.6 | 1.1 / 2.6 | 1.1 / 2.6 | 1.1 / 2.6 | 1.0 / 2.1 | | |
| espresso | 2.2 / 10.8 | 2.1 / 10.1 | 1.7 / 9.7 | 1.7 / 9.7 | 1.7 / 9.7 | 1.7 / 9.7 | 1.6 / 8.7 | | |
| javac | 3.9 / 11.6 | 1.4 / 6.8 | 2.2 / 5.5 | 2.2 / 5.5 | 2.2 / 5.5 | 2.2 / 5.5 | | | |
| javadoc | 3.1 / 11.1 | 1.4 / 7.2 | 1.2 / 3.4 | 1.2 / 3.4 | 1.2 / 3.4 | 1.2 / 3.4 | 1.1 / 1.4 | | |

a. Shaded cells correspond to configurations that either did not complete in 24 hours or exhausted available virtual memory (450MB).

defined "constructor" method. In contrast, Java programs tend to use in-line object constructors (i.e. `new` expressions). Thus, there tends to be a much larger increase in the number of class contours under 1-1-CFA for Java than for Cecil.

- The analysis times and memory requirements for performing the various interprocedurally flow-sensitive algorithms on the larger Cecil programs strongly suggest that the algorithms do not scale to realistically sized programs written in a language like Cecil. Scalability was better for the Java programs, but analysis times still were not linear in program size. It also appears that a large percentage of the analysis time is being consumed by contour reanalysis. We suspect that the majority of these reanalysis steps (especially for algorithms such as SCS and b-CPA that do not allow a contour's incoming formal sets to be widened) are due to dependencies on the results of instance variable reads; when a new class is added to the contents of an instance variable, all accessing contours are reanalyzed. We are investigating seeding the instance variable contents with class sets derived from dynamic profile data for algorithms such as 0-CFA, SCS, b-CPA, and 1-0-CFA that perform context-insensitive analysis of instance variables. This may result in substantial reductions in contour reanalysis and thus overall analysis time, and make more sophisticated algorithms feasible on the larger Cecil programs. However, even if re-analysis time is sharply reduced, it appears that memory requirements may limit the scalability of the interprocedurally flow-sensitive algorithms.

Previous work has assessed the precision of call graph construction algorithms by reporting various metrics such as the average cardinality of class sets or the average number of callees at a call site in a contour. Although reporting these statistics at the granularity of contours can be useful for comparing various context-sensitive algorithms, it does not reflect the effective precision of the call graph unless multiple versions of each procedure are compiled, one for each of its analysis-time contours. Some previous systems [Cooper et al. 92, Plevyak & Chien 95] have used the contours created during interprocedural analysis to drive procedure specialization. However, because the Vortex compiler does not perform procedure specialization based on contours, summarizing the contour-level information to a procedure granularity will more accurately reflect the effective call graph precision seen by later stages of Vortex. Table 4 reports both the static and dynamic (computed by weighting each call site by its execution frequency in a sample program execution) number of callees per call site at a procedure-level granularity. We observe the following:

- The interprocedurally flow-sensitive algorithms (0-CFA and above) produce call graphs that are substantially more precise than the simpler linear-time algorithms, but, for the benchmarks where analysis completed, the context-sensitive algorithms did not provide much additional precision over the context-insensitive 0-CFA algorithm. The RTA algorithm provides relatively small additional precision beyond $G_{simple}$ for the Cecil programs, but was more successful for the Java programs. The high degree of average polymorphism at call sites in Cecil programs under the flow-insensitive algorithms is mostly due to inaccuracy in modeling the flow of first-class functions.
- In our benchmarks, the dynamic degree of polymorphism at call sites was usually higher than the static degree of polymorphism. Often the difference was quite large, which strongly suggests that purely static metrics may not accurately predict the impact on program execution speed.

Based on this abstract precision data, we expect flow-sensitivity (0-CFA) to provide the main improvements in bottom-line execution speed, with flow-insensitive algorithms much worse and context-sensitive algorithms not much better.

## 4.2 Overall Impact

To assess the importance of call graph precision on the bottom-line performance impact of interprocedural optimizations, we compared, for each benchmark, the performance of a pair of base configurations that did not use interprocedural optimizations against pairs of configurations performing interprocedural

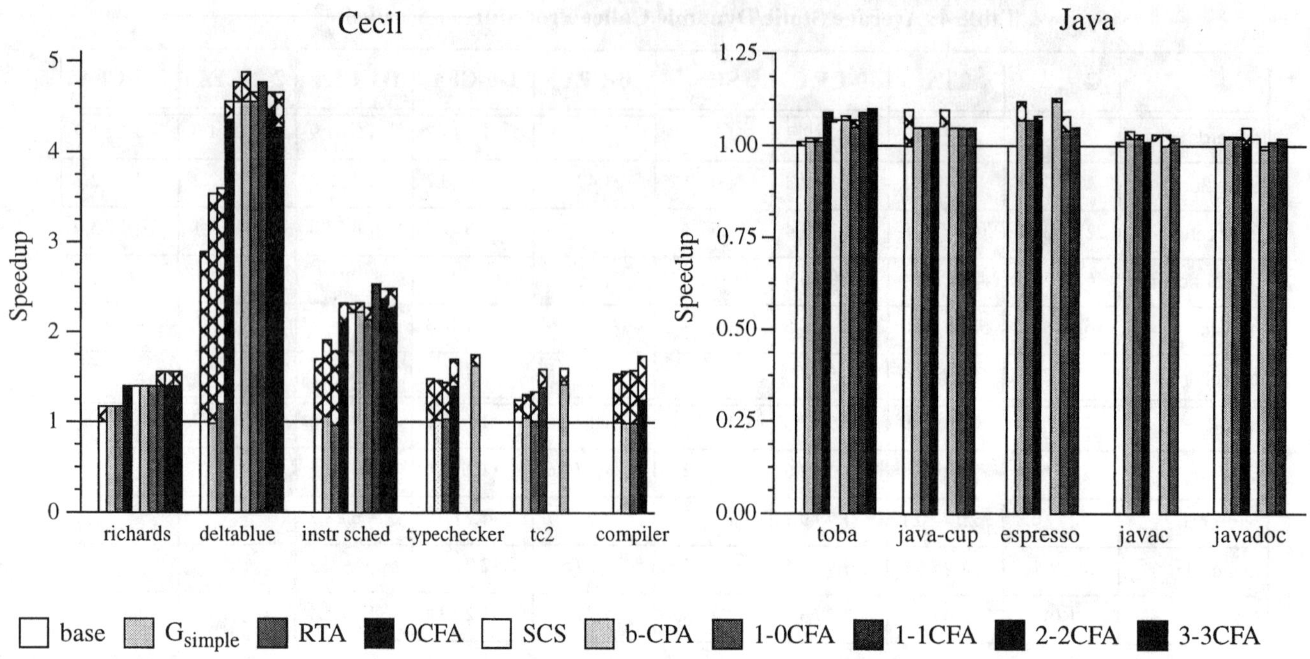


**Figure 6:** Application Execution Speed

optimizations building on the call graphs produced by the different construction algorithms.

- The **base** configuration represents an aggressive combination of intraprocedural and limited interprocedural optimizations which include: intraprocedural class analysis [Johnson 88, Chambers & Ungar 90], hard-wired class prediction for common messages (Cecil programs only) [Deutsch & Schiffman 84, Chambers & Ungar 89], splitting [Chambers & Ungar 89], class hierarchy analysis [Dean et al. 95], cross-module inlining, static class prediction [Dean 96], closure optimizations (Cecil only), and a suite of traditional intraprocedural optimizations such as common subexpression elimination, constant propagation and folding, dead assignment elimination, and redundant load and store elimination. We applied these optimizations through our Vortex compiler to produce C code, which we then compiled with `gcc -O2` to produce executable code.
- The base+profile configuration augments base with profile-guided class prediction [Hölzle & Ungar 94, Grove et al. 95].
- For each constructed call graph *G*, the base+IP$_G$ configuration augmented base with interprocedural analyses that enabled the intraprocedural optimizations in base to work better:
    - Class analysis: As a side-effect of constructing the call graph, each formal, local, global, and instance variable is associated with a set of classes whose instances may be stored in that variable. Intraprocedural class analysis exploits these sets as upper bounds that are more precise than "all possible classes," enabling better optimization of dynamically dispatched messages.
    - Mod analysis: This interprocedural analysis computes for each procedure a set of global variables and instance variables that may possibly be modified by calling the procedure. A number of intraprocedural analyses exploit this information to more accurately estimate the potential effect of procedure calls on local dataflow information.
    - Exception detection: This interprocedural analysis identifies those procedures which are guaranteed to not raise exceptions during their execution. This information can be exploited both to streamline their calling conventions and to simplify the intraprocedural control flow downstream of calls to exception-free routines.
    - Escape analysis: Interprocedural escape analysis identifies first-class functions which are guaranteed not to out-live their lexically enclosing environment, thus enabling the function objects and their environments to be stack-allocated [Kranz 88]. This optimization applied only to the Cecil benchmarks.
    - Treeshaking: As a side-effect of constructing the call graph, the compiler identifies those procedures which are unreachable during any program execution. The compiler does not compile any unreachable procedures, often resulting in substantial reductions both in code size and compile time.
- The base+IP$_G$+profile configuration augments the base+IP$_G$ configuration with profile-guided class prediction. We used the same dynamic profile data (derived from the base configuration) for all profile configurations. This methodology may slightly understate the benefits of profile-guided class prediction in the base+IP$_G$+profile configurations, but it eliminates an additional variable from our experiments.

Figure 6 displays application execution speed normalized to the speed of each application's base configuration (raw data can be found in appendix A). The bars for the various profile configurations are shown behind the bars for the corresponding non-profile versions, highlighting any additional benefit from dynamic profile data in that configuration. Each pair of bars is labeled with the call graph construction algorithm used to produce the call graph used in that algorithm, or base for the non-interprocedural version. We draw the following conclusions from this data:

- For most programs, the simple interprocedurally flow-insensitive algorithms, $G_{simple}$ and RTA, produced little improvement in execution speed, as foreshadowed by the high average degree of polymorphism at call sites shown in table 4.
- For the Cecil programs, interprocedurally flow-sensitive algorithms (0-CFA and better) provided a significant boost in performance, with speeds ranging from 1.25 to 4.5 times faster. For the three smaller Cecil programs, interprocedurally flow-sensitive static analysis subsumed profile-guided class prediction, but profile data remained important for the larger Cecil programs. Context-sensitivity was less important, although it did have a measurable impact on the typechecker benchmark. This suggests that if it were feasible to apply context sensitive analysis to even larger Cecil programs, one might see additional benefit.
- For the Java programs, interprocedural optimizations enabled modest improvements of between 0% and 13% over the base configuration. It should be emphasized that these speedups are relative to an already well-optimized base configuration; for comparison*, the base configuration is on average 7.6 times faster than Sun's JDK1.0.2 interpreter, 3.8 times faster than Sun's JDK1.0.2 just-in-time dynamic compiler, 2.0 times faster than Toba 1.0.5, an unoptimizing translator from Java to C, and 1.5 times faster than our own Vortex implementation [Dean et al. 96] without any optimizations other than those due to our `gcc -O2` back-end.

The treeshaking optimization shrank executable sizes for all the interprocedural analysis configurations. For the Java programs, executables were 10% to 20% smaller with treeshaking than the base configuration; the flow-sensitive algorithms typically reduced executable size by 0% to 3% more than the flow-insensitive algorithms. For the Cecil programs, decreases in executable size ranged from 15% on the compiler benchmark to 40% on the instr sched benchmark. Interprocedurally flow-sensitive algorithms enabled reductions of an additional 10% over the flow-insensitive algorithms. Context-sensitive call graphs did not measurably improve the effectiveness of treeshaking on any of the benchmark programs.

### 4.3 Relative Value of the Interprocedural Analyses

The results presented in the previous section summarize the impact of a number of interprocedural analyses and optimizations into a single data point. Determining how much of the total speedup was attributable to each optimization would be useful in deciding which of the analyses would be most valuable to include in future compilers. To partially answer this question we built and measured several variations on the base+$IP_{SCS}$ configuration for the instr sched and javac benchmarks; each variation excluded one of the interprocedural analyses. By comparing the execution time of each variant against that of the full base+$IP_{SCS}$ configuration we can identify those analyses which have substantial performance impact. We found that virtually all of the improvement in execution speed was due to class analysis. The version of base+$IP_{SCS}$ that excluded class analysis was significantly slower than the version with all interprocedural optimizations enabled. The versions that excluded the other interprocedural optimizations showed slight decreases in execution time over the version with all optimizations enabled, but the differences were too small to be considered significant.

Interprocedural escape analysis had little impact for the Cecil programs because the Vortex Cecil implementation allows programmers to annotate closures as LIFO (and thus non-escaping); virtually all of the closures in our benchmarks were annotated LIFO. When Vortex compiles ignoring these annotations, the modified base configurations run at half the speed of the base configurations used in this paper, but the base+$IP_{SCS}$ configurations run at essentially the same speed as reported previously. Thus, interprocedural escape analysis is sufficient to enable virtually all of the closure allocation optimizations enabled by the source level annotations. We chose to use the faster base configuration in the previous section to avoid overstating the benefits of interprocedural analysis; the cost of non-LIFO closures in the non-annotated base configuration could be somewhat reduced without resorting to interprocedural analysis by some simple intraprocedural techniques that Vortex does not implement due to the prevalence of LIFO annotations in the Cecil source code.

## 5 Other Related Work

In addition to the prior work studying particular algorithms for call graph construction already discussed in section 3, there exists a large body of prior work in interprocedural analysis and optimization. Typically this work has studied the impact of a single interprocedural analysis in the context of a single language.

Closely related to ours is a trio of parameterized algorithms for interprocedural flow analysis of higher-order functional languages [Stefanescu & Zhou 94, Jagannathan & Weeks 95, Nielson & Nielson 97]. All three of these frameworks are similar to ours in that they support the construction of context-sensitive contour-based call graphs and are parameterized over *ContourKeys*, allowing them to express a variety of algorithms. Both Jagannathan & Weeks and Nielson & Nielson model formally the program's semantics and treat interprocedural analysis as an abstract interpretation, while we formalize only the solution space of interprocedural analysis. All three frameworks are less general than ours in that they do not directly support non-monotonic improvement, initial call graphs other than $G_T$, or object-oriented features such as message passing, or context-sensitive analysis of instance variable and class contours. We also extend their work by considering the issue of cross-algorithm precision comparisons and by implementing our framework in an optimizing compiler and assessing the impact of interprocedural analysis empirically. Additionally, the framework of Stefanescu and Zhou appears to be limited to only using various flavors of dynamic call chain information as contour keys. Agesen used *templates* as an informal explanatory device in his description of constraint-graph-based instantiations of 0-CFA, *k*-CFA, and Plevyak's algorithm [Agesen 94]. Templates are similar to contours in that they serve to group and summarize all of the local constraints introduced by a procedure. Agesen does not formally define templates and only considers context-sensitivity in the *ProcKey* domain.

Hölzle and Agesen compared the effectiveness of interprocedural class analysis based on the Cartesian Product Algorithm and profile-guided class prediction for the optimization of Self programs [Hölzle & Agesen 96]. They found that there was very little performance difference (less than 15%) between three optimizing configurations: one using only profile-guided class prediction, one using only interprocedural class analysis, and one

* Our Java system does not currently implement null pointer dereference checks, multithreading, or dynamic class loading, so these comparisons to other Java implementations should only be used as evidence that our base configuration is efficient.

using both techniques. Our results for Cecil (a language similar to Self) differ in that flow-sensitive interprocedural class analysis alone appears significantly better than profile-guided class prediction alone.

## 6 Conclusions

We developed both a conceptual model and an implementation framework that encompasses a wide range of algorithms for call graph construction in object-oriented languages. Using this framework, we empirically assessed a variety of algorithms, applying them to a suite of medium-sized applications written in two different object-oriented languages. We found that interprocedural analyses, especially interprocedural class analysis, enabled substantial speedups for Cecil programs but only modest speedups for Java programs. In both languages, the additional precision of the call graphs constructed by the interprocedurally flow-sensitive algorithms had a large impact on the effectiveness of client interprocedural analyses and subsequent optimizations. However, the more precise contour-level call graphs constructed by the context-sensitive algorithms did not yield correspondingly large increases in application performance, in the absence of producing separate specialized compiled code for each procedure contour. Larger Cecil programs may benefit from context-sensitivity, but our experiments demonstrated that scalability problems prevent the context-sensitive algorithms from being applied beyond the domain of small benchmark programs. Thus the search for a scalable and effective call graph construction algorithm for programs that make heavy use of polymorphism and dynamic dispatching remains an open problem.

We are hopeful that one of the new algorithmic instantiations presented in section 3, such as extensions of $G_{unif}$, local non-monotonic improvement, or using $G_{prof}$ as the initial call graph will result in an algorithm that offers both scalability and reasonable precision. Another important area of future work is investigating techniques to support incremental reconstruction of the program call graph and derived interprocedural information in the presence of program changes. Incremental algorithms would widen the applicability of interprocedural analysis by enabling it to be applied in new domains such as day-to-day program development and in environments that support dynamic class loading.

## Acknowledgments

Michael Ernst, Urs Hölzle, and the anonymous OOPSLA reviewers provided valuable feedback on earlier drafts of this paper. David Bacon encouraged us to develop the precision comparisons of context-sensitive algorithms depicted in figure 5. The use of exact unions during local non-monotonic improvement is due to Chris Colby. Finally, we wish to thank Bjarne Steensgaard for several helpful discussions of the area. This research is supported in part by an NSF grant (number CCR-9503741), an NSF Young Investigator Award (number CCR-9457767), a grant from the Office of Naval Research (contract number N00014-94-1-1136), an Intel Foundation Graduate Fellowship, and gifts from Sun Microsystems, IBM, Xerox PARC, Pure Software, and Edison Design Group.

## References

[Agesen 94] Ole Agesen. Constraint-Based Type Inference and Parametric Polymorphism. In *First International Static Analysis Symposium*, September 1994.

[Agesen 95] Ole Agesen. The Cartesian Product Algorithm: Simple and Precise Type Inference of Parametric Polymorphism. In *Proceedings ECOOP '95*, Aarhus, Denmark, August 1995. Springer-Verlag.

[Agesen 96] Ole Agesen. *Concrete Type Inference: Delivering Object-Oriented Applications*. PhD thesis, Stanford, January 1996. SLMI TR 96-52.

[Alt & Martin 95] Martin Alt and Florian Martin. Generation of efficient interprocedural analyzers with PAG. In *Proceedings of the Second International Symposium on Static Analysis*, pages 33–50. Springer-Verlag, September 1995.

[Bacon & Sweeney 96] David F. Bacon and Peter F. Sweeney. Fast Static Analysis of C++ Virtual Function Calls. In *OOPSLA'96 Conference Proceedings*, San Jose, CA, October 1996.

[Bracha & Griswold 93] Gilad Bracha and David Griswold. Strongtalk: Typechecking Smalltalk in a Production Environment. In *Proceedings OOPSLA '93*, pages 215–230, October 1993. Published as ACM SIGPLAN Notices, volume 28, number 10.

[Callahan et al. 90] David Callahan, Alan Carle, Mary W. Hall, and Ken Kennedy. Constructing the Procedure Call Multigraph. *IEEE Transactions on Software Engineering*, 16(4):483–487, 1990.

[Chambers & Ungar 89] Craig Chambers and David Ungar. Customization: Optimizing Compiler Technology for Self, A Dynamically-Typed Object-Oriented Programming Language. *SIGPLAN Notices*, 24(7):146–160, July 1989. In Proceedings of the ACM SIGPLAN '89 Conference on Programming Language Design and Implementation.

[Chambers & Ungar 90] Craig Chambers and David Ungar. Iterative Type Analysis and Extended Message Splitting: Optimizing Dynamically-Typed Object-Oriented Programs. *SIGPLAN Notices*, 25(6):150–164, June 1990. In Proceedings of the ACM SIGPLAN '90 Conference on Programming Language Design and Implementation.

[Chambers 93] Craig Chambers. The Cecil Language: Specification and Rationale. Technical Report TR-93-03-05, Department of Computer Science and Engineering. University of Washington, March 1993.

[Cooper et al. 92] Keith D. Cooper, Mary W. Hall, and Ken Kennedy. Procedure Cloning. In *Proceedings of 1992 IEEE International Conference on Computer Languages*, pages 96–105, Oakland, CA, April 1992.

[Cousot & Cousot 77] Patrick Cousot and Radhia Cousot. Abstract Interpretation: A Unified Lattice Model for Static Analysis of Programs by Construction or Approximation of Fixpoints. In *Conference Record of the Fourth ACM Symposium on Principles of Programming Languages*, pages 238–252, Los Angeles, California, January 1977.

[Dean 96] Jeffrey Dean. *Whole Program Optimization of Object-Oriented Languages*. PhD thesis, University of Washington, November 1996. TR-96-11-05.

[Dean et al. 95] Jeffrey Dean, David Grove, and Craig Chambers. Optimization of Object-Oriented Programs Using Static Class Hierarchy Analysis. In *Proceedings ECOOP '95*, Aarhus, Denmark, August 1995. Springer-Verlag.

[Dean et al. 96] Jeffrey Dean, Greg DeFouw, Dave Grove, Vassily Litvinov, and Craig Chambers. Vortex: An Optimizing Compiler for Object-Oriented Languages. In *OOPSLA'96 Conference Proceedings*, San Jose, CA, October 1996.

[DeFouw et al. 97] Greg DeFouw, David Grove, and Craig Chambers. Fast Interprocedural Class Analysis. Technical Report TR-97-07-02, Department of Computer Science and Engineering. University of Washington, July 1997.

[Deutsch & Schiffman 84] L. Peter Deutsch and Allan M. Schiffman. Efficient Implementation of the Smalltalk-80 System. In *Conference Record of the Eleventh Annual ACM Symposium on Principles of Programming Languages*, pages 297–302, Salt Lake City, Utah, January 1984.

[Diwan et al. 96] Amer Diwan, Eliot Moss, and Kathryn McKinley. Simple and Effective Analysis of Statically-typed Object-Oriented Programs. In *OOPSLA'96 Conference Proceedings*, San Jose, CA, October 1996.

[Emami et al. 94] Maryam Emami, Rakesh Ghiya, and Laurie J. Hendren. Context-Sensitive Interprocedural Points-to Analysis in the Presence of Function Pointers. *SIGPLAN Notices*, 29(6):242–256, June 1994. In Proceedings of the ACM SIGPLAN '94 Conference on Programming Language Design and Implementation.

[Gosling et al. 96] James Gosling, Bill Joy, and Guy Steele. *The Java Language Specification*. Addison-Wesley, Reading, MA, 1996.

[Grove et al. 95] David Grove, Jeffrey Dean, Charles Garrett, and Craig Chambers. Profile-Guided Receiver Class Prediction. In *OOPSLA'95 Conference Proceedings*, pages 108–123, Austin, TX, October 1995.

[Hall & Kennedy 92] Mary W. Hall and Ken Kennedy. Efficient Call Graph Analysis. *ACM Letters on Programming Languages and Systems*, 1(3):227–242, September 1992.

[Hölzle & Agesen 96] Urs Hölzle and Ole Agesen. Dynamic vs. Static Optimization Techniques for Object-Oriented Languages. *Theory and Practice of Object Systems*, 1(3), 1996.

[Hölzle & Ungar 94] Urs Hölzle and David Ungar. Optimizing Dynamically-Dispatched Calls with Run-Time Type Feedback. *SIGPLAN Notices*, 29(6):326–336, June 1994. In Proceedings of the ACM SIGPLAN '94 Conference on Programming Language Design and Implementation.

[Jagannathan & Weeks 95] Suresh Jagannathan and Stephen Weeks. A Unified Framework of Flow Analysis in HIgher-Order Languages. In *Conference Record of POPL '95: 22nd ACM SIGPLAN-SIGACT Symposium on Principles of Programming Languages*, pages 393–407, January 1995.

[Johnson 88] Ralph Johnson. TS: AN Optimizing Compiler for Smalltalk. In *Proceedings OOPSLA '88*, pages 18–26, November 1988. Published as ACM SIGPLAN Notices, volume 23, number 11.

[Kam & Ullman 76] John B. Kam and Jeffrey D. Ullman. Global data flow analysis and iterative algorithms. *Journal of the ACM*, 23(1):158–171, January 1976.

[Kildall 73] Gary A. Kildall. A Unified Approach to Global Program Optimization. In *Conference Record of the ACM Symposium on Principles of Programming Languages*, pages 194–206, Boston, Massachusetts, October 1973.

[Kranz 88] David Kranz. *ORBIT: An Optimizing Compiler for Scheme*. PhD thesis, Yale University, February 1988. Department of Computer Science, Research Report 632.

[Lakhotia 93] Arun Lakhotia. Constructing Call Multigraphs Using Dependence Graphs. In *Conference Record of the Twentieth Annual ACM SIGPLAN-SIGACT Symposium on Principles of Programming Languages*, pages 273–284, Charleston, South Carolina, January 1993.

[Landi et al. 93] William Landi, Barbara G. Ryder, and Sean Zhang. Interprocedural Side Effect Analysis With Pointer Aliasing. *SIGPLAN Notices*, 28(6):56–67, June 1993. In Proceedings of the ACM SIGPLAN '93 Conference on Programming Language Design and Implementation.

[Nielson & Nielson 97] Flemming Nielson and Hanne Riis Nielson. Infinitary Control Flow Analysis: a Collecting Semantics for Closure Analysis. In *Conference Record of POPL '97: 24th ACM SIGPLAN-SIGACT Symposium on Principles of Programming Languages*, pages 332–345, Paris, France, January 1997.

[Odersky & Wadler 97] Martin Odersky and Philip Wadler. Pizza into Java: Translating theory into practice. In *Conference Record of POPL '97: 24th ACM SIGPLAN-SIGACT Symposium on Principles of Programming Languages*, pages 146–159, Paris, France, January 1997.

[Oxhøj et al. 92] Nicholas Oxhøj, Jens Palsberg, and Michael I. Schwartzbach. Making Type Inference Practical. In O. Lehrmann Madsen, editor, *Proceedings ECOOP '92*, LNCS 615, pages 329–349, Utrecht, The Netherlands, June 1992. Springer-Verlag.

[Palsberg & Schwartzbach 91] Jens Palsberg and Michael I. Schwartzbach. Object-Oriented Type Inference. In *Proceedings OOPSLA '91*, pages 146–161, November 1991. Published as ACM SIGPLAN Notices, volume 26, number 11.

[Plevyak & Chien 94] John Plevyak and Andrew A. Chien. Precise Concrete Type Inference for Object-Oriented Languages. In *Proceedings OOPSLA '94*, pages 324–340, Portland, OR, October 1994.

[Plevyak & Chien 95] John Plevyak and Andrew A. Chien. Type Directed Cloning for Object-Oriented Programs. In *Proceedings of the Workshop for Languages and Compilers for Parallel Computing*, pages 566–580, 1995.

[Plevyak 96] John Plevyak. *Optimization of Object-Oriented and Concurrent Programs*. PhD thesis, University of Illinois at Urbana-Champaign, 1996.

[Ryder 79] Barbara Ryder. Constructing the Call Graph of a Program. *IEEE Transactions on Software Engineering*, 5(3):216–225, 1979.

[Shivers 88] Olin Shivers. Control-Flow Analysis in Scheme. *SIGPLAN Notices*, 23(7):164–174, July 1988. In Proceedings of the ACM SIGPLAN '88 Conference on Programming Language Design and Implementation.

[Shivers 91a] Olin Shivers. *Control-Flow Analysis of Higher-Order Languages*. PhD thesis, Carnegie Mellon University, May 1991. CMU-CS-91-145.

[Shivers 91b] Olin Shivers. Data Flow Analysis and Type Recovery in Scheme. In *Topics in Advanced Language Implementation*. MIT Press, 1991. Edited by Peter Lee.

[Steensgaard 94] Bjarne Steensgaard. A Polyvariant Closure Analysis with Dynamic Abstraction. Unpublished manuscript, 1994.

[Steensgaard 96] Bjarne Steensgaard. Points-to Analysis in Almost Linear Time. In *Conference Record of POPL '96: 23rd ACM SIGPLAN-SIGACT Symposium on Principles of Programming Languages*, pages 32–41, St. Petersburg, Florida, January 1996.

[Stefanescu & Zhou 94] Dan Stefanescu and Yuli Zhou. An Equational Framework for the Flow Analysis of Higher-Order Functional Programs. In *Proceedings of the ACM Symposium on Lisp and Functional Programming*, pages 190–198, June 1994.

[Wilson & Lam 95] Robert P. Wilson and Monica S. Lam. Efficient Context-Sensitive Pointer Analysis for C Programs. *SIGPLAN Notices*, pages 1–12, June 1995. In Proceedings of the ACM SIGPLAN '95 Conference on Programming Language Design and Implementation.

## Appendix A Performance Data

The table below reports program execution times on a Sun Ultra 1 model 170 with 256MB of memory. Figure 6 is derived from this data.

**Table 5: Execution Time (secs)**

| | | Base | $G_{simple}$ | RTA | 0-CFA | SCS | b-CPA | 1-0-CFA | 1-1-CFA | 2-2-CFA | 3-3-CFA |
|---|---|---|---|---|---|---|---|---|---|---|---|
| Without Profile-Guided Receiver Class Prediction | richards | 0.14 | 0.13 | 0.12 | 0.10 | 0.10 | 0.10 | 0.10 | 0.10 | 0.10 | 0.10 |
| | deltablue | 2.05 | 2.01 | 1.72 | 0.47 | 0.45 | 0.45 | 0.45 | 0.43 | 0.46 | 0.48 |
| | instr sched | 1.09 | 1.03 | 1.14 | 0.52 | 0.49 | 0.49 | 0.51 | 0.54 | 0.52 | 0.49 |
| | typechecker | 9.83 | 9.60 | 9.54 | 7.02 | | | 6.04 | | | |
| | new-tc | 9.68 | 9.20 | 9.57 | 6.94 | | | 6.80 | | | |
| | compiler | 193 | 195 | 195 | 155 | | | | | | |
| | toba | 1.78 | 1.76 | 1.76 | 1.64 | 1.68 | 1.66 | 1.71 | 1.63 | 1.62 | |
| | java-cup | 0.22 | 0.21 | 0.21 | 0.21 | 0.21 | 0.21 | 0.21 | 0.21 | | |
| | espresso | 1.76 | 1.65 | 1.65 | 1.65 | 1.55 | 1.57 | 1.69 | 1.68 | | |
| | javac | 1.12 | 1.10 | 1.10 | 1.11 | 1.11 | 1.12 | 1.11 | | | |
| | javadoc | 1.23 | 1.21 | 1.21 | 1.23 | 1.20 | 1.24 | 1.22 | 1.20 | | |
| With Profile-Guided Receiver Class Prediction | richards | 0.12 | 0.12 | 0.12 | 0.10 | 0.10 | 0.10 | 0.010 | 0.09 | 0.09 | 0.09 |
| | deltablue | 0.71 | 0.58 | 0.57 | 0.45 | 0.43 | 0.42 | 0.44 | 0.43 | 0.44 | 0.44 |
| | instr sched | 0.64 | 0.57 | 0.61 | 0.47 | 0.47 | 0.47 | 0.48 | 0.49 | 0.46 | 0.46 |
| | typechecker | 6.65 | 6.72 | 6.83 | 5.80 | | | 5.61 | | | |
| | new-tc | 7.75 | 7.39 | 7.20 | 6.08 | | | 6.04 | | | |
| | compiler | 125 | 123 | 122 | 111 | | | | | | |
| | toba | 1.76 | 1.75 | 1.75 | 1.63 | 1.66 | 1.65 | 1.67 | 1.63 | 1.61 | |
| | java-cup | 0.20 | 0.21 | 0.21 | 0.21 | 0.20 | 0.21 | 0.21 | 0.21 | | |
| | espresso | 1.80 | 1.57 | 1.65 | 1.63 | 1.55 | 1.55 | 1.68 | 1.68 | | |
| | javac | 1.11 | 1.08 | 1.09 | 1.12 | 1.09 | 1.09 | 1.10 | | | |
| | javadoc | 1.27 | 1.20 | 1.20 | 1.19 | 1.22 | 1.23 | 1.22 | 1.21 | | |

# Efficient Dynamic Dispatch without Virtual Function Tables. The SmallEiffel Compiler.

Olivier ZENDRA, Dominique COLNET and Suzanne COLLIN
E-mail: {zendra, colnet, collin}@loria.fr

Centre de Recherche en Informatique de Nancy
Campus Scientifique, Bâtiment LORIA,
54506 Vandoeuvre-lès-Nancy BP 239 Cedex
France

## Abstract

SmallEiffel is an Eiffel compiler which uses a fast simple type inference mechanism to remove most late binding calls, replacing them by static bindings. Starting from the system's entry point, it compiles only statically living code, which saves compiling and then removing dead code. As the whole system is analyzed at compile time, multiple inheritance and genericity do not cause any overhead.

SmallEiffel features a coding scheme which eliminates the need for virtual function tables. Dynamic dispatch is implemented without any array access but uses a simple static binary branch code. We show that this implementation makes it possible to use modern hardware very efficiently. It also allows us to inline more calls even when dynamic dispatch is required. Some more dispatch sites are removed after the type inference algorithm has been performed, if the different branches of a dispatch site lead to the same code.

The advantage of this approach is that it greatly speeds up execution time and considerably decreases the amount of generated code.


**OOPSLA '97 10/97 GA, USA**


## 1 Introduction

Object-oriented programming has become a major trend both in computer science and computer engineering. Indeed, heavy use of inheritance and dynamically-bound messages is likely to make code more extensible and reusable. However, some concern still exists about performance of object-oriented systems, especially because of dynamic dispatch.

In order to reach performance similar to that of traditional languages like C, object-oriented systems must implement message dispatch efficiently. Recent work on type inference is a first step in this direction, since it allows the replacement of many polymorphic call sites by monomorphic direct call sites. The method used to implement remaining polymorphic call sites also has a significant impact on speed. Furthermore, optimization techniques for object-oriented programs must be fast enough not to be used only for application delivery. Fast compilers are needed to match the incremental nature of object-oriented languages.

In this study, we present the results obtained during the SmallEiffel project, started three years ago. This real-size project brought us to the somewhat surprising following conclusion: separate compilation doesn't outperform whole system compilation, even for incremental development. We indeed claim that global system type inference combined with a powerful implementation of dynamic dispatch can be used for incremental development.

The SmallEiffel compiler was designed to validate existing assumptions and offer new ideas. A powerful type inference algorithm was implemented and validated on a large-scale (50,000 lines) project, as well as some more specialized benchmarks. The method consists in completely removing all Virtual Function Tables (VFTs) or similar structures, replacing them by simple but efficient type tests. Since all indirect calls have been replaced by direct ones, this implementation of dispatch sites allows code inlining even inside polymorphic call sites.

The method described here is not limited to Eiffel [Mey94], but can also be used for any class-based language [MNC+91] without dynamic class creation or modification: for example, it is possible to apply the same method to C++ [Str86] but not to Self [US87].

The remainder of this paper is organized as follows. Section 2 provides some background material on type inference and Virtual Function Tables (VFTs). Section 3 describes the method used to remove as many polymorphic call sites as possible and efficiently implement remaining dispatches. Results and the benchmarks they were obtained from are presented in section 4. Section 5 reviews related work and section 6 concludes.

# 2 Background

Object-oriented languages derive significant expressive power from *polymorphism*, the ability to use an object of any concrete type, as long as it conforms to the required abstract type.

The overall purpose of type inference applied to object-oriented languages is information extraction, type checking and application optimization. Ole Agesen's PhD thesis [Age96] contains a complete survey of type inference systems. Reviewed systems range from purely theoretical ones [VHU92] to systems in regular use by a large community [Mil78], with partially implemented systems [Suz81, ST84] and systems implemented on small languages [GJ90, PS91, PS92].

While much research has been done on type inference [CF91, APS93, PC94, AH95, DGC95, EST95], with interesting results, common production compilers don't seem to take advantage of powerful type inference algorithms. Indeed, implementations of such algorithms are sometimes not fast enough for incremental development, especially since they require knowledge of the whole system, which often prevents separate compilation.

Most previously published dispatch techniques have been studied by Driesen et al. [DHV95]. There are two major kinds of dispatch techniques: dynamic and static. Dynamic dispatch techniques rely on run time or profile-guided information [HCU91, AH96]. They consist of various forms of caching at run time [DS84, UP87]. Static dispatch techniques precompute their data and code structure at compile time in order to minimize the work performed at runtime. Typically, the dispatch code retrieves the address of the target function by indexing into a table — the VFT — and performs an indirect jump to that address. There are variants of the VFT method (see section 4 in [DHV95]). Most of them use at least one array access and a function pointer.

Previous papers [DH96] have shown that the VFT mechanism doesn't schedule well on modern processors, since unpredictable conditional branches as well as indirect branches break control flow and thus are expensive on superscalar architectures. Another drawback of use of VFTs is that a polymorphic call site can never be inlined, because function pointers are required in all cases, including simple operations like attribute accesses. For example, an access to an attribute value via a VFT implies an access function definition. The method studied in this paper allows us to inline monomorphic and polymorphic call sites similarly. Thus, access functions do not need to be defined.

Since for application delivery, executable size is of some importance, dead-code elimination [Dha91, KRS94] is also a factor to be considered.

# 3 Method

This section describes the whole compilation process we used: type inference, implementation of dispatch, inlining, extra polymorphic call sites removal and finally the recompilation strategy.

## 3.1 Type inference

The first stage of this method consists in removing as many polymorphic sites as possible, replacing them by direct calls. This is done by a type inference algorithm, previously described in [CCZ97]. It can be considered as the combination of RTA (Rapid Type Analysis [BS96]) and customization [CU89] algorithms. SmallEiffel's type inference algorithm can be qualified as *polyvariant* (which means each feature may be analyzed multiple times) and *flow insensitive* (no data flow analysis).

Briefly, our algorithm builds and analyzes the call graph of the whole system and computes the set of all possible concrete types at run time. Dead code is never reached and thus never compiled, which avoids the cost of unnecessary compilation followed by code removal. Each living routine is duplicated and customized according to the concrete type of the target. Genericity as well as multiple inheritance are taken into account by our algorithm. This analysis doesn't imply any run time overhead since it is done during compilation.

In previous experiments [CCZ97], we showed this type inference mechanism was able to replace many occurrences of polymorphic sites by direct calls: more than 80% is a usual score. As the whole system is explored, efficient dead code removal is performed, since only living methods of a class are customized. This results in a significant speedup of the application execution and compilation times. For example, compiling SmallEiffel itself — which represents about 50,000 lines of Eiffel code — takes less than 10 seconds on a Pentium Pro (200MHz, 32Mb RAM).

Even when a polymorphic call (multiple possible target types) cannot be replaced by a direct call (one target), the number of possible target types is reduced.

No data flow analysis is performed in the current version. However, since class instantiation information seems to be more important than the flow-based information [BS96], the cost of such an analysis appears to be too high for the expected gain.

Obviously, the 100% limit cannot be reached for all programs whatever the quality of the inference algorithm used: a simple array filled with different mixed objects typed in is enough to break down any type inference system.

Most programs are thus likely to contain polymorphic sites, even after the best type inference analysis. When considering all the benchmarks of [DMM96], one may notice that polymorphic sites are called 26 times more frequently than monomorphic sites. Therefore, optimization of remaining polymorphic sites is crucial.

### 3.2 Removing Virtual Function Tables

Removing Virtual Function Tables (VFTs) is the solution we have chosen to optimize remaining dispatch sites.

Indeed, VFTs is the most common way to implement dynamic dispatch. However, compilers as well as modern architectures require a substantial amount of control flow information to fully exploit the hardware. As pointed out in [DH96, DMM96], VFT dispatch sequences do not schedule well on superscalar processors because they cause frequent unknown control transfers.

The method we use to implement dynamic dispatch is closely linked to Polymorphic Inline Caches (PICs) [HCU91]. PICs extend dynamic inline caching [DS84] to handle polymorphic call sites, by caching for a given polymorphic call site all lookup results, instead of only the last one. Shared PICs consists in using the same PIC for several call sites, caching for a given message name all receiver types known so far.

Our implementation of dynamic dispatch is a statically computed variation of shared PICs. As suggested in [HCU91], we use binary search to check the receiver type. To our knowledge, this method has never been tested before in Eiffel, at least on such a large scale.

Removing VFTs implies modifying the run time object structure. Generally each object structure contains a pointer to the appropriate VFT. SmallEiffel's method replaces this pointer by a statically computed integer value to identify the corresponding concrete type. This integer ID allows us to explicitly test the dynamic type of the target.

With VFT-like methods, a dispatch site is mapped as at least one array access to get a function pointer, followed by the call to this function. Our method is a direct call to a specialized dispatch function, which spares both array accesses and function pointer. There is thus no need for any array, and the associated table compaction burden [DHV95] becomes irrelevant. All the information used to discriminate concrete types as well as selectors is in the code area. Obviously, direct function calls are also faster than indirect ones.

Thus, one function is specially defined for each kind of polymorphic site: its definition is done for one given selector with a statically known set of concrete types. This scheme applies similarly to single and multiple inheritance, with no increase in complexity, unlike VFT-based methods [DHV95, DH96].

For example, assume `x.f` is a polymorphic site whose target has four possible concrete types $T_A$, $T_B$, $T_C$ and $T_D$. A dispatch function is especially defined to handle both the selector `f` and the set $\{T_A,T_B,T_C,T_D\}$. In another polymorphic call site, the same dispatch function can be used only when both the selector and the concrete type set are exactly the same. Using a dispatch function instead of directly inlining the dispatch code allows an important factorization of code. Without such factorization, the total size of the generated code would be much more important, as we shall see later in this paper.

The body of the dispatch function contains static multi-branch selection code with hard-coded type ID numbers. To avoid costly sequential inspection code inside the dispatch function, the set of possible concrete IDs is sorted at compile time. Obviously, this method is possible because the type inference algorithm is applied to the whole system.

The body of the dispatch function is efficient binary branching code. Assuming ID of $T_A$, $T_B$, $T_C$ and $T_D$ are respectively 19, 12, 27 and 15, the following dispatch scheme is produced for our last **x.f** example:

```
if id_x ≤ 15 then
      if id_x ≤ 12 then f_B(x)
            else f_D(x)
      endif
   else
      if id_x ≤ 19 then f_A(x)
            else f_C(x)
      endif
endif
```

Obviously $f_A(x)$, $f_B(x)$, $f_C(x)$ and $f_D(x)$ are not always function calls. As the concrete dynamic type of the target is known inside each selected branch, the corresponding behavior may be inlined.

## 3.3 Inlining

Because of the efficient type inference algorithm and also the way we implement dynamic dispatch, a lot of inlining sites are detected. One must keep in mind that classical VFT-based methods are an obstacle to inlining, since the compiler doesn't know which function will be called.

Most of SmallEiffel's inlining patterns are presented in this section. The label given to each inlining pattern will be used in some figures of the result section.

**ARI** Attribute Reader Inlining is done when the function is a simple attribute access: the function has only one instruction which returns an attribute. All call sites of such a function are inlined and there is no need to define the function. Monomorphic sites are directly inlined, whereas for polymorphic sites, inlining occurs in the branch of the corresponding type ID. As a consequence, attribute reader functions entail no overhead at all.

**AWI** Attribute Writer Inlining is performed when the procedure is only defined to set an attribute with the value passed as an argument. Such a procedure has only one argument with only one instruction and the argument is used to write an attribute. As for ARI, all sites are inlined and attribute writer functions do not entail any overhead.

**DRI** Direct Relay Inlining is used when the routine body has only one instruction to relay another routine directly applied to the same target. Such a case occurs when someone wants to alias a routine. For example, assume we have in class `COLLECTION[X]` the following Eiffel definition:

```
push(element: X) is
   do
      Current.add_first(element);
   end;
```

As `add_first` is called with the same target as `push` (Eiffel `Current` is equivalent to `this` in C++ or to `self` in Smalltalk [GR83]), the `push` procedure is inlined. All direct relay sites are inlined, and this kind of aliasing doesn't create any overhead or relay function definition.

DRI is also applied when arguments of the relayed call are statically computable. For example, this routine from class `STRING` of SmallEiffel's standard library is also inlined:

```
first: CHARACTER is
   do
      Result := Current.item(1);
   end;
```

Calling `first` has the same cost as calling directly `item(1)`. Thus improving readability does not cost anything.

**DARI** Direct Attribute Relay Inlining uses the fact that if the concrete type of `Current` is known, the concrete types of its attributes may be known as well. This is the case when the three following conditions hold. First, the routine has only one instruction which is a call. Second, the target of this call is an attribute of `Current`. Third, this call is monomorphic (the target attribute has only one possible concrete type).

For example, the function `item` of class `STRING` is defined as follows in SmallEiffel's standard library:

```
item(index: INTEGER): CHARACTER is
   do
      Result := storage.item(index - 1);
   end;
```

The call to `item` is monomorphic since attribute `storage` has only one possible concrete type (it is always an array of characters). As for previous inlinings, DARI sites are inlined and this kind of relay routine has no overhead.

**PRI** Predictable Result Inlining is used when the result of a function has a value known at compile time. The result may be any statically computable expression including nested function calls. For example, the following functions are both inlined:

```
two: INTEGER is
    do
        Result := 1 + 1;
    end;
three: INTEGER is
    do
        Result := 1 + Current.two;
    end;
```

The previous examples are trivial, but one must keep in mind that each living routine is customized for each concrete living type [CCZ97]. Thus, the call to `two` — which is currently statically computable — may be redefined in a subclass. The new definition will be considered separately and may be statically computable too.

**RCI** Result is Current Inlining is done when a function body has only one instruction to return the `Current` value. The following function is thus inlined:

```
foo(bar: Y): X is
    do
        Result := Current;
    end;
```

As we will show in the results section, this kind of strange function is not very common, though it exists.

**EPI** Empty Procedure Inlining is performed when a procedure has an empty body. Surprisingly, we have noticed that such a case is more frequent than expected (for example, the common Eiffel standard `do_nothing` is an EPI case).

**OEI** Other Eiffel Inlinings are performed by the SmallEiffel compiler. We do not describe those inlinings here because they are closely linked to the Eiffel language (e.g. inlining of pre-computable `once` functions). Unlike previous inlinings, OEI is not directly mappable to C++ or Java [JGS96].

### 3.4 Removing some more dispatch sites

Removing some more dispatch sites is still possible even after the type inference algorithm is finished. When all branches of the dispatch have exactly the same behavior — the code produced inside each branch has the same effect — no dispatch is needed. The polymorphic call site becomes a monomorphic one. Here is the classification of removed polymorphic sites.

**ARR** Attribute Read Removal is performed when the two following conditions hold. First, each branch of the dispatch is an ARI. Second, all attributes have the same common offset for all possible concrete types of the polymorphic site. Even when all attributes have the same name, it is important to check for the second condition because of multiple inheritance: one concrete type may inherit different attributes. For single inheritance languages, the second condition may be omitted.

**AWR** Attribute Write Removal is performed when the two following conditions hold. First, each possible concrete type of the polymorphic call is an AWI. Second, each attribute has the same common displacement. As for the previous removal pattern (ARR), the second condition may be omitted when the source language has no multiple inheritance.

**DARR** Direct Attribute Relay Removal is performed when all branches drive to the same relayed routine: all branches are DARI and the relayed routine is the same.

**OER** Other Eiffel Removals allow some other polymorphic calls to be removed. They are not described here because they are closely linked with the SmallEiffel interface with low level arrays. Like OEI, OER may not be applicable to C++ or Java.

### 3.5 Recompilation

Whole system analysis is likely to raise some concerns about compilation times. As we will show in section 4, the Eiffel to C translation from scratch is extremely fast. In order to avoid recompiling all C files, we use an amazingly simple and efficient process. It consists of the three following stages.

First, all C files and object files produced during the previous compilation are saved. Assume the saved C files are named $old_1.c$, $old_2.c$, ..., $old_n.c$. Next, the whole Eiffel source code is analyzed and all new C files are generated as $new_1.c$, $new_2.c$, ..., $new_n.c$. Note that each C file contains a bunch of code which is unrelated to the class hierarchy. Finally, for each pair ($new_i.c$, $old_i.c$), file contents are compared byte to byte. If the C file has not changed, the old object file is used, thus avoiding a C compilation.

The — very fast — Eiffel to C compilation is thus non-incremental, whereas the C compilation is. An advantage of this trivial technique is to avoid maintaining a project database with information that is implicitly in the C code. The Eiffel to C compiler work is thus reduced, which contributes to its speed.

# 4 Results

## 4.1 The SmallEiffel benchmark

The SmallEiffel benchmark is the most significant benchmark we have. SmallEiffel is fully bootstrapped in Eiffel and represents about 50,000 lines of Eiffel for about 300 classes. Everything is written in pure Eiffel: lexical analysis, parsing, semantic analysis, type inference, code generation and code optimization [AU77]. The standard library distributed with SmallEiffel (`ftp://ftp.loria.fr/pub-/loria/genielog/SmallEiffel`) is the one used by the compiler itself. One may check that everything is full Eiffel even for very basic objects like `STRING` or `ARRAY`. The public `DICTIONARY` class is used for all symbol tables of SmallEiffel.

The compiler makes extensive use of dynamic dispatch to analyze Eiffel source code. For example, the abstract class `EXPRESSION` has no less than 48 concrete living types to implement all kinds of Eiffel expressions. Obviously, dynamic dispatch is used to select the appropriate behavior for each expression. The following table gives some other examples of the "Object-Orientedness" [DDG+96] of the SmallEiffel benchmark:

| Concrete types | Abstract class |
|---|---|
| 48 | EXPRESSION |
| 27 | CALL |
| 20 | TYPE |
| 17 | FEATURE |
| 16 | INSTRUCTION |
| 12 | NAME |
| 8 | ROUTINE |
| 8 | CONSTANT_ATTRIBUTE |
| ... | ........ |

One must also keep in mind that Eiffel is a pure Object-Oriented language [Mey88] (ie. every routine is virtual, using C++ terminology).

In [CCZ97], we show some early results[1] related to the bootstrap process. We present here new benchmarks and analyses[2] that take into account more complete and optimized algorithms (especially those described in sections 3.3 and 3.4).

As SmallEiffel analyzes the whole system to produce code, one may be worried about compilation time. Figure 1 gives a survey on various architectures of the bootstrap process: SmallEiffel compiles itself with all previously described optimizations enabled. The total compilation time is divided in two parts. The upper part gives the time to produce the C code from the Eiffel source starting from scratch including the comparison of new and old C files. The middle part gives the time to produce the executable file from C code using `gcc -O6`.

This figure shows that SmallEiffel's Eiffel to C compilation is extremely fast: for example it takes less than 10 seconds on a Pentium Pro 200 to translate 50,000 lines of Eiffel into 65,000 lines of C code. This first stage — which contains all the previously described techniques — is about 10 to 20 times faster than the translation from C code to executable.

Total time from scratch to executable is only 2 minutes on a Pentium Pro 200. Furthermore, when one does not compile from scratch, only some C files need to be recompiled. Thus, with a minor change in a program of 50,000 lines of Eiffel, it takes only about 15 seconds to build the new executable on a Pentium Pro 200. This demonstrates that whole system analysis can be used for incremental development.

Figure 1 also gives the size of the executable file produced (the SmallEiffel compiler). Compared with other commercial Eiffel compilers or with gcc, the SmallEiffel executable is small (655Kb on a Pentium Pro 200). This demonstrates that extensive inlining and method customization combined with an efficient dead code removal do not increase the size of executables.

For the whole compiler, the type inference analysis final score is very good. There are 24975 monomorphic call sites and only 3983 polymorphic call sites:

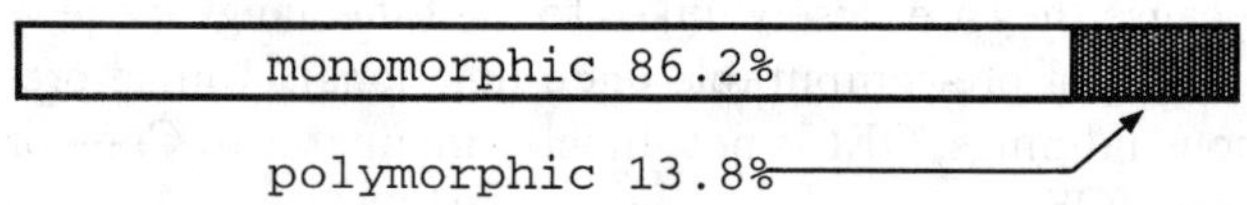


As seen previously, some polymorphic sites are removed because each branch would produce the same code (ARR, AWR, DARR, OER). The gain is 1098 polymorphic sites.

[1] which come from the first public version of SmallEiffel, numbered `-0.99`

[2] obtained with the 14th version, named SmallEiffel `-0.86`

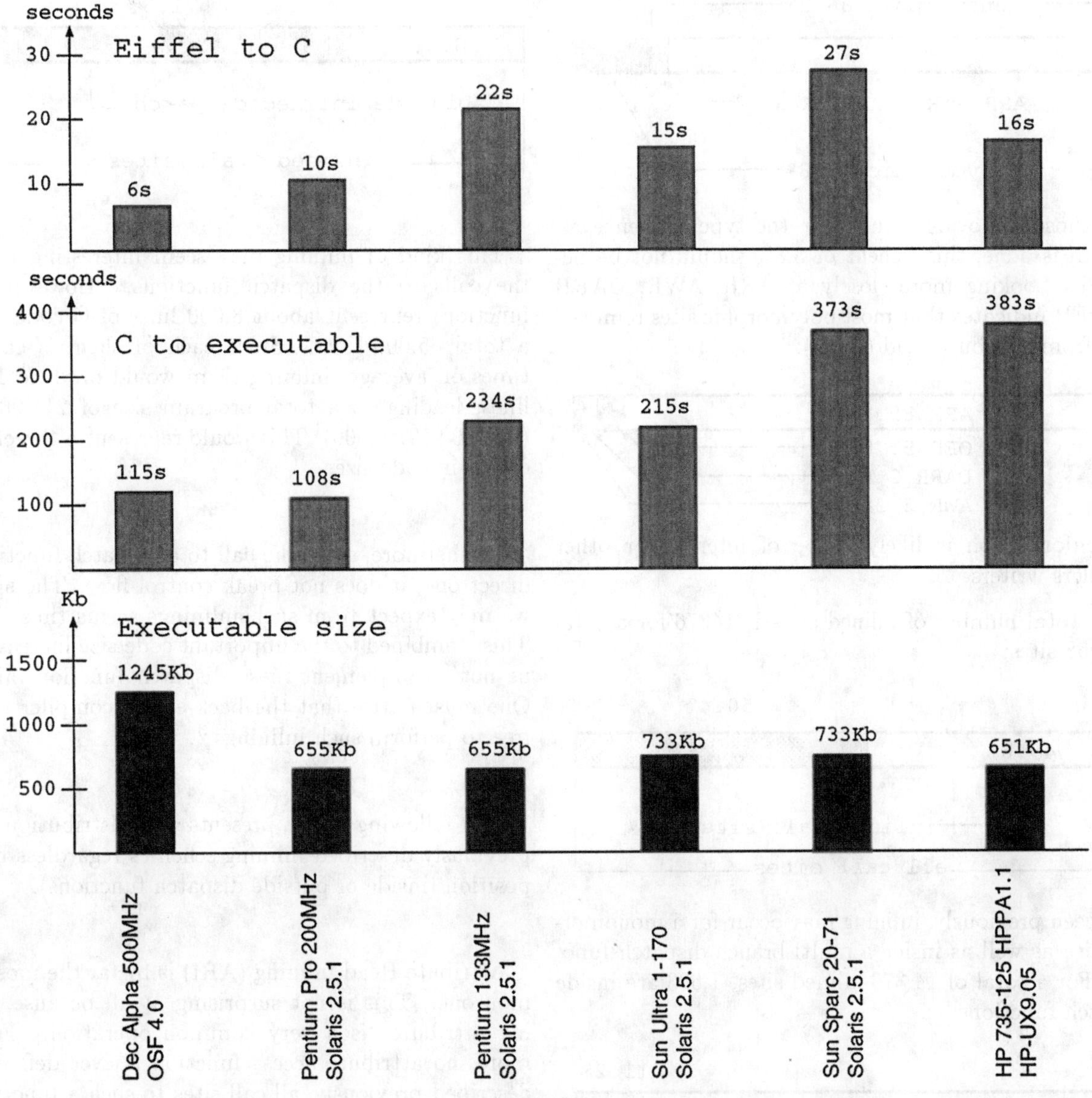


Figure 1: Bootstrapping SmallEiffel on various architectures.

The upper graph gives the total time from scratch to obtain 65,000 lines of optimized C from 50,000 lines of Eiffel. The middle graph shows the total time from C code to executable (link time is included). The lower graph gives the size of stand-alone executables.

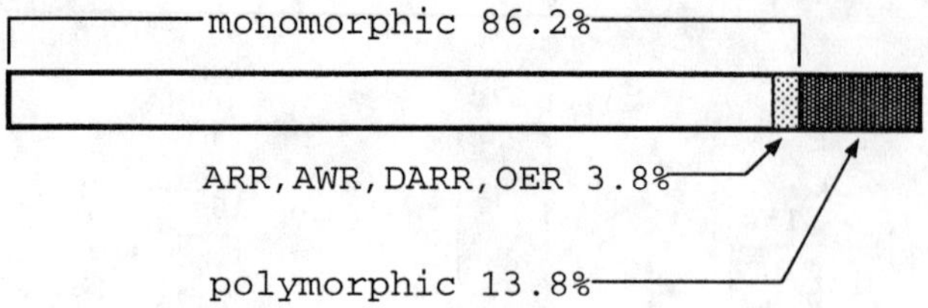


As those removals occur after the type inference algorithm is done, this benefit of 3.8% should not be neglected. Looking more closely at ARR, AWR, DARR and OER indicates that most polymorphic sites removed come from attribute read (ARR):

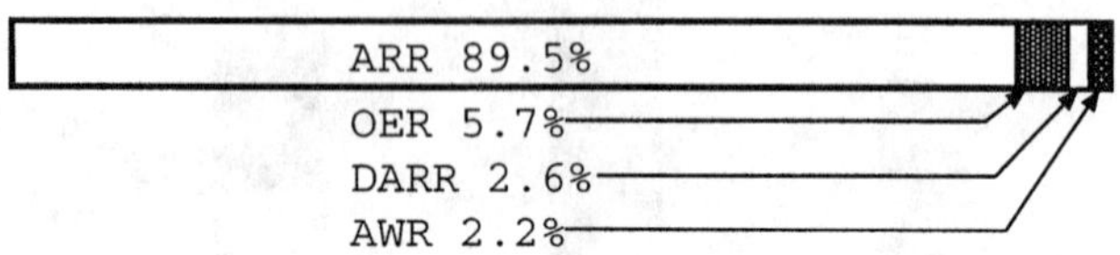


This information is likely to be of interest for other compilers writers.

The total number of inlined sites is 14376 for a total of 28958 sites:

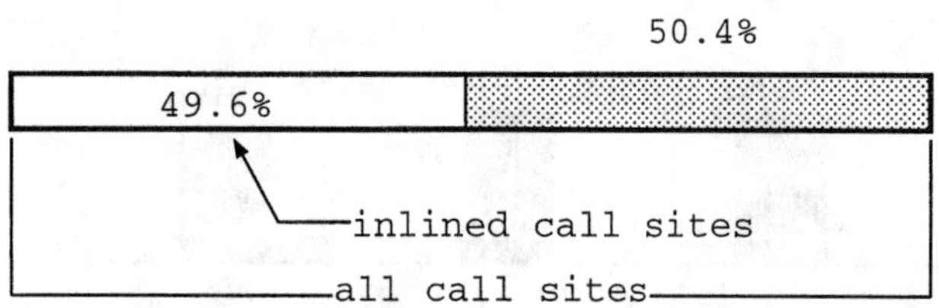


As seen previously, inlining may occur for a monomorphic site as well as inside a multi-branch dispatch function. For a total of 14,376 inlined sites, 1,603 are inside dispatch functions:

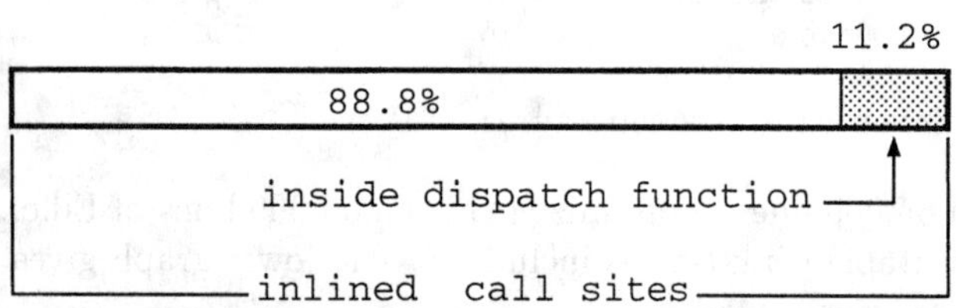


For 3,983 polymorphic call sites, there are 199 dispatch functions: the average number of calls per function is thus about 20. Consequently, the impact of one inlining inside a dispatch function may be considered 20 times more important than that of an inlined monomorphic call site.

Assuming that dispatch functions themselves are inlined gives the following ratio:

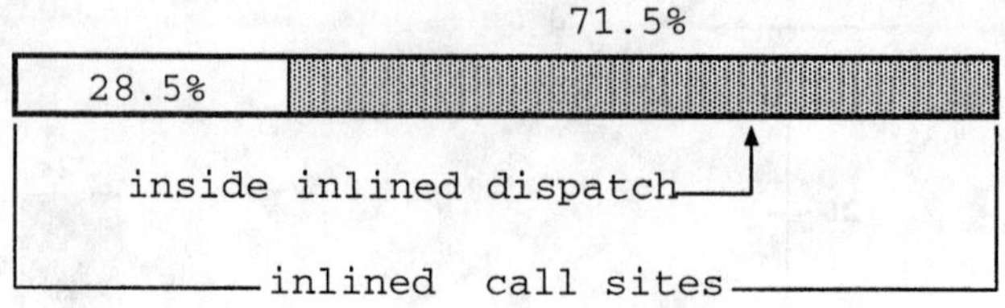


This kind of inlining may seem interesting to avoid the calls to the dispatch functions. However, these functions represent about 8,000 lines of C code, among a total 65,000 lines. Since each of them is called 20 times on average, inlining them would produce 160,000 lines, leading to a total program size of 217,000 lines (65,000+19×8,000). This would represent a threefold increase in code size.

Furthermore, since the call to a dispatch function is a direct one, it does not break control flow. The speedup we may expect from such inlinings seems thus limited. This, combined to the important code size increase, lead us not to implement these dispatch function inlinings. One must notice that the back-end C compiler remains free to perform such inlinings [3].

The following figure presents the distribution of the previously described inlining schemes regardless of their position (inside or outside dispatch functions).

Attribute Read Inlining (ARI) is by far the most common one. This is not surprising at all because accessing attributes is a very common operation. Furthermore, no attribute access function is ever defined. As described previously, all call sites to such a function are always inlined. As a consequence, there is no run time penalty when reading an attribute through an access function: maximum performance and encapsulation can be achieved simultaneously.

[3] For example, we have checked that gcc version 2.7.2 did inline small dispatch functions, as expected.

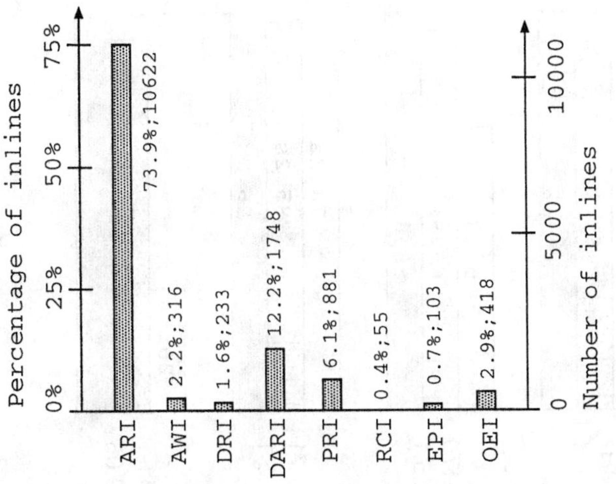


Conversely, the VFT method implementation of polymorphic call sites requires function pointers, which prevent any polymorphic function from being inlined.

Direct Attribute Relay Inlining (DARI) and Predictable Result Inlining (PRI) also represent a non-negligible part of inlinings. After looking at the generated code, we noticed that DARI often comes from encapsulation. Indeed, an encapsulating class often serves as a simple relay to services provided by private attributes.

An explanation of the importance of PRI can be deduced from the following figure, which shows — for each inlining scheme — the ratio of inlinings inside dispatch functions to the total number of inlinings.

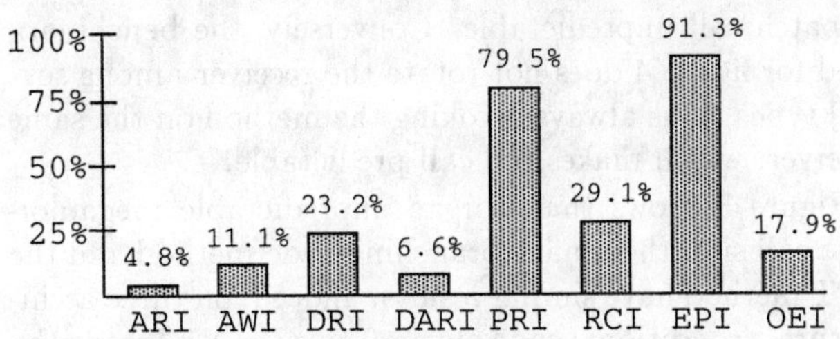


Inlining inside dispatch functions

Most PRI are inside dispatch functions. A closer examination of the generated code reveals that this phenomenon is linked to a common use of inheritance in object-oriented programming: a virtual function in some abstract class is implemented with a constant result in most of its concrete subtypes. For example, function **number_of_wheels** of class VEHICLE has the constant value 4 in subclass CAR and 2 in subclass MOTORCYCLE.

The importance of Empty Procedure Inlinings (EPI) inside dispatch functions results from a similar cause. It is indeed not uncommon to redefine a selector **do_something** with an empty function body, or, conversely, to have an empty default behavior which is redefined to actually do something in only a few subtypes.

## 4.2 Dynamic Dispatch and VFT overhead

In order to quantify the impact of binary branch code compared with VFTs, we ran a simple benchmark written both in Eiffel and in C++. It only comprises one polymorphic dispatch site, embedded in a long-time loop. There is one abstract class X with three concrete subclasses A, B and C. The virtual abstract function **do_it** of X is redefined differently for each concrete class. Redefinition in each class is chosen to avoid any possibility of removal (section 3.4) by SmallEiffel.

Consequently, the following benchmark still has one remaining dispatch call site after type inference has been performed, which allows us to actually measure the cost of the dispatch method. Here is the loop given in C++:

```
{X *x;
 A *a = new A();
 B *b = new B();
 C *c = new C();
 int i;
 for (i = 100000000; i != 0; i--) {
   switch (i % 3) {
   case 0 : x = a; break;
   case 1 : x = b; break;
   default: x = c;
   }
  x->do_it(); // The Polymorphic Call Site
 }
};
```

Since it rotates between the three branches, this benchmark prevents any target prediction.

This C++ version (g++) implements the dispatch with a VFT, whereas SmallEiffel standard generated C code uses a multi-branch dispatch function. In order to ascertain the only difference we could notice came from the dispatch implementation, we added a third version. It was obtained by manually modifying the C code produced by SmallEiffel, to replace the dispatch call site by a VFT call written in C, everything else remaining unchanged.

Figure 2 shows the execution times of those three benchmarks on various architectures. Of course, our purpose is not to compare processors, but to show that the results are not linked to a specific architecture.

The unmodified C code produced by SmallEiffel is always the fastest one. On the architectures we tested on,

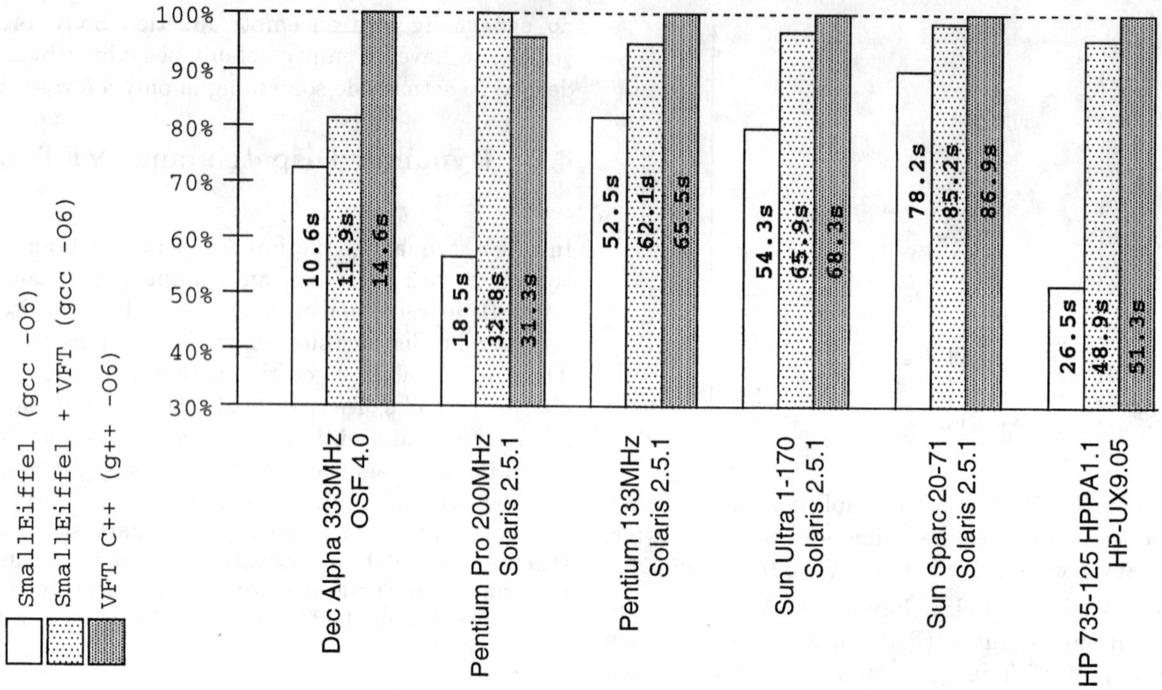


Figure 2: Execution time comparison for a 3 branch unpredictable call site: VFT vs. multi-branch.

SmallEiffel is in the worst case 10% faster than the C++ version, and 48% faster in the best case. This clearly shows that SmallEiffel's dispatch implementation is better for polymorphic call sites with few possibilities. Furthermore, times obtained with C++ and the modified SmallEiffel C code are consistent. Since they both implement dispatches with VFTs, this seems to confirm that VFT implementation of dynamic dispatch is less efficient than the method presented in this paper.

The VFT dispatch method has a constant execution time regardless of the number of possible concrete types of a polymorphic call site. Conversely, SmallEiffel's method cost is not constant because the number of branches inside the dispatch function grows with the number of possible concrete types. As we have chosen a binary branching code to test among various possible concrete types, the number of branches is given by $log_2(N)$ where $N$ is the number of possible concrete types. In order to compare execution time for a *megamorphic* call site — i.e. a polymorphic call site with many possible receivers [DHV95] — we have extended the previous benchmark to 50 subclasses. According to [AH96], a total of 17 possible concrete types may be considered as megamorphic. One may also note that the most polymorphic call site of SmallEiffel (50,000 lines) has 48 possible concrete types (class **EXPRESSION**).

The previously described class **X** now has 50 subclasses, which leads to a 50 branch dispatch. Figure 3 shows results obtained with a benchmark where the code rotates the receiver among the 50 possiblities, making the dispatch call unpredictable. Conversely, the benchmark used for figure 4 does not rotate the receiver among several types, thus always invoking the method on the same receiver, which makes the call predictable.

Figure 3 shows that, for an unpredictable megamorphic call site, the binary branching code method and the VFT method have similar results. Indeed, on three architectures, conditional code outperforms the VFT code (by 4% to 31%), whereas on the three others VFTs are faster (by 4% to 7%). Consequently, the binary branching code method appears to be quite scalable. Since all branches are equiprobable, profile guided techniques [AH96] or inline caching [DS84, UP87] do not seem to be able to improve results.

Figure 4 shows that results are even better on a predictable call site, since conditional code now outperforms the VFT code on four architectures.

A closer look at the assembly code generated for the binary branching code and for the VFT mechanism leads to some interesting observations. First, data dependen-

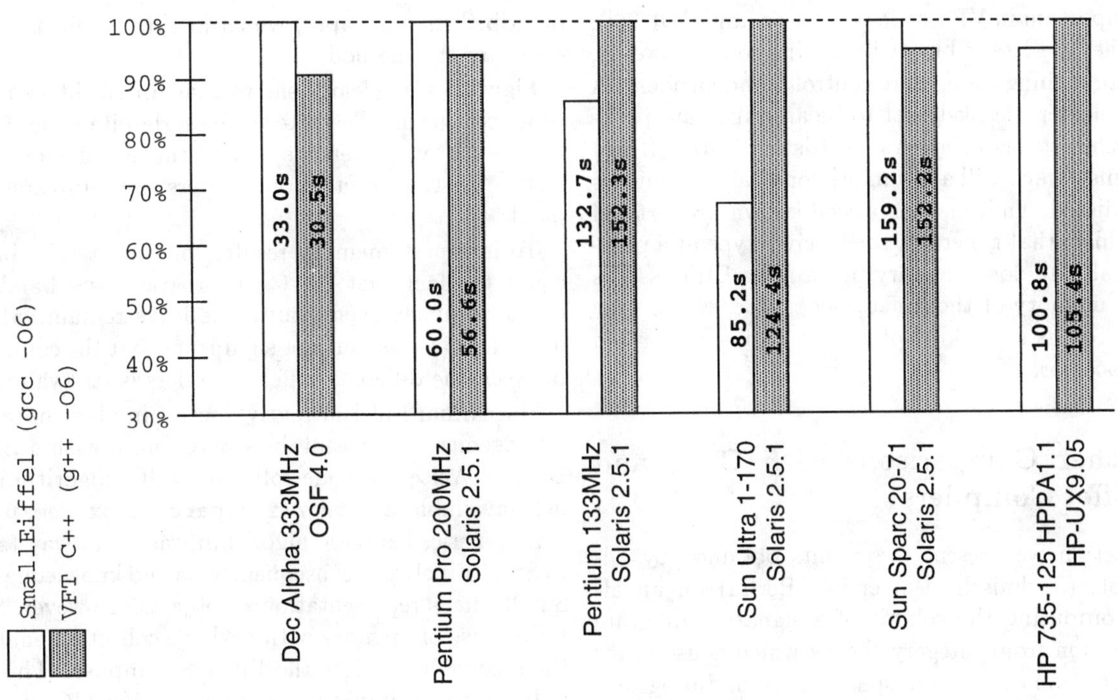


Figure 3: Execution time comparison for a 50 branch unpredictable megamorphic call site.

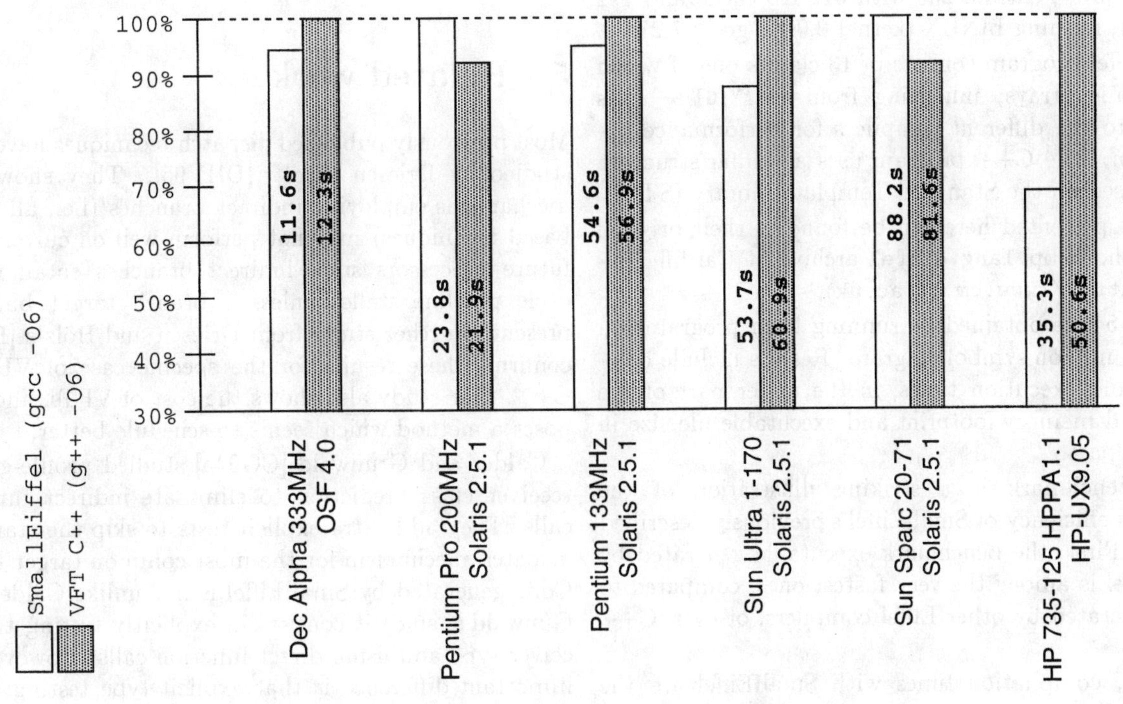


Figure 4: Execution time comparison for a 50 branch predictable call site.

cies are important in VFT code (see for example [DH96]), whereas they are less in binary branching code. However, in binary branching code, more control flow dependencies arise. The latter are likely not to be an important problem on architectures using Branch History Table (BHT) mechanisms, which will allow many conditional branches to be predicted. Indeed, it is a well-known property of polymorphism that generally, the receiver type at a polymorphic call site does not vary much. The BHT is thus used as a memory of the last receiver type, which may be considered as some kind of inline caching performed by the processor.

### 4.3 Other Comparisons with C++ and Eiffel Compilers

In this section we present the results obtained by Dietmar Wolz (Technische Universität Berlin) on an algorithm computing the colimit of a signature diagram (a construction from category theory which is useful for parameterization concepts in specification and programming languages and for graph transformations).

This algorithm was implemented both in Eiffel and in C++, and benchmarked with different compilers and/or libraries, on a Pentium 200 with 512 Kb cache and 192 Mb RAM, running LINUX (kernel 2.0.12, gcc 2.7.2).

The Eiffel program consists of 13 classes one of which — dynamic arrays, inheriting from `ARRAY[G]` — was adapted to the different compilers for performance optimization. The C++ program uses a similar structure and is based on the Standard Template Library (STL).

Results presented here can be found in their original form in the `comp.lang.eiffel` archive at Cardiff University (`http://www.cm.cf.ac.uk`).

Figure 5 was obtained by running both programs on a large, 2 million symbol diagram. Results include compilation and execution times, in the upper part of the graph, and memory footprint and executable file size in the lower part.

This benchmark is a striking illustration of the speed and efficiency of SmallEiffel's previously described method. First, the benchmark executable generated by SmallEiffel is among the very fastest ones, compared to those generated by other Eiffel compilers, or even C++ compilers.

Second, compilation times with SmallEiffel are the best, whether compared to those of other Eiffel or C++ compilers. Since SmallEiffel has been bootstrapped, its executable code itself was produced using the method described in this paper, which in turn confirms the efficiency of the method.

Figure 5 also clearly shows that SmallEiffel's method produces the smallest executables, despite code duplication — for type inference — and the use of explicit type tests — instead of function pointers — to implement dispatch.

To interpret memory results, one must take into account the fact that the C++ program uses hand-made memory management, but some leaks remain. Memory usage for C++ is thus not significant, but the comparison between the different Eiffel compilers is still valid.

Since SmallEiffel currently doesn't implement memory management, its executables were linked with a Boehm-Demers-Weiser garbage collection (GC) algorithm, publicly available at `ftp://ftp.parc.xerox.com/pub/gc`. This generic, heuristic algorithm was in no way tailored to SmallEiffel, and consequently has no knowledge about SmallEiffel's representation of objects. However, SmallEiffel's use of memory with garbage collection enabled is the second best, after the Eiffel/S compiler. This score is likely to be improved when a specific GC algorithm is implemented in SmallEiffel. Indeed, with garbage collection turned off, SmallEiffel makes the sparest use of memory.

## 5 Related work

Most previously published dispatch techniques have been studied by Driesen et al. [DHV95]. They show that mechanisms employing indirect branches (i.e., all table-based techniques) may not perform well on current and future processors since indirect branches entail multi-cycle pipeline stalls, unless a branch target buffer is present. Further study from Driesen and Hölzle [DH96] confirms these results for the specific case of VFTs in C++. Our study also shows the cost of VFTs, and proposes a method which seems to schedule better.

Calder and Grunwald [CG94a] studied profile-guided receiver class prediction to eliminate indirect function calls. They add extra explicit tests to skip the standard dispatch mechanism for the most common target types. Code generated by SmallEiffel is not unlike Calder and Gunwald's, since it consists in explicitly testing the receiver type and using direct function calls. However, an important difference is that explicit type testing is extended to all possible receiver types, and not only the most common ones. This allows a complete removal of any VFT-like standard dispatch mechanism.

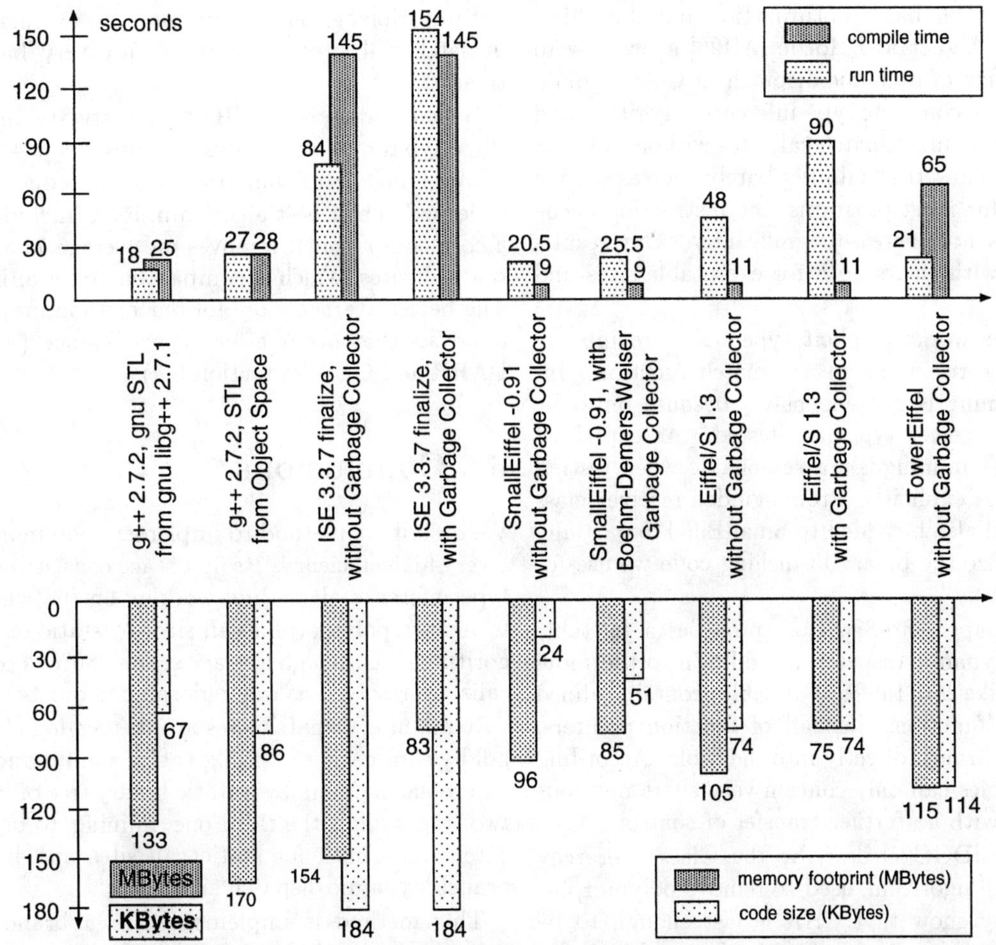


Figure 5: Overall performances of SmallEiffel vs. other compilers.

Using both profile-based optimization and class hierarchy analysis, Aigner and Hölzle [AH96] show how to improve efficiency of dynamic dispatch in C++. SmallEiffel uses a more complete type inference algorithm and implements remaining dispatch call sites without VFT at all. They also show that inlining barely increases code size, and that for most programs, the instruction cache miss ratio does not increase significantly. Our results are consistent with theirs both for executable sizes and execution time.

In both prior works, explicit type tests are inlined, whereas we factorize them in a dispatch function. Indeed, such inlining is not expensive, because only the most frequent receiver types are tested. As explained in section 4, this inlining is not reasonable when testing all receiver types explicitly. Profile-guided receiver class prediction could also be added to SmallEiffel to partially sort and optimize the binary branching code we use for dispatch.

In an early paper [Ros88], Rose proposes a *fat* table technique for dynamic dispatch in addition to the more classical VFT-like *thin* tables. Fat tables contain inlined code for small functions, instead of function pointers, thus allowing a branch directly into the table. According to Rose, fat tables can only contain very short methods which execute with no further transfer of control.

Dean et al. [DGC95] describe the Class Hierarchy Analysis (CHA) algorithm, used to remove polymorphic call sites. They show that CHA is fast enough to be supported in an interactive programming environment. They also indicate that despite the fact CHA needs information on the whole program, it can be adapted to allow incrementality. Our results also confirm this, thanks to the high speed of the SmallEiffel compiler.

Though SmallEiffel's type inference algorithm is more developed than CHA alone, Ole Agesen's Cartesian Product Algorithm (CPA, [Age95]) is an even more powerful one. Indeed, SmallEiffel currently doesn't perform any data flow analysis [CG94b] (neither intra- nor interprocedural). Using CPA in SmallEiffel would allow us to eliminate even more dispatch call sites, thus further increasing the speed of the generated code. Further studies are needed to precisely estimate the resulting speedup and extra cost.

Hölzle and Ungar [HU95] raise an interesting question: whether object-oriented languages need special hardware. They conclude that dispatch tests cannot easily be improved with special-purpose hardware, and that the most promising way to reduce dispatch overhead is via compiler optimizations. As an exemple, SmallEiffel's optimizations generally eliminate an average of 80% of dispatch call sites, generating only very basic instructions.

Bacon and Sweeney [BS96] investigate the ability of three types of static analyses to improve C++ programs by resolving virtual function calls and reducing compiled code size. Their best algorithm, RTA (including CHA as a core component), removes on average 71% of the virtual call sites, which is comparable to SmallEiffel's 80%. The better average score for our method may come from removals that occur after type inference (ARR, AWR, DARR and OER, of section 3.4)

# 6 Conclusions

We describe a method to implement polymorphism with a very high efficiency. Its first stage consists in a powerful type inference algorithm, working on the whole system, to replace polymorphic call sites by static ones. This algorithm reaches high average scores: 80% of polymorphic calls are resolved as monomorphic in our benchmarks.

Remaining dispatch sites are then coded efficiently, by boldly eliminating VFT-like tables and function pointers, and replacing them by a static binary tree of tests. These two stages allow the third one, inlining, to be performed extensively, both for static call sites and inside multi-branch dynamic dispatch sites.

This method is implemented in a brand-new Eiffel compiler, started three years ago. To our knowledge, it is the first time such a method is applied to a full-scale project (a 50,000 line Eiffel compiler).

We demonstrate the validity of the method both in terms of speed and size of the generated code, even in the pathological cases of unpredictable or highly polymorphic (megamorphic) calls. We show the VFT overhead is avoided by this method, with no other extra cost.

The compilation technique we describe here for Eiffel may apply to any class-based language — even with genericity and multiple inheritance — but without dynamic class creation or modification. This is the case for C++ while it is not completely clear whether the method can be applied to Java, because of some more dynamic aspects. This issue seems worth investigating.

The major drawback of our method is that it requires knowledge of the whole system, which prevents separate compilation as well as the production of precompiled libraries. This may appear to be a problem for incremental development, but the most relevant aspect for the developer is compilation speed. Since the method allows very high compilation speed, as shown in section 4, we are convinced it is possible to easily integrate it in incremental production compilers.

The impossibility to deliver precompiled libraries seems to be a problem when their source code is confidential, e.g. for commercial reasons. However, a trivial solution consists in using encryption techniques. Of course this solution does not address the issue of run time shared libraries. Indeed, programs generated by SmallEiffel are able to interact with existing shared libraries (e.g made with C/C++ compilers), but it is currently impossible to create such libraries with SmallEiffel.

We think the technique can be easily adapted to produce precompiled libraries. However, precompiled library code is very likely to be less specific, hence less optimized, than the code of a standalone executable compiled from a complete system. We hope to address this in future work.

Our method uses only static information to improve code — especially dynamic dispatch — efficiency. Adding flow sensitivity to our compiler would increase performance of the generated code, since it would allow some more dispatch sites to be replaced by static calls. However, this may significantly increase compilation times.

As seen previously in section 3.4, when all branches of a dispatch function lead exactly to the same code, the corresponding polymorphic call sites are completely removed. It is also possible to further optimize the binary tree of tests by merging branches when only several of them lead to the same code. A coarse analysis of the generated dispatch trees seems to confirm that a lot of branches should be merged. In order to merge the largest number of dispatch functions properly, type ID assignment is a crucial issue. This is a rather complex problem that we have not adressed yet.

Other improvements may also come from heuristic methods, based on dynamic, run time information, such as inline caching.

## Acknowledgments

We would like like to thank the anonymous reviewers for their helpful comments and suggestions, and Dietmar Wolz who allowed us to include his benchmark results. We are also grateful to Richard M. Washington, Philippe Ribet and Charles Després for proofreading early versions of this paper.

## References

[Age95] Ole Agesen. The Cartesian Product Algorithm: Simple and Precise Type Inference of Parametric Polymorphism. In *Proceedings of the 9th European Conference on Object-Oriented Programming (ECOOP'95)*, volume 952 of *Lecture Notes in Computer Sciences*, pages 2–26. Springer-Verlag, 1995.

[Age96] Ole Agesen. *Concrete Type Inference: Delivering Object-Oriented Applications.* PhD thesis, Department of Computer Science of Stanford University, Published by Sun Microsystem Laboratories (SMLI TR-96-52), 1996.

[AH95] Ole Agesen and Urs Hölzle. Type Feedback vs. Concrete Type Inference: A Comparison of Optimization Techniques for Object-Oriented Languages. In *Proceedings of 10th Annual ACM Conference on Object-Oriented Programming Systems, Languages and Applications (OOPSLA'95)*, pages 91–107, 1995.

[AH96] Gerald Aigner and Urs Hölzle. Eliminating Virtual Function Calls in C++ Programs. In *Proceedings of the 10th European Conference on Object-Oriented Programming (ECOOP'96)*, volume 1098 of *Lecture Notes in Computer Sciences*, pages 142–166. Springer-Verlag, 1996.

[APS93] Ole Agesen, Jens Palsberg, and Michael I. Schwartzbach. Type Inference of SELF. Analysis of Objects with Dynamic and Multiple Inheritance. In *Proceedings of the 7th European Conference on Object-Oriented Programming (ECOOP'93)*, volume 707 of *Lecture Notes in Computer Sciences*, pages 247–267. Springer-Verlag, 1993.

[AU77] Alfred V. Aho and Jeffrey D. Ullman. *Principles of Compiler Design.* Addison-Wesley, Reading, Massachusetts, 1977.

[BS96] David F. Bacon and Peter F. Sweeney. Fast Static Analysis of C++ Virtual Function Calls. In *Proceedings of 11th Annual ACM Conference on Object-Oriented Programming Systems, Languages and Applications (OOPSLA'96)*, pages 324-341, 1996.

[CCZ97] Suzanne Collin, Dominique Colnet, and Olivier Zendra. Type Inference for Late Binding. The SmallEiffel Compiler. In *Joint Modular Languages Conference*, volume 1204 of *Lecture Notes in Computer Sciences*, pages 67–81. Springer-Verlag, 1997.

[CF91] Robert Cartwright and Mike Fagan. Soft Typing. In *Proceedings of the ACM SIGPLAN '91 Conference on Programming Language Design and Implementation*, pages 278–292, 1991.

[CG94a] Brad Calder and Dirk Grunwald. Reducing Indirect Function Call Overhead In C++ Programs. In *21st Annual ACM Symposium on the Principles of Programming Languages*, pages 397–408, January 1994.

[CG94b] Diane Corney and John Gough. Type Test Elimination using Typeflow Analysis. In *PLSA 1994 International Conference, Zurich*, volume 782 of *Lecture Notes in Computer Sciences*, pages 137–150. Springer-Verlag, 1994.

[CU89] Craig Chambers and David Ungar. Customization: Optimizing Compiler Technology for SELF, a Dynamically-Typed Object-Oriented Language. In *Proceedings of the ACM SIGPLAN '89 Conference on Programming Language Design and Implementation*, volume 24 of *SIGPLAN notices*, pages 146–160, 1989.

[DDG+96] Jeffrey Dean, Greg DeFouw, David Grove, Vassily Litvinov, and Craig Chambers. Vortex: An Optimizing Compiler for Object-Oriented Languages. In *Proceedings of 11th Annual ACM Conference on Object-Oriented Programming Systems, Languages and Applications (OOPSLA'96)*, pages 83–100, 1996.

[DGC95] Jeffrey Dean, David Grove, and Craig Chambers. Optimization of Object-Oriented Programs Using Static Class Hierarchy Analysis. In *Proceedings of the 9th European Conference on Object-Oriented Programming (ECOOP'95)*, volume 952 of *Lecture Notes in Computer Sciences*, pages 77–101. Springer-Verlag, 1995.

[DH96] Karel Driesen and Urs Hölzle. The Direct Cost of Virtual Function Calls in C++. In *Proceedings of 11th Annual ACM Conference on Object-Oriented Programming Systems, Languages and Applications (OOPSLA'96)*, pages 306–323, 1996.

[Dha91] D.M. Dhamdhere. Practical Adaptation of the Global Optimization Algorithm of Morel and Renvoise. *ACM Transactions on Programming Languages and Systems*, 13(2):291–294, 1991.

[DHV95] Karel Driesen, Urs Hölzle, and Jan Vitek. Message Dispatch on Pipelined Processors. In *Proceedings of the 9th European Conference on Object-Oriented Programming (ECOOP'95)*, volume 952 of *Lecture Notes in Computer Sciences*, pages 253–282. Springer-Verlag, 1995.

[DMM96] Amer Diwan, J. Eliot B. Moss, and Kathryn S. McKinley. Simple and Effective Analysis of Statically-Typed Object-Oriented Programs. In *Proceedings of 11th Annual ACM Conference on Object-Oriented Programming Systems, Languages and Applications (OOPSLA'96)*, pages 292–305, 1996.

[DS84] Peter L. Deutsch and Alan Schiffman. Efficient Implementation of the Smalltalk-80 System. In *11th Annual ACM Symposium on the Principles of Programming Languages*, 1984.

[EST95] Jonathan Eifrig, Scott Smith, and Valery Trifonov. Sound Polymorphic Type Inference for Objects. In *Proceedings of 10th Annual ACM Conference on Object-Oriented Programming Systems, Languages and Applications (OOPSLA'95)*, pages 169–184, 1995.

[GJ90] J. Graver and R. Johnson. A Type System for Smalltalk. In *17th Annual ACM Symposium on the Principles of Programming Languages*, pages 139–150, 1990.

[GR83] A. Goldberg and D. Robson. *Smalltalk-80, the Language and its Implementation.* Addison-Wesley, Reading, Massachusetts, 1983.

[HCU91] Urs Hölzle, Craig Chambers, and David Ungar. Optimizing Dynamically-Typed Object-Oriented Languages With Polymorphic Inline Caches. In *Proceedings of the 5th European Conference on Object-Oriented Programming (ECOOP'91)*, volume 512 of *Lecture Notes in Computer Sciences*, pages 21–38. Springer-Verlag, 1991.

[HU95] Urs Hölzle and David Ungar. Do Object-Oriented Languages Need Special Hardware Support ? In *Proceedings of the 9th European Conference on Object-Oriented Programming (ECOOP'95)*, volume 952 of *Lecture Notes in Computer Sciences*, pages 283–302. Springer-Verlag, 1995.

[JGS96] Bill Joy James Gosling and Guy Steele. *The Java Language Specification.* Addison Wesley, 1996.

[KRS94] Jens Knoop, Oliver Ruthing, and Bernhard Steffen. Partial Dead Code Elimination. In *Proceedings of the ACM SIGPLAN '94 Conference on Programming Language Design and Implementation*, pages 147–10000, 1994.

[Mey88] Bertrand Meyer. *Object-oriented Software Construction.* Prentice Hall, 1988.

[Mey94] Bertrand Meyer. *Eiffel, The Language.* Prentice Hall, 1994.

[Mil78] R. Milner. A Theory of Type Polymorphism in Programming. In *Journal of Computer and System Sciences*, pages 348–375, 1978.

[MNC+91] G. Masini, A. Napoli, D. Colnet, D. Léonard, and K. Tombre. *Object Oriented Languages.* Academic Press Limited, London, 1991.

[PC94] John Plevyak and Andrew A. Chien. Precise Concrete Type Inference for Object-Oriented languages. In *Proceedings of 9th Annual ACM Conference on Object-Oriented Programming Systems, Languages and Applications (OOPSLA'94)*, pages 324–340, 1994.

[PS91] Jens Palsberg and Michael I. Schwartzbach. Object-Oriented Type Inference. In *Proceedings of 6th Annual ACM Conference on Object-Oriented Programming Systems, Languages and Applications (OOPSLA'91)*, pages 146–161, 1991.

[PS92] J. Palsberg and M.I. Schwartzbach. Safety Analysis Versus Type Inference for partial Types. *Information Processing Letters*, pages 175–180, 1992.

[Ros88] John R. Rose. Fast Dispatch Mechanisms for Stock Hardware. In *Proceedings of 3rd Annual ACM Conference on Object-Oriented Programming Systems, Languages and Applications (OOPSLA'88)*, pages 27–35, 1988.

[ST84] N. Suzuki and M. Terada. Creating Efficient System for Object-Oriented Languages. In *11th Annual ACM Symposium on the Principles of Programming Languages*, pages 290–296, 1984.

[Str86] B. Stroustrup. *The C++ Programming Language.* Addison-Wesley Series in Computer Science, 1986.

[Suz81] N. Suzuki. Inferring Types in Smalltalk. In *Eighth Symposium on Principles of Programming Languages*, pages 187–199, 1981.

[UP87] David Ungar and David Patterson. What Price Smalltalk ? *IEEE Computer*, 20(1), 1987.

[US87] David Ungar and Randall B. Smith. Self: The Power of Simplicity. In *Proceedings of 2nd Annual ACM Conference on Object-Oriented Programming Systems, Languages and Applications (OOPSLA'87)*, pages 227–241, 1987.

[VHU92] Jan Vitek, R. Nigel Horspool, and James S. Uhl. Compile-Time Analysis of Object-Oriented Programs. In *International Conference on Compiler Construction*, volume 641 of *Lecture Notes in Computer Sciences*, pages 237–250. Springer-Verlag, 1992.

# Efficient Type Inclusion Tests

Jan Vitek
Object Systems Group, CUI,
Université de Genève,
Geneva, Switzerland
Jan.Vitek@cui.unige.ch

R. Nigel Horspool
Dept. of Computer Science,
University of Victoria,
Victoria, BC, Canada
nigelh@csr.uvic.ca

Andreas Krall
Institut für Computersprachen,
Technische Universität Wien,
Wien, Austria
andi@complang.tuwien.ac.at

## Abstract

A type inclusion test determines whether one type is a subtype of another. Efficient type testing techniques exist for single subtyping, but not for languages with multiple subtyping. To date, the only fast constant-time technique relies on a binary matrix encoding of the subtype relation with quadratic space requirements. In this paper, we present three new encodings of the subtype relation, the *packed encoding*, the *bit-packed encoding* and the *compact encoding*. These encodings have different characteristics. The bit-packed encoding delivers the best compression rates: on average 85% for real life programs. The packed encoding performs type inclusion tests in only 4 machine instructions. We present a fast algorithm for computing these encoding which runs in less than 13 milliseconds for PE and BPE, and 23 milliseconds for CE on an Alpha processor. Finally, we compare our results with other constant-time type inclusion tests on a suite of 11 large benchmark hierarchies.

## 1 Introduction

Many modern programming languages, particularly object-oriented ones, have been built around the notion of type conformance to allow for a form of polymorphism and code reuse. The idea is that, if a type $A$ conforms to a type $B$, then $A$ can be used in any context where $B$ is expected. This notion is essential for the code inheritance advocated by most object-oriented languages. Conformance is usually summarized by a transitive, reflexive, anti-symmetric subtype relation (<:) between the types of a hierarchy.

A type inclusion test determines if a pair of types is in the subtyping relation. Such tests are performed frequently during compilation. Most object-oriented language implementations are also able to perform tests at runtime. In SMALLTALK the *isKindOf:* method tests whether an object's class is a subclass of the class given as argument, OBERON provides type tests and type guards, JAVA *instanceof, etc.* Type tests need not always be explicitly requested by the programmer, they may also be inserted by the compiler, either as an optimization ([14]) or for safety. For example, in the JAVA code fragment shown below, the assignment to the local variable `b` is checked to ensure that the actual, runtime, type of the argument to the method is effectively a subtype of `B`:

```
class B extends A {
    void foo( A a ) {
        B b = (B) a ;
    }
}
```

Since the subtype relation is a partial order on the types of the program, type inclusion testing is more than the mere comparison of type tags. Depending on the implementation of the type test algorithm and on the dynamic frequency of tests, the cost of dynamic typechecking can strain the overall system performance.

This paper discusses the implementation of type inclusion tests in languages that allow multiple subtyping[1]. We present and compare different encodings of the subtype relation, as well as algorithms to compute these encodings and perform the type inclusion test. Our exploration of the design space of algorithms and encodings was driven by three requirements:

1. Runtime efficiency: Type tests should be fast. Our original motivation for this research was to optimize method dispatch ([15], [14]). To this end, the cost of testing for type inclusion had to be comparable to the cost of dispatch in statically typed languages (5 machine instructions, but see [8]). We also insist on constant-time tests[2] as we believe that the cost of language primitives should be predictable.

[1]Note that we make a difference between subtyping and inheritance. JAVA is a single inheritance language with multiple subtyping.

[2]In this context, constant means *constant number of instructions*, we did not explore cache behavior.


OOPSLA '97 10/97 GA, USA

2. Space efficiency: The runtime data structures that encode the subtype relation must be small. Furthermore, the code sequence emitted by the compiler for each static occurrence of a subtype test must be short.

3. Incremental hierarchy modifications: Support for runtime updates of the subtype relation. The concern here is that the cost in space and time of recomputing the encoding must not be prohibitive.

To the best of our knowledge no existing technique meets our requirements. Algorithms based on dynamic data structures such as linked lists and hash tables are slow and exhibit unpredictable behavior. Constant-time techniques either require large amounts of space, as for the bit matrix encoding, or are quite complex to compute, as for the hierarchical encoding [2], [12].

In this paper, we present three new encodings of the subtype relation, the *packed encoding*, the *bit-packed encoding* and the *compact encoding*. We describe how they are computed and how they are used to implement constant-time tests. The packed encoding extends to multiple subtyping an algorithm first described by Cohen [3] and rediscovered independently by Queinnec [13]. When multiple subtyping is not used our solution is the same as Cohen's. We improve on the runtime performance of tests by removing a bound check advocated by Cohen. The code sequence that implements the type test is short enough to be inlined and thus avoid the cost of an extra call. The computation of the packed encoding is very fast and requires little memory. Thus, it is well suited for on-the-fly updates of the hierarchy. Furthermore, there are categories of updates that do not require recomputing the encoding. The second new encoding, called bit-packed encoding, reduces further the space requirement of the packed encoding at the cost of slower type inclusion tests. The last encoding, compact encoding, adapts the compact dispatch table technique of Vitek and Horspool [16]. It is designed for very large hierarchies. For small and medium-sized ones, it is less efficient than the packed encoding. We compare the new encodings and algorithms to the bit matrix encoding and the near optimal hierarchical encoding of [12] and conclude with guidelines for choosing an encoding of the subtype relation.

The remainder of this paper is organized as follows. Section 2 introduces terminology, important definitions, and a running example. Section 3 briefly reviews previous work in the field, including the binary matrix encoding, Cohen's encoding and the near optimal hierarchical encoding. Section 4 presents the packed encoding, the type inclusion test and the encoding construction algorithm. Section 5 presents the bit-packed encoding. Section 6 presents the compact encoding. Section 7 compares time and space requirements of the techniques on a set of 11 benchmark programs. Finally, section 8 presents our conclusions.

## 2 Definitions and Example Hierarchy

A type hierarchy $H = \langle \mathcal{T}, <: \rangle$ is a set of types $\mathcal{T}$ and a reflexive, transitive, anti-symmetric subtype relation $<:$. If $A <: B$ holds, then we say that $A$ is a subtype of $B$ and $B$ is a supertype of $A$. In class-based languages this hierarchy is defined explicitly by the programmer through the subclassing relationship between classes. In languages with structural subtyping, the subtype relation is derived automatically.

We also define an anti-reflexive, anti-symmetric direct subtype relation $<:_d$

$$
\begin{aligned}
<:_d \;\equiv\; & \{\langle x \in \mathcal{T}, y \in \mathcal{T}\rangle | x <: y \wedge \\
& (\nexists z \in \mathcal{T} | x \neq z \wedge y \neq z \wedge x <: z <: y)\}
\end{aligned}
$$

The subtype relation is represented by a directed acyclic graph, shown in fig. 1, with vertices for types and edges for the subtype relation. By convention, we draw supertypes above their subtypes and draw only edges in $<:_d$. We also need the following definitions:

$$
\begin{aligned}
roots(\mathcal{T}) &\equiv \{x \in \mathcal{T} |\ \nexists y \in \mathcal{T} : x <: y\} \\
parents(x) &\equiv \{y \in \mathcal{T} | x <:_d y\} \\
children(x) &\equiv \{y \in \mathcal{T} | y <:_d x\} \\
ancestors(x) &\equiv \{y \in \mathcal{T} | x <: y\} \\
descendants(x) &\equiv \{y \in \mathcal{T} | y <: x\} \\
multis(\mathcal{T}) &\equiv \{x \in \mathcal{T} | card(parents(x)) > 1\}
\end{aligned}
$$

where $card(\mathcal{S})$ is the cardinality of a set $\mathcal{S}$. *Roots* is the set of top level types. *Parents* and *children* are sets of direct supertypes and subtypes, respectively. *Ancestors* and *descendants* are sets of all subtypes and supertypes of a type. *Multis* is the set of all types with more than a single direct supertype.

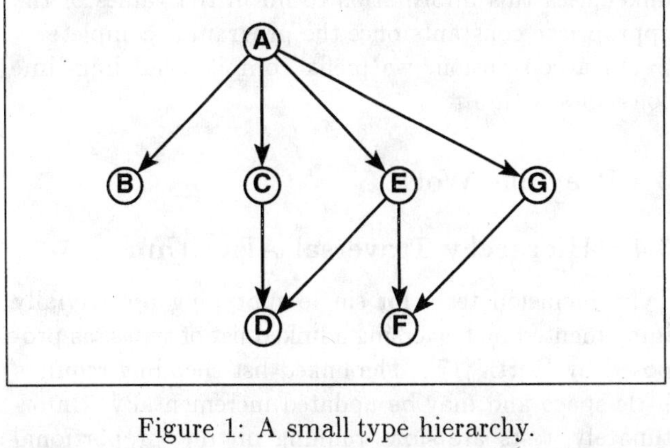


Figure 1: A small type hierarchy.

```
class Object_rep {
      Type_rep type_rep
      ...
}
```

Figure 2: Object runtime representation.

A *single subtyping* type hierarchy restricts the number of direct parents to one, $card(parents(x)) \leq 1$. We assume single rooted hierarchies, *i.e.* $card(roots(\mathcal{T})) = 1$. In practice, we fix hierarchies that do not fulfill this assumption by adding an extra root type $R$ so that $children(R) = roots(\mathcal{T})$. The hierarchy of figure 1 is a multiple subtyping hierarchy, with $roots(\mathcal{T}) = \{A\}$, $multis(\mathcal{T}) = \{D, F\}$, $parents(F) = \{E, G\}$ and $ancestors(F) = \{A, E, G\}$.

We define the *level* of a type in a hierarchy as the length of its longest path to the root:

$$level(x) \equiv \begin{cases} 0 & \textbf{if } parents(x) = \{\} \\ max(L) + 1 & \textbf{otherwise} \end{cases}$$
$$\textbf{where} \quad L \equiv \{level(y) | y \in parents(x)\}$$

For the runtime representation of objects, we assume they are implemented by data structures with, as a common prefix, a reference to a type information data structure, the `Type_rep` field of fig. 2. In many implementations this field can be merged with the dispatch data structure (*e.g.* the `vtbl` of C++).

Unless explicitly stated, the type test instruction sequences check subtyping against a type known at compile-time. This corresponds to a test of the form

```
obj instanceof A
```

where `A` is a type constant. This is the most frequent use of a subtype test. We assume that the compiler or linker uses this information to fill in the values of the appropriate constants once the program is complete.

As a convention, we prefix compile- and link-time constants with a `#`.

## 3 Previous Work

### 3.1 Hierarchy Traversal Algorithms

Type inclusion tests for single subtyping are trivially implemented by traversing a linked list of types, as proposed by Wirth [17]. The linked list encoding requires little space and may be updated incrementally. Unfortunately, tests are slow, running in time proportional to the distance between the two types in $<:_d$. This led Wirth to switch to a constant-time scheme for OBERON [18]. Linked data structures for multiple subtyping only increase the cost of type tests. We have experimented with linked representations as well as with other non-constant-time schemes based on hashing while working on this paper. Non-constant-time techniques are much slower than the algorithms discussed in the remainder of the paper. We decided to concentrate on constant-time solutions.

### 3.2 Constant-time Algorithms

#### 3.2.1 Binary Matrix (BM)

Type inclusion tests can be performed in constant-time if the subtype relation is encoded as a binary matrix. If $N = card(\mathcal{T})$, and $\gamma : \mathcal{T} \rightarrow [1 \ldots N]$ is a one-to-one mapping from types to indices, we build a $N \times N$ binary matrix $M_{BM}$ such that:

$$M_{BM}[\gamma(x), \gamma(y)] \equiv \begin{cases} 1 & \textbf{if } x <: y \\ 0 & \textbf{otherwise} \end{cases}$$

The binary matrix encoding for the hierarchy of fig. 1 is shown in fig. 3(a).

The runtime representation of types decomposes the matrix into rows corresponding to a type and stores each row into a `Type_rep` data structure, fig. 3(b). Every type representation has the same layout. This data structure has two fields: a position, `pos`, and a sequence of $(N + 31)$ **mod** 32 words, `row`. The position field encodes $\gamma$ and is used during type inclusion testing to compute a word index and a bit index. If we assume 32 bit words, the word index is `pos >> 5` and the bit index is `pos & 31`.

With BM, a type inclusion test is simply an array access, a bit shift and a comparison. Figure 3(c) tests whether the type of an object `obj` is a subtype of a type with known `word_pos` and `bit_pos`. The machine instruction sequence for this test is given in the appendix.

This encoding is trivial to compute. Its main drawback is that it has quadratic space requirements. For large programs, half megabyte matrices are easily conceivable. Nevertheless, the simplicity of the binary matrix has motivated its use in practice [11], [4].

The other constant-time algorithms presented in this paper use encodings which can be viewed as compressed forms of the binary matrix. The constraint on the compression is that very fast random access to elements must be guaranteed. In this view, the works on parse table optimization and dispatch table optimization are closely related, as, in both cases, their aim is to compress sparsely populated matrices. The parse table compression techniques discussed by Dencker, Dürre and

|   | $\gamma$ |
|---|---|
| A | 0 |
| B | 1 |
| C | 2 |
| D | 3 |
| E | 4 |
| F | 5 |
| G | 6 |

$\gamma$

|   | | | | | | | |
|---|---|---|---|---|---|---|---|
| A | 1 | 0 | 0 | 0 | 0 | 0 | 0 |
| B | 1 | 1 | 0 | 0 | 0 | 0 | 0 |
| C | 1 | 0 | 1 | 0 | 0 | 0 | 0 |
| D | 1 | 0 | 1 | 1 | 1 | 0 | 0 |
| E | 1 | 0 | 0 | 0 | 1 | 0 | 0 |
| F | 1 | 1 | 0 | 0 | 0 | 1 | 1 |
| G | 1 | 0 | 0 | 0 | 0 | 0 | 1 |
| $\gamma$ | 0 | 1 | 2 | 3 | 4 | 5 | 6 |

$M_{BM}$

(a) The encoding of figure 1.

```
class   Type_rep  {
        int32  pos
        array [1...N] of int32  row
}
```

(a) Runtime data structures.

```
Type_rep  type := obj.type_rep
int32  word := type.row[#word_pos]
if  (bit_extract(word, #bit_pos) = 1)
```

(c) Type inclusion test.

Figure 3: Binary Matrix (BM).

Heuft [5] have influenced works in the field of dispatch table compression [7], [15]. The compact encoding is in fact a straightforward adaptation of compact dispatch tables of [15].

### 3.2.2 Cohen's Algorithm

Cohen proposed the first practical algorithm for performing subtype tests in constant-time [3]. Cohen's idea is a variation of Dijkstra's "displays" [6]. Each type is identified by a unique type identifier, **tid**, which is simply a number. The runtime type information data structure also records each type's complete path to the root as a sequence of type identifiers. The key trick is to build, for each type $x$, an array of $card(ancestors(x))$ type identifiers so that for each ancestor $y$, the **tid** of $y$ is stored at an offset equal to $level(y)$ in the array. The Cohen encoding for sample hierarchy of fig. 4(a) is given in fig. 4(b).

With this encoding, type inclusion tests reduce to a bound-checked array access and a comparison operation. The bound check is necessary as array sizes are not uniform. The runtime data structure, shown in fig. 4(c), consists of a level field, **level** and a sequence of $L$ type identifiers, **row**, where $L$ is equal to the value of the current type's **level**. Note that the type identifier of a type $x$ is stored at $x$**.row[**$x$**.level]**. The code sequence that tests whether an object's type is a subtype of some known type is shown in fig. 4(d).

The advantages of Cohen's algorithm are that it is both easy to understand and easy to implement, it performs tests in constant-time and requires little space. The packed algorithm of section 4 extends the algorithm to multiple subtyping and proposes a type inclusion test that is faster than the one outlined above.

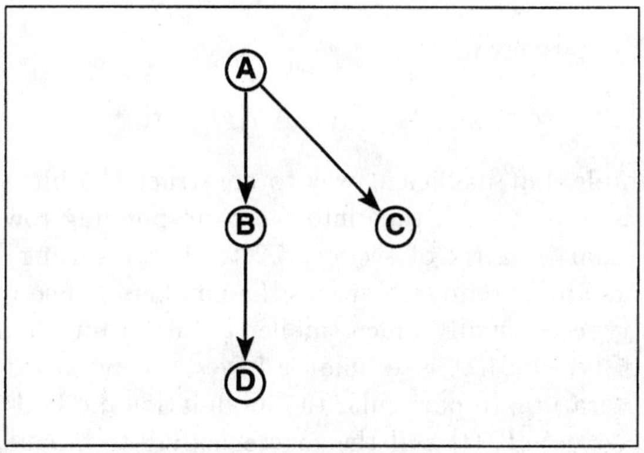


(a) A small single subtyping hierarchy.

|   | tid | *lvl* |
|---|---|---|
| A | 1 | 0 |
| B | 2 | 1 |
| C | 3 | 1 |
| D | 4 | 2 |

|   | | | |
|---|---|---|---|
| A | 1 | | |
| B | 1 | 2 | |
| C | 1 | 3 | |
| D | 1 | 2 | 4 |

(b) The encoding of figure 4(a).

```
class  Type_rep  {
       int16  level
       array [0...L] of int16  row
}
```

(c) Runtime data structures.

```
Type_rep type := obj.type_rep
if    (type.level ≤ #level
   &&  type.row[#level] = #tid )
```

(d) Type inclusion test.

Figure 4: Cohen's encoding.

### 3.2.3 Hierarchical Encodings (NHE)

Hierarchical encoding represents each type with a set of integers. This set must be chosen so that

$$x <: y \quad \Leftrightarrow \quad \gamma(x) \subseteq \gamma(y)$$

where $\gamma(x)$ maps type $x$ to its set representation. Thus, the set of a subtype has to be a superset of the set representing its parent. The sets have a natural representation as bit vectors; an example is shown in fig. 5(a). In the bit vector representation the test function becomes

$$x <: y \quad \Leftrightarrow \quad \gamma(x) \vee \gamma(y) = \gamma(x)$$

or alternatively

$$x <: y \quad \Leftrightarrow \quad \gamma(x) \wedge \gamma(y) = \gamma(y)$$

A simple, but inefficient way to construct the bit vectors is to map each type into the corresponding row of the binary matrix of section 3.2.1. The resulting bit vectors are extremely sparse as the number of ancestors of a type is usually much smaller than the total number of types. Better techniques have been proposed in the literature, in particular the modulation method[3] of Aït-Kaci *et al.* [1] and the gene encoding technique of Caseau [2], which try to minimize the range of integers used to construct the sets, thus shortening the corresponding bit vectors. It is well known that finding an optimal bit vector encoding for partial ordered sets is NP-hard [10] and that there exist classes of partial ordered sets (distributive and simplicial lattices) where an optimal encoding is as large as the number of types with only one supertype [10]. Fortunately, type hierarchies can be encoded much more compactly than distributive lattices. In a previous paper, we have developed a new and improved version of the Caseau approach [2] which we call Near Optimal Hierarchical Encoding (NHE) [12]. This version generalizes Caseau's algorithm by expressing it as a graph coloring problem. It is able to encode arbitrary partially ordered sets rather than just lattices [2]. Our algorithm generates the sets faster and generates much smaller sets (about 50% percent smaller than our implementation of [2]), thus making type inclusion tests more efficient.

A complete description of the algorithm can be found in [12], we will summarize it briefly here. A simple version of the technique would assign a set element (*i.e.* a position of a bit in the bit vector) to each node in the type hierarchy graph. This element distinguishes the node from other nodes. This distinguishing element is called a gene by Caseau. The set representation for a type is formed as the union of all its ancestor's sets of genes plus its own gene. However, if the set of ancestors of a type $x$ with more than one immediate parent is not a subset of another ancestor set, then $x$ does not need a gene. We can construct a conflict graph where the nodes represent types and the edges connect types which are not allowed to use the same gene. Graph coloring is then used to assign different genes to conflicting nodes. A crucial part of the technique, performed prior to computing the conflict graph, is inserting extra nodes into the hierarchy in order to balance the graph – the aim is to reduce the maximum number of children possessed by any node and that will tend to reduce the number of nodes that require distinct genes. Fig. 5(a) shows the NHE encoding of the example hierarchy (fig. 1). The algorithm uses only four genes as $D$ and $F$ are able to reuse the genes of their parents, the root $A$ does not need a gene as it encodes the empty set. This technique yields the optimal encoding for single subtyping and near optimal encoding for multiple subtyping hierarchies.

The bit vector is of fixed size and can be stored at any fixed position inside the class object. The runtime data structure is shown in fig. 5(b), `row` is a sequence of $H$ integers, $H$ is the length of the bit string in words.

| | |
|---|---|
| A | 0000 |
| B | 1000 |
| C | 0100 |
| D | 0110 |
| E | 0010 |
| F | 0011 |
| G | 0001 |

(a) The encoding fig. 1.

```
class Type_rep {
    array [1...H] of int32 row
}
```

(b) Runtime data structures.

```
Type_rep type := obj.type_rep
if ( (type.row[i] & #row_i) = #row_i)
  // repeated for i from 1 to H
```

(c) Type inclusion test.

Figure 5: Near Optimal Hierarchical Encoding (NHE).

[3] The modulation method is an efficient encoding of lattices which is used to perform lattice operations such as finding the least upper bound or greatest lower bound, as well as relative complementation. Type hierarchies are not necessarily lattices.

The comparison part of the test function has to be replicated for each machine word used in the bit vector. This leads to the problem that with increasing code length both execution time and instruction space increase. The number of unrollings is only known at link time when the entire hierarchy is at hand, so the algorithm is constant-time at run-time but not constant-time at compile-time[4]. The implementation of the run-time test against a known bit vector (**#row**) is shown in fig. 5(c).

This implementation will be referred to as inline near optimal hierarchical encoding, INHE. It has three drawbacks: first it requires varying numbers of instructions, second, even in the best case, the instruction sequence is longer than for the other algorithms. This causes code bloat as discussed in sect. 7.3. A slightly slower alternative is to wrap the test in a function, we refer to this solution as the generic near optimal hierarchical encoding, or GNHE. GNHE is implemented by coding a number of similar type test functions, one for each unrolling factor. Then, depending on the length of the bit vector, the appropriate test function will be called. The third drawback of the method is that it is computationally intensive and that the full encoding must be regenerated after any change to the type hierarchy.

### 3.3 Relative Numbering

We mention briefly one last encoding of the subtype relation based on relative numbering of trees. In a tree it is possible to find out if a node is a child of another node as follows. For each node store two numbers, *left* and *right*. Traverse the tree in order, for each new node increment a counter $c$. When a node is first encountered, store $c$ in *left*. When the traversal leaves the node store the current value of $c$ in *right*. A node $n_1$ is a child of a node $n_2$ if

$$n_2.left \leq n_1.left \;\wedge\; n_1.left \leq n_2.right$$

A single subtyping hierarchy is a tree; relative numbering is therefore a very compact and elegant representation of the single subtyping relation. This scheme is used in the DEC SRC MODULA-3 system. Unfortunately, there is no obvious way to extend the technique to multiple subtyping.

[4] This use of "constant" is a slight abuse of language. In our set of benchmark programs the maximal number of unrollings is 3 as the longest bit vector length is 96, [12]. The longest test takes 18 machine instructions. The shortest test is performed in 8 machine instructions. Note also that the number of instructions is solely determined by the supertype. So, if the supertype is known at link-time (this accounts for the overwhelming majority of type tests in real programs) the number of instructions needed is also known statically.

## 4 Packed Encoding (PE)

Experience with binary matrices shows that they are always sparse. It is therefore not surprising that they can be compressed. We propose a technique which works well in practice and manages to reduce the size of encodings of real type hierarchies.

In the binary matrix encoding, $\gamma$ is a one-to-one mapping from types to matrix indices. Each type has a column and a row of the matrix. In the packed encoding, we propose to reuse columns for unrelated types. This reuse of columns is similar in spirit to the reuse of genes in hierarchical encoding and to the levels of Cohen's algorithm.

### 4.1 The encoding

For the packed encoding of a hierarchy $\langle \mathcal{T}, <: \rangle$ with $N$ types, we construct a $N \times P$ bucket matrix $M_{PE}$

$$M_{PE} : \mathcal{T} \times [1 \ldots P] \rightarrow tid$$

so that

$$x <: y \;\Leftrightarrow\; M_{PE}[x, \gamma(y)] = M_{PE}[y, \gamma(y)]$$

where $\gamma : \mathcal{T} \rightarrow [1 \ldots P]$ maps types to columns indices (*N.B.* we call columns of $M_{PE}$, *buckets*), and $\tau : \mathcal{T} \rightarrow tid$ maps types to identifiers, which are simply small numbers. The number of columns $P$ is computed by the bucket assignment algorithm of sec. 4.3. For an example of packed encoding, consider fig. 6 which encodes the hierarchy of fig. 1.

The type inclusion test to determine whether $A$ is a subtype of $B$ proceeds as follows:

$$\begin{aligned} A <: B \;\equiv\; & M_{PE}[A, \gamma(B)] = M_{PE}[B, \gamma(B)] \\ & M_{PE}[A, 1] = M_{PE}[B, 1] \\ & 1 = 1 \\ & true \end{aligned}$$

Buckets partition the set of types according to a simple rule: no two types in the same bucket may have

| | $\gamma$ |
|---|---|
| A | 1 |
| B | 2 |
| C | 2 |
| D | 3 |
| E | 4 |
| F | 3 |
| G | 2 |

| | $\tau$ |
|---|---|
| A | 1 |
| B | 1 |
| C | 2 |
| D | 1 |
| E | 1 |
| F | 2 |
| G | 3 |

| $M_{PE}$ | | | | |
|---|---|---|---|---|
| A | 1 | 0 | 0 | 0 |
| B | 1 | 1 | 0 | 0 |
| C | 1 | 2 | 0 | 0 |
| D | 1 | 2 | 1 | 0 |
| E | 1 | 0 | 0 | 1 |
| F | 1 | 3 | 2 | 1 |
| G | 1 | 3 | 0 | 0 |
| $\gamma$ | 1 | 2 | 3 | 4 |

Figure 6: Packed encoding of fig. 1.

common descendants. Thus a valid packed encoding must abide by the following *bucket assignment rule.*

**Rule 1** *Bucket assignment. Types in the same bucket can not have common subtypes.*

$$\gamma(x) = \gamma(y) \quad \Rightarrow \quad descendants(x) \cap descendants(y) = \{\}$$

*where* $x \in \mathcal{T} \ \wedge \ y \in \mathcal{T} \ \wedge \ x \neq y.$

Clearly, this rule implies that in pathological cases the packed encoding may degenerate into a binary matrix. This occurs for a flat hierarchy with a bottom element that is a subtype of every other type. Fortunately, such a hierarchy is unlikely as it implies that some type has all the operations and attributes of all other types in the program.

Identifiers are assigned so as to ensure that two types in the same bucket will not have the same identifier. A valid encoding must abide by the following *identifier assignment rule.*

**Rule 2** *Identifier assignment rule. Types in the same bucket have different identifiers.*

$$\gamma(x) = \gamma(y) \quad \Rightarrow \quad \tau(x) \neq \tau(y)$$

*where* $x \in \mathcal{T} \ \wedge \ y \in \mathcal{T} \ \wedge \ x \neq y.$

## 4.2 Implementing type inclusion tests

The runtime representation of a type assumed by the packed encoding is shown in fig. 7(a). It is composed of a short integer `bucket` which represents the bucket to which the type was assigned, *i.e.* the value of $\gamma$, and an array of bytes, `row`, which contains the identifiers of all ancestors of the type—each array is a row of $M_{PE}$. The type identifier (*i.e.* the value of $\tau$) does not need to be stored explicitly as it can be fetched from `row`. Furthermore, type identifiers can be small numbers as the assignment rule (rule 2) does not require them to be globally unique. Identifiers need only be unique within a bucket. In our set of benchmarks, only a few buckets contain more than 255 types. So, we chose to limit identifiers to a byte and create additional buckets when necessary.

The type inclusion test for checking whether an object `obj` is a subtype of a type with identifier `#tid` and bucket `#bucket` is shown in fig. 7(b). The type test is faster than Cohen's encoding; it is not necessary to perform a bound check since all `row` arrays have the same length. The machine instruction sequence, shown in the appendix, is four instructions long. This is shorter than any known multiple inheritance dispatch sequence[5] and probably short enough to be inlined.

[5]Single inheritance dispatch in a statically typed language can be done in three instructions [8]. Note also, that multiple subtyping dispatch in JAVA can be done in 3 instructions [11].

```
class Type_rep {
    int8  bucket
    array [1 ...P] of int8  row
}
```

(a) Runtime data structures.

```
Type_rep   type := obj.type_rep
if  (type.row[ #bucket ]  =  #tid )
```

(b) Type inclusion test.

Figure 7: Implementing the Packed Encoding (PE).

## 4.3 Computing the packed encoding

The bucket assignment rule can be turned into an algorithm without too much effort. It suffices to associate with every type the set of its descendants, and to maintain, for every bucket, a set that is the union of the descendant sets of all of the types it contains. The algorithm is then to build a list of types sorted by their level, to guarantee that we visit parents before children. Then, for each type in the list, the algorithm must find a bucket for which the intersection between the bucket's set of descendants and the type's set of descendants is empty. If no such bucket can be found, a new bucket is added. This is what we did in an earlier version of this paper. Unfortunately, the result is an extremely inefficient algorithm which spends most of its time performing intersections and unions of large sets—the sets are arbitrary subsets of $\mathcal{T}$.

We present a more sophisticated algorithm which is an order of magnitude faster and yet remains simple and easy to implement. The crucial idea is to separate the single subtyping portion of the hierarchy from the multiple subtyping portion and to use this to refine the bucket assignment rule. We start by defining three disjoint subsets of $\mathcal{T}$. The first subset is the set of *join* types. A join type is a type with multiple parents (*i.e.* direct supertypes) which has only single subtyping descendants.

$$join(\mathcal{T}) \equiv \ \{x \in multis(\mathcal{T}) | \ \nexists y \in multis(\mathcal{T}) : y <: x\}$$

The second subset is the set of *spine* types. Any ancestor of a join type belongs to this set.

$$spine(\mathcal{T}) \ \equiv \ \{x \in ancestors(y) | y \in join(\mathcal{T})\}$$

The last subset is the set of *plain* types, these are types which are neither in spine nor in join. A plain type is a type that has a single parent, and whose descendants are also plain types.

$$plain(\mathcal{T}) \equiv \mathcal{T} - (spine(\mathcal{T}) \cup join(\mathcal{T}))$$

We will also use two list building functions *level_order* and *rev_level_order*. Each of them returns a list of types sorted by their level.

$$\begin{aligned} level\_order(\mathcal{S}) &\equiv [x_1, \ldots, x_N] \\ &\quad \textbf{where } N \equiv card(\mathcal{S}), \\ &\quad \textbf{and } level(x_i) \leq level(x_{i+1}) \end{aligned}$$

$$\begin{aligned} rev\_level\_order(\mathcal{S}) &\equiv [x_1, \ldots, x_N] \\ &\quad \textbf{where } N \equiv card(\mathcal{S}), \\ &\quad \textbf{and } level(x_i) \geq level(x_{i+1}) \end{aligned}$$

**Rule 3** *Bucket assignment (plain and join). Plain and join types may be assigned the same bucket only if they are not related by* <:.

$$\gamma(x) = \gamma(y) \Rightarrow x \notin ancestors(y) \qquad (a)$$

$$\gamma(x) = \gamma(y) \Rightarrow y \notin ancestors(x) \qquad (b)$$

*where* $x \in join(\mathcal{T}) \cup plain(\mathcal{T}) \wedge y \in join(\mathcal{T}) \cup plain(\mathcal{T}) \wedge x \neq y$.

This rule is trivial since, for single subtyping, the only way for two types to have a common descendant is that either $x <: y$ or $y <: x$.

**Rule 4** *Bucket assignment (spine). Two spine types may be assigned the same bucket only if they have no join type in common.*

$$\gamma(x) = \gamma(y) \Rightarrow joins(x) \cap joins(y) = \{\}$$

*where* $x \in spine(\mathcal{T}) \wedge y \in spine(\mathcal{T}) \wedge x \neq y \wedge joins(z) \equiv descendants(z) \cap join(\mathcal{T})$.

This rule is equivalent to rule 1. By construction, every spine type has one or more join nodes in its descendants list. If $x <: y$ then $joins(x) \cap joins(y) = joins(x) \neq \{\}$. If $y <: x$ then $joins(x) \cap joins(y) = joins(y) \neq \{\}$. If $x \not<: y$ and $y :\not> y$ then if the types have common descendants at least one of them must be in $spine(\mathcal{T})$.

The bucket assignment algorithm, shown in fig. 8 starts by assigning buckets to spine types, as the other types depend on them. Spine types are visited in reverse topological order as the lower types are less likely to conflict with each other. A spine type is added to a bucket if the bucket is not full (fewer than 255 types) and if adding the type to the bucket does not violate rule 4. Checking the validity of the rule requires types and buckets to have a set of join types. The set of join types of the bucket is updated each time a type is added. Note that the size of these sets is limited by the number of join nodes in the hierarchy. If there is no bucket where to put the type, a new bucket must be created. Another reason for visiting join types in reverse level order is that we can build the join sets while

```
T := load_hierarchy()
Buckets := {}

foreach(x ∈ T)
   x.joins := {}
   x.used := {}
foreach(x ∈ join(T))
   foreach(y ∈ parents(x))
      y.joins := y.joins ∪ {x}

foreach(x ∈ rev_level_order(spine(T)))
   found := false
   foreach(b ∈ Buckets)
      if(card(b.elements) ≤ 255
         ∧ x.joins ∩ b.joins = {})
         found := true
         b.elements := b.elements ∪ {x}
         b.joins := b.joins ∪ x.joins
         break
   if(found = false)
      b := newBucket
      Buckets := Buckets ∪ {b}
      b.elements := b.elements ∪ {x}
      b.joins := x.joins

   foreach(y ∈ parents(x))
      y.joins := y.joins ∪ x.joins

foreach(x ∈ level_order(plain(T) ∪ join(T)))
   found := false
   foreach(b ∈ Buckets)
      if(card(b.elements) < 255 ∧ b ∉ x.used)
         found := true
         b.elements := b.elements ∪ {x}
         x.used := x.used ∪ {b}
         break
   if(found = false)
      b := newBucket
      Buckets := Buckets ∪ {b}
      b.elements := b.elements ∪ {x}
      x.used := x.used ∪ {b}
   foreach(y ∈ children(x))
      y.used := y.used ∪ x.used
```

Figure 8: Bucket assignment algorithm.

assigning buckets. After assigning a bucket to a type, the join sets of the parents of the type are updated with the joins of the current type. The second part of the algorithm deals with non-spine types. These types are visited in level order to ensure that buckets are assigned to parents before children. All that needs to be done is to compute for every type, the set of buckets that have already been used by its ancestors. Any bucket not in this set can be used for the type. This implements rule 3.

Building the runtime data structures once the buckets have been assigned is merely a matter of traversing the bucket set in any order and creating `Type_rep` objects. We maintain a counter $n$ that indicate the column index of the bucket, this is used for setting `bucket` ($\gamma$) and an intra bucket counter $c$ which is used for type identifiers ($\tau$). The size of the rows, $P$, is the cardinality of the set of buckets. The last stage of the algorithm is to traverse the hierarchy in level order and set the `row` fields of all types to their correct values.

```
P = card(Buckets)
n := 0
foreach(b ∈ Buckets)
    c := 0
    n := n + 1
    foreach(x ∈ b.elements)
        c := c + 1
        x.type := new Type_rep
        x.type.bucket := n
        x.type.row :=
                newArray [1...P] of int8
        foreach(i ∈ [1...P])
            x.type.row[i] := 0
        x.type.row[x.type.γ] := c

foreach(x ∈ level_order(T))
    foreach(y ∈ children(x))
        foreach(i ∈ [1...P])
            y.type.row[i] :=
                y.type.row[i] | x.type.row[i]
                // | is the logical-or operator
```

Figure 9: Building the PE type representation.

## 4.4 Discussion

The bucket construction algorithm is quite fast (see sec. 7.2), but does not guarantee an optimal bucket assignment. In some cases it may allocate too many buckets. Consider the type hierarchy of fig. 10, The optimal assignment is

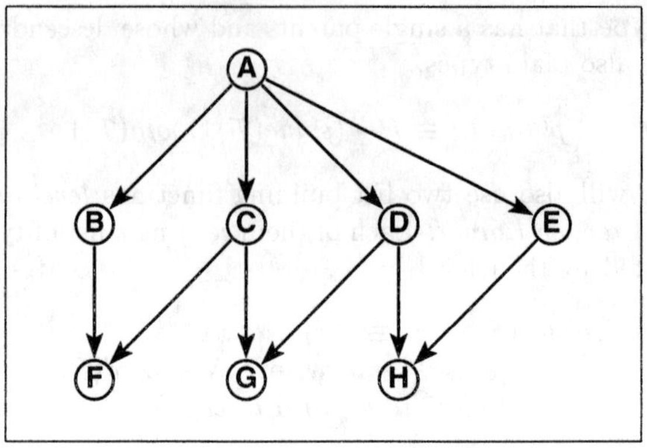


Figure 10: Type hierarchy.

| Bucket | 1 | 2 | 3 | 4 |
|---|---|---|---|---|
| Types | $A$ | $B, D$ | $C, E$ | $F, G, H$ |

Depending on the order in which level–1 types are visited the algorithm may return the following bucket assignment:

| Bucket | 1 | 2 | 3 | 4 | 5 |
|---|---|---|---|---|---|
| Types | $A$ | $B, E$ | $C, H$ | $D, F$ | $G$ |

This assignment requires one extra bucket. Because $B$ and $E$ were put in the same bucket, $C$ and $D$ had to be placed in different buckets.

The obvious approach for finding the optimal assignment would require graph coloring, which we wanted to avoid, as one of the strong points of this algorithm is its speed. But, before looking for more complex solutions, it is a good idea to evaluate what there is to gain. One way to do this is to compute an approximation of the lower bound on the number of buckets needed in our set of benchmark programs and compare that with the number of buckets generated by the bucket assignment algorithm. A very simple lower bound is the largest value of *ancestors*($x$) for each hierarchy. It is guaranteed by the bucket assignment rules that the optimal encoding will have at least that many buckets. We have done that for our benchmark programs. The results are summarized in table 1. The only three programs where we actually lose are GEO, EDE and LOV; all three are the output of a code generator which makes extensive use of multiple subtyping—see 7.1 for a description

| *Hierarchy* | VW2 | DG3 | NXT | ET+ | UNI | SLF |
|---|---|---|---|---|---|---|
| *max ancestors* | 15 | 14 | 8 | 9 | 10 | 41 |
| *comp. buckets* | 15 | 14 | 8 | 9 | 10 | 41 |

| *Hierarchy* | GEO | LOV | EDE | LAU | JAV |
|---|---|---|---|---|---|
| *max ancestors* | 50 | 24 | 23 | 16 | 7 |
| *comp. buckets* | 51 | 27 | 26 | 16 | 7 |

Table 1: Assessing the quality of bucket assignments.

of the benchmark suite. The difference in the case of GEO is one bucket and, for LOV and EDE, three buckets. Such small numbers do not warrant complicating the algorithm. We also believe that these examples are atypical in their heavy use of multiple subtyping.

## 5 Bit-Packed Encoding (BPE)

The choice of an uniform bucket length for the packed encoding was motivated by an emphasis on speed of type inclusion tests. If data size is the issue, the encoding can be compressed further by allowing variable bucket lengths. A length of 8 bits is used for PE which allows 255 types to share the same bucket. In practice, the number of types that actually share a bucket is much lower. In fact, for the multiple subtyping hierarchies of our benchmark suites, 33% of the buckets contain a single type. These buckets actually need a single bit. The *bit-packed encoding* (BPE) uses variable sized representations for buckets. With this simple change it improves the compression rate of all multiple subtyping examples of the benchmark suite (see section 7.3).

The BPE encoding is generated by an algorithm which is run after PE generation and which simply packs as many buckets as possible in a single word. Fig. 11(a) shows the result for the hierarchy of fig. 1. The value of $\gamma$ is the offset in the bit string, $\tau$ is the type identifier bit string. For practical purposes, the BPE algorithm will not split type identifiers across word boundaries. Thus words may be padded to 32 bits if needed. In fig. 11(a), the identifier of type A requires single bit while those of all the other type require 2 bits.

The main differences between PE and BPE are their runtime data structures and type inclusion tests. With the bit-packed encoding, each `Type_rep` contains an array of $B$ 32 bit words, `row`, where $B$ is obtained by packing the PE encoding. Type identifiers are represented by numbers no larger than 8 bits at an arbitrary offset in a word. To be able to extract a type identifier, it is thus necessary to know its word, its position in a word and its length. Thus, a `Type_rep` contains a `bucket_word` field, a `bucket_pos` field and a `bucket_mask`. The last field is used to mask irrelevant bits out of a byte. The runtime data structure is shown in fig. 11(b). The type inclusion test, shown in fig. 11(c), extracts the type identifier by shifting by `bucket_pos` and masking with `bucket_mask`.

We refer to the machine instruction sequence for the BPE test of fig. 11(c) as *inline bit-packed encoding* (IBPE). The IBPE type test takes 6 machine instructions. Similarly to the INHE, long instruction sequences may lead to code bloat. This can be avoided by performing most of the type test out of line, in a separate procedure. This variant of BPE is called *generic bit-packed encoding* (GBPE). It reduces the per test site overhead to 3 instructions. The GBPE type test is given in the appendix.

The BPE has another advantage over PE. For the worst case scenario of a flat hierarchy described in section 4.1, the space needed for BPE is exactly the same as for the binary matrix. With PE's uniform bucket lengths, the encoding is 8 times as large.

| | $\gamma$ |
|---|---|
| A | 1 |
| B | 2 |
| C | 2 |
| D | 4 |
| E | 6 |
| F | 4 |
| G | 2 |

| | $\tau$ |
|---|---|
| A | 1 |
| B | 01 |
| C | 10 |
| D | 01 |
| E | 01 |
| F | 10 |
| G | 11 |

| | $M_{BPE}$ |
|---|---|
| A | 100000 |
| B | 101000 |
| C | 110000 |
| D | 110010 |
| E | 100001 |
| F | 111101 |
| G | 111000 |
| $\gamma$ | 123456 |

(a) Encoding of fig. 1.

```
class  Type_rep  {
       int8    bucket_word
       int5    bucket_pos
       int8    bucket_mask
       array [1 ...B] of int32  row
}
```

(b) Runtime data structures.

```
Type_rep type := obj.type_rep
int32 word := type.row[#bucket_word]
word := word >> #bucket_pos
word := word & #bucket_mask
if  (  word  =  #tid )
```

(c) Type inclusion test.

Figure 11: Bit-Packed Encoding (BPE).

## 6 Compact Encoding (CE)

A notable characteristic of all constant-time encodings is redundancy. In Cohen's encoding, a row differs from its parent in only one position. With multiple subtyping, more than one position may differ as each type may have more than one parent. Yet, in general, rows remain fairly constant from one generation to the next.

The compact encoding is a straightforward adaption of the compact dispatch table technique of Vitek and

Horspool [15]. It reduces repetition by introducing sharing between rows of a type matrix. The idea is simple, start with a $N \times M$ matrix (either a binary matrix or the packed encoding, in the following we take the packed encoding) and break it into a number, $m$, of chunks. Each chunk is composed of $N$ rows and $M_i$ columns. Then, for each chunk, compare all rows and merge equal rows.

| | $\gamma_i$ | |
|---|---|---|
| $A$ | $\gamma_1$ | 1 |
| $B$ | $\gamma_2$ | 1 |
| $C$ | $\gamma_2$ | 1 |
| $D$ | $\gamma_3$ | 2 |
| $E$ | $\gamma_2$ | 1 |
| $F$ | $\gamma_3$ | 2 |
| $G$ | $\gamma_2$ | 1 |

| | $\tau$ |
|---|---|
| $A$ | 1 |
| $B$ | 1 |
| $C$ | 2 |
| $D$ | 1 |
| $E$ | 1 |
| $F$ | 2 |
| $G$ | 3 |

$M_{1CE}$

| | |
|---|---|
| $A, B, C, D, E, F, G$ | 1 |
| $\gamma_1$ | 1 |

$M_{2CE}$

| | |
|---|---|
| $A, E$ | 0 |
| $B$ | 1 |
| $C, D$ | 2 |
| $F, G$ | 3 |
| $\gamma_2$ | 1 |

$M_{3CE}$

| | | |
|---|---|---|
| $A, B, C, G$ | 0 | 0 |
| $D$ | 1 | 0 |
| $E$ | 0 | 1 |
| $F$ | 2 | 1 |
| $\gamma_3$ | 1 | 2 |

(a) The encoding of fig. 1.

```
class  Type_rep  {
       short    chunk
       short    bucket
       array [1...M]  of Row   row
}
class  Row  {
       array [1...mi]  of int8   elem
}
```

(b) Runtime data structures.

```
Type_rep  type := obj.type_rep
Row  row := type.row[ #chunk ]
if  (row.elem[ #bucket ] = #tid )
```

(c) Type inclusion test.

Figure 12: Compact Encoding (CE).

This yields a set of smaller, $N_i \times M_i$, matrices where $N_i \leq N$ and $M_i \leq M$ for each of the chunks. The choice of the chunk size and of the column in which to put in a chunk relies on heuristics as discussed in [15].

The compact encoding for the small type hierarchy of fig. 1 is shown in fig. 12(a). In this encoding the packed matrix ($7 \times 5$) is split into three chunks. So, with $m = 3$, the three chunks have dimensions $1 \times 1$, $4 \times 1$, and $4 \times 2$.

The runtime data structure for each **Type_rep** consists of a short integer **chunk** which indicates which $\gamma_i$ to use, a second short integer **bucket** which is the value of $\gamma$ and an array of rows, **row**. An element in this array of rows is a chunk, a portion of one of the rows of the original matrix. The actual **Row** objects are shared by multiple **Type_rep** objects. Fig. 12(b) shows these data structures. As before, the type identifier may be recovered from the type, so the identifier of type $x$ is stored at **$x$.row[$x$.chunk].elem[$x$.bucket]**. The type inclusion test against a type with chunk **#chunk**, bucket **#bucket** and identifier **#tid** is shown in fig. 12(c).

## 7 Evaluation

This last section evaluates the different constant-time type inclusion test techniques according to four criteria: the runtime characteristics of the type test algorithms, space requirements of the associated encoding, generation time of the encoding and suitability for incremental hierarchy modifications.

We compare five algorithms: the binary matrix (BM) of section 3.2.1, the near optimal hierarchical encodings (NHE) of section 3.2.3, the packed encoding (PE) of section 4, the bit-packed encoding (BPE) of section 5, and the compact encoding (CE) of section 6. Type tests with NHE and BPE can be either performed inline (INHE and IBPE) or in a separate function (GNHE and GBPE). We refer to the algorithms by the above mentioned acronyms.

### 7.1 Benchmark data sets

Choosing data sets to compare encodings is a tricky task. While it is fairly easy to generate arbitrary directed acyclic graphs, they seldom resemble those of real programs. For example, the degree of multiple subtyping that humans seem to be comfortable with is usually quite low; the average number of direct supertypes is very close to 1 in all large programs we have been able to study. The encodings that we want to compare have been designed to be space efficient representation of type hierarchies, we thus feel that it is necessary to compare them on real-life data sets.

| Library | Lang. | Types num. | Level max. | Parent (max./avg.) | Ancestor (max./avg.) |
|---|---|---|---|---|---|
| VW2 | SMALLTALK | 1956 | 15 | 1 / 1 | 15 / 6.40 |
| DG3 | SMALLTALK | 1357 | 14 | 1 / 1 | 14 / 6.40 |
| NXT | OBJ.-C | 311 | 8 | 1 / 1 | 8 / 3.94 |
| ET+ | C++ | 371 | 9 | 1 / 1 | 9 / 4.30 |
| UNI | C++ | 614 | 10 | 2 / 1.01 | 10 / 4.02 |
| SLF | SELF | 1802 | 18 | 9 / 1.05 | 41 / 30.88 |
| GEO | EIFFEL | 1319 | 14 | 16 / 1.89 | 50 / 14 |
| EDE | EIFFEL | 434 | 11 | 7 / 1.66 | 23 / 7.99 |
| LOV | EIFFEL | 436 | 10 | 10 / 1.71 | 24 / 8.50 |
| LAU | LAURE | 295 | 12 | 3 / 1.07 | 16 / 8.13 |
| JAV | JAVA | 225 | 7 | 3 / 1.04 | 7 / 3.43 |

Table 2: Benchmark type hierarchies.

Another consideration is whether to include single subtyping hierarchies. Since single subtyping is a special case of multiple subtyping, and it is fairly common to find single subtyping hierarchies in languages with multiple subtyping (*e.g.* ET++, see below), we must include single subtyping in this evaluation. Furthermore, as the packed encoding (PE) reduces to Cohen's encoding in the single subtyping case, it is interesting to compare its space requirements with those of the hierarchical encoding.

We use a collection of 11 medium to large type hierarchies to evaluate encodings[6] [9].

Some descriptive data about the hierarchies is given in table 2. *Level* indicates the depth of each hierarchy, *parent* gives both the largest and average number of direct supertypes, and, finally, *ancestors* gives largest and average number of supertypes for each hiearchy.

VW2 and DG3 are both large SMALLTALK-80 class libraries, respectively VisualWork2 and Digitalk3. Each class corresponds to a type, the subtype relation is the inheritance relationship between classes. VW2 is our largest hierarchy with almost 2000 types. VW2 is also quite deep with 15 levels. NXT contains types extracted from the NeXTStep class library. ET+ is the ET++ graphical user interface library. UNI is the Unidraw C++ toolkit. SLF contains data extracted from the SELF system[7]. This is our largest multiple subtyping example, it is also the deepest hierarchy (18 levels). Notice that the maximum number of parents is 9 which is rather high. The largest number of ancestors 41 and the average number of ancestors is more than 30. Both values are much larger than in class-based languages. GEO, EDE and LOV are EIFFEL applications produced by a code generator. They exhibit very large amounts of multiple subtyping, up to 16 parents for GEO. Their average number of parents is also way higher than that of the other hierarchies. LAU is the Laure language of Caseau. Finally, JAV is the JAVA JDK 1.02 library. We refer to the data sets by their acronyms.

We consider these hierarchies to be fairly large, but expect to see much larger hierarchies for big systems. Another source of large hierarchies is the growing number of code generators that use object-oriented languages (JAVA for example) as their target. Generated code may use multiple subtyping more extensively as automatic tools are better at keeping track of complex hierarchies than human programmers.

### 7.2 Runtime behavior of type tests

Based on the machine code sequences given in the appendix, the different algorithms are compared with respect to their speed, instruction count and register usage. The comparison is based on a generic RISC architecture which executes one instruction every cycle with a load latency of 2 cycles and no penalty for correctly predicted branches. The variable $H$ for INHE and GNHE is a factor of the length of the bit string encoding the hierarchy. If the word size is 32 bits and the encoding is $n$ bits, $H = (n+31) \textbf{ mod } 32$. In our set of programs the largest $H$ was 3. For GNHE, we count the number of instructions at the call site only. All algorithms under consideration guarantee constant-time type tests. In the case of the INHE and GNHE, the time is determined at link-time when the entire hierarchy is known. The, perhaps surprising, result of table 3 is that type tests with PE are as efficient as type tests that use a binary matrix. The other techniques are slower, require more registers and have higher instruction counts.

| Resources | BM | INHE | GNHE |
|---|---|---|---|
| Cycles | 6 | $3 + 6H$ | $5 + 6H$ |
| Instructions | 4 | $3 + 5H$ | 4 |
| Registers | 1 | 4 | 5 |

| Resources | PE | IBPE | GBPE | CE |
|---|---|---|---|---|
| Cycles | 6 | 8 | 11 | 8 |
| Instructions | 4 | 6 | 3 | 5 |
| Registers | 1 | 1 | 3 | 1 |

Table 3: Comparing runtime characteristics.

### 7.3 Space requirements

Table 4 summarizes space requirements of the different encodings relative to the binary matrix encoding. Compression rates are computed as $1 - (sizeX/sizeBM)$. These measurements assume 32 bit pointers and 32 bit alignment of the data and do not include the size of the machine code sequences.

[6] We thank Yves Caseau (LAU) and Karel Driesen (VW2, DG3, ET+, UNI, SLF). The benchmark data set is available from `http://www.cs.ucsb.edu/oocsb/classhierarchies/`.

[7] In SELF shared behavior is implemented by maps, for our purpose each map represents a type.

The space requirements of the naive approach (BM) can come close to 0.5MB and these get compressed down to 16 KB with NHE and 30 KB with PE and BPE. The size of BM depends on the number of types, we get equally large hierarchies with single (VW2) and multiple subtyping (SLF). NHE has consistently better compression rates. It performs slightly worse on inputs containing multiple inheritance like EDE, LOV and JAV, but interestingly enough performs very well on SLF and GEO. PE demonstrates good compression rates for single subtyping and only adequate compression rates multiple subtyping. BPE improves on PE for all multiple subtyping hierarchies. For instance for SLF, the encoding size drops from 77 KB to 28 KB. CE fails to improve on the PE, except for LOV and EDE where it performs slightly better. The reason for this poor performance is that gains due to sharing parts of bit vectors are offset by the cost of the additional pointers in each type data structure. These numbers suggest that CE needs larger hierarchies to become profitable.

| Lib. | BM | NHE | PE | BPE | CE |
|---|---|---|---|---|---|
| VW2 | 485.3 | 16.0 | 30.5 | 30.5 | 39.3 |
| | | (96.7%) | (93.7%) | (93.7%) | (91.9%) |
| DG3 | 233.4 | 10.9 | 21.2 | 15.9 | 24.0 |
| | | (95.3%) | (90.9%) | (93.2%) | (89.7%) |
| NXT | 12.4 | 1.2 | 2.4 | 2.4 | 3.7 |
| | | (90.3%) | (80.6%) | (80.6%) | (70.2%) |
| ET+ | 17.8 | 1.4 | 4.3 | 2.8 | 4.8 |
| | | (92.1%) | (75.8%) | (84.3%) | (73.0%) |
| UNI | 49.1 | 2.4 | 7.2 | 4.8 | 8.5 |
| | | (95.1%) | (85.3%) | (90.2%) | (82.7%) |
| SLF | 410.8 | 14.7 | 77.4 | 28.1 | 85.0 |
| | | (96.4%) | (81.2%) | (93.2%) | (79.3%) |
| GEO | 221.5 | 15.9 | 66.9 | 25.7 | 67.1 |
| | | (92.8%) | (69.8%) | (88.4%) | (69.7%) |
| EDE | 24.3 | 3.4 | 11.9 | 5.1 | 10.5 |
| | | (86.0%) | (51.0%) | (79.0%) | (56.8%) |
| LOV | 24.4 | 3.4 | 11.9 | 5.1 | 10.8 |
| | | (86.1%) | (51.2%) | (79.1%) | (55.7%) |
| LAU | 11.8 | 1.1 | 4.6 | 2.3 | 6.2 |
| | | (90.7%) | (61.0%) | (80.5%) | (47.5%) |
| JAV | 7.2 | 0.9 | 1.8 | 0.9 | 2.7 |
| | | (87.5%) | (75.0%) | (87.5%) | (62.5%) |

Table 4: Space requirements (KB/compression rate).

### 7.3.1 Considering instruction space

We were able to obtain the number of static type check calls (3861) for the Java library (JDK 1.0.2). If the space requirements for both the table and the instructions are considered, the rankings of the algorithms are completely reversed. The results are presented in table 5. The generic algorithms (GPBE and GNHE) win as they require fewer instructions per test site. The size of the tables actually is irrelevant, code space dominates the size requirements. Nevertheless, the code size measures should be taken with caution: (1) it is not clear how representative this data is, (2) many of these type tests will be inlined away by an optimizing compiler, and (3) the JDK1.0.2 hierarchy was quite small. These numbers should be considered as upper bounds on size requirements.

| Space | BM | INHE | GNHEE |
|---|---|---|---|
| code only | 60.3 | 123.4 | 60.3 |
| data + code | 67.6 | 124.3 | 61.2 |

| Space | PE | IBPE | GBPE | CE |
|---|---|---|---|---|
| code only | 60.3 | 90.5 | 45.2 | 77.1 |
| data + code | 62.1 | 91.4 | 46.1 | 79.6 |

Table 5: Space requirements with instructions (KB).

## 7.4 Encoding generation

The time needed to generate the encoding can not be neglected as it will lengthen the overall compile and link cycle time or even play a role at runtime in the case of incremental hiearchy updates.

We have measured the speed of all four algorithms on a 500 MHz 21164 Alpha processor. The running times in milliseconds are shown in table 6. These times were obtained by computing the encoding 100 times for each hierarchy.

The difference between BM, PE, BPE and CE is quite small, all three algorithms run fast. The worst time for BM is 10 msecs for VW2 which is the largest

| | BM | (B)PE | CE | NHE |
|---|---|---|---|---|
| VW2 | 10 | 12 | 13 | 890 |
| DG3 | 6 | 8 | 9 | 426 |
| NXT | 1 | 2 | 2 | 30 |
| ET+ | 1 | 2 | 2 | 39 |
| UNI | 2 | 3 | 4 | 93 |
| SLF | 9 | 11 | 14 | 1367 |
| GEO | 8 | 13 | 23 | 1902 |
| EDE | 2 | 4 | 5 | 136 |
| LOV | 1 | 4 | 5 | 168 |
| LAU | 1 | 2 | 2 | 21 |
| JAV | 1 | 1 | 2 | 19 |

Table 6: Encoding generation times (msecs).

hierarchy. PE and CE take 13 and 23 msecs, respectively, for GEO which is large and features heavy multiple inheritance. NHE is slower, yet it still generates encodings in less than 2 seconds.

### 7.5 Incremental hierarchy updates

Dealing with changes in the subtyping relation is difficult. As for most table compression algorithms small changes in the input can result in widely different compressed outputs. Thus it is not always possible to avoid recomputing the entire encoding.

There are two kinds of changes to the subtype relation: *destructive changes*, changes that modify the type graph either by adding or removing edges between existing vertices, and *additive changes*, changes that only add new vertices and new edges to a type graph. The first kind is usually restricted to programming environments during software development. The second kind may actually occur at runtime when new software components are dynamically linked. In class-based languages, such as JAVA, new classes and interfaces can be loaded at arbitrary points during program execution. The new types thus created are always subtypes of already existing types. In languages with structural subtyping, new types may also be supertypes of existing types.

Supporting dynamic changes to the subtype relation implies that the information dependent on a particular encoding must be localized to some well defined portion of the program and easy to change or update to reflect the new situation. This comes at a cost in efficiency. For one, compile- or link-time constants can not be updated. In general that would prove too costly. Thus type inclusion tests must be wrapped in function calls to a generic test function that expects two `Type_rep` objects and is able to extract the necessary information for a type test out of their fields.

Another trick to speed up recomputation of the encodings is not to recompute them. Or, at least, to wait until the last possible time before doing so. The motivation is that changes often come in batches. As it is economical to recompute for as many types as possible, we must try to wait until all the types in the batch have been added before starting the update. What is the latest time? It is either the first subtype test, or, if we want to be more precise, the first subtype test that involves a new type. So, we can either modify—by overwriting code—the type test function to trigger recomputation, or add extra information to type representations to indicate whether they have been initialized and add an extra check to each type test to verify that both types already have been installed.

In any case, the next question is what to do when recomputing is necessary. Assume that we have batched a group of updates. If the batch contains destructive updates the encoding will have to be recomputed. If the batch contains no destructive updates, the binary matrix does not have to be updated. For a new type, each row has to be extended by an entry and a new row must be added. The cost of extension can be reduced by pre-allocating longer rows with some unused entries. In the case of the hierarchical encoding, recomputing can not be avoided easily. For the packed and compact encodings, adding new subtypes does not necessarily mean recomputing the encoding. Recomputing is only necessary if we add new join types of previously existing types. Otherwise the update can be performed by extending rows. For the bit-packed encoding, the same comments as for PE apply, except that the encoding must also be recomputed if the number of bits required to represent a bucket changes.

When the encoding has to be recomputed, generation time and memory requirements become important. BM, PE and BPE have the fastest generation times. CE follows close behind PE. Finally, NHE is most computationally intensive algorithm and thus less suited to frequent encoding generation.

## 8 Conclusions

In this paper we have looked at the problem of testing for type inclusion in object-oriented programming languages with multiple subtyping. We evaluated five main techniques for computing type inclusion with different trade-offs. Which is the best type test method? If run-time speed is the primary concern, the Packed Encoding is a clear winner. It ties with the Binary Matrix as achieving the fastest type test times, it is almost as fast to compute, yet it requires much less storage for tables. The packed encoding is thus suited for statically compiled programming languages as well as to environments that permits dynamic addition of new types (as with SMALLTALK and JAVA). If space and speed of tests are equal concerns, the Bit-Packed Encoding is the best choice as it is consistently more compact than the Packed Encoding, yet it is fast to compute and guarantees constant time type inclusion tests. If space is the major concern, our generic Near Optimal Hierarchical Encoding method will give the best results. Finally, we believe that the Compact Encoding may compress some very large hierarchies better than the other encodings but we were not able to substantiate this hypothesis with the data at our disposal.

Source code for the algorithms described in this paper is available from:
*http://www.complang.tuwien.ac.at/andi/typecheck/*
*http://cuiwww.unige.ch/~jvitek/fcttit/*

## Acknowledgments

The authors wish to thank Ole Agesen, Laurent Dami, Karel Driesen and Manuel Serrano for thoughtful comments on earlier versions of this paper; Christian Queinnec for interesting discussions of alternative techniques and uses of type inclusion tests; and the OOPSLA reviewers as their technical comments helped us improve this paper.

## References

[1] H. Aït-Kaci, R. Boyer, P. Lincoln, and R. Nasr. Efficient implementation of lattice operations. *ACM Transactions on Programming Languages and Systems*, 11(1):115–146, 1989.

[2] Y. Caseau. Efficient handling of multiple inheritance hierarchies. In *Proc. Conference on Object Oriented Programming Systems, Languages & Applications, OOPSLA'93*, Published as SIGPLAN Notices 28(10), pages 271–287. ACM Press, September 1993.

[3] N. H. Cohen. Type-extension type tests can be performed in constant time. *ACM Transactions on Programming Languages and Systems*, 13(4):626–629, 1991.

[4] J. Dean, G. DeFouw, D. Grove, V. Litvinov, and C. Chambers. Vortex: An optimizing compiler for object-oriented languages. In *Proc. Conference on Object Oriented Programming Systems, Languages & Applications, OOPSLA'96*. ACM Press, October 1996.

[5] P. Dencker, K. Dürre, and J. Heuft. Optimization of parser tables for portable compilers. *ACM Transaction on Programming Languages and Systems*, 6(4):546–572, October 1984.

[6] E. W. Dijkstra. Recursive programming. *Numer. Programming*, (2):312–318, 1960.

[7] K. Driesen. Selector table indexing and sparse arrays. In *Proc. Conference on Object Oriented Programming Systems, Languages & Applications, OOPSLA'93*, Published as SIGPLAN Notices 28(10), pages 259–270. ACM Press, September 1993.

[8] K. Driesen, U. Hölzle, and J. Vitek. Message dispatch on pipelined processors. In *Proc. European Conference on Object-Oriented Programming, ECOOP'95*, Lecture Notes in Computer Science. Springer-Verlag, 1995.

[9] K. Driesen, U. Hölzle, and J. Vitek. The OOCSB class heterarchy benchmark suite. Technical Report TRCS97-09, Dept. of Computer Science, University of California, Santa Barbara, July 1997.

[10] M. Habib and L. Nourine. Tree structure for distributive lattices and its applications. *Theoretical Computer Science*, 165:391–405, 1996.

[11] A. Krall and R. Grafl. CACAO – a 64 bit JavaVM just-in-time compiler. In G. C. Fox and W. Li, editors, *PPoPP'97 Workshop on Java for Science and Engineering Computation*, Las Vegas, June 1997. ACM.

[12] A. Krall, J. Vitek, and R. N. Horspool. Near optimal hierarchical encoding of types. In *Proc. European Conference on Object-Oriented Programming, ECOOP'97*, Lecture Notes in Computer Science. Springer-Verlag, June 1997.

[13] C. Queinnec. Designing MEROON v3. In C. Rathke, J. Kopp, H. Hohl, and H. Bretthauer, editors, *Object-Oriented Programming in Lisp: Languages and Applications. A report on the ECOOP'93 Workshop*, September 1993.

[14] C. Queinnec. Fast and compact dispatching for dynamic object-oriented languages. *Information Processing Letters (accepted for publication)*, 1997.

[15] J. Vitek. Compact dispatch tables for dynamically-typed object-oriented languages. M.sc. thesis, University of Victoria, April 1995.

[16] J. Vitek and R. N. Horspool. Taming message passing: Efficient method look-up for dynamically-typed languages. In *Proc. European Conference on Object Oriented Programming, ECOOP'94*, Lecture Notes in Computer Science. Springer-Verlag, 1994.

[17] N. Wirth. Type extensions. *ACM Transactions on Programming Languages and Systems*, 10(2):204–214, 1988.

[18] N. Wirth. Reply to "type-extension type tests can be performed in constant time". *ACM Transactions on Programming Languages and Systems*, 13(4):630, 1991.

## Appendix: Implementations in Generic RISC Assembly Code

In all four code sequences below, control transfers to the label FAIL if the type inclusion test fails and drops through to the following instruction if it succeeds.

BINARY MATRIX

```
    load   [object + #type_rep], type_rep
    load   [type_rep + #word_pos], bit
    lshift bit, 31 - #bit_pos,    bit
    bgez   bit, #FAIL
```

PACKED ENCODING

```
    load  [object + #type_rep], type_rep
    load  [type_rep + #bucket],    tid
    cmp   tid, #tid
    bne   #FAIL
```

INLINE BIT-PACKED ENCODING

```
    load   [object + #type_rep], type_rep
    load   [type_rep + #bucket_word], tid
    rshift tid, #bucket_pos, tid
    and    tid, #bucket_mask, tid
    cmp    tid, #tid
    bne    #FAIL
```

GENERIC BIT-PACKED ENCODING

```
    load   [object + #type_rep], type_rep
    add    #0, #par_tid, par_tid
    call   check_n
check_n:
    load   [type_rep + #bucket_word], tid
    rshift tid, #bucket_pos, tid
    and    tid, #bucket_mask, tid
    cmp    tid, par_tid
    bne   #FAIL
    ret
```

COMPACT ENCODING

```
    load [object + #type_rep], type_rep
    load [type_rep + #chunk],  chunk
    load [chunk + #bucket],    tid
    cmp  tid, #tid
    bne  #FAIL
```

INLINE NEAR OPTIMAL HIERARCHICAL ENCODING

```
    load  [object + #type_rep], type_rep
    sethi high(#parent_type), parent
    setlo low(#parent_type),  parent
    // repeated H times:
    load  [type_rep], this_tid
    load  [parent],   parent_tid
    and   this_tid,   parent_tid, this_tid
    cmp   this_tid,   parent_tid
    bne   #FAIL
```

GENERIC NEAR OPTIMAL HIERARCHICAL ENCODING

```
    load  [object + #type_rep ], type_rep
    sethi high(#parent_type),    parent
    setlo low(#parent_type),     parent
    call  GNHE_H

GNHE_H:
    // comparison of one machine word
    load  [type_rep], this_tid
    load  [parent],   parent_tid
    and   this_tid,   parent_tid, this_tid
    cmp   this_tid,   parent_tid
    bne   #FAIL
    // repeated H times:
    ret
```

# Changing the engine of the car? While driving 60 miles an hour!

## Panel Session

Moderator: Jim Coplien

Panelists: Luke Hohmann, Norm Kerth, John Rae-Grant, Eileen Strider

**Abstract:** Most software development projects don't practice what is usually considered "proper" software engineering practices: well-documented, traceable requirements do not exist, formal inspections are non-existent, analysis and design models are incomplete or not even done at all, and so forth. We know that many of these projects fail, and it is easy to blame the failure of the project on the lack of good software engineering practices ("If we only had well-documented requirements, a complete and thorough test plan, and formal schedules then we would have been successful!")

But many projects that do not practice what many consider to be good software engineering practices succeed, and succeed famously. Examples include the startup introducing a revolutionary new product, the skunkworks project of an established firm that succeeds in changing the status quo, and selecting a mission critical application as the first OO application of a group just beginning to make the transition to the new technology.

Gaining a deeper understanding of success and failure on software projects is absolutely essential for the continued maturation of our industry, and object technology in particular.

*Key Issues*:

- What enables software projects to be successful withoutstringent adherence to software engineering practices?
- What specific software engineering practices should beapplied on any project? What evidence exists to support answers to this question?
- Are successful practices mostly sociological or arethey mostly technical?
- What practices should be avoided at all cost? Why?

**Format:** Each panelist will be given 5 minutes to answer the questions above. This will take roughly half the allotted time. The remaining time will be spent answering and addressing audience comments and questions. The moderator will take questions from audience members at fixed microphones. The panel will conclude with brief closing remarks from the panelists.

*Jim Coplien is is a member of the Software Production Research Department in Bell Laboratories. He holds a BS in Electrical and Computer Engineering, and an MS in Computer Science, both from the University of Wisconsin at Madison. He is currently studying organization communication patterns to help guide process evolution.*

### Richard Gabriel

I have run a number of successful software projects, all with an eye toward innovation and high productivity, and all in a context where watching the bottom line was important. I have also helped rescue a couple of projects from disaster. I have never worked in an environment in which a team was writing software using what I would call a mainstream process. I have also observed a number of unsuccessful software projects and seen what set them wrong. This position statement lists what works for and against success.

*Things To Do*:

- You need a team that has both a lot of experience and a lot of youthful developers - the experience can be embodied in a small number of developers, and youthful developers can be any age as long as they are full of playfulness - and enthusiasm.
- You need a charismatic leader who has the respect of the developers and who is interested in creating a team whose members are more talented than is he or she. It helps if the leader is the embodiment of experience and wisdom.
- The leader must have the respect of upper management and must take up the role of shielding the team from upper management, marketing, and sales.
- You need a project with reasonable time schedules - tight but flexible if necessary.
- The project must have a lot of decision-making authority over the system it's building.
- The surrounding parts of the project - sales, marketing, and upper management - must be competent and have faith in the team. The strategy of the company must be well understood and well articulated by marketing and upper management.
- The project must have an individual who is expert at tracking progress, coordinating tasks, and understanding how people and parts of the project interact. This includes understanding the release process, packaging, testing, documentation, and collateral material.
- It is impossible to specify a system or capture all its requirements before it is built - in other words, you cannot design it before you build it, and you probably don't know exactly what it is until it is completed. You cannot do this for a 1-bedroom house, so why do you think you can do it for software? People act as though it is possible, and you certainly can design something and then built something, but what you get probably has no life and contributes to the post modern death of the human spirit. Therefore, the team and its schedule should have in mind small, frequent releases in order to understand the system's evolving design and requirements.
- As soon as possible and as frequently as possible, the team should produce a running version of the software. A release a day is a good target.

- The team must have team members who represent the end-users so that the running system can be constantly evaluated.
- The team should exhibit playfulness, and the environment of work should be whimsical.
- The team should exhibit its own culture: Myth and stories should be prevalent, the team should have a place that it has marked as its own, conservative executives should worry they have a cult on their hands.
- It is best if there is an enemy or evil force against whom to rail. When in doubt, use Microsoft for this.
- At most, 20% of the success of a project like this has to do with process. That is, almost any process should work, but it should be adapted to the project, the team, the company situation, and market forces. The process must support frequent releases and the unfolding of design.
- If there is a designer, he or she should have the complete faith of each developer and the leader.

*Things To Avoid:*

- Bozos. Observe the team in action closely; if someone rubs the other team members the wrong way, remove him or her. Particular people to watch closely are those with more authority than the developers: the leader, the project manager, and the designer. A team can succeed with a bozo, but the experience and the results will show traces of his or her presence.
- Stupid management. If the schedule is cast in stone, if the CEO can't articulate the strategy or the strategy seems to change from week to week, if fingers are pointed to account for failures, if communication seems poor, if roles aren't clear, or if anything about management seems wedged, then don't even try a project like this. Use a mainstream methodology and its inevitable limited success and protect your reputation; then move on. Other particularly devastating problems are called out below.
- Desperation projects. If this project is required to save the company, run.
- Market ignorance. If the company doesn't seem to understand the customers for the system, then give up on the project and maybe the company.
- Overambitious goals. This goes with stupid management. If the project seems to be over-encompassing, as if it tries to solve every problem, give up. A successful new product provides minimal good functionality that is improved upon.

*Richard P. Gabriel holds a PhD from Stanford University. In 1984 he founded Lucid, Inc., a software company specializing in programming environments and language implementations. In 1994 he joined ParcPlace Systems, Inc., and in 1995 and 1996 was its Vice President of Development. Since then he has been a Management Consultant and writer. Among his publications is "Patterns of Software" (Oxford University Press), a collection of essays on patterns, pattern languages, and software development. He's done a lot of CS stuff over the years, and it's unlikely you can totally stump him on any CS-related topic.*

## Luke Hohmann

I don't know much about changing the engine of a car while driving 60 miles an hour. It sounds rather dangerous, and the chances of success seem dubious at best. However, it doesn't sound all that different from what I know about most software development, especially the software development often associated with the adoption and use of object technology. Specifically, object technology is commonly used to replace part or all of a legacy system that must itself be maintained and extended while the new system (based on objects, Java, the web, or some other new technology) is being written. And then the new system itself must be maintained and extended until it too is replaced. Transforming systems is a messy process, no less messier than changing the engine in a car.

When most people think about software development teams, they think only about the team. By itself, this is not bad, for it is indeed the efforts of the developers that produce the work. But focusing solely on the team denigrates the legitimate role a manager has in any project. A "good" manager provides several essential services to the team. These include:

- Provide an appropriate structure for the work environment. By "structure" I mean relatively stable characteristics of the work environment, including the composition of the team, the topology of the team, the tools and resources at the disposal of the team (such as source code control or fast computers), and the physical and organizational setting in which the team works. By "appropriate" I mean structures that directly support the processes of the team and materially contribute to the creation of desired outcomes.
- Guide the creation of a functional culture. By "functional", I mean a culture that is characterized by sharing, openness, mutual support, and honest communication.
- Assist the team in creating their own methodology without giving up their legitimate authority to enforce, when necessary, the processes required to produce a stated or necessary outcome.
- Assume responsibility for the quality of the final system. (This does not mean developers are excluded from this process).
- Support the current and future needs of the team by reflecting on what was, assessing what is is, and reflecting on what needs to be, and then sharing this decision making process with the team. Such current and future needs might be planning for new equipment, new space, training courses, the adoption of a new language, and aspects of structure.
- Understand that "self-managed" teams are a myth, and that simply throwing a lot of smart people together does not imply success.

Certainly "poor management" can kill a project. My position is that "good management" does far more to help a project succeed than is commonly thought. Thinking back to the car analogy, if all of the mechanics are hard at work tending to the needs of the car, who is hard at work tending to the needs of the mechanics? If the answer is "no one", then the entire team--mechanics or software developers--are likely to crash.

*Luke Hohmann is Vice President of Engineering at SmartPatents, Inc., the leading provider of analytical software tools for intellectual property management. Mr. Hohmann has extensive experience in object-oriented analysis and design, software engineering, user interface design, and project management. Author of "Journey of the Software Professional: A Sociology of Software Development" (Prentice Hall) he especially enjoys his mission of consulting, writing, and speaking about the sociology of software development and graphical user interface design. Mr. Hohmann has a B.S.E. in*

*Computer Engineering and an M.S.E. in Computer Science and Engineering from the University of Michigan.*

## John Rae-Grant

The challenge of shipping great software on time is one of getting an arbitrarily large group of relative strangers to attain and sustain a state of creative intimacy for long enough to create ground breaking functional art.

Methodologies fail because the people employing them usually have little to no understanding of the underlying psychodynamics of a creative team. Most methodologies try to remove the human factors of intuition, emotion, creative struggle, and conflict from the software process. This is not only impossible, it is the opposite of what great teams continually demonstrate.

Great teams are powered by integrity, conflict, and passion. Top down management, including the tyranny of academic and theoretical ideals, can kill the desire to think, experiment, take risks, and succeed. Methodologies which actually work will grow and change in response to a team's deep understanding of its needs, not a hypothetical desire for efficiency.

Most processes, end up processing software teams the same way that Kraft processes cheese. Remove all the flavor, and what do you end up with?

*John Rae-Grant is currently employed at McCarthy TeamworX. A partner of Jim McCarthy's (author of "Dynamics of Software Development", Microsoft Press), John is a ten year Microsoft veteran. While at Microsoft, John participated in, and lead numerous software development tool projects as a developer, program manager, group program manager, quality assurance manager, development manager and general manager. As QA Manager for Visual C++ from version 1.5 through 2.1, John oversaw the evolution of VC++'s shipping cycle from one product per eighteen months to a minimum of one multiple language product per four months. John's final position at Microsoft was as Business Unit Manager of the Microsoft Developer Network (MSDN), where he managed MSDN's emerging use of the web. John also managed the team which produced the "Mastering Series" CD-ROM training products on Microsoft's Development Tools and Platforms. At TeamworX, John is primarily responsible for the content of our training products, primarily the Software Development Bootcamp.*

## Norm Kerth

Changing the engine of a car while driving 60 miles an hour is dangerous. If your team plans to attempt this, then they had better be very disciplined, very experienced and very practiced.

Most likely, to get good at this, your team will have practiced on cars that were stationary. And then over time, they would work on cars that were moving rather slowly and eventually they increase the speed. During this learning period, your team would learn what works well and what not to do.

They would come to understand, trust and use each other's strengths and weaknesses. They would learn to adapt to emergencies, to openly discuss problems and manage risks. They would have studied the books on changing engines at high speed, but they would not follow the wisdom of any one author. Nor would they follow any engine changing standard, written for changing engines on stationary automobiles. Instead, they would have created their own way of changing engines, adapted from the wisdom from many sources. They might borrow a few ideas of changing engines at sea or in outer space. Thus they would have their own process, and their own methodology, which is taught to anyone who joins the team.

A team that does not work learn to work together to change engines at high speed, is likely to have a serious accident: the car is likely to be damaged, team members are likely to get hurt, and the engine may never work as expected.

Software is built by groups of people, not individuals. Sometimes these groups of people become highly effective teams. In these top performance teams you discover that the team owns their own methodology — they have adapted from a number of experts but they have put their own twists on the process that best fit their work. They will take short-cuts where there is no risk, and use discipline where needed. They are no different than the team that know how to change engines in moving automobiles.

Groups of people who do not take the time to learn how to work as a team flounder. Without practice, learning and growing together, these groups are at the mercy of all the demons that can attack a project. The blind acceptance of a book published methodology will most certainly lead to excess attention spent on irrelevant models and light treatment of the material that is crucial to the success of a project. Thus the folk wisdom is spread that methodologies, procedures and discipline don't work.

The premise of this panel session is that running a software project without "proper" software engineering practice is not only common but also acceptable. IT IS NOT!

I know of no faster way to get software "out the door" than by using effective software engineering discipline. By effective, I don't mean rigid, by the book, mindlessly filling out forms and adhering to standards that have little baring on reality. Effective discipline is designed by the team that will use it, to help, not hinder in the successful development of software. The team will find ways to assure that all:

- are all working together focused on the same goal;
- have enough visibility of the project to see problems before they are major ones;
- know who is good at what and when to call upon that expertise;
- handle emergencies and adapt to strange cases naturally as part of the development process;
- know when it is safe to take short-cuts; and
- own the responsibility for the success/failure of the project.

The team owns this discipline and can change it as necessary.

*Norm Kerth is a consultant working with companies interested in ensuring that they make a successful transition to using object-oriented technologies, postmorta and pattern languages. He includes the wider issues of specification and design activities, quality assurance, continuous process improvement, project management and building effective teams. He is particularly interested in building large, distributed object-oriented systems and growing system architects.*

*Prior to starting his company, Elite Systems, he was a professor and researcher at the University of Portland. He has a decade of engineering experience with Tektronix and is a master teacher, with over 25 years of experience in front of students and computer professionals.*

### Eileen Strider

I believe the most critical ingredients in a software project are within the people on the project. Not just technical people, but all the people can either make or break a project. But let me be more specific than that. It's not just "people" on the project; it's you!

You are your most valuable tool in terms of helping a project succeed. You with your brain power, your technical ability, your physical being and your emotional capabilities. The project needs all of you to succeed. Your brain and technical expertise for obvious reasons (although apparently not on some projects), your ears to listen, your fingers to write the specs or key the strokes of code, your energy to sustain the project, etc..

The part I'm most interested in you contributing to the project is your emotional energy and feedback. I think of your feelings as your own personal project barometer. They give you information about what's going well and what you're worried about. If listened to and examined carefully, they provide you with very accurate information about the project, as experienced through your own personal values and beliefs. If voiced with a helpful intent, they can have a profound influence on the project's success.

Yes, I know that many will reject this concept. "Leave your feelings checked outside the project's door. They don't belong on the project." Well, I disagree. They most certainly do belong on the project; nevermind the fact that it's impossible to leave them at the door. They come in with you whether they are invited or not. I think when people say these things, what they mean is "I don't know how to deal with feelings if they show up on the project, especially when they are very strong feelings." It's true that they are perhaps the most scary thing with which you have to deal on a project. They may tell you things rather not have to hear, let alone cope with during an already stressful time on a project. It's very understandable why people would rather not allow feelings on projects. But I propose, if you can find the strength and courage to listen to them, their intentions are good and they will help you succeed. After all, they are part of you and they are real. I find that denying them leads to higher stress, health problems and gradual decay of people's belief and hope in the project.

Sometimes, it takes real personal courage to listen privately to what your feelings are trying to tell you. I think this is because once your allow yourself to acknowledge your feelings, then you can no longer pretend they don't exist. And, even more scary, you may feel obligated to take some action to help the project move in a different direction. I think this is a crucial step where projects can go wrong. If you strongly feel there is an issue on the project and you don't take action, you may be denying the project your best effort.

Yes, I know what I'm saying can be very hard to do. Learning how to use your physical voice to express your feelings in a way that they will be heard and understood is not easy. It takes a lot of hard work to build your skills in this area. It's critical that as you express them, you also let people know why you are doing so. If they know and believe that your intentions are to help the project succeed, you greatly increase your chances of being heard. It is certainly possibe that you still may not be heard. If this happens, then you have to decide what to do next. Just remember, you always have a choice.

So, how can I say all of these things so freely when they are so hard to do? Because I've been there personally on many occasions. I've had to admit to myself that a project is beyond saving and cancel it. I've had to publicly take the heat for projects in trouble and figure out how to make course corrections. I've stood in front of senior executives and told them the hard truths and survived (sometimes, just barely). I would not lightly give you my perspective on this subject if I did not believe it and practice it myself. I think the most valuable contribution I can make to a project is to be emotionally honest with myself and the project team.

I encourage you to explore your own reactions to this view and see where they lead you on your projects.

*Eileen Strider is a principal in Strider & Cline, an IT consulting firm she and Wayne Strider founded in 1989. She recently joined Strider & Cline full time, after four years as the CIO for a mid-western insurance company where she lead the IT organization in signficant improvements in software engineering capability.*

*She is an experienced IS executive wth over 28 years in the information technology field. She has worked as a consultant, a technical developer and in numerous management positions in business applications, engineering applications, operating system support, telecommunications, PC/LAN, software engineering process and quality assurance, product development and advanced scientific technologies. She has lead and consulted in the areas of IT management practice, strategic planning, capabilitiy development, project management, change management, curriculum development, process improvement and organization and project reviews.*

*With Wayne Strider, she jointly leads Strider & Cline's annual IT Leaders Forum as well as Actionshop, an executive development series. She is a faculty member of the Weinberg & Weinberg Problem Solving Leadership Workshop. She has been featured in articles in Computerworld, Information Week and CIO magazines.*

# Garbage Collecting the World: One Car at a Time

Richard L. Hudson,[¥] Ron Morrison,[†] J. Eliot B. Moss,[¥] & David S. Munro[†]

[¥]Department of Computer Science, University of Massachusetts,
Amherst, MA 01003, U.S.A.
Email: {hudson, moss}@cs.umass.edu

[†]School of Mathematical and Computational Sciences, University of St Andrews, North Haugh, St Andrews, Fife, KY16 9SS, Scotland
Email: {ron, dave}@dcs.st-and.ac.uk

**Abstract**

A new garbage collection algorithm for distributed object systems, called DMOS (Distributed Mature Object Space), is presented. It is derived from two previous algorithms, MOS (Mature Object Space), sometimes called the train algorithm, and PMOS (Persistent Mature Object Space). The contribution of DMOS is that it provides the following unique combination of properties for a distributed collector: safety, completeness, non-disruptiveness, incrementality, and scalability. Furthermore, the DMOS collector is non-blocking and does not use global tracing.

## 1 Introduction

Automatic storage management is an essential property of high level programming systems providing an error-free abstraction with which the programmer may manipulate space without regard to the inessential details of physical storage. The abstraction holds only until the store becomes full. Thus it is important for the storage management system to distinguish useful data from garbage, so that the space occupied by the garbage may be reused. The technique used to identify the unreferenced space automatically is called *garbage collection* (see Wilson [Wilson92] for a survey of these techniques).

Here we are concerned with garbage collection in a distributed system where each node in the system has its own local storage and may communicate with other nodes only by passing messages. The problem is difficult because of asynchrony, implying lack of knowledge of global state, and lack of globally atomic operators on that state.

We present a new garbage collection algorithm for distributed object systems, called DMOS (Distributed Mature Object Space). It derives from both the MOS (Mature Object Space) [HM92], sometimes known as the train algorithm, and PMOS (Persistent Mature Object Space) [MMH96] collectors.


OOPSLA '97 10/97 GA, USA


The MOS collector is an incremental main memory copying collector specifically designed to collect large, older generations of a generational scheme in a non-disruptive manner. The PMOS collector extends MOS to ensure incrementality in a persistent context, while also limiting the I/O overhead.

The contribution of the DMOS collector is the following unique combination of properties for a distributed collector without the need for global tracing:

- **Safety**: the collector does not collect live (reachable) objects.
- **Completeness**: the collector is complete in that all garbage, including cyclic garbage that spans nodes, is collected within a finite number of invocations.
- **Non-disruptiveness**: the collector bounds the amount of collection work, thereby bounding the time and space requirements, for each invocation.
- **Incrementality**: the collector reclaims space incrementally without global knowledge of reachability.
- **Scalability**: the collector is potentially scalable in that it is decentralised, uses asynchronous communication, and has no protocols that demand the involvement of all nodes.
- **Non-blocking**: the collector at a node need only synchronise with other nodes in a few cases. Application computation never need wait for such collector synchronisation.

The collector assumes the following support in delivering the above:

- Each node in the system has its own local storage and may communicate with other nodes only by passing messages.
- Ordered delivery of messages is guaranteed without omission, corruption, or duplication. Causal delivery is not assumed.
- Nodes appear to operate correctly, without crashes or Byzantine behaviour.
- No bounds are placed on the relative rates of computation of the nodes.
- Events and actions at a given node are totally ordered, yielding a partial ordering of events in the system as a whole.

As presented, the collector is well suited to distributed memory multiprocessors and to applications that do not require fault-tolerance. To widen the applicability of the collector, fault-tolerance may be provided by lower levels of the system. While others have chosen to build some of this support into garbage collectors, we regard these facilities as being provided by lower level protocols, upon which the garbage collector can be built, in order to separate policy and mechanism and to keep the levels of abstraction relatively understandable.

### 1.1 The Computational Model

Our distributed computational model is made up of computation, objects, and pointers.

Computation consists of one logical *process*, perhaps with concurrent threads, per (logical) node with the processes communicating via *messages*. Computation proceeds by creating and mutating *objects*. A physical node may support more than one logical node.

A (physical) object resides on a single node, which we term the object's *home*, and may contain any number of pointers (references to other objects) as well as non-pointer data. DMOS moves (logical) objects within nodes and allows applications to move objects across nodes, so it includes algorithms to *substitute* one physical object for another and to update the affected references.

Each node has zero or more *root pointers* to objects, which we can view as being part of the node's process's state. If an object is not reachable via a chain of pointers through objects originating from some root then the object is garbage and may be reclaimed. Pointers may propagate to other nodes, and be stored there, by being included in messages.

### 1.2 Overview

Our goal is a fully distributed algorithm that will, concurrently and incrementally, eventually detect and reclaim all garbage while computation continues. Since DMOS builds on MOS and PMOS, we describe it first by giving a concise summary of the MOS collector, indicating how DMOS differs at a high level but omitting details of distribution. The high level description is followed by presentations of several detailed protocols, for keeping track of pointers to objects (and detecting when objects are unreachable), for adjusting pointers when objects are moved within (or across) nodes, and for managing the internal data structures (trains and cars) of the DMOS collector.

Since object migration is a policy decision in a distributed computation that mutators may not wish imposed upon them, we will not consider it as a fundamental technique required by the garbage collector. However, our collector does allow objects to migrate.

## 2 The DMOS Collector

The DMOS collector is described, in the manner similar to the MOS and PMOS descriptions, using the metaphor of *trains* made up of *cars*. The address space of each node is divided into a number of disjoint blocks (cars). One car is collected in each local invocation of the collector, by copying its potentially reachable objects into other cars. Since only potentially reachable data is copied, all garbage contained within one car will be collected immediately. The number of cars per node and the individual size of the cars is a matter of implementation policy, but for each invocation of the collector the car size bounds the time and space required for that invocation.

To collect cyclic garbage that spans more than one car, cars are grouped together into trains. Each car resides on a single node but a train may span more than one node. It is again a matter of policy as to how many trains there are (there must be at least two) and when new trains are created. By ensuring that all the cars in a train are collected by copying the potentially reachable data into other trains, cyclic garbage will be left behind and can be collected, if it can be marshalled into the same train. The trick is to find the minimum constraint on the order of collection to guarantee completeness. For this it is sufficient to order the trains in terms of the (logical) time they are created. Hence we will refer to trains being *older* or *younger* than other trains.

The DMOS collector uses the following rules for copying data from a car during collection:

1 Data locally reachable1 from roots is copied to a younger train, adding a car to that train if required.

2 Data locally reachable from younger trains is copied to those trains, adding a car if required. If an object is reachable from more than one younger train, it may be copied to any younger train from which it is reachable.

3 Data locally reachable from older trains is copied to any other car of its current train, adding a car if required.

4 Data locally reachable from other cars of the same train is copied to any other car of the train, adding a car if required.

5 The remaining data is unreachable and is reclaimed immediately.

It should be noted that the above rules are followed in order. To complete the collection of cyclic garbage one more rule is required:

0 If no object in a train is reachable from outside the train, reclaim the entire train. If necessary, create another train to ensure that there are always at least two trains.

The algorithm allows any car from any train to be selected for collection.[2]

Figure 1 illustrates the algorithm, showing a sequence of four collections, which collects intra-train and inter-train cycles of garbage, and reclusters the live objects.

Since in DMOS trains may span nodes,[3] in following Rule 2 the collector may find that it wishes to add a car to a train which is not represented on this node. Thus Rule 2 must be amended as follows:

2 Data locally reachable from younger trains is copied to those trains, adding a car if required. If an object is reachable from more than one younger train, it may be copied to any younger train from which it is reachable. If the destination train is not represented on this node, then the node should *join* the train and create a new car in that train.

This, as we will see later, requires a distributed protocol as does the detection of an empty train, Rule 0.

The completeness of the algorithm is based on four constraints:

- Objects never move from a younger train to an older one,
- garbage can never move to a train younger than its youngest referent (as of some time), and
- each car is eventually collected, which implies that
- the oldest train is eventually evacuated.

A completeness argument for the distributed collector, which also addresses the anomaly discovered by Seligmann and Grarup [SG95], is given later.

1 Object Y is locally reachable from pointer X if X refers to Y, or there is a chain of pointers, all within the car, that leads from X to Y.

2 The work of Cook, Wolf, and Zorn [CWZ94] suggests that a flexible selection policy allowing a collector to choose which partition to collect can significantly increase the amount of space reclaimed and, in an OODB context, reduce the amount of I/O.

3 An alternative is to restrict trains to a single node. This, however, has the consequence to making object migration compulsory if distributed cyclic garbage is to be marshalled into a single train.

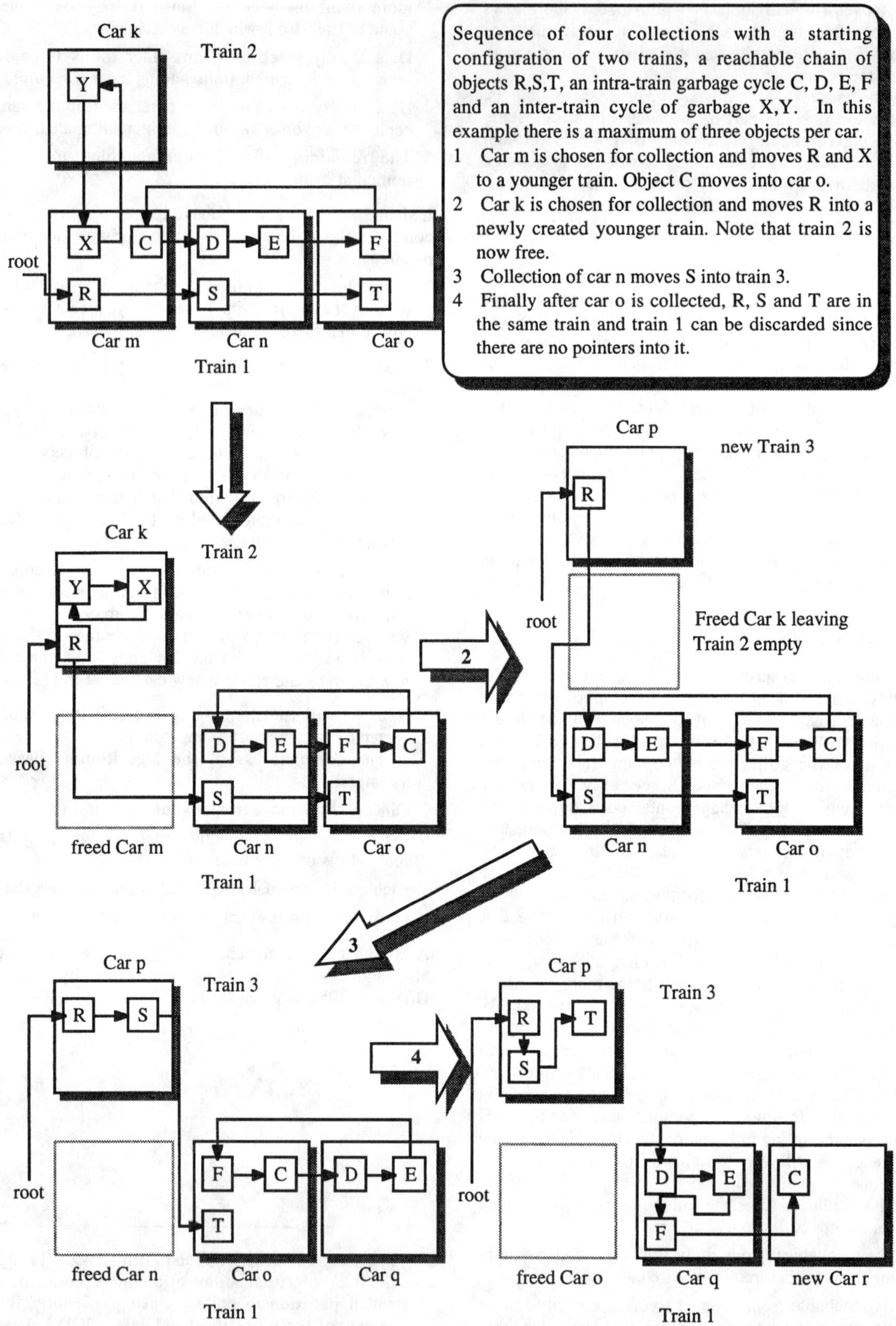


**Figure 1: Example Sequence of Mature Object Space Collection**

## 3 Addressing Objects

Since DMOS is a copying collector, it moves objects, and is thus involved in issues of object addresses and locations. Put another way, in DMOS objects are referred to with addresses that encode at least a logical location, because location (e.g., within a car or train) is fundamental to how the collector works. The MOS collector assumes that each object reference somehow encodes the car and train containing the referent object. This might be accomplished using tables that map regions of address space to cars and trains. DMOS assumes that references also somehow encode the home node of the referent object.

Object references might include an absolute address, or might be based more on a location independent object identifier. However, when an object is moved, references to its old copy may survive for some time, so one must either defer reusing the address space containing the old copy (not an attractive alternative), or arrange that a complete object reference includes information beyond a node and absolute address at that node. We assume that car numbers at a node are not reused, or else reused quite slowly. The car number can then distinguish different periods of use for the same portion of absolute address space allowing prompt reuse of vacated memory.

## 4 Pointer Tracking

Collecting a car requires knowing external references (from objects outside the car to objects inside the car). To avoid global synchronisation we cannot demand that such knowledge be entirely up-to-date. On the other hand, safety requires that the collector never treats a reachable object as unreachable, and completeness requires that a node eventually discovers when there are no longer external references to a local object.

The pointer tracking algorithm is designed to meet the above criteria by ensuring that the home node H, of an object o, is informed of any relevant manipulation of a pointer to o by another node. This ensures that H has sufficient information to allow for either object substitution or reclamation of the object. As we will see, object substitution requires H to know which other nodes refer to o, and for reclamation H must know that there are no pointers to o from other nodes.[4]

### 4.1 Events Related to Pointer Tracking

Our pointer tracking mechanism consists of handling five events. The home node, H, is informed of these events via asynchronous messages. Our initial description of these events will be presented with a virtual message being generated for each event in the system. This will be followed by an optimisation strategy describing how the number of messages and the size of each message may be reduced. The five events are detailed in Table 1.

| Event | Description |
|---|---|
| <s, n, o, A, B> | This (send) event indicates that node A has sent to node B a pointer to o. The number n is chosen such that no other event <s, m, o, A, B> has m = n, i.e., n, o, A, and B together uniquely identify the *s* event for all time and space. This event is said to *happen at* A (the sender), hence it is A's responsibility to inform H.<br>Intuition: This indicates that a new pointer to o has been created in the virtual channel A→B. The number n is used to match *s* events with their corresponding *r* events. |
| <r, n, o, A, B> | This (receive) event indicates that node B has received a pointer to o sent by node A. The number n is chosen to match the corresponding *s* event. This event happens at B.<br>Intuition: An *r* event indicates that the pointer has been deleted from the virtual channel A→B and has been created in a message receive buffer at B. |
| <d, n, o, A, B> | This (delete) event indicates that node B has deleted from its message buffers the received pointer to o uniquely identified by n, A, and B. The number n corresponds to the *s* and *r* messages previously described. This event happens at B. |
| <+, m, o, A> | This event indicates that node A has created a new pointer, uniquely identified by m, to object o. This event happens at A. |
| <–, m, o, A> | This event indicates that node A has deleted the specific pointer, uniquely identified by m, to object o. This event happens at A. |

**Table 1: Pointer Tracking Events**

Figure 2 illustrates a possible scenario of events in which a pointer is sent from one node to another. Messages sent are drawn as broken arrows and object pointers signified by unbroken arrows. Node A sends a copy of the pointer to node B and eventually informs H of the *s* event. Node B receives the pointer in its receive buffer, and informs H of the *r* event. Node B puts the pointer into its heap,[5] eventually informing H of the + event. Finally, B deletes the pointer from its receive buffer and eventually informs H of the *d* event.

There is no specific requirement for rapid delivery to H of information about events at A and B. This is intentional, since such information can normally be piggy-backed on other communication, thereby reducing the overhead of the scheme. Messages 2, 3, and 4 in Figure 2 arrive at H in that order. There is, however, no constraint on the arrival of message 1, relative to messages 2, 3, and 4.

4 The protocol is designed specifically to avoid any need for causal messaging [Fidge96].

5 Note that this is optional, and hence the * in the diagram.

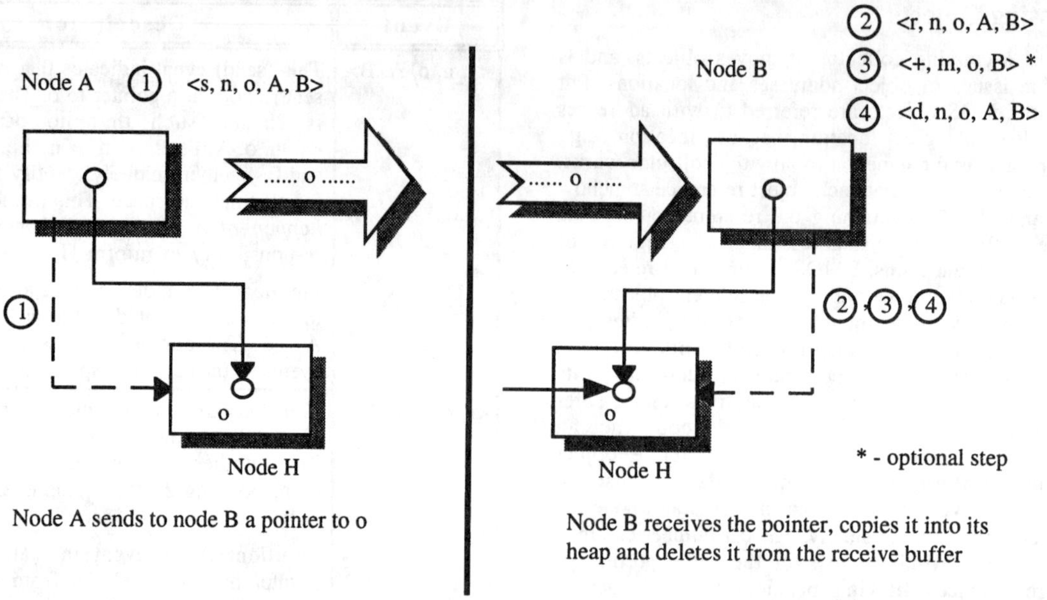


**Figure 2: Node A Sends to Node B a Pointer to o**

In Table 1, either A or B can be the home node, H. We assume, however, that H is informed immediately of events that happen at H.

## 4.2 Constraints on Ordering of Events

It is useful to have some definitions relating to events and the existence of pointers. First, we define the predicate any(o, Y, E), which indicates whether node Y has any pointers to object o in the situation described by the set of events E.

**Definition**: Given a set of events E, where each event is of the form described in Table 1, any(o, Y, E) for an object o and node Y holds iff E contains an event <r, n, o, X, Y> but not the event <d, n, o, X, Y>, or E contains an event <+, n, o, Y> but not the event <–, n, o, Y>.

The intuition is that a node has a pointer if it has received it in a message buffer but not yet deleted it, or created it in the heap but not yet destroyed it.

Using the *any* predicate we define *absence*, which indicates when there are no pointers to an object o, except possibly on o's home node.

**Definition**: *absence(o, E)* is true iff any(o, X, E) is false for all nodes X other than H, the home node of o, and E has no event <s, n, o, A, B> such that the corresponding receive event <r, n, o, A, B> is not in E.

**Claim**: Let E be the set of events known at H involving o; we call this H's view. If absence(o, E) then no node other than H has a pointer to o.

A detailed correctness argument appears in [HMMM97]. The intuition is that absence(o, E) is a stable condition if no pointers are being sent in messages, and thus H's view is up-to-date.

## 4.3 Pointer Tracking Optimisations

We consider six optimisations to the pointer tracking algorithm: removing unique numbers in events; reducing the number of messages; reducing the bookkeeping at H; piggy-backing messages; compressing multiple event information into messages; and combining *d* and – events.

### 4.3.1 Removing the unique numbers from events

We argue that the unique numbers (*n* and *m* in Table 1) can be removed by counting the number of events of similar form to obtain an equivalent pointer tracking algorithm.

For *s* and *r* events related to any given virtual channel A→B, the *r* events occur in exactly the same order as the *s* events, because the channel preserves message order. We now require that H is informed of events that happen at any node in the order in which they happen at that node.[6] Thus, all events are matched in H's view if the number of <r, o, A, B> events equals the number of <s, o, A, B> events.

For *r* and *d* events, the number of pointers to o in receive message buffers at B is exactly the number of <r, o, A, B> events minus the number of <d, o, A, B> events. It does not matter that the order of receives may differ from the order of deletes, only that for any(o, B, E) to be false, the number of *r* and *d* events for o at B must be equal.

For + and – events, as for the *r* and *d* events, the net number of heap pointers to o at B is the number of + events minus the number of – events, and again, for any(o, B, E) to be false, the number of + events must equal the number of – events.

This optimisation depends on the fact that *d* events occur only after their corresponding *r* events, and likewise for – events after + events.

### 4.3.2 Referring fewer events to H

We need to inform H of a + (respectively, –) event only if it causes any(o, B, E) to change from false to true (respectively, true to false). This is correct since H does not need to know the actual number of pointers at B, only whether or not there are any.

For future purposes, we observe that we can tell H independently about whether or not each *car* has any pointers to the object in question. Again, the key point is that H will correctly know whether or not there are any pointers at all.

---

6 This is simplified by our assumption of in-order message delivery.

### 4.3.3 Further reducing the detail required at H

Incorporating the first optimisation means that H will keep only net counts based on (o, A→B) for pointers to o sent from A to B, net counts inHeap(o, B) for pointers to o in the heap at B, and inBuffers(o, B) for pointers in message receive buffers. Can we reduce the number of counts further? It turns out that we need counts of sends and receives (only) for each receiving node, and counts of numbers of pointers at each node (see [HMMM97] for details).

### 4.3.4 Piggy-backing and compressing messages

As previously observed, messages informing home nodes of pointer events can be held and piggy-backed on other communications. Further, sequences of events can be compressed, especially if they are guaranteed to be delivered all at once. For example, an *r* event, then a + event, then a *d* event can be processed to compress the *r* and *d* events together. We will not pursue the issue further here, since it does not relate to correctness or completeness of our algorithms, though the performance improvements may be important in practice.

### 4.3.5 Combining events

It is possible to combine the *d* and – events as long as it is remembered that the *r* event acts as both a + event at the receiver and a balance for *s* in the virtual channel.[7] The effect of this is to alter the counts kept at H for pointer tracking and to reduce the *any* predicate from $(\#r \neq \#d) \vee (\#+ \neq \#-)$ to $\#+ \neq \#-$. While this optimisation does not reduce the number of events generated dynamically, it does simplify the calculation of *any* by reducing the number of kinds of events from five to four and it reduces the size of the bookkeeping data.

If we incorporate all the optimisations above, then only two counts for each object and node are required: an *inTransit*(o, →B) count to record the number of pointers to object o sent out to node B but not yet received, and a *pointersTo*(o, B) count to record whether node B has any pointers to object o. The effect on these counts of messages arriving at H is summarised in Table 2.

| Event | Effect at H | |
|---|---|---|
| | **inTransit(o, →B)** | **pointersTo(o, B)** |
| <s, o, B> | + | |
| <r, o, B> | – | + |
| <+, o, B> | | + |
| <–, o, B> | | – |

**Table 2: Optimised Counts at H**

The inTransit count can take on any integer value including negative numbers. The pointersTo count can be only 0 or 1, and the collection of these counts for a single object o encodes what we will call the *current remembered set*, the set of nodes currently known to possess pointers to o.

## 5 Object Substitution Protocol

DMOS is a copying collector. When it copies an object, all references to the old copy must be updated to refer to the new copy. While DMOS does not need to make copies across nodes, we have designed the *object substitution* protocol to support cross-node copying (object migration). A mutator, or a collector with a different policy, may take advantage of this capability.

Any object substitution protocol must

- work while references are being updated (safety), and
- find and update all references eventually (completeness).

The above must be combined with our goal of asynchrony.

The specific goal of object substitution is to replace object o, home node H, with object o', home node H' (where H' may or may not be H), and to have all pointers to o in the entire system eventually replaced with pointers to o'.

To support object substitution, home nodes, H, maintain for each moved object o, KnownNodes(o), the set of nodes that H knows have had pointers to o since the decision was made to substitute o' for o. Likewise, all nodes maintain *object relocation tables* with entries of the form o⇒o', meaning that o has been substituted by o'.

The algorithm is described through the messages required to support it and how nodes should respond to those messages:[8]

- When o is substituted by o', H adds o⇒o' to its relocation table, and initialises KnownNodes(o) to contain those nodes X for which any(o, X, E) is true in H's current view E. Then H sends a message [m, o, o'] (m is for *move*) to each node in KnownNodes(o). Note that the *m* message should be considered an *s* event for o', but not for o, in the pointer tracking algorithm.
- When a node X receives a message [m, o, o'], it adds o⇒o' to its object relocation table. The *m* message should be treated as an *r* event of o' but not o, and the relocation table entry should count as an occurrence of o' but not of o.
- Once X has inserted a relocation table entry o⇒o', it should (at its leisure, but before deleting the table entry) replace any receive buffer or heap pointers to o with pointers to o'. Such replacement is considered a <–, o', X> event and a <+, o, X> event.
- If X receives a pointer to o while it has o⇒o' in its relocation table, it should replace o with o', causing events <r, o, X>, <+, o', X>, and <–, o, X>.
- If H has o⇒o' in its relocation table and is informed of an event of the form <s, o, X>, <r, o, X>, <–, o, X>, or <+, o, X> then it should check whether X is in KnownNodes(o); if it is not, then it should be added and an *m* message sent to X.
- Since H deletes the contents of o during the substitution, a <–, ...> event is induced at H for each pointer in o. Likewise a <+, ...> event is induced at H' for each pointer in o'. If H ≠ H' then appropriate *s* and *r* events are also induced. As soon as the contents of o have been copied either directly into o' or into a message to H' then the space occupied by o may be reclaimed. This works since the object identifier o is unique and will not be reused.
- If H ≠ H', then the creation and management of the copy requires more steps. H sends a message to H' indicating that it would like to migrate o and requesting a pointer to the copy o' that H' will allocate. This message includes the contents of o, and is considered an *s* event at H for each pointer in the contents of o, but this communication to H'

7 Note that the *r* and + events cannot be combined since the *r* event is required to balance the *s* event.

8 From now on we will use the optimisations given in Section 4.

should not be considered an *s* event of o to H'. H' sends back a response to H with the new pointer, which is considered an *s* event of o'. H proceeds as described above. This protocol does not allow H' to reject the request.

- If H ≠ H', and H receives a message to manipulate o, then in addition to the protocol steps above, H forwards the request to H'.

## 5.1 Cleaning up the Tables

Upon detection of absence(o, E) using the pointer tracking algorithm and completion of substitution of o' for o at H, H sends [e, o, o'] (e is for *end move*) to each node X in KnownNodes(o), deletes KnownNodes(o), and removes o⇒o' from its relocation table. This last step is a <–, o', H> event. An [e, o, o'] message is not an *s* event for either o or o'.

When node X receives [e, o, o'], it removes o⇒o' from its relocation table which is a <–, o', A> event.

Note that the substitution protocol is entirely asynchronous and never delays computation.

## 5.2 Multiple Substitutions

Suppose we have a series of substitutions in progress for the same object, e.g., o⇒o' and o'⇒o''. It is simplest if we maintain multiple relocation table entries and view the substitutions as happening one after the other. However, we need not notify H' of the pairs of <+, o', ...> and <–, o', ...> events, and in effect we directly substitute o'' for o. With care one could flag this directly in the relocation table.

## 5.3 Opaque Addressing

An obvious optimisation to the basic DMOS collector can be made if object addressing is opaque or semi-opaque, that is, if nodes maintain a mapping from external references to local addresses. Substituting an object within the node becomes a matter only of updating the local map. This is a simple operation if an indirection table is employed but may be slightly more complicated in the presence of pointer swizzling. In either case it does not entail the participation of other nodes since the external address does not change. Thus the object substitution protocol may be greatly simplified. Note also, however, that since the substituted object usually resides in a different car, appropriate – and + events usually occur for every pointer in the contents of the substituted object.

The solution does not, however, work for object migration, where we have to revert to our original method.

# 6 Car and Train Management

To support the DMOS collector, we refine the pointer tracking algorithm to indicate at o's home node H which *cars* have pointers to o at H. That is, H will maintain tables indicating the cars C that have one or more pointers to o, and + and – messages will indicate the cars gaining and losing any pointers to o. Another way of understanding this is that the pointer tracking algorithm is the DMOS correlate of remembered set maintenance.

In order to solve a completeness problem that we explain later, we distinguish between the current remembered set for o and the *sticky remembered set* for o. The current remembered set is as previously described in the pointer tracking algorithm, as refined to track on a per car basis. The sticky remembered set accumulates every car that is ever known by H to point to o and is deleted when o is substituted by another object. The current remembered set will thus always be a subset of the sticky remembered set.

The DMOS collector rules constrain the choices of where to move objects from a car C in order to evacuate C. DMOS uses the object substitution algorithm to accomplish those movements. C is evacuated and its space can be reclaimed once all of C's reachable objects have been copied.

DMOS does require some additional protocols, described in more detail below. Firstly, it must be able to create and delete cars and trains, and clean up any associated data structures. Secondly it must be able to detect when a *train's* sticky remembered set is empty (i.e., there are no pointers to objects in the train from outside of the train), to reclaim the entire train.

## 6.1 Basic Train Management

We identify each train with a pair n:A, where the positive integer n indicates the logical *birth date*[9] of the train (i.e., higher numbers are younger), and A is the node that created the train (we term it the train's *master* node). The number n is unique within the master node, thus n:A is unique within the whole system. We assume that nodes are also ordered (e.g., by some kind of node numbers), and n:A < m:B iff n < m or (n = m and A < B), i.e., lexicographic ordering. The master node A of train n:A is responsible for creating, managing, and cleaning up the train.

Although node A created train n:A, any number of nodes may contain cars of n:A. All nodes holding cars of n:A are linked together in a logical token passing ring, where each node X in the n:A ring knows its successor, written successor(X, n:A), at any given time. Initially successor(A, n:A) is A. Nodes may join or leave the train independently.

**Joining a ring**: If a node X wishes to create a car at X in n:A but is not currently in the n:A ring, it sends a [join, X, n:A] message to A. When A receives that message, it sends the message [succ, successor(A, n:A), n:A] to X and updates successor(A, n:A) to be X. That is, A inserts X after A in the circularly linked list of nodes in the n:A ring.

**Leaving a ring**: If node X has no cars of n:A but is still in the n:A ring, it can send a message [leave, X, successor(X, n:A), n:A] to its successor, to start exiting the ring. The general idea is that the [leave, ...] message propagates around the ring to X's predecessor, which then cuts X out of the ring (using the knowledge of X's successor that X thoughtfully provided in the leave message) and informs X that it has in fact been removed. In the meantime X must continue to pass messages around the ring.

However, multiple nodes may be trying to exit the ring at the same time, so the complete algorithm is a little more complicated, and we describe it according to how nodes should process leave messages. Suppose the message [leave, Y, Z, n:A] arrives at node X; X responds according to these cases and actions:

**Case 1**: Y = successor(X, n:A), i.e., X is Y's predecessor: X sets successor(X, n:A) to be Z (Y's successor) and sends the message [left, n:A] to Y.

**Case 2**: Z = X and X is not in the process of leaving the ring: X sends the message [leave, Y, Z, n:A] to successor(X, n:A).

**Case 3**: Z = X and X is in the process of leaving the ring: X sends a [leave, Y, successor(X, n:A), n:A] message to successor(X, n:A).

---

9 The *birth date* need not indicate a date or time but is used only to indicate relative ages of trains.

The first two cases are fairly obvious, but the third one is more subtle because it passes a modified message further along the ring. It pertains when X's predecessor, Y in this case, starts to remove itself from the ring while X is being removed. Modifying the message guarantees that Y's predecessor will cut both Y and X from the ring. The technique is general and will work for any number of simultaneous deletions from the ring. The algorithm depends on the fact that messages flowing around the ring cannot pass one another.

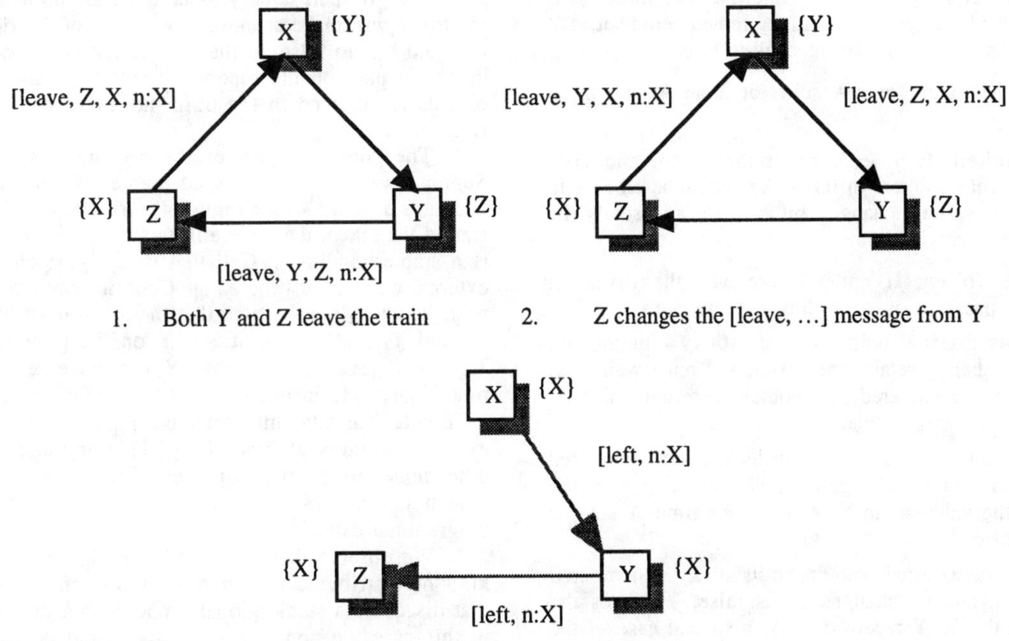


1. Both Y and Z leave the train

2. Z changes the [leave, ...] message from Y

3. Y sends [left, ...] message to Z and changes its successor.
X sends [left, ...] message to Y and changes its successor

**Figure 3: Two Nodes Leave a Train Ring at the Same Time**

Figure 3 shows the sequence of [leave, ...] messages when two adjacent nodes leave a train ring at the same time. In the diagram there are three nodes X, Y, and Z, with X as the master node. The successor of a node is indicated in braces beside the node. Nodes Y and Z each send a [leave, ...] message to their respective successors. Node Z is in the process of leaving when the [leave, ...] message arrives from Y, so it alters Y's successor in the message to its own successor X and sends the amended message to X. Y knows that its successor is Z, so when Y receives Z's [leave, ...] message it changes its successor to the successor in the message and sends a [left, ...] message to Z thereby cutting Z out of the ring. Similarly the [leave, ...] message from Y arrives at X (Y's predecessor) and X sets its successor to the one in the message, cutting Y from the ring, and sends a [left, ...] message to Y.

We do need one special rule, though: A may not delete itself from the n:A ring unless and until it is the only node in n:A. This is because A is the authority for adding nodes to n:A. If A could delete itself before n:A is otherwise empty then we could end up with two independent rings.

Note that while a node is in the process of being deleted from the n:A ring, it cannot create cars in n:A. We will return to this point in the discussion of the train reclamation algorithm.

The approach we have described allows any node to create new trains without synchronising with other nodes. It also requires minimal synchronisation (with a train's master node, and only if the train is not locally represented) to add cars to existing trains. A train can even come into existence, be reclaimed, and be created again, with no ill effect.

When are trains created in DMOS? New young trains can be created at any time; we do not specify any particular policy. However, each node should have at least two trains and should work to move objects reachable from local roots to younger trains. Other than new trains, the collector may create a new representative of an existing (or previously existing) train T at a node, if local objects have references from T in their sticky remembered set. These are the only ways in which trains are created in DMOS. Note that after a certain point, the DMOS collector will not create trains of a given birth date, i.e., once that date is earlier than the birth date of any train currently in the system. In our approach, trains are cleaned up without any global knowledge. Thus, we have achieved train management that is simple, fully distributed, and minimally synchronised.

## 6.2 Train Reclamation

The original MOS algorithm, as well as the PMOS and DMOS algorithms, depends on being able to detect when there are no pointers into a train from outside of the train, allowing the whole train to be reclaimed at once. Such detection is trivial for MOS and PMOS because they are neither distributed nor asynchronous; as might be expected, we need a more subtle algorithm for DMOS.

The basic idea in detecting that there are no pointers into a train is to pass a *token* around the train's ring. We first describe a protocol that works if no objects can be created in the train or added to the train during detection. We later describe a problem with that restriction, and extend the basic algorithm to relax the restriction.

At any given time the token resides at a single node in the ring, and under specific circumstances is passed from the current token holder to that holder's successor in the ring. The token also bears a *value*, which indicates a node in the ring where a current round of detection of absence of external pointers began. An *external pointer* is a pointer from outside the train to an object in the train; significantly, a root pointer is considered external.

Each node X in n:A maintains a *changed bit* related to n:A, which indicates whether X has been aware of any external pointers to objects in n:A at X, since the last time the token was held by X. When X joins the ring, its changed bit is initialised to true. A's changed bit is likewise true initially. If an external pointer is entered into a sticky remembered set at X then X will set the appropriate changed bit to true.

**Initial state**: The token for n:A starts at node A; its initial value is A.

**Starting the token**: If node X holds the token, and goes from having external pointers in its sticky remembered sets to having none,[10] it sets its changed bit to false and sends the token to its successor, with value X.

**Receiving the token**: If node Y receives the token, it either holds it or passes it on, according to these rules:

**Rule 1**: If Y has external pointers in its sticky remembered sets for the train, then Y retains the token, and must wait until none of its sticky remembered sets contain external pointers, at which time Y will start the token.

**Rule 2**: If Y has no external pointers in its sticky remembered sets for the train, but its changed bit is true, Y passes the token, but with the value set to Y. At the same time, Y sets its changed bit to false.

**Rule 3**: If Y has no external pointers in its sticky remembered sets for the train, and its changed bit is false, Y passes the token with the value as Y received it. As a special case, if the received value is Y, then we have detected that there are no external pointers to the train, at any node of the train, and the train can be reclaimed.

Though we will need to extend this algorithm, let us first gain understanding of how it works under the assumption that no new objects are added to the train. We want to demonstrate that we *detect* no external pointers if and only if there *are* in fact no external pointers. Note that if at some instant of time there are no external pointers to a given train, none will be created in the future: since the objects are unreachable, the mutator will not create external pointers; since the collector moves objects to other trains only if they are reachable from a root or pointed to from another train, the collector will not create external pointers either.

The "if" part is easy: once there are no external pointers, the token will make at most two circuits of the ring, setting the changed bits to false on the first circuit and accomplishing its detection pass on the second circuit. Note also that since no objects are created in the train, no nodes will be joining the ring, etc.

The "only if" part of the argument is a little harder. Suppose we detect no external pointers via a token that starts and ends at node X (see Figure 4). We claim that at the time X started the token, there were in fact no external pointers (which is a stable condition). Call that time $X_{n-1}$; clearly X had no external pointers at time $X_{n-1}$. Consider any other node on the ring, Y; let $Y_n$ be the time that the token most recently passed Y, and $Y_{n-1}$ the time it left Y on the previous pass. Now $Y_{n-1} < X_{n-1} < Y_n$. Further Y had no external pointers at time $Y_{n-1}$, and, since Y's changed bit is false at time $Y_n$, Y had no pointers at any time between $Y_{n-1}$ and $Y_n$, so Y had no external pointers at time $X_{n-1}$. This argument holds for all other nodes in the ring, so none of the nodes in the ring had external pointers at time $X_{n-1}$. Figure 4 argues this diagrammatically.[11]

We observe that our token ring algorithm is a particular kind of distributed termination algorithm, i.e., an algorithm that discovers a stable global property in a distributed system, in this case the non-existence of external pointers to objects on a set of nodes. There have been many distributed termination algorithms published [DFG83, CM86, Mattern87], and we suspect that just about any of them could be adapted and used to solve the train reclamation problem. Why, then did we choose this one? We felt that a token passing ring would be

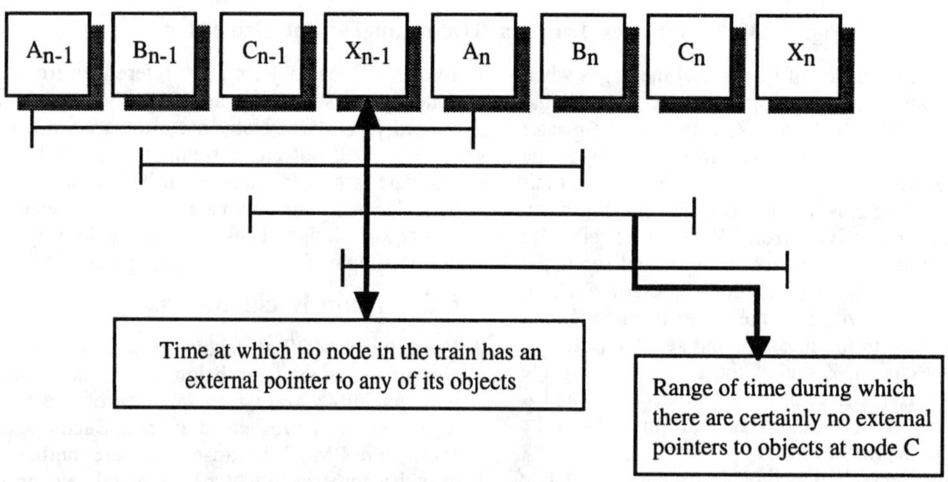


**Figure 4: Illustration of Correctness of the Train Reclamation Algorithm**

10 While no individual sticky remembered set has pointers removed, car collection causes entire sets to be deleted, thus possibly removing external pointers in sticky remembered sets at the node.

11 The time argument does not rely on any notion of global time, but only on the inherent causal ordering of events in the system.

simple and convincing, even in the face of changing membership in the train. Also, we believe that the token ring's overhead is low and that its latency is not problematic in this case since train reclamation is not urgent. In any case, the particular distributed termination algorithm used is not of importance to the completeness of the DMOS collector.

### 6.2.1 The Unwanted Relative Problem

The token ring algorithm just described assumes that no objects are added to the train while the algorithm is running. To prevent new objects from being added, each node always marks one or more of its oldest trains as *closed*, meaning no new objects may be created in the train, and starts or passes a train's token only if the train is closed at the node.[12] It is hard to prevent the collector from trying to move objects into a train, as shown by the following scenario (illustrated in Figure 5), which we term the *unwanted relative*:

In Figure 5, train n:A has no external pointers in its sticky remembered set but has a pointer to an object in an older train m:B. Train i:C is younger than train n:A and also has a pointer to the same object. When collecting the car in train m:B the collector moves the object into train n:A thereby creating an external pointer from i:C to n:A.

- Since the problem does not occur if n:A is the oldest train, attempt to reclaim a train only if it is the oldest. This would delay train reclamation needlessly; it would also require a global protocol to determine when a train is oldest.

The alternative we adopt is to introduce the notion of *epochs* of object creation in a train. Each node in the train ring associates each of its cars in the train with either the *old epoch* or the *new epoch*. When node X starts the token for n:A, it associates all of its n:A cars with the old epoch and sets its changed bit to false. Cars added at node X when the changed bit is false are added to the new epoch; cars added when the changed bit is true are added to the old epoch. Further, if the changed bit switches from false to true at X, all n:A cars at X become associated with the old epoch. The changed bit for n:A at X is set only if X sees an external pointer to an object in an old epoch car of n:A at X.

We claim that the token ring algorithm, modified as just described, correctly detects that the old epoch n:A cars are not reachable and can be discarded. The only way in which the previous arguments could fail is if a new epoch object n points to an old epoch object o (and n is itself reachable). Since the train was closed, n was moved into the train from outside and had a pointer to o. So there was an external pointer to o at a

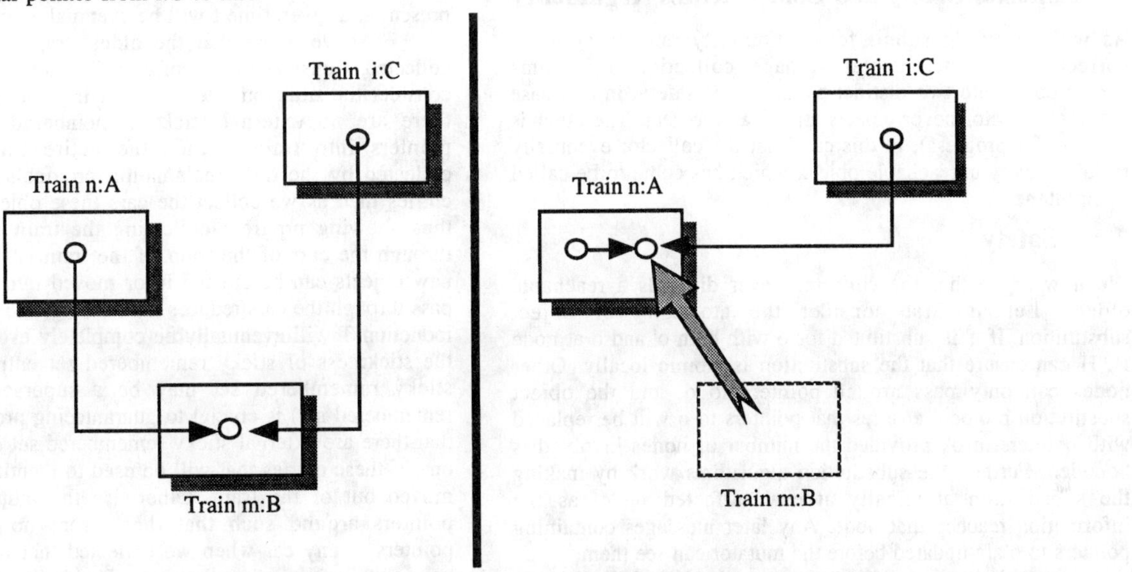


**Figure 5: The "Unwanted Relative" Problem**

Further, note that n:A need no longer actually point to the object in m:B, since m:B's information can be out of date because of asynchrony in the system.

We considered the following design options, rejecting each for the reasons indicated:

- Disallow moving unwanted relatives into n:A. This is undesirable since it implies a synchronous inter-node protocol for the collector to check whether a relative is unwanted.
- Delay moving the relative in until the train's status is better determined. This is messy, and the delay cannot be bounded. Again, it introduces delays and dependencies into a collection process where we prefer to avoid inter-node interaction.

time o was unreachable, a contradiction.

A key observation here is that at the time the token starts its last circuit, not only do all of the nodes in the n:A ring believe that there are no external pointers to their (old epoch) n:A objects, it is in fact true. That is, their perception is up to date. The reasoning is similar to that used in arguing the correctness of the pointer tracking algorithm.

### 6.2.2 Cleaning up Trains

Once the old epoch has been detected as unreachable, the new epoch becomes the old one, the new one becomes empty, and the system starts all over. This is accomplished by sending an [end-of-epoch, X] message around the ring, where X is the node that started the token. As each node receives the message, it deletes its old epoch cars, marks any new epoch ones as old, and passes on the end-of-epoch message. When X receives the end-of-epoch message, it restarts the token passing algorithm on the new epoch.

---

12 Receiving the token may indicate that the train is a good one to close.

But this leaves the question: how do we ever get rid of a train if we can keep creating new epochs in it? One answer is that, as previously mentioned, eventually the train will become the oldest in the system and will no longer have objects moved into it. However, we believe that taking advantage of this fact requires a protocol to detect the oldest train.

The problem is somewhat easier than that since the collector can be designed so that when it moves an object from one train to another, it does so only within a single node.[13] Thus, we can decide to remove a node X (other than A) from the n:A ring if X has no objects in n:A or older trains. Once we start removing X from n:A, we disallow moving objects into n:A at X until X receives the [left, X, n:A] message, at which time it can rejoin n:A if necessary or desired. So, we prohibit some object substitutions temporarily. This temporary prohibition will not affect the collector's completeness since it merely slows the collector down.[14]

If we reach a situation where A is the only node in the n:A ring, and the n:A train is empty at A, we can delete n:A entirely. Due to asynchrony, it is possible that another node X might later request to join n:A, and we can simply recreate n:A at A at that time.

# 7 Collector Safety and Completeness Arguments

As with many algorithms for continuously running systems, correctness of incremental garbage collection algorithms breaks down into two distinct parts. One is safety, in this case that the collector never deletes a reachable object. The other is liveness (or progress), in this case that the collector eventually reclaims every unreachable object, which has come to be called completeness.

## 7.1 Safety

We now argue that the collector never discards a reachable object. Let us first consider the atomicity of object substitution. If o' is substituted for o with both o' and o at node H, H can ensure that the substitution is atomic locally. Other nodes can only pass around pointers to o, and the object substitution protocol ensures that pointers to o will be replaced with pointers to o', provided the number of nodes involved is bounded. Further, the substitution algorithms work by making the substitution atomically at each affected node, as the information reaches that node. Any later messages containing pointers to o are updated before the mutator can see them.

If o and o' are on different home nodes H and H', H' takes over responsibility for the migrated object as soon as the information arrives at H', and H gives up manipulating o as soon as it sends it to H'. There is a period of time during which H does not know the new identifier o' for o at H', and will have to refer application requests concerning o to H' under the identifier o, but H' will use its relocation table to rewrite the incoming pointer to o', so everything works out without indefinite waits.

Our point is that object deletion related to object substitution is not a problem. Observe also that since object relocation tables are considered to contain pointers to the new objects (o' in the example), the new object will not be deleted until we have cleaned up all pointers to the old one, or the new object is itself substituted.

Where else does the algorithm delete objects? In car collection and train reclamation. The car collection algorithm discards only objects not reachable from outside the car. These objects must be in the absence(o, E) condition as used in the pointer tracking algorithm. Therefore, they can be reached only through other objects on the same node; but remembered sets are always accurate with respect to references from our own node, so there is no path to the objects deleted.

The train reclamation algorithm was separately argued: the old epoch objects in the train were unreachable from outside the train, and also unreachable from new epoch objects in the train, and so are unreachable and it is correct to discard them.

## 7.2 Completeness

The completeness argument is similar to those found in Bishop [Bishop77], Hudson and Moss [HM92], Moss et al. [MMH96], and Seligmann and Grarup [SG95]. The argument proceeds in two main steps. Firstly, we show that the oldest train will eventually be evacuated and secondly that all garbage in trains present at a given time t will be eventually collected.

First we argue that the oldest train will be eventually collected. Consider the set of cars C in a train T at time t, and consider the situation after each car in C has been collected. If there are no external sticky remembered set entries with pointers into train T then the entire train is eventually collected by the train reclamation protocol. If there are such entries then as we collect the cars these objects are evacuated thus showing progress collecting the train during each pass through the cars of the train. If the train is the oldest then no new objects can be created in or moved into the train so each pass through the cars reduces the number of objects in T and by induction T will eventually be completely evacuated. Note that the stickiness of sticky remembered set entries (i.e., that the sticky remembered set may be a superset of the current remembered set) is crucial to guaranteeing progress in the case that there are external sticky remembered set entries, since it is one of these entries that will be used to identify an object to be moved out of the train. Otherwise the mutator could move pointers around such that there were no current external pointers at any car when we collected that car, but that there were such pointers for other cars. This is the problem identified by Seligmann and Grarup [SG95].

We now argue that garbage is eventually reclaimed. Consider a time t; let G be the set of unreachable objects at t, and S be the set of trains existing at that time. Remembered set entries at time t can only be from trains in S. Since garbage is immutable, remembered set entries for objects in G will *never* mention trains not in S so garbage will not move to trains not in S. Eventually the oldest train in S will be evacuated, and then the next oldest and thus eventually every train in S will be evacuated, and at that point all objects in G will have been collected. The final inductive step in the argument depends on two additional properties: that mutators do not allocate new objects in the oldest train, and that only a finite number of trains can be created of ages intermediate between two trains (which is ensured because train numbers n:A are formed from positive integers n, and node names A from a finite set of nodes).

# 8 Related Work

Work in distributed garbage collection has become increasingly active as distributed systems become increasingly

---

[13] The only constraint this imposes is that inter-node migration of objects must be done by having the new and old versions of the object in the same train, which in no way inhibits migration from node to node.

[14] Alternatively, we can thread the n:A ring through the *cars* of n:A (instead of the nodes), which supports adding new cars (at a possibly different position in the ring) while old cars are being deleted.

important; we do not attempt to cover all related work, but focus on the most relevant contributions. Plainfossé and Shapiro [PS95] offer a survey. Previous and ongoing research in this area falls into three categories: object migration, reference counting, and tracing. Some proposed algorithms are hybrids that combine these techniques. We will discuss the approaches one at a time and indicate how they have been combined.

## 8.1 Migration

Bishop presents a non-distributed garbage collection algorithm that divides the heap into multiple areas [Bishop77]. Users specify the area in which each object is allocated. These areas are designed to be garbage collected individually so that the collections do not interfere with processes that do not use the area being collected. In order to allow independent collection, each area keeps track of pointers both into the area and out of the area. Referencing an object in another area is accomplished using a level of indirection.

Bishop points out that related areas could be collected at the same time. He handles multiple area cycles of garbage either by collecting all areas involved in the cycle at the same time, or by moving objects to consolidate the cycle of objects into one area. He presents an inductive proof to show that his technique of moving objects guarantees that all unreachable objects are collected. Bishop does not bound the size of an area or provide ways to collect individual areas incrementally. The obvious distributed version of Bishop's algorithm uses one area per node, which requires object migration to collect inter-node cyclic garbage. Our algorithm does not require migration and is also incremental.

## 8.2 Reference Counting

Reference counting has been used to collect distributed objects. The advantage of reference counting is that the rules appear simple; but reference counting alone cannot guarantee completeness (because of cyclic data structures), and making a copy of a reference requires contacting the owner of the referent object.

Bevan [Bevan87] and Watson and Watson [WW87] introduce a refinement to traditional reference counting called *weighted reference counting* where each reference count is divided into a partial weight and a total weight. Unlike the DMOS collector, weighted reference counting avoids the need to send a message to the owner of an object whenever an object reference is passed from node to node. However, it is still a reference counting scheme and suffers from inability to collect cycles.

In *reference listing* [BEN+93] an entry is maintained for each node holding a reference to an object, while reference counting maintains only the count of such references. Reference listing uses more space than reference counting, but messages are idempotent so the system is resilient against message duplication and loss. Again reference listing does not handle cyclic garbage.

Both reference listing and reference counting schemes require that cyclic garbage be rare and sufficient memory be provided to tolerate the leakage. Extensions to reference listing to handle cycles include *optimised weighted reference counting* augmented with background global tracing [Dickman91], and reference listing with partial tracing [RJ96].

## 8.3 Tracing

Hughes [Hughes85] uses time stamps based on global time to trace live objects. Each trace initiated on a node uses the time stamp to mark objects. Each outgoing pointer uses the time stamp whenever it propagates the trace to other nodes. The algorithm requires a globally synchronised clock, and message delivery time must be bounded. Given these requirements, Hughes shows that any object with a time stamp older than a certain time is garbage and can be collected. The termination algorithm used by Hughes is not scalable and reclamation of distributed garbage can be blocked until the slowest node in the system performs a local garbage collection.

Liskov and Ladin [LL86] propose using a centralised server to calculate global accessibility of objects. The idea is that each node informs the centralised (but possibly replicated) server of any pointers into and out of the node. The local collector is responsible for determining the connectivity between the incoming and outgoing references. Rudalics [Rudalics90] points out an error in the original algorithm that is corrected by Ladin and Liskov [LL92] using an adaptation of Hughes's time stamp algorithm. Their solution also uses the centralised server clock to simplify Hughes's termination algorithm.

Lang, Queninnec, and Piquer [LQP92] propose a technique where spaces (or nodes) are grouped. Any garbage cycle completely within a group is collected using a mark/sweep algorithm. The groups can be hierarchically ordered so that increasingly large groups are traced. Ultimately, the entire system needs to be traced in order to collect garbage not located entirely within a previously associated group. This is therefore not scalable and requires a considerable amount of co-ordination between the nodes. Maheshwari and Liskov [ML97] claim that the algorithm will not terminate correctly if the object graph is mutated concurrently with tracing.

Ferreira and Shapiro [FS96] propose a system that allows replication of segments at multiple sites. Each segment maintains a list of incoming and outgoing pointers and is traced using these pointers as roots. Segments that appear at the same site are collected together so cyclic structures that span segments can be collected only if they are gathered at a single site. The co-ordination of segments is not a problem since replication is assumed.

Maheshwari and Liskov [ML97] describe a partitioned garbage collector that piggy-backs global marking with the marking of partitioned data. Their scheme is guaranteed to terminate correctly, and while not as yet distributed, is optimised for efficient tracking of a partition's incoming and outgoing pointers.

## 8.4 Garbage Tracing

Vestal [Vestal87] suggests selecting objects suspected of being part of a cyclic garbage structure, and on a trial basis decrementing the reference count. If this causes all connected objects' counts to drop to zero, then the structure is garbage.

Lins and Jones [LJ91] propose combining weighted reference counting with mark and sweep where the marking is not started with roots but with any object that experiences a reference deletion. The reference count is copied and then decremented. If the trace returns to the start then the object is part of a cyclic graph and can be deleted. While this does collect cyclic garbage it appears to be expensive.

Maeda et al. [MKI+95] and Fuchs [Fuchs95] suggest techniques where potentially cyclic garbage is traced to see if it reaches a root. Fuchs traces the inverse graph to see if it reaches a root while Maeda et al. trace potential garbage to see if it forms an isolated cycle.

All these schemes attempt to discover garbage and suffer from the same difficulty: they need a heuristic to select suspected cyclic garbage. There are no completeness arguments for any of these schemes and all could result in much tracing of live objects.

## 9 Conclusions

We have presented a new garbage collection algorithm for distributed systems, DMOS (Distributed Mature Object Space). It is unique among distributed collectors in that it is safe, complete, non-disruptive, incremental, scalable, and non-blocking, as defined in the introduction. DMOS is an advance in that no prior distributed collector has possessed all these desirable properties. DMOS thus overcomes significant limitations in previous collectors: it is complete (unlike reference counting and partial tracing techniques), it is non-disruptive, incremental, and scalable (unlike global tracing), and it does not require object migration.

Like the MOS and PMOS algorithms on which DMOS is based, each collection processes a bounded size region of objects, in this case on a single node, copying them to other regions, according to a set of rules that ultimately guarantee that all garbage is collected. We track cross-region and cross-node pointers, using a distributed termination algorithm to detect when an object has no more references. We also introduce a distributed termination algorithm to detect when a distributed set of regions (a train) has no pointers into it from outside, and distributed algorithms for managing trains.

Interesting work remaining to be done including implementation and practical evaluation, algorithmic performance analysis, and extensions to tolerate node and communications failures, which we intend to address in future work.

## 10 Acknowledgements

We thank Peter Bailey, Huw Evans, Al Dearle, and anonymous OOPSLA referees for their constructive comments regarding this paper. The work was supported by NSF grants IRI-9632284 and INT-9600216 and by EPSRC Grant GR/J67611.

## 11 References

[Bakker+87] W. Jacobus Bakker, L. Nijman, and Philip C. Treleaven, editors. *Parallel Architectures and Languages Europe*, numbers 258, 259 in *Lecture Notes in Computer Science*, Springer-Verlag, June 1987.

[BC92] Bekkers and Cohen, editors. In *Proceedings of the International Workshop on Memory Management*, St. Malo, France, 1992. Published as number 637, *Lecture Notes in Computer Science*, Springer-Verlag, 1992.

[BEN+93] Andrew Birrell, David Evers, Greg Nelson, Susan Owicki, and Edward Wobber. Distributed garbage collection for network objects. Digital Equipment Corporation, Systems Research Center Tech. Rep. 116, 15 December 1993.

[Bevan87] David I. Bevan. Distributed garbage collection using reference counting. In [Bakker+87].

[Bishop77] Peter B. Bishop. Computer systems with a very large address space and garbage collection. Ph.D. thesis, published as Technical Report MIT/LCS/TR-178, Massachusetts Institute of Technology, 1977.

[CM86] K. M. Chandy and J. Misra. An example of stepwise refinement of distributed programs: quiescence detection. ACM Trans. on Prog. Lang. and Systems 8,326 (1986).

[CWZ94] Johnathan E. Cook, Alexander L. Wolf, and Benjamin G. Zorn. Partition selection policies in object database garbage collection. In *Proceedings of the 1994 ACM SIGMOD International Conference on Management of Data (SIGMOD '94)* (Minneapolis, MN, May 1994), pp. 371-382.

[DFG83] E. W. Dijkstra, H. H. J. Feijen, and A. J. M. van Gasteren. Derivation of a termination detection algorithm for distributed computation. Information Processing Letters 16,217 (1983).

[Dickman91] Peter Dickman. Distributed object management in a non-small graph of autonomous networks with few failures. PhD thesis, University of Cambridge, United Kingdom, September 1991.

[Fidge96] C. J. Fidge. Fundamentals of distributed system observation. IEEE Software, 13(6):77-83, November 1996.

[FS96] Paulo Ferreira and Marc Shapiro. Larchant: Persistence by reachability in distributed shared memory through garbage collection. In *Proceedings of the 16th International Conference on Distributed Computing Systems*, IEEE Press, 1996.

[Fuchs95] Matthew Fuchs. Garbage collection on an open network. In [IWMM95], pp. 251-266.

[HM92] Richard L. Hudson and J. Eliot B. Moss. Incremental garbage collection for mature objects. In [BC92].

[HMMM97] Richard L. Hudson, Ron Morrison, J. Eliot B. Moss, David S. Munro. Training distributed garbage: The DMOS collector. Submitted for publication. Also available as a University of St Andrews, Dept. of Computer Science Technical Report (http://www-fide.dcs.st-and.ac.uk/Publications/1997.html#dmos).

[Hughes85] R. John M. Hughes. A distributed garbage collection algorithm. In *Proceedings of the 1985 Conference on Functional Programming and Computer Architecture*, number 201, *Lecture Notes in Computer Science*, pp. 256-272, Springer-Verlag, 1985.

[IWMM95] *Proceedings of the 1995 International Workshop on Memory Management* (Kinross, Scotland, United Kingdom). Published as number 986, *Lecture Notes in Computer Science*, Springer-Verlag.

[LJ91] Rafael D. Lins and Richard E. Jones. Cyclic weighted reference counting. Technical Report 95, University of Kent, Canterbury, United Kingdom, December 1991.

[LL86] Barbara Liskov and Rivka Ladin. Highly-available distributed services and fault-tolerant distributed garbage collection. In *Fifth ACM Symposium on the Principles of Distributed Computing*, pp. 29-39, 1986.

[LL92] Rivka Ladin and Barbara Liskov. Garbage collection of a distributed heap. In *Proceedings of the International Conference on Distributed Computing Systems*, IEEE Press, 1992.

[LQP92] Bernard Lang, Christian Queinniec, and Jose Piquer. Garbage collecting the world. In *Proceedings of the ACM Symposium on Principles of Programming Languages*, pp. 39-50, ACM Press, 1992.

[MKI+95] M. Maeda, H. Konake, Y. Ishikawa, T. Tomokiyo, A. Hori, and J. Nolte. On the fly global garbage collection based on partly mark-sweep. In [IWMM95], pp. 283-296.

[Mattern87] F. Mattern. Algorithms for distributed termination detection. Distributed Computing, 2,161 (1987).

[ML97] Umesh Maheshwari and Barbara Liskov. Partitioned garbage collection of a large object store. In *Proceedings of ACM SIGMOD '97*, Phoenix, Arizona, 1997.

[MMH96] J. Eliot B. Moss, David S. Munro, and Richard L. Hudson. PMOS: A complete and coarse-grained incremental garbage collector for persistent object stores. In *Proceedings of the 7th International Workshop on Persistent Object Systems*, pp. 140-150, Morgan Kaufmann, 1996.

[PS95] David Plainfossé and Marc Shapiro. A survey of distributed garbage collection techniques. In *Proceedings of International Workshop on Memory Management*, Kinross, Scotland, pp. 211-249, September 1995.

[RJ96] Helena Rodrigues and Richard Jones. A cyclic distributed garbage collector for Network Objects. In *Proceedings of 10th International Workshop on Distributed Algorithms* (WDAG '96) Bologna (Italy) 9-11 October 1996.

[Rudalics90] Martin Rudalics. Correctness of distributed garbage collection algorithms. Technical Report 90-40.0, Johannes Kepler Universitat, Linz Austria, 1990.

[SG95] Jacob Seligmann and Steffen Grarup. Incremental mature garbage collection using the train algorithm. In *Proceedings of the European Conference on Object-Oriented Programming (ECOOP '95)* (Aarhus, Denmark, August 1995), no. 952 in *Lecture Notes in Computer Science*, Springer-Verlag, pp. 235-252.

[Vestal87] S. C. Vestal. Garbage collection: An exercise in distributed, fault-tolerant programming. PhD thesis, University of Washington, Seattle, Washington, January 1987.

[WW87] P. Watson and I. Watson. An efficient garbage collection scheme for parallel computer architecture. In [Bakker+87], pp. 432-443.

[Wilson92] Paul R. Wilson. Uniprocessor garbage collection techniques. In [BC92].

# *Ephemerons*: A New Finalization Mechanism

**Barry Hayes**[1]

1.BHayes@placeware.com, 2037 Landings Drive, Mountain View, CA 94043 Phone 415 944 0900, Fax 415 944 0929

## ABSTRACT

*Finalization* occurs when a garbage collector informs an application that an object is "almost collectable." It is used to help an application maintain its invariants. To make finalization more useful, this paper defines "almost collectable" in terms of a new class of objects, called *ephemerons*. Ephemerons are similar to weak pairs, but an object in an ephemeron's key field may be classed as "almost collectable" even if it is reachable from the epehemeron's value fields.

### Keywords

garbage collection, finalization, weak pointers, resource management

## INTRODUCTION

Languages with garbage collection have had ardent followers since early Lisp systems, and forms of *weak references* have been around since at least the early 1980's [RAM84, Xer85]. Weak references allow a collector to free certain objects, even when there are some bookkeeping pointers to them, as will occur with object caching or property associations.

Objects requiring type-specific clean-up activity at deallocation benefit when *finalization* is added to the collector. Finalization just requires that the collector notify the application when designated objects are collected [Rov85, Par90].

### Road map

In this paper, we first discuss garbage collection and finalization in more detail, with a focus on using finalization to manage external resources. Using a certain class of finalization, involving *non-resurrecting* collectors, we show a problem case where objects needing finalization are being inappropriately retained by pointers contained in information needed for their own finalization.

A variant of this problem, independent of resurrection, is then demonstrated in implementations of *property tables* using weak references. Simply associating an object with a property is enough to keep it from being collected, based only on the external semantics of property tables. Both of these problems are known in the garbage collection community, but do not seem to have been discussed in the literature.

Finally, we introduce *ephemerons* as a variant on weak pairs, a traditional structure using weak references, and show how the garbage collector can trace ephemerons to solve both of the problems presented. A pseudo-code implementation of an ephemeron-aware garbage collector is presented at the end of this paper.

For a comprehensive overview of uniprocessor garbage collection and automatic memory management, see Paul Wilson's excellent survey article [Wil92]. For an overview of finalization, see [Hay92].

### Clarification

The author of this paper is just that, and is not the inventor of ephemerons. George Bosworth invented ephemerons and designed the algorithms presented in this paper.

## GARBAGE COLLECTION

Dynamically garbage collected languages avoid many common errors that occur when deallocation must be explicit. There are situations where explicit deallocation might be more efficient, clearer, or easier, but garbage collection is becoming ever more common.

The concepts presented in this paper could be implemented in a reference counting collector, but not with great ease. All further discussion will assume that the garbage collector is some variant of a tracing collector, perhaps generational [FY69, LH83], and conservative [BW88].

In one view, the garbage collector's purpose is to supply information of a global nature concerning how objects are connected to one another. The simple case is that it is being asked to locate and deallocate those objects that have become unreachable from some specified set of root objects.

Given the view of the collector as the source of topological information, it's natural to ask what other services can be driven by this supply of information. As with simple garbage collection, the information could be gathered by other mechanisms, such as reference counting [Col60, DB76]. This discussion will assume that the collector is the only source of the topology, and the goal is to find other services that require the same sort of view of the global topology as the garbage collector. In other words, we are looking for problems that could be addressed by a solution like reference counting, and trying to see if the garbage collector's traversal of memory can be used instead.

## FINALIZATION

While garbage collection can handle the deallocation of unneeded objects, there are situations where a little more help from the garbage collector makes life much easier for the designer of an application.

The garbage collector can be augmented to provide information to the application, through a *finalization interface*, to let the application know when an object of interest is *"almost collectable."* The precise definition of the finalization interface is directly linked to the definition of "almost collectable."[1]

One canonical example where finalization is useful is in handling objects that are proxies for externally allocated resources, like files supplied by an operating system. In this case, the operating system has a protocol it expects users of the file to follow: a file is opened, it is read and written, and then it is closed.

If the garbage collector simply discards the proxy object that represents this system resource, the protocol isn't strictly followed because the proxy might be discarded before the file is closed. This may lead to unflushed buffers, files that are unavailable to other processes, and may even cause the operating system to run out of resources associated with open files.

If the proxy object were somehow special, the garbage collector could be modified to notice when a file was about to be collected and close the file before the proxy's memory is deallocated. Some Lisp systems have explicitly allowed files to have this behavior [AAB+91, RAM84], but without generally making it available for other application objects.

The mechanisms in this paper are a variant of *container-based finalization.*[2] In these schemes, the proxy objects are seen as special not because of any feature of their own, but because they are in some special kind of container recognized by the garbage collector.

For example, to make sure that all files are closed when the application is done with them, the file manager could maintain a special "open-file container," known to the collector and the file manager, but not to the file manager's clients. The file manager can put every file proxy into that container when it is first opened, and pass a pointer to the proxy back to the client opening the file.

As long as there is a client actively using the file, there will be a pointer to the proxy other than the pointer in the open - file container. When the client deletes the last pointer to the proxy there will still be a pointer in the file manager's open-file container. If the manager knew that the proxy was "almost collectable," by this definition, it could know to close the file and free the resource, and could then collect the proxy.

This is precisely the kind of "global topology" information that the garbage collector is in a position to discover and communicate.

## THE PROBLEM

There are two actions that are indicated for an object that is "almost collectable:" one is to run the specific code to free the system resource, the other is to free the proxy. Some collectors take the view that proxies should be collected first, before the application is notified. The pointers to the proxy from the special containers are replaced by some special *tombstone* (or perhaps a null pointer) to avoid dangling pointers to the deallocated proxy. Once the tombstones are in place, there are no pointers to the object and it can be deallocated. Only then will the application be notified. This avoids having the "almost collectable" proxies *resurrected,* since the "almost collectable" objects are collected before the application is notified.[3]

In the open-file example, the proxy would be freed by a non-resurrecting garbage collector before the file manager would be notified that the proxy was "almost collectable." This means that information needed to close the file (the file ID number, for example) must be separate from the proxy itself, since the proxy will have been deallocated by the time the file manager is notified that a file proxy was collected. The information needed throughout the lifetime of the resource is factored into the proxy and the *executor,* with the executor holding the information that will be needed after the proxy has been collected.

Proxies are known to the garbage collector, and are the internal object representing some external resource. Executors are not known to the garbage collector, but are a conventional name used for an object that holds information about an external resource that is needed to finalize the external resource after the proxy has been garbage collected.

In most cases the factoring is simple, and a shallow copy of the object can be used as its own executor. But if the object

---

1.In modern collectors, not all unreachable and "almost collectable" objects will be detected by each collection. This can happen due to the presence of *conservative pointers*, data values which must be assumed to be pointers, but might not be, as well as generational collection, where not all objects are targeted for collection at all times.
These collectors may assume that certain objects are reachable when they are not, and unreachable and "almost collectable" objects may be treated as live by the collector. Finalization is not prompt in that a finalization action may be triggered long after the event that made the object "almost collectable."

2.As opposed to *object-based finalization*. In a simple form of object-based finalization, seen in Java, the collector arranges that proxies receive a special message when they become unreachable from the roots [GJS96]. This also typically makes them reachable again.

3. A non-resurrecting collector is supposed to make it easier to form and check some invariants, but this opinion is not universal.

contains a pointer to itself the executor ends up with a pointer to the proxy, and as long as the executor is reachable the proxy will never be "almost collectable." The path from the executor to the proxy need not be short -- any indirect path that leads from the proxy to itself will induce a path from the executor to the proxy, and thwart finalization.

The factoring of proxies and executors can get complex. If there are two finalizable objects, each may prevent the other from being finalized by referring to the other's proxy in its executor. The factoring to avoid this may require more global knowledge that can easily be expressed in interfaces, since an interface typically does not indicate that an object is a proxy for an external resource that will require finalization Loops of finalizable objects present difficult problems outside the scope of this paper.[1]

Only non-resurrecting collectors force the issue of proxy/ executor factoring. In a collector that does not tombstone the pointers from the special containers, the proxy and executor can be collapsed.

The problems associated with factoring into proxies and executors is associated with non-resurrecting collectors. There is a more general problem involving circular references to "almost collectable" objects that is present in any collector supporting container-based finalization: freeing of objects from property tables.

## A BASIC WEAK CONTAINER

Container-based finalization requires special constructs known to the collector in order to define "almost collectable." One early and elegant solution was to define "almost collectable" in terms of a new construct called *weak pointers*[2] [RAM84, Xer85, ADH+89, Par90].

A weak pointer can be traversed just like any other pointer, but is treated specially by the collector. When a collector supporting finalization traces to find all reachable objects, it traces in two phases, rather than one. The first phase does not trace through weak pointers, but queues them for later processing. The second phase starts at the enqueued pointers and traces through all pointers. The objects that are not reached in the first phase, but are reached in the second are "almost collectable." These are just those objects that can be reached from the roots, but would be unreachable if all the weak pointers were replaced by tombstones.

As a concrete example, consider implementing a *weak pair* with a special Lisp *cons cell* where the *car* (the first element of the pair) is weak but the *cdr* (the second element) is not, as in Figure 1. The double box is a cons cell, and the first field, the *car*, is shaded to show that it contains a weak pointer. If the weak pair in the figure is reached in the first tracing phase, the tracing will continue along the *cdr* of the pair, the second field, to the unshaded circle, but the *car* will not be traced. In the second tracing phase, if the object represented by the black circle has not been reached, that object is "almost collectable." The collector will notify the application, and then tombstone the pointer or trace into and through the object represented by the black circle.

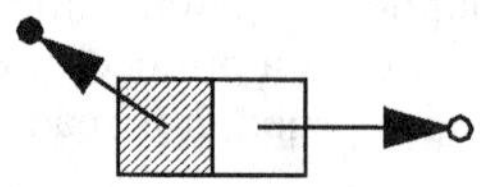

Figure 1
A weak pair

The notification to the application may take many forms; the method chosen is of no consequence in this paper.[3] But the notification must be exact enough that an application can determine which objects are "almost collectable." For concreteness, we will assume that the collector sends a message to a weak pair when it detects that its *car* is not reachable except via this link and other *cars* of weak pairs, and we will also assume that the method invoked by that message can be overridden to provide the particular behavior needed by any particular weak pair.

Weak pairs can be used to build an open-file container that allows management of proxies. In Figure 2, a group of weak pairs is acting to create a *weak collection*. File proxies (represented by the black circles) are chained on to this list when they are opened by the file manager. When the last client pointer to a proxy is dropped, the collector will send a message to the weak pair, which can close the file, and remove the weak pair from the collection.

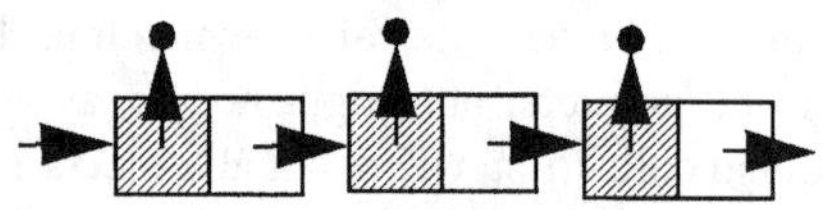

Figure 2
A weak collection

1.When a group of finalizable objects that point to one another are all are found to be "almost collectable" there is no general agreement as to which, if any, should be informed. The difficulty is that one may need another at finalization time, and if an inappropriate order is chosen, it may find that the needed object has already been finalized. When the connectivity among the objects contains cycles, the collector needs extra information to make a reasonable choice. *Guardians* [DBE93] are one attempt to supply that information, but this approach has not been widely accepted.

2.Weak pointers have gone under many other names, including *xpointers, soft pointers, and hashed pointers*.

3.Implementations differ in how they notify the application to identify the set of "almost collectable" objects. The notification must contain enough information to identify a particular weak slot. For a weak pair, having just one slot, the identity of the pair would suffice. For a structure having many weak slots, an object/index pair would be needed.

## PROPERTY TABLES

Weak pairs can also be used to construct tables of key/value pairs to add arbitrary properties to arbitrary objects. The added benefit of using weak pointers to build these tables is that in most cases adding a property to an object does not change the time when it is garbage collected. When the property tables act in concert with the collector, the added property can work more or less as an added instance variable as far as reasoning about objects' lifetimes.

For a concrete implementation, we could have a property table use two cons cells per entry, one containing a key in a weak slot and the other containing a value in a strong slot, as in Figure 3. When a queried object is found in the "key" position, the probe returns the value from the associated "value" cell. This will make a perfectly respectable property table.

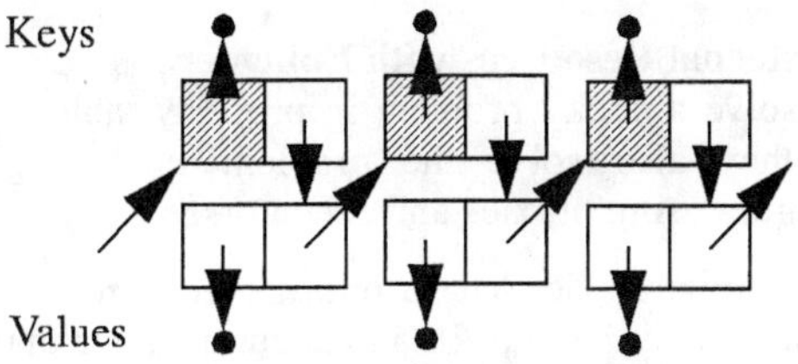


Figure 3
A property table

If all of the pointers in the property table were strong pointers, then simply entering a key/value pair in the table would ensure that they would never be garbage collected without extra effort. When the keys are held by weak pairs, finalization lets the table purge itself of keys and values that are no longer useful.[1]

If the only pointers to some key are from the weak pairs of property tables, the garbage collector will not find the key in phase one, but will find it in phase two. The weak pair will be notified that the key is "almost collectable" and can arrange that the key and value be removed from the table. The key is released when the garbage collector discovers that no client external to the tables will be able to get the key, and thus no query on the tables with that key is possible.

### A problem

The problem comes about when the "values" slot of some entry contains a direct or indirect reference to a key. An object might have itself as the property value, as do the first two cells in Figure 4. The implementation of a property with a value still works -- when the object is queried in the property table, it returns itself as its value. But when all other references to the object are deleted, the reference from the "value" slot lets the garbage collector find the key in phase one of the trace. The definition of "almost collectable" is not quite what is wanted, since the presence of an object in a value slot makes the object uncollectable.

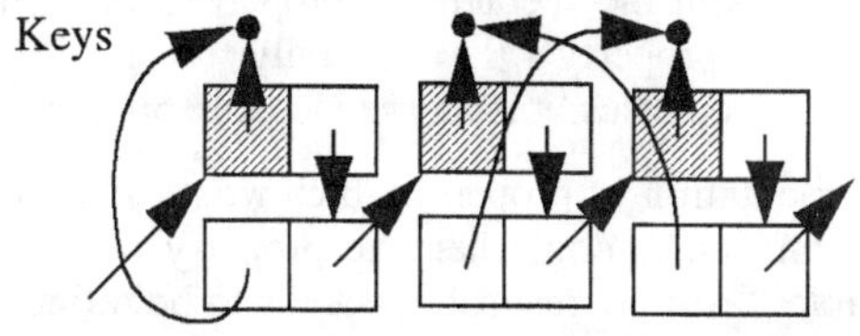


Figure 4
Some problems with weak pairs

Making the "value" slots weak doesn't help either. If some object only exists as a value in a property table, the table must keep that entry, since the key that maps to that value may not have been collected, and so a query on that key is still possible.

### Other Weak Variants

Weak pairs and this implementation of property tables were chosen as a simple way to get weak pointers and notification into the system, and there are many variants we could have chosen instead. Perhaps some other simple variant of weakness would not have this problem.

Unfortunately, the problem is inherent in two-phase tracing and the definition of "almost collectable" that it imposes. Without considering the implementation of property tables, we can discuss their characteristics. For example, given a property table and a key, there must be a "get value" operation to recover the key's value, if it has one.

Likewise, the relationship to garbage collection can be well defined. We would like a key/value pair to be collected when no series of "get value" operations starting with an object reachable without the tables could reach the key. In these situations, no application can reach the key, even though it is in a table.

But how can a two-phase collector trace property tables to construct proofs that a key/value pair should be collected? Consider an object that has itself as its own property value, when there are no other pointers to the object. This object should be "almost collectable." If the table's values are traced in the first phase, then this object would not be "almost collectable," as desired.

If the table's values are not traced in the first phase, consider an object which is a value in a property table when there are no other pointers to it. This object should not be "almost collectable" but would not be traced in the first phase.

The definition of "almost collectable" that two-phase tracing generates doesn't jibe with how property tables should be garbage collected.

## EPHEMERONS

The case where a property table contains the same object as its key and value fields, and the object is not stored anywhere else, is one example of an *unreachable property.* This is an abstract quality of properties independent of implementation.

---

1.This presupposes what it means to be "useful." In particular, we assume that there is no way to ask the table for the keys. So, for example, there is no "which keys have this value" operator.

Another example is two properties, each with the other's key as its value, as in the second two properties in Figure 5. In general, if a property's key is only reachable through unreachable properties, it is an unreachable property.

An implementation of property tables would like to know it may free an association when the property it represents is unreachable. "Almost reachable" needs to be refined to take these unreachable properties into account.

*Ephemerons* are a refinement of weak pairs that solve this "unreachable property" problem. The first slot of an ephemeron is used to hold the key of a property, while the second slot holds the value, but the slots are neither "weak" nor "strong" in the previous sense.

**Tracing Ephemerons in the Garbage Collector**

An ephemeron-aware collector traces objects in three phases rather than two. The first phase traces up to ephemerons, but traces none of their fields. The second phase repeatedly traces ephemerons that can be classed as not maintaining unreachable properties. At the end of the second phase, the remaining ephemerons all represent unreachable properties. The third phase traces all remaining reachable objects (or tombstones the pointers to them).

Ephemerons are classed by the garbage collector as either maintaining a "reachable property" or not. When an ephemeron is encountered in the course of the first phase of a garbage collector trace, the collector does not immediately trace *either field* in the ephemeron, but puts it on a queue. Ephemerons in this queue might maintain reachable or unreachable properties.

In the second phase, the collector scans the queue of delayed ephemerons. Any ephemeron that has a key that has already been reached maintains a property that could be requested -- the ephemeron is reachable, and the key is reachable, so some code might ask for the value. These are classed as "reachable properties."

Any ephemeron that has a key that has not been reached may or may not maintain a reachable property -- that remains to be seen. These ephemerons are requeued for future inspection.

The first group of ephemerons, those maintaining reachable properties, are now traced in the same way that any non-ephemeron would be. Since the key is known to have already been reached, it has been traced, and only the value field needs to be traced.

But tracing these value fields may make it clear that some ephemeron in the queue maintains a reachable property. Ephemerons on the queue must be inspected again to see if they now can be clearly classified as maintaining a reachable property. Also, more ephemerons may be discovered as the value fields are traced. When they are discovered, they are added to the queue.

This continues until the queue contains only ephemerons that have keys that have not yet been reached. This is a set of ephemerons that maintain unreachable properties. It is not possible to request the value field of one of these ephemerons without first having the key or value field of some other ephemeron in the set. At this point the collector arranges that all of these ephemerons in the set will be notified. If the ephemerons are maintaining a collection of property tables, deleting all of these ephemerons will release the storage associated with the unreachable properties, just as if the properties had been added as instance variables.

In the third phase, the collector traces the remaining objects, beginning at the ephemerons still on the queue. Any ephemerons encountered in this phase are treated as ordinary objects, and all fields traced[1].

The portion of the algorithm presented that traces ephemerons adds running time $O(nd)$ where $n$ is the number of ephemerons and $d$ is the length of the longest chain of ephemerons. In practice, $d$ is small and the algorithm is linear in the number of ephemerons[2].

**Managing External Resources with Ephemerons**

Ephemerons solve a sticky problem in property tables, but surprisingly they also solve the problem in managing external resources using proxies and executors.

Recall that information needed to return a resource to its external manager may be kept in an executor rather than a proxy. When this occurs, the split between executor and proxy must be carefully managed. With only weak pairs, the executor cannot keep a strong reference to the proxy itself or any indirect path that leads to the proxy, since that would cause the collector to find the proxy in phase one of the trace.

If the executor is in a value field of an ephemeron that has the proxy as its key, it may contain references to the proxy without interfering with the finalization. The proxy in the key field guards the executor in the value field. The collector will not trace the executor unless the proxy is reachable anyway. The value fields are traced only after the key is shown to be otherwise reachable, in which case finalization should not occur, or after the collector has decided that the ephemeron maintains an unreachable property, in which case the application will be notified to finalize the resources.

**Further Variants of Ephemerons**

A simple extension to ephemerons is to allow flexibility in the number of "value" fields. The first field of an ephemeron is the "key," and all other fields are treated the same way as the "value" field in a simple ephemeron[3].

This extension applies even if there is only a single field. A one-field Ephemeron simply has the "key" slot, and is a one-element weak container. It can be used to mimic traditional

---

1.It is unclear if they should also be sent a message. Strictly speaking, they are maintaining unreachable properties, and if they had been discovered in phase one or two, because of a conservative pointer for example, they would not effect the results of the trace, but would have been included in the set. Of course, if in addition their keys had been discovered due to another conservative pointer, they would not have been so notified.

two-phase weak tracing.

Three-phase tracing and ephemerons offer a slight variation on what most container-based finalization systems already do, and so most variants of two-phase tracing can be retooled for three-phase tracing. The ephemeron's references may be tombstoned rather than traced, the notification to the application may be synchronous, and so on.

## CONCLUSIONS

Ephemeron tracing, as is implemented with the three-phase algorithm described, solves some long-standing problems with finalization.

- Packages responsible for management of external resources can maintain pointers to the proxies for those resources without interfering with the collector's ability to decide when a proxy indicates a resource that needs to be returned to its external manager.
- Objects can be removed from property tables when they are no longer useful, even if they are used as values of properties of other objects.

## LEGAL NOTICE

I am not a lawyer, and this section should not be taken as legal advice.

Ephemerons have been a trade secret in some Digitalk and ParcPlace-Digitalk products shipped more than one year ago, and ParcPlace-Digitalk has allowed publication of this paper, making this trade secret public knowledge. It is my understanding that because more than a year has passed since shipping those products, a valid United States patent for ephemerons would not be issued to the inventor.

I do not know if any other obstacles, such as foreign patent rights, should discourage anyone else from implementing ephemerons.

Java, VisualWorks, and VisualSmalltalk, are trademarks.

---

2.Ephemerons can be recovered in time strictly proportional to the number of ephemerons. To do this, build distinct delay queues for each unique key that has not yet been visited. When the trace encounters an ephemeron, if the key has already been traced, there will be no delay queue, and the ephemeron should be traced immediately. If the key has not been traced, there will be a delay queue and the ephemeron should be enqueued.
When any object which is a key for some delayed ephemerons is found to be reachable, its associated queue of delayed ephemerons should be traced at that time, and the queue deleted.
Any ephemeron that is left on any queue after this single trace phase maintains an unreachable property. These ephemerons need to be traced in a second phase.

3.This extension is allowed in VisualWorks's and VisualSmalltalk's implementation of ephemerons.

## ACKNOWLEDGMENTS

Ephemerons were developed by employees of Digitalk, Inc, and this paper was written with the support of many people at ParcPlace-Digitalk, Inc.

Ephemerons were designed by George Bosworth. They were first implemented for VisualSmalltalk by Roger Thayer. Barry Hayes implemented them for VisualWorks.

## REFERENCES

[AAB+91] H. Abelson, N. I. Adams IV, D. H. Bartley, G. Brooks, R. K. Dybvig, D. P. Friedman, R. Halstead, C. Hanson, C. T. Haynes, E. Kohlbecker, D. Oxley, K. M. Pitman, G. J. Rozas, G. L. Steele JR., G. J. Sussman, and M. Wand. Revised(4) Report on the Algorithmic Language Scheme. ACM Lisp Pointers, IV(3), November 1991.

[ADH+89] R. Atkinson, Alan Demers, Carl Hauser, Christian Jacobi, Peter Kessler, and Mark Weiser. Experiences creating a portable Cedar. SIGPLAN Notices, 24(7):261-269, July 1989.

[BW88] Hans-Juergen Boehm and Mark Weiser. Garbage collection in an uncooperative environment. *Software Practice and Experience*, 18(9):807-820, 1988.

[COL60] George E. Collins. A method for overlapping and erasure of lists. *Communications of the ACM*, 3(12):655-657, December 1960.

[DB76] L. Peter Deutsch and Daniel G. Bobrow. An efficient incremental automatic garbage collector. Communications of the ACM, 19(9):522-526, September 1976.

[DBE93] R. Kent Dybvig, Carl Bruggeman, and David Eby. Guardians in a generation-based garbage collector. In *Proceedings of SIGPLAN'93 Conference on Programming Languages Design and Implementation*, volume 28(6):207-216 of ACM SIGPLAN Notices, Albuquerque, New Mexico, June 1993. ACM Press.

[FY69] Robert R. Fenichel and Jerome C. Yochelson. A Lisp garbage collector for virtual memory computer systems. Communications of the ACM, 12(11):611-612, November 1969.

[GSJ96] James Gosling, Bill Joy, and Guy Steele. *The Java Language Specification*, Addison -Wesley, August, 1996.

[Hay92] Barry Hayes "Finalization in the Collector Interface" in *Memory Management, Proceedings of The International Workshop on Memory Management, 1992, St. Malo, France, September, 1992*, Y. Bekkers and J. Cohen, editors, LNCS 637:277-298, Springer-Verlag.

[LH83] Henry Lieberman and Carl E. Hewitt. A real-time garbage collector based on the lifetimes of objects. Communications of the ACM, 26(6):419-29, 1983. Also report TM-184, Laboratory for Computer Science, MIT, Cambridge, MA, July 1980 and AI Lab Memo 569, 1981.

[Par90] ParcPlace Systems. *ObjectWorks/Smalltalk User's Guide, Release 4*. ParcPlace Systems, Inc, Mountain View, CA, 1990.

[RAM84] Jonathan A. Rees, Norman I. Adams, and James

R. Meechan. The T Manual. Technical report, Yale University, January 1984.

[Rov85] Paul Rovner. On adding garbage collection and runtime types to a strongly-typed, statically-checked, concurrent language. Technical Report CSL-84-7, Xerox PARC, Palo Alto, CA, July 1985.

[Wil92] Paul R. Wilson. "Uniprocessor Garbage Collection Techniques" in *Memory Management, Proceedings of The International Workshop on Memory Management, 1992, St. Malo, France, September, 1992*, Y. Bekkers and J. Cohen, editors, LNCS 637:1-42, Springer-Verlag.

[Xer85] Xerox Corporation. Interlisp Reference Manual, Volume 1. Xerox Corporation, Palo Alto, CA, October 1985.

## EPHEMERON COLLECTION CODE

Send the mark message to every object that's reachable from the roots.

```
Heap::garbageCollectMark
  self markPhase1.
  self markPhase2.
  self markPhase3
```

Mark all of the objects from the roots up to any ephemerons. Place the ephemerons in the global collection EphemeronQueue.

```
Heap::markPhase1
  EphemeronQueue makeEmpty.
  self enumerateRoots: [:rootPointer |
    rootPointer tracePointerQueueingEphemerons]
```

Mark all of the objects reachable from this pointer, queueing all of the ephemerons encountered.

```
Pointer::tracePointerQueueingEphemerons
  self deref isMarked
    return.

  self deref markObject.
  self deref isEphemeron
    EphemeronQueue add: self.
  else
    self deref enumeratePointers: [:pointer |
      pointer tracePointerQueueingEphemerons]
```

Identify a set of ephemerons with reachable keys, and trace them. Since that might cause other ephemerons' keys to become reachable, recurse until all the ephemerons on the queue have unreachable keys.

```
Heap::markPhase2
  | reachableProperties otherProperties |

  otherProperties <- Collection new.
  reachableProperties <- Collection new.
  EphemeronQueue enumerate: [:ephemeron |
    ephemeron deref key isMarked
      reachableProperties add: ephemeron.
    else
      otherProperties add: ephemeron].
  EphemeronQueue <- otherProperties.

  reachableProperties empty not
    reachableProperties enumerate: [:reachableProperty |
      | value |
      value <- reachableProperty deref valueField.
      value tracePointerQueueingEphemerons].
    self markPhase2
```

The queue contains a collection of ephemerons that maintain unreachable properties. Notify the ephemerons, and trace through.

```
Heap::markPhase3
  EphemeronQueue enumerate: [:ephemeron |
    ephemeron deref signal: almostCollectable.
    ephemeron deref keyField tracePointer.
    ephemeron deref valueField tracePointer]
```

Mark all of the objects reachable from this pointer, paying no attention to ephemerons.

```
Pointer::tracePointer
  self deref isMarked
    return.

  self deref markObject.
  self deref enumeratePointers: [:pointer |
    pointer tracePoiner]
```

# The Design and Performance of a Real-time CORBA Event Service

Timothy H. Harrison, David L. Levine, and Douglas C. Schmidt

{harrison,levine,schmidt}@cs.wustl.edu
Department of Computer Science, Washington University
St. Louis, MO 63130, USA

## Abstract

*The CORBA Event Service provides a flexible model for asynchronous communication among objects. However, the standard CORBA Event Service specification lacks important features required by real-time applications. For instance, operational flight programs for fighter aircraft have complex real-time processing requirements. This paper describes the design and performance of an object-oriented, real-time implementation of the CORBA Event Service that is designed to meet these requirements.*

*This paper makes three contributions to the design and performance measurement of object-oriented real-time systems. First, it illustrates how to extend the CORBA Event Service so that it is suitable for real-time systems. These extensions support periodic rate-based event processing and efficient event filtering and correlation. Second, it describes how to develop object-oriented event dispatching and scheduling mechanisms that can provide real-time guarantees. Finally, the paper presents benchmarks that demonstrate the performance tradeoffs of alternative concurrent dispatching mechanisms for real-time Event Services.*

## 1 Introduction

There is a widespread belief in the embedded systems community that object-oriented (OO) techniques are not suitable for real-time systems. In particular, the dynamic binding properties of OO programming languages seem antithetical to real-time systems, which require deterministic execution behavior and low latency. However, many real-time application domains (such as avionics, telecommunications, process control, and distributed interactive simulation) can benefit from flexible and open distributed object computing architectures, such as those defined in the CORBA specification [1].

### 1.1 Overview of CORBA

CORBA is a distributed object computing middleware standard being defined by the Object Management Group (OMG).


OOPSLA '97 10/97 GA, USA
© 1997 ACM 0-89791-908-4/97/0010...$3.50

CORBA is designed to support the development of flexible and reusable distributed services and applications by (1) separating interfaces from remote implementations and (2) automating many common network programming tasks (such as object registration, location, and activation; request demultiplexing; framing and error-handling; parameter marshalling and demarshalling; and operation dispatching).

Figure 1 illustrates the primary components in the OMG Reference Model architecture [2]:

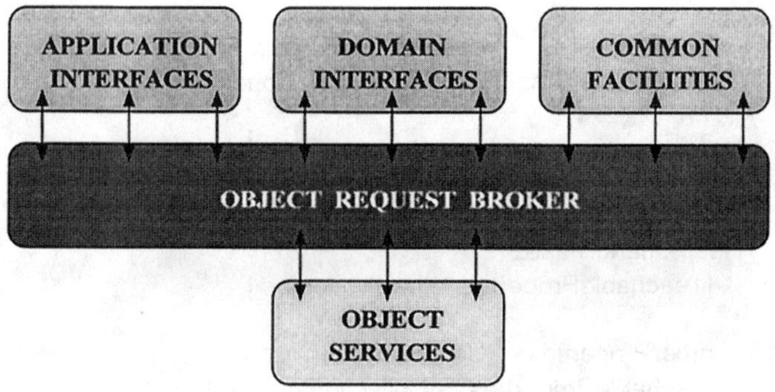


Figure 1: **OMG Reference Model Architecture.**

At the heart of the OMG Reference Model is the *Object Request Broker* (ORB). ORBs allow clients to invoke operations on target object implementations without concern for where the object resides, what language the object is written in, the OS/hardware platform, or the type of communication protocols and networks used to interconnect distributed objects [3].

This paper focuses on the *CORBA Event Service*, which is defined within the CORBA Object Services (COS) component in Figure 1. The COS specification [4] presents architectural models and interfaces that factor out common services for developing distributed applications.

Many distributed applications exchange asynchronous requests using *event-based* execution models [5]. To support these common use-cases, the CORBA Event Service defines **supplier** and **consumer** participants. Suppliers generate events and consumers process events received from suppliers. In addition, the CORBA Event Service defines an **Event Channel**, which is a mediator [6] that propagates events to consumers on behalf of suppliers.

The OMG Event Service model simplifies application software by allowing decoupled suppliers and consumers, asynchronous event delivery, and distributed group communication [7]. In theory, this model seems to address many common needs of event-based, real-time applications. In practice, however, the standard CORBA Event Service specification lacks other important features required by real-time applications such as *real-time event dispatching and scheduling, periodic event processing*, and *efficient event filtering and correlation mechanisms.*

To alleviate the limitations with the standard COS Event Service, we have developed a *Real-time Event Service* (RT Event Service) as part of the TAO project [3] at Washington University. TAO is a real-time ORB endsystem that provides end-to-end quality of service guarantees to applications by vertically integrating CORBA middleware with OS I/O subsystems, communication protocols, and network interfaces. Figure 2 illustrates the key architectural components in TAO and their relationship to the real-time Event Service.

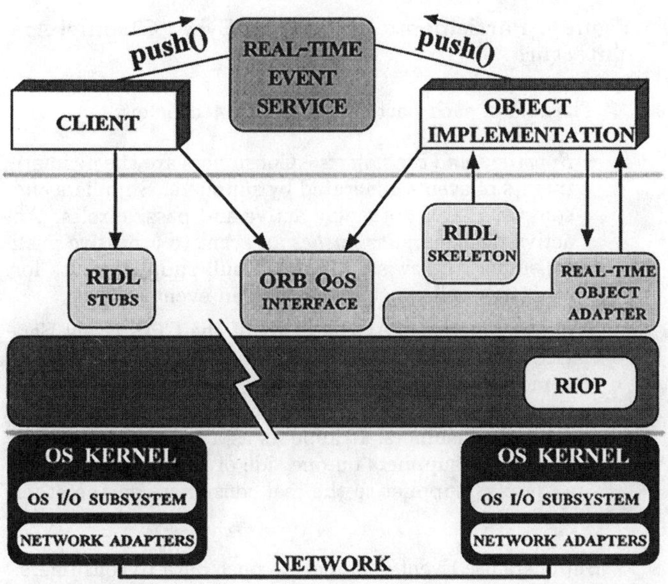


Figure 2: **TAO: An ORB Endsystem Architecture for High-Performance, Real-time CORBA.**

TAO's RT Event Service augments the CORBA Event Service model by providing source-based and type-based filtering, event correlations, and real-time dispatching. To facilitate real-time scheduling (*e.g.*, rate monotonic [8]), TAO's RT Event Channels can be configured to support various strategies for priority-based event dispatching and preemption. This functionality is implemented using a real-time dispatching mechanism that coordinates with a system-wide real-time Scheduling Service.

TAO's RT Event Service runs on real-time OS platforms (*e.g.*, VxWorks and Solaris 2.x) that provide real-time scheduling guarantees to application threads. Windows NT also provides real-time threads, though it lacks certain features required for hard real-time systems [9].

## 1.2 Related Work

Conventional approaches to quality of service (QoS) enforcement have typically adopted existing solutions from the domain of real-time scheduling, [8], fair queuing in network routers [10], or OS support for continuous media applications [11]. In addition, there have been efforts to implement new concurrency mechanisms for real-time processing (such as the real-time threads of Mach [12] and real-time CPU scheduling priorities of Solaris [13]).

However, QoS research at the network and OS layers has not necessarily addressed key requirements and usage characteristics of distributed object computing middleware. For instance, research on QoS for network infrastructure has focused largely on policies for allocating bandwidth on a per-connection basis. Likewise, research on real-time operating systems has focused largely on avoiding priority inversions and non-determinism in synchronization and scheduling mechanisms. In contrast, the programming model for developers of OO middleware focuses on invoking remote operations on distributed objects. Determining how to map the results from the network and OS layers to OO middleware is a major focus of our research.

There are several commercial CORBA-compliant Event Service implementations available from multiple vendors (such as Expersoft, Iona, Sun Systems, and Visigenic Software). Iona also sells OrbixTalk, which is a messaging technology based on IP multicast. Unfortunately, since the CORBA Event Service specification does not address issues critical for real-time applications, these implementations are not acceptable solutions for many domains.

The OMG has issued a request for proposals (RFP) on a new Notification Service [14] that has generated several responses [15]. The RFP specifies that a proposed Notification Service must be a superset of the COS Event Service with interfaces for the following features: event filtering, event delivery semantics (*e.g.*, at least once, at most once, *etc.*), security, event channel federations, and event delivery QoS. The organizations contributing to this effort have done some excellent work in addressing many of the shortcomings of the CORBA Event Service [16]. However, the OMG RFP documents do not address the implementation issues related to the Notification Service.

Although there has been research on formalisms for real-time objects [17], relatively little published research on the design and performance of real-time OO systems exists. Our approach is based on emerging distributed object computing standards (*i.e.*, CORBA) - we focus on the design and performance of various strategies for implementing QoS in real-time ORBs [3].

The QuO project at BBN [18] has defined a model for communicating changes in QoS characteristics between applications, middleware, and the underlying endsystems and network. The QuO architecture differs from our work on RT Event Channels, however, since QuO does not provide hard real-time guarantees of ORB endsystem CPU scheduling. SunSoft [19] describes techniques for optimizing the performance of CORBA Event Service implementations. As with QuO, their focus also was not on guaranteeing CPU processing for events with hard real-time deadlines.

Rajkumar, *et al.*, describe a real-time publisher/subscriber prototype developed at CMU SEI [5]. Their Publisher/Subscriber model is functionally similar to the COS Event Service, though it uses real-time threads to prevent priority inversion within the communication framework. One interesting aspect of the CMU model is the separation of priorities for subscription and event transfer so that these activities can be handled by different threads with different priorities. However, the model does not utilize any QoS specifications from publishers (suppliers) or subscribers (consumers). As a result, the message delivery mechanism does not assign thread priorities according to the priorities of publishers or subscribers. In contrast, the TAO Event Service utilizes QoS parameters from suppliers and consumers to guarantee the event delivery semantics determined by a real-time scheduling service.

## 1.3 Organization

This paper is organized as follows: Section 2 describes how the CORBA Event Service model can help to simplify application development in real-time domains like avionics; Section 3 discusses the real-time extensions we added to the CORBA Event Service; Section 4 outlines the OO framework for real-time event dispatching and scheduling that forms the core of TAO's Real-time Event Service; Section 5 shows how different implementations of the dispatching and scheduling mechanisms perform under different workloads on VxWorks running real-time threads; Section 6 discusses our experiences using OO techniques in a real-time context; and Section 7 presents concluding remarks.

# 2 Overview of the OMG CORBA Event Service

## 2.1 Background

The standard CORBA operation invocation model supports twoway, oneway, and deferred synchronous interactions between clients and servers. The primary strength of the twoway model is its intuitive mapping onto the `object->operation()` paradigm supported by OO languages. In principle, twoway invocations simplify the development of distributed applications by supporting an implicit request/response protocol that makes remote operation invocations transparent to the client.

In practice, however, the standard CORBA operation invocation models is too restrictive for real-time applications. In particular, these models lack asynchronous message delivery, do not support timed invocations or group communication, and can lead to excessive polling by clients. Moreover, standard oneway invocations might not implement reliable delivery and deferred synchronous invocations require the use of the CORBA Dynamic Invocation Interface (DII), which yields excessive overhead for most real-time applications [20].

The Event Service is a CORBA Object Service that is designed to alleviate some of the restrictions with standard CORBA invocation models. In particular, the COS Event Service supports asynchronous message delivery and allows one or more suppliers to send messages to one or more consumers. Event data can be delivered from suppliers to consumers without requiring these participants to know about each other explicitly.

## 2.2 Structure and Participants for the COS Event Service

Figure 3 shows the key participants in the COS Event Service architecture:

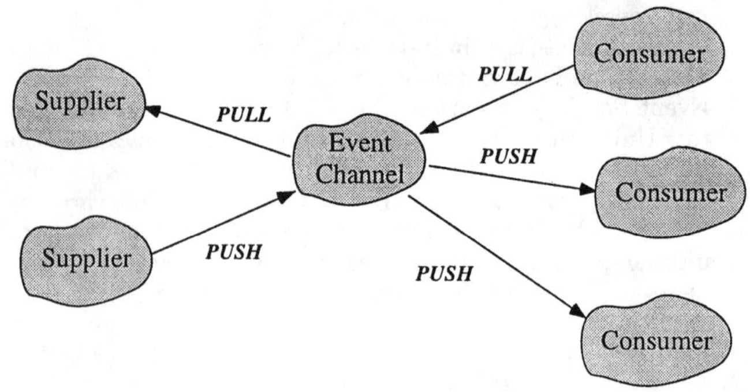


Figure 3: **Participants in the COS Event Channel Architecture.**

The role of each participant is outlined below:

- *Suppliers and consumers* – Consumers are the ultimate targets of events generated by suppliers. Suppliers and consumers can both play active and passive roles. An active push supplier *pushes* an event to a passive push consumer. Likewise, a passive pull supplier waits for an active pull consumer to *pull* an event from it.
- *Event Channel* – At the heart of the COS Event Service is the Event Channel, which plays the role of a mediator between consumers and suppliers. The Event Channel manages object references to suppliers and consumers. It appears as a "proxy" consumer to the real suppliers on one side of the channel and as a "proxy" supplier to the real consumers on the other side.

Suppliers use Event Channels to push data to consumers. Likewise, consumers can explicitly pull data from suppliers. The push and pull semantics of event propagation help to free consumers and suppliers from the overly restrictive synchronous semantics of the standard CORBA twoway communication model. In addition, Event Channels can implement group communication by serving as a replicator, broadcaster, or multicaster that forward events from one or more suppliers to multiple consumers.

There are two models (*i.e.*, *push* vs. *pull*) of participant collaborations in the COS Event Service architecture. This paper focuses on real-time enhancements to the push model, which allows suppliers of events to initiate the transfer of event data to consumers. Suppliers push events to the Event Channel, which in turn pushes the events to consumers.

## 2.3 Applying TAO's Real-time Event Service to Real-time Avionics Systems

Modern avionics systems are characterized by processing tasks with deterministic and statistical real-time deadlines, periodic processing requirements, and complex data dependencies. Building flexible application software and OO middleware that meets these requirements is challenging because the need for determinism and predictability often results in tightly coupled designs. For instance, conventional avionics mission control applications consist of closely integrated responsibilities that manage sensors, navigate the airplane's course, and control weapon release.

Tight coupling often yields highly efficient custom implementations. As the example below shows, however, the inflexibility of tightly coupled software can substantially increase the effort and cost of integrating new and improved avionics features. For example, navigation suites are a source of continual change, both across platforms and over time. The specific components that make up the navigation suite (*e.g.*, sensors) change frequently to improve accuracy and availability. Many conventional avionics systems treat each implementation as a "point solution," with built-in dependencies on particular components. This tight coupling requires expensive and time consuming development effort to port systems to newer and more powerful navigation technologies.

## 2.4 Overview of Conventional Avionics Application Architectures

Figure 4 shows a conventional architecture for distributing periodic I/O events throughout an avionics application:

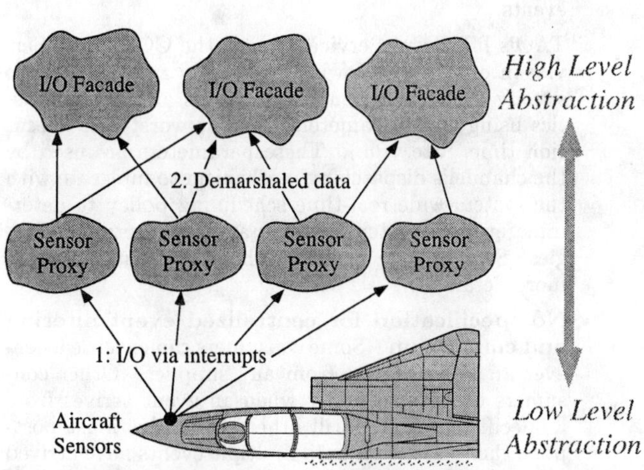


Figure 4: **Example Avionics Mission Control Application.**

This example has the following participants:

- *Aircraft Sensors* – Aircraft-specific devices generate sensor data at regular intervals (*e.g.*, 30 Hz (*i.e.*, 30 times a second), 15 Hz, 5 Hz, *etc.*). The arrival of sensor data generates interrupts that notify the mission computing applications to receive the incoming data.
- *Sensor Proxies* – Mission computing systems must process data to and from many types of aircraft sensors, including Global Position System (GPS), Inertial Navigation Set (INS), and Forward Looking Infrared Radar. To decouple the details of sensor communication from the applications, Sensor Proxy objects are created for each sensor on the aircraft. When I/O interrupts occur, data from a sensor is given to an appropriate Sensor Proxy. Each Sensor Proxy object demarshals the incoming data and notifies I/O Facade objects that depend on the sensor's data. Since modern aircraft can be equipped with hundreds of sensors, a large number of Sensor Proxy objects may exist in the system.
- *I/O Facade* – I/O Facades represent objects that depend on data from one or more Sensor Proxies. I/O Facade objects use data from Sensor Proxies to provide higher-level views to other application objects. For instance, the aircraft position computed by an I/O Facade is used by the navigation and weapon release subsystems.

The *push*-driven model described above is commonly used in many real-time environments, such as industrial process control systems and military command/control systems. One positive consequence of this push-driven model is the efficient and predictable execution of operations. For instance, I/O Facades only execute when their event dependencies are satisfied (*i.e.*, when they are called by Sensor Proxies).

In contrast, using a *pull*-driven model to design the mission control application would require I/O Facades that actively acquire data from the Sensor Proxies. If the data was not available to be pulled, the calling I/O Facade would need to block awaiting a result. In order for the I/O Facade to pull, the system must allocate additional threads to allow the application to make progress while the I/O Facade task is blocked. However, adding threads to the system has many negative consequences (such as increased context switching overhead, synchronization complexity, and complex real-time thread scheduling policies). Conversely, by using the push model, blocking is largely alleviated, which reduces the need for additional threads. Therefore, this paper focuses on the push model.

## 2.5 Drawbacks with Conventional Avionics Architectures

A disadvantage to the architecture shown in Figure 4 is the strong coupling between suppliers (Sensor Proxies) and consumers (I/O Facades). For instance, in order to call back to I/O Facades, each Sensor Proxy must know which I/O Facades depend on its data. As a result, changes to the I/O Facade layer (*e.g.*, addition/removal of a consumer) require the modification of Sensor Proxies. Likewise, consumers that register for callbacks are tightly coupled with suppliers. If the availability of new hardware (such as Forward Looking Infrared Radar) requires a new Sensor Proxy, I/O Facades must be altered to take advantage of the new technology.

## 2.6 Alleviating Drawbacks with Conventional Avionics Architectures

Figure 5 shows how an Event Channel can alleviate the disadvantages of the tightly coupled consumers and suppliers shown above in Figure 4.

In Figure 5, Sensor Proxy objects are suppliers of I/O events that are propagated by an Event Channel to I/O Facades, which consume the demarshalled I/O data. Sensor Proxies push I/O events to the channel without having to know which I/O Facades depend on the data. The benefit of using the Event Channel is that Sensor Proxies are

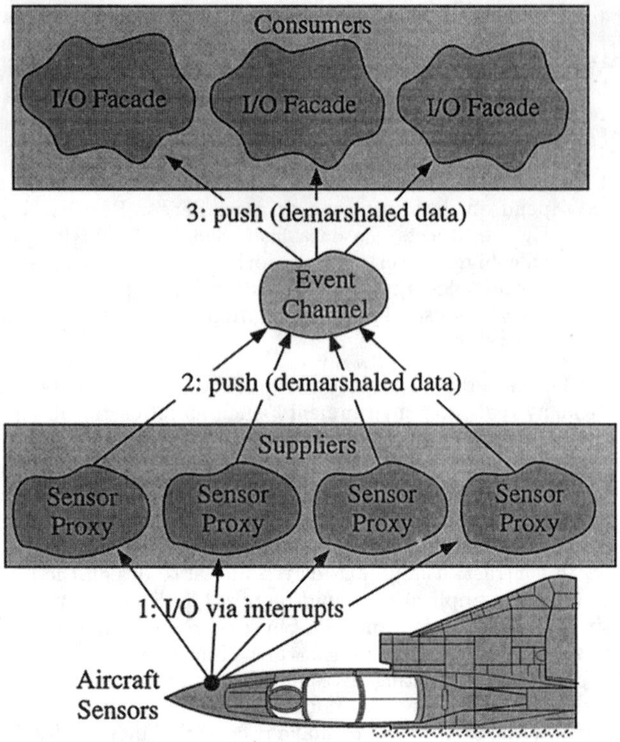


Figure 5: **Example Avionics Application with Event Channel.**

unaffected when I/O Facades are added or removed. This architectural decoupling is described concisely by the Observer pattern [6].

Another benefit of an Event Channel-based architecture is that an I/O Facade need not know which Sensor Proxies supply its data. Since the channel mediates on behalf of the Sensor Proxies, I/O Facades can register for certain types of events (*e.g.*, GPS and/or INS data arrival) without knowing which Sensor Proxies actually supply these types of events (Section 3.2 discusses typed-filtering). Once again, the use of an Event Channel makes it possible to add or remove Sensor Proxies without changing I/O Facades.

# 3 Overview of the Real-time Event Service

## 3.1 Motivation

As shown in the previous section, the CORBA COS Event Service provides a flexible model for transmitting asynchronous events among objects. For example, it removes several restrictions inherent in synchronous twoway communication. Moreover, it frees application programmers from the tedious and error-prone details of handling registrations from multiple consumers and suppliers. In addition, the COS Event Service interfaces are fairly intuitive and the consumer/supplier connections and event delivery models are symmetrical and straightforward.

However, the standard COS Event Service Specification lacks several important features required by real-time applications. Chief among these missing features include real-time event dispatching and scheduling, periodic event processing, and centralized event filtering and correlations. To resolve these limitations, we have developed a Real-time Event Service (RT Event Service) as part of the TAO project [3]. TAO's RT Event Service extends the COS Event Service specification to satisfy the quality of service (QoS) needs of real-time applications in domains like avionics, telecommunications, and process control.

The following list summarizes the features missing in the COS Event Service and outlines how TAO's Real-time Event Service supports them:

- **No guarantees for real-time event dispatching and scheduling** – In a real-time system, events must be processed so that consumers can meet their QoS deadlines. For instance, the Sensor Proxies shown in Figure 5 generate notification events that allow the I/O Facades who depend on the sensor data to execute. To enforce a real-time scheduling policy, higher priority I/O Facades must receive events and be allowed to run to completion before lower priority I/O Facades receive events.

  The COS Event Service has no notion of QoS, however. In particular, there is no Event Channel interface that consumers can use to specify their execution and scheduling requirements. Therefore, standard COS Event Channels provide no guarantee that they will dispatch events from suppliers with the correct scheduling priority, relative to the consumers of these events.

  TAO's RT Event Service extends the COS Event Service interfaces by allowing consumers and suppliers to specify their execution requirements and characteristics using QoS parameters (such as worst-case execution time, rate, *etc.*). These parameters are used by the channel's dispatching mechanism to integrate with the system-wide real-time scheduling policy to determine event dispatch ordering and preemption strategies. Section 4.2.1 describes these QoS parameters in more detail.

- **No specification for centralized event filtering and correlation** – Some consumers can execute whenever an event arrives from any supplier. Other consumers can execute only when an event arrives from a specific supplier. Still other consumers must postpone their execution until multiple events have arrived from a particular set of suppliers (*e.g.*, a correlation of events).

  For instance, an I/O Facade may depend on data from a subset of all Sensor Proxies. Furthermore, it may use data from many Sensor Proxies in a single calculation of aircraft position. Therefore, the I/O Facade can not make progress until all of the Sensor Proxy objects receive I/O from their external sensors.

  It is possible to implement filtering using standard COS Event Channels, which can be chained to create an event filtering graph that consumers to register for a subset of the total events in the system. However, the filter graph defined in standard COS increases the number of hops that a message must travel between suppliers and consumers. The increased overhead incurred by traversing these hops is typically unacceptable for real-time applications with low latency requirements. Furthermore, the COS filtering model does not address the event correlation needs of consumers that must wait for *multiple* events to occur before they can execute.

To alleviate these problems, TAO's RT Event Service provides filtering and correlation mechanisms that allow consumers to specify logical OR and AND event dependencies. When those dependencies are met, the RT Event Service dispatches all events that satisfy the consumers' dependencies. For instance, the I/O Facade can specify its requirements to the RT Event Service so that the channel only notifies the Facade object after all its Sensor Proxies have received I/O. At that time, the I/O Facade receives an aggregate of all the Sensor Proxies it depends on via a single `push`.

- **No support for periodic processing** –

  Consumers in real-time systems typically require $C$ units of computation time every $P$ milliseconds. For instance, some avionics signal processing filters must be updated periodically or else they will spend a substantial amount of time reconverging. Likewise, an I/O Facade might guarantee regular delivery of its data to higher level components, regardless of whether its Sensor Proxy objects actually generate events at the expected rate.

  In both cases, consumers have strict deadlines by which time they must execute the requested $C$ units of computation time. However, the COS Event Service does not permit consumers to specify their temporal execution requirements. Therefore, periodic processing is not supported in standard COS Event Service implementations.

  TAO's RT Event Service allows consumers to specify event dependency timeouts. It uses these timeout requests to propagate temporal events in coordination with system scheduling policies. In additional to the canonical use of timeout events (*i.e.*, receiving timeouts at some interval), a consumer can request to receive a timeout event if its dependencies are not satisfied within some time period (*i.e.*, a real-time "watchdog" timer). For instance, an I/O Facade can register to receive a timeout event if its Sensor Proxy dependencies are not satisfied after some time interval. This way, it can make best effort calculations on the older sensor data and notify interested higher level components.

## 3.2 RT Event Service Architecture

Figure 6 shows the high-level architecture of TAO's RT Event Service implementation.

The role of each component in the RT Event Service is outlined below:

- *Event Channel* – In the RT Event Service model, the Event Channel plays the same role as it does in the conventional COS Event Service. Externally, it provides two factory interfaces, `ConsumerAdmin` and `SupplierAdmin`, which allow applications to obtain consumer and supplier administration objects, respectively. These administration objects make it possible to connect and disconnect consumers and suppliers to the channel. Internally, the channel is comprised of

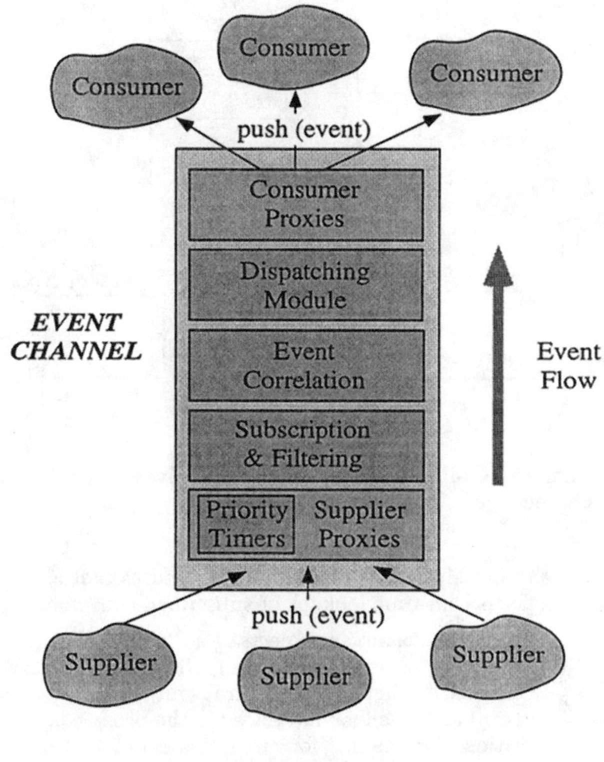


Figure 6: **RT Event Service Architecture.**

  several processing modules based on the ACE Streams framework [21]. As described below, each module encapsulates independent tasks of the channel.

- *Consumer Proxy Module* – The interface to the Consumer Proxy Module is identical to `ConsumerAdmin` interface defined in the COS Event Service `CosEventChannelAdmin` module. It provides factory methods for creating objects that support the `ProxyPushSupplier` interface. In the COS model, the `ProxyPushSupplier` interface is used by consumers to connect and disconnect from the channel.

  TAO's RT Event Service model extends the standard COS `ProxyPushSupplier` interfaces so that consumers can register their execution dependencies with a channel. Figure 7 shows the types of data exchanged and the inter-object collaborations involved when a consumer invokes the `ProxyPushSupplier::connect_push_consumer` registration operation.

- *Supplier Proxy Module* – The interface to this module is identical to `SupplierAdmin` interface defined in the COS Event Service `CosEventChannelAdmin` module. It provides factory methods for creating objects that support the `ProxyPushConsumer` interface. Suppliers use the `ProxyPushConsumer` interface to connect and disconnect from the channel.

  TAO's RT Event Service model extends the standard COS `ProxyPushConsumer` interface so that suppliers can specify the types of events they generate. With this information, the channel's Subscription and Fil-

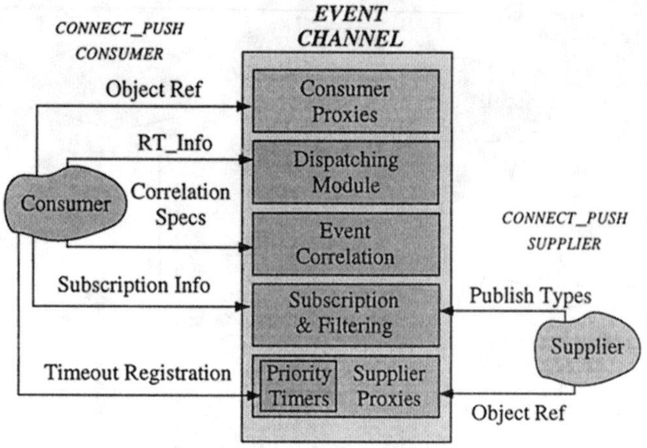


Figure 7: **Collaborations in the RT Event Service Architecture.**

tering Module can build data structures that allow efficient run-time lookups of subscribed consumers.

`ProxyPushConsumer` objects also represent the entry point of events from suppliers into an Event Channel. When Suppliers transmit an event to the `ProxyPushConsumer` interface via the proxy's `push` operation the channel forwards this event to the `push` operation of interested consumer object(s).

- *Subscription and filtering* –

  The CORBA Event Service defines Event Channels as broadcasters that forward all events from suppliers to all consumers. This approach has several drawbacks. If consumers are only interested in a subset of events from the suppliers, they must implement their own event filtering to discard unneeded events. Furthermore, if a consumer ultimately discards an event, then delivering the event to the consumer needlessly wastes bandwidth and processing.

  To address these shortcomings, TAO's RT Event Service extends the COS interfaces to allow consumers to subscribe for particular subsets of events. The channel uses these subscriptions to filter supplier events, only forwarding them to interested consumers.

  There are several reasons why TAO implements filtering in the channel. First, the channel relieves consumers from implementing filtering semantics. Second, it reduces communication channel load by eliminating filtered events in the channel instead of at consumers. Furthermore, to implement filtering at the suppliers, the suppliers would require knowledge of consumers. Since this would violate one of the primary motivations for an event service (that is, decoupled consumers and suppliers), TAO integrates filtering into the channel.

  Adding filtering to the Event Channel requires a well-defined type system for events. Although the complete schema for this type system is beyond the scope of this paper, it includes source ID, type, data, and timestamp fields (the schema is fully described in [22]). The RT Event Channel uses the event type system in the following ways:

  1. *Supplier-based filtering* – Not all consumers that connect to an Event Channel are interested in the same events. In this case, consumers only register for events generated by certain suppliers. The event type system includes a source ID field that allows applications to specify unique supplier identifiers with each event. The Subscription and Filtering Module uses this field to locate consumers that have subscribed to particular suppliers in *O(1)* worst-case time.
  2. *Type-based filtering* – Each event contains a type field. This allows consumers to register for events of a particular type. Since the type field is represented as an enumerated type, the subscription and Filtering Module utilizes a lookup structure to find type-based subscribers in *O(1)* worst-case time.
  3. *Combined supplier/type-based filtering* – Consumers can register for any combination of supplier and type-based filtering (*e.g.*, only supplier-based, only type-based, or supplier-based and type-based). To implement this efficiently, the Subscription and Filtering Module maintains type-based subscription tables for every supplier in the system.

     When an event enters the Subscription and Filtering Module, consumers that subscribe to combined supplier/type-based IDs are located with two table lookups. The first lookup finds all the type-based subscription tables corresponding to the event's source ID. The second lookup finds the consumers subscribed to the event's type ID.

  The Subscription and Filtering Module permits consumers to temporarily disable event delivery by the channel through `suspend` and `resume` operations. These are lightweight operations that have essentially the same effect as de-registering and re-registering for events. Therefore, `suspend` and `resume` are suitable for frequent changes in consumer sets, which commonly occur during mode changes. By incorporating suspension and resumption in the module closest to the suppliers, Event Channel processing is minimized for suspended consumers.

- *Priority Timers Proxy* – The Supplier Proxy Module contains a special-purpose *Priority Timers Proxy* that manages all timers registered with the channel. When a consumer registers for a timeout, the Priority Timers Proxy cooperates with the Run-time Scheduler to ensure that timeouts are dispatched according to the priority of their corresponding consumer.

  The Priority Timers Proxy uses a heap-based callout queue [23]. Therefore, in the average and worst case, the time required to schedule, cancel, and expire a timer is *O(log N)* (where *N* is the total number of timers). The timer mechanism preallocates all its memory, which eliminates the need for dynamic memory allocation at run-time. Therefore, this mechanism is well-suited for real-time systems requiring highly predictable and efficient timer operations.

- *Event correlation* – A consumer may require certain events to occur before it can proceed. To implement this functionality, consumers can specify conjunctive

("AND") or disjunctive ("OR") semantics when registering their filtering requirements (*i.e.*, supplier-based and/or type-based). Conjunctive semantics instruct the channel to notify the consumer when *all* the specified event dependencies are satisfied. Disjunctive semantics instruct the channel to notify the consumer(s) when *any* of the specified event dependencies are satisfied. Consumers can register their filtering requests with a channel multiple times. In this case, the channel creates a disjunction relation for each of its consumer registrations.

Mechanisms that perform filtering and correlation are called *Event Filtering Discriminators* (EFDs). EFDs allow the run-time infrastructure to handle dependency-based notifications that would otherwise be performed by each consumer as *all* events were pushed to it. Thus, EFDs provide a "data reduction" service that minimizes the number of events received by consumers so that they only receive events they are interested in.

- *Dispatching* – The Dispatching Module determines when events should be delivered to consumers and pushes the events to them accordingly. To guarantee that consumers execute in time to meet their deadlines, this module collaborates with the system-wide Scheduling Service (discussed in Section 4.2). TAO's Off-line Scheduler initially implements the rate monotonic scheduling policy. Section 4 illustrates how adding new dispatching implementations is straightforward since this module is well-encapsulated from other components in the Event Channel's OO real-time event dispatching framework.

### 3.3 Static and Dynamic Event Channel Configuration

The performance requirements of an RT Event Service may vary for different types of real-time applications. The primary motivation for basing the internal architecture of the TAO Event Channel on the ACE Streams framework is to allow static and dynamic channel configurations. Each module shown in Figure 7 may contain multiple "pluggable" strategies, each optimized for different requirements. The Streams-based architecture allows independent processing modules to be added, removed, or modified without requiring changes to other modules.

TAO's Event Channel can be configured in the following ways to support different event dispatching, filtering, and dependency semantics:

- The modules implementing a "full" TAO Event Channel include the Dispatching, Correlation, Filtering, and Consumer/Supplier Proxy modules. Configuring a channel with all of these modules supports type and source-based filtering, correlations, and priority-based queueing and dispatching.
- As discussed in Section 4, TAO's Event Channel Dispatching Module implements several concurrency strategies. Each strategy caters to the type and availability of system resources (such as the OS threading model and the number of CPUs). TAO's Event Channel framework is designed so that changing the number of threads in the system, or changing to a single-threaded concurrency strategy, does not require modifications to unrelated components in a channel.

The following configurations can be achieved by removing certain modules from an Event Channel:

  - Removing the Dispatching Module from the Event Channel results in an *Event Forwarding Discriminator* (EFD) configuration that supports event filtering and correlations. An EFD configuration is shown in Figure 9(C). Since TAO's Filtering and Correlation Modules have been implemented to guarantee deterministic run-time performance, the EFD configuration is applicable for real-time applications that do not require priority-based queueing and dispatching in the Event Channel. As discussed in Section 4.1.1 below, such systems might implement real-time dispatching in the ORB's Object Adapter level, thereby simplifying the channel.
  - Removing the Correlation Module from a full TAO Event Channel yields a *Subscription and Filtering* configuration. This configuration is useful for applications that have no complex inter-event correlation dependencies, but simply want to receive events when they match a simple filter.
  - A *Broadcaster Repeater* configuration can be achieved by removing the Correlation and Dispatching Modules. This configuration supports neither real-time dispatching nor filtering/correlations. In essence, this implements the semantics of the standard COS Event Channel push model.

In static real-time environments (such as conventional avionics systems), the configuration of an Event Channel is generally performed off-line to reduce startup overhead. In dynamic real-time environments (such as telecommunication call-processing), however, component policies may require alteration at run-time. In these contexts, it may be unacceptable to completely terminate a running Event Channel when a scheduling or concurrency policy is updated. In general, therefore, an RT Event Channel framework must support dynamic reconfiguration of policies without interruption while continuing to service communication operations [24]. Basing TAO's RT Event Channel on the ACE Streams framework supports both static and dynamic (re)configuration.

## 4 An Object-Oriented Framework for Real-time Event Service Dispatching and Scheduling

Applications and middleware components using a real-time Event Service have deterministic and statistical deadlines. As a result, TAO's RT Event Channel utilizes a real-time Scheduling Service to ensure that events are processed before deadlines are missed. Most real-time scheduling policies (such as rate monotonic and earliest deadline first) require priority-based event dispatching and preemption. To maximize reuse and allow flexibility between multiple scheduling policies, TAO's Event Channel framework separates the dispatching mechanism from the scheduling policy. The dispatching mechanism implements priority-based dispatching and preemption, but consults a Run-time Scheduler to determine the priorities of objects and events.

This section discusses the Dispatching Module and Scheduling Service in TAO's RT Event Channel.

## 4.1 The Dispatching Module

The Dispatching Module is responsible for implementing priority-based event dispatching and preemption. When the Dispatching Module receives a set of supplier events from the Event Correlation Module, it queries the Run-time Scheduler to determine the priority of the consumers that the events are destined for. With that information, the Dispatching Module can either (1) insert the events in the appropriate priority queues (which are dispatched at a later time) or (2) preempt a running thread to dispatch the new events immediately.

The following figure shows the structure and dynamics of the Dispatching Module in the context of the Event Channel.

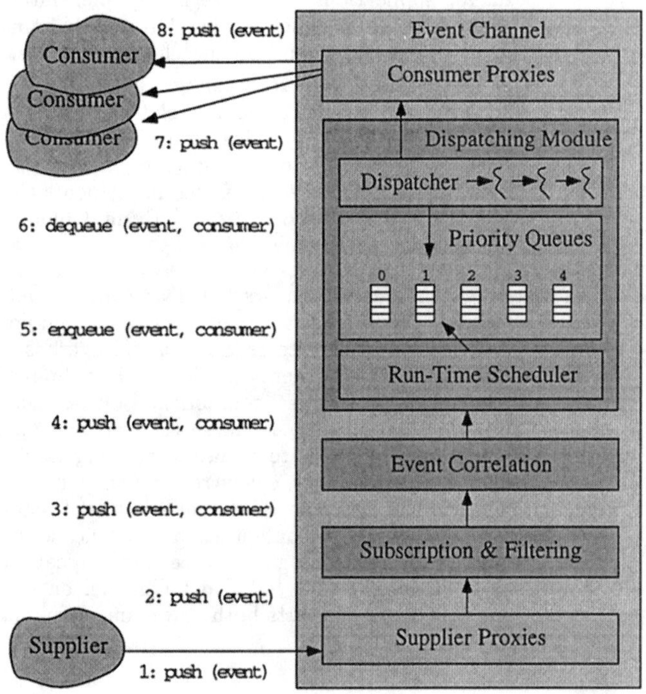


Figure 8: **Event Channel Dispatching.**

The participants in Figure 8 include the following:

- *Consumer and Supplier Proxies* – The Event Channel utilizes proxies to encapsulate communication with the consumers and suppliers. For a distributed consumer or supplier, a proxy manages the details of remote communication.
- *Event filtering and correlation* – When events arrive from consumers, the Event Filtering and Correlation Modules determine which consumers should receive the events and when to dispatch the events. These modules forward the events to the Dispatching Module, which handles the details of dispatching each event to its consumer(s) in accordance with the priority of the event/consumer(s) tuple.
- *Run-time Scheduler* – The Dispatching Module collaborates with the Run-time Scheduler to determine priority values of the event/consumer tuples. Given an event and the target consumer, the Run-time Scheduler determines the priority at which the event should be dispatched to the consumer.

  The motivation for decoupling the Run-time Scheduler from the Dispatching Module is to allow scheduling policies to evolve independently of the dispatching mechanism. TAO's Run-time Scheduler was initially implemented with a rate monotonic scheduling policy that used the consumer's rate to determine the tuple's priority. Subsequent Run-time Scheduler implementations use an Earliest Deadline First (EFD) policy, where the deadline of the event (or consumer) determines the priority of the tuple. Thus, by separating the responsibilities of scheduling from dispatching, the Run-time Scheduler can be replaced without affecting unrelated components in the channel.
- *Priority Queues* – Given an event/consumer tuple, the Run-time Scheduler returns a preemption priority and a sub-priority. The Dispatching Module maintains a priority queue of events for each preemption priority used by the Run-time Scheduler. When an event/consumer tuple arrives, it is inserted onto the queue corresponding to the preemption priority returned by the scheduler. The sub-priority is used by the Dispatcher to determine where in the Priority Queue the tuple is placed (described below).
- *Dispatcher* – The Dispatcher is responsible for removing event/consumer tuples from the priority queues and forwarding the events to the consumers by calling their push operation. Depending on the placement of each tuple in the Priority Queues, the Dispatcher may preempt a running thread in order to dispatch the new tuple.

  For instance, consider the arrival of an event/consumer tuple in a Dispatching Module implemented with real-time preemptive threads. If the Run-time Scheduler assigns the tuple a preemption priority higher than any currently running thread, the Dispatcher will preempt a running thread and dispatch the new tuple. Furthermore, assuming that lower numbers indicate higher priority, the Dispatcher in Figure 8 would dispatch all tuples on queue 0 before dispatching any on queue 1. Similarly, it would dispatch all tuples on queue 1 before those on queue 2, and so on.

  To remove tuples from Priority Queues, the Dispatcher always dequeues from the head of the queue. The Run-time Scheduler can determine the order of dequeueing by returning different sub-priorities for different event/consumer tuples. For instance, assume that an implementation of the Run-time Scheduler must ensure that some event $E_1$ is always dispatched before event $E_2$, but does not require that the arrival of $E_2$ preempt a thread dispatching $E_1$. By assigning a higher sub-priority to event/consumer tuples containing $E_1$, the tuple will always be queued before any tuples containing $E_2$. Therefore, the Dispatcher will always dequeue and dispatch $E_1$ events before $E_2$ events.

  A benefit of separating the functionality of the Dispatcher from the Priority Queues is to allow the implementation of the Dispatcher to change independently of the other channel components. TAO's RT Event Channel has been implemented with four different dispatching mechanisms, as described in the following subsection.

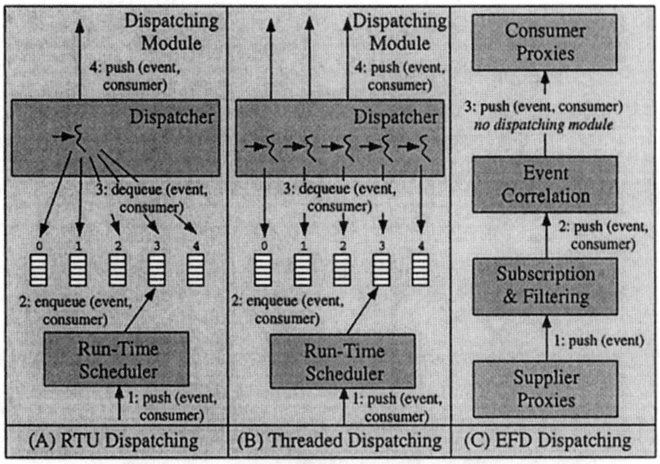


Figure 9: **Dispatcher Implementations.**

### 4.1.1 Dispatcher Preemption Strategies

An important responsibility of the Event Channel's Dispatcher mechanism is *preemption*. Most real-time scheduling policies require preemption. For example, if consumer A with a priority of 2 is executing when consumer B with a priority of 1 becomes runnable, consumer A should be preempted so that B can run until it completes or is itself preempted by a consumer with a priority of 0. As shown in Figure 9, TAO's Event Channel Dispatching Module supports several levels of preemption via the following strategies:

- *Real-time upcall (RTU) dispatching (with deferred preemption)* – Figure 9(A) shows a single-threaded implementation where one thread is responsible for dispatching all queued requests. This requires that consumers cooperatively preempt themselves when a higher priority consumer becomes runnable. This model of "deferred preemption" is based on a Real-time Upcall (RTU) concurrency mechanism [25].

  The primary benefit of the RTU model is its ability to reduce the context switching, synchronization, and data movement overhead incurred by preemptive multi-threading implementations. However, preemption is delayed to the extent that consumers check to see if they must preempt themselves. This latency may be unacceptable in some real-time applications.

- *Real-time preemptive thread dispatching* – An increasing number of OS platforms (*e.g.*, VxWorks, Solaris 2.x, and DEC UNIX) support real-time threads. Figure 9(B) shows an implementation of the Dispatching Module that allocates a Real-time thread (or pool of threads) to each priority queue.

  The advantage of this model is that the dispatcher can leverage kernel support for preemption by associating appropriate OS priorities to each thread. For instance, when a thread at the highest priority becomes ready to run, the OS will preempt any lower priority thread that is running and allow the higher priority thread to run. The disadvantages are that this preemption incurs thread context switching overhead, and that applications must identify, and synchronize access to, data that can be shared by multiple threads.

- *Single-threaded priority-based dispatching* – The Dispatching Module can also be implemented with no support for preemption. This is similar to the RTU dispatching mechanism in the sense that a single-thread is used to dispatch events based on priority. However, once a consumer receives an event, it can run to completion regardless of the arrival of events for higher priority consumers.

  As with the RTU model, single-threaded dispatching exhibits lower context switching overhead than the real-time thread dispatching model. Moreover, since the channel maintains its own thread of control, it does not borrow supplier threads to propagate events. As a result, the channel is an asynchronous event delivery mechanism for suppliers. However, since the channel's dispatching thread does not implement preemption, consumers run to completion regardless of priority. As a result, single-threaded dispatching can suffer from priority inversion, which results in lower system utilization and non-determinism.

- *EFD dispatching* – As discussed in Section 3.3, the Dispatching Module can be removed from the channel, yielding a purely EFD-based Event Channel. This configuration is shown in Figure 9(C). An EFD channel forwards all events to the consumers without any priority queueing, real-time scheduling, or context switching. Events are dispatched without attention to priority, and there is no preemption of consumers when higher priority event/consumer tuples become available.

  EFD channels are appropriate in systems that do not have significant priority-based requirements. In these cases, there is no overhead incurred by a Dispatching Module. However, EFD channels are not always suitable when real-time scheduling policies must be enforced. As shown in Section 5, our performance results show that these drawbacks can cause missed deadlines even under relatively low loads.

The current design of the Dispatching Module is motivated largely from need to support a single host, real-time event propagation mechanism. To allow all CORBA applications to utilize the ORB's real-time scheduling and dispatching features, we are integrating the role of the Dispatching Module into TAO's Real-time Object Adapter [3]. However, this paper focuses on an implementation that integrates real-time dispatching into TAO's Real-time Event Service.

### 4.1.2 Scheduling Enforcement

The real-time scheduling for the version of TAO's Event Channel described in this paper is performed off-line. Therefore, no mechanisms for enforcing component behavior are provided. Consequently, tasks that overrun their allotted resource allocations can cause other tasks to miss their deadlines. An advantage of this "trusting" policy is there is no overhead incurred by QoS enforcement mechanisms that would otherwise be necessary to monitor and enforce the scheduling behavior at run-time. A disadvantage is that all components must behave properly, *i.e.*, they must use only the resources allotted to them. Though the architecture of our Event Service framework supports QoS enforcement, the decision not to include this mechanism in the Event Channel is motivated by the static scheduling characteristics and stringent performance requirements of real-time avionics applications.

#### 4.1.3 Visualization of Dispatching Module Implementations

To visualize the semantic differences between the four Dispatching Module implementations outlined in Section 4.1.1, we implemented a timeline visualization tool in Java. The timeline tool reads event logs from RT Event Service test runs and displays a timeline of supplier and consumer activity. Figures 10 and 11 show timelines from multi-threaded and single-threaded implementations of the Dispatching Module, respectively. Each test run consists of 3 suppliers and 3 consumers, which are listed on the y-axis. Supplier$_2$ and consumer$_2$ run at the highest frequency (40 Hz), supplier$_1$ and consumer$_1$ run at the next highest frequency (20 Hz), and supplier$_0$ and consumer$_0$ run at the lowest frequency (10 Hz).

The x-axis denotes time in $\mu$seconds. Each consumer and supplier outputs a point when it receives an event from the Event Channel. Another point is output when it finishes processing the event. Suppliers receive timeouts and generate a single event for each timeout. Each consumer registers for events from a single supplier. A horizontal line indicates the time span when the respective consumer or supplier runs on the CPU.

Each figure is explained below:

- *Real-time thread dispatching* – Figure 10 shows how OS real-time thread support for preemption results in supplier$_0$ and consumer$_0$ being preempted whenever higher priority tasks become runnable. Our performance results (discussed in Section 5) demonstrate that Dispatching Module implementations (such as the real-time thread dispatching) that support more responsive preemption mechanisms yield higher resource utilization without missing deadlines.
- *Single-threaded dispatching* – Figure 11 shows how a single-threaded dispatching module can result in deadlines being missed if lower priority tasks hold the CPU for excessive periods of time. The negative values next to the end times of supplier$_2$ and consumer$_2$ show the number of $\mu$secs the deadlines were missed. In other words, consumer$_0$ held the CPU too long, so that higher rate suppliers and consumers were unable to execute in time to preserve correct application behavior.

### 4.2 Real-time Scheduling Service

The RT Event Service must guarantee that consumers receive and process events with sufficient time to meet their

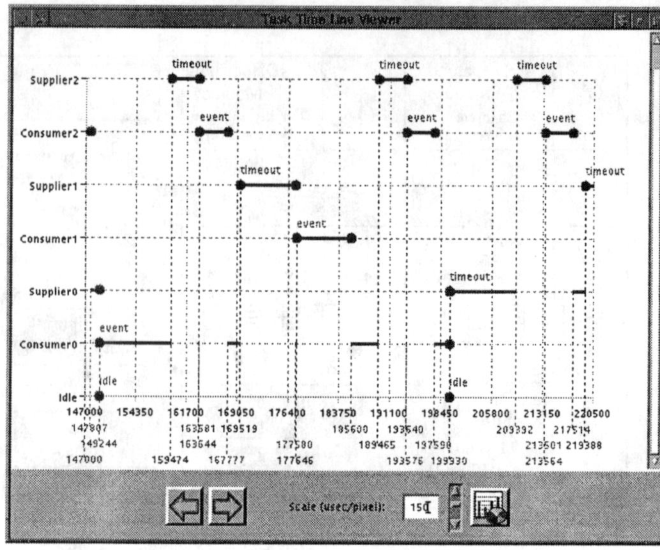


Figure 10: **Timeline from Multi-Threaded Channel.**

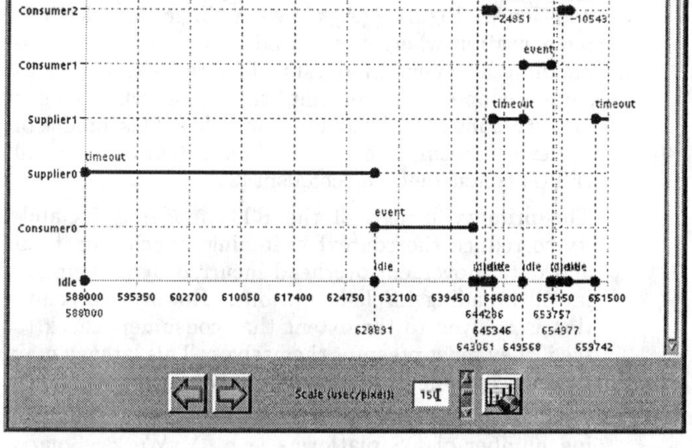


Figure 11: **Timeline from Single-Threaded Channel.**

deadlines. To accomplish this, we have developed a Real-time Scheduling Service. The two primary components in the Real-time Scheduling Service are the Run-time Scheduler and Off-line Scheduler. Although a complete discussion of these components is beyond the scope of this paper, their responsibilities are summarized below ([22] describes these components in detail).

### 4.2.1 Run-time Scheduler

The Run-time Scheduler associates priorities with target object implementation operations at run-time. The implementation of the Real-time Scheduling Service described in this paper uses a static scheduling policy. Therefore, thread priorities are determined prior to run-time by the Off-line Scheduler.

Our Real-time Scheduling Service requires that if an object is to be scheduled, each of its operations must export an `RT_Info` data structure describing the operation's execution properties. During scheduling *configuration runs* (described in Section 4.2.2 below), `RT_Infos` contain execution times and rate requirements. At run-time, the static Scheduler need not know any information about an operation's execution characteristics. Only the operation's priority is needed, so the scheduler can determine how the operation should be dispatched. Thus, at run-time, each operation's `Rt_Info` need only contain priority values for the operation.

At run-time, the Dispatching Module queries the Run-time Scheduler for the priority of a consumer's push operation. The Run-time Scheduler uses a static repository that identifies the execution requirements (including priority) of each operation. The Event Channel's Dispatching Module uses the operation priority returned by the Run-time Scheduler to determine which priority queue an event/consumer tuple should be inserted onto.

All scheduling and priority computation is performed off-line. This allows priorities to be computed rapidly (*i.e.*, looked up in *O(1)* time) at run-time. Thus, TAO's Run-time Scheduler simply provides an interface to the results of the Off-line Scheduler, discussed below.

### 4.2.2 Off-line Scheduler

The Off-line Scheduler has two responsibilities. First, it assigns priorities to object operations. Second, it determines whether a current Event Channel configuration is schedulable given the available resources and the execution requirements of supplier and consumer operations. Both responsibilities require that operation interdependencies be calculated by a *Task Interdependency Compilation* process during during a *configuration run*. Task Interdependency Compilation builds a repository that records which objects' operations call each other. This can be visualized as a directed graph where the nodes in the graph are object operations and directed edges indicate that one operation calls another, as shown in Figure 12.

Once Task Interdependency Compilation is complete, the Off-line Scheduler assigns priorities to each object operation. The implementation of the Event Service described in this paper utilizes a rate monotonic scheduling (RMS) policy [8, 26]. Therefore, priorities are assigned based on task rates, *i.e.*, higher priorities are assigned to threads with faster rates. For instance, a task that needs to execute at

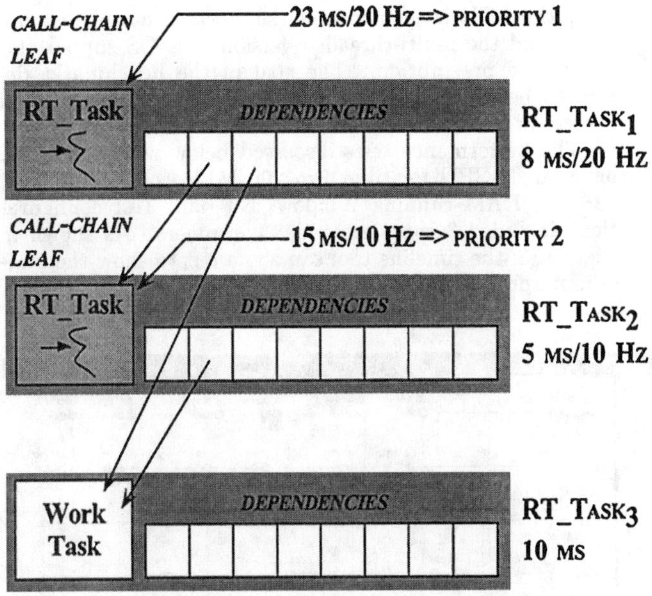


Figure 12: **Scheduling Service Internal Repository.**

30 Hz would be assigned to a thread with a higher priority than a task that needs to execute at 15 Hz.

Most operating systems that support real-time threads guarantee higher priority threads will (1) preempt lower priority threads and (2) run to completion (or until higher priority threads preempt them). Therefore, object operations with higher priorities will preempt object operations with lower priorities. These priority values are computed by the Off-line Scheduler and are stored in a table that is queried by the Run-time Scheduler at execution time.

## 5 Performance Tests

### 5.1 Utilization Measurements

For non-real-time Event Channels (*e.g.*, EFD-based), correctness implies that consumers receive events when their dependencies are met (*i.e.*, source/type subscriptions and correlations). Conversely, for real-time Event Channels (*e.g.*, RTUs and real-time threads), correctness implies that deadlines are met. Therefore, correct RT Event Service behavior requires that (1) consumers receive events when their dependencies are satisfied *and* (2) consumers receive these events in time to meet their deadlines.

An important metric for evaluating the performance of the RT Event Service is the *schedulable bound.* The schedulable bound of a real-time schedule is the maximum resource utilization possible without deadlines being missed [25]. Likewise, the schedulable bound of the RT Event Service is the maximum CPU utilization that supplier and consumers can achieve without missing deadlines.

For TAO's Real-time Scheduling Service to guarantee the schedulability of a system (*i.e.*, all tasks meet their deadlines), high priority tasks must preempt lower priority tasks. With RMS, higher rate tasks preempt lower rate tasks.

Each of the RT Event Channel's Dispatching Module strategies support varying degrees of preemption. The EFD and Single-Threaded implementations support no preemption; the RTU implementation supports deferred preemptions; and the multi-threaded version uses OS support for immediate preemption. The goal of the benchmarks described below is to measure the utilization implications of each approach.

The performance tests discussed below were conducted on a single-CPU Pentium Pro 200 MHz workstation with 128 MB RAM running Windows NT 4.0. Test configurations included 3 suppliers and 3 consumers. As shown in Figure 13, the timeline tool can zoom out to show the periodic nature of the test participants.

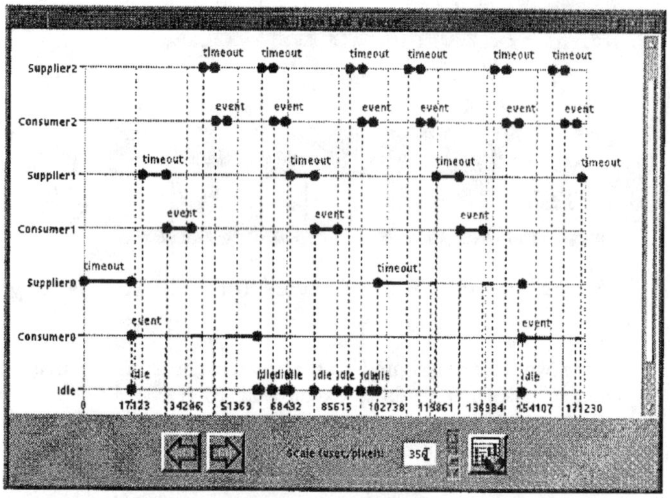


Figure 13: **Wide view of test run.**

The view in Figure 13 shows the relative frequencies of the participants. $\text{Supplier}_2$ generates events for $\text{consumer}_2$ at the highest frequency (40 Hz). Likewise, $\text{supplier}_1$ generates events for $\text{consumer}_1$ at 20 Hz, and $\text{supplier}_0$ generates events for $\text{consumer}_0$ at 10 Hz.

Figure 14 shows the total CPU utilization achieved (y-axis) by each Event Channel implementation (*i.e.*, multi-threaded, RTU, single-threaded, and EFD), as the workload configuration was changed (x-axis).

More specifically, the x-axis in Figure 14 represents the percentage workload given to the 40 Hz supplier and consumer. For instance, at the 10 percent x-axis column, the 40 Hz supplier and consumer were given relatively small amounts of work (10 percent of the total possible) to perform each iteration (40 times second). Then the workload for the 20 Hz and 10 Hz participants was repeatedly increased (thus increasing overall CPU utilization) until deadlines started to be missed. The maximum utilization achieved was then plotted relative to the y-axis.

As the values along the x-axis increase, the workload of the 40 Hz participants increases and the workload of the 20 Hz and 10 Hz participants decreases. Likewise, for lower values on the x-axis, the workload of the 20 Hz and 10 Hz participants are larger. For each value on the x-axis, the maximum utilization achieved without any missed deadlines was then plotted on the y-axis. The graph in Figure 14 illustrates how the utilization of different channel implementations can vary as the configuration of the system changes.

The results of our performance benchmarks show that the RTU and multi-threaded implementations of the chan-

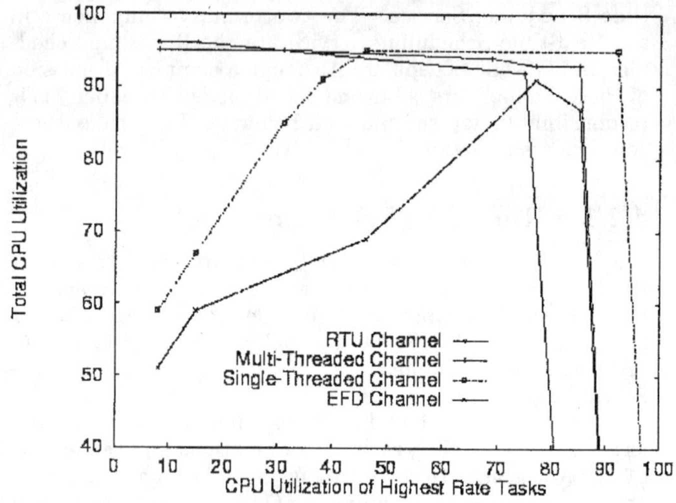


Figure 14: **CPU Utilization for RTU, Multi-Threaded, Single-Threaded, and EFD channel implementation.**

nel achieve approximately 95 percent utilization for all workload configurations. That these implementations fell 5 percent behind the maximum utilization results from the overhead imposed by the Event Channel. Although the RTU and multi-threaded implementations performed consistently for all configurations, utilizations for the single-threaded and EFD implementations vary significantly as the workload configurations change. These results show how the increased support for preemption provide greater stability across workloads.

The differences between the single-threaded and EFD channels can be accounted for by the fact that the single-threaded channel provides minimal support for preemption. After each event is propagated to a consumer in the single-threaded channel, the channel's thread (in the Dispatching Module) dispatches the next highest priority event/consumer tuple. Thus, if while an event is being dispatched, a higher priority event/consumer tuple arrives in the channel (*e.g.*, a timeout for a high priority consumer), the new tuple will be dispatched as soon as the currently running event completes.

Alternatively, when a supplier generates an event in the EFD channel, it is dispatched immediately to all consumers. If the EFD channel is dispatching an event to consumers when a timeout occurs for a higher priority consumer, the timeout will not be dispatched until all other consumers have completed. In the single-threaded channel, the timeout would be dispatched after the next consumer completed. The EFD's semantics increase the chances of missed deadlines and consequently reduce utilization.

It is also instructive to note that the single-threaded implementation performs optimally when the workload of 40 Hz participants is the greatest. For higher x-axis values, the workload of the 20 Hz and 10 Hz participants is lower. This reduces the demand for preemption since lower priority suppliers and consumers only use the thread of control for a very short time (since they are doing less work). Therefore, the graph shows that as the demand for preemption decreases (x values become greater), the lack of support for preemption becomes less crucial.

Table 1: **Event Latency, $\mu$secs, Through Event Channel, 250 millisec Event Interval.**

| Suppliers | Consumers | Events | Average per Event, millisec | Latency, $\mu$sec First Consumer | Latency, $\mu$sec Last Consumer |
|---|---|---|---|---|---|
| 1 | 1 | 100 | 250.035 | 90 | – |
| 1 | 10 | 100 | 250.057 | 331 | 603 |
| 1 | 50 | 100 | 250.050 | 1247 | 2073 |
| 2 | 1 | 100 | 250.203 | 197 | – |
| 2 | 10 | 100 | 250.587 | 337 | 531 |
| 2 | 50 | 100 | 250.379 | 1250 | 2330 |
| 50 | 1 | 100 | 251.117 | 393 | – |
| 50 | 10 | 100 | 250.859 | 473 | 1831 |
| 50 | 50 | 100 | 250.626 | 501 | 2092 |
| 50 | 50 | 1000 | 250.074 | 356 | 1020 |

## 5.2 Latency Measurements

Another important measure of Event Channel performance is the latency it introduces between suppliers and consumers. To determine Event Channel latency, we developed an Event Latency Test. This test timestamps each event as it originates in the supplier and then subtracts that time from the arrival time at the consumer to obtain the end-to-end supplier $\rightarrow$ consumer latency. The consumer does not do anything with the event other than to keep track of the minimum, maximum, and average latencies.

The Minimum Event Spacing Test looks at the average event delivery time for all of the events that a supplier delivers to its consumers. As before, consumers do not do anything with events that are pushed to them. The average event delivery time includes the event interval (spacing) and Event Channel overhead. Ideally, it should be as close as possible to the event interval. As the event interval is reduced, however, the Event Channel overhead starts to become significant. This test finds that minimum event interval.

These tests were run on a Sun UltraSPARC 2 with two 167 Mhz CPUs, running SunOS 5.5.1. The Event Channel and test applications were built with g++ 2.7.2 with –02 optimization. Consumers, suppliers, and the Event Channel were all co-located in the same process to eliminate ORB remote communication overhead. Furthermore, there was no other significant activity on the workstation during testing. All tests were run in the Solaris real-time scheduling class, so they had the highest software priority (but below hardware interrupts) [13].

With the single-threaded Event Channel, we measured a best-case supplier-to-consumer latency of ~90 $\mu$secs. "Best-case" refers to a single supplier and single consumer registered with Event Channel. The supplier received a timeout every 250 milliseconds and then sent a timestamped event to the consumer. As the number of suppliers and/or consumers increased, the latency increased as well, as shown in Table 1.

Under these conditions, the average event delivery time was comparable to the event timeout interval of 250 milliseconds. The supplier timeout value was progressively reduced to find the point at which the Event Channel overhead significantly affected the average delivery time. That timeout interval was ~20 millisec; below that value, the average event delivery time increased significantly.

We have investigated optimizations for this Event Channel implementation to improve these performance numbers. Probes were inserted to track the progress of an event through the Event Channel components. The detailed latency breakdown is shown in Table 2.

Table 2: **Breakdown of Event Latency.**

| Event Channel Operation | Time, $\mu$sec |
|---|---|
| delivery to Supplier Module (thru Supplier Proxy) | 5.4 |
| delivery to Subscription Module | 0.9 |
| Subscription Module: | |
| push_source | 7.9 |
| push_source_type: Correlation Module | 34.8 |
| push_source_type: Dispatching Module enqueuing | 7.9 |
| dispatch (dequeue) the event | 29.7 |
| decode the event | 0.9 |
| deliver event to consumer proxy | 6.4 |
| push event to consumer | 3.4 |
| total | 97.3 |

The probes measure the time spent by an event in each of the major Event Channel components shown in Figure 6. Most of the time is spent in the Subscription Module. Therefore, we inserted additional probes into it to precisely pinpoint its latency contribution. The two functions, `push_source` and `push_source_type`, correspond to consumer event registration for events from a particular supplier and for events from a particular supplier of a specified type, respectively.

In the Latency Test, the consumers registered only for events from a particular supplier of a specified type. So, the time spent in `push_source` was not used to deliver the event. Additional probes were inserted into `push_source_type`. They show the time spent in the major Event Channel components that contribute to actual event delivery, in this case.

Performance analysis revealed the following potential areas for improvement:

- Bypassing the Correlation Module for uncorrelated events;
- Optimizing internal data structures (there is a fixed-size table that, when initialized, constructs each of its slots individually whether or not they will be used);
- Eliminating dynamic allocation and deallocation;
- Streamlining the Dispatching Module to bypass queueing when possible. There are some cases when the Dispatching Module queuing can be eliminated. For ex-

ample, if the supplier thread has the same priority as the target consumer, and there are no events queued for that priority, the supplier thread can be used to dispatch the event.

To estimate the event latency with these optimizations applied, we developed the estimated latency breakdown shown in Table 3

Table 3: **Estimated Breakdown of Optimized Event Latency.**

| Event Channel Operation | Estimated Time, $\mu$sec |
|---|---|
| delivery to Subscription module (thru Supplier proxy) | 6 |
| Subscription module | 8 |
| Dispatching Module enqueue | 8 |
| check env | 2 |
| Dispatching Module dequeue | 30 |
| delivery to Consumer (thru Consumer proxy) | 10 |
| total (estimated) | 64 |

This estimate is based on removal of the overhead of "unused" subscriptions, (*e.g.*, **push_source** for a **push_source_type** message), and the overhead of correlation when not used.

# 6 Evaluating the Use of OO for Real-time Systems

While applying OO technologies to real-time systems we encountered two issues regarding polymorphism that threatened to compromise the predictability and performance of our systems. This section briefly discusses each of the issues and how our systems address the potential problems.

## 6.1 The Cost of Dynamic Binding Mechanisms

Since our systems are developed using C++, dynamic binding is implemented via virtual function tables (VFTs). As a result, compilers can implement highly optimized virtual function call mechanisms that impose constant-time overhead. These algorithms typically involve loading the *this* pointer, adjustment of the *this* pointer (for multiple inheritance), lookup of the function offset in the VFT, and final calculation of the address before invoking the function. However, these steps still have bounded completion times allowing predictable virtual function call performance regardless of the degree of inheritance used by applications.

We measured the cost of virtual function calls on three real time platforms: VxWorks 5.3 on a 60 MHz Pentium with Cygnus g++ 2.7.2-960126, Solaris 2.5.1 on a dual-CPU 168 MHz Sun UltraSPARC 2 with g++ 2.7.2, Irix 6.4 on a dual-CPU 180 MHz SGI Origin200 with SGI C++ 7.10, and Windows NT 4.0 on a 200 MHz PentiumPro with Microsoft Visual C++ 5.0. As shown in Table 4, the a virtual function call costs roughly 2 to 5 times that of a global or member function call. While these ratios seem high, for some platforms, the absolute time penalty (relative to a global function call) for a virtual function call was less than 0.6 $\mu$sec on the tested platforms. Our experience has been that this is not an impediment to real-time system performance, though we avoid virtual functions where not needed. Furthermore, modern compilers implement strategies for replacing indirect virtual function calls with direct function calls [27]. The results for the IRIX C++ and Microsoft VC++ compilers indicate well-optimized virtual function calls.

## 6.2 The Cost of Polymorphism

Polymorphism facilitates run-time changes in object behavior. Real-time systems often require predictable behavior of all components. Initially, the flexibility of polymorphism seems to be at odds with the requirement for real-time predictability. We resolved this issue using the Off-line Scheduler discussed in Section 4.2. Since scheduling is performed off-line, all objects and operations must be known in advance. Therefore, it is the responsibility of the Off-line Scheduler to determine whether a particular system configuration will meet all of its deadlines. As a result, when a virtual function is called at run-time, the system is not concerned with the actual implementation being invoked. The Off-line Scheduler has already guaranteed that its deadline will be met, based on the published parameters of each schedulable operation.

One advantage of our approach is that operation invocations only pay the overhead of the C++ virtual function call. If the schedule was not determined off-line, a run-time (dynamic) scheduler would need to intercede before any abstract operation was invoked, which incurs additional overhead. For instance, if a rate monotonic scheduling policy is used, the scheduler must determine the rate that each object operation executes in order to calculate its priority. Furthermore, this type of dynamic scheduler must make some type of guarantee, either weak or strong, that deadlines will be met.

One way a scheduler could make strong guarantees is to perform admission control, which permits operations to execute when the necessary resources are available. Admission control requires that object operations export execution properties such as worst-case execution time. Alternatively, the scheduler might implement a weaker, "best-effort" admission policy. For example, if an Earliest Deadline First policy is used, object operations with the nearest deadlines are given priority over operations with later deadlines. Such a policy would require that object operation deadlines be exported or calculated by the scheduler. This type of support for dynamic scheduling can incur significant overhead, and thus decrease effective resource utilization. As a result, dynamic scheduling solutions are sometimes not viable solutions for systems with hard deadlines and constrained resources.

Since all objects and operations in TAO's Real-time Event Service are determined off-line, one could argue that no real polymorphism exists. Although this is true to a certain extent, there are more benefits to dynamic binding than just changing behavior at run-time. In particular, we found that the ability to develop components independently of applications that use them significantly increases the potential for reuse in the avionics domain. For instance, since the Event Channel pushes to abstract `PushConsumer` interfaces, the code for the Event Channel remains decoupled from the number and type of application `PushConsumer` objects.

Table 4: **Cost of Virtual Function Calls.**

| Call type | VxWorks 5.3.1 Pentium 60 MHz Cygnus g++ | Solaris 2.5.1 Sun UltraSPARC 2 168 MHz g++ 2.7.2 | IRIX 6.4 SGI Origin200 180 MHz CC 7.10 | Windows NT 4.0 PentiumPro 200 MHz MS VC++ 5.0 |
|---|---|---|---|---|
| global function call time, μsec | 0.300 | 0.069 | 0.061 | 0.030 |
| member function call time, μsec | 0.450 | 0.061 | 0.061 | 0.035 |
| virtual function call time, μsec | 0.900 | 0.173 | 0.084 | 0.035 |
| ratio, virtual to global function call | 3.0 | 2.5 | 1.4 | 1.2 |
| ratio, virtual to member function call | 2.0 | 2.8 | 1.4 | 1.0 |

## 7 Concluding Remarks

The CORBA COS Event Service provides a flexible OO model where Event Channels dispatch events to consumers on behalf of suppliers. TAO'S Real-time Event Service described in this paper augments this model with Event Channels that support source and type-based filtering, event correlations, and real-time event dispatching. TAO's Event Channels can be configured with multiple scheduling policies (*e.g.*, rate monotonic scheduling and earliest deadline first) by configuring different Run-time Scheduler strategies. Similarly, channels can be built with varying levels of support for preemption by configuring different Dispatcher preemption strategies (*e.g.*, EFD, single-threaded, RTU, and real-time thread Dispatchers). This flexibility allows applications to adapt their scheduling and dispatching policies to obtain optimal utilization for different application requirements and platform resource characteristics.

Our performance results demonstrate that dispatching mechanisms with finer-grained support for preemption yield more consistent CPU utilization across different application configurations. These results also indicate that the dynamic binding mechanisms used by our C++ compilers are not fundamentally at odds with the deterministic execution behavior required by real-time applications. In addition, our results illustrate that it is feasible to apply CORBA Object Services to develop real-time systems. TAO's Real-time Scheduling Service architecture was submitted as a response to the OMG Real-time Special Interest Group *Request for Information* on Real-time CORBA [22].

The current implementation of TAO's Real-time Event Service is written in C++ using components from the ACE framework [21]. ACE is a widely used communication framework that contains a rich set of high-performance components. These components automate common communication software tasks such as connection establishment, event demultiplexing and event handler dispatching, message routing, dynamic configuration of services, and flexible concurrency control for network services. ACE has been ported to a variety of real-time OS platforms including VxWorks, Solaris, Win32, and most POSIX 1003.1c implementations.

The RT Event Service is currently deployed at McDonnell Douglas in St. Louis, MO, where it is being used to develop operation flight programs for next-generation avionics systems.

## 8 Acknowledgments

This work was funded in part by McDonnell Douglas Aerospace (MDA). We gratefully acknowledge the support and direction of the MDA Principal Investigator, Bryan Doerr. In addition, we would like to thank Brian Mendel for designing and implementing the single-processor ORB that was used for our Event Channel tests, and Seth Widoff for building the Java visualization tool that generated the time lines shown in Sections 4 and 5.

## 9 References

## References

[1] Object Management Group, *The Common Object Request Broker: Architecture and Specification*, 2.0 ed., July 1995.

[2] S. Vinoski, "CORBA: Integrating Diverse Applications Within Distributed Heterogeneous Environments," *IEEE Communications Magazine*, vol. 14, February 1997.

[3] D. C. Schmidt, A. Gokhale, T. Harrison, and G. Parulkar, "A High-Performance Endsystem Architecture for Real-time CORBA," *IEEE Communications Magazine*, vol. 14, February 1997.

[4] Object Management Group, *CORBAServices: Common Object Services Specification, Revised Edition*, 95-3-31 ed., Mar. 1995.

[5] R. Rajkumar, M. Gagliardi, and L. Sha, "The Real-Time Publisher/Subscriber Inter-Process Communication Model for Distributed Real-Time Systems: Design and Implementation," in *First IEEE Real-Time Technology and Applications Symposium*, May 1995.

[6] E. Gamma, R. Helm, R. Johnson, and J. Vlissides, *Design Patterns: Elements of Reusable Object-Oriented Software.* Reading, MA: Addison-Wesley, 1995.

[7] S. Maffeis, "Adding Group Communication and Fault-Tolerance to CORBA," in *Proceedings of the Conference on Object-Oriented Technologies*, (Monterey, CA), USENIX, June 1995.

[8] C. Liu and J. Layland, "Scheduling Algorithms for Multiprogramming in a Hard-Real-Time Environment," *JACM*, vol. 20, pp. 46–61, January 1973.

[9] M. Timmerman and J.-C. Monfret, "Windows NT as Real-Time OS?", *Real-Time Magazine*, 2Q 1997. http://www.realtime-info.be/encyc/magazine/97q2/-winntasrtos.htm.

[10] L. Zhang, "VirtualClock: A New Traffic Control Algorithm for Packet Switched Networks," in *Proceedings of the Symposium on Communications Architectures and Protocols (SIGCOMM)*, (Philadelphia, PA), pp. 19–29, ACM, Sept. 1990.

[11] G. Coulson, G. Blair, J.-B. Stefani, F. Horn, and L. Hazard, "Supporting the real-time requirements of continuous media in open distributed processing," *Computer Networks and ISDN Systems*, pp. 1231–1246, 1995.

[12] H. Tokuda, T. Nakajima, and P. Rao, "Real-Time Mach: Towards Predictable Real-time Systems," in *USENIX Mach Workshop*, USENIX, October 1990.

[13] S. Khanna and et. al., "Realtime Scheduling in SunOS5.0," in *Proceedings of the USENIX Winter Conference*, pp. 375–390, USENIX Association, 1992.

[14] Object Management Group, *Notification Service Request For Proposal*, OMG Document telecom/97-01-03 ed., January 1997.

[15] Object Management Group Telecommunications Domain Task Force, "Notification Service RFP (Telecom RFP3)," 1997.

[16] D. C. Schmidt and S. Vinoski, "Object Interconnections: Overcoming Drawbacks in the OMG Events Service," *C++ Report*, vol. 9, July-August 1997.

[17] I. Satoh and M. Tokoro, "Time and Asynchrony in Interactions among Distributed Real-Time Objects," in *Proceedings of 9th European Conference on Object-Oriented Programming*, Aug. 1995.

[18] J. A. Zinky, D. E. Bakken, and R. Schantz, "Architectural Support for Quality of Service for CORBA Objects," *Theory and Practice of Object Systems*, vol. 3, no. 1, 1997.

[19] Y. Aahlad, B. Martin, M. Marathe, and C. Lee, "Asynchronous Notification Among Distributed Objects," in *Proceedings of the 2nd Conference on Object-Oriented Technologies and Systems*, (Toronto, Canada), USENIX, June 1996.

[20] A. Gokhale and D. C. Schmidt, "The Performance of the CORBA Dynamic Invocation Interface and Dynamic Skeleton Interface over High-Speed ATM Networks," in *Proceedings of GLOBECOM '96*, (London, England), pp. 50–56, IEEE, November 1996.

[21] D. C. Schmidt, "ACE: an Object-Oriented Framework for Developing Distributed Applications," in *Proceedings of the 6th USENIX C++ Technical Conference*, (Cambridge, Massachusetts), USENIX Association, April 1994.

[22] D. C. Schmidt, D. L. Levine, and T. H. Harrison, "An ORB Endsystem Architecture for Hard Real-Time Scheduling," Feb. 1997. Submitted to OMG in response to RFI ORBOS/96-09-02.

[23] R. E. Barkley and T. P. Lee, "A Heap-Based Callout Implementation to Meet Real-Time Needs," in *Proceedings of the USENIX Summer Conference*, pp. 213–222, USENIX Association, June 1988.

[24] J.-B. Stefani, "Requirements for a real-time ORB," tech. rep., ReTINA, 1996.

[25] R. Gopalakrishnan and G. Parulkar, "Bringing Real-time Scheduling Theory and Practice Closer for Multimedia Computing," in *SIGMETRICS Conference*, (Philadelphia, PA), ACM, May 1996.

[26] M. H. Klein, T. Ralya, B. Pollak, R. Obenza, and M. G. Harbour, *A Practitioner's Handbook for Real-Time Analysis: Guide to Rate Monotonic Analysis for Real-Time Systems*. Norwell, Massachusetts: Kluwer Academic Publishers, 1993.

[27] S. Porat, D. Bernstein, Y. Fedorov, J. Rodrigue, and E. Yahav, "Compiler Optimization of C++ Virtual Function Calls," in *Proceedings of the 2nd Conference on Object-Oriented Technologies and Systems*, (Toronto, Canada), USENIX, June 1996.

# UML: the language of blueprints for software?

## Panel Session

Moderator: Derek Coleman

Panelists: John Artim, Viktor Ohnjec, Erick Rivas, Jim Rumbaugh, Rebecca Wirfs-Brock

**Abstract:** The Unified Method was launched by Grady Booch and Jim Rumbaugh at an OOPSLA'95 Conference Fringe meeting organised by Rational Software Corporation. In 1996 the Unified Method was re-scoped to a notation, and renamed the Unified Modeling Language (UML).

Earlier this year, UML was submitted to the Object Management Group for standardisation and has been endorsed by Microsoft, IBM, HP, Platinum Technologies, ObjectTime and many other corporations. No wonder UML is the leading contender as the *de facto* standard notation for object-oriented analysis and design.

The panel will take a sanity check, and will go beyond the hype and newsgroup flames and attempt to form an objective view of UML and its prospects.

The members of the panel have been working closely with UML in many different roles, including that of UML language designer, end-user, consultant, CASE tool expert, and object-oriented methodologist. The discussion will focus on how UML matches up in practice against one of its original raisons d'etre as "the language of blueprints for software".

Specific issues to be addressed include:

- What is the advantage of UML over existing OOA/D notations?
- Can UML be used on real projects today?
- Is the language sufficiently simple, and well-enough defined, to become the *de facto* standard?
- Will UML lead to improved OOA/D methods and CASE tools?
- What is the importance of the meta-model in UML?

*Derek Coleman is currently Professor and Head of Department of Computer Science at King's College, University of London, UK. Prior to this Derek was a manager at HP Laboratories in Palo Alto and Bristol (England) where he lead the development of the Fusion OOA/D method. He has extensive experience as a consultant transitioning projects to using object-oriented methods, both in Hewlett-Packard and in financial services and telecommunications companies. He has authored many research papers on software engineering and object technology and is currently co-authoring a book on a new version of Fusion using UML.*

### John Artim

I would like to evaluate the state of the Unified Modeling Language and its prospects through the following questions.

1) "Does UML embody sufficient notational richness and meta-model flexibility to support a wide range of in-house and commercial development?" UML is the first method I know of to publish a meta-model in its own notation — in itself a significant sign of technical fitness. UML includes notation to express most of the requirements, analysis, or design information I have come across. Though diverse, UML does have its limitations.

With Responsibility Driven Design and Object Behavior Analysis, among others, preferred by a significant number of practitioners, larger projects will, based on methodological preference, continue to experience communication issues and outright schisms among colleagues. Until the strengths and semantics of these complementary notations and methods have been incorporated into UML, it will remain difficult to unite a diverse group of practitioners behind UML. It is especially important that UML's creators look further into the role of cognitive differences in choice of preferred notation and method. The human factors issues behind these preferences must be better understood.

2) "Does UML include or accommodate organizing constructs such as framework and design pattern?" Though Booch[1] discusses the concept of framework and how it relates to class, I was unable to find a formalized definition of a framework within UML's meta-model. From a standpoint of engineering pragmatics, I am troubled that UML appears not to aid in coordinating the representation of frameworks. This reflects on UML's completeness but also on the viability, or at least the timeliness, of OMG coming forward as a means of integrating vertical and horizontal frameworks. This deficit may, however, be offset by the advantage of a published meta-model. I would hope to see future discussions of OO concepts expressed in terms of this meta-model.

3) "Is there an on-going dialog between UML's creators and the broad ranks of day-to-day practitioners?" In publishing a detailed meta-model and description, UML has significantly raised the bar for technical communication of OOAD issues. Unfortunately, the dialog seems to have become one-sided. A quick scan of OOPSLA workshop offerings over the past couple of years shows an absence of UML-specific discussion. OOPSLA workshops I have attended often seem to end up discussing the use and relative merits of various methods, including UML. I do not know of any systematic way this information is getting back to UML's organizers. Nor does there seem to be, at least at this point, much effort to solicit detailed feedback through other than the OMG review process. Participation in this approval process is resource intensive and therefore tends to exclude many practitioners. The same discussion mechanisms that laid the groundwork for the predecessor methods of UML seem to no longer function to ensure its continuing evolution.

4) Can UML embrace co-evolving standards of practice in disciplines allied with object-oriented technology such as user interface or documentation design?" The only place in the UML submissions I could find a modeled notion of software engineering process and the flow of artifacts was in the

business process modeling extensions needed by Objectory. Expanding these extensions into a development process meta-model, would, in principle, enable UML to integrate development artifacts across the software engineering lifecycle. There was a discussion of this topic at a CHI 97 workshop on the use of object-oriented methods in user interface design [5].

The workshop's participants are relying on one participant's company status as an OMG reviewer to relay feedback on UML's meta-model design. A mechanism for submitting technical review commentary by non-OMG participants would guarantee a more reliable means of providing feedback but at the cost of an increase in volume of review comments. Note that this is not an issue of approval but rather it is an issue of communication regarding UML and its place in a larger and evolving technical community.

5) "Is there a comprehensive (with respect to UML), complete (with respect to an example domain and system) and publicly accessible sample model(s) documenting intended usage of UML notations and techniques?" I do not think such a model is within the scope of an OMG proposal. I would turn, instead, to the published works of UML's three creators ([1], [2], and [4]). The model snippets used throughout each of their initial texts fall short of satisfying these criteria. Rumbaugh's "OMT Insights" [3] clears up much ambiguity with its comprehensive set of examples but these are examples in isolation. The utility of a more elaborate reference model would be in illustrating some of the many engineering decisions that must be made when modeling a real-world system. Probably the two most important kinds of decisions to illustrate are appropriate levels-of-detail within a model and the trade-off between problem complexity, model complexity and reader comprehension. This is especially needed given that UML is a standard meta-model and notation but not a standard methodology. Illustrations of each of the three principal architect's methodologies would help clarify the range of intended use of UML.

What do I believe the state of UML to be? I recommended UML as the basis for our development center's standard process and I see no reason to change that recommendation. The UML OMG proposal has considerably clarified UML's content and notation. Serious gaps remain in the areas of development process meta-modeling and framework description support.

These missing pieces are not immediately necessary but a viable standard in this area must demonstrate that it can grow to fill these gaps. Finally, the on-going evolution of UML seems much less open than much of the discussion that led up to its creation. Ultimately, this may increase UML's risk of premature obsolescence.

*For the past 3 years John Artim has worked at Orient Overseas Container Lines, a global container shipping company, in the Information Services Development Center in San Jose, California. He is the user interface architect for an enterprise-wide system of applications supporting customer service and the shipment life cycle. In addition to working on the current phase of application delivery, John is interested in putting into shop practice a user interface style guide based on user task descriptions corresponding to the content of an application's use cases. Prior to 1995 John spent 6 years working at IBM, primarily at the Santa Teresa Laboratory in San Jose, California. He worked in development, user interface architecture and human factors. The principal products he worked on included various CASE and development tools supporting structured and object-oriented programming. He holds an M.A. in Experimental Psychology and a B.A. in Psychobiology from the University of California at Santa Cruz.*

## Viktor Ohnjec

Genesis will specifically offer comments on the following issues:

- Can UML be used on real projects today?
- How well suited is UML to addressing the issues of distributed object systems and the Internet?
- Is the language sufficiently simple, and well enough defined, to become the *de facto* standard?
- Will UML lead to improved OOA/D methods and CASE tools?

As an organization, Genesis refers to itself as "object transition specialists". As such, we target the transfer of technology and knowledge for our clients in a variety of object technology related areas. These areas include analysis and design methodology usage. We see the OMG OOAD standardization effort as a very positive move for the industry that develops both the methodologies and tools to support software development and see the evolution of UML as a very positive example of what submissions into the standardization effort should be. There are issues that we must contend with and that are not, in our opinion, sufficiently covered with the current version of UML. We hope to discuss those issues during the panel discussion.

*Q*: Can UML be used on real projects today?
*A*: Genesis believes the answer is yes, because we have to date already used UML in a variety of client specific situations. UML is very reasonable as a notation and although there are some inconsistencies in the semantics and notation, they are minor in comparison to the benefit that using a modeling language brings to organizations. We look at methodologies and at UML as a mechanism to assist communication of ideas between team members on a project. As such, we look at whether UML can help team members to describe the requirements, analysis, and design ideas that they feel are important. We have seen that UML can do this and specifically have focused on Use Cases, class diagrams, state diagrams and interaction diagrams(collaboration and sequence diagrams to be specific) as the most important elements of our modeling efforts.

Where we feel that UML is lacking is in the area of process. In many ways, the UML is a fine notation, with reasonable syntax and semantics; clever use of stereotypes to reduce complexity, and as a general rule, the language is well received by both the vendors, the end-users and the standardization effort. What it is not, and admittedly, it does not claim to be, is process rich. We have found that clients are eagerly awaiting some guidance from the "three amigos" on a suggested approach for how to use UML. We find that although many approaches are reasonable, having a single approach that is suggested would make the convergence effort even more rapid.

We at Genesis have also noted that methodologies like Team Fusion or some of the areas of OPEN may in fact add the most value add to end-users through the suggestion of process. Team Fusion is already incorporating UML as the notation, and essentially offering the updated Fusion process around UML.

As a company that assists end-users through pragmatic use of OOAD, we consider such efforts very important.

*Q*: How well suited is UML to addressing the issues of distributed object systems and the Internet?
*A*: Few methodologies can truly be used throughout the entire lifecycle in creating a solutions based on distributed object technology-UML is no different. The challenge faced by all methodologies is to break out of the notion of application development to move more towards infrastructure and component development. These new directions are not trivial, however, and must be undertaken with extreme care.

First, a standard mechanism must be identified and adopted for the definitions necessary in creating any solution with object technology. UML is already well on the way to providing this as we have already discussed here. But we as an industry need to continue to encourage the that it is in fact sufficient as the *de facto* standard today. Again, having additional process-related information available is about the only real area that should be improved upon. Note however that we do expect further refinements to be shown (most likely through stereotypes of some form) especially in the way that UML will support business process engineering activities and distributed object computing activities. At present, we see the current version of UML being reasonable in its support of these areas (so long as the approach that an organization chooses to take in supporting BPE or DOC remains self-consistent within all groups that are working together in the organization).

*Q*: Will UML lead to improved OOA/D methods and CASE tools?
*A*: Regarding improved OOA/D methods, Genesis sees convergence on a single method (or smaller set of methods) as positive and UML is already helping to reduce the number of methods available. So, yes, we think this will help, but we believe that the main help is to reduce the "religious wars" rather than suddenly make developer so much more intelligent in their use of OOAD methods. It will, however, allow the issues to deal with to be raised from "how can I learn the method?" to "how do I use the method effectively?" more quickly. This is good.

As a consulting organization that is unbiased by what specific tool or vendor an organization chooses, we consider the question "will UML lead to improved CASE tools" from a service perspective. We expect that the CASE tool organization that will become most dominant, will be the one that has good services available to support not only their tool (through internal resources), but most importantly, the effective use of the method and the tool to bring projects to fruition. As such, we look for the organization that will partner with other groups that have pragmatic experience, and that can offer experience through mentoring to be the vendor that will see the most dominance. This is especially true since the area of process, that we feel so strongly about, is one that the service side of the CASE tool usage must support.

We also see the need for greater levels of integration between the "so called" CASE tools and products that support the remaining aspects of object or component based development, namely requirements capture tools, documentation tools, configuration management and version control tools and testing tools. We feel that end-users will become more and more sophisticated in their development and component assembly approaches and thus UML will need to ensure that it and the tools that support its use, will be easily integrated through-out the software lifecycle.

Incidentally, we wonder out loud if any of the CASE tool vendors plan to formalize mappings from UML to areas beyond. In such cases, and although work has definitely been published in these areas already, we expect to see things like formal Use Case to Test Case mapping, formal simulation of distributed components and debuggers, and automatic component "producer and consumer" models where it is expected that business objects will be assembled from base objects and that "infrastructural objects" will in essence be present to support the "foundation" that all business objects will require for an application to run. In such a model, we see an evolution in how people would present models that they built using UML rather than a necessary evolution in UML.

In closing, Genesis believes that standardization is a positive activity and since UML has shown the ability to gather momentum and support, it has in essence helped to accelerate the standardization effort. Is it the absolute best that it can be today? Probably not, but that isn't as important as the enthusiasm that it has generated and therefore the interest that people once again have in performing proper analysis and design prior to attempting to code away at a project!

*Viktor Ohnjec is Vice President, Professional Services, at Genesis Development Corporation. Viktor is responsible for ensuring customer satisfaction in training and consulting engagements through the management of technical resources and courseware development for Genesis. With 12 years of Object Technology experience, Viktor has been directly involved in planning, mentoring and leading teams through large systems development in military, aerospace, commercial, manufacturing, financial and petrochemical areas.*

*Viktor has introduced Object Technology to executives, middle managers and developers and influenced organization, infrastructure, object architecture, object modeling, development and integration in both distributed and non-distributed computing projects worldwide.*

*Viktor has presented at numerous conferences on a variety of technology and management topics. As a participating member of OMG, he chairs the Test Special Interest Group and is a member of the Architecture Group and Analysis and Design Task Force.*

*As an author, Viktor has written articles on emerging technology trends including the Application Development Trends February, 1997 cover story "Converging on OOAD Agreement" and June, 1997 titled "The Brave New World of Distributed Object Computing". A book by Viktor is expected by late-1997.*

### Erick Rivas

*Erick Rivas works for Platinum Technologies.*

### Jim Rumbaugh

UML is intended to consolidate the experience of the OO modeling community by providing a set of semantic modeling concepts and a corresponding notation that can provide a standard general-purpose modeling language for expressing most kinds of models. Its main advantage over other OOAD notations is the opportunity to end the petty wars over minor differences in semantics and notation by adopting a broad consensus developed by a number of methodologists and vendors. UML contains some newer features, but its core is based on years of experience with several of the leading OO methods. Yes, UML can be used on real projects today.

UML is not a tiny language, but neither are C++, Smalltalk, Java, or Eiffel. It needs to accommodate analysis and design, large and small projects, be compatible with many programming languages but dependent on none. In particular, it needs to embrace the systems of today (they are no longer in the future) that are inherently concurrent, distributed, and multilingual. We have made UML as simple as possible subject to these needs, but we don't expect someone to learn it in a day. We have structured the core concepts of UML to be straightforward; however; users of most popular methods SHOULD learn enough in a day to continue working productively in UML.

We feel that UML is better defined than any other comparable modeling language. It has a self-referential meta-model (any general purpose modeling language should be able to model itself) as well as a built-in constraint language for defining non-syntactic restrictions. We have tried to strike a balance between formality and pragmatism. People will find flaws, of course; nothing of this size is ever perfect, but that is no different from most software products. We feel that the language is robust and can be repaired or extended easily, if the need arises.

By providing a standard, comprehensive definition of a modeling language covering all major areas of concern we feel that UML can lead to a great increase in quality and quantity of modeling tools. Vendors can develop more effective tools if they can count on a widely accepted standard, rather than having to choose among dozens of potential candidates, and users benefit from being able to choose the best implementation rather than worrying about which notation is supported.

*Jim Rumbaugh works for Rational Software Corporation in Santa Clara, California. He received his Ph.D. from MIT in 1975. He has been involved in software modeling for almost 30 years, as well as software development including an operating system, a parallel machine architecture, a compiler, a transaction management system, an X-ray tomography system, an object-oriented programming language, and an OOAD CASE tool. He is the lead developer of the OMT method and the book "Object-Oriented Modeling and Design" with colleagues from GE and Calma. Since 1994 he has been working with Grady Booch and later Ivar Jacobson at Rational Software Corp. to unify their methods into a single approach. The UML is the first fruit of that collaboration, but they continue to work on process unification also.*

### Rebecca Wirfs-Brock

I have spent a dozen years exploring informal techniques and ways of thinking about object system development. I see notation as an aid to conceptualizing, specifying and communicating various aspects of object models. Unified Modeling Language is becoming the lingua-franca for object modeling in the 1990As. One of the more subtle, but important characteristics of UML is its formal underpinning — there are semantics behind each modeling construct. UML was also designed to be formally extended. These good intentions remain to be proven.

I am still getting used to speaking this object modeling Esperanto. It takes a bit of effort for me to distinguish between an instance and a class (underlined names are a pretty subtle distinction). The notion of drawing objects as squares also seems alien. I have always equated circles with objects! I am getting over my ingrained notion of "circle" as "object", because I too wish to communicate and be understood by others, without translation. This is important. In the process of adopting a modeling language standard, we give up colloquialisms to gain common understanding.

UML isn't pretty or elegant; however I think it is utilitarian. It won't meet everyone's aesthetics, but in the end this does not matter. I intend to make serious attempts to be UML compliant when it expresses the constructs I need. But when I must color outside the lines to communicate an idea, I will do so. I still conceptualize object responsibilities on CRC cards, then transform them to individual operations, attributes and associations to fit into UML. I augment use case models with quite a few embellishments and believe that UML can be woven into a process that incorporates a rich set of informal techniques and modeling constructs.

However, I want to caution you — don't become complacent with these new standards! The notation war may be over, but UML falls far short of expressing all we need to understand about object-oriented software systems! UML does not address many intrinsically non object-oriented details that are important to describe. And UML doesn't speak to extended use case models nor does it particularly well describe dynamic relationships between objects, patterns, algorithmic hot-spots, event models, object subassemblies or subsystems, Bertrand Meyer's notion of contracts, invariants, business rules, or many of the artifacts of our own Responsibility-Driven Design process.

I have difficulty distinguishing between levels of detail, precision and abstraction when looking at models expressed in UML. The basic constructs of object, interface, class, sequence diagram, etc. are used to express analysis, design and implementation models. Some may argue that this is a virtue, it's objects from the top to the bottom. But you really haven't communicated with me if I can't discriminate between various levels of abstraction. I leave it to object development processes and forward-thinking modelers to provide us guidance in this area.

Is the state of modeling with UML so bad? On my worst days, I fear that people will stop thinking about their objects once they have sketched a few UML diagrams, and that future object modeling innovations will be ignored by those biased towards a rigid standard. However, I ask you to put UML into its proper perspective. UML shouldn't be burdened with having to be all things to all people for all times. I hope UML continues to remain a living language, adapted by people to create new modeling idioms appropriate to the task at hand.

*Rebecca has been active in the object community for over a dozen years. Her object experience began in 1984, when she managed the Tektronix software team that developed the first commercial Smalltalk. Rebecca was the lead author of the popular Designing Object-Oriented Software, Prentice-Hall, 1990 and has written columns for the Smalltalk Report and the Report on Object Analysis and Design. Rebecca left Tektronix in 1991 to pursue her object analysis and design passion full-time and to direct the consulting and training practice at*

*Instantiations. Through two high tech mergers, she came to be the Director of Frameworks and Methods at ParcPlace-Digitalk. She is an internationally recognized author, teacher and speaker on object analysis and design and co-inventor of the Responsibility-Driven development method.*

**References**


1. Booch, G. (1994). *Object-Oriented Analysis and Design*. Redwood City, California: The Benjamin/Cummings Publishing Company, Inc.

2. Jacobson, I., M. Christerson, P. Jonsson, and G. Overgard (1995). *Object-Oriented Software Engineering: A Use Case Driven Approach*. Menlo Park, California: Addison-Wesley Publishing Company.

3. Rumbaugh, J. (1996). *OMT Insights*. New York, New York: SIGS Books.

4. Rumbaugh, J., M. Blaha, W. Premerlani, F. Eddy, and W. Lorenson (1991). *Object-Oriented Modeling and Design*. Englewood Cliffs, New Jersey: Prentice Hall.

5. van Harmelen, M., J. Artim, K. Butler, A. Henderson, D. Roberts, M. B. Rosson, J. Tarby, and S. Wilson (1997). Object Models in User Interface Design: CHI'97 Workshop Summary. In preparation for *SIGCHI Bulletin*, October 1997.

# Tiling Design Patterns
# —A Case Study Using the Interpreter Pattern

DAVID H. LORENZ

The Faculty of Computer Science,
Technion—Israel Institute of Technology,
Technion City, Haifa 32000, ISRAEL;
Email: david@CS.Technion.AC.IL

## Abstract

This paper explains how patterns can be used to describe the implementation of other patterns. It is demonstrated how certain design patterns can describe their own design. This is a fundamental reflexive relationship in pattern relationships. The process of assembling patterns by other patterns is named pattern tiling. Tiling enables us to interweave simple understood concepts of patterns into their complex real-life implementation. Several pattern tilings for the Interpreter design pattern are illustrated.

## 1 Introduction

Tilings are sets of physical objects ("tiles"), typically made of stone or ceramic, which fit together in a recurring motif ("pattern") to cover surfaces without gaps or overlaps. The art of tiling and the relevance of its technology extends from early days uses to applications in modern engineering (e.g., VLSI design [36]) and in modern science (a study of their mathematical properties can be found in [18].) This paper presents tilings of non-physical objects: design patterns [14, 15] as declarative *entities* that fit together.

One of the nice features that Prolog [33] beginners struggle with at first is its declarative semantics. Declaring, for example, that conc($L_1, L_2, L_3$) if $L_3$ is the concatenation of $L_1$ and $L_2$, allows the functor conc/3 to be used in more than one way. The obvious use is to concatenate two lists, $L_1$ and $L_2$, into $L_3$. But it may also be used to split a given list $L_3$. Likewise, the *intent* of a pattern and the manipulation of its *participants* can be taken declaratively.

The pattern *name* is perhaps its most profound declarative form. The names associated with design patterns enrich our vocabulary for reasoning about design at higher levels of abstraction. Their rapid growth threatens to become a language for design. One indication of a language's expressive power is its ability to describe itself. BNF (Backus-Naur-Form [29])–a formal notation to describing the context-free syntax of a given language, for example, can describe its own grammar. This begs a question: can design patterns describe their own design?

Design patterns improve considerably the manner in which object-oriented experience is communicated. But, no matter how well a design pattern is written, there will always remain a gap between comprehending a pattern and applying it. This gap is revealed in the complexity and cost of putting certain design patterns into practice. Implementing the *Interpreter* [15] pattern, for instance, is limited to *simple* grammars, since "for complex grammars, the class hierarchy for the grammar becomes large and unmanageable" [15, page 245]; changing the structure traversed by a *Visitor* [15] "requires redefining the interface to all visitors, which is potentially costly" [15, page 333].

This paper shows how patterns can be used to describe the implementation of other patterns. It is demonstrated how certain design patterns can describe their own design. This is a fundamental reflexive relationship in pattern relationships. The process of assembling patterns by other patterns is named *pattern tiling*. Tiling patterns reduces the comprehension-application gap. For example, we shall see how one Interpreter helps with implementing another Interpreter pattern, and that a Visitor to the first interpreter can generate a family of visitors to the second.


OOPSLA '97 10/97 GA, USA

Yet another gap is stretched between applying each pattern individually and integrating several patterns. Knowing the catalogue of patterns by heart is prudent perhaps but unfortunately not a sure recipe for successfully applying them. For example, one may fully understand both the Interpreter [15] and the *Reflection* [35, Sect. 17] patterns and yet not see how an implementation of an interpreter implicitly possesses a reflective architecture, as shall be shortly demonstrated.

The issue of pattern relationship is one of the difficult aspects of patterns. In [15] this is addressed by classifying patterns into groups according to their *purpose* and *scope*, specifying related patterns, and providing a *spaghetti-diagram* that shows graphically the relationships between patterns. For example, the Interpreter is a *behavioral* pattern. It applies primarily to *classes*, and can use the *Composite* [15] pattern in defining the grammar, the Visitor for adding operations, and the *Flyweight* [15] pattern for sharing terminal symbols. As informative as it is, this is far from satisfactory, albeit hard to improve, as indicated by attempts for improved classifications ([8, Sect. 18] is a good example) that followed. Noticeably, the spaghetti-diagram for showing related patterns contains no loops. The possible *reflexive* relationships between patterns seem to be missing.

An implementation of a pattern can simultaneously be (or share large portions with) an implementation of several other patterns. A special case of this is integrating several implementations of the *same* pattern. Integrating a pattern with itself is conceptually simpler than integrating two different patterns but just as powerful, (though somewhat more confusing). To this extent, *tiling* design patterns is one of many *reflexive* relationships between patterns.

Tiling is neither genericity nor inheritance. Inheritance is a form of abstraction that promotes reuse. Tiling is a form of reuse that promotes abstraction. Delegating requests along adjacent tiles brings inheritance and tiling to the same conceptual level. Tiling is different from templates in the same way grammars are different from regular expressions. A template can instantiate simple tiles. The tiles we shall be concerned with, however, are design patterns for which a template that generates them is something to be desired. Tilings compare to other techniques for pattern application, like automatic code generation [6]. Patterns can be classified by whether or not they can be tiled by other patterns.

The symmetry art works of Maurits Cornelis Escher [12], a Dutch graphic artist, (also the cover art on the design patterns book [15]), should serve as the motivation for this work. The main observation is that the Interpreter pattern and the Visitor pattern have a common interesting characteristic–they are building blocks capable of constructing themselves. Repeating Interpreter tilings result in a reflective Interpreter. A tessellation of Visitors molds a Visitor mosaic. In design patterns, as in Escher's work, what you see the first time is most certainly not all there is to see.

The outline of the paper is the following. The next section describes a systematic approach to implementing the Interpreter pattern. Section 3 demonstrates several tilings of the Interpreter pattern (reflective, mirror, in-out, and execution.) Section 4 presents tessellations of primitive visitors (null, exception, inheritance, and composition) that form more complex ones (e.g., known variants of the Visitor pattern.) Section 5 describes related work and offers conclusions.

## 2 Interpreter Pattern Making

*"If a particular kind of problem occurs often enough, then it might be worthwhile to express instances of the problem as sentences in a simple language. Then you can build an interpreter that solves the problem by interpreting these sentences"* [15, page 243].

At the heart of the Interpreter pattern is the class-based observation, shown in Figure 1, in which programs relate to grammars as objects relate to classes. An analogy is drawn between writing a program in a context-free language and instantiating an object from a class. A program is perceived as an instantiation of its grammar, just as an object is an instantiation of its class.

More precisely, let *InstanceTypeOf*$(c)$ (following the conventions in [1]) indicate the *type* of objects of class $c$ and, analogically, *ProgramTypeOf*$(g)$ the

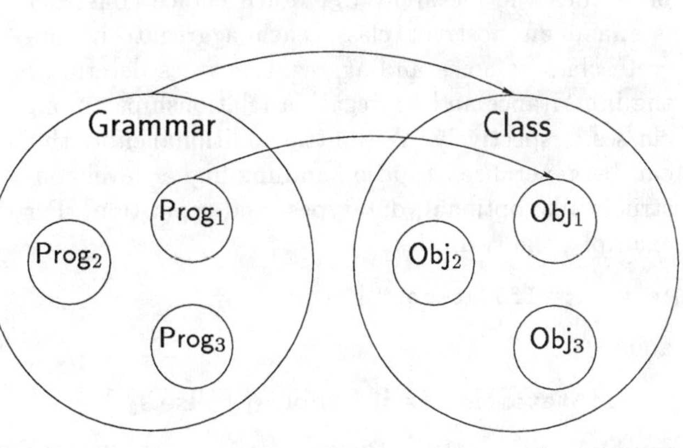


Figure 1: Class based approach to the Interpreter pattern

programs in the language generated by the context-free grammar $g$. We indicate by $\mathcal{L}$ the language in which the program is written, and by $\mathcal{G}_{\mathcal{L}}$ a context-free grammar for $\mathcal{L}$. The Interpreter pattern takes the approach of viewing a program in $\mathcal{L}$ as an instance of $\mathcal{G}_{\mathcal{L}}$, just as an object is an instance of a class, as follows. First, $\mathcal{G}_{\mathcal{L}}$ is transformed into a class definition $\mathcal{C}_{\mathcal{L}}$. Then, both $\mathcal{G}_{\mathcal{L}}$ and $\mathcal{C}_{\mathcal{L}}$ are used (with the help of a parser generator) to produce a parser capable of compiling any program $\mathcal{P}: \mathit{ProgramTypeOf}(\mathcal{G}_{\mathcal{L}})$ into an object $\mathcal{O}_{\mathcal{P}}: \mathit{InstanceTypeOf}(\mathcal{C}_{\mathcal{L}})$.

### A Systematic Approach to Implementing an Interpreter

Figure 1 is, of course, an over simplification. The Interpreter pattern actually takes an *object-oriented* approach, in which the class definition $\mathcal{C}_{\mathcal{L}}$ is a hierarchy of classes, just like the grammar $\mathcal{G}_{\mathcal{L}}$ is a group of related rules. It's left to the pattern implementer to make the leap from the simple understood metaphor to its detailed implementation. Orderly done, though, the hierarchy $\mathcal{C}_{\mathcal{L}}$ can be systematically obtained in a relatively straightforward manner.

If $\mathcal{L}$ is a nonempty context-free language then it can be generated by a context-free grammar $\mathcal{G}_{\mathcal{L}}$ with the following properties. Every production of $\mathcal{G}_{\mathcal{L}}$ is of one of the forms: (1) A *choice* of having a number of given variants, $B \rightarrow A_1|\cdots|A_n$, where $A_i$ and $B$ are variables; or (2) an *aggregate* made of a fixed number of parts, $A \rightarrow \alpha$, where $\alpha$ is a nonempty string of variables and terminals. Furthermore, any variable $A$ appears at most once as the left-hand-side construct of a rule, and at most once at the right-hand-side of a choice rule. This restricts the format of productions without reducing the generative power of the grammar [38].

Once $\mathcal{G}_{\mathcal{L}}$ conforms to the above canonical form, it prescribes the hierarchy $\mathcal{C}_{\mathcal{L}}$: Each choice construct is made an abstract class, each aggregate–a concrete class. Choice and aggregation rules determine the inheritance and aggregation relationships among classes, respectively. With little additional effort this can be generalized to also handling higher level constructs like optional, datatypes, and repetition. For example, the two rules:

$s$ ::= `IfStatement` | $\cdots$;

and

`IfStatement` ::= **if** $b$ **then** $s_1$ [ **else** $s_2$ ];

would determine that **`IfStatement`** is a concrete subclass of the abstract class $s$, and that it has three components: a condition, and two statements of which the second may be void. (See [16] for a complete example.)

## 3 Tiling a Reflective Interpreter

Whether systematic or not, interpreting $\mathcal{G}_{\mathcal{L}}$ and producing the class hierarchy $\mathcal{C}_{\mathcal{L}}$, especially for a long grammar like that of a programming language, is a chore. The description in [15] acknowledges this implicit complexity. The book even warns, as quoted above, that the Interpreter's application is therefore limited to simple grammars. In doing so the pattern has missed the point of its own design. Such an interpretation is the bread and butter of the Interpreter pattern itself.

Let $\mathcal{G}_{\mathcal{B}}$ be the context-free description of BNF itself. Then, the grammar $\mathcal{G}_{\mathcal{L}}$ is no more than a program in $\mathcal{B}$. By re-applying the Interpreter pattern to transform the BNF grammar $\mathcal{G}_{\mathcal{B}}$ into a class hierarchy $\mathcal{C}_{\mathcal{B}}$, we can compile our original grammar $\mathcal{G}_{\mathcal{L}}: \mathit{ProgramTypeOf}(\mathcal{G}_{\mathcal{B}})$ into an instance $\mathcal{O}_{\mathcal{L}}: \mathit{InstanceTypeOf}(\mathcal{C}_{\mathcal{B}})$ in the precise same way we compiled $\mathcal{P}$. The procedure can be repeated for compiling $\mathcal{G}_{\mathcal{B}}$ into $\mathcal{O}_{\mathcal{B}}: \mathit{InstanceTypeOf}(\mathcal{C}_{\mathcal{B}})$. Since $\mathcal{G}_{\mathcal{B}}: \mathit{ProgramTypeOf}(\mathcal{G}_{\mathcal{B}})$ is a "fixed point" of this process, it does not result in an infinite sequence. Rather, it stops at $\mathcal{O}_{\mathcal{B}}$, as illustrated in Figure 2.

### 3.1 A Universal Interpreter Generator

To better understand the dynamics of this process, suppose there were a universal machine for generating Interpreter patterns. We could configure this machine with Eiffel's grammar so that it would accept an Eiffel [28] program and generate an object encapsulating the program. This object would then serve as an *agent* for performing miscellaneous analyses on the program (e.g., pretty printing, type checking, testing, and computing software metrics).

Suppose further that the machine model we've got requires, for the process of configuration, an expert on Eiffel's grammar rather than a textual description. We could first configure our universal machine with BNF's grammar and use it to translate Eiffel's grammar into a knowledgeable object, an agent of Eiffel, which in turn we'll use for our original configuration purposes. But before we do that we use the machine once more to translate the textual description of BNF to a BNF agent, and we can do that, putting the issue of bootstrapping aside for a moment, because BNF uses BNF to describe itself.

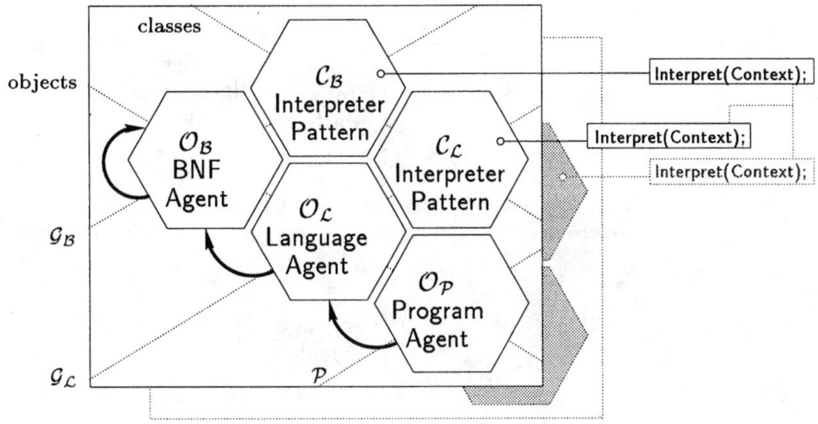


Figure 2: Tiling a Reflective Interpreter

We end up substituting our textual description $\mathcal{P}$ with three objects, tiled as depicted in Figure 2: an object $\mathcal{O_P}$ which is an instance of the class $\mathcal{C_L}$, its corresponding metaclass object $\mathcal{O_L}$ which is an instance of $\mathcal{C_B}$, and a meta-metaclass object $\mathcal{O_B}$. In Figure 2, a class object which represents a class $x$ is named an *x agent*, to distinguish it from an *x object* which is simply some object of type *InstanceTypeOf*$(x)$. Our Eiffel agent is hence a BNF-instance, and an Eiffel-program agent would be an Eiffel-instance.

Along the dashed diagonal lines sketched in Figure 2, we can observe an information trinity $\langle text, instance, type \rangle$ for each kind of knowledge: The BNF language described by $\mathcal{G_B}$ is also represented by both the agent $\mathcal{O_B}$ and the Interpreter pattern class hierarchy $\mathcal{C_B}$. Similarly, $\mathcal{G_L}$, $\mathcal{O_L}$, and $\mathcal{C_L}$, each in its own way, represent the programming language. The letters: $\mathcal{G}$, $\mathcal{O}$, and $\mathcal{C}$, were chosen to emphasize the shape of the description. If you need a reminder of the contents, just look at the subscripts.

The objects $\mathcal{O_P}$, $\mathcal{O_L}$, and $\mathcal{O_B}$ form together a reflective architecture. For example, generating $\mathcal{C_L}$ could be a **once** routine, in Eiffel's terminology, for $\mathcal{O_B}$. This reflective structure lends itself to various degree of reuse.

## 3.2 Tiling as Means of Reuse

In order for the program agent $\mathcal{O_P}$ to compute something, we need to place appropriate interpret routines in $\mathcal{C_L}$ to do the job. If several interpretations perform a common computation, or if similar ones are parameterized by only a syntactical property, even if these interpretations belong to entirely different interpreters, then this commonality can be placed as a computation in the meta-interpreter, as depicted in Figure 2. A resemblance between tiling and inheritance is apparent in the figure.

### Computing Syntax-Based Metrics

A simple example showing how to compute basic software metrics ([7, 4, 23, 19]) will make this clearer. Syntax-based metrics are the most common software metrics. They measure how the source code is written, differing in what they measure as size. Lines-of-Code (LOC), for example, is an elementary syntax-based metric. Nonetheless, computing it properly requires a non-trivial analysis. It is a misnomer since it really refers to executable statements. In C, for instance, counting semicolons (";") would not provide the accurate measure, since it would count *lines* instead of *statements*. A `for` statement contains two semicolons but should count as one, whereas an `if` should count as two but contains only one semicolon.

By placing a counter in the interpret routine associated with the class `Statement` of an Interpreter pattern for the C language, we can accurately compute the LOC measurement. More generally, a meta-routine in the meta-Interpreter can count all constructs of a particular type. We can use such a general routine to count statements as well as other kinds of repeated constructs (the number of class declarations, the number of functions, etc.) Moreover, this general routine would be just as applicable in an entirely different Interpreter. Having an Interpreter pattern for Eiffel, for example, we'll be able to count the LOC of Eiffel programs.

Complex metrics can be handled in much the same way. Computing the deepest static nesting-level of class declarations, for instance, can be abstracted to a general metric routine in $\mathcal{C_B}$ that computes the deepest level of a given kind of syntactical construct. As a consequence, getting, for example, the deepest static

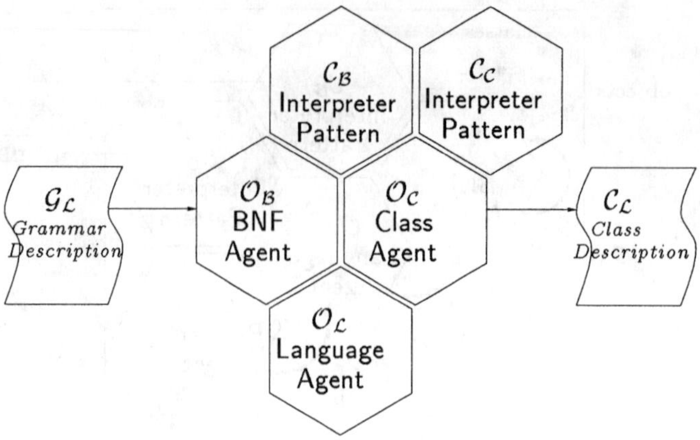


Figure 3: Tiling an In-Out Interpreter

level of conditional statements is obtained for free. More sophisticated analysis can be carried out by delegating requests back and forth between the base and meta-levels, resembling perhaps method invocations up and down the class hierarchy due to inheritance.

### 3.3 The Interpreter's Mirror

A tile can also be flipped over. A design pattern tells you how, given a right problem, to arrange your classes and objects in order to solve it. Conversely, an arrangement of classes and objects can remind you of a pattern you know, putting them in a totally new light.

The concept of a grammar, that ordinarily designates (formal) languages, is used by the Interpreter patterns to designate a class hierarchy. But the *grammar* metaphor works both ways. The Interpreter views a grammar $\mathcal{G}$ in terms of a class $\mathcal{C}_\mathcal{G}$. The Interpreter's mirror would view any given class hierarchy $\mathcal{C}$ in terms of a grammar $\mathcal{G}_\mathcal{C}$. Concepts taken from the theory of languages would then bring new meanings into the system's class structure.

For example, a grammar definition is associated with a special variable $S$ called the start symbol. This symbol would correspond to the set of classes that can instantiate composition roots (i.e., *standalone* [17] objects.) In grammars, a symbol $X$ is useful if there is a derivation in which it appears. Otherwise it is *useless* [20]. If $X$ is useful then some terminal string must be derived from $X$ and $X$ must occur in some string derivable from $S$. We can compare usefulness of classes to other class traits provided by the programmer and supported by the programming language, such as abstract, concrete, interface, implementation, and so on.

*Environmental acquisition* [17] refers to the ability of objects to acquire properties in a *type safe* manner from the classes of objects in their environment. As such, it may be viewed as a generalization over class traits. Had environmental acquisition been an established design pattern, it would have been the Interpreter's mirror.

In the next section, we will make use of a flipped Interpreter tile in refining the tiling of the Reflective Interpreter.

### 3.4 Tiling an In-Out Interpreter

Given a language, the Interpreter usually [1] interprets sentences in the language. It can also generate sentences instead of interpreting them. The role of the grammar changes then from determining how the program is parsed to being a *synthesizing grammar* [16].

Returning to our Eiffel example, if the analyzed program is to be processed by a Java application on the Web, then we would like the class representation of the Eiffel grammar to be in Java. By implementing an Interpreter pattern for Java, we can decouple the process of translating Eiffel from the act of generating classes in Java. The Eiffel program will be compiled into an Eiffel object. The Eiffel object will create a Java object, and the Java object will generate the desired class description in Java.

Generally, two Interpreters can be tiled back-to-back such that one implementation of the pattern interprets the input, shares the interpretation with the other, which in turn outputs the desired translation. Figure 3 gives an example. Let $\mathcal{G}_\mathcal{C}$ be a context-free grammar such that $\mathcal{C}_\mathcal{L} : ProgramTypeOf(\mathcal{G}_\mathcal{C})$. ($\mathcal{G}_\mathcal{C}$ is the mirror of $\mathcal{C}_\mathcal{L}$.) Then, an Interpreter for $\mathcal{G}_\mathcal{B}$ and an Interpreter for $\mathcal{G}_\mathcal{C}$ can cooperate in translating $\mathcal{G}_\mathcal{L}$ into $\mathcal{C}_\mathcal{L}$.

[1] A notable exception is a *Reversible Interpreter* [26] which is an interpreter capable of running programs backwards.

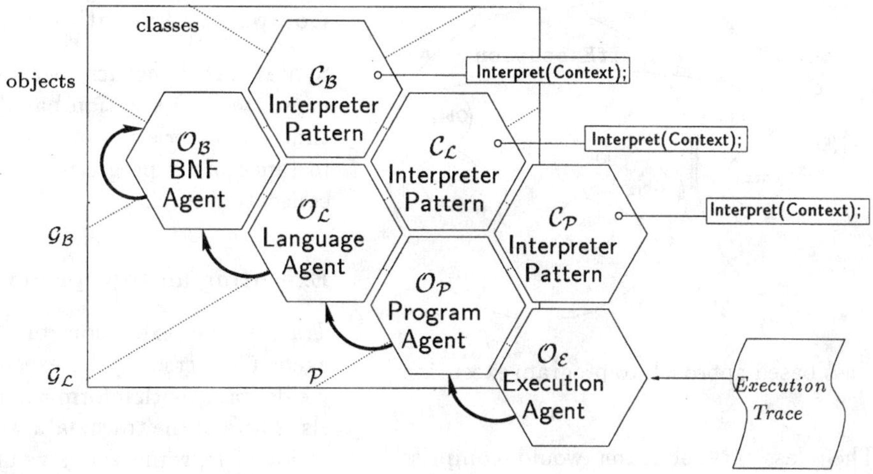


Figure 4: Tiling an Execution Interpreter

We see that two Interpreters can help bring to life a third one. Being themselves Interpreter patterns, they may be subjected to the same treatment. Of course, eventually some "fixed-point" Interpreter would need to be handled manually. Hopefully, its corresponding grammar, i.e., its mirror, would fit in the category of "simple grammars".

It is possible to merge Figures 2 and 3, applying the construction applied to $\mathcal{C_L}$ in Figure 3 to $\mathcal{C_B}$ and $\mathcal{C_C}$ also, but presenting it requires a true graphic artist.

### 3.5 Tiling an Execution Interpreter

Recall that the Reflective Interpreter in Figure 2 established a duality between objects and types. $\mathcal{O_B}$ is an agent representing the BNF Interpreter pattern. $\mathcal{O_L}$ is an agent representing the language Interpreter pattern. A natural question that comes about is: does the program agent $\mathcal{O_P}$ have a dual Interpreter pattern too (which we would denote $\mathcal{C_P}$, as shown in Figure 5)? Tiling the Reflective Interpreter from

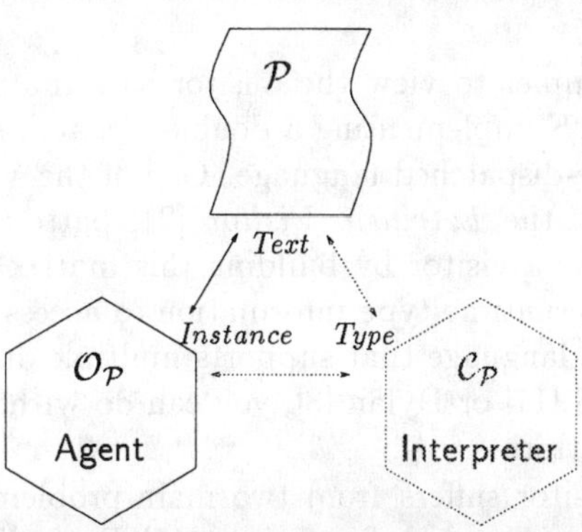


Figure 5: Program representations

the base up to the meta-level has reached its limit in $\mathcal{O_B}$ being its own type. The concern raised here is whether we may add tiles at the other end of the Reflective Interpreter. Answering this question in the affirmative raises another one regarding the nature of a program's instantiations. Viewing a program as a type makes a program's execution (which we shall denote $\mathcal{O_E}$) one of its values. Figure 4 illustrates how the Reflective Interpreter of Figure 2 can be extended to deal with program executions.

Generating $\mathcal{C_P}$ is harder than it seems. For generating the language Interpreter pattern $\mathcal{C_L}$ we needed knowledge about the language *syntax*. A separation of abstract and concrete syntax was required. For example, a syntax rule for a conditional `IfStatement` of the form

$$\texttt{IfStatement} ::= \textbf{if } b \textbf{ then } s_1 \text{ [ } \textbf{else } s_2 \text{ ];}$$

is regarded a triple $\langle b, s_1, s_2 \rangle$ (the keywords ignored but the order preserved), and implemented as a class with three data members.

```
struct IfStatement:
    public Statement {
  Expression condition_;
  Statement then_;
  Statement* else_;
  //..
};
```

Generating now the Interpreter pattern of a certain *program* requires knowledge of the *semantics* of the programming language. For example, a particular `IfStatement` instance in $P$, $\texttt{If}_1$, would be mapped to a type `IfExecution` that designates the regular expression $b[s_1|s_2]$. Each time $\texttt{If}_1$ is executed, an `IfExecution` object will be instantiated

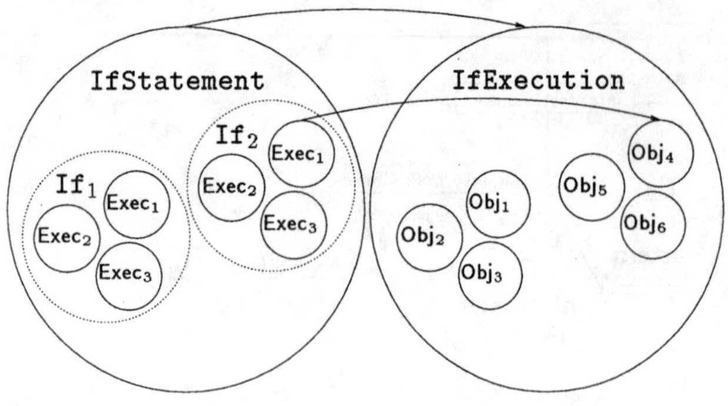


Figure 6: Class based approach to program execution

in $\mathcal{O}_{\mathcal{E}}$. The class **IfExecution** would comprise only two slots, as opposed to the three of its metaclass **IfStatement**: A slot of type expression that contains the execution of the condition $b$, and another of type statement, which would contain either the execution of $s_1$ or the execution of $s_2$.

```
struct IfExecution:
    public StatementExecution {
  ExpressionExecution condition_;
  union {
      StatementExecution then_;
      StatementExecution else_;
  } action_;
  //..
};
```

A point of interest regarding the Execution Interpreter is that although, in principle, an $\texttt{If}_2$ in $P$ is a different type than $\texttt{If}_1$, it makes sense that both instantiate the same kind of objects. That is, **IfExecution** should be a type shared by all **IfStatement** executions, as shown in Figure 6. The meta-object representing this type could be implemented as a shared Flyweight whose meta-information link is extrinsic.

The Interpreter design pattern reflects primarily the *static* design of the program interpreted. It captures static relationships embodied in code. Applying the Interpreter pattern seamlessly to program execution captures also *dynamic* behavior of the program. Some useful implications of this are listed here.

### Object-Oriented Visualization

The class definition $\mathcal{C}_{\mathcal{P}}$ may model only selective parts of the program execution. For example, if $\mathcal{C}_{\mathcal{P}}$ contains classes just for method invocation and nothing else, then an Annotalk [9, 10] trace of method calls in runtime will correspond to an object instantiation of this class definition.

### Computing Execution-Based Metrics

Syntax-based metrics measure how the source code is written. Execution-based metrics measure runtime characteristics. Perceiving an execution as an instance of its program puts these two at the same conceptual level.

### Executing an Interpreter Pattern

Tracing the execution of $P$ yields an execution agent $\mathcal{O}_{\mathcal{E}}$. Tracing the execution of $\mathcal{O}_{\mathcal{P}}$, $\mathcal{O}_{\mathcal{L}}$ or $\mathcal{O}_{\mathcal{B}}$, yields traces with information from several source levels. Parts of the trace data would reflect the interpretation of $P$, while others would reflect the interpretation process itself and its meta processings, somewhat like what Smalltalk [13] traces look like.

## 4 Visitor Pattern Tessellations

The Interpreter and Visitor patterns play the role the syntax and the semantics play in a programming language, respectively. The Interpreter is concerned with the grammatical structure of programs. The Visitor is concerned with the meaning of grammatically correct programs. Unlike the nature of programming languages, the Visitor makes it possible to interpret a parsed program in new ways by simply changing the semantics of the language.

Given an interpret method invocation the Visitor pattern provides a lookup scheme for identifying the appropriate interpretation to be executed. Without the Visitor, the Interpreter's *interpret* routine is associated with a unique object. It is a mapping $m : C \to S$ from the set of element types $C$ into the set of semantic actions $S$. The Visitor turns this mapping into a *curried* mapping $m : C \xrightarrow{\text{accept}} V \xrightarrow{\text{visit}} S$, where $V$ is the set of visitors. In doing so, "Visitor lets you define a new operation without changing the classes of the elements on which it operates" [15, page 331].

It is simpler to view the Visitor as a matrix $m : C \times V \to S$ implementing a double-dispatch scheme in a single-dispatched language. One of the Visitor's variations, the *Extrinsic Visitor* [21] pattern, even implements a visitor by building this matrix explicitly, using runtime type information to access it. Indeed, in a language that supports multiple dispatch, like CLOS [11] or Dylan [3], you can do without the Visitor pattern.

The Visitor suffers from two main problems that can be put in terms of matrices: (1) Extending the matrix with a new row (class) affects all the columns (visitors), and consequently all the other rows (making, for example, re-compilation necessary). (2) We are forced to write a method for each entry $m(c, v)$, $c \in C$, $v \in V$, regardless if we need it or not. These are especially problematic in large matrices, the ones we shall take interest in.

The *Acyclic Visitor* [27] variation provides, at the cost of multiple inheritance and dynamic casting across the visitor hierarchy, a partial solution to the cyclic dependency problem: The type of the visitor is temporarily forgotten and reclaimed using dynamic casting (see also [34]). We, on the other hand, shall focus on decreasing the complexity of implementing visitors whose matrix is *sparse* (i.e., only few classes really need special handling.) We shall see that some of the visitor variations (e.g., [21]) can be imitated by a mosaic of primitive visitors.

## 4.1 Primitive Visitors

The description of the Visitor pattern as it appears in [15] applies a single level of *subtyping*. An abstract `NodeVisitor` defines an interface to the `Node` hierarchy, and we can provide as many concrete visitor implementations as necessary as long as they conform with the `NodeVisitor` interface. A further degree of reuse in the Visitor pattern can be gained by allowing also *class inheritance*, that is, letting visitors refine and extend other visitors.

We can make it the Interpreter's responsibly to supply, on demand, a set of primitive visitors for that purpose. The following scheme is proposed using a Reflective Interpreter. A meta-visitor to the meta-interpreter systematically generates a group of simpler visitors to the base-interpreter. Then, these visitors serve as building blocks in constructing more complex visitors. A visitor's matrix is tessellated by inherited entries.

For example, a primitive *Null Visitor*, that does nothing at all (taking after the *Null Object* pattern [37]) is generated as following. The language agent $\mathcal{O}_{\mathcal{L}}$ is visited by a meta-visitor defined over $\mathcal{C}_{\mathcal{B}}$. This meta-visitor generates, for each encountered *rule* named `X`, an empty `NullVisitor::Visit_X` routine. [2]

For our `IfStatement` example we might get a definition like:

[2] It's a recurring pattern that whenever Visitor is discussed a footnote about overloading the visit routine appears. In [15, page 337] and [21, page 3] *function overloading* is regarded an option when implementing a Visitor in C++, only an unrecommended option. However, in C++, overriding an overloaded method hides all other overloaded definitions (unless explicitly re-`using` [22, Sect. 7.3.3] them.) Hence, if you wish visitors to be refined and you're not careful, overloading might change the semantics of not providing an implementation.

```
class NullVisitor {
public:
  NullVisitor() {}
  virtual ~NullVisitor() {}
  class VisitException {};

  virtual void
    Visit_IfStatement (const IfStatement& it) {}
  //...
};
```

By placing in each routine a `throw` statement, a different primitive visitor is generated, which we may call an *Exception Visitor*.

```
class ExceptionVisitor {
public:
  ExceptionVisitor() {}
  virtual ~ExceptionVisitor() {}
  class VisitException {};

  virtual void
    Visit_IfStatement (const IfStatement& it) {
      throw VisitException();
  }
  //...
};
```

The usefulness of these visitors will be made apparent immediately, but first let us introduce two additional building blocks, namely an *Inheritance Visitor* and a *Composition Visitor*.

For each superclass `Y` of `X`, an `InheritanceVisitor::Visit_X(X& it)` routine explicitly calls `Visit_Y(it)`, implementing one possible kind of refinement (element hierarchy). A second kind of refinement (visitor hierarchy) is achieved, for example, by overriding only `Visit_Y(it)` in a sub-visitor. Figure 7 illustrates this for `IfStatement` and `Statement`.

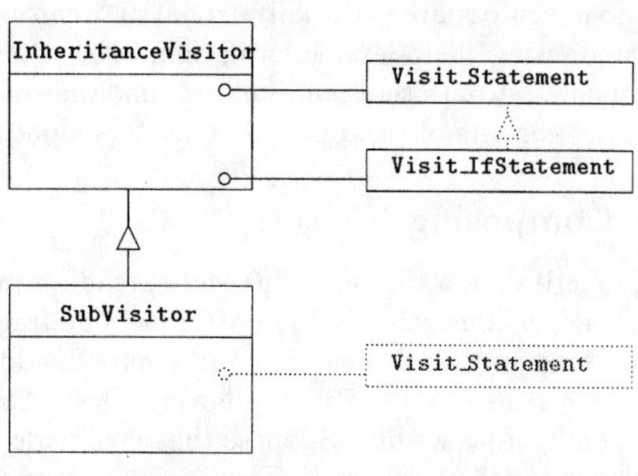


Figure 7: Inheritance Visitor

```
template <class SuperVisitor>
class InheritanceVisitor: public SuperVisitor {
public:
  InheritanceVisitor() {}
  virtual ~InheritanceVisitor() {}
  class VisitException:
    public SuperVisitor::VisitException {};

  virtual void
    Visit_IfStatement (const IfStatement& it) {
      SuperVisitor::Visit_IfStatement(it);
      //visit the sub-object
      Visit_Statement(it);
  }
  //...
};
```

A `CompositionVisitor::Visit_X(X& it)` routine explicitly calls `Visit_Z(it)` for each component `Z` of `X`.

```
template <class SuperVisitor>
class CompositionVisitor: public SuperVisitor {
public:
  CompositionVisitor() {}
  virtual ~CompositionVisitor() {}
  class VisitException:
    public SuperVisitor::VisitException {};

  virtual void
    Visit_IfStatement (const IfStatement& it) {
      SuperVisitor::Visit_IfStatement(it);
      it.condition_.Accept(*this);
      it.then_.Accept(*this);
      if (it.else_)
        it.else_->Accept(*this);
  }
  //...
};
```

All four visitors are essentially trivial and can be generated using meta-level information. Nevertheless, for the rest of this section, we'll assume that our set of tiles consists of these primitive visitors alone.

## 4.2 Composing Visitors

Using inheritance, a tile can refine and extend an inherited tile, as illustrated in the preceding code fragments. Genericity, as demonstrated in Figure 8, adds a *subject-oriented* [30] flavor in allowing tiles to be glued in any order we like. Suppose that $v$ is made a subclass of another visitor $v'$. Then, in the absence of a handler for $m(c, v)$ the inherited entry $m(c, v')$ will be called. This rather standard mechanism of inheritance can be exploited in several ways. If $v'$ defines a default action for each $c$, then $v$ is exempt from providing an implementation for element types it will never visit. Inheriting from `ExceptionVisitor` would provide runtime checking that $v$ indeed does not visit elements it's not supposed to. If $v$ inherits from `NullVisitor`, $v$ need not check beforehand whether an element is visitable.

```
template <class SuperTile>
class Tile: public SuperTile {
  //...
};
```

```
template <class SuperTile>
void Tile<SuperTile>::Visit_X(const X& it)
{
  SuperTile::Visit_X(it);
  //...
};
```

Figure 8: Gluing tiles using genericity and inheritance

Another possibility is that $v$ will rely on $v'$ for delegating the interpret request to some other matrix entry. For example, if $v$ wishes that an implementation for $m(c', v)$ is "inherited" by all entries $m(c, v)$ for which $c$ is a subclass of $c'$, then $v$ should inherit from an instantiation of the `InheritanceVisitor` class template. Similarly, by inheriting from an instantiation of the `CompositionVisitor`, a call $m(c, v)$ recursively calls $m(c'', v)$ for each component $c''$ of $c$. This results in a complete scanning of the containment subtree.

Derive your visitor from `InheritanceVisitor<NullVisitor>` if you wish `YourVisitor::Evaluate_Y` to be called whenever you do not specify a handler for `X`, and `Y` is a superclass of `X`. If you do define `YourVisitor::Evaluate_X` you may still force a call to `YourVisitor::Evaluate_Y` by calling `SuperVisitor::Evaluate_X(it)`. Note that the Visitor `InheritanceVisitor<NullVisitor>` is precisely the *Default Visitor* proposed in [21].

Use `CompositionVisitor<InheritanceVisitor<NullVisitor> >` if you wish to perform a Depth-First Scan (DFS) of the tree (Figure 9). `YourVisitor`'s `Evaluate_X` routine, if it exists, is called for nodes of type `X`, and should have in its body a call to the `SuperVisitor` routine `Evaluate_X`, otherwise the DFS is not pursued.

The DFS Visitor mimics the operation of a class default constructor. This also emphasizes the power of tilings over templates. We can generate a *Copy*

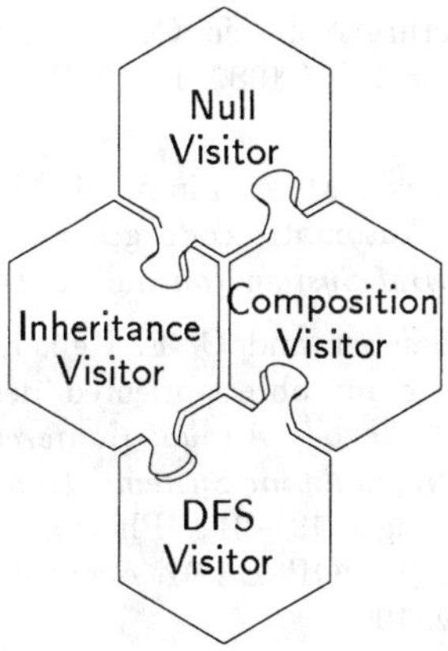


Figure 9: DFS Visitor tessellation

*Visitor* that will mimic the operation of the default copy constructors generated by the C++ compiler. We cannot, however, write a C++ template that would do the same.

## Example

The following examples illustrates the relative simplicity of tiling visitors (although the details of application are secondary at best.) First, a visitor V that counts program statements is implemented in C++.

```
typedef CompositionVisitor<InheritanceVisitor<
  NullVisitor> > DFSVisitor;

// counting statements
class V: public DFSVisitor {
public:
  int counter;
  V(): counter(0) {}
  virtual void
    Visit_Statement(const Statement& it) {
      //invoked for all statements
      ++counter;
      DFSVisitor::Visit_Statement(it);
  }
};
```

That's the entire class. Sending an instance of V to visit a particular program p will yield the overall number of statements in that program:

```
V v;
p->Accept(v);
cout << v.counter << " statements." << endl;
```

Next, the visitor named V_only_if counts only if-statements.

```
// counting if-statements
class V_only_if:
  public CompositionVisitor<NullVisitor> {
public:
  int counter;
  V_only_if(): counter(0) {}
  virtual void
    Visit_Statement(const Statement& it) {
      //never invoked since Statement
      //is an abstract class
      assert(0);
  }
  virtual void
    Visit_IfStatement(const IfStatement& it) {
      ++counter;
      CompositionVisitor<NullVisitor>::
        Visit_IfStatement(it);
  }
};
```

Note that Visit_Statement is never called, because InheritanceVisitor is left out.

If we refine the first visitor V and add a handler also for IfStatement, we can count all statements except if-statements, as following:

```
// counting non-if statements
class V_sans_if: public V {
public:
  V_sans_if(): V() {}
  virtual void
    Visit_IfStatement(const IfStatement& it) {
      //invoked only for if-statements
      --counter; //undo ++counter
      V::Visit_IfStatement(it);
  }
};
```

# 5 Conclusions

The concept of tiling design patterns is a novel twist on pattern application. Tiling enables us to interweave simple understood concepts of patterns into their complex real-life implementation. With the help of tilings we've seen implementations of the Interpreter and Visitor patterns in a more concise and accurate manner.

Tessellations help us adapt more easily to changes (e.g., in the class hierarchy.) Similar considerations rooted the work on *propagation patterns*, later incorporated into *adaptive programming* [25, 2]. The *class dictionary graph* approach in the Demeter system, [24] which allows integrated definition of classes and syntactic forms, is of particular relevance. Tiling match the benefits, that the *Adaptive* variants, proposed by Lieberherr and colleagues (e.g., [32]), have with respect to the traditional patterns, but without requiring language extensions.

Efforts of abstraction over design patterns have taken many directions. For example, attempts to discover patterns of patterns, or looking for recurring mini-patterns. The danger in that kind of abstractions is in becoming either obvious or too abstract. Tilings is a form of abstraction that restricts us to design pattern as wholes. As such, the building blocks at least are a solid foundation.

Some tiles fit nicely together (e.g., the Interpreter and the Visitor.) Some tiles may have the same shape but a different purpose (e.g., the *Adapter* [15] and the *Bridge* [15].) Some tiles may always need to work together (e.g., perhaps the Interpreter and the Visitor?) In that case, they may simply be parts of the same pattern. If a subset of the patterns can tile all the others, then that group would be a *basis* that can span the rest. If a set of pattern fractions can do the jobs, those would be mini-patterns. We have seen two related patterns that can tile themselves.

This work has focused on a particular design pattern, the Interpreter. Even in that limited scope, tiling has shown insight into the Interpreter's own design. Whether or not this phenomena is found in other patterns, is left for future work.

**Acknowledgments** I thank Harold Ossher, Yuval Sherman, Ricardo Szmit, and the anonymous referees for thoughtful comments on drafts of this paper.

## References

[1] M. Abadi and L. Cardelli. *A Theory of Objects.* Monographs in Computer Science. Springer Verlag, 1996.

[2] Workshop on adaptable and adaptive software. In S. C. Bilow and P. S. Bilow, editors, *Addendum to the Proceedings of the $10^{th}$ Annual Conference on Object-Oriented Programming Systems, Languages, and Applications*, pages 149–154, Austin, Texas, USA, Oct. 15-19 1995. OOPS Messenger 6(4) Oct. 1995. Reported by K. Lieberherr.

[3] Apple Computer, Inc., Cupertino, CA. *Dylan: An object-oriented dynamic language*, 1992.

[4] G. M. Barnes and B. R. Swim. Inheriting software metrics. *Journal of Object-Oriented Programming*, pages 27–34, November-December 1993.

[5] J. Bézivin, J.-M. Hullot, P. Cointe, and H. Lieberman, editors. *Proceedings of the $1^{st}$ European Conference on Object-Oriented Programming*, number 276 in Lecture Notes in Computer Science, Paris, France, June 15-17 1987. ECOOP'87, Springer Verlag.

[6] F. J. Budinsky, M. A. Finnie, J. M. Vlissides, and P. S. Yu. Automatic code generation from design patterns. *IBM System Journal*, 35(2), 1996.

[7] S. R. Chidamber and C. F. Kemerer. Towards a metrics suite for object-oriented design. In *Proceedings of the $6^{th}$ Annual Conference on Object-Oriented Programming Systems, Languages, and Applications*, pages 197–211, Phoenix, Arizona, USA, Oct.6-11 1991. OOPSLA'91, Acm SIGPLAN Notices 26(11) Nov. 1991.

[8] J. O. Coplien and D. C. Schmidt, editors. *Pattern Languages of Program Design.* Addison-Wesley, 1995.

[9] W. De Pauw, R. Helm, D. Kimelman, and J. Vlissides. Visualizing the behavior of object-oriented systems. In *Proceedings of the $9^{th}$ Annual Conference on Object-Oriented Programming Systems, Languages, and Applications*, pages 326–337, Portland, Oregon, USA, Oct. 23-27 1994. OOPSLA'94, Acm SIGPLAN Notices 29(10) Oct. 1994.

[10] W. De Pauw, D. Kimelman, and J. Vlissides. Modeling object-oriented program execution. In M. Tokoro and R. Pareschi, editors, *Proceedings of the $8^{th}$ European Conference on Object-Oriented Programming*, number 821 in Lecture Notes in Computer Science, pages 163–182, Bologna, Italy, July 4-8 1994. ECOOP'94, Springer Verlag.

[11] L. G. DeMichiel and R. P. Gabriel. The common lisp object system: An overview. In Bézivin et al. [5], pages 151–170.

[12] K. U. Erven. *The Graphic Work of M. C. Escher.* Macdonald & Co., London, new, revised and expanded edition, Oct. 1967.

[13] B. Foote and R. E. Jonson. Reflective facilities in smalltalk-80. In N. K. Meyrowitz, editor, *Proceedings of the $4^{th}$ Annual Conference on Object-Oriented Programming Systems, Languages, and Applications*, pages 327–335, New Orleans, Louisiana, Oct. 1-6 1989. OOPSLA'89, Acm SIGPLAN Notices 24(10) Oct. 1989.

[14] E. Gamma, R. Helm, R. Johnson, and J. Vlissides. Design patterns: Abstraction and reuse of object-oriented design. In O. M. Nierstrasz, editor, *Proceedings of the $7^{th}$ European Conference on Object-Oriented Programming*, number 707 in Lecture Notes in Computer Science, pages 406–431, Kaiserslautern, Germany, July 26-30 1993. ECOOP'93, Springer Verlag.

[15] E. Gamma, R. Helm, R. Johnson, and J. Vlissides. *Design Patterns: Elements of Reusable Object-Oriented Software.* Professional Computing. Addison-Wesley, 1995.

[16] J. Gil and D. H. Lorenz. SOOP – A synthesizer of an object-oriented parser. In *Proceedings of the 16$^{th}$ International Conference on Technology of Object-Oriented Languages and Systems*, pages 81–96, Versailles, France, Mar. 6-10 1995. TOOLS 16 Europe Conference, Prentice-Hall.

[17] J. Gil and D. H. Lorenz. Environmental Acquisition—A new "inheritance"-like abstraction mechanism. In *Proceedings of the 11$^{th}$ Annual Conference on Object-Oriented Programming Systems, Languages, and Applications*, San Jose, California, Oct. 6-10 1996. OOPSLA'96, Acm SIGPLAN Notices 31(10) Oct. 1996.

[18] B. Grünbaum and G. Shephard. *Tilings and Patterns*. Mathematical Sciences. W. H. Freeman and Company, New York, 1987.

[19] B. Henderson-Sellers. *Object Oriented Metrics*. Object-Oriented Series. Prentice-Hall, 1996.

[20] J. E. Hopcroft and J. D. Ullman. *Introduction to Automata Theory, Languages and Computation*. Addison-Wesley, 1979.

[21] M. E. N. III. Variations on the visitor pattern. In *PLoP '96* [31]. Group 5: Design Patterns.

[22] A. Koenig. *C++ Standard Draft Proposal X3J16/96-0225*. American National Standards Institute, Digital Equipment Corporation 1996.

[23] H. F. Li and W. K. Cheung. An empirical study of software metrics. *IEEE Transactions on Software Engineering*, 13(6):697–708, June 1987.

[24] K. J. Lieberherr. *Adaptive Object-Oriented Software: The Demeter Method with Propagation Patterns*. PWS Publishing Company, Boston, 1996.

[25] K. J. Lieberherr, I. Silva-Lepe, and C. Xiao. Adaptive object-oriented programming using graph-based customization. *Communications of the ACM*, 37(5):94–101, May 1994.

[26] H. Lieberman. Reversible object-oriented interpreters. In Bézivin et al. [5], pages 11–19.

[27] R. C. Martin. Acyclic visitor. In *PLoP '96* [31]. Group 5: Design Patterns.

[28] B. Meyer. *EIFFEL the Language*. Object-Oriented Series. Prentice-Hall, 1992.

[29] P. Naur. Revised report on the algorithmic language ALGOL 60. *Communications of the ACM*, 3(5):229–314, May 1960.

[30] H. Ossher, M. Kaplan, W. Harrison, A. Katz, and V. Kruskal. Subject-oriented composition rules. In *Proceedings of the 10$^{th}$ Annual Conference on Object-Oriented Programming Systems, Languages, and Applications*, pages 235–250, Austin, Texas, USA, Oct. 15-19 1995. OOPSLA'95, Acm SIGPLAN Notices 30(10) Oct. 1995.

[31] PLoP '96. *Proceedings of the 3$^{rd}$ Annual Conference on the Pattern Languages of Programs*, Robert Allerton Park and Conference Center, University of Illinois at Urbana-Champaign, Monticello, Illinois, Sept. 3-6 1996. Washington University, Technical Report WUCS-97-07.

[32] L. M. Seiter, J. Palsberg, and K. J. Lieberherr. Evolution of object behavior using context relations. In D. Garlan, editor, *Proceedings of the 4$^{th}$ ACM SIGSOFT Symposium on the Foundations of Software Engineering*, pages 46–57, San Francisco, California, Oct. 16-18 1996. SIGSOFT'96, Acm Software Engineering Notes 21(6) Nov. 1996.

[33] E. Y. Shapiro and L. Sterling. *The Art of Prolog*. Logic Programming. MIT Press, Cambridge, Mass, second edition, 1994.

[34] J. Vlissides. Pattern hatchig: The trouble with observer. *C++ Report*, June 1996.

[35] J. M. Vlissides, J. O. Coplien, and N. L. Kerth, editors. *Pattern Languages of Program Design 2*. Addison-Wesley, 1996.

[36] N. H. E. Weste and K. Eshraghian. *Principles of CMOS VLSI Design - A System Perspective*. VLSI Systems. Addison-Wesley, 1988.

[37] B. Woolf. The null object pattern. In *PLoP '96* [31]. Group 5: Design Patterns.

[38] P.-C. Wu and F.-J. Wang. An object-oriented specification for compiler. *ACM SIGPLAN Notices*, 27(1):85–94, Jan. 1992.

# Composite Design Patterns

Dirk Riehle
Ubilab, Union Bank of Switzerland, Bahnhofstrasse 45, CH-8021 Zurich
Phone: +41-1-234-2702, fax: +41-1-236-4671
E-mail: Dirk.Riehle@ubs.com or riehle@acm.org
WWW: http://www.ubs.com/ubilab + staff/riehle

## Abstract

Software design patterns are the core abstractions from successful recurring problem solutions in software design. *Composite design patterns* are the core abstractions from successful recurring frameworks. A composite design pattern is a pattern that is best described as the composition of further patterns the integration of which shows a synergy that makes the composition more than just the sum of its parts. This paper presents examples of composite patterns, discusses a role-based analysis and composition technique, and demonstrates that composite patterns extend the pattern idea from single problem solutions to object-oriented frameworks.

## 1 Introduction

A developer versed in software design patterns might explain the Model-View-Controller paradigm (MVC, [KP88, Ree96a]) for designing interactive software systems like this: "(a) MVC helps you design applications with graphical user interfaces. Its core are three collaborating objects: a Model object which represents an instance of a domain concept, a View object which realizes a specific user interface representation of the Model, and a Controller object which handles user input in order to work with the Model. (b) These objects interact according to the Observer, Strategy and Composite pattern: A View observes a Model—thus the View is an Observer of the Model which is its Subject. A View does not handle user input but leaves this to the Controller—thus the Controller is a Strategy for handling user input. Moreover, Views can have Subviews which represent smaller parts of the user interface and which can have Subviews themselves—thus the View is a Component in the Composite pattern and different Views can be either Leafs or Composites."

From MVC's overall point of view (described in (a) above), the use of each of the design patterns (described in (b) above) is of a tactical nature: every pattern is used to solve a specific problem at hand. Taken together and directed towards the goal of designing a reusable and flexible user interface architecture, the patterns achieve a synergy which constitutes a whole that is larger than just the sum of some patterns. *MVC is a composite design pattern.*

A composite pattern is first of all a pattern: It is a design theme that keeps recurring in specific contexts as a solution to a problem. It is a composite pattern, because it can best be explained as the composition of some other patterns. However, a composite pattern goes beyond a mere composition: It captures the synergy which arises from the integration of several patterns into an overall composition structure. A composition of some patterns turns into a composite pattern, if and only if (a) a relevant synergy between the pattern interactions arises, and (b) this synergy can be observed as a recurring design theme.

This paper discusses the notion of composite pattern. It introduces a notation based on roles to better describe and compose patterns. It presents an analysis and composition technique to better cope with the complexity of composite patterns. The notation and technique cover patterns based on object collaborations which constitute the majority of patterns known today. Eventually, the paper compares composite patterns with object-oriented frameworks and pattern languages.

Composite patterns and frameworks are orthogonal concepts. However, analyzing and understanding successful recurring frameworks as composite patterns helps us better capture the core abstraction behind such frameworks, much like atomic design patterns help us capture the solution to a recurring design problem. Not every composite pattern constitutes a framework, but behind every successful recurring framework there must be a core abstraction that can be captured as a pattern, usually a composite pattern. As such, composite patterns hold the same promise as atomic patterns, but on a much larger scale.

Section 2 examines the notion of composite pattern more closely, presents a first example, and lists further ones. Section 3 introduces role diagrams and composition constraints as a means for describing patterns. This prepares the way to section 4, which presents an elaborate example of a composite pattern. Doing so, it introduces an analysis and composition technique based on the concepts of prototypical pattern application and role relationship matrix. In section 5, the definition of composite pattern is compared with frameworks and pattern languages. Section 6 discusses related work and section 7 presents some final conclusions.

## 2 Composite Patterns

This section examines and defines the notion of composite design pattern and sets up a proper terminology. An example further illustrates the idea of composite pattern. This prepares the way to the analysis and composition technique of the following sections.


**OOPSLA '97 10/97 GA, USA**
**© 1997 ACM 0-89791-908-4/97/0010...$3.50**

## 2.1 Definition

A *composite design pattern* is first of all a design pattern: It is the abstraction from a concrete recurring solution that solves a problem in a certain context [GOF95, POSA96, RZ96]. A pattern is a *composite* pattern, if it can be best explained as the composition of further atomic or composite patterns. An atomic pattern is a pattern that, on a given level of abstraction, cannot sensibly be described as the composition of further patterns.

In a composite pattern, the constituting patterns integrate with each other to achieve a synergy that gives the composite pattern its own identity beyond being just the sum of some patterns. This distinguishes a composite pattern from an arbitrary pattern composition, which may be a suitable solution for a specific design problem, but which does not recur as a pattern of its own.

Usually, a pattern can be described as the abstraction from a recurring form that consists of several elements which interact with each other and their context in specific ways [RZ96]. A composite pattern's synergy emerges from the interaction of different elements from different patterns. This interaction can take on many shapes, depending on the kind of pattern. Generally speaking, each pattern element interacts with further elements from other patterns. If these non-trivial element interactions keep recurring, they constitute the synergy that motivates the composite pattern.

## 2.2 Active Bridge

As a first example, consider the Active Bridge pattern [Rie97a]. This pattern represents a recurring type of frameworks which is used to connect an application to underlying event-driven resources like window-system widgets or inter-process communication channels. This pattern has been used in ET++ [WG95], Geo (our current project), and the newly redesigned VisualWorks window-system framework presented at OOPSLA '96 [Yel96].

Figure 1 presents the role diagram of the pattern. It shows the five object roles Application, Abstraction, Implementor, Resource and Factory. A role defines a view on an object within a given object collaboration. The use of roles will be discussed in more detail in the next section. For the Active Bridge pattern it suffices to know that each of the aforementioned roles maps directly on a single object in a pattern instantiation.

The Active Bridge pattern can best be understood as the composition of the five patterns Bridge, Proxy, Observer, Abstract Factory and Factory Method, all of which are described in [GOF95].

- At the heart of the Active Bridge pattern is the *Bridge* pattern which serves to decouple an Abstraction from a number of different Implementors. For instance, a Window abstraction can be implemented based on a lower-level Implementor interface.
- Each Implementor acts as a *Proxy* for an underlying resource like a window-system native window widget [Yel96]. The Proxy is implemented based on the resource and acts as an object-oriented placeholder for it.
- Communication flows in both directions. An application directly uses an Abstraction which uses an Implementor which uses a Resource. A Resource may cause events due to user interactions or incoming communication requests. It forwards them to the Implementor. The Implementor informs the Abstraction using the *Observer* pattern, thus becoming the Subject of the Abstraction which is its Observer.
- The configuration of such a subsystem requires some thought and is therefore delegated to an *Abstract Factory*. The Factory creates the Implementor instances and thereby ensures that the chosen implementations can coexist, meet the applications' needs, and work with the available resources.
- The creation operations of the Abstract Factory are implemented using *Factory Methods*. Factory Methods are the best choice because the Factory is chosen once at startup time and there is no need to reconfigure it.

Each of the five patterns defines a set of roles for its elements. Every object in an instance of the Active Bridge pattern plays several roles from the constituting patterns. Figure 2 groups the roles from the atomic patterns into composite roles. Composite

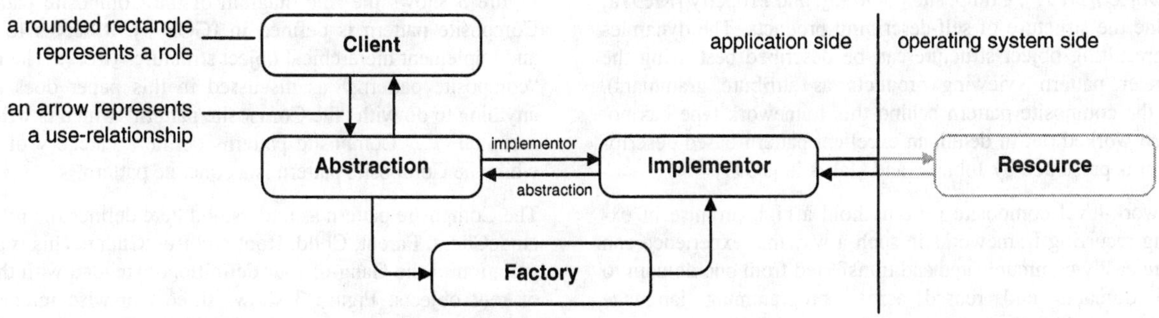


Figure 1: Role diagram of the Active Bridge pattern

$$
\begin{aligned}
\mathtt{Client}_{AB} &= \{\ \mathtt{Client}_{B}\ \} \\
\mathtt{Abstraction}_{AB} &= \{\ \mathtt{Abstraction}_{B},\ \mathtt{Client}_{P},\ \mathtt{Observer}_{O},\ \mathtt{Client}_{AF}\ \} \\
\mathtt{Implementor}_{AB} &= \{\ \mathtt{Implementor}_{B},\ \mathtt{Proxy}_{P},\ \mathtt{Subject}_{O},\ \mathtt{Product}_{AF},\ \mathtt{Product}_{FM}\ \} \\
\mathtt{Factory}_{AB} &= \{\ \mathtt{Factory}_{AF},\ \mathtt{Client}_{FM},\ \mathtt{Creator}_{FM}\ \} \\
\mathtt{Resource}_{AB} &= \{\ \mathtt{Subject}_{P}\ \}
\end{aligned}
$$

Figure 2: Composite roles of the Active Bridge pattern

roles are the roles of the composite pattern; they are a composition of some atomic roles. The index of a role name in figure 2 indicates the pattern in which it is defined. AB stands for Active Bridge, B for Bridge, P for Proxy, O for Observer, AF for Abstract Factory, and FM for Factory Method.

Active Bridge is a fairly simple composite pattern, because the patterns it consists of are fairly simple. The constituting patterns' roles can be grouped easily to form the composite roles.

It is easy now to prove that Active Bridge is a composite pattern according to the definition of section 2.1: Active Bridge can be observed to recur; it is described in [WG95, Yel96] and has been used in many other frameworks. As has just been demonstrated, it can be explained well as a composition of some patterns. Finally, the composite roles defined in figure 2 are a visible expression of the synergy achieved by the composite pattern. This synergy stems from integrating different roles from different constituting patterns in a composite role played by a single object at runtime.

## 2.3 Further examples

The Active Bridge pattern is described in some more depth in [Rie97a], where further composite patterns can be found (Bureaucracy, Model-View-Controller and Role Object). The Bureaucracy pattern will be discussed in section 4. The Role pattern serves to adapt a core abstraction to different contexts by means of role objects, as it is ubiquitously needed in many complex domains. Further composite patterns can be abstracted from recurring frameworks for such topics as product specification, resource allocation or order management.

Another concrete example of a such a framework-level composite pattern is the user-defined product specification pattern, the abstraction from product specification frameworks. A product specification framework lets users dynamically define banking or insurance products (like loans, financial instruments, or insurance contracts). Because the number of different products is large, constantly changes and must be adapted (to some extent) for every customer, a naive approach like modeling each product as a class of its own is doomed to fail.

Instead, product specification frameworks repeatedly compose Type Object [JW97], Composite [GOF95], and Property [Rie97a] to define the structure of self-describing products. The dynamics of the resulting object structure can be described best using the Interpreter pattern (viewing products as attribute grammars). While the composite pattern behind this framework type has not yet been worked out in detail, an excellent pattern-based description of it is presented by Johnson and Oakes in [JO97].

Framework-level composite patterns hold a high promise of explaining recurring frameworks in such a way that experience can be more easily communicated and transferred from one domain to related domains and reused across programming language boundaries. A high leverage can be expected from uncovering, describing and communicating these composite business patterns.

# 3 Pattern Description

If all composite patterns were as simple as the Active Bridge pattern, this paper would probably end here. However, many composite patterns are much more complex than the introductory pattern. To cope with this complexity, we need proper concepts, techniques and tools to support human intuition and experience while defining a pattern.

This section presents a new notation for describing patterns, the role diagram notation. Role diagrams are based on Reenskaug's role models [Ree96a], but extend them with the notion of composition constraint [Rie96, Rie97a]. The next section discusses an analysis and composition technique for composite patterns based on role diagrams.

Choosing role diagrams as the primary means for describing patterns ignores class inheritance based patterns for which further techniques have to be developed. This is justified, because role diagrams can be used more effectively than class diagrams when dealing with patterns based on object collaborations.

## 3.1 Role diagrams

Almost all pattern descriptions today use class diagrams to describe patterns [CS95, VCK96, MRB97]. The reason is that classes have long been the primary means for modeling object-oriented software systems. In addition, they are explicitly represented in today's object-oriented programming languages. However, class diagrams often mix the actual problem solution in terms of the distribution of responsibilities between objects with efficient ways of implementing it. Role diagrams in turn are better suited for describing object collaboration based patterns than class diagrams, because they better focus on the actual problem solution as a set of collaborating objects.

A *role diagram* describes how some collaborating objects, each one playing one or more *roles*, achieve a common goal. A *role* represents the view some objects in the collaboration hold on another object playing that role [Rie96, KO96]; it captures the responsibilities of an object with respect to achieving the purpose defined by the role diagram. An object can play several roles at once, and the same role can be played by several objects. An object collaboration usually serves several purposes—it can be viewed as a set of overlapping role diagrams. Thus, role diagrams can be composed easily, which makes them attractive for describing composite patterns.

Figure 3 shows the role diagram of the Composite pattern. The Composite pattern is defined in [GOF95]; it serves to describe and implement hierarchical object structures (trees). The notion of "composite patterns" as discussed in this paper does not have anything to do with "the Composite pattern" which is written with a capital "C." Composite patterns define a category of patterns, while the Composite pattern is a concrete pattern.

The Composite pattern as understood here defines the roles Node, NodeClient, Parent, Child, Root and RootClient. This is a reinterpretation of the Gang-of-four definition, extended with the notion of root objects. Figure 3 shows three pair-wise interactions: a NodeClient makes use of a Node, a Parent has several Child objects, and a RootClient makes use of the Root object. These interactions are linked together by *composition constraints:* An object playing the Root role also always plays the Parent role which also always plays the Node role. On an implementation level, this type of composition constraints frequently maps well on class inheritance.

Role diagrams are more abstract than class diagrams. Role diagrams can be mapped on several class diagrams. The use of class inheritance often introduces important implementation twists that help handle the instantiated pattern more easily. [Rie96] discusses the resulting levels of abstraction, and shows how the general role diagram of the Observer pattern depicted in figure 6 maps on at least three different class diagrams that make it more concrete.

## 3.2 Role relationships

Figure 3 does not fully show how the roles can be mapped on objects. The mapping of roles on objects may be subject to composition constraints. A *composition constraint* is a binary relationship between roles which may take on one of three different values: Two roles *may be played* by the same object, or they *must be played* by the same object, or they *must not be played* by the same object.

The set of composition constraints can be expressed as a role relationship matrix which relates every role with every other role. Figure 4 shows the role relationship matrix of the Composite pattern. It uses the three aforementioned different values for a matrix entry (A, B) which defines a relationship between the two roles. These three values are:

- An object playing role A also always plays role B in the same collaboration. Thus role A implies role B. This is depicted by a black rectangle for the matrix entry (A, B).
- An object playing role A never plays role B in the same collaboration. Thus, role A prohibits role B. This is depicted by a white rectangle for the matrix entry (A, B).
- Two roles A and B arbitrarily mix and match ("don't care"). Thus, role A may or may not go with Role B; nothing can be said. This is depicted by a gray rectangle for the matrix entry (A, B).

In the Composite pattern, two examples of "A implies B" are the pairs (Parent, Node) and (Child, Node) which specify that an object playing the Parent or Child role also always plays the Node role. The relationship is not symmetric: One cannot conclude that an object playing the Node role also plays the Parent or Child role. An example of "A prohibits B" is the pair (Child, Root) which specifies that a Child object never plays the Root role.

The role relationship matrix depicted in figure 4 is a visual representation of a propositional calculus formula. Part of the description of an object's behavior within a collaboration is the set of roles it may play, and the constraints which define valid sets can be described well and in simple terms using propositional logic.

The meaning of the matrix entries is as follows: The "implies" relationship between two roles corresponds to a logical implication between two roles "($A \Rightarrow B$)," the "prohibits" relationship between two roles corresponds to "$\neg(A \wedge B)$" (due to its symmetry) and the "don't care" relationship corresponds to "true." The

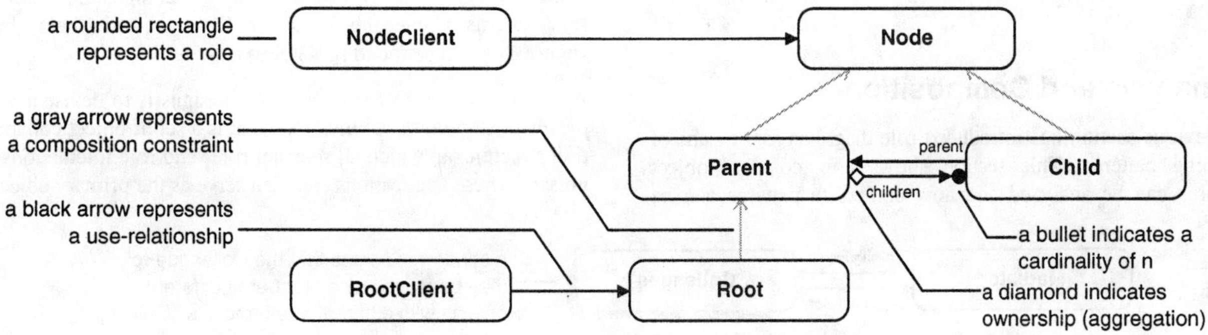


Figure 3: Role diagram of the Composite pattern

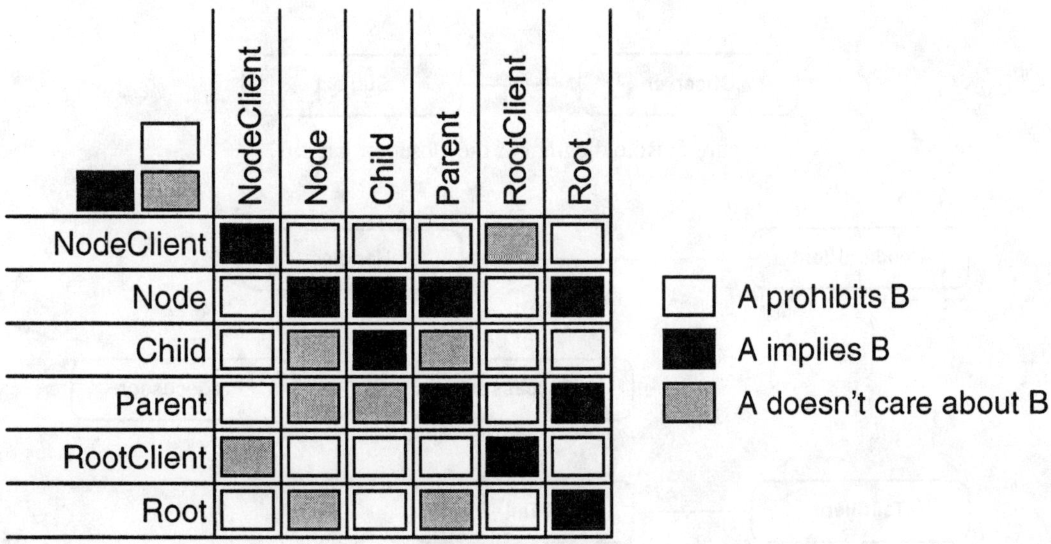


Figure 4: Role relationship matrix of the Composite pattern

overall matrix represents a conjunction of its entries. An object's role set is valid within a collaboration if the binding of the variables makes the formula evaluate to true.

### 3.3 Further examples

Figures 5 to 7 show three further patterns needed for this paper.

- The *Mediator pattern* (figure 5) serves to decouple, manage and integrate several Colleague objects by means of a coordinating Mediator.
- The *Observer pattern* (figure 6) serves to decouple Observer objects from a Subject object while maintaining state dependencies. The maintenance is achieved by using events for inter-object communication.
- The *Chain of Responsibility pattern* (figure 7) serves to define an object chain along which requests are passed until they are handled. Thus, by configuring the chain, the receiver of a request can be defined dynamically.

These examples are taken from [Rie97a] where more atomic and composite patterns are described using role diagrams. Some of these descriptions are simpler than the original from [GOF95], and some are more complex. In particular, descriptions of patterns with a recursive structure like Composite or Chain of Responsibility are more complex, because satisfying the boundary conditions increases the number of roles and composition constraints.

## 4 Analysis and Composition

The previous section has introduced role diagrams as a means of describing patterns. This section shows how complex object structures can be analyzed and how composite patterns can be derived and defined. The key concepts are the set of prototypical pattern applications and the role relationship matrix. I use the Bureaucracy pattern [Rie97b] as an example of a complex composite pattern.

### 4.1 Prototypical pattern application

Patterns grow from experience. Thus, every effort to devise a new pattern should be based on previously known pattern instantiations, that is concrete designs in which the patterns have been applied (albeit implicitly). The documentation of existing systems is a good starting point. However, concrete designs and implementations often vary greatly, even if a common core indicates a potential composite pattern.

In a Bureaucracy pattern instantiation, the objects form a hierarchy, with each parent-node object being a manager to its child-node objects. This management and integration task conforms to the Mediator pattern. Child objects, like subordinates in a bureaucratic hierarchy, inform their parent about state changes, for example when they have finished a task they had to fulfill. This is done according to the Observer pattern. Moreover, if an external client requests a task from an object in the hierarchy which exceeds this object's context information, the object forwards the request up the hierarchy until it can be satisfied by a node that has enough context information to do so. This interaction is handled according to the Chain of Responsibility pattern. Finally, the hierarchical structure itself is defined using the Composite pattern. All four patterns, Composite, Mediator, Observer and Chain of Responsibility can be found in [GOF95].

A first step to abstract from concrete designs is to devise a *set of prototypical pattern applications,* that is a set of object collaboration structures in which all relevant roles and role interactions are present. These applications can then serve as the primary object of

Figure 5: Role diagram of the Mediator pattern

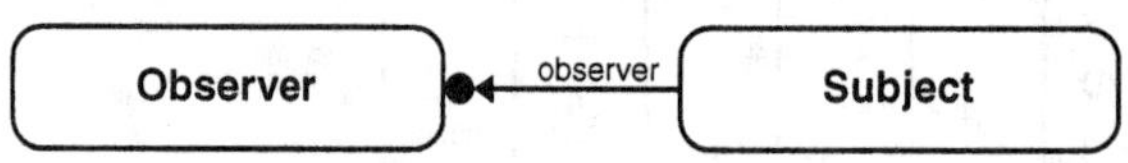


Figure 6: Role diagram of the Observer pattern

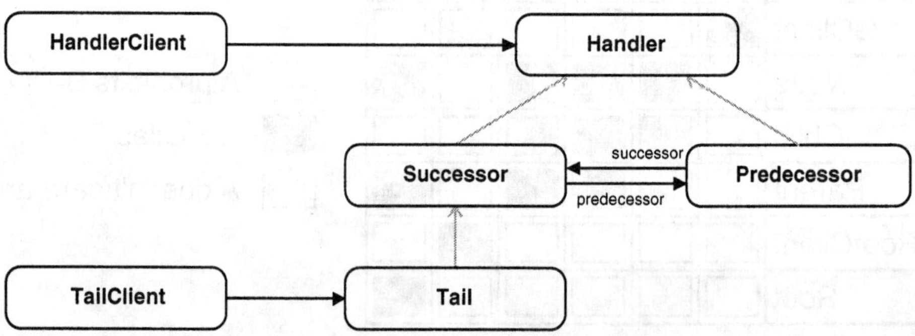


Figure 7: Role diagram of the Chain of Responsibility pattern

study. Frequently, a single prototypical pattern application is sufficient to capture all relevant configurations. If not, further applications must be devised until all relevant configurations are covered. This forms the set of prototypical pattern applications.

Figure 8 shows a prototypical pattern application of the Bureaucracy pattern, as it can be found in graphical editors like HotDraw [Joh92], ET++Draw [WG95], and Sane [RZ95]. It shows a hierarchy of visual objects which represent the elements of a drawing. They are displayed in an editor window, ready for being manipulated by the user. The visual objects communicate with each other in order to keep the hierarchy in a consistent state as well as to perform user initiated actions. This section's analysis of the collaboration structure will show that its driving force is a recurring design theme which can be captured as the Bureaucracy pattern.

## 4.2 Involved patterns

An analysis of the prototypical pattern application identifies four patterns: Composite, Mediator, Chain of Responsibility, and Observer.

- The *Composite pattern* is used to define the hierarchy. Every visual object in the hierarchy plays the role of Node, some play the role of Parent (aFigure, aGroup), some play the role of Child (aCircle, aGroup, aRectangle, anArrow, aTriangle), and one plays the role of Root (aFigure). A user plays the role of NodeClient and anApplication plays the role of RootClient.
- The *Mediator pattern* is used to let a Parent in the hierarchy manage its Child objects. The roles of Mediator in the Mediator pattern maps on Parent and the role of Colleague maps on Child in this pattern. For example, aGroup plays the role of a Mediator for aRectangle, anArrow, and aTriangle which it coordinates to behave like a group.
- The *Chain of Responsibility* pattern is used to handle client requests. Every Node is a Handler which can receive client requests. Child objects are Predecessors which forward requests up the hierarchy if they cannot handle them. If aCircle is manipulated, for example moved, it sends an invalidate drawing region request to its Successor. Thus, aCircle is both a Handler and a Predecessor, and aFigure is both aNode and a Successor as well as a Tail for the Chain.
- The *Observer pattern* is used to keep up with changes that are not explicitly forwarded up the hierarchy. Every Parent in the hierarchy is an Observer of its Child objects which are its Subjects. If aCircle is not constrained by its Parent aFigure to ask first before letting a user change its label, it can do so on its own. Nevertheless, further objects, either inside or outside the hierarchy, might have to change accordingly, so aCircle informs its Observers about the change.

In short, the Composite pattern defines the hierarchical structure, the Mediator pattern shows how each hierarchy node manages its subordinate nodes, the Chain of Responsibility pattern shows how client requests are forwarded up the hierarchy, and the Observer pattern shows how nodes observe their subordinate nodes in order to readjust the hierarchy in case of unanticipated changes.

Working together, these patterns achieve a synergy that goes beyond their individual purposes: Their integration helps to design hierarchical structures which can maintain their inner stability (invariants) themselves while still allowing clients to interact with every hierarchy level. Client requests may cause a complex control flow inside the hierarchy which it uses to readjust itself.

## 4.3 Role relationship matrix

Figure 9 shows how the different roles of the constituting patterns are assigned to objects. Every role was taken and assigned to those objects which play that role. This defines the set of all roles an object may play in a collaboration.

Now the role relationship matrix can be derived. As defined, a role relationship matrix specifies how the roles objects play in an

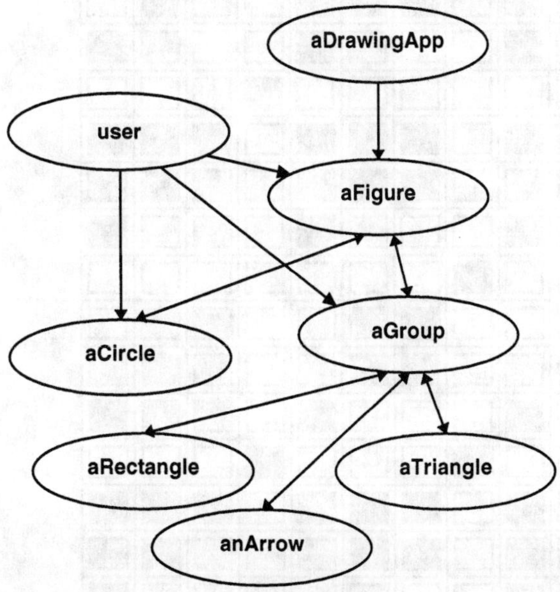


Figure 8: A prototypical pattern application of the Bureaucracy pattern

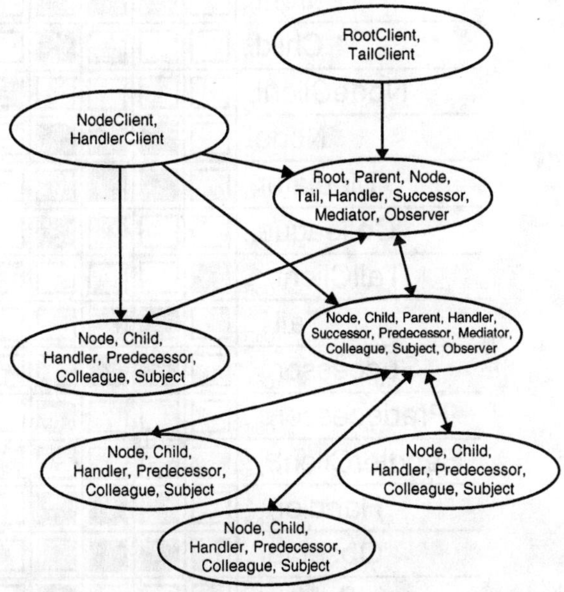


Figure 9: The roles objects in the prototypical pattern application play

object collaboration relate to each other. Its purpose here is to describe the pattern interaction synergies and help uncover hidden composite roles. Figure 10 shows the preliminary non-consolidated role relationship matrix of the Bureaucracy pattern, as derived from figure 9.

If it were not for the "implies" and "prohibits" relationship between roles, there would be no composite patterns. If it were possible to arbitrarily map roles on objects, anything would be possible but nothing could be said about pattern interaction synergies. However, it is exactly the set of *composition constraints,* which represents the synergy the composition achieves and which turns it from an arbitrary composition into a composite pattern.

The role relationship matrix is represented visually rather than as a large formula, because the visual presentation is more accessible to human perception and lets us much easier recognize composite roles and interaction synergies, as discussed now.

### 4.4 Pattern derivation

Analysis of the role relationship matrix reveals that several columns (and rows, the matrix is symmetric with respect to this) are equivalent. Thus, grouping equivalent columns lets us partition the overall role set into equivalence sets, each one representing a composite role. Why? Because if an object plays a role it always also plays any other role from its equivalence set so that in an instantiation of the composite pattern the roles are always played together. Thus, they constitute the pattern's composite roles.

Figure 11 shows the composite roles of the Bureaucracy pattern. It is based on the roles DirectorClient, Director, Manager, Subordinate, ClerkClient and Clerk, each of which represents an equivalence set of roles from the composed patterns. The index B stands for Bureaucracy, C for Composite, M for Mediator, CoR for Chain of Responsibility, and O for Observer.

Figure 12 shows a consolidated role relationship matrix which is solely based on composite roles. The redundancy of the equivalence sets has been eliminated. This leaves us with a matrix in which only the composition constraints between the composite roles are present (for example, every Director is a Manager, which in turns is always a Clerk—in accordance with the textbook definition of bureaucracy [Web47]).

Figure 13 shows the role diagram of the Bureaucracy pattern, as it conforms to the role relationship matrix of figure 12. The structure is isomorphic to the Composite pattern's structure of figure 3 and 4, but the dynamics are more elaborate. This role diagram is the result of this section's work.

This section has presented an analysis, composition and derivation technique for composite patterns based on object collaborations. The set of prototypical pattern applications serves to abstract from concrete designs. The role relationship matrix serves to analyze the interaction of different roles from the involved

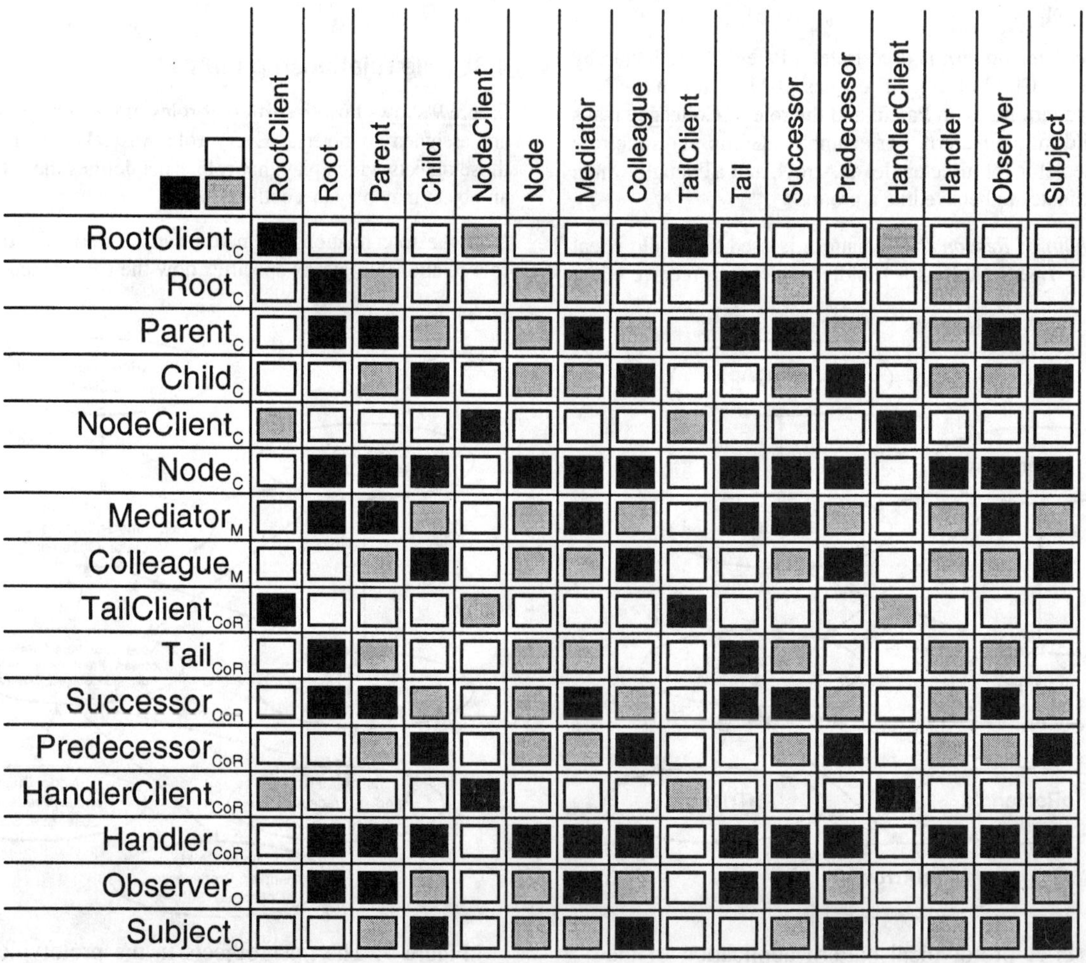


Figure 10: Role relationship matrix of the Bureaucracy pattern before consolidation

patterns. Starting with the role relationship matrix, role equivalent sets are defined which stand for composite roles. Based on composite roles, the preliminary role relationship matrix can be consolidated and the final role diagram can be defined.

The process demonstrated in this section is an after-the-fact rationalization [PC86]. The creative process of working out the pattern did not proceed in the linear fashion as implied by the steps taken in this section.

# 5 Comparison

This section discusses the relationship between composite patterns, frameworks and pattern languages. It shows that recurring frameworks can be abstracted into patterns and demonstrates that composite patterns are different from pattern languages.

## 5.1 Frameworks

A framework is a set of classes which model and solve a specific domain problem. Usually, this set of classes contains some abstract classes which define the design of the framework and the interaction of their instances, and some concrete classes which provide implementations for the abstract classes [JF88, GOF95, Lew95]. As already pointed out in [GOF95], patterns are abstractions from concrete designs and therefore are to be seen on a different level. In this paper I have claimed and illustrated that composite design patterns are the abstractions from concrete recurring frameworks. This point will now be clarified further.

Both patterns and frameworks can be described using class or role diagrams [Rie96, Rie97a, Ree96a]. Both frameworks and pattern instances can be understood well as solving a particular problem. A framework, which keeps recurring and which solves a specific problem, can be abstracted into a pattern. Thus, the abstraction

$$
\begin{aligned}
\texttt{DirectorClient}_B &= \{\ \texttt{RootClient}_C,\ \texttt{TailClient}_{CoR}\ \} \\
\texttt{Director}_B &= \{\ \texttt{Root}_C,\ \texttt{Tail}_{CoR}\ \} \\
\texttt{Manager}_B &= \{\ \texttt{Parent}_C,\ \texttt{Mediator}_M,\ \texttt{Successor}_{CoR},\ \texttt{Observer}_O\ \} \\
\texttt{Subordinate}_B &= \{\ \texttt{Child}_C,\ \texttt{Colleague}_M,\ \texttt{Predecessor}_{CoR},\ \texttt{Subject}_O\ \} \\
\texttt{ClerkClient}_B &= \{\ \texttt{NodeClient}_C,\ \texttt{HandlerClient}_{CoR}\ \} \\
\texttt{Clerk}_B &= \{\ \texttt{Node}_C,\ \texttt{Handler}_{CoR}\ \}
\end{aligned}
$$

Figure 11: Definition of the composite roles of the Bureaucracy pattern

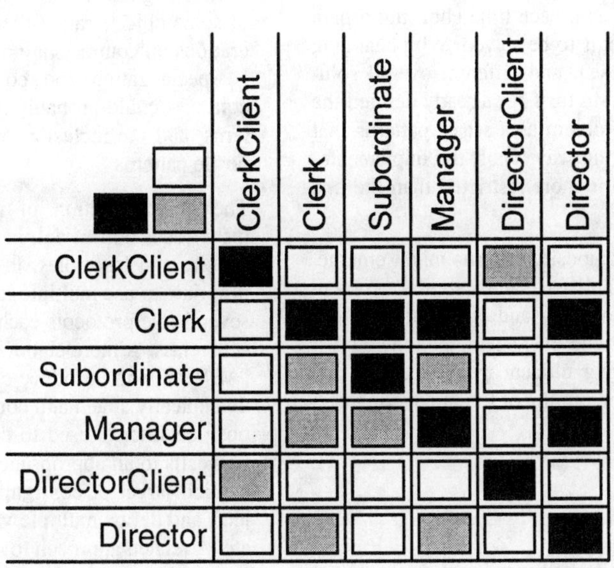


Figure 12: Role relationship matrix of the Bureaucracy pattern

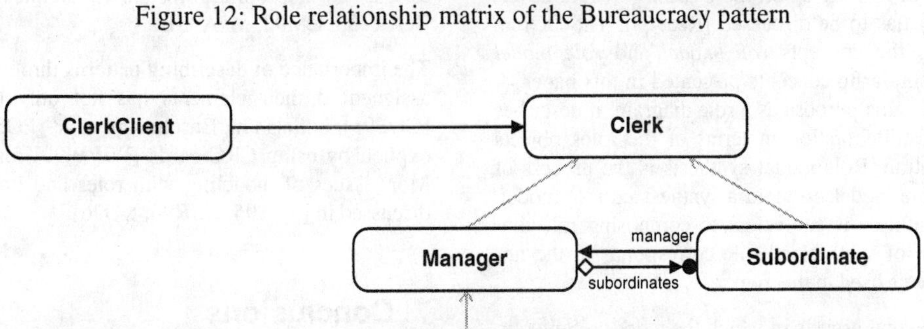


Figure 13: Role diagram of the Bureaucracy pattern

from a set of similar recurring frameworks is a pattern, and the concrete frameworks are its instances.

A framework, in which several patterns have been applied and in which these pattern instances interact in always the same way, can be abstracted into a composite pattern. The definition of composite pattern is pragmatic: Describing a composite pattern as the composition of several patterns helps to explain it better and makes clear that the way the pattern instances interact in a given framework keeps recurring as a pattern of its own.

### 5.2 Pattern languages

A pattern language is a collection of patterns which refer to each other in such a way that users can use the patterns to build software systems in a similar way as they use natural language to create sentences, paragraphs and books [Ale79, Cop97]. The power of a pattern language emerges from being "generative" in the sense that it helps users with going back and forth between patterns, describing the pattern relationships and interactions. Alexander has given up pattern languages [Gab94] because it did not meet his hopes and expectations, but the software and organizational patterns community discusses them as a possible means for effectively supporting software development activities.

A pattern language offers more freedom of choice than a composite pattern. When using a pattern language, users actually traverse paths in the language's pattern graph, each time choosing a path specific to the overall problem that is to be solved. With changing problems, different paths are chosen, and different overall solutions emerge. A composite pattern in turn has already defined the one single solution space for a problem as a set of patterns that interact in always the same recurring way. Thus, the implementation space of a composite pattern is more restricted than the one of a pattern language.

From using a pattern language, composite patterns might emerge. If a user of a pattern language notices that in similar problem contexts he or she is actually traversing and applying a pattern language using the same path over and over again, then there must be some hidden theme, a recurring hidden agenda behind that traversal path. This might be the beginning of the uncovering of a new composite pattern.

## 6 Related Work

First of all, the work of Reenskaug on the OOram software development methodology has to be discussed [Ree96a]. The OOram methodology defines the concepts *role model* and *role model synthesis* which are similar to concepts presented in this paper. A role model serves the same purpose as a role diagram: it describes an archetypal object collaboration in terms of the roles objects play in the collaboration. Role model synthesis is the process of composing several role models to yield a synthesized role model. Thus, role model synthesis is equivalent to composing role diagrams and the notion of synthesized role corresponds to the notion of composite role as used in this paper.

However, there are several aspects in which the work presented in this paper is different or goes beyond his work. On the concrete role modeling level, it introduces the notions of composition constraint and role relationship matrix to address issues of describing role interactions. Reenskaug suggests to directly synthesize role models instead of preserving the individual roles and annotating them with composition constraints [Ree96b]. Using composition constraints helps to keep independent roles separate while preserving important information about their relationship.

On page 260pp of [Ree96a], Reenskaug shows that design patterns can be described using role models. He presents a sequence of patterns for the MVC pattern and shows how to construct software tools from them. Effectively, he documents a framework using patterns described as role models, in a similar vain as Johnson has already done using class diagrams [Joh92]. This is a different issue than what this paper tries to achieve: To understand recurring frameworks as composite patterns, that is not to document them (although this is an important issue), but to abstract from them to make them reusable across notation, language and domain boundaries.

Moreover, this paper presents means for analyzing object collaboration structures with respect to involved patterns. Such analytical means are necessary to cope with the increasing complexity as we turn to more challenging patterns which promise increased leverage.

The importance of *behavioral compositions* has been acknowledged for some time. The work of Helm et al. [HHG90] used the notion of *contract* to describe the formal semantics of a behavioral composition, that is a collaboration of some objects. Similar to role diagrams and role models, the focus is on the collaboration of some objects rather than on single objects. Two important operations on contracts are discussed, refinement and inclusion, that is specialization and composition. With some enhancements, contracts could probably be used to formally describe design patterns, and the inclusion operation could be used to define composite patterns.

The implementation of collaboration-based composite pattern instances is non-trivial, in particular if an object may dynamically acquire and lose roles. In the simple static case, it might be appropriate to use multiple inheritance to derive a class which offers several role protocols each of which is represented by an abstract superclass. A more elaborate approach is presented by Aksit et al. [ABV92] who introduce *composition filters* which can be used to dynamically attach and control views (roles) on an object. A composition filter is used to control the dispatch of incoming operation calls to an appropriate target. Making the method dispatch an explicit target of configuration at runtime helps to compose objects and define multiple views on the resulting object conglomerate. A related approach to control the dispatch of operation calls is to use an appropriate metalevel architecture, exemplified in [KAR+93, CM93, McA95].

The importance of describing patterns through the responsibilities assigned to their elements has not only been emphasized by [GOF95], but also by Buschmann et al. [POSA96] who made this explicit by using CRC cards [WWW90] for describing patterns. More issues of modeling with roles and implementing them are discussed in [WJS95, GSR96, KO96].

## 7 Conclusions

This paper defines the notion of composite pattern and illustrates it using one elaborate and further small examples. It demonstrates that composite patterns can be understood to be the abstraction from successful recurring object-oriented frameworks. To support this, an analysis and derivation technique is presented that helps pattern authors work out the essence of complex composite patterns.

The discussion is restricted to deal with patterns based on object collaborations which represent the majority of software design patterns known today. This restriction serves to introduce a more effective description, analysis and composition technique than is possible without.

In particular, the patterns are described using role diagrams, an extension of Reenskaug's role models. The most important aspect of this extension is the definition of composition constraints which specify the set of roles an object may, has to, or must not play. Composition constraints can be expressed visually as a role relationship matrix. Such a matrix supports the analysis of complex object structures as needed when defining the core of a potential composite pattern.

These concepts and techniques are to be seen as tools which pattern authors use to attack ever more complex patterns. First evaluations show that frameworks for such topics as user-defined product specifications, resource allocation, and order management share a common repeating design core. I believe that abstracting these cores into composite patterns will help software developers communicate more effectively about their frameworks and will make learning from each other easier.

## Acknowledgements

I wish to thank Walter Bischofberger, Thomas Gross, Kai-Uwe Mätzel, Trygve Reenskaug, and Antonio Rito da Silva for discussing the topics of this paper as well as the paper itself with me.

## References

**ABV92** Mehmet Aksit, Lodewijk Bergmans and Sinan Vural. "An Object-Oriented Language-Database Integration Model: The Composition-Filters Approach." ECOOP '92, *Conference Proceedings.* Springer-Verlag, 1992.

**Ale79** Christopher Alexander. *A Pattern Language.* Oxford University Press, 1979.

**CM93** Shigeru Chiba and Takashi Masuda. "Designing and Extensible Distributed Language with a Metalevel Architecture." ECOOP '93, *Conference Proceedings.* LNCS 707. Springer-Verlag, 1993. Page 482-501.

**Cop97** James O. Coplien. "Pattern Languages." *C++ Report* 9, 1 (January 1997): 15-21.

**CS95** James O. Coplien and Douglas Schmidt (editors). *Pattern Languages of Program Design.* Addison-Wesley, 1995.

**Gab94** Richard P. Gabriel. "The Failure of Pattern Languages." *Journal of Object-Oriented Programming* 5, 9 (February 1994): 84-88.

**GOF95** Erich Gamma, Richard Helm, Ralph Johnson and John Vlissides. *Design Patterns: Elements of Reusable Design.* Addison-Wesley, 1995.

**GSR96** Georg Gottlob, Michael Schrefl, and Brigitte Röck. "Extending Object-Oriented Systems with Roles." *ACM Transactions on Information Systems* 14, 3 (July 1996): 268-296.

**HHG90** Richard Helm, Ian M. Holland and Dipayan Gangopadhyay. "Contracts: Specifying Behavioral Compositions in Object-Oriented Systems." OOPSLA '90, *Conference Proceedings.* ACM Press. Page 169-180.

**JF88** Ralph E. Johnson and Brian Foote. "Designing Reusable Classes." *Journal of Object-Oriented Programming* 1, 2 (June/July 1988): 22-35.

**JO97** Ralph E. Johnson and Jeff Oakes. "The User-Defined Product Framework." *In preparation.*

**Joh92** Ralph E. Johnson. "Documenting Frameworks using Patterns." OOPSLA '92, *ACM SIGPLAN Notices* 27, 10 (October 1992): 63-70.

**JW97** Ralph E. Johnson and Bobby Woolf. "Type Object." *In MRB97.* Chapter 4.

**KAR+93** Gregor Kiczales, J. Michael Ashley, Luis H. Rodriguez Jr., Amin Vahdat and Daniel G. Bobrow. "Metaobject Protocols: Why We Want Them and What Else They Can Do." *Object-Oriented Programming: The CLOS Perspective.* MIT Press, 1993. Page 101-118.

**KO96** Bent Bruun Kristensen and Kasper Osterbye. "Roles: Conceptual Abstraction Theory and Practical Language Issues." *Theory and Practice of Object System* 2, 3 (1996): 143-160.

**KP88** Glenn E. Krasner and Stephen T. Pope. "A Cookbook for Using the Model-View-Controller User Interface Paradigm in Smalltalk-80." *Journal of Object-Oriented Programming* 1, 3 (August/September 1988): 26-49.

**Lew95** Ted Lewis. *Object-Oriented Application Frameworks.* Manning, 1995.

**McA95** Jeff McAffer. "Metalevel Programming with CodA." ECOOP '95, *Conference Proceedings.* Lecture Notes in Computer Science 952. Berlin, Heidelberg: Springer-Verlag. Page 190-214.

**MRB97** Robert C. Martin, Dirk Riehle, and Frank Buschmann (editors). *Pattern Languages of Program Design 3.* Addison-Wesley, 1997.

**PC86** David L. Parnas and Paul C. Clements. "A Rational Design Process: How and Why to Fake It." *IEEE Transactions on Software Engineering*, 12, 2 (February 1986): 251-257.

**POSA96** Frank Buschmann, Regine Meunier, Hans Rohnert, Peter Sommerlad and Michael Stal. *Pattern-Oriented Software Architecture.* Wiley & Sons, 1996.

**Ree96a** Trygve Reenskaug, with Per Wold and Odd Arild Lehne. *Working with Objects.* Manning: 1996.

**Ree96b** Trygve Reenskaug. *Personal communication,* 1996.

**Rie96** Dirk Riehle. "Describing and Composing Patterns Using Role Diagrams." WOON '96 (1st Int'l Conference on Object-Orientation in Russia), Conference Proceedings. St. Petersburg Electrotechnical University, 1996. Reprinted in *Proceedings of the Ubilab Conference '96, Zürich.* Edited by Kai-Uwe Mätzel and Hans-Peter Frei. Konstanz, Universitätsverlag Konstanz, 1996. Page 137-152.

**Rie97a** Dirk Riehle. *A Role-Based Design Pattern Catalog of Atomic and Composite Patterns Structured by Pattern Purpose.* Ubilab Technical Report 97.1.1. Zürich, Switzerland: Union Bank of Switzerland, 1997.

**Rie97b** Dirk Riehle. "Bureaucracy." *In MRB97.* Chapter 11.

**RZ95** Dirk Riehle and Heinz Züllighoven. "A Pattern Language for Tool Construction and Integration Based on the Tools and Materials Metaphor." *In CS95.* Chapter 2, page 9-42.

**RZ96** Dirk Riehle and Heinz Züllighoven. "Understanding and Using Patterns in Software Development." *Theory and Practice of Object Systems* 2, 1 (1996). Page 3-13.

**VCK96** John Vlissides, James O. Coplien and Norm Kerth. *Pattern Languages of Program Design 2.* Reading, MA: Addison-Wesley, 1996.

**Web47** Max Weber. *The Theory of Social and Economic Organization*. Oxford University Press, 1947.

**WG95** Andre Weinand and Erich Gamma. "ET++ A Portable Homogeneous Class Library and Application Framework." *In Lew95.* Chapter 7, page 154-194.

**WJS95** Roel Wieringa, Wiebrien de Jonge and Paul Spruit. "Using Dynamic Classes and Role Classes to Model Object Migration." *Theory and Practice of Object Systems* 1, 1 (1995): 61-83.

**WWW90** Rebecca Wirfs-Brock, Brian Wilkerson und Lauren Wiener. *Designing Object-Oriented Software.* Prentice-Hall, 1990.

**Yel96** Phillip M. Yelland. "Creating Host Compliance in a Portable Framework." OOPSLA '96, *Conference Proceedings.* ACM Press, 1996. Page 18-29.

# An Open Implementation Analysis and Design for Lightweight Threads

Matthew Haines*
Department of Computer Science
University of Wyoming

## Abstract

Open Implementation Analysis and Design (OIA/D) has been introduced as a design methodology for object-oriented software systems, and in particular for substrate software. In this paper we detail our experiences with using OIA/D to design and implement a common substrate component for parallel language runtime systems: a lightweight threads package. We show how existing thread packages employ a "black-box" design, hiding crucial design decisions that drastically reduce their ability to be re-used. We detail these design decisions (dilemmas) and show how an implementation based on OIA/D principles results in a thread package that is flexible, efficient, portable, and re-usable.

**Keywords**: reflection and metaobject models, analysis and design methods, parallel systems.



*Supported in part by National Science Foundation Career Award ASC-9623904

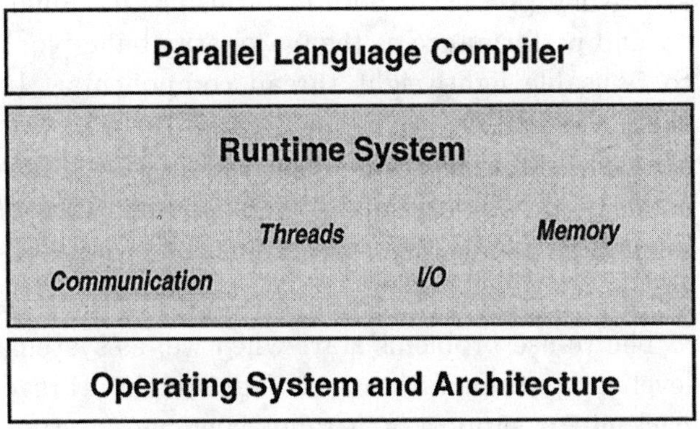


Figure 1: A parallel language runtime system

## 1 Introduction

As depicted in Figure 1, parallel language runtime systems bridge the gap between the functionality required by the parallel language compiler and the functionality provided by the native operating system. Many parallel languages map the notion of a *parallel task* onto a lightweight thread which can then be scheduled for execution when and where the language compiler and runtime system see fit. For this reason, most parallel language runtime systems [3, 6, 7, 9, 11, 20] contain a component that supports lightweight threads. Additional components often include communication, I/O, and memory management.

From the perspective of a parallel language runtime system designer, the opportunity to re-use the threads component seems exceptional. First, a lightweight threads component supports a very well-know and well-defined set of abstractions, such as threads, mutexes, and condition variables. Second, there are well-established standards and implementations for lightweight threads [15, 28]. These correspond to two of Goguen's four requisites for re-usable software [12]: finding the parts you need and understanding these parts. However, re-using a lightweight thread module is difficult when we consider the other two requisites for re-usable software: getting the parts to do what you need and putting them together correctly. In particular, getting a thread component to do exactly what you need, both in terms of functionality and performance, is the major stumbling block to re-usable lightweight thread components. In short, the inability to re-use existing thread packages stems from one or more of the following shortcomings of a lightweight thread module: *lack of flexibility*, *lack of performance*, or *lack of portability*.

The re-use problems start when we, as system-level programmers using a lightweight thread package to support a parallel language runtime system, want to change the *implementation decisions* of one or more of the component's abstractions to suit our needs. For example, to implement a load balancing scheme a designer will need to change the thread scheduler so that it can gather load information and make balancing decisions in cooperation with other processors. Since most thread modules provide little to no support for altering the scheduler, the designer is forced to write a new thread module just to gain control over the implementation of the scheduler. The inability to accommodate a range of implementation strategies is the downfall of all substrate components designed with strict "black box" principles, and the problem with most thread components in general.

In response to the problems of a traditional black box design, Kiczales put forth an alternative design approach called Open Implementation Analysis and Design (OIA/D) [17, 22]. The goals of an Open Implementation (OI) are "to ensure that suitable implementation strategies are available for a range of clients, to ensure that the appropriate strategy be selected for or by a client, and to ensure that the benefits associated with black box abstraction are not unreasonably compromised" [22].

This paper provides a case-study of the OIA/D process by presenting an Open Implementation for a lightweight thread module called OpenThreads. Our goals for this paper are twofold. First, we provide an Open Implementation Analysis and Design of a lightweight thread module. We focus on identifying the design dilemmas and the implementation options, and report on the performance of our resulting system with respect to flexibility, performance, and portability. Second, we review our analysis and design of OpenThreads with respect to the Open Implementation design guidelines [19] and comment on the OIA/D process as a whole.

The remainder of this paper is divided into six sections. Section 2 provides background on OIA/D and lightweight threads. Section 3 provides an analysis of lightweight threads that will provide the information required for our OI design. Section 4 outlines the design of OpenThreads using the information provided from the analysis. Section 5 provides an evaluation of the OpenThreads design. Section 6 outlines related research projects, and we conclude in Section 7.

## 2 Background

In this section we provide background information for readers unfamiliar with either OIA/D or lightweight threads.

### 2.1 Open Implementation

*Decomposition* and *abstraction* are the two principles that drive conventional software engineering. The basic idea is simple: decompose large problems into well-defined modules that interact with one-another through interfaces that hide the details of their implementation. Together, decomposition and abstraction produce "black boxes" (see Figure 2) that allow us to build larger software components from smaller components without having to know the details of how each of component is implemented.

Exposing only the functionality of a module in its interface, however, can lead to difficulties when either i) there are multiple implementation strategies and no single strategy favors all known uses, or ii) a module is used in a way in which it was

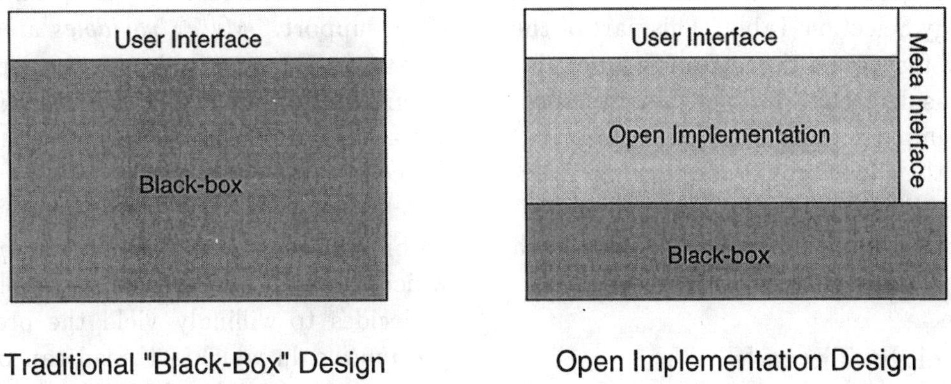


Figure 2: Black-box and Open Implementation designs

never envisioned. For example, consider the implementation of a byte stream from a file. Given the tremendous difference in time between accessing a memory block and accessing a disk block, block caching will almost certainly be useful. The question is, which caching policy will be the most efficient? Since the answer depends on how the file stream will be used, a black box module that supports a single policy and hides this decision from the client will fail to perform optimally for certain clients [21]. So, while a black-box abstraction is effective at hiding unnecessary details from a user, it also hides these key design decisions that need to be altered depending on how the module is to be used.

When faced with a black-box design that does not select the correct implementation strategies for each of the important design decisions, the programmer is forced to work around the given interface in one of two ways.

1. A *hematoma of duplication* occurs when a programmer writes an equivalent abstraction that duplicates the functionality of the black-box interface, but with different implementation strategies for the key design decisions.

2. *Coding between the lines* occurs when a programmer uses the black-box interface in a particularly contorted way to get the desired performance or functionality.

OIA/D recognizes that while it is beneficial to hide unnecessary implementation details for a module, there are some design decisions (*dilemmas*) that should be accessible to a system-level programmer with domain-specific knowledge about how the module is to be used. Therefore, the traditional black-box is divided into two implementation sections (see Figure 2):

- An "open" implementation that exposes implementation strategies for the key design decisions through a special interface called the *meta interface*. The "meta" term comes from the recognition that this is an interface that describes how the abstractions defined in the user interface should behave.

- A black box implementation that hides the remaining details.

Thus, OIA/D boils down to the design of the meta interface: give programmers a *principled* way to alter the implementation strategies that matter to them without opening the details of the entire implementation. To enable such a design, OIA/D consists of two phases [19]: an *analysis* phase in which a model of the module is constructed, and a *design* phase in which the interfaces for the module are designed.

The analysis phase of OIA/D produces an Internals Model that captures the abstract functionality of the module, the properties that determine how it is to be implemented, and the decisions that require information about client behavior in order to be implemented well. In addition, a Strategy Selection Table gives the range of client behaviors that must be supported and the corresponding range of implementations to support these behaviors.

The design phase of OIA/D produces the client (user) and meta interfaces for the module based on the information gathered in the Internals Model and the Strategy Selection Table. This part of the OIA/D process focuses on the *style* of the meta interface, either as declaring client behavior or specifying module implementation strategies. For example, should the client provide declarative information such as "I'll sequentially scan the next file" or select a module implementation strategy such as "I'll use LRU caching for the next file."

## 2.2 Lightweight Threads

Lightweight threads are useful for a variety of purposes. An application-level programmer will typically use threads to facilitate asynchronous scheduling for a number of related tasks. For example, consider an event-driven application such as Xlib [27], where lightweight threads are used to schedule tasks for execution based on an external event. In this context, threads free the programmer from the details of dynamic scheduling.

Lightweight threads are also useful for supporting independent tasks generated by parallel or concurrent programming languages. In this context, system-level programmers use lightweight threads to create and control the many independent tasks created by a parallel language compiler.

In general, threads provide the ability for a programmer to create and control multiple, independent units of execution entirely outside of the operating system kernel (i.e., in user-space). Since the OS kernel controls addressing and scheduling for the CPU, user-level threads must be multiplexed atop one or more kernel-level entities, such as Unix processes [4], Mach kernel threads [1], or a Sun Lightweight Processes (LWP) [26]. This "multiplexing" is commonly referred to as *scheduling* of the user-level threads. The kernel-entity (hereafter referred to as a "process") also provides a common address space that is shared by all threads multiplexed onto that process, and synchronization primitives are provided to keep the memory consistent.

From this description, we can start to define the basic components of a module that supports lightweight threads. First, there are the threads themselves, which will execute the actual user code. Then, to protect shared resources, there are synchronization primitives. While many synchronization primitives exist, most thread modules have settled on two basic primitives for all of their support. *Mutex variables* are used to provide short-term mutual exclusion operations that ensure atomic execution, and *condition variables* are used to provide long-term waiting on an event (or condition).

Scheduling policies for lightweight threads can be broadly classified either as *non-preemptive*, in which a thread executes until completion or until it decides to willingly yield the processor, or as *preemptive*, in which a thread can be interrupted at an arbitrary point during its execution so that some other thread may execute. Orthogonal to the issue of preemption, thread scheduling can incorporate a wide range of capabilities, including priorities, hand-off scheduling, and arbitrary run list structures (such as trees). Clearly, there are many design choices to be made for thread scheduling, and many runtime system designers will want to switch between various policies depending on the state of the system.

# 3 Analysis

The goal of the analysis phase of an Open Implementation design is to understand what functionality the module is providing to the client, and to understand how the client's wish to use the module. As put forth in [19], the result of this understanding is then expressed in terms of a Strategy Selection Table that details each of the design dilemmas and the corresponding implementation strategies for each dilemma. However, since OpenThreads was designed and implemented prior to the publication of these formal design guidelines, we did not develop a formal Strategy Selection Table. However, we did the equivalent work of identifying all of the design dilemmas for a lightweight threads package and corresponding implementation strategies. The remainder of this section discusses these dilemmas and implementation strategies.

Before discussing the design dilemmas, it is important to have an understanding of the domain for a module. In this case, we are concerned with the domain of a lightweight thread module. This is best expressed by giving the user (or client or black box) interface that describes the functionality of the abstractions supported by

```
typedef void (ot_userf_t)(void *p0);
extern void ot_thread_init (ot_thread_t *thread, ot_userf_t *start,
                void *args, unsigned tid, ot_queue_t *runq);
extern void ot_thread_yield (void);
extern void ot_thread_yield_onto (ot_queue_t *destq);
extern void ot_thread_exit (void);
extern unsigned ot_thread_id (void);
extern ot_thread_t *ot_current_thread (void);
extern void ot_thread_setspecific (ot_thread_t *thread, void *ptr,
                void (*cleanup)(void*));
extern void *ot_thread_getspecific (ot_thread_t *thread);

extern void ot_queue_init (ot_queue_t *q);

extern void ot_mutex_init (ot_mutex_t *m, ot_queue_t *blockq);
extern void ot_mutex_lock (ot_mutex_t *m);
extern int ot_mutex_trylock (ot_mutex_t *m);
extern void ot_mutex_unlock (ot_mutex_t *m);

extern void ot_cond_init (ot_cv_t *cv, ot_queue_t *blockq,
                ot_mutex_t *m);
extern void ot_cond_wait (ot_cv_t *cv);
extern void ot_cond_bcast (ot_cv_t *cv);
```

Figure 3: OpenThreads user interface

the module. For OpenThreads, the user interface is given in Figure 3. From this interface we see that OpenThreads supports four main abstractions: threads, queues, mutex variables, and condition variables.

The following subsections provide a detailed examination of the design dilemmas for a lightweight thread module and the corresponding range of implementation decisions. These dilemmas were obtained through examination of domain knowledge regarding how threads are used to support parallel language runtime systems.

## 3.1 Thread States

The lifetime of a thread is marked by a series of transformations between different *states*. A primary set of dilemmas that are present when designing a lightweight thread package is to define the set of actions to be performed during each state transition. A common set of thread states includes: being created, being placed onto an active run list, being selected (scheduled) for execution, being blocked on a mutex or condition variable, and being terminated. The transitions that take a thread from one state to the next can differ from one thread package to the next. For example, a blocked thread can either be resumed as an active thread or as a runnable thread. Figure 4 depicts these states transitions.

The dilemma here is to decide what actions should be performed at the various thread state transitions. Choices include support for:

- thread-specific data by adding code to the *save* and *restore* states of a thread.
- profiling by adding registration statements at each state transition.
- changing the behavior of the system depending on whether it is in an active state or in an idle state (no threads on the run list).

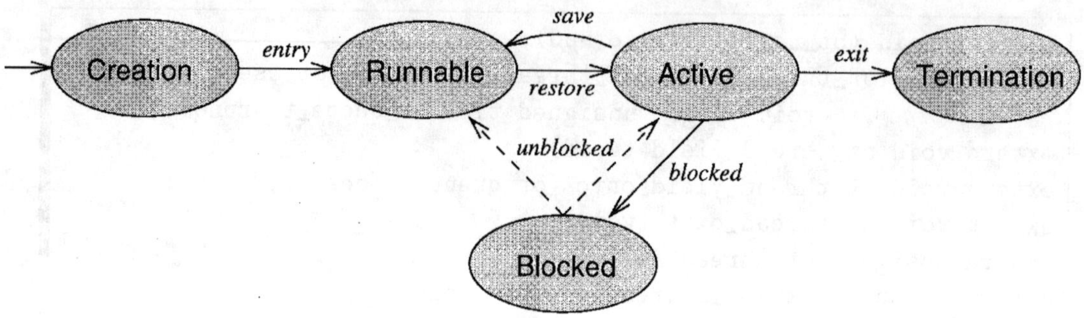


Figure 4: Thread state diagram

- timing various portions of a thread's life.
- different behavior of a specific thread in the system, such as a server thread.

### 3.2 Thread Lists and Scheduling

A *thread list* is a data structure used to hold a collection of threads. Thread lists are commonly referred to as *queues*, even if the scheduling strategy they employ is not first-in, first-out. The list may be used to hold threads that are ready to execute, called a *run list*, or may be used to hold threads in some other state, such as blocked on a mutex or condition variable. Since all threads must be on some thread list, state transitions typically involve moving a thread from one list to another. The scheduling policy for threads is therefore determined by the structure of the thread lists and the implementation of the operations that remove a thread from a list (`get`) and place a thread onto a list (`put`). For example, simple FIFO scheduling is achieved by using a FIFO queue for a run list, whereas priority scheduling might involve a tree of FIFO queues, where each leaf of the tree represents a queue of threads with the same priority.

The dilemma here is to decide i) what is the best scheduling strategy for the threads, and ii) what is the best implementation of the data structures and algorithms. Choices for scheduling algorithms include FIFO, round robin, hand-off, etc. Choices for data structures include linked lists, arrays, trees, etc.

### 3.3 Context Switching Modes

Every thread maintains *state information* that defines the thread. Minimally, this set includes the stack pointer, the instruction pointer, and the contents of the live registers. During a context switch between two threads, the state information of the current thread is saved and the state information of the new thread is restored. Some systems, such as Concert [9], use compiler analysis to store the state of a thread within its data space so that none of the registers need to be saved or restored. Other systems will require only that the integer registers be saved, and still others may require that all registers be saved and restored.

The dilemma here is to decide how much state to save during a context switch. Specifically, how many of the registers should be saved? Choices include all register, only the integer registers, or none of the registers.

### 3.4 Stack Management

Often, the most time-consuming portion of creating a new thread is allocating and aligning the thread stack. While most thread packages offer support to change the size of a thread's stack, few allow the programmer to specify the stack allocation policy. Lack of control over this dilemma is another common reason why multithreaded runtime systems abandon common thread packages. For example, the programmer may want to cache the stacks because threads are created and destroyed rapidly, but there are never more than a small number of threads alive at any one time. Another example is when the programmer wishes to enable checks on stack overflow, or to resize the stack at runtime to enable stack growth.

The dilemma here is to decide how to allocate and manage thread stacks. For allocation, choices include allocating stacks from the heap or from a shared cache of stacks, and binding stacks to threads at thread creation or during some later phase of the thread's life. For management, choices usually include whether to perform boundary checks on the stacks or not.

### 3.5 Timing and Profiling

Existing thread systems offer little or no support for thread timing and profiling. While most application-level programmers may not care about how many times a given thread is switched or what the total execution time for a thread is, most system-level programmers do care about these measures. However, because the state transitions that define these measures are hidden from the user, it is usually impossible to gather these statistics even if the user wants to.

The dilemma here is whether to pay the cost for timing and profiling information. Choices include either gathering the information or not.

## 4 Design

In this section we discuss how the design dilemmas outlined in the previous section are transformed into a meta interface, or *strategy control interface*, that permits principled modification of the implementation strategies. We begin by addressing each of the dilemmas in turn and then summarizing the resulting meta interface. For each dilemma, one of the key decisions for the meta interface will be the *interface style* for that dilemma. There are three possible interface styles [22]:

1. Client Behavior. Using this style, the client would provide information about how it will behave and the module selects an appropriate implementation strategy. For example, in the context of a file management system [21], the client might say: "I'll sequentially scan the next file."
2. Specific Implementation. Using this style the client specifies an implementation strategy from a list of supported strategies. For example, "Use LRU caching for the next file."
3. Provided Implementation. Using this style the client provides an implementation strategy. For example, "Use the following caching policy for the next file."

In the following subsections we examine how each of the design dilemmas is addressed.

### 4.1 Thread States

To enable the execution of various code segments at different thread state transitions, we provide a mechanism by which the programmer can attach functions to be executed at each of the following transitions: **entry** - when a thread first begins execution; **exit** - when a thread is about to be terminated; **save** - when a thread moves from an active state to a runnable state; **restore**, when a thread moves from a runnable state to an active state; **blocked**, when a thread moves from an active state to a blocked state; and **unblocked**, when a thread moves from a blocked state to either an active or runnable state.

Since we're not sure *what* the user wants to do at each transition, the meta interface for this dilemma uses a Provided Implementation strategy, where the user provides the code to be executed at a specific transition point. The meta interface calls for installing functions at these state transition points are `otm_push_callback` and `otm_pop_callback`. The former adds a function to a stack of routines that is called, in order, each time a thread reaches the associated state. The latter function allows a programmer to remove a function or re-arrange the order of the stack. The functions can be applied to all threads or to specific threads, and there are no limitations to the functions that can be applied.

### 4.2 Thread Lists and Scheduling

There are a couple of common thread scheduling algorithms and data structures, such as FIFO or round robin using a linked list. However, there are also many more combinations that a client may want, such as tree data structures and algorithms that perform load balancing. Thus we selected the Provided Implementation style for this dilemma and provide a couple of useful default implementations, such as FIFO and round robin.

To enable complete control over thread lists and scheduling we define the abstract notion of a thread list with `get` and `put` primitives that can be re-defined by the programmer. We also make thread lists explicit in the user interface so that programmers can simultaneously create different thread lists with different properties and arrange the threads on these lists as desired. For example, the user interface routine that creates a new thread, `ot_thread_init`, takes a thread list pointer as an explicit argument.

The meta interface call `otm_install_queue` defines a new thread list (queue) and declares the associated `init`, `get`, and `put` functions for the thread list. The `otm_install_queue` declaration can be applied to a single queue or to all queues.

### 4.3 Context Switching Modes

Since there are only a small number of possible implementation options for this dilemma, we chose the Specific Implementation style for this dilemma. The meta interface call `otm_define_switch` allows the programmer to specify one of three context switching modes: no registers, integer registers, or all registers. This allows the programmer to customize, for a single thread or for all threads, how much state will be saved and restored during each context switch.

### 4.4 Stack Management

Here again we have a situation where the user might wish to encode a fancy stack caching or stack boundary scheme, or do nothing at all. We selected a Provided Implementation style and provide the default of doing nothing. To enable flexible stack management, the meta interface call `otm_install_stackalloc` allows a programmer to install a pair of allocation and deallocation routines that will be invoked whenever a thread stack is required. These routines can then establish a boundary checking protocol or employ a cache to speed allocation.

### 4.5 Timing and Profiling

There are no special meta interface routines for timing and profiling. Instead, programmer can use the ability provided by the other routines in the meta interface to add timing and profiling capabilities. For example, per-thread context switch counts can be obtained by adding the following function to the *restore* event stack:

```
void bump () {
  ctxswCounter++;
}
```

Figure 5 provides a detailed description of the resulting meta interface for our OIA/D implementation of a lightweight thread package.

## 5 Evaluation

In this section we evaluate our OpenThreads design and implementation along four dimensions: OI design strength, flexibility, efficiency, and portability.

### 5.1 OI Design

This part of our evaluation focuses on the quality of the interfaces for OpenThreads. The guidelines for a quality Open Implementation [19] state that Open Implementation module interfaces should ...

- ... support a clear separation between client code that uses the module's functionality (use code) and client code that provides implementation strategy control (ISC).
- ... be designed to make the ISC code optional, easy to disable, and support alternative ISC codes for one piece of use code.
- ... be designed to allow the scope of influence of ISC code to be controlled in a way that is both natural and sufficiently fine-grained.
- ... be designed to pass only "essential" implementation strategy information (i.e., much of the implementation should still be a secret).

Scoring the OpenThreads user (Figure 3) and meta (Figure 5) interfaces against these guidelines:

- The use/ISC separation is clear – use code and ISC code reside in separate functions.
- The ISC code is optional – a client can use OpenThreads with the default strategies and never make a call to the meta interface.
- The ISC code is easy to disable – simple macros can remove all calls to the OpenThreads meta interface.

```
extern void otm_init (void);
extern void otm_install_stackalloc (otm_sallocf_t *salloc,
                otm_sfreef_t *sfree);
extern void otm_define_switch (otm_switch_mode_t, ot_thread_t *t);
extern void otm_push_callback (int cbid, otm_callback_t *cbfunc);
extern otm_callback_t *otm_pop_callback (int cbid);
extern void otm_install_queue (ot_queue_t *q, unsigned qlink_size,
                unsigned qimp_size, otm_qinitf_t *init,
                otm_qgetf_t *get, otm_qputf_t *put);
```

Figure 5: OpenThreads meta interface

- OpenThreads doesn't directly support multiple ISC calls for a single use call, but the effect can easily be achieved using preprocessing support such as #ifdef.
- The ISC code supports scope control – most of the OpenThreads meta interface routines can be either restricted to a single thread or applied to all threads.
- The ISC code passes only essential strategy information – much of the meta interface employs a Provided Implementation style in which the client provides the actual implementation. However, unnecessary items are still hidden, such as how a context switch is performed. So it is sufficient to tell OpenThreads to execute a user-supplied function every time a thread is restored without having the user specify how a restore is to be done.

Overall, the OpenThreads design evaluates favorably against the Open Implementation design guidelines.

## 5.2 Flexibility

The flexibility of OpenThreads is manifest by the meta interface, and the ability of a programmer to provide solutions to the design dilemmas outlined in Section 3. As a concrete example of this flexibility, we have adapted the Panda multithreaded runtime system [6] to use OpenThreads for implementing its tasks. Panda is a parallel language runtime system that supports the Orca parallel programming language. The meta interface was successful at implementing all but one of the specific implementation optimizations that Panda employs [14]. The remaining optimization required a change to the OpenThreads implementation regarding how threads can be re-entered. OpenThreads was upgraded to handle the remaining optimization, and this illustrates the necessity of re-evaluating the design of the user and meta interfaces for a software module after it has been used. For OIA/D, this implies a feedback loop in the design cycle where the domain knowledge is updated after having been through the entire analysis and design cycle.

## 5.3 Efficiency

There are various ways to report on the performance of a substrate module. First, it is useful to know how much overhead the module is responsible for (i.e., how much time does it add to the underlying software). Second, it is interesting to know how the module compares to other modules offering similar abstractions and functionality. In comparing performance for lightweight threads, two measures are commonly used: the time required to perform a single context switch from one thread to another (*ctxsw*), and the time required to create a new thread (*create*). All times are commonly measured in microseconds. Table 1 presents the results of these two experiments.

For the first experiment, OpenThreads is compared to QuickThreads [16], which is a low-level thread building toolkit upon which OpenThreads is built. From the numbers in Table 1 we see

| | MIPS R4400 | | SPARC | | ALPHA | |
|---|---|---|---|---|---|---|
| | ctxsw | create | ctxsw | create | ctxsw | create |
| QuickThreads | 0.9 | 5.6 | 6.5 | 10.5 | 1.2 | 2.7 |
| OpenThreads | 1.3 | 7.0 | 7.2 | 13.5 | 2.3 | 3.1 |
| Pthreads | 23.8 | 17.5 | 28.5 | 160.3 | — | — |

Table 1: OpenThreads raw performance on various architectures and in comparison to other thread packages; *ctxsw* is the time in microseconds for a context switch and *create* is the time in microseconds to create a single thread with default stacksize (usually 8Kb).

that OpenThreads adds very little overhead to the toolkit, which is exceptional given the level of abstraction that is supported in OpenThreads and the flexibility that is offered. Having a meta interface is slower than having hard-wired implementation decisions because function binding is typically delayed until runtime (as with virtual functions in C++). Still, with careful and efficient coding, OpenThreads imposes little overhead on top of basic thread functionality.

For the second experiment, OpenThreads is compared with Pthreads, a comparable thread module. Both OpenThreads and Pthreads support a similar level of abstraction (eg., threads, mutex variables, condition variables), though Pthreads does support more functionality for its abstractions. For example, Pthreads supports better signal handling for its threads than does OpenThreads. From the numbers in Table 1, we see that OpenThreads performs very well in comparison to a similar thread module.

A third measure of the performance of a substrate module is to measure its affect on the performance of a client. To carry out such an experiment, we measured the performance of the Panda runtime system, which requires a thread component. On the Sun Solaris platform, Panda uses Solaris threads as its thread module. On the Amoeba operating system running on a set of Sparc workstations, Panda uses a hand-coded thread module based on underlying Amoeba primitives. Amoeba is a distributed operating system with low-level support for threads and synchronization. In Table 2 we compare the performance of these two Panda implementations (labeled *Panda*) with a version of Panda that uses OpenThreads for its thread module (labeled *Panda-OT*). For the Amoeba system, where we are comparing against a hand-tuned thread module and underlying operating system support for threads, we see that Panda with OpenThreads does slightly better for context switches and worse for thread creation. The overhead in thread creation time is due to the fact that Panda-OT must allocate an additional structure in addition to doing everything that Panda needs for creating a thread. In comparing performance on Solaris, we see that Panda-OT is far superior to Panda with Solaris threads, most of which is attributable to the difference in basic thread performance (see Table 1).

### 5.4 Portability

In the published OIA/D design process [22], there is no attention given to the issue of module portability. However, given the wide array of hardware platforms and operating systems available, particularly in the area of parallel computing, substrate software that is not portable is almost useless.

An OI module has two interfaces: one for "use" code and one for and one for implementation strategy control (ISC, meta) code. To correct the deficiency of portability, we recognized the need for an additional module interface (see Figure 6). A third interface, called a *system* interface, is used to clearly identify all of the underlying dependencies for a module. Portability can then be easily defined as providing a mapping of the system interface to a new architecture platform.

The system interface for OpenThreads contains a small set of routines for thread stack initialization and context switching (via QuickThreads), a simple test-and-set instruction for implementing

| | Amoeba | | Solaris | |
|---|---|---|---|---|
| | ctxsw | create | ctxsw | create |
| Panda | 40.2 | 108.9 | 34.1 | 417.4 |
| Panda-OT | 35.4 | 262.7 | 7.4 | 62.0 |

Table 2: Performance of Panda thread packages on various platforms.

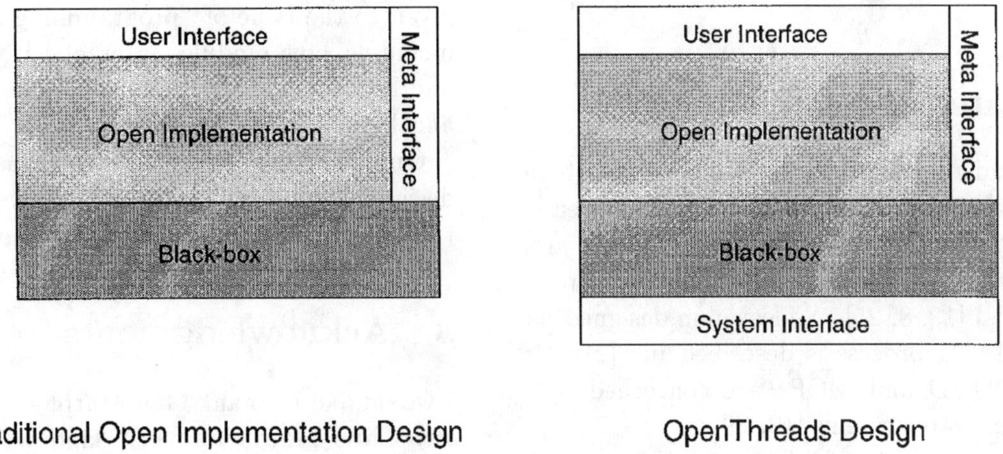


Figure 6: OpenThreads design

mutex and condition variables, a signal-handling routine, and a timer routine. In all, there are a total of 12 functions that need to be mapped onto a given architecture, 8 of which are provided by QuickThreads. Thus, given QuickThreads (which runs on almost every modern architecture), porting OpenThreads requires mapping four routines in the system interface, which can usually be done in a couple of hours.

### 5.5 Comments on OIA/D

So, did OIA/D work? Did OIA/D help us to construct a useful piece of software?

In general, yes. The idea of an Open Implementation makes perfect sense, especially for substrate software. In particular, OIA/D helped in defining what a *dilemma* was and how to organize them. However, the success of the resulting system depends not only on the identification of the design dilemmas, but on the design and implementation of the actual meta interface. For doing this, OIA/D provides some general guidelines that can be used to measure the quality of a meta interface, but the systems designer is required to make all of the actual implementation decisions. Since OIA/D is a general design methodology, it can offer little help in the specifics of the actual implementation. However, implementing the meta interface so that the programmer has control over the design decisions in a "principled way" is where the rubber meets the road for OIA/D, and there is little advice for how to do this. For OpenThreads, we decided to use callback functions as our primary vehicle for implementing our meta interface. While this approach yields excellent control over the design, it is not clear that this is a very "principled" way to do it since any piece of code can be installed.

We've also mentioned the lack of attention that OIA/D gives to portability concerns. While this can be easily rectified by applying an analysis to the underlying dependencies and using this analysis to develop a system interface, this lack of attention points to a larger problem. OIA/D discusses the design of a module that can interact with different sorts of clients. But what about modules interacting with other modules or atop multiple platforms? OIA/D does not address the "programming in the large" issues for an OI module.

One question of primary concern is how one meta interface influences another. Looking back on our picture of a parallel language runtime system (Figure 1) we see that there are several components needed, not just threads. How will the meta interface for OpenThreads be affected by the presence of an OI module for communication? This is an open question that we are in the process of pursuing.

## 6 Related Research

OpenThreads represents a proof-of-concept of the OIA/D process applied to lightweight threads. OIA/D [22] stems from earlier work in the area of reflective programming and metaobject protocols (MOPs) [18, 8, 25]. A filesystem designed using the OIA/D process is described in [21]. In general, OIA/D and MOPs are concerned with reusable software systems [10, 29].

There are a variety of lightweight thread packages currently being used as substrate software [5, 13, 23, 24]. Of these, the Awesime [13] package contains a thread class that allows customization of the thread stacks and scheduling discipline through virtual functions. Callbacks at save and restore states were supported by the original Sun user-level thread package [30] and more generally by Scheduler Activations [2].

QuickThreads [16] is a thread-building toolkit that offers platform independent micro-instructions for managing thread stacks. QuickThreads is similar to assembly language programming in terms of flexibility, speed, and complexity.

## 7 Conclusions

Open Implementation Analysis and Design (OIA/D) describes a methodology for designing reusable substrate software. The key idea is to give programmers control over implementation strategies that correspond to the most important design decisions. Without this control, programmers are forced to either re-implement the necessary abstractions or use them in a contorted way. Both are bad examples of reuse.

This paper presents experiences using OIA/D to design and implement a lightweight threads package. We found the OIA/D process beneficial in helping to organize the design dilemmas and the idea of a meta interface is certainly useful. However, the actual implementation of the meta interface as a principled method for adjusting implementation techniques requires thought and experience beyond the scope of what OIA/D can provide. We also felt that more attention needs to be given to the issue of "programming in the large," including how modules interact with one-another and how modules are ported from one platform to another.

On the whole, our goal was to use OIA/D to design a flexible, efficient, and portable lightweight threads package. In this regard we were successful.

## 8 Acknowledgments

I would like to thank Gail Murphy, Gregor Kiczales, Chris Maeda for their kind words and useful comments on earlier drafts of this paper. I would also like to thank Koen Langendoen for his patience in describing the details of the Panda runtime system, and for helping me to debug OpenThreads during the Panda port.

## References

[1] J. J. Accetta, R. V. Baron, W. Bolosky, D. B. Golub, R. F. Rashid, A. Tevanian, and M. W. Young. Mach: A new kernel foundation for UNIX development. In *Proceedings of Summer Usenix*, July 1986.

[2] Thomas E. Anderson, Brian N. Bershad, Edward D. Lazowska, and Henry M. Levy. Scheduler activations: Effective kernel support for the user-level management of parallelism. *ACM Transactions on Computer Systems*, 10(1):53–79, February 1992.

[3] Gregory R. Andrews and Ronald A. Olsson. *The SR Programming Language: Concurrency in Practice.* Benjamin/Cummings, 1993. ISBN 0-8053-0088-0.

[4] Maurice J. Bach. *The Design of the UNIX Operating System.* Software Series. Prentice-Hall, 1986.

[5] Brian N. Bershad, Edward D. Lazowska, Henry M. Levy, and David B. Wagner. An open environment for building parallel programming systems. Technical Report 88-01-03, Department of Computer Science, University of Washington, January 1988.

[6] Raoul Bhoedjang, Tim Rühl, Rutger Hofman, Koen Langendoen, Henri Bal, and Frans Kaashoek. Panda: A portable platform to support parallel programming languages. In *Symposium on Experiences with Distributed and Multiprocessor Systems IV*, pages 213–226, San Diego, CA, September 1993.

[7] F. Bodin, P. Beckman, D. Gannon, S. Yang, S. Kesavan, and B. Mohr. Implementing a parallel C++ runtime system for scalable parallel systems. In *Supercomputing*, pages 588–597, Portland, OR, November 1993.

[8] Shigeru Chiba. A metaobject protocol for C++. In *Proceedings of OOPSLA 95*, pages 285–299, Austin, TX, October 1995.

[9] Andrew Chien, Vijay Karamcheti, and John Plevyak. The concert system – compiler and runtime support for efficient, fine-grained concurrent object-oriented programs. Technical Report UIUCDCS-R-93-1815, University of Illinois at Urbana-Champaign, Urbana-Chambaign, IL, June 1993.

[10] D. Fafchamps. Organizational factors and reuse. *IEEE Software*, 11(5):31–41, September 1994.

[11] Ian Foster, Carl Kesselman, Robert Olson, and Steven Tuecke. Nexus: An interoperability layer for parallel and distributed computer systems. Technical Report Version 1.3, Argonne National Labs, December 1993.

[12] J. Goguen. Principles of parameterized programming. In T. Biggerstaff and A. Perlis, editors, *Software Reusability: Concepts and Models (Volume 1)*, chapter 7. ACM Press, 1989.

[13] Dirk Grunwald. A users guide to AWESIME: An object oriented parallel programming and simulation system. Technical Report CU-CS-552-91, Department of Computer Science, University of Colorado at Boulder, November 1991.

[14] Matthew Haines and Koen Langendoen. Platform-independent runtime optimizations using openthreads. In *Proceedings of the International Parallel Processing Symposium*, Geneva, Switzerland, April 1997. IEEE.

[15] IEEE. *Standard for Threads Interface to POSIX*, 1996. P1003.1c.

[16] David Keppel. Tools and techniques for building fast portable threads packages. Technical Report UWCSE 93-05-06, University of Washington, 1993.

[17] Gregor Kiczales. Beyond the black bok: Open Implementation. *IEEE Software*, 13(1):8 – 11, 1996.

[18] Gregor Kiczales, Jim des Rivières, and Daniel G. Bobrow. *The Art of the Metaobject Protocol.* MIT Press, 1991.

[19] Gregor Kiczales, Cristina Videira Lopes, Anurag Mendhekar, and Gail Murphy. Open implementation design guidlines. In *Proceedings of the 19th International Conference on Software Engineering*, 1996.

[20] Tim Lindholm and Frank Yellin. *The Java Virtual Machine Specification.* The Java Series. Addison-Wesley, 1997. ISBN 0-201-63452-X.

[21] Chris Maeda. A metaobject protocol for accessing file systems. In *Proceedings of ISOTAS 96*, 1996.

[22] Chris Maeda, Arthur Lee, Gail Murphy, and Gregor Kiczales. Open Implementation Analysis and Design. In *Proceedings of the 1997 ACM Symposium on Software Reusability (SSR)*, 1997. http://www.parc.xerox.com/oi.

[23] Frank Mueller. A library implementation of POSIX threads under UNIX. In *Winter USENIX*, pages 29–41, San Diego, CA, January 1993.

[24] Bodhisattwa Mukherjee, Greg Eisenhauer, and Kaushik Ghosh. A machine independent interface for lightweight threads. Technical Report CIT-CC-93/53, College of Computing, Georgia Institute of Technology, Atlanta, Georgia, 1993.

[25] Philippe Mulet, Jacques Malenfant, and Pierre Cointe. Towards a methodology for explicit composition of MetaObjects. In *Proceedings of OOPSLA 95*, pages 316–330, Austin, TX, October 1995.

[26] M.L. Powell, S.R. Kleinman, S. Barton, D. Shah, D. Stein, and M. Weeks. SunOS Multi-thread Architecture. In *Proceedings of USENIX Winter Technical Conference*, Dallas, TX, 1991.

[27] Carl Schmidtmann, Michael Tao, and Steven Watt. Design and implementation of a multithreaded Xlib. In *Winter USENIX*, pages 193–203, San Diego, CA, January 1993.

[28] SunSoft Manual Set. *Solaris Multithreaded Programming Guide*. SunSoft Press, 1996. ISBN 0-13-160896-7.

[29] W. Staringer. Constructing applications from reusable components. *IEEE Software*, 11(5):61–68, September 1994.

[30] Sun Microsystems, Inc. *Lightweight Process Library*, sun release 4.1 edition, January 1990.

# Migrating Relational Data to an ODBMS: Strategies and Lessons From a Molecular Biology Experience

**Jon Oler and Gary Lindstrom**

Department of Computer Science
University of Utah
50 S. Central Campus Drive, Rm. 3190
Salt Lake City, Utah 84112-9205 USA
{oler, gary}@cs.utah.edu

**Terence Critchlow**

Lawrence Livermore National Laboratory
P.O. Box 808 L-560
Livermore, CA 94550
critchlow@llnl.gov

## Abstract

The growing maturity of ODBMS technology is causing many enterprises to consider migrating relational databases to ODBMS's. While data remapping is relatively straightforward in most cases, greater challenges lie in economically and non-invasively adapting legacy application software. We report on a genetics laboratory database migration experiment, which was facilitated by both organization of the relational data in object-like form and a C++ framework designed to insulate application code from relational artifacts. Although this experiment was largely successful, we discovered to our surprise that the framework failed to encapsulate three subtle aspects of the relational implementation, thereby "contaminating" application code. We analyze the underlying issues, and offer cautionary guidance to future migrators.

## 1. Introduction

Relational database (RDB) management systems are the dominant database technology in use today. Initially developed in the 1970's, RDB technology is mature, robust, flexible, and broadly applicable. However, in recent years traditional RDBMS's have come to be viewed as deficient in data representational power in comparison to modern application software, which is increasingly object-oriented. This RDB shortcoming is being addressed by extended relational systems (e.g., Postgres [SK91]) and middleware such as object oriented relational database gateway products (e.g. Persistence [KJA93]). Such RDBMS extensions have been spurred by competition from object-oriented database management systems (ODBMS's), which combine comprehensive database management functionality and full-fledged OO data modeling [ABDDMZ89].

Enterprises are understandably cautious in adopting new technology such as an ODBMS due to risks including lack of prior experience in effective ODBMS use, concerns for vendor stability, slow standardization, disruption of application software development, and fear of failure --- with associated loss of investment and an embarrassing retreat to prior technology. Hence a cost effective, reversible, risk mitigating migration strategy has great appeal. In fortunate cases, the increasing OO sophistication of the enterprise's application software may have steered the enterprise's relational data design to a *de facto* object-based organization. Indeed, the database architects may have been blessed with the foresight to encapsulate RDB representation details in an OO framework, delivering to applications an ODBMS-like view on the relational data. Not surprisingly, such frameworks are a great aid to migration, in that they embody a ready solution to the first problem one encounters: converting data from relational to object form.

We report our experience in employing such a framework as a migration vehicle. In many ways, the framework fulfilled our expectations as a migration aid, especially in terms of ease of data conversion. However, the thrust of this paper is on unforeseen semantic and pragmatic issues encountered in the migration, arising from subtle aspects of RDB technology "leaking" through the framework and "contaminating" our application software. After sketching our application setting, framework-based migration strategy, and lessons learned along the way, we conclude with a chart of *dysfunctions*, *diagnoses* and *remedies* which may be instructive to other database developers contemplating a similar migration path.


**OOPSLA '97 10/97 GA, USA**
**© 1997 ACM 0-89791-908-4/97/0010...$3.50**

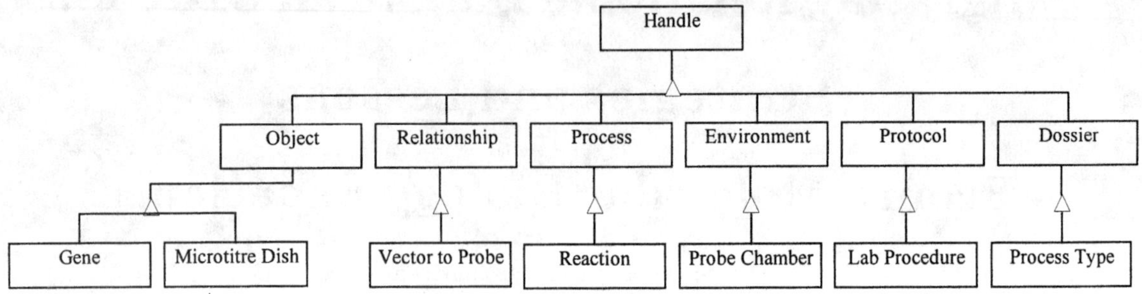


Figure 1: Simplified GORP class hierarchy

# 2. The Utah Center for Human Genome Research Database

Over the past six years, the Utah Center for Human Genome Research (UCHGR) has developed a comprehensive data model, database implementation and application suite for molecular biology laboratory information. The key characteristics of this database are: (i) an object-based meta data model comprising five fundamental concepts (*objects, relationships, processes, protocols,* and *environments*) in terms of which all concrete entities are expressed; (ii) an implementation of this model using a commercial RDBMS (Sybase), and (iii) a framework permitting application software to manipulate database contents as though they were a collection of persistent C++ objects, i.e., an ODBMS [SFCDML96].

Underlying this database design is a defensive posture with respect to the most vexing problem the UCHGR database implementers have faced over the years: frequent but unanticipatible schema evolution. Extensive use is made of meta information which guides access within a "hyper normalized" implementation by which object attributes are dispersed in individual tuples logically associated by object identifiers (OIDs) internal to the database. The result is an exceptionally supple data representation, permitting both (i) application data schema evolution by ordinary RDBMS transactions on meta data tables, and (ii) representational tolerance to data in many schema versions, both current and historical. These two features are crucial to the rapidly changing, yet archival, nature of molecular biological data.

These advantages notwithstanding, it rapidly became clear that the generality of this meta data representation, plus its lack of conventional OO structure, make it inappropriate for direct access by application programs. Hence a C++ framework was developed to act as an API to the database. This framework, called *GORP* (for *Generic Objects, Relationships* and *Processes*), presents to applications a reconstructive view of the database contents, consistent with the current concrete OO data schema expressed as C++ classes. Historical data, which is needed far less frequently, is either accessed through a lower level interface, or through GORP code specially written to do data evolution on demand. Like all class libraries worthy to be termed frameworks, GORP makes extensive use of abstract classes serving as interfaces to hidden implementation classes *completing* the framework. The production database currently comprises the GORP framework plus a completion library implementing GORP abstract methods in terms of SQL stored procedures.

# 3. Migrating the UCHGR Database to an ODBMS

Beyond its support for fluid schema evolution, the UCHGR database strategy is also defensive in that it anticipated eventual adoption of ODBMS technology, while protecting the developers from the pains of being an "early adopter" [GRS94]. The advent and commercial success of well-engineered ODBMS products, such as ObjectStore [LLOW91], indicate the time is ripe to seriously investigate migration to a true ODBMS.

The potential advantages of ODBMS's are well known, the most important to UCHGR being (i) direct storage of application-pertinent objects, eliminating the run-time overhead and the software maintenance cost of representation conversion code; (ii) faster overall performance, due to direct pointer navigation rather than multi-way joins (an unfortunate consequence of UCHGR's meta data representation); (iii) more seamless integration with C++ software development tools; (iv) more flexible data structuring representation possibilities, and (v) a true OO representation upon which application understanding can guide performance tuning and development of customized consistency and concurrency control policies.

In addition to assessing the practical merit of these potential advantages, the migration experiment provided a litmus test for GORP's representation encapsulation power. The experiment was approached through a novel migration strategy exploiting cooperating completions of the GORP framework. We describe this strategy in subsequent sections, along with some surprising pitfalls encountered, and lessons learned. Throughout, we focus on effective ODBMS exploitation by applications accessing current version (rather than historical) data. In the concluding section we offer some speculative remarks on how our migration strategy might be extended to support schema evolution.

# 4. Framework-Based Data Migration

The hypothesis underlying our experiment was simple: that GORP sufficiently encapsulated all RDB-specific aspects of the UCHGR database, such that no application software changes would be necessary if the RDBMS (Sybase) implementation were replaced by a genuine ODBMS (ObjectStore). To a first approximation, our hypothesis was validated.

| Mode | Uses |
|---|---|
| Read RDB / Write RDB | Preserves existing working RDB implementation; "benchmark" for alternate implementations |
| Read ODBMS / Write ODBMS | Complete conversion to ODBMS |
| Read RDB / Write ODBMS | Migrate data from RDB to ODBMS; populate ODBMS using real data in RDB |
| Read ODBMS / Write RDB | Migrate data from ODBMS to RDB |
| Read RDB / Write Both | Access data through RDB, maintain RDB / ODBMS consistency |
| Read ODBMS / Write Both | Access data through ODBMS, maintain RDB / ODBMS consistency |

Table 1: GORP framework: modes of operation

## 4.1 Dual Database Strategy

Our experiment began by building a dual-completion instantiation of the framework capable of operating in several modes. Table 1 summarizes how these modes might be used. We started with the *Read RDB / Write RDB* mode already implemented. Since this code is in production use, we made the baseline assumption that it is correct, and relied on it as a validation standard for other modes. This mode when will be used as a performance benchmark for the *read ODBMS / write ODBMS* mode when the latter is fully deployed..

Given the purely relational (*read RDB / write RDB mode*) completion of the framework, implementing the other modes described in Table 1 was, with the exception of several nuances described in the next section, very straightforward. The interface exported by the framework was left unchanged; in fact, the portion of the framework describing GORP database objects directly formed the basis of the ODBMS schema.

The *read RDB / write ODBMS* mode was applied on a wholesale basis to transfer data from the RDB to the ODBMS. The *read ODBMS / write both* mode allows both databases to be updated in tandem. Each database can then be read to verify that they returned the same result. In keeping with our risk mitigating strategy, this dual write mode constitutes a reassuring fallback to the fully robust relational version after deploying the ODBMS version. That is, if the ODBMS performance lags or other problems are encountered, it could be pulled from production and the RDB completion could be quickly redeployed since its associated database would be a "warm spare". The other two modes, *read ODBMS / write RDB* and *read RDB / write both*, were added for completeness but have not been extensively used.

## 4.2 Extent Sets

Since the class definitions already existed, the only work required to complete the ODBMS schema was to organize the database types into extent sets. Some ODBMS products automatically create and maintain class extents for every type in the database. While convenient, this service may be wasteful both in time and disk usage because some object types may only be accessed exclusively by navigation from another object rather than through key-based or exhaustive lookup on the extent set of the type. ObjectStore, in contrast, leaves the creation and maintenance of class extents entirely to the user.

Determining how to allocate class extents and index them for efficient access was quite challenging. We experimented with three design alternatives before identifying the one that best suited our needs. For background, we provide a simplified version of the GORP class hierarchy in Figure 1.

Under the first design we allocated class extents for every class in the database: an extent set representing all GORP database objects (the Handle extent), an extent set each comprising the Objects, Relationships, Processes, Environments, and Protocols, and finally an extent set for each of the leaves in the class hierarchy. As a result, each GORP database object was referenced from three extent sets. This led to further redundancy when indices defined on the base class were recreated in child classes. For example, an index was defined on the Handle extent with Handle's **id** attribute as key. However, this index was also duplicated on the Object extent as well as on many of the extents of classes that inherit from Object. Obviously, this approach resulted in a potentially large waste of storage.

Unfortunately, this was not the only problem we encountered with out initial approach: each time an object is created (or deleted) it had to be inserted (removed) from each of the three distinct extent sets, and more importantly, the indexes defined on each of the extents had to be updated. We discovered that this cost dominated the object's creation (deletion) time when we began to populate the database. Since the database loading process only required an extent over the Handle class with one simple index, we deferred building the other class extents and indexes until after loading the database. This dramatically reduced the time required to load the database.

The second design alternative was based on the observation that the redundancy of explicitly creating class extents for each object type is unnecessary in principle. That is,

```
objects := db.all_objects                       // Retrieve all objects
relationships := db.all_relationships           // Retrieve all relationship objects
foreach object in objects
    object.get_relationships                    // Associate each object with its relationships
foreach relationship in relationships
    relationship.get_objects                    // Associate each relationship with related objects
```

Figure 2: Pseudo-code for retrieving all GORP objects and relationships

the Process extent is simply the union of the extents of its child classes; likewise, the Handle extent is the union the Dossier, Object, Relationship, Process, Environment, and Protocol extents. Conversely, assuming the availability of run time type information, extents for any class in the GORP class hierarchy can be derived by filtering the Handle class extent.

However, neither of these options is a compelling choice. Consider the first; to derive extent sets, a class must be aware of all of its subclasses — generally bad object-oriented programming practice. For example, in order to execute a query over all processes, the Process class must either first build the Process extent from the extents of its subclasses, or ask each subclass to perform the query and combine the results. The second option is even more problematic because it is impossible to create indexes on the Handle extent based on attributes defined in subclasses of Handle. In addition, queries that deal with a single subclass will take longer to execute. For example, to find a Process with a given **id**, only Process instances need to be queried; however, if there is only one massive extent set, all instances participate in the query.

Note that completely eliminating redundancy is only one option; in fact, we utilize redundant sets to improve efficiency for common queries, while eliminating them where not needed. In our third and final design, the Handle extent is eliminated once the database is built. This does not dramatically effect query performance since interesting queries on Handle are rare and the direct subclasses of Handle are a fixed part of the framework unlikely to change. The reduction in insert/delete time as well as the space required by the database were significant. Additional savings were recognized by eliminating extent sets on classes that are accessed solely by relationships. The other extents were kept for performance reasons. Since retrieval/update is much more frequent than object creation/deletion our approach balances the extra space required by redundant extent sets and slower object creation/deletion against faster query execution speed.

## 4.3 Database Open and Close

Generic database functions such as opening and closing the database, and beginning, committing and aborting transactions were already expressed in the GORP framework and implemented in the RDB completion. The interfaces to these functions required no substantial changes to support the ODBMS completion. Their implementations, of course, were modified to perform the operations on the RDB, ODBMS, or both, depending upon the mode of operation. The lower-level database interface code of the GORP framework was extended to provide ODBMS-specific functionality such as object clustering, query facilities, and the creation/deletion of indexes. Since an API for some of these services has been defined in the ODMG standard, we wrapped the ObjectStore API within an ODMG-compliant interface where possible. This will ease porting to another ODBMS in the future, should the need arise. In all material respects, the GORP framework design proved to be adequate to encapsulate these DBMS-specific features, and hide them from applications.

The bulk of the work in implementing the ODBMS GORP completion involved modifying the query and update functions to access an ODBMS rather than an RDB. As explained earlier, the relational database employs a meta data representation which performs reconstructive querying in order to deliver concrete objects. In the RDB completion, this service is provided by SQL stored procedures, which apply meta data querying and component-wise accesses to reconstruct GORP objects for application presentation. However, because the ODBMS queries don't have to dynamically reconstruct objects and relationships between objects, the queries are much simpler than their relational counterparts. In contrast to the RDB completion where application data is stored in decomposed, meta data mediated form, the ODB completion has the luxury of retaining persistent objects in concrete application form.

## 4.4 Populating the Database

The ODBMS was populated by a transfer program using the GORP interface to traverse all objects in the database using the *read RDB / write ODBMS* mode. A simple traversal algorithm identifies each base object, and all data accessible from it. As each object is retrieved, a check is performed to see if an object with the same GORP OID has already been recorded. If the object was previously entered, it is ignored; otherwise, it is persistently allocated in the ObjectStore database. Once each object has been instantiated in the ODBMS, relationships between the objects can be established as shown in simplified form in Figure 2. Due to the simplicity of the underlying data model, less than 500 lines of C++ code were required to perform this migration.

# 5. Issues

We now examine three areas in which the migration did not proceed as smoothly as expected. In some areas, the causes can be attributed to inadequate foresight in the GORP framework design. However, since the relational completion of the GORP framework was implemented by experienced developers with extensive experience in both relational database development and object-oriented frameworks, we believe that their approach is typical of many projects exploiting an object-oriented interface to a relational database. In other areas, more fundamental semantic disparities emerge between RDBMSs and ODBMSs, and the application software architectures they commonly engender.

## 5.1 Issue 1: Object Mapping

Four basic operations on GORP database objects are exported to application programs by the GORP framework: *create*, *delete*, *retrieve*, and *update*. One of the most compelling ODBMS virtues is the elimination of object copying between application memory and the supporting database. Unfortunately, this virtue introduces subtle differences between the RDB and ODBMS semantics. This is a theme we will return to frequently throughout this paper.

There are currently a large number of commercial middleware products available to aid in mapping objects between an RDB and an object oriented programming language. These products vary widely in their approach to transactions, caching, mapping capabilities, scalability, database access (RDB-like vs. ODB-like), etc. Virtually everyone who has worked on the RDB completion of the GORP framework concurs that the necessity of writing custom code to map objects between the programming language and RDB representations is one of GORP's most unpleasant aspects. Mapping code occupies approximately 30 percent of the RDB version of the framework and must be maintained as the database schema changes. Employing middleware to do at least part of this job would provide a significant boost to productivity. Whether a project develops custom code, uses an RDB middleware product, or a true ODBMS, the mapping of objects from the database to application programs is an important issue. We now examine object mapping issues for each of the four basic GORP database operations.

### 5.1.1 Object Creation

The ODBMS completion of the framework invokes ObjectStore's rebindings of the C++ new and delete operators to create and destroy objects in persistent storage. Implementing this rebinding was facilitated by the framework design in which every persistent class has at least one static create method. This function originally allocated class instances on the application's transient heap, e.g., for containing the results of a database query. We easily modified these methods to accept a boolean flag indicating whether the object should be allocated on persistent storage instead.

Persistence-awareness also dictated that supporting classes allocate their internal data structures on persistent storage. Container classes (i.e. lists, bags) and a string class are examples of such classes. Of course, these implementation classes are part of the framework completion, rather than the GORP application interface, so their modification was completely transparent. To maintain their generality, these classes were augmented so they could allocate storage in either persistent or transient memory, depending on which creation method was invoked. These modifications were easily accomplished. For example, strings are implemented using an array of characters. The string constructor was modified to recognize whether the enclosing structure is allocated on persistent or transient memory (which is easily done using ObjectStore's os_database::of or os_segment::of operators), and to allocate the character array appropriately.

With some ODBMS products, such as the Java version of ObjectStore, object persistence may be determined at transaction commit time by identifying all objects reachable from a persistent root; with others, objects may be electively migrated from transient to persistent memory. With the C++ version of ObjectStore, persistent objects must be explicitly allocated in persistent memory when the object is created. Unfortunately, the relational completion of GORP allows applications to create a new GORP object transiently by invoking a class constructor, and subsequently confer persistence on the object by calling the object's save( ) operation. This is problematic because it is complex, costly, and perhaps ill-advised to move an object from transient to persistent memory in this version of ObjectStore. Indeed, this is particularly expensive if an entire graph of objects were created in transient memory, because a *deep* copy of this graph must occur when save( ) is invoked on a transient object.

Since all existing GORP applications know at object creation time whether an object will persist or not, we decided against implementing object migration from transient memory to the ODBMS in the GORP framework. Instead, we changed the semantics of the class constructors for GORP objects in the framework: persistent objects must be created exclusively with a call to the static create( ) method provided by each GORP class. Temporary objects may be created either through this create( ) method or through a class constructor. This allows temporary objects to still be efficiently allocated and deallocated on either the stack or the heap, and prevents applications from having to use DBMS-specific calls to persistent new. The difference between the two methods is demonstrated in Figure 3. This experience suggests that creation time determination of object transience or persistence should be mandatory in future GORP application development.

### 5.1.2 Object Deletion

Object deletion is encapsulated via destroy methods in GORP interface classes. Typically, applications (all initially written for the RDB completion of GORP) use the delete operator to free the transient memory occupied by GORP objects. The ODMG standard (as well as the ObjectStore API) overrides the delete operator to remove a persistent object from the database. We chose to reimplement the delete operator of each GORP class to be operative only if the object resides on the transient heap or the stack. If the object is persistently allocated, no action is taken. However, finessing the issue in this manner has the side effect that useless delete operations remain in the code, potentially confusing future maintenance programmers. It should be noted that this problem could be averted altogether by using an language and an ODBMS that supports persistent garbage collection.

### 5.1.3 Object Retrieval/Update

We now consider object retrieval and updating, which exposed additional, more subtle differences between the semantics of these operations in the RDB and ODBMS completions of the GORP framework. Figure 4 gives pseudo-code for a typical interaction between an application and the GORP

| RDB Implementation | ODB Implementation |
|---|---|
| transaction.begin( ); | transaction.begin( ); |
| | bool persist = true; |
| | // Make persistent when created<br>// with ODBMS |
| DNA_fragment * frag =<br>new DNA_fragment; | DNA_fragment * frag =<br>DNA_fragment::create( persist ); |
| frag->operation1( );<br>frag->operation2( );<br>frag->save( ); // Inefficient with<br>// ODBMS | frag->operation1( );<br>frag->operation2( );<br>frag->save( ); // No-op with<br>// ODBMS |
| transaction.commit( ); | transaction.commit( ); |

Figure 3: Modifications to GORP for object creation

framework. Invoking get_unprocessed_microtitre_dishes( ) in the RDB version causes the GORP framework to issue an SQL query which returns a set of tuples representing unprocessed microtitre dishes. The GORP framework maps each microtitre dish tuple returned to a transiently allocated C++ microtitre dish object. The process( ) member function of class microtitre_dish modifies the microtitre dish as a C++ object. Note, however, that the persistent representation of the microtitre dish is not affected until the microtitre dish save( ) operation is invoked. The save( ) operation performs an SQL update synchronizing the transient C++ microtitre dish representation with its persistent representation in the RDB. Thus the GORP framework, and consequently the application software it supports, fundamentally embodies a copy in, copy out view of persistent data (the "client / server" viewpoint).

By contrast, the ODBMS completion of GORP handles the interaction of Figure 4 quite differently. The method invocation get_unprocessed_microtitre_dishes( ) queries the database as before, but no translation or explicit copy is required to convert the database representation of a microtitre dish to the C++ representation. Although a transient C++ replica of each unprocessed microtitre dish object is still created (by the ObjectStore ODBMS, in the application's address space, operating as a database cache), this replication is transparent to the GORP framework and application code. In reality, modifications made to microtitre dish objects by invoking process( ) are made to the transient copies as before. However, unlike in the RDB GORP completion, the save( ) operation is an empty function in the ODBMS GORP completion. This is because the modifications made to the microtitre dish objects are automatically updated in the persistent store by the ODBMS when the surrounding transaction commits. Just as no code is required to translate the object from persistent memory to transient memory, no code is required to translate the object from transient memory to persistent memory.

## 5.2 Issue 2: Transactions and Swizzled References

As mentioned earlier, the GORP framework includes basic operations for starting, committing, and aborting transactions. However, the *copy in / modify / copy out* paradigm of the RDB version, plus ambivalence concerning the appropriateness of strict serialization of GORP applications as long running transactions, resulted in a *laissez faire* utilization of these features by UCHGR application programmers. Although database consistency issues were recognized clearly to be a concern, we encountered a different, rather subtle issue as a consequence. This issue concerns the lifetime and binding of object references, and their relationship to transaction semantics and duration. Although this problem manifests in various ways among ODBMS products, we believe them to be endemic to ODBMS technology.

Currently, and into the foreseeable future, real databases must be able to grow larger than the address space of the machines that access them. Unfortunately, this poses obstacles in fully integrating persistent data into a programming language, i.e., converting an object-oriented programming language into an ODBMS data manipulation language. If persistent objects are to be accessed in the same way as transient objects, applications must be able to access them through references native to the programming language, i.e. in *swizzled* form [EM92]. These references are bound to a block of memory into which the persistent object is mapped in the address space of the application process. However, if a process references a working set of persistent objects that exceed the size of its address space, some objects need to be removed to make way for new objects.

This requirement is benign if the evicted objects are not referenced again; however, it is difficult to determine at runtime which objects may be accessed again and which can be safely evicted. Hence it is often necessary to maintain valid swizzled references to persistent objects, even if they have been invalidated and evicted from an application's address space. To address this requirement, the API of most ODBMS products provide a "long pointer" data structure constituting a universally valid persistent object reference. This provides a reliable way for an object to be recovered and remapped into a process' address space in the event it has been evicted between references. Indeed, some ODBMS's require persistent objects to be referenced only through unswizzled pointers. Unfortunately, this encapsulated access requires an extra level of indirection each time an object is accessed. Other ODBMS products, like ObjectStore, allow both swizzled and unswizzled references.

The ObjectStore ODBMS unmaps all persistent objects from an application's address space at transaction commit time. As a result, all swizzled pointers in an application become invalid at that time. However, applications written presuming the RDB completion of GORP expect that pointers to persistent objects remain valid across transaction boundaries --- which is a reasonable assumption because the application is operating on transient copies rather than the persistent objects.

Figure 5 shows a gene object referenced in two different transactions. With the RDB completion, the framework caches a transient copy of the gene object until the application explicitly deallocates the object. Therefore, the gene reference in the second transaction is valid, but may not reflect changes to the database between the time the first transaction commits and the second transaction begins. With the ODB completion, the gene reference is invalidated when the first transaction commits. This leads to two error conditions when an attempt is made to access the gene in the second transaction: an invalid pointer dereference exception, or the worse possibility of an undetected erroneous reference to an arbitrary location in a database segment subsequently mapped into that memory region.

```
transaction.begin( );
   microtitre_dishes = GORP.get_unprocessed_microtitre_dishes( );
   foreach microtitre_dish in microtitre_dishes
      microtitre_dish.process( );                    //microtitre dish object is mutated
      microtitre_dish.save( );
transaction.commit( );
```

Figure 4: Example GORP framework operation

There were several options available to us to overcome this problem. First, we could simulate the RDB version of GORP by making transient copies of each object read from the ODBMS. References to these transiently allocated objects would not be invalidated across transaction boundaries. This approach also had the advantage of overcoming the object mapping concerns previously identified as Issue 1. However, this proposal was quickly rejected as ODBMS heresy, as well as because the additional overhead was deemed unacceptable.

A second option was to adopt longer duration transactions whereby transactions do not commit until it is no longer necessary to reference any object. Because of the programming style used to implement the applications, this amounted to wrapping the entire application within a single transaction. This approach was rejected not only due to the resulting poor throughput but also because these applications may reference more data than can fit within the application's address space. When the address space is exhausted, ObjectStore aborts the transaction.

ObjectStore's default behavior of unmapping the virtual address space occupied by persistent objects at transaction commit time can be disabled. In this case, once an object is mapped to a virtual address, the mapping is retained until the application exits. Like the previous option, the application's address space can be exhausted. Potentially, applications could free portions of the address space at appropriate times through the ODBMS API, but this is not very elegant and is difficult to do in some GORP applications with dynamic transaction boundaries.

The final and most general approach is to use the unswizzled ("long") pointers supplied by ObjectStore. The primary disadvantage of this approach is that application source code must be modified to use long pointers to persistent objects referenced across transaction boundaries. Alternatively, the GORP framework could encapsulate the swizzled pointers in a GORPPointer class and modify all GORP functions to return references to this class rather than C++ pointers. This option was rejected because it introduces at least one additional level of indirection, and resulting overhead, for every pointer deference. The prospect of changing all applications to use GORPPointer references was daunting, as well.

The approach we ultimately adopted constitutes a hybrid of the last two approaches. Where appropriate, we extended transaction boundaries to encompass multiple object references. We also modified application source code to use unswizzled pointers for the remaining database references that cross transaction boundaries.

One of the lures of ODBMS technology is that the programming language becomes the database data manipulation language. The hallmark of such a DML is uniform ("seamless") access of persistent and transient data alike. Unfortunately, native programming language pointers are not sufficient to support all references to persistent objects. Today's programming languages were not designed to support transactions and concurrent access to shared data by multiple processes. Encapsulated access through unswizzled pointers is the price to pay for such features.

## 5.3 Issue 3: Object Identity

As mentioned briefly in an earlier section, the GORP framework defines unique object identifiers for all objects in the database which may be accessed by applications. In the original specification of the RDB version of the GORP framework, GORP OIDs were defined to be opaque data types with only one valid operation, a test for equality. Concretely, the RDB completion of GORP implements OIDs as integers. Unfortunately, in the rush to push applications into production, application developers were allowed to rely on the implementation of OIDs as integers. They took advantage of OID stability and external significance, e.g., a user could retrieve an OID, jot it down in a lab notebook, and later initiate a GORP object retrieval using it as a key.

In contrast, OIDs are a hidden implementation artifact in most ODBMS's. Hence in the ODBMS completion of GORP, it is not *ipso facto* appropriate to maintain a separate, GORP specific notion of OID. Had OIDs originally been implemented correctly as opaque data types, we could have easily changed the implementation of GORP OIDs to use the ODBMS OID. Although there is never any reason for an application to do anything but compare two OIDs for equality, application programmers have used the integer representation of OIDs in their code in so many ways that it is unfeasible to undo it. Consequently we are reluctantly maintaining both forms of OID in the ODBMS version of the framework for backwards compatibility with older applications.

The lesson offered here to framework designers is that

| **RDB Implementation** | **ODB Implementation** |
|---|---|
| Gene * gene; | Gene * gene; |
| transaction_1.begin( ); | transaction_1.begin( ); |
| gene = Gene::get_gene( "X" ); | gene = Gene::get_gene( "X" ); |
| transaction_1.commit(); // framework maintains transient copy of // gene | transaction_1.commit(); // gene is now invalid |
| transaction_2.begin(); | transaction_2.begin(); |
| GeneBag * bag = gene->related(); // gene is valid, but may not be current | GeneBag * bag = gene->related(); // invalid pointer dereference // exception! |
| transaction_2.commit(); | transaction_2.commit(); |

Figure 5: Differences in lifetime of object references

the concept of OIDs and externally visible keys should be built into the framework. However, we feel strongly that these two concepts should be strictly separated from each other. That is, it is ill-advised to use OIDs to implement external keys or external keys to implement OIDs.

## 5.4 Final Remarks on Portability

When the RDB version of GORP was conceived, it was designed to accommodate an ODBMS port with relative ease. Ideally, no application code would need to be modified. For the most part, this has proved to be true. With the exception of adding transaction boundaries and some long pointers, we have not modified any application code. In short, encapsulating all data accesses to persistent objects within a framework like GORP has enabled us to port many applications with very little modification of source code between two very different DBMS products.

However, it would also be desirable to port the framework across ODBMS products with minimal effort. We believe that the GORP design sufficiently abstracted the notion of a relational database to make porting it from one RDBMS to another a fairly painless task requiring very few changes to the framework. It is important to note that one of the fundamental reasons this abstraction is successful is because of the acceptance of SQL as a standard interface to relational databases. Unfortunately, considerably more work would be required to port the current ODBMS version of GORP from ObjectStore to another ODBMS. Because a standard API does not currently exist for ODBMSs, all the queries within the GORP object completion would have to be converted from ObjectStore's proprietary query facilities to another proprietary API. We are optimistic current work by ODMG on OQL [C96] and ANSI/ISO on SQL3 [SQL3] may make ODBMS queries much more portable in the future.

# 6. Related work

The complexity of representing genomic data has been recognized by many other researchers [F91] [GRS94b]. MapBase, and its successor, LabBase, are genomic information systems developed at the Whitehead Institute similar in scope to that developed at the UCHGR [GRS94a] [RSG95] [G94]. However, both MapBase and LabBase were implemented using an ODBMS (ObjectStore) from the beginning. The fact that both the Whitehead Institute and the UCHGR have independently chosen to use an ODBMS is evidence of the difficulty in representing complex genomic data in a relational format.

The creators of Intermedia, a hypermedia framework developed at the Institute for Research in Information and Scholarship, considered porting their framework from an RDBMS to an experimental ODBMS [SZ87]. Although ODBMS technology was in its infancy at the time, the Intermedia researchers were mainly interested in overcoming the need to make transient copies of persistent objects stored in the RDBMS as well as the impedance mismatch between an object's representation in an RDBMS and an object-oriented programming language.

A comparison of performance for various pointer swizzling and non-swizzling schemes is described in [M92]. The Texas [SKW92] persistent store implemented pointer swizzling mechanisms very similar to that used by ObjectStore. The developers of Texas also recognized the problem of address space consumption and made some novel suggestions of how to deal with this problem by means other than invalidating all references to persistent objects at transaction boundaries [WK92].

As described above, the original version of the GORP framework had an ill-defined form of relaxed consistency due to the creation and manipulation of transient copies of database objects. This problem can be generalized in terms of a cache consistency problem [F96]. Efficient protocols for allowing appropriate degrees of consistency in a distributed computing environment with long running, interactive transactions remain an open research question.

# 7. Conclusions and Future Work

The lessons learned from our migration experience are summarized in Table 2, relying on a clinical metaphor. In the words of Waverly Root, *"Every virtue is accompanied by its inseparable vices"* [W66, p. 14]. For ODBMS's, the virtue is direct manipulation of persistent objects by application software. The inseparable vices are the semantic and operational burdens attending such direct manipulation. Perhaps it is too much to ask for an application framework to support deft and natural manipulation of objects in both *off line* (RDB) and *on line* (ODBMS) form. In any case, we offer the humble opinion that data representation issues --- the subject of much research in the academic database community --- are not the difficult problems. Instead, the core issues lie in areas long recognized to be among the most vexing of persistent data: object identity (copying vs. replication), transaction semantics (nature and lifetime of data ownership), and object naming (significance of OIDs and reference binding).

Despite the cautionary tone of this paper, we are pleased with the relative success of this experiment, and are encouraged to pursue several promising directions for future work. From a practical standpoint, UCHGR developers remain enthusiastic regarding the original goal of achieving a risk mitigating RDB to ODBMS migration strategy. Consequently a full-fledged port and performance comparison is underway. The project staff is particularly keen on exploiting the ODBMS version to explore relaxed concurrency control mechanisms appropriate for molecular biology applications, in which database modifications are mostly monotonic, and some degree of data inconsistency is part of daily life [BK91].

On a research level, we continue to be intrigued by the question of data evolution within this dual database environment. As remarked early on, among the many services provided by GORP framework is meta to concrete data representation conversion. The question thus arises: if the ODBMS port is a complete success, and the RDB is retired, how will data evolution be accommodated? We speculate that this dual database approach constitutes a "best of both worlds" solution: the ODBMS provides direct, fast, application-pertinent object access, and the RDB provides a generalized evolution-tolerant representation.

The long term solution thus may be a hybrid system, in which the ODBMS manages the live data, which is flushed to the RDB when data evolution is required. The GORP framework is then updated to present the new concrete data model, recompiled (along with applications, as necessary) and live data are loaded (or faulted in) as production resumes. The upshot is an ironic *denouement* of our plot: the RDB is now the cache.

| Dysfunction | Diagnosis | Remedy |
|---|---|---|
| Application code relies on low level access to database representations. | Lack of a framework providing encapsulated database access will require significant source code changes to each application. | Create a framework. |
| Creation of transient copies of database objects. | 1. Weak object identity semantics.<br>2. Uncontrolled or irregular updates to persistent objects.<br>3. Deallocating memory associated with an object is no longer the responsibility of the application.<br>4. Depending upon the ODBMS chosen, object creation model may be difficult to maintain. | In framework and application code, distinguish between object replication (same identity) and copying (new identity). Perform copying only when coherence between copies is not expected or appropriate. |
| Reliance upon object copying to implement a relaxed consistency protocol. | 1. Retaining this will require many small transactions.<br>2. Might be desirable to take advantage of ODBMS transaction facilities to devise a sound and appropriate consistency protocol. | Determine appropriate consistency and concurrency control model for application domain.<br>Implement as generalized transaction concept. |
| Amount of data accessed by applications exceeds the address space. | Individual transactions too large.. | Use of unswizzled pointers may be required. Restructure database into segments, offering finer grain control of swizzled pointer validity. |
| OIDs are manipulated by applications as a concrete data type. | OIDs may represent additional semantics, e.g., temporal creation order. | OIDs should be opaque data types.<br>May require re-engineering of application code. |
| Difficulty in porting the framework from one ODBMS to another. | Proprietary languages and inconsistent features. | Investigate industry joint or standard efforts such as OMDG's OQL or SQL3 |

Table 2: A "clinical" analysis of porting a relational database to an ODBMS

*Acknowledgments*: The authors are indebted to the designers and implementers of the UCHGR database and GORP framework: Peter Cartwright, David Fuhrman, Rob Sargent, Robert Mecklenburg, Tony Di Sera, and Chunwei Wang.

This research was funded in part by the National Institutes of Health grant *Utah Center for Human Genome Research.*

# 8. References

[ABDDMZ89] M. Atkinson, F. Bancilhon, D. DeWitt, K. Dittrich, D. Maier, and S. Zdonik. The Object-Oriented Database System Manifesto. *In Proceedings of the First International Conference on Deductive and Object-Oriented Databases*, pages 223-40, Kyoto, Japan, December, 1989.

[BK91] Naser S. Barghouti and Gail E. Kaiser, Concurrency Control in Advanced Database Applications, *Computing Surveys*, vol. 23, no. 3, September 1991.

[C96] R.G.G. Cattell, editor. *The Object Database Standard: ODMG-93*. 1996. Morgan Kaufmann Publishers, Inc.

[CMFRAD94] Judy Cushing, D. Maier, D. Feller, M. Rao, D. Abel, and M. DeVaney. Computational Proxies: Modeling Scientific Applications in Object Database, In *Proceedings of the Seventh International Working Conference on Scientific and Statistical Database Management*, p. 196-206, Portland, Oregon, September, 1994.

[EM92] J. Eliot and B. Moss. Working with Persistent Objects: To Swizzle or Not to Swizzle. *IEEE Transactions on Software Engineering*. Volume 18, Number 8, August, 1992. (pages 657-673).

[F91] Karen A. Frenkel. The Human Genome Project and Informatics. *Communications of the ACM*, Vol. 34, Number 11. (pages 41 - 51).

[F96] Michael J. Franklin. *Client Data Caching: A Foundation for High Performance Object Database Systems*. 1996. Kluwer Academic Publishers.

[G94] Nathan Goodman. An Object Oriented DBMS War Story: Developing a Genome Mapping Database in C++. In Kim, W., editor, *Modern Database Management: Object-Oriented and Multidatabase Technologies*. ACM Press.

[GRS94a] Nathan Goodman, Steve Rozen, Lincoln Stein. Building a Laboratory Information System around a C++-Based Object-Oriented DBMS. *Proceedings of the 20th VLDB Conference*, Santiago, Chile, 1994.

[GRS94b] Nathan Goodman, Steve Rozen, Lincoln Stein. A Glimpse at the DBMS Challenges Posed by the Human Genome Project. Available via anonymous ftp from genome.wi.mit.edu as file /pub/papers/Y1994/challenges.ps.Z.

[KJA93] Arthur M. Keller, Richard Jensen, and Shailesh Agarwal. Persistence software: bridging object-oriented programming and relational databases. *Proceedings of the ACM SIGMOD International Conference on Management of Data*, Washington DC, 1993, pp. 523-528.

[LLOW91] C. Lamb, G. Landis, J. Orenstein, and D. Weinreb. The ObjectStore database system. *Communications of the ACM.* Volume 34, Number 10, October, 1991. (pages 50-63).

[ODI96] Object Design, Inc., 25 Burlington Mall Rd., Burlington, MA 01803-4194, USA. Manual Set for ObjectStore Release 4.0, March, 1996.

[RSG95] Steve Rozen, Lincoln Stein, and Nathan Goodman. LabBase: Managing Lab Data in a Large-Scale Genome-Mapping Project. *IEEE Engineering in Medicine and Biology*, Volume 14, Number 6, p. 702 - 709.

[RSG94] Steve Rozen, Lincoln Stein, and Nathan Goodman. Constructing a Domain-Specific DBMS using a Persistent Object System. *Sixth International Workshop on Persistent Object Systems*. Available via anonymous ftp from genome.wi.mit.edu as file /pub/papers/Y1994/labbase-design.ps.Z.

[SFCDML96] Rob Sargent, Dave Fuhrman, Terence Critchlow, Tony Di Sera, Robert Mecklenburg, Gary Lindstrom, and Peter Cartwright. The Design and Implementation of a Database for Human Genome Research. In *Proceedings of the Eighth International Conference on Scientific and Statistical Database Systems*, IEEE Computer Society Press, p. 220-225, Stockholm, Sweden, June, 1996.

[SK91] Michael Stonebraker and Greg Kemnitz. The Postgres Next Generation Database Management System. *Communications of the ACM*. Volume 34, Number 10, October, 1991. (pages 78-92)

[SKW92] Vivek Singhal, Sheetal V. Kakkad, and Paul R. Wilson. Texas: An Efficient, Portable Persistent Store. *Proceedings of the Fifth International Workshop on Persistent Object Systems*, San Miniato, Italy, September, 1992.

[SZ87] Karen E. Smith and Stanley B. Zdonik. Intermedia: A Case Study of the Differences Between Relational and Object-Oriented Database Systems. *OOPSLA '87*, Orlando, Florida, October, 1987.

[SQL3] ISO and SQL3 working draft, available via anonymous ftp from speckle.ncsl.nist.gov in directory /isowg3.

[W66] Waverly Root. *The Food of France*. Vintage Books, 1966.

[WK92] Paul R. Wilson and Sheetal V. Kakkad. Pointer Swizzling at Page Fault Time: Efficiently and Compatibly Supporting Huge Address Spaces on Standard Hardware. *Workshop on Object Orientation in Operating Systems*, p. 364-377, Paris, France, September, 1992.

# The ODMG Object Model: Does it Make Sense? *

Suad Alagić
Department of Computer Science
Wichita State University, Wichita, KS 67260-0083, USA
e-mail: alagic@cs.twsu.edu

## Abstract

The ODMG Object Model is shown to have a number of problems. A major confusion is caused by the intended type of polymorphism and the way it is expressed in the Model. Dynamic type checking is required even in situations when static type checking is possible. There are situations in which there is no way that type checking can determine whether a particular construct is type correct or not. The model of persistence in the ODMG Standard is not orthogonal, which has undesirable pragmatic consequences on complex objects. The discrepancies between the ODMG Object Model and the particular language bindings of the ODMG Standard are non-trivial. This paper presents solutions to some of these problems together with the associated formal system. Without such a formal system the recommended ODMG bindings are open to a wide range of different, and sometimes confusing interpretations. The criticism expressed in the paper is intended to be helpful in developing future releases of the ODMG Standard.

*This material is based upon work supported in part by the U.S. Army Research Office under grant number DAAH04-96-1-0192.


OOPSLA '97 10/97 GA, USA
© 1997 ACM 0-89791-908-4/97/0010...$3.50

## 1 Introduction

The ODMG Object Model is the core of the ODMG Standard [Cat96]. As the Standard has been developed by the major vendors of object-oriented database management systems, the model deserves careful attention. Indeed, we may have to live with it for many years to come.

In this paper we show that the ODMG Object Model is behind the current state of object-oriented research. We reveal a number of problems in the Model and propose their solutions. We naturally hope that future releases will not have the problems reported in this paper.

The paper was written when the Release 1.2 [Cat96] was available. In the phase of the final preparation of the paper for the proceedings, ODMG 2.0 appeared [CBB97]. It was very difficult to make a careful account of the effects of all the changes in the new version of the Standard. Every attempt has been made to do so within the severe time constraints. Some differences between the two versions of the ODMG Standard will be pointed out in the paper. We were very pleased to see that the new version of the ODMG Standard seemed to recognize some of the problems reported in this paper.[1] But ODMG 2.0 is still far enough from a consistent standard. The core of our criticism still applies to the 2.0 version of the ODMG Standard just as well.

This paper also presents the core of a formal system which may be used to specify the intended bindings of the ODMG Object Model. Without such a formal system those bindings are open to a wide range of

[1] The first version of this paper was completed in October of 1996.

sometimes very confusing interpretations.

The difficulties in coming up with a good object model for the ODMG Standard are understandable. This paper thrives toward conceptual and even formal clarity. It aims to show that it is possible to achieve these goals, and at the same time meet the very pragmatic goals of the Standard.

A major confusion exists in the ODMG Object Model regarding the polymorphic facilities which the Model is actually supporting. The Model has a very inappropriate way of expressing situations requiring parametric polymorphism, which causes major problems in the underlying type system.

A related group of problems in the ODMG Object Model covers situations in which dynamic type checking is required in spite of the fact that static type checking is possible. Excessive dynamic checks affect efficiency and reliability of database transactions. It is unacceptable to carry out a dynamic check every time a transaction is executed if the check could have been performed once and for all when the transaction was compiled. Perhaps worse, expensive recovery procedures may have to be invoked only because of run-time type errors which could have been detected at compile time.

Yet another group of problems are those coming from the rigidity of the ODMG Object Model which makes it impossible to express frequently occurring situations in a natural way. This forces database programmers to use techniques which bypass the type system. A very likely and frequent consequence is undetected type errors that may cause database transactions to fail at run time.

A further class of problems are those in which it appears that type safety has been established by static type checking, and yet a transaction fails at run time due to a type error. Perhaps the most embarrassing are situations in which there is no way that type checking can determine whether a particular construct is type correct, no matter how sophisticated the checker may be. Such situations do exist in the ODMG Object Model. But they can be avoided, and we show how.

Particularly important are those aspects of the ODMG Object Model which are related to the model of persistence. The ODMG Standard does not have an orthogonal model of persistence. This leads to specific pragmatic problems related to complex objects. We offer an orthogonal solution for a model of persistence which is tied with the proposed formal system.

A closely related fact is that object-oriented database type systems necessarily require dynamic checks in some situations. It is essential to make those situations explicit, and not to confuse them with situations in which dynamic checks are not necessary. Our analysis is intended to eliminate such a confusion from the ODMG Object Model.

When introducing desirable features of a typed object-oriented model, one should have in mind what kind of demands those features place on the type system, and what kind of type technology is required to guarantee efficiency and reliability. This paper reveals some of such hidden subtleties in the ODMG Standard. They require advanced typing techniques, as well as a variety of reflective techniques elaborated to some extent in the paper.

This paper consists of two parts. The first part of the paper (sections 1–7) is informal. It presents the problems in the ODMG Object Model and our solutions to these problems. The second part of the paper (sections 8 – 14) presents the core of a formal system for a family of ODMG Object Models.

Many of the problems in the ODMG Object Model come from the fact that it is intended to be common for programming languages such as C++ and Smalltalk. But the underlying paradigms of these two languages are so different: C++ is strongly and mostly statically typed, and Smalltalk is mostly untyped (or dynamically typed). A reflective paradigm which treats classes as objects ([Feb89], [OPS95]) is truly object-oriented, but it defeats the whole purpose of a type system. It is thus hard to imagine that the requirement of the ODMG Standard to have a unified type system across the database and the programming language can ever be satisfied.

This paper shows that it is in fact possible to define a family of ODMG Object Models of increasing level of sophistication. Unlike the existing ODMG Object Model, each model in this family may be well and even formally defined, without any of the confusing points in the current ODMG Object Model.

## 2 The top class interface

All class interfaces in the ODMG Object Model are derived by inheritance from the interface `Object`. But in addition, the ODMG Object Model contains a mysterious type any. any stands for any type and it is used in situations where a type parameter is in fact required. This produces a type system which is not sound. Since the ODMG Object Model contains `Object`, any is redundant, and should be identified with `Object`, as illustrated below.

```
interface Collection : Object {
  unsigned long cardinality();
  boolean is_empty();
  void insert_element(in Object element);
//ODMG: void insert_element(in any element);
  void remove_element(in Object element);
  boolean contains_element(in Object
                                    element);
//ODMG: void contains _element(in any
                                    element);
  Iterator create_iterator();
};
```

With exception handling omitted, this is how the iterator class should look like:

```
interface Iterator: Object {
  void reset();
  boolean not_done();
  boolean next(out Object next_obj);
//ODMG: boolean next(out any next_obj);
  void advance();
  Object get_element();
//ODMG: any get_element();
};
```

The usage of any leads to obvious type errors that cannot be detected at compile time. Here is an example:

```
  Iterator  p;
  p.reset();
  select p.get_element().salary();
```

In our model the select clause fails a static type check. But what happens in the ODMG Object Model? The result type of `get_element` is any, where any stands for any type. Thus it is impossible for the type checker to determine whether the select clause is type correct. Does any have a method salary? All the types certainly do not.

In order to introduce a dynamic check one would have to write `((Person)(p.get_element()).salary()`. But the class indicator is intended to be used for going down the inheritance hierarchy and `Person` is not derived by inheritance from any. It is thus unclear whether this solution is even possible and correct according to the ODMG Object Model. ODMG 2.0 has an exception `InvalidCollectionType` in the interface `iterator`. When any is identified with `Object`, the problem disappears.

This simple change produces a model which requires usage of `Object` where one would use a type parameter in a model which supports parametric polymorphism. Using `Object` in place of a type parameter, as one would do in Java$^{TM}$, requires downcasting, which means dynamic checking. This is contrary to parametric polymorphism, which can be implemented with static type checking. In addition, quite contrary to the intent of parametric polymorphism, using `Object` implies heterogeneity of types of collection elements. But at least the model is consistent, unlike the current ODMG Object Model. And in fact, this basic model corresponds to the Java binding which appears in the ODMG 2.0 Standard.

## 3 Persistence

A model of persistence is orthogonal if objects of any type may be persistent or transient [ABD89], [AM95]. In a type system with orthogonal persistence, there may exist both persistent and transient objects of any type. *The model of persistence in the ODMG Standard is not orthogonal.* It is based on persistence capable classes. Objects of persistence capable classes may be persistent or transient. Objects of other classes are always transient.

In Release 1.2 persistence capable classes must be declared as such in the schema. In ODMG 2.0 persistence capable classes are eliminated from ODL, but then they reappear both in the C++ and the Java bindings (but not in the Smalltalk binding). Intriguing examples of classes the are not persistent capable according to the ODMG 2.0 are `Transaction` (this rules out long transactions), `Database` (!?) and `d_Extent` (used for managing extents of persistence capable classes in the C++ binding).

In the C++ binding of the ODMG Standard persistence capable classes, in addition to being derived from other classes, must also be derived from a distinguished class `d_Object` which enables persistence. But `d_Object` is not the top of the inheritance hierarchy. In fact, there is no such class in the C++ type system. The model of persistence is thus not orthogonal. Similar techniques are used in several extensions of C++ supporting persistence [AG89]. There are in fact even less flexible solutions. For example, E [RCS93] makes a clear distinction between database classes, whose objects are always persistent, and other classes, whose objects are transient.

ODMG 2.0 Java binding does not specify how a class becomes persistence capable.

The lack of orthogonality has its disadvantages. For example, consider a class `Shape` for which persistence capability has not been declared in the schema. If we now have a complex persistent object which has a shape, an awkward situation occurs. A persistent object has a component which cannot be persistent. Of course, we can define a new class `Persistent_shape`, equipped with persistence capabilities. But does it really make sense to have both `Shape` and `Persistent_shape` in the model?

The Java binding of the ODMG 2.0 struggles with this issue trying to reconcile non-orthogonal persistence with persistence by reachability. But the whole point is that persistence by reachability requires orthogonal persistence. Persistence by reachability is essential for object-oriented database technology, since it allows proper handling of complex objects. Support for complex objects is one of the key advantages of the object-oriented database technology over the relational database technology.

For the sake of completeness and fairness, we would also like to mention a database architecture which is object-oriented, largely untyped and reflective, and which does not support persistence by reachability [OPS95]. At the same time, a very active research and development work is under way to extend Java with orthogonal persistence. A representative project is PJava [ADJ96].

This paper offers a truly orthogonal, object-oriented model of persistence. The model is based on inheritance and on message passing. This last feature makes persistence in our model per object based. The class interface `Object` is extended by a method `persists` and a test `is_persistent`. Both are thus inherited by all other classes, and none of this disturbs any of the properties of the type system.

```
interface Object{
  boolean same_as(in Object anObject);
  boolean is_persistent();
  Object copy();
  void delete();
  void persists(in string name);
};
```

The message `persists` promotes the receiver object to longevity and makes the argument string the name of this object in the currently valid persistent scope. In a model with single, flat name space per database, this scope would correspond to the currently opened database. This binding thus corresponds to the effect of the method `bind` of the `Database` interface that follows.

Persistence capabilities are thus associated with the top of the inheritance hierarchy. This technique works well with Java, Smalltalk and Eiffel. In fact, we would argue that there is probably no other more natural way of supporting generic and orthogonal persistence capabilities in object-oriented systems. In spite of that, we are not aware of a single object-oriented model of persistence that is based on this simple observation.

An extension of the interface `Object` in ODMG 2.0 associates locking primitives with this interface. This is just yet another point of disagreement that we have with the ODMG Standard. Messages for promoting an object to longevity belong to the user interface. Locking is merely an implementation technique and should not be placed in the user model, just as persistence implementation techniques do not belong there.

Another component of a model of persistence is a binding mechanism for names of persistent objects. The ODMG Standard supports a single, flat name space which corresponds to the entire database. This is very impractical and it is expected to be changed in future revisions of the Standard. In fact, ODMG 2.0 has a very elaborate meta-level support which includes schemas, scopes and modules. We still have not been able to understand how this elaborate addition, and a single, flat name space, coexist in a single model.

The binding mechanism for names of persistent objects is given in the Database class interface. As in other models of persistence, this is an instance where explicit dynamic type checking is required.

```
interface Database: Object {
  void open(in string database_name);
  void close();
  void bind(in Object an_object,
                      in string name);
  Object lookup(in string object_name);
  // ODMG 1.2:
  // any lookup(in string object_name);
};
```

Note that the above mechanism leads naturally to orthogonality of persistence. Named objects are persistent (these are called persistence roots), and so are all their components, direct or indirect (reachability). This is essentially the approach taken in PJava [ADJ96]. Persistence by reachability or transitive persistence also appears at several places in ODMG 2.0, but it is somehow combined with persistence capable classes.

The confusion about the type any in the ODMG Object Model applies to this situation as well. Here is an illustration which shows how object lookup may be performed.

```
Database d; Person p;
p=d.lookup("John Doe");
```

According to the ODMG C++ binding `d.lookup( "John Doe")` returns a reference of type any. The object is then fetched and its type checked. If that type is not `Person`, a run-time error occurs. One problem with this is that it appears that assignments cannot be statically type checked. But that is not true. The usual rule in object-oriented languages is that the compile-time type of the right-hand side must be derived by inheritance from the compile-time type of the left-hand side. In order to guarantee type safety by static type checking, a more restrictive discipline must be adopted. The compile-time type of the right-hand side must be a subtype of the compile-time type of the left-hand side.

In the model proposed in this paper two solutions are possible. Both apply to situations in which dynamic type checking is required when retrieving a persistent object. One is based on the reverse assignment ?= as in Eiffel, which necessarily involves a dynamic type check:

```
p ?= d.lookup("John Doe");
```

If ordinary assignment were used above, it would not have type checked. The type of the right-hand side is not derived by inheritance, nor is it a subtype of the left-hand side. But the reverse assignment type checks, because it generates a mandatory run-time check. Such a check is not generated with the ordinary assignment. If the fetched object is indeed of the type `Person`, its identity will be assigned to `p`. Otherwise, `p` will be assigned a nil identifier. Testing `p` after the assignment reveals what happened.

The other solution is more in the spirit of the ODMG Standard. According to the `Database` interface, all that can be specified for the type of an object with a given name fetched from the database is that its type is any. In our type system that type is `Object`. In either case, very little can be done with such an object. A dynamic type check asserts that the fetched object is of a specific, expected type.

```
Database d; Person p;
p=(Person)(d.lookup("John Doe"));
```

But the above solution does not work according to the ODMG Standard 1.2. The class indicator `(Person)` should not be applied to the result of the method `lookup`. Indeed, the result type of `lookup` is any, and `Person` is not derived by inheritance from any. If any is identified with `Object`, the problem disappears.

To prove our point, in ODMG 2.0 the result type of the method `lookup` is indeed `Object`, as it should be. But then a new interface `Dictionary` is introduced in ODMG 2.0 with a method `lookup` whose result type is again any.

```
interface Dictionary: Collection {
  exception KeyNotFound(any key);
  void bind(in any key, in any value);
  void unbind(in any key)
                        raises(KeyNotFound);
  any lookup(in any key)
                        raises(KeyNotFound);
  boolean contains_key(in any value);
};
```

Our criticism applies just the same to this new interface, as well as to the retrieve methods of interfaces `List` and `Array` of both versions of the ODMG Standard. Furthermore, in the C++ binding of the ODMG 2.0 the result type of the method `lookup_object` of the class `d_Database` is `d_Ref_Any`, which causes even worse problems. At the same time, the class `d_Dictionary` of the C++ binding makes proper usage of parametric polymorphism in specifying the result type of the method `lookup`.

In the conclusion of this section we point out a major controversial issue related to persistence: object identifiers. It appears that in the ODMG Object Model these identifiers are hidden from the users, as they should be. But in the C++ binding of the ODMG Standard object references are explicitly present in the language.

This is contrary to years of research and experience in database systems. It is also contrary to the intent of the object-oriented data model as presented in [ABD89]. It is hard to imagine a type system that can deal with all the problems caused by the explicit availability of object identifiers to the users. We hope that this dangerous feature is not a consequence of the ideas behind the ODMG Object Model. Rather, it is a consequence of compliance with C++, which has references explicitly in the language. Regrettably, other C++ database programming languages suffer from the same problem. An example is O++ [AG89].

Java does not have this problem, and neither does the ODMG 2.0 Java binding.

# 4 Self types

In this section we show that the ODMG Object Model is in fact too rigid. This problem is not specific to the ODMG Object Model alone. This rigidity guarantees type safety in most situations. But then there are situations in which a database programmer must bypass completely the type system in order to accomplish perfectly natural tasks. The consequences may be very serious. A more flexible model is obtained by using self types [BCM93], [BSG95], [AC96], as illustrated below:

```
interface Object{
  boolean same_as(in Object anObject);
  MyType copy();
 // ODMG: Object copy();
  void delete();
};
```

This definition differs from the ODMG Object Model only in the result type of the `copy` method. But this seemingly small difference has major implications. `MyType` is a distinguished type variable denoting the type of object executing the message. `MyType` allows more flexible typing discipline in comparison with the ODMG Object Model since it changes its interpretation in a derived class. For example:

```
interface Person: Object{
  unsigned short age();
};
interface Employee: Person {
  float salary();
};
Person John; Employee Doe;
...
select John.copy().age();
select Doe.copy().salary();
```

In the class `Person`, `MyType` as the result type of the method `copy()` stands for `Person`, and in the class `Employee`, `MyType` stands for `Employee`. Because of that both select clauses type check. But according to the ODMG Object Model, neither one of them would. The reason is that the result type of `copy` is `Object`, which is not equipped with a method `age`, nor with a method `salary`.

One could argue that the problem may be solved using the class indicator as follows:

```
select ((Person)John.copy()).age();
select ((Employee)Doe.copy()).salary();
```

But according to the ODMG Object Model, the class indicator implies a dynamic check, which is not necessary in a model with self types. Besides, what is the point in making a copy of an object in such a way that the copy apparently contains only the features of the class `Object`. If a copy of a person object is created, presumably the copy should be a person object as well. Thus it appears that `copy` should be redefined in the derived classes accordingly. Although the ODMG Object Model is not specific on this point, it appears that such a redefinition is not possible. It is certainly forbidden in the Java and the C++ bindings of the ODMG Standard. Yet, if it were allowed, such a redefinition would have been known at compile time, and then the check could be static. This is an instance which shows the rigidity of the type system underlying the ODMG Object Model.

A closely related issue is the thorny problem of object creation which was completely avoided in ODMG 1.2. ODMG 2.0 attempts to deal with it, as illustrated by the following two interfaces.

```
interface ObjectFactory{
  Object new();
};

interface CollectionFactory: ObjectFactory
{
  Collection new_of_size(in long size);
};
```

ODMG 2.0 states that the operation `new` inherited by `Collection` from the interface `Object` creates a `Collection` object with system-dependent default amount of storage for its elements. But the result type of `new` is `Object`, and not `Collection`!

The C++ binding of the ODMG 2.0 contains specification of `new` based on overloading which completely bypasses the type system:

```
class d_Object {
 ...
 void* operator new(size_t size,
                    d_Database *database,
                    const char *typename);
 ...
};
```

As if the result type `void` was not enough, the physical size of the newly created object appears as the parameter of `new`, and the type name is passed at run-time as a string. If a programmer makes a mistake, the consequences may be disastrous. The whole point about the operator `new` in C++ is that it is meant to be type safe. ODMG 2.0 has an unacceptable explanation for how anomalies would be avoided in the above situation [CBB97].

In a type system which is based on self types, a distinction must be made between inheritance and subtyping. If an interface B is derived by inheritance from an interface A, contrary to the ODMG Object Model, it does not follow that B is a subtype of A. Substituting an instance of B where an instance of A is expected is allowed only if B is in fact a subtype of A. Otherwise, type safety cannot be guaranteed by static type checking. Multiple dispatch techniques must be used (see, for example, [BC96], [Ala97]) in order to guarantee type safety. A more expressive model is thus obtained at the expense of a strictly more sophisticated type technology, and even more sophisticated run-time technology. The tradeoffs must be well understood.

For example, covariant extensions of the signatures of the inherited methods are allowed in O2. With single dispatch this produces a system which is not type safe.

The formal rules for inheritance and subtyping are specified starting with section 9.

## 5 Parametric interfaces

Unlike Eiffel and C++, the ODMG Object Model does not offer general support for parametric classes. It has a roundabout way of supporting it only for collection classes, via "type generators". This view is shared by O2. The most likely reason for this controversial issue is the fact that the ODMG Standard defines bindings for both C++ and Smalltalk, as well as for Java in ODMG 2.0. The latter two of course do not support parametric polymorphism. C++ supports parametric polymorphism and thus the C++ binding of the ODMG Standard does not have many of the problems discussed in this paper. But the C++ binding has problems of its own. They include a model of persistence which is not orthogonal, and explicit presence of object identifiers in the language.

A clean solution from the viewpoint of the type system is to have explicit support for generic or parametric classes, as specified below:

```
interface Collection <T> {
 //ODMG:  interface Collection: Object {
   ....
  Iterator<T>  create_iterator();
 // ODMG: Iterator create_iterator();
};
```

Explicit support of parametric polymorphism allows type safe iterators, as illustrated below. A point of confusion in the ODMG Standard is that the ODMG Object Model does not define `Iterator` as a parametric class and its C++ binding does.

```
interface Iterator<T> {
  //ODMG: interface Iterator: Object {
      ....
      T get_element();
  //ODMG: any get_element();
};
```

Type safety can now be accomplished with static type checking, as illustrated below:

```
Iterator<Person> p;
  //ODMG: Iterator p;
  ....
select p.get_element().age();
```

The select clause type checks. In a model without parametric polymorphism one would have to introduce a dynamic check. One of the advantages of parametric classes is that they can be handled with static type checking.

The problems with the lack of parametric polymorphism and the rigid typing discipline for binary methods come up in deriving class interfaces `Set` and `Bag` from `Collection`. This is how it works in a type system with parametric polymorphism and self types:

```
interface Set <T> : Collection<T> {
  // ODMG: interface Set: Collection {
  MyType union_with(in MyType other);
  // ODMG: Set union_with(in Set other);
  MyType intersection_with(in MyType other);
  MyType difference_with(in MyType other);
  boolean is_subset_of(in MyType other_set);
  //ODMG:
  //boolean is_subset_of(in Set other_set);
  boolean is_proper_subset_of(
                    in MyType other_set);
  boolean is_superset_of(
                    in MyType other_set);
  boolean is_proper_subset_of(
                    in MyType other_set);
};
```

Consider now an example involving a class interface derived by inheritance from `Set`. It is unclear how one would accomplish this with type generators available in the ODMG Object Model for the collection classes `Collection`, `Set`, `Bag`, `List` and `Array`. There is no provision in the model to derive one type generator from another. This problem does not appear in the C++ binding of the ODMG Standard.

```
interface Bounded_Set <T> : Set<T> {
  unsigned long bound();
  void set_bound(in unsigned long
                               new_bound);
};
Bounded_Set<Person> Employees, Candidates;
...
select
Employees.union_with(Candidates).bound();
```

According to the ODMG Object Model the expression `Employees.union_with(Candidates).bound()` fails to type check. The type of the result of `union_with` is `Set<Person>` and thus does not have a bound. In our more flexible type system the type check succeeds, as one would naturally expect. Using the class indicator leads to the issues already discussed.

It is essential to note that `Bounded_Set` as derived above by inheritance from `Set` is not a subtype of `Set`. This is caused by the appearance of `MyType` in the argument position, and follows from the rules given in sections from 9 onwards. The remarks given in section 4 on the required technology which handles properly this situation apply.

## 6 Higher-order typing

The C++ binding of the ODMG Standard reveals further subtleties of the type system required by the intended ODMG Object Model. The type of elements of a collection cannot be just any type. Elements of a collection are required to be equipped with methods for the copy semantics. The type of polymorphism is thus not even parametric, it is more complicated. An example of an element type that satisfies this requirement is given below:

```
interface Person {
   unsigned short age();
   Person copy();
   boolean equal(in Person e);
};
```

The type of polymorphism which captures the intent of this ODMG requirement is either matching [BSG95] or F-bounded polymorphism [CCH89], [Ala94]. Parametric polymorphism is its particular case. This is how it works. Define the element type of a collection type as:

```
interface Element<T> {
  T copy();
  boolean equal(in T e);
 };
```

According to the ODMG Standard elements of ordered collections are also required to be equipped with a comparison method. Because of that, we also define the element type of ordered collections as follows:

```
interface Ord_element<T> : Element<T> {
  boolean less_than(in T e);
 };
```

A generic collection type whose elements are equipped with the copy semantics is now defined as follows:

```
interface Collection
     <T | T subtype_of  Element<T> >{
       ...
};
```

An F-bounded condition on the type parameter T is `T subtype_of Element<T>`. For example, `Person` as defined above satisfies this condition. A particular case of F-bounded polymorphism is bounded quantification (constraint genericity in Eiffel [Mey92]). To obtain this particular case, F-bound is replaced with a fixed class, for example `T subtype_of Ordered_element`.

A collection type whose elements are equipped both with the copy semantics and a comparison function is defined as follows:

```
interface Ordered_collection
       <T | T subtype_of Ord_element<T> >{
     ...
};
```

Note that `Person` now does not satisfy the condition `Person subtype_of Ord_element<Person>`.

F-bounded polymorphism is not just an exotic typing notion. It is in fact required for typing some very fundamental components of most database system architectures. Consider what is involved in typing the index abstraction:

```
interface Order<T> {
      boolean less_than(in T element);
 };

interface Index <T,To | T inherits_from To,
                To subtype_of Order<To>>
{ void build(Collection<T> collection);
  Iterator<T> iterator();
  T find(To key);
  void assign_iterator(Iterator<T>
                                iterator);
};
```

`Index` has two type parameters. `T` stands for the type of elements of the underlying collection, and `To` for the type of the indexing (key) attributes. There are two type constraints. The first one requires that the set of features of `To` is a subset of the set of features of `T`, hence `T inherits_from To`. The other constraint on `To` guarantees that `To` is equipped with the comparison function, hence `To subtype_of Order<To>`.

Similar subtleties are involved in typing keyed collections and dictionaries that appear in ODMG 2.0. Among the existing typed object-oriented programming languages, Eiffel is the closest to being able to deal with these subtleties.

# 7 Reflection

There are both hidden and explicit reflective features in the ODMG Standard. An elaborate meta-level extension in ODMG 2.0 is likely to be relevant to the discussion in this section. However, due to the time constraints, we have not been able to evaluate fully this new development in the Standard.

## 7.1 Type reflection

Type reflection treats types as objects of computation. This is possible only in a very restrictive fashion in order not to defeat the whole purpose of the type system. A conservative approach proposed in this paper is to allow only construction of new types at compile time. The approach is not only type safe, but also based on static type checking.

The simplest form of type computation carried out at compile time is type substitution required for parametric interfaces. Type reflective facilities in the ODMG Object Model appear in the form of type generators. The ODMG Object Model has type generators for collection classes `Collection<T>`, `Set<T>`, `Bag<T>`, `List<T>` and `Array<T>` as a roundabout way of providing limited parametric polymorphic features.

According to the ODMG 1.2 Object Model `Struct` is a type generator which allows definition of application oriented structures. Methods applicable to such structures are defined in the following interface.

```
interface Struct{
  unsigned long size();
  void set_element(in any field,
                   in any value);
  any get_element(in any field);
  void clear_element(in any field);
  Struct copy();
  void delete();
};
```

Apart from the fact that the above interface includes the usual confusion related to the type any, it also raises a question whether structures are objects. The intent of the ODMG Object Model is that structures are not objects, but according to the above ODMG interface they are. If the idea is to make structure types objects, then a type becomes a run-time notion. It is hard to imagine a type system that would offer a resolution to this confusing situation. To prove our point, this interface has been eliminated from ODMG 2.0.

The ODMG Object Model is intended to subsume the relational model. In ODMG 1.2 `Table(a1: t1, a2: t2,..., an:tn)` is defined to be equivalent to `Bag<Struct<a1 t1,a2 t2,...,an tn>>`. ODMG 2.0 states that `Table` is semantically equivalent to a collection of structures. But the ODMG Standard does not say anything about relational operators that `Table` should be equipped with, in addition to the operators on bags. Quite contrary to the ODMG Standard, a natural and truly object-oriented approach leads to a definition of `Table` as a class derived by inheritance from the class `Bag`.

With proper usage of parametric polymorphism and self types, a collection class `Bag` of the ODMG Object Model can now be defined as follows:

```
interface Bag <T> : Collection<T> {
 // ODMG: interface Bag: Collection  {
 unsigned long occurrences(in T element);
 MyType  union_with(in MyType other);
 // ODMG: Bag union_with(in Bag other);
 MyType intersection_with(in MyType other);
 MyType difference_with(in  MyType other);
 };
```

A class `Table` can now be derived from `Bag` as follows:

```
interface Table <T> : Bag<T> {
  Table<T*R> natural_join(Table<R>);
};
```

In order to illustrate the issues, only one specific database operator has been introduced in the interface `Table`: the natural join.

Typing a generic natural join function causes well-known difficulties [SFS90], [OBB89]. The solution presented above is based on type computation carried out at compile time. This computation is expressed in terms of operators on types [Car88]. Two such operators are *meet*, denoted *, and *join* of types, denoted +. Interestingly enough, typing joins requires meets of types. Type computations are necessarily very restrictive, so that they always terminate.

## 7.2 Linguistic reflection

A major step toward more general reflective facilities which typically cannot accommodate static type checking is in treating programs (transactions and queries) as objects. This is exactly what the ODMG Object Model does. Transactions are defined as objects of a particular class. The C++ binding of the ODMG Standard also treats queries as objects. In order not to obscure the main idea by C++ specifics, we will maintain the style of presentation of this paper. In our view queries may be viewed as objects of a class with the following interface:

```
interface Query<T> {
  void construct_query(in string query);
  void pass_int_arg(in unsigned short arg);
  void pass_float_arg(in float arg);
  void pass_string_arg(in string arg);
  Collection<T> execute();
    ....
};
```

The corresponding class in the C++ binding of the ODMG Standard is not parametric, which only causes further unnecessary dynamic checks. The method `construct_query` takes a string representing a query and associates this query with the object executing this message. Actual parameters can then be passed to the query using methods such as `pass_int_arg`, `pass_float_arg`, `pass_string_arg`, etc. This amounts to reconstructing a query at run time.

The method `execute` applied to a query object returns a collection which is the result of the query. It requires a compiler that can be called at run-time. Type checking will be thus carried out by the compiler as usual. But it will happen at run time. This technique is called run-time reflection [SSS92], [AM95]. The type parameter `T` stands for the type of elements selected by the query. Type checking involved in the execute message ensures that the argument query of this method indeed has this property. Here is a specific example of usage of this parametric class:

```
Query<Person> q;
..........
q.construct("select p  from Person p
  where p.age > $1 and p.salary >=  $2");
..........
q.pass_int_arg(40);
q.pass_float_arg(75,000.00);
q.execute();
...........
q.pass_int_arg(55);
q.pass_float_arg(100,000.00);
q.execute();
```

Run-time reflection based on a callable compiler has been a part of the technology of persistent programming languages such as Ps-algol [PsA87] and Napier [MBC88]. However, expressing it in a formalism of typing rules presents a real challenge. A further point is that type checking of the above argument query requires type inference [OB89], [OBB89], because of the usage of $1 and $2, as required by the ODMG Standard.

# 8 Schemas

We now proceed with a formal development. Names in a schema are bound to classes, objects and class extents. Every schema should contain at least a binding for the class `Object`. We thus have:

$$\frac{}{\{interface\ Object\ Ro\}\ schema}$$

A statement of the form $\mathcal{S}$ *schema* asserts that $\mathcal{S}$ is a schema. $dom(\mathcal{S})$ denotes the set of identifiers for which a binding is specified in a schema $\mathcal{S}$. In addition to `Object`, a schema will naturally contain other predefined bindings from the ODMG Standard, such as those for predefined simple types and collection types.

A binding for a class is introduced by a statement of the form `interface C R`, where `R` is a structure expression containing signatures of methods of the class `C`. For example, `Ro = {boolean same_as(in Object anObject); MyType copy(); void delete();}`. Every valid structure expression is formally derived from the empty structure expression. This relationship is expressed as $R \leq \{\};$, where $\leq$ is the inheritance ordering. The inheritance ordering for structures is defined in section 10 and the inheritance ordering for object types in section 9.

The rule for binding an identifier to an interface presented below is recursive since an interface (such as `Object` above) often naturally refers to itself, hence the condition $C \leq Object$. The axiom $\mathcal{S}\ schema \vdash MyType \leq Object$ is naturally a part of the formal system.

$$\frac{\mathcal{S}\ schema,\quad C \notin dom(\mathcal{S}),\quad \mathcal{S}, C \leq Object \vdash R \leq \{\};}{\mathcal{S} \cup \{interface\ C\ R\}\ schema}$$

$\mathcal{S}$ will always denote a schema, so that the statement $\mathcal{S}$ *schema* will in most cases be abbreviated to $\mathcal{S}$. Thus $\mathcal{S}$ stands for a collection of assertions about bindings of identifiers to interfaces (object types), extents and objects.

A binding for a class `C2` derived by inheritance from a class `C1` is introduced by a statement of the form `interface C2: C1 R`, hence the rule:

$$\frac{\mathcal{S}\ schema,\quad interface\ C1\ R1 \in \mathcal{S},\quad C2 \notin dom(\mathcal{S}),\quad \mathcal{S}, C2 \leq Object \vdash R2 \cup R1 \leq \{\};}{\mathcal{S} \cup \{interface\ C2:\ C1\ R2\}\ schema}$$

The expression $R2 \cup R1 \leq \{\}$; reflects the requirement that no redefinitions of the inherited signatures are allowed, other than those caused by the change of interpretation of `MyType`.

If `C` is bound to a class `C`, then `C` is necessarily derived by inheritance from the class `Object`.

$$\frac{\mathcal{S}\ schema,\quad interface\ C\ R\ \in \mathcal{S}}{\mathcal{S} \vdash C \leq Object}$$

Likewise, if a schema `S` contains a binding `interface C2:C1 R2`, then the inheritance relationship expressed as $C2 \leq C1$ is derivable from the schema `S`.

$$\frac{\mathcal{S}\ schema,\quad interface\ C2 : C1\ R2\ \in \mathcal{S}}{\mathcal{S} \vdash C2 \leq C1}$$

The rules which allow parametric interfaces to be declared in a schema are given in section 12.

An identifier `a` is bound to an object (yet unspecified) of a class `C` according to the following rule:

$$\frac{\mathcal{S}\ schema,\quad \mathcal{S} \vdash C \leq Object,\quad a \notin dom(\mathcal{S})}{\mathcal{S} \cup \{C\ a\}\ schema}$$

If a schema $\mathcal{S}$ contains a binding $C\ a$, (i.e., $(C\ a) \in \mathcal{S}$), then we can naturally deduce from $\mathcal{S}$ that $a$ is of class (type) $C$, denoted $a : C$. This rule is also a part of the formal system.

The above rules are easily extended to capture classes with extents as defined in ODMG 2.0. Unlike interfaces, classes in ODMG 2.0 are object types whose instances can be directly created. A class `C` with an extent `E` introduces an additional binding of `E` to a collection of objects of the type `C`. Two rules required to capture this idea are specified below:

$$\frac{\mathcal{S} \cup \{class\ C\ R\}\ schema,\quad E \notin dom(\mathcal{S})}{\mathcal{S} \cup \{class\ C\ (extent\ E)\ R\}\ schema}$$

$$\frac{\mathcal{S}\ schema,\quad class\ C\ (extent\ E)\ R \in \mathcal{S}}{\mathcal{S} \vdash E : Collection < C >}$$

# 9 Inheritance and subtyping

The ODMG Object Model identifies inheritance and subtyping. Thus `Employee` is a subclass and a subtype of `Person`. An instance of `Employee` may be substituted where an instance of `Person` is expected. This is a discipline from Eiffel and C++ and it causes some well-known problems [Coo89]. They do not appear in C++ because of a rigid type system. At the same time, this rigidity requires unsafe features which amount to bypassing the type system altogether. A more flexible type system requires a distinction between inheritance and subtyping ([CHC90], [BCM93]).

The collection of all object types (classes) is thus equipped with two orderings: `inherits_from`, denoted $\leq$, and `subtype_of`, denoted $<:$. If $C1 \leq C2$ holds, then C1 is derived by inheritance from C2. However, if $C1 <: C2$ holds, then an instance (object) of C1 may be substituted where an instance of C2 is expected, with type safety guaranteed by static type checking.

The class `Object` is defined in such a way that it is both the top of the inheritance and the subtyping orderings. Thus any class C derived by inheritance from `Object` ($C \leq Object$) will also be a subtype of `Object` ($C <: Object$). This explains why the type of the argument of the method `same_as` in the class `Object` is `Object`, just as in the ODMG Object Model. Another reason is that `same_as` is the object identity test and not the value equality test.

$$\frac{\mathcal{S} \vdash C \leq Object}{\mathcal{S} \vdash C <: Object}$$

### 9.1 Inheritance ordering

The inheritance ordering is reflexive and transitive. These properties are expressed in our type system as follows:

$$\frac{}{\mathcal{S} \vdash Object \leq Object}$$

$$\frac{\mathcal{S} \vdash C \leq Object}{\mathcal{S} \vdash C \leq C}$$

$$\frac{\mathcal{S} \vdash C3 \leq Object, \quad \mathcal{S} \vdash C2 \leq C3, \quad \mathcal{S} \vdash C1 \leq C2}{\mathcal{S} \vdash C1 \leq C3}$$

### 9.2 Subtyping ordering

The subtyping ordering is also reflexive and transitive:

$$\frac{\mathcal{S} \vdash C \leq Object}{\mathcal{S} \vdash C <: C}$$

$$\frac{\mathcal{S} \vdash C3 \leq Object, \ \mathcal{S} \vdash C2 <: C3, \ \mathcal{S} \vdash C1 <: C2}{\mathcal{S} \vdash C1 <: C3}$$

An important connection between the two orderings is expressed by the following rule:

$$\frac{\mathcal{S} \vdash C2 \leq Object, \ \mathcal{S} \vdash C1 <: C2}{\mathcal{S} \vdash C1 \leq Object}$$

If C1 $\leq$ C2 or C1 $<:$ C2, then an instance of C1 may be viewed as an instance of C2. In fact, safety of a type system depends critically on whether this is allowed for inheritance or subtyping.

## 10 Structures

Contrary to Smalltalk and Eiffel, class interface is not the only type structuring construct in the ODMG Object Model. A more primitive one is structure (record), as in C++ and O2. Instances of structures are not objects but values. Structures are a natural starting place for the development of the formal rules for object types in the ODMG Object Model. The relationship $R \leq \{\};$ (R is a valid structure) is defined inductively as follows:

$$\frac{\mathcal{S} \vdash C \leq Object}{\mathcal{S} \vdash \{C\ m;\}; \leq \{\};}$$

$$\frac{\mathcal{S} \vdash \{C1\ m1; C2\ m2; \ldots; Ck\ mk;\}; \leq \{\};, \quad \mathcal{S} \vdash Cl \leq Object, \ \ ml \neq mi\ for\ i = 1, 2, \ldots, k}{\mathcal{S} \vdash \{C1\ m1; C2\ m2; \ldots; Ck\ mk; Cl\ ml;\}; \leq \{\};}$$

Two more rules are needed to allow structures within structures. The only difference from the above rules is that the condition $C \leq Object$ is replaced by the condition $C \leq \{\};$, and the condition $Cl \leq Object$ is replaced by the condition $Cl \leq \{\};$. Similar remarks apply to some of the rules for structures given in the sequel.

The inheritance relationship among structures is defined simply as the subset relation:

$$\frac{\mathcal{S} \vdash R2 \leq \{\};, \mathcal{S} \vdash R1 \leq \{\};, \ \ R1 \subseteq R2}{\mathcal{S} \vdash R2 \leq R1}$$

This relationship is obviously reflexive and transitive.

The subtyping relationships among structures are much more subtle. Subtyping is certainly reflexive and transitive. Formal statements of these properties follow the pattern in the corresponding rules for object types. The general subtyping rule for structures is:

$$\frac{\mathcal{S} \vdash Ci \leq Object\ \ for\ 1 \leq i \leq k, \quad \mathcal{S} \vdash C'i \leq Object\ \ for\ k < i \leq n, \quad \mathcal{S} \vdash C'i <: Ci\ \ for\ 1 \leq i \leq k}{\mathcal{S} \vdash \{C'1\ m1; \ldots; C'k\ mk; \ldots; C'n\ mn;\}; \ <: \{C1\ m1; \ldots; Ck\ mk;\};}$$

Selecting a field of a structure is governed by the following familiar typing rule:

$$\frac{S \vdash e : \{C1\ m1; \ldots ; Ck\ mk;\};}{S \vdash e.mi : Ci}$$

In order to define the type rules for class interfaces, we extend the type expressions for structures to allow structure expressions of the form $\{C1\ m1(C11,\ldots,C1p1);\ldots;Ck\ mk(Ck1,\ldots, Ckpk);\};$. These extended structure expressions allow signatures of methods. The first two rules given below define inheritance as it applies to extended structures.

$$\frac{S \vdash Ci \leq Object,\ for\ 1 \leq i \leq k, \quad S \vdash C \leq Object}{S \vdash \{C\ m1(C1, C2, \ldots, Ck);\}; \leq \{\};}$$

$$\frac{\begin{array}{c} S \vdash \{C1\ m1(C11,\ldots,C1p1);\ldots; \\ Ck\ mk(Ck1,\ldots,Ckpk);\}; \leq \{\};, \\ S \vdash Cl \leq Object, \\ S \vdash Cli \leq Object, for\ 1 \leq i \leq pl, \\ ml \neq mi\ for\ 1 \leq i \leq k \end{array}}{\begin{array}{c} S \vdash \{C1\ m1(C11,\ldots,C1p1);\ldots \\ Ck\ mk(Ck1,\ldots,Ckpk); Cl\ ml(Cl1,\ldots,Clpl);\} \leq \\ \{\}; \end{array}}$$

The rule that follows defines subtyping for extended structures:

$$\frac{\begin{array}{c} S \vdash Ci \leq Object\ \ for\ 1 \leq i \leq k, \\ S \vdash C'i \leq Object\ \ for\ k < i \leq n, \\ S \vdash C'i <: Ci,\ \ for\ 1 \leq i \leq k, \\ S \vdash C'ij \leq Object,\ \ for\ 1 \leq i \leq n,\ 1 \leq j \leq pn, \\ S \vdash Cij <: C'ij\ \ for\ 1 \leq i \leq k,\ 1 \leq j \leq pk, \\ Cij \neq MyType \end{array}}{\begin{array}{c} S \vdash \{C'1\ m1(C'11,\ldots,C'1p1);\ldots; \\ C'k\ mk(C'k1,\ldots,C'kpk);\ldots;C'n\ mn(C'n1,\ldots, \\ C'npn);\}; <: \{C1\ m1(C11,\ldots, \\ C1p1);\ldots;Ck\ mk(Ck1,\ldots,Ckpk);\}; \end{array}}$$

## 11 Objects and messages

Object creation (as defined in OQL) is now specified by the following rule:

$$\frac{\begin{array}{c} S \vdash R \leq \{Ci\ fi;\};,\ \ 1 \leq i \leq n, \\ S \vdash ei : Ci, 1 \leq i \leq n, \\ class\ CR \in S \end{array}}{S \vdash C(f1 : e1, f2 : e2, \ldots, fn : en) : C}$$

The condition $R \leq \{Ci\ fi;\};$ guarantees that R has an attribute $fi$ of type $Ci$ for $1 \leq i \leq n$.

As an interface typically refers to itself, the subtyping rule for object types is naturally recursive. In the ODMG Object Model $C2$ is a subtype of $C1$ only if the interface $C2$ is derived by inheritance from the interface $C1$. In our type system there are additional requirements, specified in the recursive rule that follows:

$$\frac{\begin{array}{c} S \vdash interface\ C1\ R1 \in S, \\ interface\ C2 : C1\ R2 \in S, \\ S, C2 <: C1 \vdash (R2 \cup R1) < MyType/C2 > \ <: \\ R1 < MyType/C1 > \end{array}}{S \vdash C2 <: C1}$$

In the above rule $R < MyType/C >$ denotes the structure expression R in which the class C has been substituted for $MyType$.

The typing rule for messages is rather tricky. It will be given on the assumption of static type checking. The first thing that static type checking must ensure is that an object `o` executing a message `o.m(a1,a2,...,an)` is in fact equipped by an appropriate method. A further requirement is that the types of arguments `a1,a2,..,an` of the message `o.m(a1,a2,...,an)` must be subtypes of the corresponding argument types `C1,C2,...,Cn` of the method signature.

$$\frac{\begin{array}{c} S \vdash interface\ C\ R \in S, \\ S \vdash R \leq \{Cm\ m(C1, C2, ..., Cn);\}; \\ S \vdash o : Co, \quad S \vdash Co \leq C, \\ S \vdash ai : Cai,\ \ S \vdash Cai <: Ci,\ 1 \leq i \leq n \end{array}}{S \vdash o.m(a1, a2, ..., an) : Cm < MyType/Co >}$$

The conditions $R \leq \{Cm\ m(C1, C2, ..., Cn);\};$ and $Co \leq C$ ensure that the type $Co$ of the object $o$ has the required method signature. And finally, recall that $MyType$ denotes the type of the object executing the message. Thus the type of the result is not just $Cm$, but rather $Cm < MyType/Co >$, which is the result of substitution of $Co$ for $MyType$ in $Cm$.

The above rule simplifies if we identify inheritance and subtyping (and thus there is only one ordering) by disallowing usage of `MyType`. Of course, the same applies to many of the previous and the remaining rules. This simplified, but also less flexible type system, would correspond to the Java binding of the ODMG 2.0 Standard. It is in fact a particular case of the type system presented in this paper.

## 12 Parametric interfaces

The C++ binding of the ODMG Standard naturally relies heavily on parametric classes. This section provides only the basics for developing the formal rules for parametric interfaces.

The rule that follows allows interfaces with a single type parameter to be declared in a schema. A generalization to a finite number of parameters is trivial.

$$\frac{\begin{array}{c} S\ schema, C \notin dom(S), \\ S, T \leq Object, C < T > \leq Object \vdash R \leq \{\}; \end{array}}{S \cup \{interface\ C < T > R\}\ schema}$$

A binding for a parametric class `C2` derived by inheritance from a parametric class `C1` is introduced by a statement of the form `interface C2<T>: C1<T> R2`, hence the rule:

$$\frac{\begin{array}{c} S\ schema, \quad interface\ C1 < T > R1 \in S, \\ C2 \notin dom(S), \\ S, T \leq Object, C2 < T > \leq Object \vdash \\ R2 \cup R1 \leq \{\}; \end{array}}{S \cup \{interface\ C2 < T >: C1 < T > R2\}\ schema}$$

Instantiation of a parametric interface to a specific one is now governed by the following rule:

$$\frac{S \vdash A \leq Object, \quad interface\ C < T > R \in S}{interface\ C < A > R < T/A > \in S}$$

The above rule says that if a parametric interface `interface C<T>` is declared in a schema, then for any interface `A` in the schema, an interface `C<A> R<T/A>` is also available in the schema.

## 13 Queries

Space limitations make it impossible to present in this paper a complete set of typing rules for OQL. In this section we specify only the formal rules for a few characteristic forms of queries. Consider a typical OQL query of the form:

```
select projection
from e1 as x1, e2 as x2, ..., en as xn
where e'
```

The from clause determines the types of control variables `x1,x2,...,xn`. Each `ei` is required to be an expression of a collection type `Collection<Ci>`, hence the type of `xi` is `Ci`. In order to make queries on complex objects possible, each `e(i+1)` may be a component of `ei` for `i=1,...,n-1`. With the types of control variables determined this way, type checking of the qualification condition `e'` must produce `boolean`. In addition, if under the same assumption, the type of `projection` is `C`, the result of the query is of type `Bag<C>`.

$$\frac{\begin{array}{c} S \vdash e1 : Collection < C1 >, \\ S \cup \bigcup_{i=1}^{k} \{Ci\ xi\} \vdash e(k+1) : \\ Collection < C(k+1) >, 1 \leq k < n, \\ S \cup \bigcup_{i=1}^{n} \{Ci\ xi\} \vdash e' : boolean, \\ S \cup \bigcup_{i=1}^{n} \{Ci\ xi\} \vdash projection : C, \end{array}}{\begin{array}{c} S \vdash \text{select projection from e1 as x1, ..., en as xn} \\ \text{where e': Bag} < C > \end{array}}$$

If `select distinct` option is used in the above query, the result type is `Set<C>`. The typing rule for OQL queries of the form:

```
select projection
from e1 as x1, e2 as x2, ..., en as xn
where e'
order by e1',e2',...,em'
```

is just slightly more complex. Each `ej'` must be available in the result. This means that if the type of `ej'` is $C'j$, and $C$ is the type of `projection`, we must have $C \leq C'j$. In addition, the result is ordered and thus its type is `List<C>`.

$$\frac{\begin{array}{c} S \vdash e1 : Collection < C1 >, \\ S \cup \bigcup_{i=1}^{k} \{Ci\ xi\} \vdash e(k+1) : \\ Collection < C(k+1) >, 1 \leq k < n, \\ S \cup \bigcup_{i=1}^{n} \{Ci\ xi\} \vdash e' : boolean, \\ S \cup \bigcup_{i=1}^{n} \{Ci\ xi\} \vdash projection : C, \\ S \cup \bigcup_{i=1}^{n} \{Ci\ xi\} \vdash ej : C'j, \\ S \vdash C \leq C'j, 1 \leq j \leq m \end{array}}{\begin{array}{c} S \vdash \text{select projection from e1 as x1, ..., en as xn} \\ \text{where e' order by e1',e2',...,em'}: List < C > \end{array}}$$

Note how parametric polymorphism plays a crucial role in the above formal rules.

## 14 Reflection

The typing rules for type reflective facilities presented in this paper pose no particular problem. At the same time, we are not aware of a collection of formal typing rules that would capture all the subtleties involved in the general linguistic reflective facilities of the kind presented in [SSS92].

Given interfaces C1 and C2, we define their meet, denoted C1*C2, as an interface such that C1*C2 $\leq$ C1, C1*C2 $\leq$ C2. Furthermore, if C is an interface such that both C $\leq$ C1 and C $\leq$ C2 hold, then C $\leq$ C1*C2.

$$\frac{\mathcal{S} \vdash C1 \leq Object, \quad \mathcal{S} \vdash C2 \leq Object}{\mathcal{S} \vdash C1 * C2 \leq Object}$$

$$\frac{\begin{array}{ll}\mathcal{S} \vdash C1 \leq Object, & \mathcal{S} \vdash C2 \leq Object, \\ \mathcal{S} \vdash C \leq C1, & \mathcal{S} \vdash C \leq C2\end{array}}{\mathcal{S} \vdash C \leq C1 * C2}$$

The definition of join of types is symmetric and it is thus omitted. Now we can specify the typing rule for the `natural_join` operator:

$$\frac{\begin{array}{c}\mathcal{S}, T \leq Object \vdash a : Table < T >, \\ \mathcal{S}, R \leq Object \vdash b : Table < R >\end{array}}{\mathcal{S} \vdash a.natural\_join(b) : Table < T * R >}$$

It is easy to see that the meet `C1*C2`, with `interface C1 R1` and `interface C2 R2`, is well-defined if $R1 \cup R2 \leq \{\};$. Likewise, the join `C1+C2` is well defined if $R1 \cap R2 \leq \{\};$.

## 15 Conclusions

Release 1.2 of the ODMG Object Model contains major problems revealed in this paper. ODMG 2.0 attempts to avoid some of them, but makes only a modest step in that direction. In fact, the core of our criticism applies to ODMG 2.0 as well. The goal of our critical analysis is to help in making future releases better. Should that ever actually happen, the mission of this paper would have been accomplished.

In particular, it is hard to imagine a sound type system for the ODMG Object Model. No matter how sophisticated a type checker may be, there will always be situations in which the checker will not be able to decide whether a particular construct is type correct or not. One consequence of this conclusion is that extensive run-time checks are required. These checks make transactions less efficient and prone to failure at run time. It is in our opinion unacceptable to be forced to invoke expensive recovery procedures just because of run-time type errors that could have been detected at compile time.

Our analysis shows that one can define not only a single ODMG Object Model, but a family of models of the increasing level of sophistication. All the models in the family can be formally defined. These particular formal definitions appear as particular cases of the formal system presented in this paper. Vendors could start by implementing the basic model, gradually moving to the more sophisticated ones as extensions of the basic model. This approach eliminates the confusion that exists in the current model, and makes clear what level of compliance and sophistication a particular vendor is actually providing.

The most basic model is obtained by identifying any with `Object`. In addition, the Model should be equipped with orthogonal persistence. Consequently, persistence capable classes should be eliminated from the Model. In this model inheritance is identified with subtyping, just as in the ODMG Object Model.

This model corresponds to the type system underlying Java. In fact, the ODMG 2.0 Java binding corresponds to this model, except that it has a model of persistence which is not orthogonal. This model can be mapped to the type system of C++ simply because the type system of C++ is more powerful. But dealing with orthogonal persistence in C++ would remain an issue. The model is also as close as one can get to Smalltalk.

The main problem with this model is that it is too rigid. Extensive downcasting with dynamic checks is required, and even that cannot solve all the problems, as illustrated by the problems of cloning objects. But at least this way the confusion that exists at present in the ODMG Object Model is eliminated, and the model is extended with orthogonal persistence.

A strictly more sophisticated and more flexible model is obtained from the basic one by allowing limited redefinitions of method signatures using the type variable `MyType`. This produces a strictly more powerful type system in which a distinction must be made between inheritance and subtyping. The expressibility of the model is significantly increased at the expense of a strictly more sophisticated type technology. If substitutability is based on subtyping, type safety can be guaranteed by static type checking. However, if substitutability is based on inheritance, as in Eiffel, a more sophisticated implementation technology based on multiple dispatch is required.

In any case a formal definition of the ODMG Object Model is required. We have presented a collection of formal rules that have not been defined as of yet for the ODMG Object Model. Without such a formal system the recommended ODMG bindings are open to a wide range of different and sometimes contradicting interpretations. If an attempt had been made earlier to formalize such rules, the problems reported in this paper would have been discovered.

The importance of parametric polymorphism in database-oriented object models is obvious from the collection classes predefined in the ODMG Object Model. The confusion that currently exists in the ODMG Object Model regarding parametric polymorphism must be eliminated. Either the ODMG Object Model supports it, or it does not. If not, then `Object` must be used consistently instead of a type parameter. A clean solution which produces a third, strictly more sophisticated model, is to provide full support for parametric polymorphism.

Whether this family of ODMG Object Models should be extended further with more advanced features is probably a topic for debate. We have demonstrated that even a more sophisticated type system is required if we want to type properly essential components of any database architecture. Such a type system would support bounded quantification (as in Eiffel), and matching or F-bounded polymorphism.

Finally, hidden subtleties in the ODMG Object Model require all of the above features, as well as type reflection. This is the most sophisticated model in this hierarchy. Admittedly, the ODMG Standard may not want to go this far. But the fact that the ODMG Object Model is a database object-oriented model requires these sophisticated features, regardless of whether the ODMG Standard wants to be explicit about them or not. In fact, Java has limited reflective facilities related to the presence of the `Class` class in the language. And ODMG 2.0 has elaborate meta-level architecture, which is yet to become the focus of our investigations.

### Acknowledgment

I would like to thank Kennis Lai for her comments on an earlier version of this paper, and Svetlana Kouznetsova and Jose Solorzano for their comments on the final version.

## References

[AC96] M. Abadi and L. Cardelli, On Subtyping and Matching, Proceedings of ECOOP'96, *Lecture Notes in Computer Science*, Springer-Verlag, Vol. 1098, pp. 145-167, 1996.

[AG89] R. Agrawal and N. Gehani, Ode: Object Database and Environment; Rationale for the Design of Persistence and Query Processing Facilities in the Database Programming Language O++, Proceedings of the 2nd International Workshop on Database Programming Languages, Portland, Oregon, 1989.

[Ala94] S. Alagić, F-bounded Polymorphism for Database Programming Languages, Proceedings of the 2nd East-West Database Workshop, *Workshops in Computing*, Springer-Verlag, pp. 125-137, 1994.

[Ala97] S. Alagić, Constrained Matching is Type Safe, Proceedings of the 6th Int. Database Programming Language Workshop, to appear, 1997.

[ABD89] M. Atkinson, F. Bancilhon, D. DeWitt, K. Dittrich, D. and S. Zdonik: The Object-Oriented Database System Manifesto, Proceedings of the First Object-Oriented and Deductive Database Conference, Kyoto, 1989.

[ADJ96] M. Atkinson, L. Daynes, M.J. Jordan, T. Printezis and S. Spence, An Orthogonally Persistent Java$^{TM}$. ACM SIGMOD Record, No. 4, Vol. 25, pp. 68-75, 1996.

[AM95] M. Atkinson and R. Morrison. Orthogonally Persistent Object Systems, *VLDB Journal*, Vol. 4, pp. 319-401, 1995.

[BC96] J. Boyland and G. Castagna, Type-Safe Compilation of Covariant Specialization: a Practical Case, Proceedings of ECOOP '96 Conference, *Lecture Notes in Computer Science* Vol. 1098, pp. 3-25, Springer-Verlag, 1996.

[BCM93] K. Bruce, J. Crabtree, T. P. Murtagh and R. van Gent, A. Dimock and R. Muller, Safe and Decidable Type Checking in an Object-Oriented Language, Proceedings of the OOPSLA Conference, pp. 29-46, 1993.

[BSG95] K. Bruce, A. Schuett, and R. van Gent, PolyTOIL: a Type-Safe Polymorphic Object-Oriented Language, Proceedings of ECOOP '95, *Lecture Notes in Computer Science* Vol. 952, pp. 27-51, Springer-Verlag, 1995.

[CCH89] P. Canning, W. Cook, W. Hill, W. Olthoff and J.C. Mitchell, F-Bounded Polymorphism for Object-Oriented Programming, Proceedings of the ACM Conference on Functional Programming Languages and Computer Architecture, pp. 273-280, 1989.

[Car88] L. Cardelli, Types for Data Oriented Languages, In: J.W. Schmidt, S. Ceri and M. Missikoff (Eds), Advances in Database Technology - EDBT '88, *Lecture Notes in Computer Science*, 303, Springer-Verlag, Berlin, pp. 1-15, 1988.

[Cat96] R. G. G. Cattell (ed), *The Object Database Standard: ODMG-93, Release 1.2*, Morgan Kaufmann, 1996.

[CBB97] R. G. G. Cattell, D. Barry, D. Bartels, M. Berler, J. Eastman, S. Gamerman, D. Jordan, A. Springer, H. Strickland, D. Wade, *The Object Database Standard: ODMG 2.0*, Morgan Kaufmann, 1997.

[CHC90] W. R. Cook, W. L. Hill and P. S. Canning, Inheritance is not Subtyping, In: Proceedings of the Conference on Principles of Programming Languages, ACM Press, 1990, pp. 125-135.

[Coo89] W. R. Cook, A Proposal for Making Eiffel Type Safe, *The Computer Journal*, Vol. 32, no. 4, 1989, pp. 305-311.

[Feb89] J. Ferber, Computational Reflection in Class Based Object-Oriented Languages, Proceedings of the OOPSLA Conference, pp. 317–326, 1989.

[GJS96] J. Gosling, B. Joy and G. Steele, *The Java$^{TM}$ Language Specification*, Addison-Wesley, 1996.

[MBC88] R. Morrison, F. Brown, R. Connor, A. Dearle, The Napier88 Reference Manual, Universities of Glasgow and St. Andrews, PPRR-77-89, 1989.

[Mey92] B. Meyer, Eiffel: *The Language*, Prentice-Hall, 1992.

[RCS93] J. E. Richardson, M. J. Carey and D. Schuh, The Design of the E Programming Language, *ACM Transactions on Programming Languages and Systems*, Vol. 15, pp. 494-534, 1993.

[OPS95] M. T. Ozsu, R. Peters, D. Szafron, B. Irani, A. Lipka, and A. Munoz, TIGUKAT: A Uniform Behavioral Objectbase Management System, *VLDB Journal*, Vol. 4, pp. 445-492, 1995.

[OB89] A. Ohori and P. Buneman, Static Type Inference for Parametric Classes, Proceedings of the OOPSLA Conference, pp. 445-456, 1989.

[OBB89] A. Ohori, P. Buneman and V. Breazu-Tannen, Database Programming in Machiavelli: a Polymorphic Language with Static Type Inference, Proceedings of the ACM SIGMOD Conference, pp. 46-57, 1989.

[O296] ODMG C++ Reference Manual, O2 Technology, 1996.

[PsA87] The Ps-Algol Reference Manual, Persistent Programming Research Report 12, Universities of Glasgow and St. Andrews, 1987.

[SFS90] D. Stemple, L. Fegaras, T. Sheard and A. Socorro, Exceeding the Limits of Polymorphism in Database Programming Languages, In: F. Bancilhon and C. Thanos (Eds), Advances in Database Technology - EDBT '90, *Lecture Notes in Computer Science*, 416, pp. 269-285, Springer-Verlag, 1990.

[SSS92] D. Stemple, R. B. Stanton, T. Sheard, P. Philbrow, R. Morrison, G.N.C. Kirby, L. Fegaras, R.L. Cooper, R.C.H. Connor, M. Atkinson, and S. Alagić, Type-Safe Linguistic Reflection: A Generator Technology, ESPRIT Research Report CS/92/6, Department of Mathematical and Computational Sciences, University of St. Andrews, 1992.

# Class Hierarchy Specialization

Frank Tip and Peter F. Sweeney

*IBM T.J. Watson Research Center*
*P.O. Box 704, Yorktown Heights, NY 10598, USA*
*E-mail:* {tip,pfs}@watson.ibm.com

## Abstract

Class libraries are generally designed with an emphasis on versatility and extensibility. Applications that use a library typically exercise only part of the library's functionality. As a result, objects created by the application may contain unused members. We present an algorithm that *specializes* a class hierarchy with respect to its usage in a program $\mathcal{P}$. That is, the algorithm analyzes the member access patterns for $\mathcal{P}$'s variables, and creates distinct classes for variables that access different members. Class hierarchy specialization reduces object size, and is hence primarily a space optimization. However, execution time may also be reduced through reduced object creation/destruction time, and caching/paging effects.

## 1 Introduction

Class libraries are generally designed with an emphasis on versatility and extensibility. An application that uses a class library typically exercises only part of the library's functionality. Unfortunately, this leads to situations where the objects created by the program contain unused components. For example, for a member $m$ in a given class $C$, it may be the case that certain $C$-objects never use $m$. We present an algorithm that *specializes* a class hierarchy with respect to its usage in a program $\mathcal{P}$. The algorithm effectively analyzes the member access patterns for the variables in $\mathcal{P}$, and creates distinct classes for variables that access different members. The benefits of specialization can be manifold:

- The space requirements of a program are reduced at run-time, because objects no longer contain unnecessary members.
- Specialization may eliminate virtual inheritance (i.e., shared multiple inheritance) from a class hierarchy. This reduces member access time, and it may reduce object size.
- Creation and destruction of objects requires less time, due to reduced object size. Time requirements may also be reduced through caching/paging effects.
- Specialization may create new opportunities for existing optimizations such as virtual function call resolution [4, 9, 3, 8, 5].
- Specialization may be of use in program understanding and debugging tools. For example, specialization can be used as a means to suppress the output of unused parts of objects during a debugging session.

Although we expect class hierarchy specialization to be primarily of use in the context of an optimizing compiler, we present the algorithm as a source-to-source translation for the sake of illustration.

### 1.1 Scope of this paper

The motivation for this work is to reduce the overhead incurred by class library usage in C++ applications. In order to prevent our definitions and algorithms from becoming too unwieldy, the present paper will focus on a small, idealized subset of C++, which we will refer to as $\mathcal{L}$. Language $\mathcal{L}$ contains the inheritance mechanisms of C++ in their full generality, including multiple inheritance and virtual inheritance. We have omitted many C++ features from $\mathcal{L}$ because they would clutter the presentation of the algorithm. E.g., we only allow default constructors/destructors, and members are assumed to be accessible from anywhere in a program, thus ignoring all issues related to access rights. In addition, several features have been omitted from $\mathcal{L}$ because their treatment is future work (e.g., explicit type-cast operations, and nested structures). This being said, we believe that our techniques are in principle applicable to realistic languages such as C++ and Java, although much engineering work remains to be done—future work will be discussed in Section 6. The syntax and semantics of $\mathcal{L}$ are very close to those of C++, and the example programs presented below have their usual meanings. For the interested reader, details of $\mathcal{L}$ are provided in Appendix A.

### 1.2 Motivating examples

Figure 1(a) shows an example program $\mathcal{P}_1$, which contains three objects `s1`, `s2`, and `s3`, each of type `S`. Careful analysis of $\mathcal{P}_1$ reveals that member `m1` is accessed from all three objects, member `m2` is accessed from `s2`, and member `m3` is accessed from `s3`. In order to save space at run-time, we would like to remove `m2` from `s1` and `s3`, and `m3` from `s1` and `s2`. Note that this requires `s1`, `s2`, and `s3` to have *different types*, since objects of the same type contain the same members.

However, the types of `s1`, `s2`, and `s3` are not completely unrelated because the assignments `s1 = s2` and `s2 = s3` impose constraints on them. If `s1`, `s2`, and `s3` have three different, *unrelated* types, the compiler would report a type error in the assignments. Observe, however, that `s1`, `s2`, and `s3` need not necessarily have *exactly* the same type: in general, an assignment $x = y$ only


**OOPSLA '97 10/97 GA, USA**
**© 1997 ACM 0-89791-908-4/97/0010...$3.50**

```
class S {   int m1;
            int m2;
            int m3;
};

void main(){
  S s1; S s2; S s3;
  s1.m1 = 10;
  s2.m1 = 20; s2.m2 = 30;
  s3.m1 = 40; s3.m3 = 50;
  s1 = s2;
  s2 = s3;
}
```

**(a)**

```
class T_var(s1) { int m1; };
class T_var(s2) : T_var(s1) { int m2; };
class T_var(s3) : T_var(s2) { int m3; };

void main(){
  T_var(s1) s1; T_var(s2) s2; T_var(s3) s3;
  s1.m1 = 10;
  s2.m1 = 20; s2.m2 = 30;
  s3.m1 = 40; s3.m3 = 50;
  s1 = s2;
  s2 = s3;
}
```

**(b)**

Figure 1: **(a)** Example program $\mathcal{P}_1$. **(b)** Result of specialization.

requires that $y$'s type be transitively derived from $x$'s type [1]. The specialized class hierarchy of Figure 1(b) shows how this observation can be exploited, using inheritance relations between the types of s1, s2, and s3. Note that s1 and s2 now contain fewer members (the number of members of s3 remains the same) while program behavior is preserved.

Figure 2(a) shows an example program $\mathcal{P}_2$ that will be used as a running example throughout the remainder of the paper. $\mathcal{P}_2$ has a class hierarchy with two virtual functions, f() and g(). The result of specialization is shown in Figure 2(b). Note that the functions A::f(), A::g(), B::g(), and C::f() are dispersed over four classes $T_{var(\texttt{*ap})}$, $T_{var(\texttt{a})}$, $T_{var(\texttt{b})}$, and $T_{var(\texttt{c})}$, and that class $T_{var(\texttt{*ap})}$ only contains a *declaration*[2] of method g(). Observe that the use of a common base class $T_{var(\texttt{*ap})}$ with only virtual methods allows us to eliminate the x data member from b and c.

Since the size of an object is strongly implementation-dependent it is difficult to make general statements about the space savings of this operation. If we assume that $\mathcal{L}$ uses the same object model as the IBM xlC C++ compiler on the RS/6000/AIX 4.1 platform, the size of variable a would remain unchanged at 8 bytes, the size of b would be reduced from 12 to 8 bytes, and the size of c would be reduced from 16 to 12 bytes.

## 1.3 Overview of algorithm

The specialization algorithm consists of four distinct phases. In Phase I, discussed in Section 2, basic program information is collected by inspecting the source code of input program $\mathcal{P}$. This information comprises the variables, class members, assignments, and member access operations that occur in $\mathcal{P}$, as well as pointer-alias information for pointer-typed variables.

Phase II is concerned with the computation of *type constraints* that precisely capture the required subtype-relationships between the types of variables, and the visibility relations between class members and variables that must be retained in order to preserve program behavior. Phase II is presented in Section 3.

In Phase III, the type constraints of Phase II are used to construct a new class hierarchy, and the variable declarations in the program are updated to take this new hierarchy into account. This is discussed in Section 4.

In the class hierarchy that results from Phase III, redundant data members and methods have been removed from objects. This hierarchy is not optimal however, since it typically exhibits an abundance of virtual inheritance. Virtual inheritance is undesirable because it is usually implemented in a way that increases member access time, and in some cases object size as well. Phase IV addresses this problem by applying a set of semantics-preserving transformation rules that simplify the specialized hierarchy, and eliminate (virtual) inheritance. Section 5 discusses Phase IV.

[1] More precisely, for an assignment $x = y$, where $x$ has type $X$ and $y$ has type $Y$, there must be exactly one $X$-subobject inside an $Y$-object.

[2] In $\mathcal{L}$, methods only need to be defined if they are invoked. This is not the case in C++.

## 1.4 Related work

A number of categories of related work can be distinguished.

The first category consists of techniques for eliminating unused components from objects or class hierarchies. Tip, et al. [23] present a class hierarchy slicing algorithm that eliminates members and inheritance relations from a C++ hierarchy. In a sense, class hierarchy specialization can be viewed as a refinement of class hierarchy slicing. Like specialization, class slicing is concerned with eliminating unused members from hierarchies, but slicing can only remove a member from a class $C$ if it is not used by *any* instance of type $C$. In contrast, specialization is capable of making finer distinctions at the variable level: By giving different types to variables that previously had the same type, members may be eliminated from certain objects while being retained in others.

Agesen and Ungar [2, 1] describe an algorithm for the dynamically typed language Self that eliminates unused slots from objects (a slot corresponds to either a data member, a method, or an inheritance relation). This algorithm computes, for each message send that may be executed, a set of slots that is needed to preserve that send's behavior, and produces a source file in which redundant slots have been eliminated. Comparing Agesen and Ungar's work to ours is difficult due to the different nature of Self and $\mathcal{L}$. Much of the complexity of our approach is due to the fact that removing members from objects requires changing the class hierarchy. This issue does not come up in Self, because Self is a dynamically typed language without classes.

We consider class hierarchy specialization to be a technique that is largely complementary to techniques for eliminating unused *executable* code, such as methods, from object-oriented programs [4, 20, 15]. In the scenario we have in mind, unused executable code is removed from an application first, after which the class hierarchy could be specialized in order to reduce object size. The benefit of this approach is that members that are only accessed from useless code are removed from the class hierarchy altogether. A specific technique that could be used to this end is *program slicing* [25, 22], which determines the set of executable statements that may affect the values computed at some designated point(s) of interest in a program. Redundant statements can be removed from a program by slicing w.r.t. all output values.

Another view on class hierarchy specialization is that of a *type inference* algorithm, which infers a set of nonstandard types for

```
class A {
  virtual int f(){ return g(); };
  virtual int g(){ return x; };
  int x;
};
class B : A {
  virtual int g(){ return y; };
  int y;
};
class C : B {
  virtual int f(){ return g() + z; };
  int z;
};


void main(){
  A a; B b; C c;
  A *ap;
  if (...)  { ap = &a; }
  else { if (...)  { ap = &b; }
         else { ap = &c; } }
  ap->f();
}
```

**(a)**

```
class T_var(*ap) {
  virtual int f(){ return g(); };
  virtual int g(); /* declaration only */
};
class T_var(a) : T_var(*ap) {
  virtual int g(){ return x; };
  int x;
};
class T_var(b) : T_var(*ap) {
  virtual int g(){ return y; };
  int y;
};
class T_var(c) : T_var(b) {
  virtual int f(){ return g() + z; };
  int z;
};

void main(){
  T_var(a) a; T_var(b) b; T_var(c) c;
  T_var(*ap) *ap;
  if (...)  { ap = &a; }
  else { if (...)  { ap = &b; }
         else { ap = &c; } }
  ap->f();
}
```

**(b)**

Figure 2: **(a)** Example program $\mathcal{P}_2$. **(b)** Specialized program and class hierarchy.

variables, and constructs a new class hierarchy reflecting these.

For a discussion of type inference for object-oriented languages, we refer the reader to the seminal work on object-oriented type systems by Palsberg and Schwartzbach [15]. There are some interesting connections between our work and that of [15]. Since Palsberg and Schwartzbach study a language with only single inheritance, they can express an expression's type as a set of classes. In the presence of multiple inheritance, this is not possible, and a more sophisticated mechanism such as Rossie and Friedman's subobject-based types is required [18]. Our notion of a type constraint is similar in spirit to Palsberg and Schwartzbach's, but due to fact that types cannot be expressed as sets of classes, type constraints cannot be expressed using the subset operator. There is also a difference in the way type constraints are used. Palsberg and Schwartzbach submit all type constraints to an inference engine, which infers a type for each program variable. In contrast, in our case, where initial types are known for each variable, type constraints are not solved but interpreted as a new class hierarchy for the program.

O'Callahan and Jackson [12] use type inference to determine statically where the structure of a C program requires sets of variables to share a common representation. Although they are primarily interested in program understanding applications such as finding abstraction violations, their algorithm also detects unused fields of data structures. Since C does not have inheritance, O'Callahan and Jackson do not address the complex issues related to subtyping that arise in our setting. We believe that, in principle, the nonstandard types inferred by our algorithm can be used for the same program understanding applications as those mentioned in [12].

A third category of related work is that of techniques for restructuring class hierarchies for the sake of improving design, improving code reuse, and enabling reuse.

Opdyke and Johnson [13, 14] present a number of behavior-preserving transformations on class hierarchies, which they refer to as *refactorings*. The goal of refactoring is to improve design and enable reuse by "factoring out" common abstractions. This involves steps such as the creation of new superclasses, moving around methods and classes in a hierarchy, and a number of similar steps. In Opdyke and Johnson's approach, the transformation of class hierarchies is guided by the user. In contrast, class hierarchy specialization has the opposite goal: class hierarchies are *customized* for a particular application, as opposed to being generalized for the sake of reusability and maintenance. Unlike refactoring, where the programmer determines what restructurings should take place, class hierarchy specialization requires no programmer intervention.

Moore [11] presents a tool that automatically restructures inheritance hierarchies and refactors methods in Self programs. The goal of this restructuring is to maximize the sharing of expressions between methods, and the sharing of methods between objects in order to obtain smaller programs with improved code reuse. Since Moore is studying a dynamically typed language without explicit class definitions, a number of complex issues related to preserving the appropriate subtype-relationships between classes of objects do not arise in his setting. Another important difference between our work and Moore's is that while Moore's algorithm rearranges methods in a hierarchy, it is not capable of eliminating unused members.

## 2 Phase I: Information Gathering

Phase I of the specialization algorithm consists of gathering basic information about the input program $\mathcal{P}$, which we will assume to be type-correct. This information will be used in Phase II (discussed in Section 3) to compute the set of type constraints (e.g., subtype-relationships between variables) that must be preserved in the specialized class hierarchy.

In the sequel, $v$, $w$, ... denote variables in $\mathcal{P}$ whose type is a class; $p$, $q$, ... denote variables in $\mathcal{P}$ whose type is a pointer to a class (we will henceforth use the word "variables" to refer to variables as well as method parameters). In addition, $x$, $y$, ... will be used to denote expressions in $\mathcal{P}$. In the definitions that follow, $\mathit{TypeOf}(\mathcal{P}, x)$ denotes the type of expression $x$ in program $\mathcal{P}$.

### 2.1 Variables

Definition 2.1 below defines $\mathit{ClassVars}(\mathcal{P})$ and $\mathit{ClassPtrVars}(\mathcal{P})$ as the set of all variables in $\mathcal{P}$ whose type is a class, and a pointer to a class, respectively. *ClassPtrVars*($\mathcal{P}$) contains elements for variables that occur in declarations as well as elements for implicitly declared `this` pointers of methods. In order to distinguish between `this` pointers of different methods, the `this` pointer of method `A::f()` will be denoted by the fully qualified name of its method, i.e., `A::f`.

**Definition 2.1** *Let $\mathcal{P}$ be a program. Then, we define the sets of class-typed variables and the set of pointer-to-class-typed variables as follows:*

$$\begin{aligned}&\mathit{ClassVars}(\mathcal{P}) \triangleq\\ &\quad \{\, v \mid\ v \text{ is a variable/parameter in } \mathcal{P},\\ &\qquad\quad \mathit{TypeOf}(\mathcal{P}, v) = C, \text{ for some class } C \text{ in } \mathcal{P} \,\}\end{aligned}$$

$$\begin{aligned}&\mathit{ClassPtrVars}(\mathcal{P}) \triangleq\\ &\quad \{\, p \mid\ p \text{ is a variable/parameter in } \mathcal{P},\\ &\qquad\quad \mathit{TypeOf}(\mathcal{P}, *p) = C, \text{ for some class } C \text{ in } \mathcal{P} \,\}\end{aligned}$$

**Example 2.2** *For program $\mathcal{P}_2$ of Figure 2, we have:*

$$\begin{aligned}\mathit{ClassVars}(\mathcal{P}_2) &\equiv \{\, \texttt{a, b, c} \,\}\\ \mathit{ClassPtrVars}(\mathcal{P}_2) &\equiv \{\, \texttt{ap, A::f, A::g, B::g, C::f} \,\}\end{aligned}$$

□

## 2.2 Class members

For a given program $\mathcal{P}$, *Members*($\mathcal{P}$) denotes the set of unqualified names of the class members that occur in $\mathcal{P}$. In addition, the sets *DataMembers*($\mathcal{P}$), and *VirtualMethods*($\mathcal{P}$) contain the unqualified names of data members and virtual methods of $\mathcal{P}$, respectively. For convenience, we assume the intersection of *DataMembers*($\mathcal{P}$) and *VirtualMethods*($\mathcal{P}$) to be empty (if this is not the case, members can be renamed), and that there are no overloaded methods with the same name but different argument types (again, renaming is possible if this is not the case).

**Example 2.3** *For program $\mathcal{P}_2$ of Figure 2, we have:*

$$\begin{aligned}\mathit{DataMembers}(\mathcal{P}_2) &\equiv \{\, \texttt{x, y, z} \,\}\\ \mathit{VirtualMethods}(\mathcal{P}_2) &\equiv \{\, \texttt{f, g} \,\}\end{aligned}$$

□

## 2.3 Points-to analysis

We will need for each pointer-to-class-typed variable a conservative approximation of the set of class-typed variables that it may point to in some execution of $\mathcal{P}$. Any of several existing algorithms [7, 6, 16, 21, 19]) can be used to compute this information, and we do not make assumptions about the particular algorithm used to compute points-to information. Definition 2.4 uses the information supplied by some points-to analysis algorithm to construct a set *PointsTo*($\mathcal{P}$), which contains a pair $\langle p, v\rangle$ for each pointer $p$ that may point to a class-typed variable $v$.

**Definition 2.4** *Let $\mathcal{P}$ be a program. Then, the points-to information for $\mathcal{P}$ is defined as follows:*

$$\begin{aligned}\mathit{PointsTo}(\mathcal{P}) \triangleq \{\, \langle p, v\rangle \mid\ & p \in \mathit{ClassPtrVars}(\mathcal{P}),\\ & v \in \mathit{ClassVars}(\mathcal{P}),\\ & p \text{ may point to } v \,\}\end{aligned}$$

**Example 2.5** *We will use the following points-to information for program $\mathcal{P}_2$. Recall that $X{::}f$ denotes the `this` pointer of method $X{::}f()$.*

$$\begin{aligned}&\mathit{PointsTo}(\mathcal{P}_2) \equiv \{\\ &\quad \langle\texttt{ap, a}\rangle, \langle\texttt{ap, b}\rangle, \langle\texttt{ap, c}\rangle, \langle\texttt{A::f, a}\rangle, \langle\texttt{A::f, b}\rangle,\\ &\quad \langle\texttt{C::f, c}\rangle, \langle\texttt{A::g, a}\rangle, \langle\texttt{B::g, b}\rangle, \langle\texttt{B::g, c}\rangle \,\}\end{aligned}$$

□

Note that the following simple algorithm suffices to compute the information of Example 2.5: for each pointer $p$ of type $*X$, assume that it may point to any object of type $Y$, such that (i) $Y = X$ or $Y$ is a class transitively derived from $X$, and (ii) if $p$ is the `this` pointer of a virtual method $C{::}m$, no definitions of $m$ that override $C{::}m$ exist in class $Y$.

## 2.4 Assignments

Definition 2.6 below defines a set *Assignments*($\mathcal{P}$) that contains a pair of objects $\langle x', y'\rangle$ for each assignment $x = y$ that occurs in $\mathcal{P}$. For a *direct* call[3], *Assignments*($\mathcal{P}$) contains elements that model parameter-passing between corresponding formal and actual parameters whose type is a (pointer to a) class. The return value of a method is treated as an additional parameter as well if the method's return type is a class. For an *indirect* call $p \rightarrow f(y_1, \ldots, y_n)$, *Assignments*($\mathcal{P}$) contains elements that model the parameter-passing in the direct call $x.f(y_1, \ldots, y_n)$, for each $\langle p, x\rangle \in \mathit{PointsTo}(\mathcal{P})$.

**Definition 2.6** *Let $\mathcal{P}$ be a program. Then, the set of assignments between variables whose type is a (pointer to a) class is defined as follows:*

$$\begin{aligned}&\mathit{Assignments}(\mathcal{P}) \triangleq\\ &\quad \{\, \langle v, w\rangle \mid v = w \text{ occurs in } \mathcal{P},\ v,\ w \in \mathit{ClassVars}(\mathcal{P}) \,\} \cup\\ &\quad \{\, \langle *p, w\rangle \mid\ p = \&w \text{ occurs in } \mathcal{P},\ p \in \mathit{ClassPtrVars}(\mathcal{P}),\\ &\qquad\qquad w \in \mathit{ClassVars}(\mathcal{P}) \,\} \cup\\ &\quad \{\, \langle *p, *q\rangle \mid p = q \text{ occurs in } \mathcal{P},\ p,\ q \in \mathit{ClassPtrVars}(\mathcal{P}) \,\} \cup\\ &\quad \{\, \langle *p, w\rangle \mid *p = w \text{ occurs in } \mathcal{P},\ p \in \mathit{ClassPtrVars}(\mathcal{P}),\\ &\qquad\qquad w \in \mathit{ClassVars}(\mathcal{P}) \,\} \cup\\ &\quad \{\, \langle v, *q\rangle \mid\ v = *q \text{ occurs in } \mathcal{P},\ v \in \mathit{ClassVars}(\mathcal{P}),\\ &\qquad\qquad q \in \mathit{ClassPtrVars}(\mathcal{P}) \,\} \cup\\ &\quad \{\, \langle *p, *q\rangle \mid *p = *q \text{ occurs in } \mathcal{P},\ p,\ q \in \mathit{ClassPtrVars}(\mathcal{P}) \,\}\end{aligned}$$

**Example 2.7** *For program $\mathcal{P}_2$ of Figure 2, we have:*

$$\begin{aligned}&\mathit{Assignments}(\mathcal{P}_2) \equiv\\ &\quad \{\, \langle\texttt{*ap, a}\rangle, \langle\texttt{*ap, b}\rangle, \langle\texttt{*ap, c}\rangle, \langle\texttt{*A::f, a}\rangle, \langle\texttt{*A::f, b}\rangle,\\ &\qquad \langle\texttt{*C::f, c}\rangle, \langle\texttt{*A::g, a}\rangle, \langle\texttt{*B::g, b}\rangle, \langle\texttt{*B::g, c}\rangle \,\}\end{aligned}$$

□

## 2.5 Member access operations

Definition 2.8 below defines a set *MemberAccess*($\mathcal{P}$) of all pairs $\langle m, x\rangle$ such that $m$ is accessed from variable $x$. For an *indirect* call $p \rightarrow f(y_1, \ldots, y_n)$, we also include an element $\langle f, x\rangle$ in *MemberAccess*($\mathcal{P}$) for each $\langle p, x\rangle \in \mathit{PointsTo}(\mathcal{P})$.

[3] A *direct* call is an invocation of a virtual method from a non-pointer typed variable. An *indirect* call is an invocation of a virtual method from a pointer, which requires the virtual dispatch mechanism to be invoked.

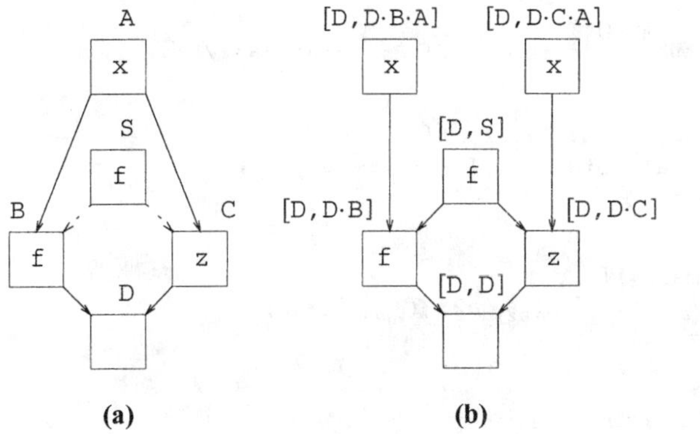


Figure 3: **(a)** Example class hierarchy graph. Solid edges indicate replicated (nonvirtual) inheritance. Dashed edges indicate virtual (i.e., shared) inheritance. **(b)** Subobject graph for type D in the class hierarchy of Figure 3(a).

**Definition 2.8** *Let $\mathcal{P}$ be a program. Then, the set of member access operations in $\mathcal{P}$ is defined as follows:*

$$
\begin{aligned}
&\mathit{MemberAccess}(\mathcal{P}) \triangleq \\
&\quad \{ \langle m, v\rangle \mid v.m \text{ occurs in } \mathcal{P},\ m \in \mathit{Members}(\mathcal{P}),\\
&\qquad v \in \mathit{ClassVars}(\mathcal{P}) \} \cup\\
&\quad \{ \langle m, *p\rangle \mid p \rightarrow m \text{ occurs in } \mathcal{P},\ m \in \mathit{Members}(\mathcal{P}),\\
&\qquad p \in \mathit{ClassPtrVars}(\mathcal{P}) \} \cup\\
&\quad \{ \langle m, x\rangle \mid p \rightarrow m \text{ occurs in } \mathcal{P},\ m \in \mathit{VirtualMethods}(\mathcal{P}),\\
&\qquad \langle p, x\rangle \in \mathit{PointsTo}(\mathcal{P}) \}
\end{aligned}
$$

**Example 2.9** *For program $\mathcal{P}_2$ of Figure 2, we have:*

$$
\begin{aligned}
&\mathit{MemberAccess}(\mathcal{P}_2) \equiv\\
&\quad \{ \langle \mathtt{x}, *\mathtt{A::g}\rangle, \langle \mathtt{y}, *\mathtt{B::g}\rangle, \langle \mathtt{z}, *\mathtt{C::f}\rangle, \langle \mathtt{g}, *\mathtt{A::f}\rangle, \langle \mathtt{g}, *\mathtt{C::f}\rangle,\\
&\qquad \langle \mathtt{f}, *\mathtt{ap}\rangle, \langle \mathtt{f}, \mathtt{a}\rangle, \langle \mathtt{f}, \mathtt{b}\rangle, \langle \mathtt{f}, \mathtt{c}\rangle, \langle \mathtt{g}, \mathtt{a}\rangle, \langle \mathtt{g}, \mathtt{b}\rangle, \langle \mathtt{g}, \mathtt{c}\rangle \}
\end{aligned}
$$

□

## 3 Phase II: Computing Type Constraints

In Phase II of the specialization algorithm, a set of *type constraints* is determined. These constraints precisely characterize the subtype-relationships between the types of variables that must be preserved in the specialized class hierarchy.

### 3.1 Member lookup and subobject graphs

The subsequent definitions of type constraints must precisely reflect the semantics of member lookup. In the presence of multiple inheritance, an object may contain multiple subobjects of a given type $C$, and hence multiple members $C::m$. In order to distinguish correctly between these subobjects and members with the same name, we need to keep track of the subobjects selected by the execution of member lookup and typecast operations. To this end, we use the formalization of subobject graphs and member lookup of [18, 23]. Here, we present this model informally; the reader is referred to [23] for details. An efficient algorithm for performing member lookups can be found in [17].

A subobject graph can be viewed as an abstract representation of the layout of an object. The subobject graph contains a distinct subgraph for each type in the class hierarchy; in what follows, we will ignore the distinction between the entire subobject graph, and the subgraph for a specific type. Figure 3(a) depicts a class hierarchy in which a class D inherits nonvirtually (replicated) from classes B and C, and classes B and C both inherit virtually (shared) from class S, and nonvirtually (replicated) from class A. Class A contains a member x, S and B contain a member f, and C contains a member z.

Figure 3(b) shows the subobject graph for D. The nodes in this graph are identified by a pair $[Y, X_1 \cdots X_n]$ where the first component, $Y$, indicates the most derived type of the subobject, and the second component is a sequence of class names, $X_1 \cdots X_n$, that uniquely identifies a subobject of type $X_n$ inside $Y$. For a subobject $\sigma \equiv [Y, X_1 \cdots X_n]$, $\mathit{mdc}(\sigma)$ denotes its most derived class $Y$, and $\mathit{ldc}(\sigma)$ denotes its least derived class $X_n$. We will say that a member $m$ occurs in subobject $\sigma$ if $m$ occurs in its least derived class $\mathit{ldc}(\sigma)$. Edges in the subobject graph of Figure 3(b) reflect the *containment* relation '$<$' between subobjects[4]. In what follows, $\Sigma(\gamma)$ denotes the set of all subobjects $\sigma$ for class hierarchy $\gamma$.

In the example of Figure 3(b), subobject [D,D] indicates the "full" D object, and subobject [D,D·B] indicates the B subobject contained in [D,D]; in other words, we have that:

$$[\mathtt{D,D\cdot B}] < [\mathtt{D,D}]$$

Due to the virtual inheritance, [D,D] contains a single shared S-subobject: [D,S]. By contrast, since B and C inherit nonvirtually (replicated) from A, [D,D] contains two distinct A-subobjects [D,D·B·A] and [D,D·C·A], each containing a distinct x.

Using the subobject graph, member lookup and typecast operations can be defined as functions from subobjects to subobjects. We will only discuss *static-lookup* and *typecast* here, which are functions that model static[5] member lookups and typecasts, respectively. Dynamic member lookups can be modeled similarly [23].

Static member lookups are modeled by way of a function *static-lookup* whose arguments are: (i) an initial subobject $\sigma$, (ii) a member $m$, and (iii) the containment relation '$<$' between subobjects. *static-lookup* returns the subobject $\sigma'$ in which the accessed member is located. As an example, we study a static lookup for an expression $e.m$ or $e \rightarrow m$ that occurs in program $\mathcal{P}$. First, an *initial subobject* $\sigma$ is associated with receiver $e$. For a static lookup, this initial subobject is simply $[T,T]$, where $T \equiv \mathit{TypeOf}(\mathcal{P}, e)$. Then, *static-lookup* determines the unique subobject $\sigma'$ such that (i) $\sigma' \leq^* \sigma$, (ii) $\sigma'$ contains member $m$, and (iii) if there is a $\sigma'' < \sigma$ that contains a member $m$, then $\sigma'' \leq^* \sigma'$ (here, '$\leq^*$' denotes the transitive and reflexive closure of '$<$').

As an example, suppose that there is a lookup d.z, where d is an object of type D. In this case, the initial subobject is [D,D], and there is one visible definition for z in subobject [D,D·C]. Consequently, the lookup function returns subobject [D,D·C] indicating that member z in the [D,D·C]-subobject of D is accessed. In other words, we have that:

$$\mathit{static\text{-}lookup}([\mathtt{D,D}], \mathtt{z}, `<`) \equiv [\mathtt{D,D\cdot C}]$$

Typecasts can be modeled as follows. For a cast from type $X$ to type $Y$ (in the present paper, we only allow the case where $Y$ is a transitive base class of $X$), the unique subobject $\sigma' \leq^* [X,X]$ for which we have that $\mathit{ldc}(\sigma') \equiv Y$ is selected. For example, suppose that the program contains an assignment b = d, where b is of type B and d is of type D, respectively. For this assignment, the compiler

[4] In the present paper, we define the contained subobject to be "less than" the containing subobject. We believe this notation to be more intuitive than that of [18, 23], where the contained subobject is "greater than" the containing subobject.

[5] We call a member lookup *static* if it corresponds to a data member access or a direct method call and *dynamic* if it corresponds to a method call that invokes the virtual dispatch mechanism.

```
class A {
  virtual void foo(){ this->x = 17; };
  int x;
};

void main(){
  A a1; A a2; A *ap;
  ap = &a1;
  *ap = a2;
  ap->foo();
  int result = a1.x;
}
```

**(a)**

```
class T_var(a2) {
  virtual void foo(); /* declaration */
};

class T_var(a1) : T_var(a2) {
  virtual void foo(){ this->x = 17; };
  int x;
};

void main(){
  T_var(a1) a1; T_var(a2) a2; T_var(a2) *ap;
  ap = &a1;
  *ap = a2;
  ap->foo();
  int result = a1.x;
}
```

**(b)**

Figure 4: **(a)** Example program illustrating the purpose of distinguishing between method declarations and method definitions. **(b)** Specialized program and class hierarchy for the program of **(a)**.

generates a typecast from type D to type B. For this typecast, we have that:

$$\textit{typecast}([\texttt{D},\texttt{D}]\,,\texttt{B},\text{`}<\text{'}) \equiv [\texttt{D},\texttt{D}{\cdot}\texttt{B}]$$

This implies that the assignment copies the [D,D·B]-subobject of d into b.

We conclude the discussion of subobjects by introducing a composition operator '$\oplus$'. Intuitively, this operator determines the subobject of a subobject. E.g., $[\texttt{D},\texttt{D}{\cdot}\texttt{B}] \oplus [\texttt{B},\texttt{B}{\cdot}\texttt{A}] \equiv [\texttt{D},\texttt{D}{\cdot}\texttt{B}{\cdot}\texttt{A}]$.

## 3.2 Declarations vs. definitions of members

We will distinguish between declarations and definitions of members. A method's *definition* models its implementation, which has a `this` pointer from which other members may be accessed. The *declaration* of a method has the sole purpose of ensuring visibility. This distinction is important because it enables elimination of spurious dependences in the presence of virtual method calls.

Figure 4 illustrates this issue by way of a simple program that uses two class-typed variables a1 and a2, and a class-pointer-typed variable ap that may point to a1, but not to a2. We will now informally discuss the type constraints induced by this program, and how the distinction between declarations and definitions of methods can be exploited to obtain a specialized class hierarchy. For convenience, we will frequently write "member $m$ must be visible/accessible[6] to variable $x$" instead of "member $m$ must be visible/accessible from the type of variable $x$" in the sequel.

Clearly, the type of ap must be a base class of the types of a1 and a2. Otherwise, the assignments ap = &a1 and *ap = a2 would not be type-correct. Since virtual method foo() is called from ap, a *declaration* of foo() must be visible to ap, and since ap may point to a1, the *definition* of A::foo() must be visible to a1. Data member x must be visible to A::foo because it is accessed from A::foo (recall that A::foo denotes the `this` pointer of method A::foo()). However, note that x need not be visible to a2. In fact, it is *undesirable* for A::foo's *definition* to be visible to ap, because that forces inclusion of x in a2.

Figure 4(b) shows the specialized program and class hierarchy for the example of Figure 4(a). Note that, while the above constraints are met, data member x has been eliminated from a2.

In the sequel, $\textit{def}(A{::}m)$ denotes the definition of member $A{::}m$, whereas $\textit{decl}(A{::}m)$ denotes its declaration. As the example of Figure 4 illustrates, it is useful to separate the declaration from the definition of virtual methods. Since a data member cannot access any other class members, we treat data members as if they only have declarations. (For nonvirtual methods, which are not treated in the present paper, distinguishing between declaration and definition is not useful, and only a definition is required.)

[6] Since we ignore access rights of members and inheritance relations in the present paper, the notions of "visible" and "accessible" are equivalent.

## 3.3 Type constraints and constraint elements

Type constraints are of the form $\langle s, \sigma, t\rangle$, where $\sigma$ is a subobject of the original class hierarchy, and $s$ and $t$ are *constraint elements*, as defined by Definition 3.1 below.

**Definition 3.1** *Let $\mathcal{P}$ be a program. Then, the set of constraint elements for $\mathcal{P}$ is defined as follows:*

$$\begin{aligned}\textit{Elems}(\mathcal{P}) \triangleq\ & \{\ \textit{var}(v) \mid v \in \textit{ClassVars}(\mathcal{P})\ \} \cup \\ & \{\ \textit{var}(*p) \mid\ p \in \textit{ClassPtrVars}(\mathcal{P}), \\ & \qquad p \textit{ is not a method's } \texttt{this} \textit{ pointer}\ \} \cup \\ & \{\ \textit{decl}(X{::}m) \mid\ m \in \textit{Members}(\mathcal{P}), \\ & \qquad m \textit{ occurs in class } X\ \} \cup \\ & \{\ \textit{def}(X{::}m) \mid\ m \in \textit{VirtualMethods}(\mathcal{P}), \\ & \qquad m \textit{ occurs in class } X\ \}\end{aligned}$$

**Example 3.2** *For program $\mathcal{P}_2$ of Figure 2, we have:*

$$\begin{aligned}\textit{Elems}(\mathcal{P}_2) \equiv \{\ & \textit{var}(\texttt{a}),\ \textit{var}(\texttt{b}),\ \textit{var}(\texttt{c}),\ \textit{var}(\texttt{*ap}),\ \textit{decl}(\texttt{A::x}), \\ & \textit{decl}(\texttt{B::y}),\ \textit{decl}(\texttt{C::z}),\ \textit{decl}(\texttt{A::f}),\ \textit{decl}(\texttt{A::g}), \\ & \textit{decl}(\texttt{B::g}),\ \textit{decl}(\texttt{C::f}),\ \textit{def}(\texttt{A::f}),\ \textit{def}(\texttt{A::g}), \\ & \textit{def}(\texttt{B::g}),\ \textit{def}(\texttt{C::f})\ \}\end{aligned}$$

□

Type constraints express subtype-relationships between constraint elements. For example, $\langle \textit{var}(v), \sigma, \textit{var}(w)\rangle$ states that $v$ has the same type as the $\sigma$-subobject of the type of $w$. Type constraints will also be used to express the "locations" of member declarations/definitions in objects. For example, the constraint $\langle \textit{decl}(A{::}m), \sigma, \textit{var}(w)\rangle$ expresses the fact that the declaration of member $A{::}m$ occurs in the $\sigma$-subobject of the type of $w$.

For reasons we will discuss shortly, `this` pointers of methods will require somewhat special treatment. Definition 3.3 below maps a variable $v$ in the program to a constraint element $\textit{var}(v)$ if $v$ is not the `this` pointer of a method, and to $\textit{def}(A{::}m)$ if $v$ is the `this` pointer of some method $A{::}m$.

**Definition 3.3** *Let $x$ be an expression such that $x \equiv v$ for some $v \in ClassVars(\mathcal{P})$ or $x \equiv *p$ for some $p \in ClassPtrVars(\mathcal{P})$. Then, the constraint element associated with $x$ is defined as follows:*

$$Elem(x) \triangleq \begin{cases} def(X::f) & \text{when } x \equiv *X::f, \\ & \text{for some method } X::f() \\ var(x) & \text{otherwise} \end{cases}$$

**Example 3.4** *For program $\mathcal{P}_2$, we have $Elem(\mathtt{a}) \equiv var(\mathtt{a})$ and $Elem(\mathtt{*A::f}) \equiv def(\mathtt{A::f})$.* □

## 3.4 Type constraints due to assignments

Consider an assignment $v = w$, where $v$ is of class type $V$ and $w$ of class type $W$. This assignment is only type-correct if [W,W] contains a unique subobject $\sigma \equiv [W,\alpha{\cdot}V]$, where $\alpha$ is some (possibly empty) sequence of class names. This subobject $\sigma$ can be defined as $\sigma \equiv typecast([W,W], V, \text{'<'})$. Definition 3.5 below defines the set of type constraints implied by assignments. These constraints are of the form $\langle var(x), \sigma, var(y)\rangle$, which can be interpreted as '$x$ must have the same type as the $\sigma$-subobject of $y$', and $\langle def(A::f), \sigma, var(y)\rangle$ which can be interpreted as 'the `this` pointer of method $A::f$ must have the same type as the $\sigma$-subobject of $y$'.

**Definition 3.5** *Let $\mathcal{P}$ be a program. Then, the set of type constraints due to assignments is defined as follows:*

$$\begin{aligned} AssignTC(\mathcal{P}) \triangleq \{\ & \langle Elem(x), \sigma, Elem(y)\rangle \mid \\ & \langle x, y\rangle \in Assignments(\mathcal{P}), \\ & X = TypeOf(\mathcal{P}, x),\ Y = TypeOf(\mathcal{P}, y), \\ & \sigma = typecast([Y,Y], X, \text{'<'})\ \} \end{aligned}$$

**Example 3.6** *For program $\mathcal{P}_2$ of Figure 2, we have:*

$AssignTC(\mathcal{P}_2) \equiv \{$
$\langle var(\mathtt{*ap}), [\mathtt{A,A}], var(\mathtt{a})\rangle$, $\langle var(\mathtt{*ap}), [\mathtt{B,B{\cdot}A}], var(\mathtt{b})\rangle$,
$\langle var(\mathtt{*ap}), [\mathtt{C,C{\cdot}B{\cdot}A}], var(\mathtt{c})\rangle$, $\langle def(\mathtt{A::f}), [\mathtt{A,A}], var(\mathtt{a})\rangle$,
$\langle def(\mathtt{A::f}), [\mathtt{B,B{\cdot}A}], var(\mathtt{b})\rangle$, $\langle def(\mathtt{C::f}), [\mathtt{C,C}], var(\mathtt{c})\rangle$,
$\langle def(\mathtt{A::g}), [\mathtt{A,A}], var(\mathtt{a})\rangle$, $\langle def(\mathtt{B::g}), [\mathtt{B,B}], var(\mathtt{b})\rangle$,
$\langle def(\mathtt{B::g}), [\mathtt{C,C{\cdot}B}], var(\mathtt{c})\rangle$ $\}$

□

## 3.5 Type constraints due to member access

Definition 3.7 below defines the set of type constraints due to member access. The definition has two cases. The first case deals with situations where only a method declaration is needed, i.e., when the accessed member $m$ is a data member, or a virtual method that is invoked from a pointer $p$. The second case addresses the situation where $m$'s definition is required, i.e., when a virtual method is invoked from a nonpointer variable $v$. As an example, consider the case where a virtual method $m$ is accessed from a pointer $p$. Assuming that $p$ has type $*Y$, there must be a unique subobject $\sigma \equiv [Y,\alpha{\cdot}X] \equiv static\text{-}lookup([Y,Y], m, \text{'<'})$ such that $X$ contains $m$. Since the virtual dispatch mechanism only requires that a *declaration* of $m$ be present in class $X$, a constraint $\langle decl(X::m), \sigma, var(*p)\rangle$ is constructed, expressing the fact that the $\sigma$-subobject of $*p$ must contain a declaration of method $X::m()$.

**Definition 3.7** *Let $\mathcal{P}$ be a program. Then, the set of type constraints due to member access operations is defined as follows:*

$$\begin{aligned} & MemberAccessTC(\mathcal{P}) \triangleq \\ & \quad \{\ \langle decl(X::m), \sigma, Elem(y)\rangle \mid Y \equiv TypeOf(\mathcal{P}, y), \\ & \qquad \langle m, y\rangle \in MemberAccess(\mathcal{P}), \\ & \qquad (y \equiv *p \text{ for some } p \in ClassPtrVars(\mathcal{P}) \\ & \qquad\quad \text{or } m \in DataMembers(\mathcal{P})), \\ & \qquad \sigma \equiv [Y,\alpha{\cdot}X] \equiv static\text{-}lookup([Y,Y], m, \text{'<'})\ \} \cup \\ & \quad \{\ \langle def(X::m), \sigma, var(y)\rangle \mid Y \equiv TypeOf(\mathcal{P}, y), \\ & \qquad \langle m, y\rangle \in MemberAccess(\mathcal{P}), \\ & \qquad (y \equiv v \text{ for some } v \in ClassVars(\mathcal{P}) \\ & \qquad\quad \text{and } m \in VirtualMethods(\mathcal{P})), \\ & \qquad \sigma \equiv [Y,\alpha{\cdot}X] \equiv static\text{-}lookup([Y,Y], m, \text{'<'})\ \} \end{aligned}$$

**Example 3.8** *For program $\mathcal{P}_2$ of Figure 2, we have:*

$MemberAccessTC(\mathcal{P}_2) \equiv \{$
$\langle decl(\mathtt{A::x}), [\mathtt{A,A}], def(\mathtt{A::g})\rangle$, $\langle decl(\mathtt{B::y}), [\mathtt{B,B}], def(\mathtt{B::g})\rangle$,
$\langle decl(\mathtt{C::z}), [\mathtt{C,C}], def(\mathtt{C::f})\rangle$, $\langle decl(\mathtt{A::g}), [\mathtt{A,A}], def(\mathtt{A::f})\rangle$,
$\langle decl(\mathtt{B::g}), [\mathtt{C,C{\cdot}B}], def(\mathtt{C::f})\rangle$, $\langle decl(\mathtt{A::f}), [\mathtt{A,A}], var(\mathtt{*ap})\rangle$,
$\langle def(\mathtt{A::f}), [\mathtt{A,A}], var(\mathtt{a})\rangle$, $\langle def(\mathtt{A::f}), [\mathtt{B,B{\cdot}A}], var(\mathtt{b})\rangle$,
$\langle def(\mathtt{C::f}), [\mathtt{C,C}], var(\mathtt{c})\rangle$, $\langle def(\mathtt{A::g}), [\mathtt{A,A}], var(\mathtt{a})\rangle$,
$\langle def(\mathtt{B::g}), [\mathtt{B,B}], var(\mathtt{b})\rangle$, $\langle def(\mathtt{B::g}), [\mathtt{C,C{\cdot}B}], var(\mathtt{c})\rangle$ $\}$

□

## 3.6 Treatment of `this` pointers

We now return to the issue of modeling `this` pointers of methods. The definitions presented above were designed with the following properties in mind:

- The treatment of `this` pointers is analogous to that of other (class-typed and pointer-to-class-typed) parameters. Both are modeled as assignments.
- Method declarations and method definitions are modeled in similar ways.
- Since the type of a `this` pointer is determined by the location of the associated method in the class hierarchy, any constraint involving the `this` pointer of some method $C::f()$ is effectively a constraint on the location of $C::f()$ in the hierarchy.

We obtain the desired properties by mapping `this` pointers to constraint elements for the associated method definitions (see Definition 3.3). As a result, assignments and member access operations involving `this` pointers give rise to constraints involving the associated method definition. For example, the access to data member `x` from `A::g`'s `this` pointer gives rise to the type constraint $\langle decl(\mathtt{A::x}), [\mathtt{A,A}], def(\mathtt{A::g})\rangle$, which can be interpreted as 'the declaration of `A::x` occurs in the [A,A]-subobject of the type containing the definition of method `A::g`.

Modeling parameter-passing of `this` pointers as assignments is consistent with the treatment of other parameters, but there is a slight drawback: identical type constraints occur in $AssignTC(\mathcal{P})$ and $MemberAccessTC(\mathcal{P})$. For example, the constraint $\langle def(\mathtt{A::f}), [\mathtt{A,A}], var(\mathtt{a})\rangle$ occurs in both $AssignTC(\mathcal{P}_2)$ and $MemberAccessTC(\mathcal{P}_2)$ (see Examples 3.6 and 3.8). Although it is possible to eliminate this duplication of type constraints by modifying the definitions slightly, we consider the present solution to be the most consistent approach. The presence of duplicate type constraints is harmless in the sense that it does not have an effect on the specialized class hierarchy.

## 3.7 Type constraints for preserving dominance

Definition 3.9 introduces a set of type constraints that model hiding/dominance relations between declarations and definitions of members with the same name. Informally, the definition states that if there are classes $A$ and $B$ in the original hierarchy that both define a member $m$, $A \neq B$, and $A$ is a transitive base class of $B$ then $def(A::m)$ must be contained in the $\sigma''$-subobject of $def(B::m)$. Similar relationships are constructed for cases where $A$ and $B$ both contain a declaration of a member, and where $A$ contains a declaration and $B$ a definition (in the latter case, a constraint is also constructed if $A = B$). These type constraints are used in Phase III to ensure that member lookup behavior is preserved in cases where multiple declarations/definitions of a member $m$ are visible to a variable.

**Definition 3.9** *Let $\mathcal{P}$ be a program. Then, the set of type constraints that reflect the hiding/dominance relations between same-named members in the original hierarchy is defined as follows:*

$$
\begin{aligned}
&\mathit{DominanceTC}(\mathcal{P}) \triangleq \\
&\quad \{ \ \langle decl(A::m), \sigma, def(B::m)\rangle \mid \\
&\qquad A = B \text{ or } A \text{ is a transitive base class of } B, \\
&\qquad \text{class } A \text{ contains a declaration of member } m, \\
&\qquad \text{class } B \text{ contains a definition of member } m, \\
&\qquad \sigma \equiv typecast([B,B], A, `<') \} \cup \\
&\quad \{ \ \langle decl(A::m), \sigma, decl(B::m)\rangle \mid \\
&\qquad A \neq B, \ A \text{ is a transitive base class of } B, \\
&\qquad \text{class } A \text{ contains a declaration of member } m, \\
&\qquad \text{class } B \text{ contains a declaration of member } m, \\
&\qquad \sigma \equiv typecast([B,B], A, `<') \} \cup \\
&\quad \{ \ \langle def(A::m), \sigma, def(B::m)\rangle \mid \\
&\qquad A \neq B, \ A \text{ is a transitive base class of } B, \\
&\qquad \text{class } A \text{ contains a definition of member } m, \\
&\qquad \text{class } B \text{ contains a definition of member } m, \\
&\qquad \sigma \equiv typecast([B,B], A, `<') \}
\end{aligned}
$$

**Example 3.10** *For program $\mathcal{P}_2$ of Figure 2, we have:*

$$
\begin{aligned}
&\mathit{DominanceTC}(\mathcal{P}_2) \equiv \{ \\
&\quad \langle def(\texttt{A::f}), [\texttt{C,C}\cdot\texttt{B}\cdot\texttt{A}], def(\texttt{C::f})\rangle, \\
&\quad \langle def(\texttt{A::g}), [\texttt{B,B}\cdot\texttt{A}], def(\texttt{B::g})\rangle, \\
&\quad \langle decl(\texttt{A::f}), [\texttt{C,C}\cdot\texttt{B}\cdot\texttt{A}], decl(\texttt{C::f})\rangle, \\
&\quad \langle decl(\texttt{A::g}), [\texttt{B,B}\cdot\texttt{A}], decl(\texttt{B::g})\rangle, \\
&\quad \langle decl(\texttt{A::f}), [\texttt{A,A}], def(\texttt{A::f})\rangle, \\
&\quad \langle decl(\texttt{A::f}), [\texttt{C,C}\cdot\texttt{B}\cdot\texttt{A}], def(\texttt{C::f})\rangle, \\
&\quad \langle decl(\texttt{A::g}), [\texttt{A,A}], def(\texttt{A::g})\rangle, \\
&\quad \langle decl(\texttt{A::g}), [\texttt{B,B}\cdot\texttt{A}], def(\texttt{B::g})\rangle, \\
&\quad \langle decl(\texttt{B::g}), [\texttt{B,B}], def(\texttt{B::g})\rangle, \\
&\quad \langle decl(\texttt{C::f}), [\texttt{C,C}], def(\texttt{C::f})\rangle \}
\end{aligned}
$$

□

# 4 Phase III: Generating a Specialized Hierarchy

In Phase III, a subobject graph for the specialized class hierarchy is constructed. Then, the specialized hierarchy itself is derived from the new subobject graph, and variable declarations in the program are updated to take the new hierarchy into account.

## 4.1 Classes of the specialized hierarchy

Definition 4.1 below defines the types of the specialized class hierarchy. The specialized hierarchy contains a class $T_e$, for each constraint element $e$ in *Elems*($\mathcal{P}$) (see Definition 3.1).

**Definition 4.1** *Let $\mathcal{P}$ be a program. Then, the classes of the specialized class hierarchy are defined as follows:*

$$\mathit{NewClasses}(\mathcal{P}) \triangleq \{ \, T_e \mid e \in \mathit{Elems}(\mathcal{P}) \, \}$$

**Example 4.2** *For program $\mathcal{P}_2$ of Figure 2, we have:*

$$
\begin{aligned}
&\mathit{NewClasses}(\mathcal{P}_2) \equiv \{ \\
&\quad T_{var(\texttt{a})}, T_{var(\texttt{b})}, T_{var(\texttt{c})}, T_{var(\texttt{*ap})}, T_{decl(\texttt{A::x})}, T_{decl(\texttt{B::y})}, \\
&\quad T_{decl(\texttt{C::z})}, T_{decl(\texttt{A::f})}, T_{decl(\texttt{A::g})}, T_{decl(\texttt{B::g})}, T_{decl(\texttt{C::f})}, \\
&\quad T_{def(\texttt{A::f})}, T_{def(\texttt{A::g})}, T_{def(\texttt{B::g})}, T_{def(\texttt{C::f})} \ \}
\end{aligned}
$$

□

## 4.2 The specialized subobject graph

Definitions 4.3 through 4.6 below together define the subobject graph $\langle N, \sqsubset \rangle$ of the specialized class hierarchy as a set of nodes $N$ on which a containment ordering '$\sqsubset$' is defined. In the following definitions $s$, $t$, and $u$ denote constraint elements in *Elems*($\mathcal{P}$).

Definition 4.3 uses the type constraints in *AssignTC*($\mathcal{P}$) and *MemberAccessTC*($\mathcal{P}$) to construct the set of nodes $N$ of the specialized subobject graph.

**Definition 4.3** *Let $\mathcal{P}$ be a program. Then, the set of nodes $N$ of the specialized subobject graph is inductively defined as follows:*

$$
\begin{aligned}
&T_{var(v),\sigma,var(v)} \in N \ \ when \\
&\quad v \in \mathit{ClassVars}(\mathcal{P}), \ V \equiv \mathit{TypeOf}(\mathcal{P}, v), \ \sigma \equiv [V,V]
\end{aligned}
$$

$$
\begin{aligned}
&T_{s,\sigma_2 \oplus \sigma_1,u} \in N \ \ when \ T_{t,\sigma_2,u} \in N, \\
&\quad \langle s, \sigma_1, t\rangle \in (\mathit{AssignTC}(\mathcal{P}) \cup \mathit{MemberAccessTC}(\mathcal{P}))
\end{aligned}
$$

Definition 4.4 below defines the most derived class and the least derived class for nodes in $N$.

**Definition 4.4** *Let $n \equiv T_{s,\sigma,u}$ be a node in $N$. Then, we define the most derived class* mdc($n$) *of $n$ and the least derived class* ldc($n$) *of $n$ as follows:*

$$ldc(T_{s,\sigma,u}) \triangleq T_s \quad mdc(T_{s,\sigma,u}) \triangleq T_u$$

Definition 4.5 below defines a mapping from subobjects in the specialized class hierarchy to subobjects in the original class hierarchy.

**Definition 4.5** *Let $N$ be the set of nodes of the specialized subobject graph. Then, we define a function $\psi$ that maps nodes in $N$ to subobjects in the original subobject graph as follows:*

$$\psi(T_{s,\sigma,u}) \triangleq \sigma, \ where \ T_{s,\sigma,u} \in N$$

Definition 4.6 below defines a relation '$\sqsubset$' on subobjects in $N$. The '$\oplus$' operator used in this definition was introduced in Section 3.1. The inclusion-relationships (cf. subtype-relationships) between the nodes in $N$ are determined by the constraints in *AssignTC*($\mathcal{P}$), *MemberAccessTC*($\mathcal{P}$), as well as those in *DominanceTC*($\mathcal{P}$). This approach has the effect of selecting the appropriate subset of dominance relationships from *DominanceTC*($\mathcal{P}$) that is needed to preserve the behavior of typecasts and member lookups in $\mathcal{P}$.

**Definition 4.6** *Let $N$ be the set of nodes in the new subobject graph. Then, the containment ordering '$\sqsubset$' on subobjects in $N$ is defined as follows: For nodes $n$, $n' \in N$ we have that:*

$$
\begin{aligned}
n \sqsubset n' \ \ when \ \ & \psi(n) = \psi(n') \oplus \sigma, \\
& T_s \equiv ldc(n), \ T_t \equiv ldc(n'), \\
& \langle s, \sigma, t\rangle \in ( \ \mathit{AssignTC}(\mathcal{P}) \cup \\
& \qquad \mathit{MemberAccessTC}(\mathcal{P}) \cup \\
& \qquad \mathit{DominanceTC}(\mathcal{P}) \ )
\end{aligned}
$$

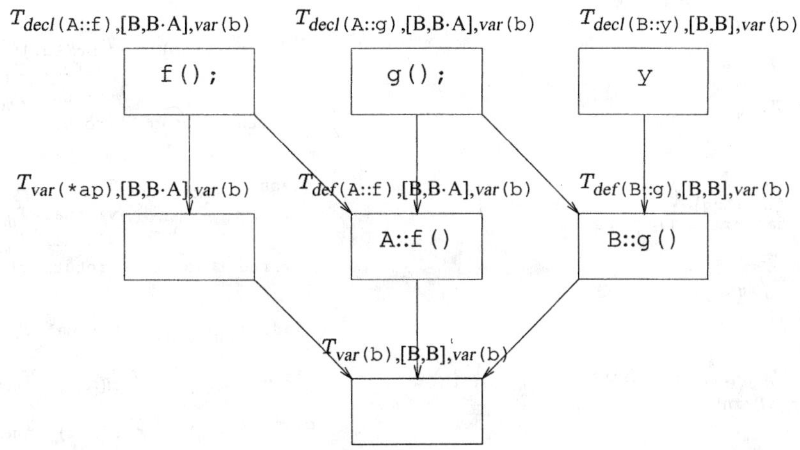


Figure 5: Specialized subobject graph for object b of example program $\mathcal{P}_2$ of Figure 2.

Figure 5 shows the specialized subobject graph for object b. Nodes in this graph correspond to subobjects in the specialized subobject graph, and edges in the graph reflect the '$\sqsubset$'-containment relation between nodes.

## 4.3 The specialized class hierarchy

We already defined the set of classes of the specialized class hierarchy in Section 4.1. In this section, we complete the construction of the specialized hierarchy by defining the members of these classes, and the inheritance relationships among these classes, using the subobject graph $\langle N, \sqsubset \rangle$ that was constructed in Section 4.2:

1. Class $T_{var(x)}$ does not contain any members.
2. Class $T_{decl(X::m)}$ contains a declaration of member $m$, similar to the declaration of $m$ in class $X$ of the original hierarchy.
3. Class $T_{def(X::m)}$ contains a definition of member $m$, similar to the definition of $m$ in class $X$ of the original hierarchy.
4. For two subobjects $n$, $n' \in N$ such that $n \sqsubset n'$, class $ldc(n)$ is an immediate base class of class $ldc(n')$. This inheritance relation is virtual if: (i) there is a node $n_1 \in N$ such that $ldc(n_1) \equiv ldc(n)$, (ii) $n_1 \sqsubset n_2$, for some $n_2 \in N$ with $ldc(n_2) \equiv ldc(n')$, (iii) $n_1 \sqsubset n_3$, for some $n_3 \in N$ such that $n_3 \neq n_2$, and (iv) $n_2 \sqsubset^* n_4$ and $n_3 \sqsubset^* n_4$, for some $n_4$ in $N$. Otherwise, the inheritance relation is nonvirtual.

## 4.4 Updating variable declarations

The final part of Phase III consists of updating the declarations in the program in order to reflect the new class hierarchy. This is accomplished by giving type $T_{var(v)}$ to each variable $v$ in *ClassVars*($\mathcal{P}$), and type $*T_{var(p)}$ to each variable $p$ in *ClassPtrVars*($\mathcal{P}$) which is not the `this` pointer of a method. The type of a `this` pointer is determined by the location of the associated method definition in the hierarchy; no declaration needs to be updated in this case.

## 4.5 Example

Figure 6 shows the new program and hierarchy that are constructed for program $\mathcal{P}_2$ of Figure 2. The behavior of this program is identical to that of the original program, and the reader may verify that certain members have been eliminated from certain objects, e.g., objects b and c no longer contain member x. However, due to an abundance of virtual inheritance in the transformed hierarchy, the objects in the transformed program may have become larger than before the transformation (virtual inheritance increases member access time, and may increase object size). Assuming that the object model of the IBM `xlC` C++ compiler would be used, object a would now be 52 bytes (was 8), object b would be 68 bytes (was 12), and object c 76 bytes (was 16).

Phase IV of the algorithm addresses this problem by applying a set of transformation rules that simplify the class hierarchy, and reduce object size by eliminating virtual inheritance. These transformations are discussed in Section 5.

## 4.6 Representability issues

There are two kinds of situations in which the specialization algorithm generates inheritance structures that cannot be represented directly in terms of the inheritance mechanisms of $\mathcal{L}$ (or C++).

The first kind of situation that gives rise to an irrepresentable inheritance structure arises in the presence of a set of assignments of the form:

$$x_1 = x_2;\ x_2 = x_3;\ \ldots;\ x_{n-1} = x_n;\ x_n = x_1$$

(the same situation arises in the presence of recursive method calls). Each assignment $x_i = x_{i+1}$ implies that the type of $x_i$ is a base class of the type of $x_{i+1}$. Since the assignment $x_n = x_1$ implies that the type of $x_n$ is a base of the type of $x_1$, there will be a cycle in the inheritance graph unless precautions are taken.

Another situation that leads to irrepresentable inheritance structures has to do with the fact that the specialization may effectively transform any replicated subobject into a shared subobject. In the presence of nonvirtual multiple inheritance, this may give rise to multiple, distinct shared subobjects of the same type—something that cannot be expressed in terms of the inheritance mechanisms of $\mathcal{L}$ (or C++). Figure 7(a) shows a program that illustrates this situation. Note that the specialized subobject graph for this program, shown in Figure 7(b), contains two distinct nodes $T_{decl}$(A::x),[D,D·B·A],var(d) and $T_{decl}$(A::x),[D,D·C·A],var(d)

```
class T_decl(A::x) {
  int x;
};

class T_decl(A::f) {
  virtual int f();
};

class T_decl(A::g) {
  virtual int g();
};

class T_decl(B::y) {
  int y;
};

class T_decl(B::g) :  virtual T_decl(A::g) {
  virtual int g();
};

class T_decl(C::z) {
  int z;
};

class T_def(A::g) :  T_decl(A::x), virtual T_decl(A::g) {
  virtual int g(){ return x; };
};

class T_def(A::f) :  virtual T_decl(A::g),
                     virtual T_decl(A::f) {
  virtual int f(){ return g(); };
};

class T_def(B::g) :  T_decl(B::y),
                     virtual T_decl(A::g),
                     virtual T_decl(B::g) {
  virtual int g(){ return y; };
};

class T_def(C::f) :  T_decl(C::z),
                     virtual T_decl(A::f),
                     virtual T_decl(B::g) {
  virtual int f(){ return g() + z; };
};

class T_var(*ap) :  virtual T_decl(A::f) { };

class T_var(a) :  T_def(A::f), T_def(A::g), T_var(*ap) { };

class T_var(b) :  T_def(A::f), T_def(B::g), T_var(*ap) { };

class T_var(c) :  T_def(C::f), T_def(B::g), T_var(*ap) { };

void main(){
  T_var(a) a; T_var(b) b; T_var(c) c;
  T_var(*ap) *ap;
  if (...)  { ap = &a; }
  else if (...)  { ap = &b; }
  else { ap = &c; }
  ap->f();
}
```

Figure 6: Result of Phase III for program $\mathcal{P}_2$ of Figure 2.

```
class A { int x; };
class B : A { ··· };
class C : A { ··· };
class D : B, C { ··· };

void main(){
  D d;
  B *bp1, *bp2;
  C *cp1, *cp2;
  bp1 = &d; bp2 = &d;
  cp1 = &d; cp2 = &d;
  bp1->x = 10;
  bp2->x += 10;
  cp1->x = 40;
  cp2->x += 10;
  int result;
  result = bp1->x;
}
```

(a)

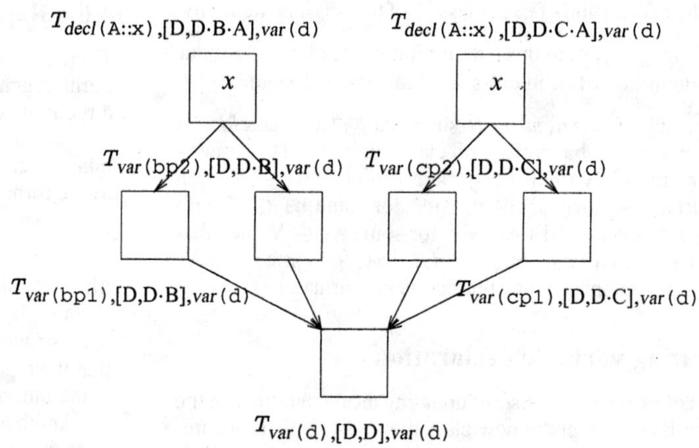


(b)

Figure 7: **(a) Example program. (b) Generated specialized subobject graph.**

with the same least derived class: $T_{decl(\texttt{A::x})}$. Unless countermeasures are taken, the algorithm of Section 4.3 will construct a specialized hierarchy where class $T_{decl(\texttt{A::x})}$ is a shared base class of classes $T_{var(\texttt{*bp1})}$, $T_{var(\texttt{*bp2})}$, $T_{var(\texttt{*cp1})}$, and $T_{var(\texttt{*cp2})}$. However, this implies that there would be a single subobject of type $T_{decl(\texttt{A::x})}$ inside an object of type $T_{var(\texttt{d})}$, and therefore, program behavior would not be preserved: the specialized version of the program would compute the value 50 for variable `result`, whereas the original program would compute the value 20.

Lack of space prevents us from presenting our approach to these problems in detail, but the essence of our solution consists of merging the types of variables in such a way that no irrepresentable structures can arise (this mechanism will be discussed in [24]). To this end, we add a phase to the algorithm where constraint elements are partitioned into equivalence classes; elements that occur in the same equivalence class must have the same type. Roughly speaking, two variables $x$ and $y$ occur in the same equivalence class if (i) $\mathcal{P}$ contains assignments such that $x$ is transitively assigned to $y$, and vice versa, or (ii) if a (member in) a replicated class $A$ (see Appendix A) is accessed from both $x$ and $y$. In addition, the type constraints of Section 3 need to be modified slightly to take equivalence classes into account.

Representability issues such as the ones discussed above become much more prominent for object-oriented languages with more limited facilities for expressing inheritance than $\mathcal{L}$, such as Java [10]. The inheritance structures that result from specialization are derived from the member access and assignment operations that occur in a program, and do not "naturally" conform to a language's limitations on inheritance. This implies that for a language without, e.g., support for multiple inheritance, classes in the specialized inheritance structures must be merged until all use of multiple inheritance is eliminated.

### 4.7 Justification

In this section, we argue that class hierarchy specialization is a semantics-preserving program transformation. Due to space limitations, we only state the essential properties here, without proofs (details may be found in [24]).

In order to show that behavior is preserved, we need to reason about "corresponding" lookup and typecast operations in the original and the specialized subobject graphs. To this end, we use the $\psi$ mapping that was introduced in Section 4.2: we will say that a subobject $n$ in $N$ *corresponds to* a subobject $\sigma \in \Sigma(\gamma)$ if $\psi(n) \equiv \sigma$.

The following theorem states that assignment behavior is preserved. Informally, the theorem states that if (i) $\sigma$ and $n$ are corresponding subobjects in $\Sigma(\gamma)$ and $N$, respectively, (ii) the least derived class of $\sigma$ and $n$ correspond to the type of object $y$, and (iii) there is an assignment $\langle x, y\rangle \in$ *Assignments*($\mathcal{P}$), then execution of the assignment will result in the selection of corresponding subobjects in $\Sigma(\gamma)$ and $N$.

**Theorem 4.7 (preservation of assignment behavior)** *Let $\mathcal{P}$ be a program with initial subobject graph $\langle \Sigma(\gamma), `<' \rangle$ and specialized subobject graph $\langle N, `\sqsubset' \rangle$. Let $n$ be a subobject in $N$ such that $ldc(n) = T_{[var(y)]}$, and let $\langle x, y\rangle \in$ Assignments($\mathcal{P}$). Then:*

$$\phi(typecast(n, T_{[var(x)]}, `\sqsubset')) = typecast(\phi(n), TypeOf(\mathcal{P}, x), `<')$$

Here, $[var(x)]$ denotes the equivalence class for variable $x$, as was alluded to in Section 4.6.

The following theorem states that lookup behavior is preserved. Informally, the theorem states that if (i) $\sigma$ and $n$ are corresponding subobjects in $\Sigma(\gamma)$ and $N$, respectively, (ii) the least derived class of $\sigma$ and $n$ correspond to the type of object $y$, and (iii) member $m$ is accessed from object $y$, then execution of the lookup will result in the selection of corresponding subobjects in $\Sigma(\gamma)$ and $N$.

**Theorem 4.8 (preservation of lookup behavior)** *Let $\mathcal{P}$ be a program with initial subobject graph $\langle \Sigma(\gamma), `<' \rangle$ and specialized subobject graph $\langle N, `\sqsubset' \rangle$. Let $n$ be a subobject in $N$ such that $ldc(n) = T_{[var(y)]}$, and let $\langle y, m\rangle \in$ MemberAccess($\mathcal{P}$). Then:*

$$\phi(lookup(n, m, `\sqsubset')) = lookup(\phi(n), m, `<')$$

## 5 Phase IV: Simplification

Phase IV of the algorithm consists of the application of a set of simple transformation rules to the specialized class hierarchy[7]. The effect of these transformations is a simplification of the inheritance structure, which may result in a reduction in the number of compiler-generated fields in objects, and hence in a reduction of object size. It is important to realize that the number of explicit (i.e., user-defined) members contained in each object is *not* affected by the transformations, with the exception that a member's declaration and definition may be merged.

In the rules below, the "merging" of two classes $X$ and $Y$ (where $X$ is a base class of $Y$) involves the following steps:

1. A new class $Z$ is created that (virtually, nonvirtually) inherits from all (virtual, nonvirtual) base classes of $X$ and $Y$, and that contains all members of $X$ and $Y$,
2. Each class $Z'$ that inherits from $X$ or $Y$ is made to inherit from $Z$ instead. This inheritance relation is virtual if the inheritance relation between $X$ and $Y$ or the inheritance relation between $Y$ and $Z'$ is virtual; otherwise it is nonvirtual.
3. All variables of type $X$ and $Y$ are given type $Z$, and all variables of type $X*$ and $Y*$ are given type $Z*$.
4. Classes $X$ and $Y$ are removed from the hierarchy.

The conditions of the rules presented below are designed in such a way that classes are only merged if no object in the program becomes larger (i.e., contains more members) as a result of the merge.

**Rule 1: Merge a base class $X$ with a derived class $Y$ if:**

1. $X$ and $Y$ have no members in common, except for the fact that for any member $m$, $X$ may contain a declaration of $m$, and $Y$ a definition of $m$.
2. There is no class $Z$ which is a direct nonvirtual base class of both $X$ and $Y$.
3. If there is a direct base class $X' \neq X$ of $Y$, and a direct derived class $Y' \neq Y$ of $X$, then $X'$ is an indirect base class of $Y'$.
4. If there are any variables in the program whose type is $X$, or any type $Y' \neq Y$ directly or indirectly derived from $X$, then neither $Y$ nor any direct or indirect base class $X' \neq X$ of $Y$ contains any data members.

[7] Alternatively, the set of type constraints could be simplified before the specialized class hierarchy is generated. However, since we believe that these transformations are of interest in their own right (e.g., as an optimization performed subsequent to class hierarchy slicing [23]), we have chosen to present them as general transformations that may be applied to *any* class hierarchy.

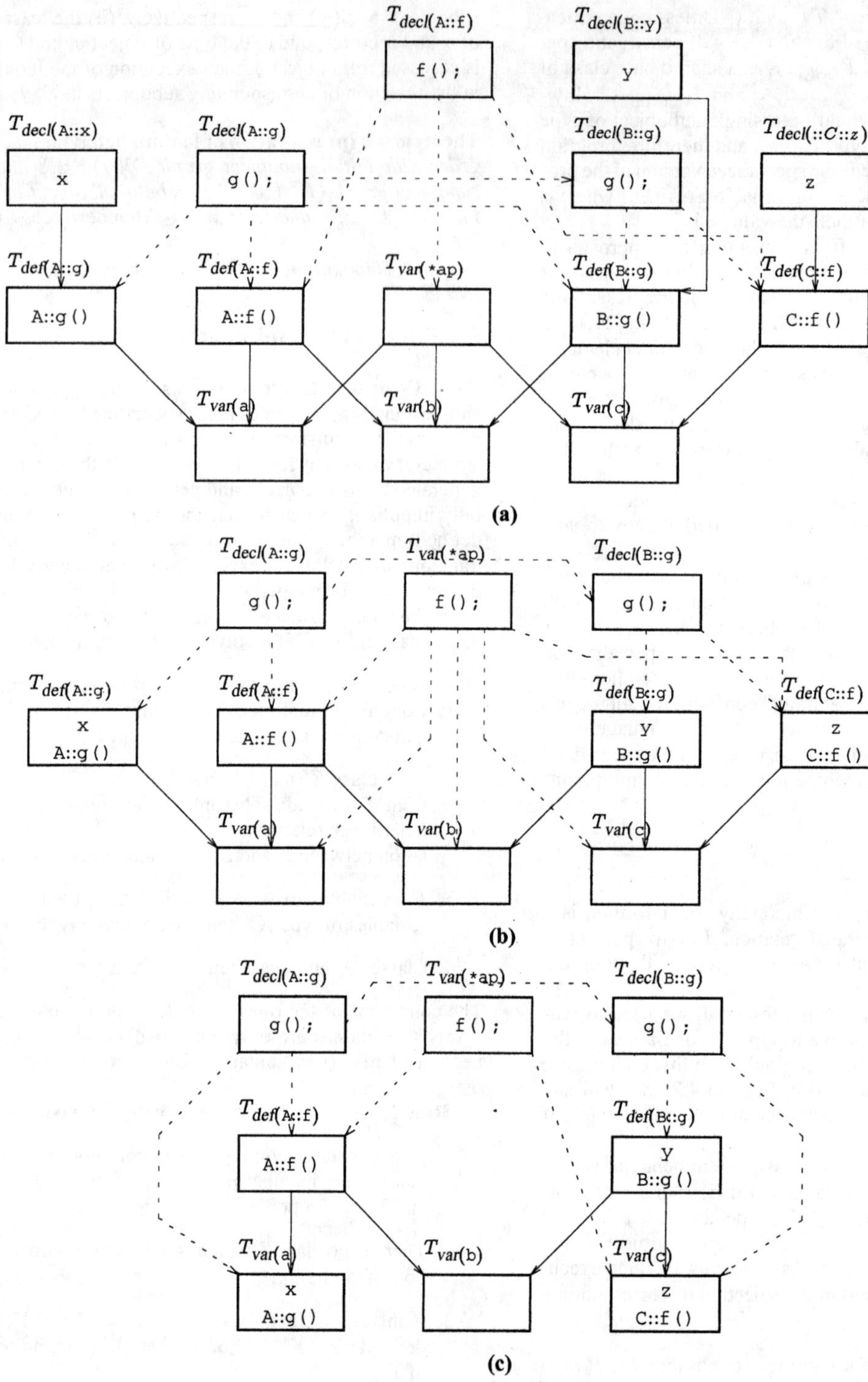


Figure 8: Illustration of the class hierarchies that result from applying the simplification rules of Section 5 to the specialized class hierarchy of Figure 6. In the figure, boxes indicate classes, solid arrows indicate nonvirtual (replicated) inheritance, and dashed arrows indicate virtual (shared) inheritance. An unqualified member name inside a box (e.g., `f();`) indicates that a declaration of that member occurs in the class. A qualified member name (e.g., `A::g()`) indicates a member definition and the class in the original hierarchy from where it originated (`A`).

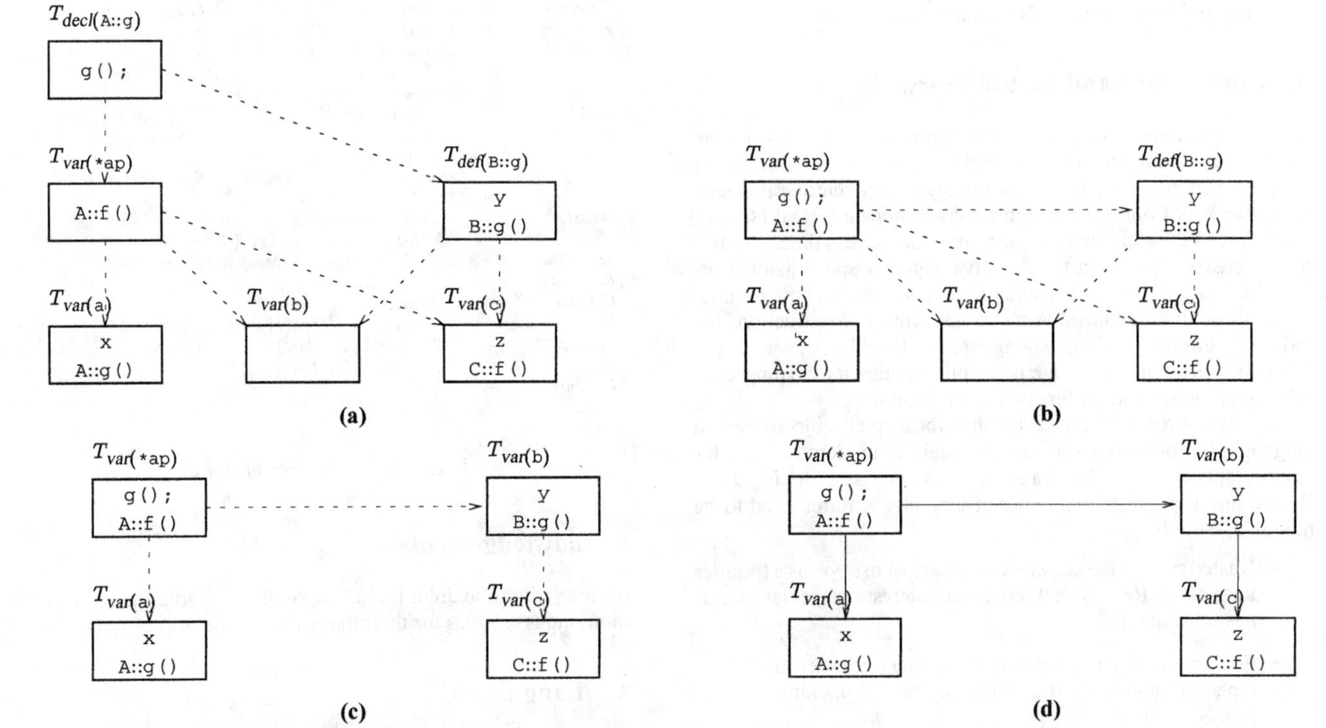


Figure 9: Illustration of the class hierarchies that result from applying the simplification rules of Section 5 to the specialized class hierarchy of Figure 6 (continuation of Figure 8).

5. If there are any variables in the program whose type is $X$, or any type $Y' \neq Y$ directly or indirectly derived from $X$, and if $Y$ or any direct or indirect base class $X' \neq X$ of $Y$ contains a declaration/definition of a virtual method, then $X$ contains a declaration/definition of a virtual method.

Conditions (1)–(3) of Rule 1 ensure that the class hierarchy is still valid after the merge, whereas conditions (4) and (5) ensure that no object becomes larger as a result of the merge.

**Rule 2: Remove the virtual inheritance relation between classes $X$ and $Z$ when:**

1. $X$ is an immediate virtual base class of $Y$,
2. $X$ is an immediate virtual base class of $Z$,
3. $Y$ is a (direct or indirect) base class of $Z$.

**Rule 3: Replace virtual inheritance between classes $X$ and $Y$ by nonvirtual inheritance when:**

1. $X$ is an immediate virtual base class of $Y$, and
2. there is no class $Y' \neq Y$ such that (i) $X$ is an immediate virtual base class of $Y'$, and (ii) there is a class $Z$ that directly or indirectly inherits from both $Y$ and $Y'$.

As an example, we will study the simplification of the specialized class hierarchy that was shown in Figure 6. Figure 8(a) depicts this class hierarchy before any simplifications have been performed. In Figure 8(b), the class hierarchy is shown after merging class $T_{decl(\texttt{A::x})}$ with class $T_{def(\texttt{A::g})}$ (Rule 1), merging class $T_{decl(\texttt{B::y})}$ with class $T_{def(\texttt{B::g})}$ (Rule 1), merging class $T_{decl(\texttt{C::z})}$ with class $T_{def(\texttt{C::f})}$ (Rule 1), eliminating the inheritance relation between class $T_{decl(\texttt{A::g})}$ and class $T_{def(\texttt{B::g})}$ (Rule 2), and merging class $T_{decl(\texttt{A::f})}$ with class $T_{var(\texttt{*ap})}$ (Rule 1). Figure 8(c) depicts the class hierarchy after eliminating the inheritance relation between class $T_{var(\texttt{*ap})}$ and class $T_{var(\texttt{a})}$ (Rule 2), eliminating the inheritance relation between class $T_{var(\texttt{*ap})}$ and class $T_{var(\texttt{b})}$ (Rule 2), eliminating the inheritance relation between class $T_{var(\texttt{*ap})}$ and class $T_{var(\texttt{c})}$ (Rule 2), merging class $T_{def(\texttt{A::g})}$ with class $T_{var(\texttt{a})}$ (Rule 1), and merging class $T_{def(\texttt{C::f})}$ with class $T_{var(\texttt{c})}$ (Rule 1).

Figure 9(a) shows the hierarchy after eliminating the inheritance relation between class $T_{decl(\texttt{A::g})}$ and class $T_{var(\texttt{a})}$ (Rule 2), eliminating the inheritance relation between class $T_{decl(\texttt{B::g})}$ and class $T_{var(\texttt{c})}$ (Rule 2), merging class $T_{decl(\texttt{B::g})}$ and class $T_{def(\texttt{B::g})}$ (Rule 1), and merging class $T_{var(\texttt{*ap})}$ and class $T_{def(\texttt{A::f})}$ (Rule 1). Figure 9(b) shows the hierarchy after merging class $T_{decl(\texttt{A::g})}$ and class $T_{var(\texttt{*ap})}$ (Rule 1). Figure 9(c) shows the hierarchy after eliminating the inheritance relation between class $T_{var(\texttt{*ap})}$ and class $T_{var(\texttt{b})}$ (Rule 2), eliminating the inheritance relation between class $T_{var(\texttt{*ap})}$ and class $T_{var(\texttt{c})}$ (Rule 2), and merging class $T_{def(\texttt{B::g})}$ and class $T_{var(\texttt{b})}$ (Rule 1). The final result, shown in Figure 9(d) is obtained by replacing all virtual inheritance relations by nonvirtual inheritance relations (three applications of Rule 3). This is the same hierarchy that was shown earlier in Figure 2.

While the simplification rules introduced above are sufficient for the examples presented in this paper, further research is needed to determine if more simplification rules are needed to cover other cases. In addition, simplification rules would ideally allow for certain time/space tradeoffs. For example, one might think of a situation where a virtual inheritance relation can be eliminated if an unused data member is added to a certain class. Other issues related to simplification rules such as proofs of correctness, termination behavior, and completeness also require further research.

## 6 Conclusions and Future Work

We have presented an algorithm that computes a new class hierarchy for a program, and updates the declarations of variables in the program accordingly. This transformation may remove unnecessary members from objects, and it may eliminate virtual (shared) inheritance (a feature that increases member access time, and that may increase object size). The advantages of specialization are reduced space requirements at run-time, and reduced time requirements through the reduced cost of object creation/destruction, and indirectly through caching/paging effects. In addition, we believe that specialization may create new opportunities for existing optimizations such as virtual function call resolution.

We have presented our techniques for a small object-oriented language, but our intentions are ultimately to implement class hierarchy specialization for real languages such as C++ and Java. Before this is feasible, a number of language features need to be modeled, including:

- Nested structures, i.e., class members whose type is a (pointer to a) class. Recursive types are an interesting special case of nested structures.
- Features that bypass the standard typing rules such as explicit typecasts, and method calls that use the '::' operator.
- User-defined constructors and destructors. Typically, a constructor initializes all members of a class. The algorithm presented in the present paper would not be able to omit any members accessed from a constructor's `this` pointer.
- Static members. Although member lookup works somewhat differently for static members [17], we do not think that there are any conceptual difficulties here. From a space savings point of view, static members are not very interesting because there is only one such member per class.

Handling these, and the other features that we currently do not treat will be a major effort, but we foresee no fundamental obstacles. Since the algorithm only inspects the code, we believe that it can be implemented efficiently. However, an in-depth complexity analysis of the algorithm is future work.

In addition to extending the algorithm to accommodate various language features, we intend to study the following:

- Although the simplification rules of Section 5 are sufficient for our current examples, more simplification rules may be needed in general. We intend to develop a complete system of simplification rules that allows for tradeoffs based on the compiler's object model.
- Since $\mathcal{L}$ has a very rich inheritance structure, expressing the inheritance structures that result from specialization in terms of a valid $\mathcal{L}$-hierarchy is relatively easy. For languages with more restricted forms of inheritance such as Java, this step will require more work.
- The primary application we have in mind for specialization is that of space/time optimization. It would be interesting to investigate whether specialization could be used as a basis for class hierarchy design/maintenance tools.
- In order to make class hierarchy specialization practical for real applications, several pragmatic issues related to separate compilation and the use of class libraries for which only object code is available need to be addressed.

```
Program     ::=  Hierarchy void main() { S_List }
Hierarchy   ::=  ClassDef | ClassDef Hierarchy
ClassDef    ::=  class Id [ : I_List] { M_List };
I_List      ::=  [virtual] Id | [virtual] Id, I_List
M_List      ::=  Member; | Member; M_List
Member      ::=  virtual int Id([D_List]) [ { S_List } ] |
                 virtual Id Id([D_List]) [ { S_List } ] | int Id
S_List      ::=  Stat; | Stat; S_List
Stat        ::=  Decl | IfStat | AssignStat | ReturnStat | CallStat
Decl        ::=  int Id | Id[ * ] Id
D_List      ::=  Decl | Decl, D_List
IfStat      ::=  if (Id) { S_List } [else { S_List } ]
AssignStat  ::=  [ * ] Id = Exp | Id M_Op Id = Exp
ReturnStat  ::=  return Exp
CallStat    ::=  CallExp
Exp         ::=  IntConst | Id | *Id | &Id | Exp + Id | CallExp
CallExp     ::=  Id M_Op Id ( [ Exp_List ]) | Id M_Op Id | Id ( [ Exp_List ])
Exp_List    ::=  Exp | Exp, Exp_List
IntConst    ::=  ... | -1 | 0 | 1 | ...
M_Op        ::=  . | ->
```

Figure 10: BNF grammar for $\mathcal{L}$.


## Acknowledgements

We are grateful to John Field, Yossi Gil, G. Ramalingam, and the anonymous referees for their many invaluable suggestions.


## A Language $\mathcal{L}$

Language $\mathcal{L}$ is a small C++-like language with virtual (shared) and nonvirtual (replicated) multiple inheritance. We omitted many C++ features from $\mathcal{L}$, including user-specified constructors and destructors, nonvirtual methods, pure virtual methods and abstract base classes, access rights (for members and inheritance relations; members and subobjects are accessible from anywhere within an $\mathcal{L}$-program), multi-level pointers, functions, operators, overloading, dynamic allocation, pointer arithmetic, pointers-to-members, the '::' direct method call operator, explicit casts, typedefs, templates, exception handling constructs. Furthermore, we assume that data members are of a built-in type. For convenience, we allow classes to contain the declaration of a method without an accompanying definition if the method under consideration is not called. All variable/parameter types are either `int` or a class, data members are always of type `int`, and members may only be accessed a variable. Figure 10 shows a BNF grammar for $\mathcal{L}$.

Without loss of generality we assume that the program does not contain variables, parameters, members, and classes with the same name (if this is not the case, some name-mangling scheme can be applied). The only exception to this rule is that we allow a virtual method to override another virtual method with the same name.

We make two assumptions concerning the member lookup expressions and typecasts in $\mathcal{L}$-programs. If a class hierarchy contains classes $X$ and $Y$ such that a $Y$-object contains multiple $X$-subobjects, we call $X$ a *replicated* class. We will assume that:

- If the program contains an (implicit) typecast from a class $Z$ to a replicated class $X$, then $X$ is an immediate base of $Z$.
- If the program contains a member access $v.m$ or $v \rightarrow m$ that statically resolves to a member $m$ in a replicated class $X$, then $v$'s type is $X$.

These assumptions are nonrestrictive: any $\mathcal{L}$-program that does not conform to these assumptions can be trivially transformed into an equivalent $\mathcal{L}$-program that meets our requirements. The reason for imposing these restrictions is to avoid the generation of irrepresentable inheritance structures, as is discussed in Section 4.6.

## References


[1] AGESEN, O. *Concrete Type Inference: Delivering Object-Oriented Applications*. PhD thesis, Stanford University, December 1995. Appeared as Sun Microsystems Laboratories Technical Report SMLI TR-96-52.

[2] AGESEN, O., AND UNGAR, D. Sifting out the gold: Delivering compact applications from an exploratory object-oriented programming environment. In *Proceedings of the Ninth Annual Conference on Object-Oriented Programming Systems, Languages, and Applications (OOPSLA'94)* (Portland, OR, 1994), pp. 355–370. *SIGPLAN Notices* 29(10).

[3] AIGNER, G., AND HÖLZLE, U. Eliminating virtual function calls in C++ programs. In *Proceedings of the Tenth European Conference on Object-Oriented Programming (ECOOP'96)* (Linz, Austria, July 1996), vol. 1098 of *Lecture Notes in Computer Science*, Springer-Verlag, pp. 142–166.

[4] BACON, D. F., AND SWEENEY, P. F. Fast static analysis of C++ virtual function calls. In *Proceedings of the Eleventh Annual Conference on Object-Oriented Programming Systems, Languages, and Applications (OOPSLA'96)* (San Jose, CA, 1996), pp. 324–341. *SIGPLAN Notices* 31(10).

[5] CALDER, B., AND GRUNWALD, D. Reducing indirect function call overhead in C++ programs. *Conference Record of the Twenty-First ACM Symposium on Principles of Programming Languages* (January 1994), 397–408.

[6] CARINI, P. R., HIND, M., AND SRINIVASAN, H. Flow-sensitive type analysis for C++. Tech. Rep. RC 20267, IBM T.J. Watson Research Center, 1995.

[7] CHOI, J.-D., BURKE, M., AND CARINI, P. Efficient flow-sensitive interprocedural computation of pointer-induced aliases and side effects. In *Conference Record of the Twentieth ACM Symposium on Principles of Programming Languages* (1993), ACM, pp. 232–245.

[8] DEAN, J., GROVE, D., AND CHAMBERS, C. Optimization of object-oriented programs using static class hierarchy analysis. In *Proceedings of the Ninth European Conference on Object-Oriented Programming (ECOOP'95)* (Aarhus, Denmark, Aug. 1995), W. Olthoff, Ed., Springer-Verlag, pp. 77–101.

[9] DIWAN, A., MOSS, J. E. B., AND MCKINLEY, K. S. Simple and effective analysis of statically-typed object-oriented programs. In *Proceedings of the Eleventh Annual Conference on Object-Oriented Programming Systems, Languages, and Applications (OOPSLA'96)* (San Jose, CA, 1996), pp. 292–305. *SIGPLAN Notices* 31(10).

[10] GOSLING, J., JOY, B., AND STEELE, G. *The Java Language Specification*. Addison-Wesley, 1996.

[11] MOORE, I. Automatic inheritance hierarchy restructuring and method refactoring. In *Proceedings of the Eleventh Annual Conference on Object-Oriented Programming Systems, Languages, and Applications (OOPSLA'96)* (San Jose, CA, 1996), pp. 235–250. *SIGPLAN Notices* 31(10).

[12] O'CALLAHAN, R., AND JACKSON, D. Lackwit: A program understanding tool based on type inference. In *Proceedings of the 1997 International Conference on Software Engineering Programming Systems, Languages, and Applications (ICSE'96)* (Boston, MA, May 1997).

[13] OPDYKE, W., AND JOHNSON, R. Creating abstract superclasses by refactoring. In *ACM 1993 Computer Science Conference* (1993).

[14] OPDYKE, W. F. *Refactoring Object-Oriented Frameworks*. PhD thesis, University Of Illinois at Urbana-Champaign, 1992.

[15] PALSBERG, J., AND SCHWARTZBACH, M. *Object-Oriented Type Systems*. John Wiley & Sons, 1993.

[16] PANDE, H. D., AND RYDER, B. G. Static type determination and aliasing for C++. Report LCSR-TR-250-A, Rutgers University, October 1995.

[17] RAMALINGAM, G., AND SRINIVASAN, H. A member lookup algorithm for C++. In *Proceedings of the ACM SIGPLAN'97 Conference on Programming Language Design and Implementation* (Las Vegas, NV, 1997), pp. 18–30.

[18] ROSSIE, J. G., AND FRIEDMAN, D. P. An algebraic semantics of subobjects. In *Proceedings of the Tenth Annual Conference on Object-Oriented Programming Systems, Languages, and Applications (OOPSLA'95)* (Austin, TX, 1995), pp. 187–199. *SIGPLAN Notices* 30(10).

[19] SHAPIRO, M., AND HORWITZ, S. Fast and accurate flow-insensitive points-to analysis. In *Conference Record of the Twenty-Fourth ACM Symposium on Principles of Programming Languages* (Paris, France, 1997), pp. 1–14.

[20] SRIVASTAVA, A. Unreachable procedures in object oriented programming. *ACM Letters on Programming Languages and Systems 1*, 4 (December 1992), 355–364.

[21] STEENSGAARD, B. Points-to analysis in almost linear time. In *Proceedings of the Twenty-Third ACM Symposium on Principles of Programming Languages* (St. Petersburg, FL, January 1996), pp. 32–41.

[22] TIP, F. A survey of program slicing techniques. *Journal of Programming Languages 3*, 3 (1995), 121–189.

[23] TIP, F., CHOI, J.-D., FIELD, J., AND RAMALINGAM, G. Slicing class hierarchies in C++. In *Proceedings of the Eleventh Annual Conference on Object-Oriented Programming Systems, Languages, and Applications (OOPSLA'96)* (San Jose, CA, 1996), pp. 179–197. *SIGPLAN Notices* 31(10).

[24] TIP, F., AND SWEENEY, P. F. Class hierarchy specialization. Technical report, IBM, 1997. Forthcoming.

[25] WEISER, M. *Program slices: formal, psychological, and practical investigations of an automatic program abstraction method*. PhD thesis, University of Michigan, Ann Arbor, 1979.

# Declarative Specialization of Object-Oriented Programs

Eugen N. Volanschi, Charles Consel, Gilles Muller

IRISA/INRIA University of Rennes
Campus Beaulieu,
F-35042 Rennes Cedex, France
e-mail: {volanski,consel,muller}@irisa.fr
http://www.irisa.fr/compose/

Crispin Cowan

Department of Computer Science and Engineering
Oregon Graduate Institute of Science and Technology
e-mail: crispin@cse.ogi.edu

## Abstract

Designing and implementing generic software components is encouraged by languages such as object-oriented ones and commonly advocated in most application areas. Generic software components have many advantages among which the most important is reusability. However, it comes at a price: genericity often incurs a loss of efficiency.

This paper presents an approach aimed at reconciling genericity and efficiency. To do so, we introduce declarations to the Java language to enable a programmer to specify how generic programs should be specialized for a particular usage pattern. Our approach has been implemented as a compiler from our extended language into standard Java.

## 1 Introduction

The object-oriented paradigm has well-recognized advantages for application design, and more specifically for program structure. It makes it possible to decompose an application in terms of well-defined, generic components, closely corresponding to the structure of the modeled problem. This structuring leads to a number of important software engineering improvements regarding maintainability and reusability of code. However, these advantages often translate to a loss in performance.

The conflict between software generality and performance has long been recognized in areas such as operating systems [9] and graphics [28]. This conflict is being increasingly addressed, with success, using forms of *program specialization*. This approach consists of adapting a generic program component to a given usage context. Program specialization can lead to considerable performance gains, by eliminating from the specialized code all the aspects which do not directly concern that precise context.

Often, specialization has been performed manually by adapting critical program components to the most common usage patterns [36, 35, 6]. This manual approach solves the efficiency problem, but has a limited applicability, because of the complexity of such a task. Recently, some tools have been developed to automatically specialize programs [1, 3, 11, 4, 26, 27, 10]. Applications of such tools are emerging in a number of fields, including scientific code [4, 5, 12], systems software [19, 30], computer graphics [22, 2], with already very promising results.

In essence, these automatic tools are transformation engines: they implement a set of program transformations which may be directly accessible to the programmer [18] or generated by some program analyses based on the usage context of the program [3, 11, 27, 1]. Programs can now be efficiently specialized at either compile time [1, 11] or run time [27, 3, 11].

The variety of options now available to the programmer drastically broadens the applicability of program specialization. However, it also makes it difficult to use for a non-expert.

Some steps towards helping the programmer control specific aspects of specialization have been achieved. In some systems, annotations are introduced in the original program to delimit code fragments to be specialized, or to indicate how to manage specialized code at run time [3, 21]. In other systems, some programming constructs in the language are overloaded to specify potential stages at which specialization can occur [27]. Although these existing strategies make specialization more usable for non-expert programmers they address very specific aspects of program specialization; many issues remain unexplored.

## This paper

We present a complete declarative approach for program specialization in the context of the object-oriented paradigm. Our approach addresses some important open issues:

- *Separated, declarative support.* Declaring the specialization behavior of a program should not cause the disturbance of the source of this program. We advocate that declaring specialization should be seen as adding information just as one would declare different aspects of a software component in an Aspect-Oriented language [25]. In fact, in our approach, a separate specialization declaration can be associated with any class.

- *A uniform approach.* As previously noted, progress in program specialization has considerably increased the number of parameters of this process (manual, automatic, incremental, run-time, compile-time, ...). Our declarative support offers a uniform way of exploiting these various strategies.


OOPSLA '97 10/97 GA, USA

- *Flexible execution support.* Introducing specialization in an existing application often requires mechanisms to be integrated in the run-time environment. These mechanisms include: triggering the specialization, detecting when a specialized component can no longer be used because the usage context has changed, deciding which specialized versions should be kept and how long. In our approach, some of these aspects are automatically inferred from the declarations; others are explicitly specified in the declarations.

## Overview of our Approach

We have developed language extensions for object-oriented languages aimed at expressing program specialization in a separate and declarative way. In our approach, the user does not need to know how a specializer works, but only has to declare what program components should be specialized and for which usage contexts. For an object-oriented language, this amounts to specifying what methods should be specialized and what variables should be used for specialization. Given these declarations, a special-purpose compiler determines how the specialized methods will be generated and managed. The result of the compilation is an extended version of the source program, able to trigger specialization when needed, and to replace the specialized components in a transparent way.

Our unit of declaration is a *specialization class*. It enriches information regarding an existing class. The relationship between regular classes and specialization classes is defined by a form of inheritance, based on *predicate classes* as developed by Chambers [8]. An important consequence of this technique is the ability to perform incremental specialization [14] based on class inheritance. That is, the specialization of a class is not fixed, it evolves as specialization values become available.

Configuring an application for a given usage context now amounts to separately declaring a set of specialization classes. From these declarations, the specialized behavior is derived.

Our declarative approach to program specialization has been implemented for Java. It has been introduced as a preprocessing phase. Our implementation produces standard Java programs which integrate a customized execution support for specialization.

## Example

Let us briefly illustrate our approach by showing how it can be applied to optimize a fragment of existing code. We compare the result with that of a manual approach. The next sections will describe a more complete example dealing with a filesystem.

Our first example is the `DirectColorModel` class taken from the standard library `java.awt.image`. A color model is a representation of a color pixel as a 32-bit integer. The default model uses 8 bits for each primary color (red, green, blue), and the extra 8 bits for an attribute called transparency. The user can define a custom color model in which a different pattern of bits is used for each color component. The `DirectColorModel` class converts a pixel in a user-defined color model into the default color model.

A new color model is defined by creating a new instance of `DirectColorModel` with arguments specifying the data layout. The constructor (see figure 1) computes from these arguments a value for each local variable of the instance. These values are invariant throughout the lifetime of the instance. Method `getRGB()` uses these values to convert a single pixel from the custom color model to the default color model. Typically this method is applied to every pixel of an image. Therefore, it is useful to specialize this method to the invariant conversion parameters.

Considering a user-defined color model for low-resolution colors which uses only 4 bits per color component, method `getRGB()` can be specialized quite drastically, resulting in the code shown in figure 2. Compared to the original version in figure 1, the four helper functions have been unfolded and all the computations based on local variables have been performed, including some arithmetic operations and test eliminations.

A manual approach to specialize this example would consist of the following steps. First, the user has to extract the code of `getRGB()` from the library, and produce the specialized version. In a second step, the user must define a new subclass of `DirectColorModel` which overrides `getRGB()` with the specialized version obtained previously (the library class `DirectColorModel` must be rewritten too, to get rid of the `final` keywords). Finally, any code requiring this specialization needs to be changed to use the new subclass whenever appropriate. The user is responsible for using the right version.

In contrast, our declarative approach to specialization only requires the user to specify the specialization opportunity, via the specialization class shown in figure 3. The specialization class lists the invariants corresponding to a low-resolution color model, and indicates the method to be specialized with respect to these invariants. Based on this specification, a program specializer is automatically invoked to produce the specialized version of method `getRGB()`. The library class `DirectColorModel` is also automatically rewritten to check, whenever a new instance is created, whether all the specified invariants are satisfied. If so, the specialized version of method `getRGB()` is "installed" in that instance[1]; otherwise, the generic version is installed instead. As a consequence, user code does not require any change, since the choice of the version to be used is transparently taken by the library class itself.

We have applied our specialization tools to this example and measured a speedup of 1.7, when using the Java interpreter from Sun (version 1.0.2) on a 200 MHz UltraSPARC Sun 4 machine running under Solaris.

## Contributions of this paper

Our contributions can be summarized as follows:

- We introduce a high-level language for declaring program specialization aspects of programs. This language is fully integrated in the object-oriented paradigm.
- This integration allows us to introduce incremental specialization based on the class hierarchy. As a result, classes exploit specialization values as they become available.

[1] Later sections describe in detail how our compiler installs different methods in different instances.

```
/* Copyright (c) 1994 Sun Microsystems, Inc. All Rights
Reserved. */
public class DirectColorModel extends ColorModel {
    private int red_mask;
    private int green_mask;
    private int blue_mask;
    private int alpha_mask;
    private int red_offset;
    private int green_offset;
    private int blue_offset;
    private int alpha_offset;
    private int red_scale;
    private int green_scale;
    private int blue_scale;
    private int alpha_scale;

    /* Constructor */
    public DirectColorModel(int bits, int rmask,
                int gmask, int bmask, int amask) {
        super(bits);
        red_mask = rmask;
        green_mask = gmask;
        blue_mask = bmask;
        alpha_mask = amask;
        CalculateOffsets();
    }

    final public int getRGB(int pixel) {
        return (getAlpha(pixel) ≪ 24)
            | (getRed(pixel) ≪ 16)
            | (getGreen(pixel) ≪ 8)
            | (getBlue(pixel) ≪ 0);
    }

    final public int getAlpha(int pixel) {...}
        if (alpha_mask == 0) return 255;
        int a = ((pixel & alpha_mask) ⋙ alpha_offset);
        if (alpha_scale ≠ 0) {
            a = a * 255 / alpha_scale;
        }
        return a;
    }

    final public int getRed(int pixel) {...}
    final public int getGreen(int pixel) {...}
    final public int getBlue(int pixel) {...}
}
```

Figure 1: The original definition of class `java.awt.image.DirectColorModel`

```
final public int getRGB(int pixel) {
    return ((((pixel & 0x0f000000) ⋙ 24) * 17) ≪ 24)
        | ((((pixel & 0x000f0000) ⋙ 16) * 17) ≪ 16)
        | ((((pixel & 0x00000f00) ⋙ 8) * 17) ≪ 8)
        | ((pixel & 0x0000000f) * 17);
}
```

Figure 2: The specialized code for method `getRGB()`

```
specclass LowResolutionModel specializes DirectColorModel {
    red_mask == 0x000f0000;
    green_mask == 0x00000f00;
    blue_mask == 0x0000000f;
    alpha_mask == 0x0f000000;
    red_offset == 16;
    green_offset == 8;
    blue_offset == 0;
    alpha_offset == 24;
    red_scale == 15;
    green_scale == 15;
    blue_scale == 15;
    alpha_scale == 15;

    getRGB();
}
```

Figure 3: A specialization class for a low-resolution color model representing each color components on 4 bits

- Processing these declarations both produces directives to perform various forms of specialization (compile time, run time, ...) and generates the run-time support to manage the specializations. As a result, our declarative approach brings together a variety program specialization techniques, usually used in isolation.
- Our approach is implemented for the Java language. Processing of specialization declarations produces standard Java programs.

The rest of this paper is organized as follows. In section 2 we examine the aspects that should be covered by a declarative approach to specialization. In section 3, the syntax and the semantics of specialization classes are presented, a complete example of specialization classes is given, and our compilation scheme to Java is outlined. Section 4 describes specific aspects of specialization classes involving run-time specialization. Section 5 discusses related work, and Section 6 presents some perspectives and conclusions. The complete compilation algorithm is given in Appendix A.

## 2 Issues in Declaring Specialization

A declarative approach to defining the specialization behavior of a program component must address all the aspects of specialization. More specifically, it should make it possible to express *what* should be specialized and *how* it should be specialized. Before presenting the details of our approach, let us first examine these aspects.

### 2.1 What to Specialize

Declaring specialization involves identifying the program components that should be specialized, and describing the usage contexts for which the components should be adapted. Components associated with multiple usage contexts may require incremental specialization to best exploit all available specialization values.

**Program components.** Traditionally, the program components considered for specialization are: the whole program, a set of procedures, a procedure, or a block of code (within a procedure). The choice of a particular entity depends on the language structure, and more importantly, on the power of a given specializer — for example, whether the specialization process is intra/inter-block or intra/inter-procedural.

**Specialization context.** The usage context for which a program component is specialized is a set of predicates over some parts of the program state, which hold over some period of time. Program specializers usually consider predicates consisting of equalities, that is, specialization is performed given some variables having some specific values. In general, a predicate is said to be compile-time if it can be evaluated at this early stage. Otherwise it is said to be run-time.

Besides its stage, a predicate must be classified with respect to its lifetime, *i.e.*, whether or not the predicate can change its value during run time. If its value can never change, the predicate is said to be stable. If it can be invalidated because of some state changes, it is said to be unstable. Both stable and unstable predicates correspond to actual situations found in real experiments [36, 35, 39].

**Incremental specialization.** A set of predicates may not be satisfied all at once. Usually, all predicates do not become true at once. Therefore, it is useful to be able to describe a sequence of specialization contexts for a given program component so that it can be specialized further as more values become available.

### 2.2 How to Specialize

The operational aspects of specialization involve applying specialization and integrating the specialized components into the program.

**Triggering specialization.** An important issue in using specialization is when to produce the specialized code. For contexts depending only on compile-time predicates, specialization can be applied either at compile time or at run time. For the other contexts, specialization must be applied at run time. In this latter case, some run-time support must detect when all the predicates in the context become valid, trigger the specialization, and replace the component (either immediately or when the component is used).

**Preserving the validity of specializations.** For contexts depending on unstable predicates, the run-time support must preserve the validity of the specializations. This implies detecting when the predicates are invalidated, and replacing the specialized component by one compatible with the current state.

**Caching specializations.** Run-time specialization requires a run-time cache to associate specialized components to their contexts, so that no duplicate specializations are produced. Due to limited space resources, one may only want to keep a few frequently used specialized components. As a result, caching techniques need to be used to manage run-time specialized components.

## 3 Specialization Classes

Now that we have detailed the issues involved in specializing programs, let us present our declarative approach to addressing these issues.

Specialization classes separately define the specialization behavior of existing classes. A specialization class

- defines a context for specialization,
- indicates which program components should be specialized for this context, and
- possibly selects some options for the specialization support.

We choose the granularity of a specializable program component to be the set of methods associated with a (regular) class. Each specialization class is attached to a class in the target program. Multiple specialization classes can be attached to a single class, capturing different opportunities for specialization. If these opportunities define a sequence of incremental specialization stages, the specialization classes can be extended step by step, instead of being all defined from scratch.

```
sc_decl = [runtime] specclass sc_name parent_decl [cache_decl]
        { (pred_decl ;)+ (method_decl ;)* }
parent_decl = specializes [class] class_name |
              extends [specclass] sc_name
pred_decl = variable_name == value |
            variable_name |
            sc_name variable_name
method_decl = method_prototype |
              method_definition
cache_decl = cached cache_strategy [[ integer ]]
cache_strategy = LRU |
                 Amortization |
                 Priority |
                 BestFit |
                 ...
sc_name = identifier
```

Figure 4: The syntax of Specialization Classes

The syntax of specialization classes is given in figure 4. The syntax is given as a Java extension: the undefined non-terminals (*identifier, integer, class_name, variable_name, method_name, method_prototype* and *method_definition*) are those defined by Java.

### 3.1 Semantics of Specialization Classes

In this section, we describe informally the semantics of specialization classes. The compilation scheme from a Java program with specialization classes to a standard Java program is discussed in section 3.3.

In Java, there are already two forms of inheritance. First, a class (or an interface) can *extend* another class (or interface, respectively). Second, a class may also *implement* some interfaces. We tried to keep the same spirit, by attaching a specialization class to a (regular) class via a new form of inheritance, *specialize*.

All the specialization classes attached to a regular class $C$ form a hierarchy of possible specialization states. Class $C$ is called the *root class*. Each specialization class either specializes a regular class, or extends another specialization class.

All the fields (variables and methods) occurring in a specialization class must exist in the corresponding root class. In other words, a specialization class cannot add new fields to a class. This is because specialization classes are not meant to add functionality to a class, but to adapt it to a particular context. To define this specialization context, a specialization class $S$ adds some constraints over existing variables of some class $C$, by defining a list of predicates on the object's state. An object of class $C$ is considered to be "in specialization state $S$" whenever *all* the predicates of specialization class $S$ are valid. When this is the case, the specialized methods defined by $S$ override the generic versions defined in class $C$.

A special case arises when an object of class $C$ satisfies all the predicates in two different specialization classes $S'$ and $S''$ at the same time. In principle, the specialization class can be chosen randomly, since both are applicable. In practice, our compiler guarantees that, if the inheritance relation defines an order between $S'$ and $S''$, then the more specialized state is always chosen.

The predicates can either refer to the local state, if they involve an instance variable of non-object type, or to non-local state, if they include an instance variable of object type. For the moment, we do not consider array instance variables, nor class variables[2].

A predicate on a variable of non-object type can be either compile-time or run-time. The syntax for compile-time predicates is "*variable_name==value;*", where the value is a compile-time constant. The syntax for run-time predicates is simply "*variable_name;*" without giving any value for the variable. This predicate is true for any value and is valid as long as the value does not change.

A predicate on a variable of some object type `class` *C1* constrains that sub-object to be in a specific specialization state *S1* (where *S1* is a specialization class for `class` *C1*). The predicate is written "*S1 variable_name;*", similar to a Java type declaration. In fact, it can be considered that the variable was redefined to be of a more precise type.

We made a deliberate design choice to restrict predicates to these simple forms, which are directly usable by a program specializer. This restriction allows the specialized method to be automatically derived from the generic definition by the program specializer. However, the syntax allows the user to specify a complete method definition for the case when the method is specialized manually.

Note that there is no distinction between stable and unstable predicates, at the syntactic level. Indeed, in an object-oriented language such as Java, it is simple to determine statically which predicates can never be invalidated — it suffices to check that the corresponding variables are assigned only in the constructors.

The syntactic constructs described so far allow the user to declare what specialization to do. There are some other syntactic constructs through which the user can influence how the specialization is achieved (keywords `runtime` and `cached`). They relate to run-time specialization, and are discussed in section 4.

### 3.2 Specializing a Filesystem

In a previous study [35], Pu *et al.* motivated the need for incremental specialization in the context of adaptive operating systems. This experiment focused on the HP-UX file system. A number of stable and unstable predicates were identified[3], under which specialization was performed by hand with very good results. The validity of specialized versions was managed by hand-written pieces of code called *guards*, manually inserted in the modified file system source, which both installed specialized versions and restored unspecialized ones.

The example presented below is a Java program, directly inspired by the HP-UX experiment. We define the specialization classes for the main objects, and we show how our approach makes the management of specialized versions automatic.

The key concepts of a Unix-like file system are the *file* and the *i-node* (for the sake of simplicity, we do not take v-nodes into account). Two data structures implement these entities: the file descriptor and the i-node descriptor. In fact, the file concept in Unix is an abstraction for character streams. It covers much more than regular disk files, as it

[2] The target Java program can contain any array or class variables; the only restriction is that they cannot be involved in a predicate.

[3] In that study, stable predicates are called invariants, and unstable predicates are called quasi-invariants.

includes: sockets, devices, pipes, etc. The actual type of the file is stored in an i-node descriptor — there is one for each device, disk file, or pipe — that is referenced in the file descriptor.

An i-node descriptor (see figure 5) contains, among other elements, type information and access permissions. In fact, the type information (partially in the `pipe` flag and partially in the `mode` bit-mask) never changes once the i-node is created. The access permissions (also part of the `mode` bit-mask) may be changed via the `chmod()` method. The most important methods of an i-node are the read and write methods (for conciseness, `write()` is omitted). The read method is generic in that it covers functionality belonging to all types of i-nodes.

Figure 6 shows a specialization class which specializes the generic i-node definition for the case where the i-node refers to a read-only, disk file. It declares that whenever an i-node has the specified values for the variables `pipe` and `mode`, a read operation should invoke a read method specialized with respect to these values. Whenever the state changes (*i.e.*, the i-node is no longer read-only), the generic version should be used again.

One could advocate for a different design of the filesystem, which consists of creating a static i-node sub-hierarchy, with a different class for pipes or devices; this would make it possible to separate the read functionality into distinct, overloaded methods. This design is seldom adopted, because the different read functionalities are quite complex and closely intertwined; such a separation would create a lot of hand-written versions of the same methods, and increase the risk of errors. Program specialization is an appropriate solution here, because it allows to derive the specialized functionality for each i-node type, directly from the generic version. Program specialization can furthermore eliminate other checks which cannot be encoded in a static hierarchy, like testing the access permissions at each read operation.

### 3.3 Compiling Specialization Classes

The compilation scheme takes as input a Java class definition and a set of specialization classes. It creates a new Java class definition that incorporates all the specialization behavior. We detail the compilation process for the i-node example. The complete compilation algorithm is given in Appendix A.

As a naming convention, notice that new field names (variables or methods) introduced by the compiler are prefixed with `'sc'`.

The compiler splits the functionality of the original i-node into several objects (see figure 7). An *enclosing* object (shown in figure 8) reproduces the basic functionality of the original i-node, but delegates the evolving part of its behavior to an *implementation* object. Actually, two implementations are created: a generic one (shown in figure 9) and a specialized one (shown in figure 10), corresponding to the specialization class `ReadFileInode` (see figure 6).

Such an object, which changes its implementation dynamically is abstracted by an *interface*, named `Mutable` in figure 11. Therefore, the compiled i-node is enriched to support this level of abstraction. It includes a new variable, named `scImpl`, that refers to the current implementation object. The "specializable" method `read()` in the enclosing object is replaced with a forwarding method, which simply invokes the current implementation object. Note that the

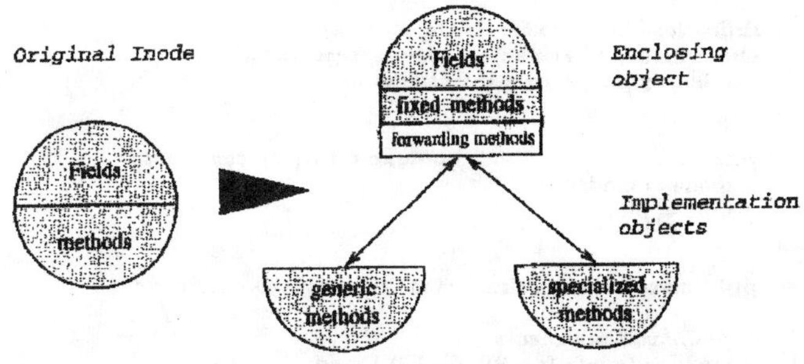


Figure 7: The compiled i-node

implementation object must execute all the methods as if they were executed by the original i-node object. To do so, the implementation object maintains a pointer (called `scEncl`) to the enclosing object. Any self reference that occurred in the original object methods (via `this`) is replaced by a reference to the enclosing object (via `scEncl`).

In order to detect state changes, which may affect the current implementation, assignments to variable `mode` are *guarded*: every assignment to this variable is replaced by a call to a new method, named `scSet_mode()`. Besides doing the assignment, this method checks whether the new value invalidates specialized methods. If an assignment has invalidated the current specialization state, the `scNotify()` method is invoked to determine a new specialization class. More precisely, it proceeds by taking every specialization class related to the i-node, and checks whether all its predicates are satisfied. When a specialization class is found (possibly the generic class), the current implementation is updated by invoking the private method `scSwitchToImpl()`.

In fact, moving to a new specialization class may change the set of guarded variables since it may rely on predicates involving different variables. Note that assignments to the `pipe` variable are not guarded; a trivial static analysis determined that this variable is never assigned outside the constructors.

When changing the implementation, `scSwitchToImpl()` method produces a new instance of either `InodeImpl` or `ReadFileInodeImpl`. In the i-node example, all the specialized methods are produced at compile time, but in case of run-time specialization, creating a new implementation invokes the run-time specializer on the fly.

Assignments in the constructor(s) are *not* guarded, since the state is not yet completely initialized. The constructor(s) are only extended to call the `scNotify()` method right before returning. Indeed, at this stage the state is complete and the implementation corresponding to this initial state may be selected.

### 3.4 Extending the Filesystem Example

We now present a complete example, where both the file object and the i-node object are specialized. The example shows how the two specializations are *composed*, by defining a predicate on non-local state, and by preserving its validity at run time. It also covers the use of run-time predicates and an example of incremental specialization.

The original definition of the file descriptor is given in figure 13. A file descriptor is created each time a file is opened. The descriptor contains a reference to the corresponding i-node, an opening mode (which cannot be more

```
public class Inode extends Object {
  short mode; // rwx info + device/regular file
  boolean pipe; // true if i-node is pipe
  // ...

  public Inode(short mod, boolean pip) { // constructor
    mode = mod;
    pipe = pip;
  }

  public void chmod(short mod) { /* change access mode
                                   (rwx bits) */
    // ... various checks
    mode = (mode & ~RWX_BIT) | mod;
  }

  public int read() { // read one byte
     // Generic version: file or pipe or device
     // ... check if readable
  }
};
```

Figure 5: The original i-node definition

```
specclass ReadFileInode specializes class Inode {
  mode == I_REGULAR | R_BIT;
  pipe == false;

  read(); /* produce a simpler version:
             disk file, read-only */
}
```

Figure 6: A specialization class for an i-node

```
import sclib.*;

public class Inode extends Object implements Mutable {
  // copy original fields:
  short mode; // rwx info + device/regular file
  boolean pipe; // true if i-node is pipe
  // ...

  // add some new fields:
  InodeImpl scImpl; // current implementation
  List scClients; // list of Mutable clients

  // rewrite constructors:
  public Inode(short mod, boolean pip) {
    // copy original body:
    mode = mod;
    pipe = pip;

    // add initialization code:
    scClients = null;
    scNotify();
  }

  // copy original methods
  // and rewrite assignments to Mutable fields inside:
  void chmod(short mod) {
    // ... various checks
    scImpl.scSet_mode((mode & ~RWX_BIT) | mod);
  }

  // add Mutable behavior:
  public void scNotify() {
    // Determine the new specialization class
    // & switch to it
    if (mode == (I_REGULAR | R_BIT) && !pipe)
      scSwitchToImpl("ReadFileInode");
    else
      scSwitchToImpl("Inode");
    if(scClients ≠ null) // to all clients:
      scClients.scNotify(); // propagate the notification
  }
  protected void scSwitchToImpl(String spec) {...}
  public void scAttach(Mutable m) {...} // add client
  public void scDetach(Mutable m) {...} // delete client
  public boolean scIsA(String spec) {...} // inspect state

  // forward specializable methods to the implementation
  public int read() { return scImpl.read(); }
};
```

Figure 8: The enclosing i-node class

```
class InodeImpl extends Impl {
  // fixed part for a generic implementation:
  protected Inode scEncl; // the "enclosing" instance
  public InodeImpl(Inode i) { // constructor
    scEncl = i;
  }

  // set methods:
  short scSet_mode(short new_mode) { // guarded
    scEncl.mode = new_mode; // perform the assignment
    if(new_mode ≠ I_REGULAR | R_BIT)
      scEncl.scNotify(); // inform the Inode
    return new_mode;
  }

  // specializable methods:
  int read() {
     // Generic version: file or pipe or device
     // ... check if readable
     // with 'scEncl' substituted for 'this'
  }
};
```

Figure 9: The generic i-node implementation

```
class ReadFileInodeImpl extends InodeImpl {
  // redefine (some) set methods:
  // (none here)

  // redefine (some) specializable methods:
  int read() {
    // ... simpler version: disk file, read-only
  }
};
```

Figure 10: The specialized i-node implementation

```
package sclib;

public interface Mutable {
   public void scNotify();
   private void scSwitchToImpl(String spec);
   public void scAttach(Mutable m);
   public void scDetach(Mutable m);
   public boolean scIsA(String spec);
};
```

Figure 11: The Mutable interface

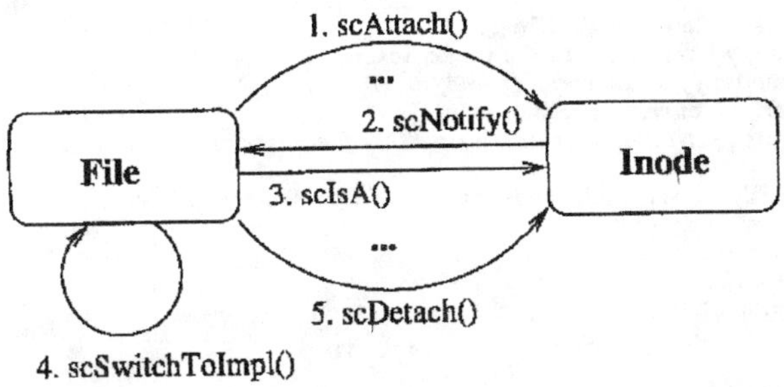


Figure 12: The protocol between `File` and `Inode`

permissive than the access mode of the i-node), the current position in the file, and a reference counter (indicating how many processes are using the file). Variables `ino` and `mode` never change after the file is opened. Variable `count` can only be changed if the file is duplicated (method `dup()`). In practice, this operation is executed quite rarely. The file position is incremented at every read.

The specialization for the i-node is the same as previously. For the file, two specialization stages are defined, as described in figure 14. The first stage (specialization class `ReadFile`) defines an open disk file: the predicate on the mode is a run-time predicate, since it holds for any value. In fact, any open mode triggers useful specialization. Variable `ino` is redefined to be of specialization class `ReadFileInode`. Thus, it requires the corresponding i-node to be in specialization state `ReadFileInode`. As a result, specialization happens inter-procedurally, that is, not only does the read method of the file object get specialized, but also the read method of the embedded i-node object. In our example, the specialized version eliminates the access test and in-lines the call to the (specialized) i-node's read method.

The second specialization stage for a file adds a new constraint: the disk file should be accessed *exclusively* by one process. In this case, the read method is even simpler, because the concurrency constraints on the file level can be ignored. Therefore, the `synchronized` branch is removed in the specialized version.

To keep the specialization states coherent between two inter-dependent objects (such as the file and its i-node), there is a simple protocol between the two objects via the `Mutable` interface (see figure 11). Each mutable object, such as the i-node, maintains a list of references to other mutable objects which depend on its state. When a file is connected to an i-node, by an assignment to its `ino` variable, the file declares itself as a client of the i-node object, by invoking the `ino.scAttach()` method (see figure 12). The `ino.scAttach()` method records the file in a list of clients (variable `scClient`). Consequently, if some predicates in i-node do not hold anymore, the file object is notified (`scNotify()`) that its i-node cannot be used for specialization anymore. Method `scNotify()` inspects the current state of the file, including the state of the i-node — by calling `ino.scIsA("ReadFileInode")`. The boolean method `scIsA("state_name")` allows a client to check if a mutable object has at least reached a given specialization state. Finally, when a file is closed, it invokes `ino.scDetach()`, which deletes that file from the `scClient` list.

Let us examine how the whole example works with a simple main program (file's `main()` method), as shown in figure 13. The program creates an i-node for a disk file, initially with read/write permissions, and opens a file object on this i-node in read-only mode. The constructors for both objects inspect their states. The i-node selects the generic implementation, because the access permissions are *not read-only*. The file selects the generic implementation too, because its i-node is not in state `ReadFileInode`.

Afterwards, the access permissions of the i-node are changed to read-only. Since the assignment to the `mode` variable is guarded, the predicate defined on `mode` is checked. Because it now holds, the i-node object switches to a `ReadFileInode` implementation, and notifies the file object. The file notices that the i-node is now specialized, and switches directly to `ExlcReadFile`, because the value of variable `count` is 1.

Finally, a `dup()` operation applied to the file triggers an un-specialization of the file up to the `ReadFile` specialization class. When the i-node returns to a read-write mode, both objects return to the generic implementation: first the i-node object, and then, by propagation, the file object too.

## 4 Run-time Specialization Issues

When a specialization class defines a run-time predicate (like the predicate on the mode in a `ReadFile`), the specialized implementations for this class cannot be generated before execution because the precise constant values are not known in advance.

In contrast, compile-time predicates can be exploited either at compile time or at run time. Usually, compile-time specialization is preferred because it does not incur the run-time code generation cost. However, run-time specialization may have other advantages. For example, if $N$ specialization classes are defined for a given root class, specialization at compile time has to speculatively generate $N$ implementations. Run-time specialization generates only the implementations used at a given moment. Either choosing compile-time or run-time specialization is a tradeoff between time and space; this choice is usually driven by the application. As explained below, our solution consist of using a default behavior, and provide the user with declaration support to overwrite it.

Our compiler computes for any specialization class a *specialization time* attribute, which can be either run-time or compile-time. This attribute is attached to the whole specialization class (instead of to every predicate), because predicates are not exploited individually. By default, if a specialization class contains only compile-time predicates, the compiler infers a "compile-time" attribute; any other specialization class is run-time. The user can force a

```
public class File extends Object {
  Inode ino; // reference to the inode descriptor
  short mode; // open mode (r and/or w)
  long pos; // current position in file
  int count; // No. of processes using this file descriptor

  public File(short mod, Inode inod) { // constructor
    mode = mod;
    ino = inod;
    count = 1;
    pos = 0;
  }

  File dup() {
    count++;
    return this;
  }

  public static void main(String argv[]) {
    Inode i = new Inode(Inode.I_REGULAR |
                        Inode.R_BIT | Inode.W_BIT,
                        false);
    File f = new File(R_BIT, i);

    i.chmod(Inode.R_BIT);
    f.dup();
    i.chmod(Inode.R_BIT | Inode.W_BIT);
  }

  public int read() {
    if((mode & R_BIT) == 0)
      return new FileAccessError();
    if(count > 1)
      synchronized(this) { // lock the file descriptor
        pos += 4; // Advance with the size of an integer
      }
    else pos +=4; // avoid lock when possible
    return ino.read();
  }
};
```

Figure 13: The original File definition and the main program

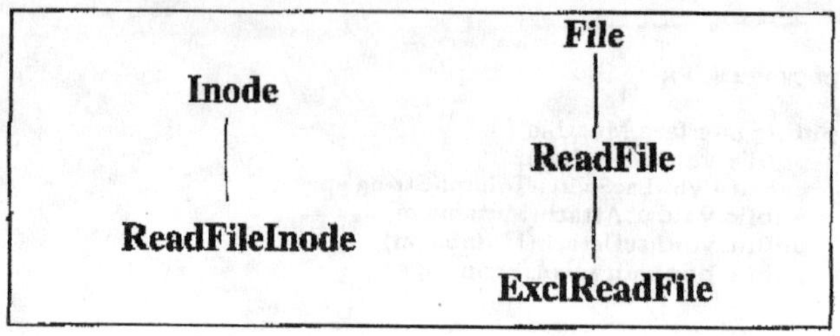


```
// Inode hierarchy:

specclass ReadFileInode specializes class Inode {
  mode == I_REGULAR | R_BIT;
  pipe == false;

  read(); /* produce a simpler version:
             disk file, read-only */
}


// File hierarchy:

specclass ReadFile specializes class File {
  mode; /* any value is good */
  ReadFileInode ino; /* restriction on the inode's state */

  read(); /* produce a simpler version:
             disk file, mode is known */
}

specclass ExclReadFile extends specclass ReadFile
        cached Amortization[20] {
  count == 1;

  read(); /* produce an even simpler version:
             no more locking */
}
```

Figure 14: The specialization classes for the filesystem

*compile-time* class to be classified *run-time* by prefixing the specialization class declaration with the keyword `runtime`. There is no possible keyword for compile-time, because run-time predicates cannot be exploited at compile time.

The run-time attribute is inherited. That is, any specialization class $D$ derived from a run-time specialization class $R$, is run-time as well. This is because class $D$ inherits all the predicates from class $R$, which are (or were forced to be) run-time.

Within a single program, run-time specialization classes can coexist with compile-time ones. Furthermore, different implementations of the same root class can have different specialization times. For example, the generic implementation is always generated at compile-time, while some of its descendants can be generated at run time. In our example, the i-node implementations are compile-time, whereas the two specialized file implementations are run-time.

## 4.1 Caching Specialized Implementations

Caching run-time specialized implementations consists of keeping the generated implementations in a data structure of bounded size. Besides limiting the code growth, this organization has two potential benefits. The first one is to save space by avoiding to duplicate an existing implementation, whenever possible. For example, two different files which are in specialization state `ReadFile` can share the same implementation if they have the same mode.

The second benefit of caching is to save time by keeping specialized implementations that are not currently used, but are likely to be reused. For example, a directory file is likely to be opened several times. Keeping its implementation for some time after the file is closed may pay off.

Different applications may need different caching strategies. Our compiler gives a default strategy, and provides a number of alternatives. The user can choose between these alternatives, allocate new caches, and define some new strategies. To select a specific cache behavior for some specialization class $S$, the declaration fragment "`cached` *strategy*`[`*size*`]`" must be included in $S$'s definition (see figure 14). This fragment specifies that a cache of `size` elements is reserved for class $S$. Cache behavior is also inherited, so that this cache is also used for classes derived from $S$ (unless they redefine it).

Our implementation is extensible (see figure 15). There is a `Specializer` interface, which defines the specialization functionality (method `spec()`). The run-time specializer implements this interface. A cache is a "filter" for the run-time specializer. That is, the cache both implements the interface, and contains a reference to the run-time specializer. It satisfies some of the specialization requests by itself, if it can reuse an existing implementation from the cache; if not, it invokes the runtime specializer. In this scheme, the user can provide its own cache strategy by extending the `Cache` abstract class.

## 4.2 Some Caching Strategies

A number of general cache strategies (*e.g.*, LRU, multi-way associative, *etc.*) can be used for the specialization caches. However, caching of run-time specialized implementations raises some specific issues:

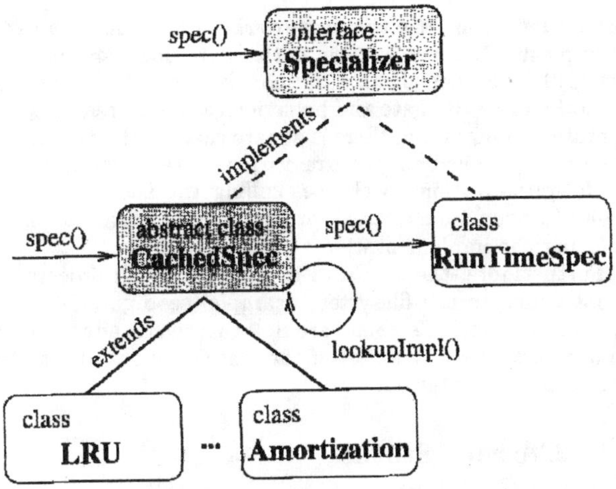


Figure 15: The cache hierarchy

- Specialization must be *amortized.* Failing to take this constraint into account may trigger frequent specializations which will never pay off.
- Specialization classes are *ordered* by the "more specialized than" relation. The most specialized implementation is intended to give the best performance gain. There is also some compatibility between ordered implementations. That is, an implementation for a given specialization class is applicable to any derived specialization classes.
- A specialization request can be refused, when resources are unavailable, by defaulting to the generic implementation.

Taking these issues into account, some novel, domain-specific strategies can be studied. Let us outline some examples.

- *Amortization:* Considers the amortization effect as the most important aspect. Therefore, a specialized implementation is never evicted from the cache until it is no more referenced. This strategy can cause some specialization opportunities to be neglected when space is exhausted.
- *Depth-most priority:* Specialization classes are prioritized upon their "depth" (or degree) of specialization in the inheritance tree. In case of an eviction from the cache, the least specialized implementations is chosen. This strategy makes highly specialized methods more likely to be available
- *First fit:* In response to a specialization request, this strategy searches in the cache until if finds any implementation compatible with the requested one. Implementations are evicted only when no approximate fit is found. This strategy encourages re-use of implementations, at the price of approximate fitting.

## 4.3 Overhead of the Execution Support

Managing specialized version at run time imposes some overhead, both in terms of time and space. Our execution support tries to minimize the time overhead in frequently executed paths. Namely, as long as the state does not change, each call of a specializable method incurs only one extra method call to delegate the behavior to the current implementation. Only when there is a state change, the execution support is invoked to perform various tasks: determining which specialization to choose, calling the specializer on-the-fly (for run-time classes), propagating notifications, and replacing the implementation.

Furthermore, the overhead is not paid by all objects of a root class. In the filesystem example (see figure 14), assignments to variable `count` are not guarded in any generic file object because this part of the state does not affect the current implementation.

### 4.4 Current Status

We have implemented a compiler prototype for specialization classes, written in Java. Our prototype directly implements the compilation algorithm given in Appendix A, using the JavaCC parser generator from Sun [38]. We are currently working on a specializer for Java code which is not yet fully functional. The idea is to use our existing Java-bytecode to C compiler, called Harissa [29], as a front-end to our existing specializer for C programs, called Tempo [12, 24]. Specialized programs may then be translated back to Java.

In the meantime, one can use specialization classes in two ways. First, Tempo can be directly used for specializing *native* methods in Java programs, both for compile-time and run-time specialization classes. Second, the user can supply manually specialized code, by supplying a complete definition for each specializable function in a specialization class. Note that this manual strategy only works when the code can be specialized statically (*i.e.*, only for compile-time specialization classes).

## 5 Related Work

Predicate classes [8] are a form of dynamic inheritance, which complements the static inherintace of an object-oriented language. They offer support for defining an object with several implementations, which are dynamically selected based on arbitrary predicates on the object's state. Implementations are not restricted to specialization of an existing behavior; they can add completely new functionalities. All implementations must be defined statically, by hand. Part of the interface checking must be done at run time, unless avoided by some user annotations. The dynamic selection of implementations is based on multi-dispatching.

Specialization classes are based on predicates classes, but are tailored for a particular goal: program specialization. Our predicates have some simple forms, which allows us to automatically derive implementations, even at run-time. As the interface of specialized objects never changes, static interface checking can still be done without any user guidance. The assumption that unstable predicates seldom change allows us to optimize the implementation, and to fully integrate it into a single-dispatched language such as Java.

Dean *et al.* explore a specific form of program specialization, which is aimed at eliminating most of the virtual method calls in an object-oriented language [17]. To eliminate a virtual method call on a receiver object, a clone of the caller method is produced for each possible type of both the receiver and the arguments. Special care is taken to avoid an uncontrolled code growth by selectively performing this optimization. The selection algorithm estimates the impact of a potential specialization based on profiling information. In their approach, methods are specialized only with respect to the *type* of the objects. Our specialization is with respect to the state of the objects. An interesting direction would be to explore a selection algorithm for (general) program specialization. This algorithm would compute the most useful specialization classes, based on profiling information.

Existing program specializers offer different levels of support for expressing and guiding specialization. In CMix [1], a specializer for C programs, the transformations are guided by command line parameters to the specializer. The management of specialized components is not addressed, because the program is always specialized as a whole. In Tempo [11], (our specializer for C programs) both run-time and compile-time specialization can be done [13], based on a separate description of the specialization context. This description is flat and somewhat limited, due to the lack of sufficient structure in C programs. The run-time specialized versions must be entirely managed by the user. In Fabius [27], a specializer for ML programs, the user guides the transformations by rewriting the program to expose two execution stages, using currying. The specializable component is a function, and it is up to the programmer to generate and manage the specialized functions. In the C dynamic compiler developed by University of Washington [3, 21], the programmer can mark replaceable components by directly annotating the program, using a few syntax extensions. The management of specialized blocks is done automatically.

Cowan *et al.* describe some execution support for managing several versions of the same procedure, in the context of adaptive operating systems [15]. Their work focuses on a re-plugging algorithm able to deal with the concurrency issues of an operating system.

Finally, let us note that our compiling scheme for generating the execution support generalizes some programming patterns found in object-oriented applications dealing with forms of dynamic adaptivity. As an example, in the standard Java library, several objects offer some adaptivity to security restrictions. The `java.net.Socket` class delegates part of its functionality to an implementation object called `SocketImpl`. These implementation objects are created by a `SocketImplFactory` object, which can be replaced by a user-defined one. This adaptivity is irreversible in that once a socket is created, its implementation cannot change anymore.

## 6 Future Work and Conclusions

Specialization classes provide a complete declarative approach to describe the specialization behavior of program components. As a result, specialization can better adapt a program to a specific usage pattern. Specialization classes allow the programmer to declare what program components should be specialized and how they should be specialized. This approach uniformly captures the numerous emerging alternatives to perform specialization (compile time, run time, incremental, automatic, ...).

Specialization classes are fully integrated in the object-oriented paradigm. It declares specialization aspects of existing classes without disturbing the source program.

Specialization classes define a specialization context

which can be applied at both compile time and run time. If a specialization context changes because of some state updates, this situation is automatically detected and the corresponding specialization methods are either specialized with more values or made more generic if some specialization values become unavailable. Because specialization classes form a class hierarchy, objects can be specialized incrementally as more specialization values become available.

Specialization classes allow the programmer to specify what run-time support a class should include to manage its specializations. In particular, various cache strategies can be declared to better fit the specialization needs of the application.

We have implemented a compiler from extended Java, with specialization classes, to standard Java. We are currently completing a program specializer for Java programs. It will then be interfaced with our specialization class compiler. It will allow a programmer to specify both compile-time and run-time specialization aspects of classes.

We are studying the generalization of the form of predicates used in specialization classes. In particular, we plan on introducing disjunctions and class variables to improve the expressive power of predicates.

Regarding applications of specialization classes, we are continuing the effort initiated by Cowan *et al.* in the area of adaptive operating system components [16]. We would like to use specialization classes to specify a number of systems optimizations that have been described in the litterature (*e.g.*, [23, 7, 37, 20]). In particular, we are redesigning a part of the CHORUS IPC subsystem, to exploit opportunities for run-time optimization that have not been addressed so far because of a lack of appropriate methodologies and tools.

## Acknowledgements

The research presented here was partially supported by SEPT/France Telecom grant CTI 951W009.

We would like to thank Gregor Kiczales, the anonymous OOPSLA referees, and the members of the Compose group, for their helpful comments and feedback. Special thanks to Julia Lawall for many discussions on earlier drafts of this paper. The original ideas for specialization classes arose from discussions with Jonathan Walpole and Calton Pu on the need for guarding, and interactions with Andrew Black.

## References

[1] L. Andersen. *Program Analysis and Specialization for the C Programming Language.* PhD thesis, DIKU, University of Copenhagen, Denmark, 1994. DIKU Research Report 94/19.

[2] P. Andersen. Partial evaluation applied to ray tracing. DIKU Research Report 95/2, DIKU, University of Copenhagen, Denmark, 1995.

[3] J. Auslander, M. Philipose, C. Chambers, S. Eggers, and B. Bershad. Fast, effective dynamic compilation. In PLDI96 [33], pages 149–159.

[4] R. Baier, R. Glück, and R. Zöchling. Partial evaluation of numerical programs in Fortran. In *ACM SIGPLAN Workshop on Partial Evaluation and Semantics-Based Program Manipulation*, pages 119–132, Orlando, FL, USA, June 1994. Technical Report 94/9, University of Melbourne, Australia.

[5] A. Berlin. Partial evaluation applied to numerical computation. In *ACM Conference on Lisp and Functional Programming*, pages 139–150, Nice, France, 1990. ACM Press.

[6] B. Bershad, T. Anderson, E. Lazowska, and H. Levy. Lightweight remote procedure call. *ACM Transactions on Computer Systems*, 8(1):37–55, February 1990.

[7] R. Campbell, N. Islam, P. Madany, and D. Raila. Designing and implementing Choices: an object-oriented system in C++. *Communications of the ACM*, 1993.

[8] C. Chambers. Predicate classes. In *Proceedings of the ECOOP'93 European Conference on Object-oriented Programming*, volume 707 of *Lecture Notes in Computer Science*, pages 268–296, Kaiserstautern, Germany, July 1993.

[9] W. Cheung and L. A. Exploring issues of operating systems structuring: from microkernel to extensible systems. *ACM Operating Systems Reviews*, 29(4):4–16, Oct. 1995.

[10] C. Consel. A tour of Schism. In PEPM93 [31], pages 66–77.

[11] C. Consel, L. Hornof, F. Noël, J. Noyé, and E. Volanschi. A uniform approach for compile-time and run-time specialization. In O. Danvy, R. Glück, and P. Thiemann, editors, *Partial Evaluation, International Seminar, Dagstuhl Castle*, number 1110 in Lecture Notes in Computer Science, pages 54–72, Feb. 1996.

[12] C. Consel, L. Hornof, F. Noël, J. Noyé, and E. Volanschi. A uniform approach for compile-time and run-time specialization. Rapport de recherche 2775, INRIA, Rennes, France, Jan. 1996.

[13] C. Consel and F. Noël. A general approach for run-time specialization and its application to C. In POPL96 [34], pages 145–156.

[14] C. Consel, C. Pu, and J. Walpole. Incremental specialization: The key to high performance, modularity and portability in operating systems. In PEPM93 [31], pages 44–46. Invited paper.

[15] C. Cowan, T. Autrey, C. Krasic, C. Pu, and J. Walpole. Fast concurrent dynamic linking for an adaptive operating system. In *International Conference on Configurable Distributed Systems*, Annapolis, MD, May 1996.

[16] C. Cowan, A. Black, C. Krasic, C. Pu, J. Walpole, C. Consel, and E. Volanschi. Specialization classes: An object framework for specialization. In *Fifth IEEE International Workshop on Object-Orientation in Operating Systems*, Seattle, Washington, Oct. 1996.

[17] J. Dean, C. Chambers, and D. Grove. Selective specialization for object-oriented languages. In *Proceedings of the ACM SIGPLAN '95 Conference on Programming Language Design and Implementation.* ACM SIGPLAN Notices, 30(6), June 1995.

[18] D. Engler, W. Hsieh, and M. Kaashoek. 'C: A language for high-level, efficient, and machine-independent dynamic code generation. In POPL96 [34], pages 131–144.

[19] D. Engler and M. Kaashoek. DPF: Fast, flexible message demultiplexing using dynamic code generation. In *SIGCOMM Symposium on Communications Architectures and Protocols*, Stanford University, CA, Aug. 1996. ACM Press.

[20] M. Gien. Evolution of the CHORUS open microkernel architecture: The STREAM project. In *Proceedings of Fifth IEEE Workshop on Future Trends in Distributed Computing Systems (FTDCS'95)*, Cheju Island, Korea, Aug. 1995. IEEE Computer Society Press. Also Technical Report CS/TR-95-107, Chorus Systemes.

[21] B. Grant, M. Mock, M. Philipose, C. Chambers, and S. Eggers. Annotation-directed run-time specialization in C. In PEPM97 [32], pages 163–178.

[22] B. Guenter, T. Knoblock, and E. Ruf. Specializing shaders. In *Computer Graphics Proceedings*, Annual Conference Series, pages 343–350. ACM Press, 1995.

[23] G. Hamilton and P. Kougiouris. The Spring nucleus: A microkernel for objects. Technical Report SMLI TR-93-14, Sun Microsystems Laboratories, Inc., Apr. 1993.

[24] L. Hornof and J. Noyé. Accurate binding-time analysis for imperative languages: Flow, context, and return sensitivity. In PEPM97 [32].

[25] G. Kiczales. Aspect-oriented programming. http://-www.parc.xerox.com/spl/projects/aop/, 1996.

[26] P. Kleinrubatscher, A. Kriegshaber, R. Zöchling, and R. Glück. Fortran program specialization. In U. Meyer and G. Snelting, editors, *Workshop Semantikgestützte Analyse, Entwicklung und Generierung von Programmen*, pages 45–54. Justus-Liebig-Universität, Giessen, Germany, 1994. Report No. 9402.

[27] P. Lee and M. Leone. Optimizing ML with run-time code generation. In PLDI96 [33], pages 137–148.

[28] B. Locanthi. Fast bitblt() with asm() and cpp. In *European UNIX Systems User Group Conference Proceedings*, pages 243–259, AT&T Bell Laboratories, Murray Hill, Sept. 1987. EUUG.

[29] G. Muller, B. Moura, F. Bellard, and C. Consel. JIT *vs.* offline compilers: Limits and benefits of bytecode compilation. Rapport de recherche 1063, IRISA, Rennes, France, Dec. 1996.

[30] G. Muller, E. Volanschi, and R. Marlet. Scaling up partial evaluation for optimizing a commercial RPC protocol. Rapport de recherche 1068, IRISA, Rennes, France, Dec. 1996. Also published in ACM SIGPLAN Conference on Partial Evaluation and Semantics-Based Program Manipulation, 1997.

[31] *Partial Evaluation and Semantics-Based Program Manipulation*, Copenhagen, Denmark, June 1993. ACM Press.

[32] *ACM SIGPLAN Symposium on Partial Evaluation and Semantics-Based Program Manipulation*, Amsterdam, The Netherlands, June 1997. ACM Press.

[33] *Proceedings of the ACM SIGPLAN '96 Conference on Programming Language Design and Implementation.* ACM SIGPLAN Notices, 31(5), May 1996.

[34] *Conference Record of the* $23^{rd}$ *Annual ACM SIGPLAN-SIGACT Symposium on Principles Of Programming Languages*, St. Petersburg Beach, FL, USA, Jan. 1996. ACM Press.

[35] C. Pu, T. Autrey, A. Black, C. Consel, C. Cowan, J. Inouye, L. Kethana, J. Walpole, and K. Zhang. Optimistic incremental specialization: Streamlining a commercial operating system. In *Proceedings of the 1995 ACM Symposium on Operating Systems Principles*, pages 314–324, Copper Mountain Resort, CO, USA, Dec. 1995. ACM Operating Systems Reviews, 29(5),ACM Press.

[36] C. Pu, H. Massalin, and J. Ioannidis. The Synthesis kernel. *Computing Systems*, 1(1):11–32, Winter 1988.

[37] V. Rozier, V. Abrossimov, F. Armand, I. Boule, M. Gien, M. Guillemont, F. Herrmann, C. Kaiser, S. Langlois, P. Léonard, and W. Neuhauser. Overview of the Chorus distributed operating system. In *USENIX - Workshop Proceedings - Micro-kernels and Other Kernel Architectures*, pages 39–70, Seattle, WA, USA, Apr. 1992.

[38] Sun. JavaCC — the Java compiler compiler. http://-www.suntest.com/JavaCC/, 1997.

[39] E. Volanschi, G. Muller, and C. Consel. Safe operating system specialization: the RPC case study. In *Workshop Record of WCSSS'96 – The Inaugural Workshop on Compiler Support for Systems Software*, pages 24–28, Tucson, AZ, USA, Feb. 1996.

# A The Compilation Algorithm

**Input:** a Java class $X$, and a set of $N$ specialization classes which *specialize* class $X$.
**Output:** a new class $X$ (the enclosing class), and a set of $N+1$ implementation classes for $X$.

1. Preliminary operations:
   a) Compute the set $V_{obj}$ of all variables which:
      - belong to class $X$, and
      - are of reference type, and
      - occur in some specialization class.

   b) for each specialization class $S$
      - for each predicate $P$ in $S$
        compute a specialization time for $P$:
        - if $P$ is of the form "$v$ == *const_expr*;" then $P$ is compile-time
        - if $P$ is of the form "$v$;" then $P$ is run-time
        - if $P$ is of the form "$S'$ $v$;" then $P$ has the specialization time of $S'$
          *Note:* cycles are not allowed.
      - compute a specialization-time attribute for $S$:
        if
        - $S$ is user-annotated `runtime`, or
        - $S$ `extends` a run-time specialization class, or
        - there exists a run-time predicate in $S$

        then $S$ is run-time
        otherwise $S$ is compile-time
      - if $S$ is compile-time
        then for each method $m$ in $S$, specialize $m$ as follows:
        - call the compile-time specializer for $m$ with specialization values derived from the predicates in $S$ and its specialization super-classes (if any)
        - collect the specialized method $m_S$

        otherwise for each method $m$ in $S$, prepare run-time specialization for $m$:
        - call the preprocessing phase of the specializer for $m$ with specialization description from $S$ and its specialization super-classes (if any)
        - collect the run-time specializer for $m_S$
      - compute stable/unstable information:
        for each predicate $P$ in $S$
        if the variable $v$ occurring in $P$ is never assigned outside the constructors and the finalizer
        then $P$ is stable
        otherwise $P$ is unstable
        *Note:* variable $v$ is also said to be stable, respectively unstable.

   c) Build a decision tree, following the hierarchy tree of specialization classes. This decision tree will be used to compute a new specialization state, in response to a state change. Each node in the tree corresponds to a specialization class $S$, and checks for a conjuction of the following predicates:
      - for each predicate $P$ in $S$ of the form "$v$ == *const_expr*;":
        $v$ == *const_expr* (*i.e.*, $P$ itself)
      - for each predicate in $S$ of the form "$S'$ $v$;":
        $v$`.scIsA(`$S'$`)`
        *Note:* run-time predicates are always true, so they are not included in the tests.

2. Construct the enclosing class $X$:
   a) Add to the parents of $X$ `implements Mutable`.
   b) Copy all variables of $X$ (whether instance or class variables).
   c) Add the following new variables:
      - $X$`Impl scImpl;`
      - `List scClients;`

   d) Define the following initialization code, in a `private void scInit()` method:
      - initialize clients list to empty:
        `scClients = null;`
      - for each variable $v \in V_{obj}$, subscribe to the clients list of $v$:
        `if(`$v$`!=null)` $v$`.scAttach(this);`
      - compute initial state:
        `this.scNotify();`

   e) Rewrite the constructors:
      for each constructor of $X$
      - *copy original* body (do not guard assignments here)
      - add a call to the initialization code: `scInit();`

   f) Rewrite the finalizer:
      - for each variable $v \in V_{obj}$, detach from $v$:
        `if(`$v$`!=null)` $v$`.scDetach();`
      - copy original body

   g) *Copy original instance methods*, by rewriting assignments to unstable variables $v$ as follows:
      $v$ `=` *expr*`;` $\longrightarrow$ `scImpl.scSet_`$v$`(`*expr*`);`
   h) Copy original class methods unchanged.
   i) Add `Mutable` behavior:
      - a `public void scNotify()` method, which recomputes the current state, using the decision tree previously built, and switches to the corresponding implementation
      - a method for changing the implementation:

```
protected void scSwitchToImpl(String state)
{
  Specializer s = getTheSpec(state);
     // either CT or RT specializer
     /* create a new implementation
        for the current object,
        specialized for the givem state: */
  scImpl = s.spec(this, state);
}
```

        *Note:* The compile-time specializer just creates a new instance of an existing specialized implementation. The run-time specializer takes an existing template implementation class, creates a new class by copying the template, runs the code generators to create a native library, loads this library into the new class, and instantiates this class to get an implementation.
      - three methods for the interface with the clients:

```
public void scAttach(Mutable m)
   // register m as client
   { scClients.insert(m); }
public void scDetach(Mutable m)
   // unregister m
   { scClients.delete(m); }
public boolean scIsA(String state)
   /* check if the object has reached at
      least the given specialization state
   { ... }
```

   j) for each specializable method $m$, replace it with a forwarding method:
      *type* $m$`(`*args*`) { return scImpl.`$m$`(`*args*`) }`

3. Construct the $N+1$ implementations for $X$:

   a) Construct a generic implementation for $X$, **class** *X*`Impl` **extends** `Impl`:

   - define a back-pointer to the enclosing instance: `protected` *X* `scEncl;`
   - define a constructor: *X*`Impl(Mutable m) { scEncl = m; }`
   - define update methods:

     **for** each specialization class $S$
       **for** each unstable variable $v$ (of type $T$) occurring in $S$
         **if** $S$ is a specialization sub-class of $X$
         **then** add:

```
T set_v(T val)
// 'enabler' update method:
{
  scEncl.v = val;
  if(P_v) scEncl.scNotify();
  return val;
}
```

         **otherwise** add:

```
T set_v(T val)
// plain assignment:
{
  scEncl.v = val;
  return val;
}
```

   - **for** each specializable method, copy the original (generic) body, in which `scEncl` has been substituted for `this`.

   b) **for** each specialization class $S$, construct a specialized implementation **class** *S*`Impl` **extends** *C*`Impl` (where $C$ is the parent of $S$ — either the class $X$ or some specialization class $S_{up}$):

   - define a constructor: *S*`Impl(Mutable m) { scEncl = m; }`
   - **if** the specializer is not the one inherited from $C$, **then** add: `static { theSpec = new` *strategy*`(`*size*`); }`
     *Note:* The specializer needs to be redefined if $S$ is run-time and $C$ is compile-time, or $S$ defines its own cache. In the former case, the cache *strategy* and *size* take some default values. In the latter case, they are those defined by $S$.
   - redefine some update methods:
     - **for** each unstable variable $v$ (of type $T$) occurring in $S$, add:

```
T set_v(T val)
// 'disabler' update method:
{
  scEncl.v = val;
  if(¬P_v) scEncl.scNotify();
  return val;
}
```

     - **for** each specialization sub-class $S_{down}$ of $S$
       **for** each unstable variable $v$ (of type $T$) occurring in $S_{down}$, add:

```
T set_v(T val)
// 'enabler' update method:
{
  scEncl.v = val;
  if(P_v) scEncl.scNotify();
  return val;
}
```

   - **for** each method $m$ occuring in $S$
     **if** $S$ is compile-time
     **then** add the specialized version of $m$, in which `scEncl` has been substituted for `this`
     **otherwise** declare method $m$ `native`; its implementation will be dynamically generated and loaded into the class.

*Note:* `Impl` is an abstract class, defined in the specialization support library (omitted). It defines a class variable which refers to the default specializer (namely, the compile-time specializer):

```
protected final
  class Specializer theSpec = CtSpecializer.theSpec;
```

*Note:* The update method for any variable $v \in V_{obj}$ contains some additional code to detach from the old object and attach to the new object. This code is not shown for simplicity.

# The OT Idea Life-cycle: From Eureka! to Shrink Wrap

## Panel Session

Moderator: Laura Hill

Panelists: Bruce Anderson, Adele Goldberg, Gregor Kiczales, Colin Scott, Kevin Tyson

**Abstract:** Over the past years, the Object Technology community has seen the birth of a number of new technology ideas that have changed the way we do computing. These ideas have affected compiler design, analysis approaches, project management techniques, user interface design, deployment strategies and implementation tactics. But where do these ideas come from? And how do they evolve? Do they address the needs as specified by members of the Object Community? Is there a way we can nurture the introduction and assimilation of these ideas to and by the community at large? And what are the market forces that bend ideas to their will. This panel will look at new ideas in Object Technology from a variety of perspectives and will attempt to get to the heart of the way that we, as technologists, create, buy, sell and grow ideas.

**Format:** The format will be a round table discussion, with each facet of the topic (described below) discussed for 15 minutes. Each topic will be introduced by a five minute presentation by one panelist, followed by a 10 minute discussion by all panelists. Audience questions will be taken at the end of the session.

*Laura Hill is Vice President for Application Development at Robertson, Stephens & Co.*

### Gregor Kiczales

*What is an idea?* "What is an idea" is something that changes over time. Take for example Java — some communities look at it and say "there's nothing new there". Others look at it and say "wow this is great new stuff". Why does that happen, and what can we learn from it?

In part I think this has to do with the changing context around ideas. As an idea matures, and the world becomes more and more ready to hear it, what people evaluate about the idea shifts. An idea which the research community sees as "old" another community can see as "new". What's happening is that they are looking at different parts of the idea.

Inventors of new ideas can exploit this, by understanding all the different parts of an idea that must "work" before the idea can be successful: technology, market niche, channel and being well attuned to which of those fronts they are attempting to cross at any one time.

My perspective then is a variant of Haldane's "usual four stages" (1963) of the process of acceptance of a scientific idea:

1. This is worthless nonsense
2. This is an interesting but perverse point of view
3. This is true, but quite unimportant
4. I always said so

What I would add is that these four stages must be traversed for each of the communities that need to buy into the idea, and that in the process the idea has to evolve to become "obvious" to that community. Only then can the kind of rapid take-up we often shoot for with new ideas happen.

*Gregor Kiczales is a principal scientist at the Xerox Palo Alto Research Center. His primary interests are in software architecture, programming languages and software engineering. He has done extensive work in object-oriented programming language design and implementation. He is one of the designers of the Common Lisp Object system (CLOS), and the implementor of PCL, a high-performance portable implementation of CLOS. He is the designer of the CLOS metaobject protocol, and the author (with Jim des Rivieres and Danny Bobrow) of "The Art of the Metaobject Protocol," a key work in the development of metaobject protocol and reflection technology. He is the inventor of aspect-oriented programming (AOP), and is the leader of a team of people developing AOP technology at PARC.*

*He has spoken extensively on a wide range of issues in software, at research and industrial conferences, as well as universities and private companies.*

### Bruce Anderson

Bruce Anderson will comment on the process of developing ideas.

*Bruce Anderson is a Senior Architect in the IBM European Object Technology Practice. Bruce has been instrumental in raising the profile of work at the architecture and pattern level. He has published many papers in the field of object technology and architecture, and is well-known in the international object technology community.*

### Adele Goldberg

Adele Goldberg will comment on the psychology of ideas.

*Dr. Adele Goldberg is currently a founder of Neometron, Inc., a Texas-based company working towards Intranet support for self-managed teams. Until April, 1996, she served as Chairman of the Board and a founder of ParcPlace-Digitalk, Inc. Prior to the creation of ParcPlace, Adele received a Ph.D. in Information Science from the University of Chicago and spent 14 years as researcher and laboratory manager of Xerox Palo Alto Research Center. From 1984-1986, Adele served as president of the ACM. Solely and with others, Adele wrote the definitive books on the Smalltalk-80 programming system and has authored numerous papers on project management and analysis methodology using object-oriented technology. Dr. Goldberg edited "The History of Personal Workstations," published jointly by the ACM and Addison-Wesley in 1988 as part of the ACM Press Book Series on the History of Computing which she organized, and co-edited "Visual Object-Oriented Programming" with Margaret Burnett and Ted Lewis. In 1995, a new book on software engineering appeared entitled*

*"Succeeding With Objects: Decision Frameworks for Project Management" with Kenneth S. Rubin.*

*She was recipient of the ACM Systems Software Award in 1987 along with Dan Ingalls and Alan Kay, PC Magazine's 1990 Lifetime Achievement Award for her significant contributions to the personal computer industry, is a Fellow of the ACM, and was honored in 1995 with the Reed College Howard Vollum Award for contributions to science and technology. She is currently a member of the scientific advisory board of the German National Research Centers, is a director of the San Francisco Exploratorium, and is a member of the Board of Directors of two private technology companies.*

## Kevin Tyson

*The Market for Ideas.* Economics, the dismal science, has provided insight into the process of technology adoption in a number technical fields. Notions such as subject marginal utility and time preference assist us in reasoning about changes in technology adoption in fields as diverse as transportation and health, e.g., inexpensive safe automobiles and alternative medicine.

Software has been largely immune to such insights. The subjective margin of utility provided by techniques such as modularity, be it the structured programming form or the more recent object-technology incarnation, are hard to quantify in most software development environments. The level of rigor present in most software engineering practices makes it almost impossible to quantify these benefits. Nonetheless they are perceived as beneficial. In the case of object-technology the actual benefits mainly accrue to developers through the presence of OT tools on their resumes. Managers are no less at fault. The number of Dilbert cartoons in which the pointy-haired boss chooses red databases or imposes a paperless office bear witness to this.

The discrepancy between the impact of economics and technology adoptions is most apparent in financial services software development efforts. Exotic derivative processing systems in which rather advanced mathematics is used for pricing and arbitrage are developed by people using engineering techniques not dissimilar to those used by the "engineers" who built the great European Medieval cathedrals, e.g. "We'll put up the framework and if the wind doesn't blow it down then we'll finish it".

I hold the position that this dysfunctional arrangement is one of the key factors affecting software development in general and OT in particular. The existence of the OSF, OMG and MOMA testify to the fact that the market for software is broken. In other commercial endeavors, the creation of standards bodies follows the establishment of the basic economic and engineering trends. Only by facing the genuine economic drivers in our field can we hope to deliver on the promise of OT.

*Kevin Tyson is the Principal Systems Architect of Enterprise Engineering Associates. He has been developing software for most of the last three decades and has worked in fields as diverse as statistical analysis, social science research, patient record management, technology R&D and financial services. For most of the last 15 years he has concentrated on the application of distributed processing technology in the financial services market. His abiding concern in all of this has been software engineering as a discipline.*

*Mr. Tyson represents his firm in the OMG where he is very active in the Common Facilities Task Force and the Financial Domain Task Force. In addition he has co-authored the OMG's DCE/CORBA Interworking RFP and is very active in the New York DCE Users Group*

## Colin Scott

*Case Studies.* From an industry perspective, innovation in an organization does not necessarily imply the development of new technology. Often, the challenge is to deploy, on a substantial scale, technology that is already well understood, or even to apply existing technology to new areas in the enterprise.

Innovation can be applied to three key dimensions of an organization:

- Technology
- Processes
- People

Often it is necessary to address all of these dimensions in order to make, say, a technological innovation successful. For example, the acceptance of OO technology inside an organization also depends on the availability of development processes at least as good as those they are replacing, and the ability of the people within the organization to assimilate the changes.

Why should an organization embrace innovative technology? An organization may find itself at any point in a spectrum that ranges from the "burning platform" at one end to the "fully satisfied with the status quo" at the other. The strategy of innovators should take account of this positioning.

Innovators often adopt the "push" approach. This assumes that the benefits of the innovation are as "obvious" to the rest of the organization as they are to their champions. This is seldom the case. Rather the innovator must try to create "pull". That is to say, create demand, or a compelling reason for the organization to adopt the innovation. That a technology is "cool" is usually insufficient.

Scale is often a major hindrance to the adoption of innovative approaches. By their nature innovative projects often tend to be on a small scale and will be criticized as such by their opponents. Getting that second client/project, the one that demonstrates the larger scale applicability is key to the success. The innovator can then use the success of that project to pull new clients towards the new technology.

Innovative approaches must live within the context of existing systems. If the new approach is sufficiently different from the rest of the environment or marketplace, it will usually fail or be slow in its adoption. Innovators must concern themselves with how the majority will get "there" from here.

The following characteristics are typical of successful innovations/innovators:

- A unique, compelling value proposition: How does this new technology contribute to the success of the organization or the buyers of the product.
- Anticipation of new sources of demand: The innovation should gather strength as the market evolves. It is not sufficient to meet demand at a single point in time.

- Collaboration through alliance networks: Linking other aproaches, organization, products into the innovation strengthens its position long-term.
- Foster an entrepreneurial culture: The people within the organization should be encouraged to think about the business they're in and consider how what they do can be successful. Not simply build based upon the specification they're given.

*Dr. Colin T. Scott has a B.Sc. and a Ph.D. in Computer Science from the University of Edinburgh, Scotland. He was a tenured member of staff at Stirling University, Scotland where he taught Computer Architecture and Operating Systems. After leaving the university, Colin took up the role of Software Development Director for Spider Systems — a networking hardware and software start-up firm. During his time there, he was responsible for the development of the first Streams-based TCP/IP protocol stack implementation. This implementation was subsequently sold to a number of computer hardware and software vendors including Microsoft. Colin next joined Reuters, a financial information systems provider. His most senior post was that of Director of Architecture and Research for Reuters' trading room information architecture (TRIARCH) network. Colin was principal architect on a number of major trading floor installations including the worldwide trading information network for Deutsche Bank. He was also responsible for the introduction of object-oriented technology to Reuters.*

*Colin joined Andersen Consulting as an Associate Partner working on Project Eagle. He worked as distributed object architect on this project and was responsible for the design of Eagle's ORB-based infrastructure. His next project was the design of NGTA, a heterogeneous component-based architecture for distributed applications. His current role is that of Program Manager for the Andersen-led Rapid Object Application Development consortium. This consortium is partially funded by the US government under the auspices of the ARPA Technology Reinvestment Project (TRP). The goal of this TRP is to transfer second-generation commercial distributed object-oriented processes and tools to the defense sector. The Andersen team is developing knowledge-based domain analysis tools, component specification and integration tools, as well as a distributed agent-based collaborative development environment.*

*Colin is Andersen's representative on the Board of Directors of the Object Management Group. He has also been an invited speaker at Object World on a number of occasions and has published papers on distributed component architectures and distributed object-oriented development.*

# Query-Based Debugging of Object-Oriented Programs

Raimondas Lencevicius, Urs Hölzle, and Ambuj K. Singh
Department of Computer Science
University of California
Santa Barbara, CA 93106
{raimisl,urs,ambuj}@cs.ucsb.edu
http://www.cs.ucsb.edu/{~raimisl,~urs,~ambuj}

**Abstract.** Object relationships in modern software systems are becoming increasingly numerous and complex. Programmers who try to find violations of such relationships need new tools that allow them to explore objects in a large system more efficiently. Many existing debuggers present only a low-level, one-object-at-a-time view of objects and their relationships. We propose a new solution to overcome these problems: query-based debugging. The implementation of the query-based debugger described here offers programmers an effective query tool that allows efficient searching of large object spaces and quick verification of complex relationships. Even for programs that have large numbers of objects, the debugger achieves interactive response times for common queries by using a combination of fast searching primitives, query optimization, and incremental result delivery.

## 1. Introduction

As the complexity of object-oriented systems increases, and as the number of objects in a program increases, debugging becomes more and more difficult. Similarly, object relationships become more numerous and complex. Consequently, a graph of objects and their relationships in a large program resembles a giant tangled web. When debugging a program, the programmer must find the few objects that violate their invariants in this giant web, a process that can resemble a search for the proverbial needle in the haystack. For example, assume that a graphical widget references its parent window, and that this parent window must in turn reference the enclosed widget. How can a programmer detect violations of this relationship?

Current debuggers offer little assistance to the programmer when it comes to solving such problems. While some debuggers (e.g., the debuggers in Smalltalk [Gol84, GR91] or ET++ [GWM89, WG94]) provide at least some assistance by finding all instances of a particular class on demand, these debuggers cannot determine the correctness of object relationships. Many graphical debuggers allow an interactive exploration of individual data structures; for example, clicking on a reference displays the referenced object. However, such manual object-by-object exploration does not significantly improve the programmer's productivity in situations where hundreds or even thousands of objects must be tediously inspected.

An alternative way to test object relationships involves using special testing code written for each application. For example, an application could keep track of all created widgets and include methods that iterate over the list of widgets and verify their correctness. Although this approach is more effective for large data structures than is the manual "display-and-click" approach, writing test code may still consume a considerable amount of time. For example, the Self virtual machine [HU96] contains over 10,000 lines of testing-related C++ code. Such testing code can be used only to answer very particular questions while tracking a bug, consequently the effort spent writing this code is considerable compared to the number of times it can be used. In addition, testing code might be inefficient, especially if the constraints are complex. For example, a relatively straightforward assertion, such as "no widget is contained in more than one window," may require the creation of reference counts to be verified efficiently. With large programs containing thousands of objects, naive testing code might take minutes to execute.

We propose a new solution to overcome these problems: query-based debugging. The approach that we describe here offers programmers an effective query tool that allows complex relationships to be formulated easily and evaluated efficiently. Such queries can be formulated during debugging, or stored as a library of predefined debugging queries together with the program's normal code. In our system, verifying that all widgets are referenced back by their containing windows is as simple as entering the query

```
widget wid; window win.
(wid window = win) &&
(win widget_collection includes: wid) not
```


OOPSLA '97 10/97 GA, USA

(The current implementation of the system is based on Self, so query expressions use Self syntax.) This query identifies all objects that violate the containment constraint. Not only does this query save programming time, the query evaluator also applies sophisticated optimization algorithms to speed the execution of the query and to deliver the results incrementally. Typical queries execute in seconds, even for programs involving thousands of objects.

The rest of this paper is structured as follows. Section 2 introduces the query model and demonstrates its usefulness by giving some examples of queries that we used while developing and testing our system. Section 3 discusses the implementation techniques we used to obtain efficient query execution. Section 4 then provides experimental results verifying that the query-based debugger is efficient enough to be a useful tool during program debugging. Finally, we discuss related work and possible future extensions of the system.

## 2. Query Model and Examples

Our basic premise is that programmers need to verify relationships among objects during debugging. However, any tool for verifying relationships must be both expressive and simple to be widely applicable and to save debugging time. In our system, query expressions look just like expressions in the underlying programming language, Self [US87], so that programmers can use queries without learning a new syntax or language. (Accordingly, we would expect query-based debuggers for different languages to choose a syntax close to that language.) Queries consist of two parts, the *search domain* and the *constraint*. Let us revisit the widget and window query:

```
widget wid; window win.
(wid window = win) &&
(win widget_collection includes: wid) not
```

The first part of the query defines the *search domain* of the query using universal quantification. The domain part of the above example should be read as "for all widgets wid and all windows win...". With Self being a prototype-based language, widget is the name of the widget prototype, and its domain is all objects that contain the same fields as this prototype†; in a class-based language, widget would be a class name and its domain would be all instances of the class.

The second part of the query specifies the constraint expression to be evaluated for each tuple of the search domain. Constraints are arbitrary Self expressions that evaluate to a boolean result. In particular, they can contain message sends. Semantically, the expression will be evaluated for each tuple in the Cartesian product of the query's individual domains, and the query result will include all tuples for which the expression evaluates to true (similarly to an SQL select query).

† See section 3 for a more precise definition.

The general form of a query is

$X_1\ x_{11} \ldots x_{1n}; \ldots ; X_m\ x_{m1} \ldots x_{mn}.$
$\text{Constraint}_1\ \&\&\ \ldots\ \&\&\ \text{Constraint}_k$

where $x_{ij}$ is a domain variable whose domain is $X_i$. The definition of domain variables can have single-type domains or domains including subtypes. For example, the widget single-type domain contains widgets but does not contain colorWidgets. In other words, a domain does not include objects of any subclass or subtype (or, in classless Self, subobject). However, using a different syntax, the user can also specify domains that include instances of subtypes, subclasses, or subobjects. In this case the widget domain would contain both widgets and colorWidgets.

We express the constraint part as a conjunction of a number of individual constraints only because this conjunctive form allows a number of optimizations to the query evaluation order as described in section 3. Constraints not in conjunctive form are perfectly valid and can be specified, but our current system performs no optimizations on them. Conjunctive queries occur frequently and are natural to use, so this restriction has not yet proved to be unreasonably limiting.

### 2.1 Assumptions

Our query model is based on several assumptions. First, it is the programmer's responsibility to ensure that queries are side-effect free—just as expressions in C/C++ assertions must be side-effect free. Second, the programmer must ensure that the queried objects are in a consistent state when the query is evaluated (i.e., that expression evaluation will succeed). Finally, to use efficient hash joins (see section 3.5), we assume that the "=" method in queries has equality semantics; since all methods can be redefined in Self, this is not guaranteed. However, the Self programming guidelines strongly suggest such semantics, and the current Self system contains no method that violates it.‡

### 2.2 Discussion

We chose this particular query model primarily because of its simplicity: a query is a boolean expression prefixed by a search domain specification. Originally we anticipated having to extend the model once its shortcomings would become clear during experimentation, but so far we have not encountered such situations.

An alternative way of specifying queries would use iterators such as Smalltalk's allInstancesDo: method; by predefining more of these iterators, one could potentially avoid

‡ For environments where this assumption is not valid, section 4.5 shows the effect of not using hash joins.

introducing any query language at all and just use the base language. We rejected this approach for two main reasons. First, it is language-dependent—languages without closures cannot express such iterators succinctly. Second, we felt that declarative domain specification was simpler and more flexible, putting the burden of choosing an efficient iteration and evaluation order on the query optimizer instead of the programmer.

Object-oriented databases typically contain more sophisticated query models [AK89, BKK88, NOT96, SZ90]. Our solution was specifically designed for query-based debugging, and we deliberately traded off some completeness and expressive power in exchange for simplicity and ease of use because we deemed these attributes to be of primary importance.

### 2.3 Examples

We now discuss several examples of queries that we used to understand large programs written by others.

#### 2.3.1 The Self Graphical User Interface

We implemented our debugger prototype using the Self user interface which is based on morphs [SMU95]. Morphs are user interface objects (usually having a visual representation) that can perform specified actions and can be moved on the desktop. Morphs can contain other morphs and hierarchically build complex interface objects. Some morphs are primitive. For example, row and column morphs arrange objects horizontally or vertically, frame morphs surround other morphs, and button morphs trigger actions. More complicated morphs such as object outliners are composed of a number of simpler morphs.

During the development of the debugger we encountered numerous questions about the accepted use of morphs. Using our debugger we could easily answer many of these questions. For example, initially we wondered whether one morph could be a part of more than one composite morph. Intuitively, we felt that such a structure would be incorrect, so we asked the debugger to "find all morphs directly contained in at least two morphs":

```
morph a b c.
(a morphs includes: b) && (c morphs includes: b) && (a != c)
```

An empty answer set showed no such morphs in the entire Self system.

Another interesting question arose when we tried to construct "table" morphs. Are row morphs usually embedded into column morphs or vice versa? We looked at the object outliner class that already implements a similar structure, and asked the following two queries:

```
objectOutliner a; rowMorph b; columnMorph c.
(a morphs includes: b) && (b morphs includes: c)
```

```
objectOutliner a; columnMorph b; rowMorph c
(a morphs includes: b) && (b morphs includes: c)
```

The output of the first query was empty, whereas the output of the second query had 23 results, leading us to conclude that object outliners contain column morphs that in turn contain row morphs. However, the query output contained only 23 of the 132 object outliners present in the system at that point; maybe some of them did not contain column morphs or row morphs at all. The query

```
objectOutliner a; columnMorph b.
(a morphs includes: b)
```

returned 130 results. That is, all but two object outliners contained column morphs, but apparently most of these column morphs did not include row morphs. Two outliners were still unaccounted for; perhaps they did not even contain column morphs. The query

```
objectOutliner a.  (a morphs size = 0)
```

confirmed this guess and showed that the two remaining object outliners were special prototype objects. This example demonstrates how our debugger can help to understand both the structure of objects as well as the interactions among them. As we have shown, the debugger can reveal anomalous objects, which might not always be erroneous as witnessed in the last query.

#### 2.3.2 Understanding the Cecil compiler

Because our debugger helped us to understand Self GUI objects, we decided to look at a complex system which we had no previous experience with—a prototype Cecil [Cha93] compiler written in Self by Craig Chambers, Jeff Dean, and David Grove. Here the main goal was to understand the system and in particular to understand relationships among objects in the system. During compilation of a Cecil program, the compiler creates a large number of internal objects representing Cecil language constructs: declaration contexts, Cecil objects and their bindings, methods, and so on.

First, we explored parts of the compiler by finding compiler objects corresponding to Cecil constructs in the compiled Cecil program. We discovered a number of properties of the Cecil types. For example, the simple Cecil program we compiled did not have named types with instantiations:

```
cecil_named_type a.  (a instantiations size != 0)
```

Also, the query below showed that only three Cecil types had subtypes:

```
cecil_named_type a.  (a subtypes size != 0)
```

Can Cecil programs have formals with the same name in different methods?

```
cecil_method a b; cecil_formal c d.
(a formals includes: c) && (b formals includes: d) &&
(c name = d name) && (c != d) && (a != b)
```

The query result was nonempty, confirming the notion that formals with the same name can indeed occur in different methods.

We made a number of other queries about the compiler objects. Overall, the debugger proved to be a valuable tool in understanding the Cecil compiler. This experience leads us to believe that query-based debuggers will be useful for other programmers trying to understand complex OO systems.

# 3. Implementation

We implemented the query-based debugger in Self [US87], a prototype-based, pure, object-oriented programming language. We chose Self as our experimental platform because it is a demanding platform for debugging due to the large number of objects in the system, as well as the numerous complex object relationships. In addition, Self provides several features that simplify the implementation of the prototype system. In particular, Self allows run-time (on-the-fly) code generation [CUL89]. Finally, we had access to the Self Virtual Machine source code, which required modification for the purposes of the debugger.

In section 3.1, we present the general structure of the system. In the remainder of section 3, we discuss in more detail the most important parts of the debugger.

## 3.1 General structure of the system

Figure 1 shows a data flow diagram of the debugger. A parser extracts the domain variables from the query string and passes their types to the collection module which then finds all objects of domain types (see section 3.2) and returns them in separate arrays to the execution module. The parser also transforms the query string into an intermediate form, which is a collection of constraints, each of which in turn corresponds to one constraint of the conjunctive form of the query. The parser then passes this intermediate form to the optimizer which performs order and method optimizations using the knowledge about query constraints and domain sizes (see section 3.4). The code generator module then generates Self source code for the query-specific constraint-checking methods and integrates it with prefabricated constraint evaluation code. In the last phase the execution module sets up the run-time environment for the query evaluation, runs the query code, and finally sends the result back to the user.

The rest of this section discusses the most important parts of the debugger in more detail.

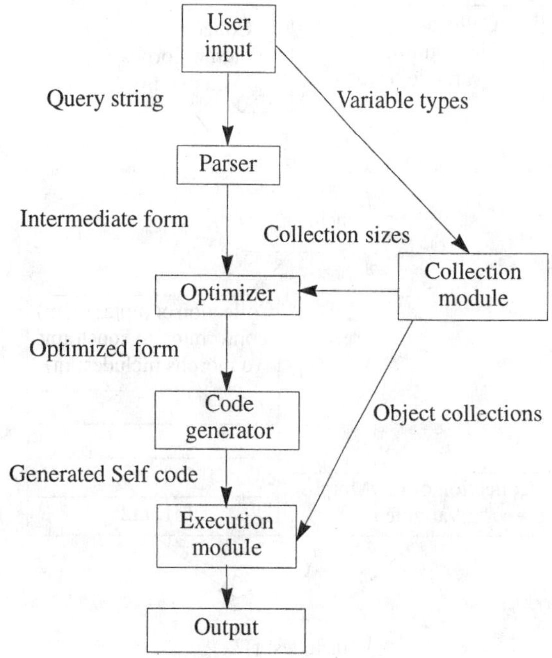


**Figure 1.** Overview of the query-based debugger

## 3.2 Enumerating all objects in a domain

To enumerate all objects in a domain, we extended the Self virtual machine with a new primitive that scans the entire heap and returns a vector containing all matching objects. Since the Self implementation already canonicalizes its internal type descriptors (*maps* [CUL89]), it ensures that all objects with the same object layout (i.e., the same slot names and, for constant slots, slot contents) have the same type descriptor. Therefore, the primitive merely needs to find all references to a particular type descriptor, a task that can be accomplished fairly quickly. The cost of the primitive is dependent on the total size of the heap and the number of matches (i.e., the size of the result). On our test machine (a 200 MHz UltraSPARC workstation) the primitive searches about 110 Mbytes per second and can return about 700,000 objects per second. Given this speed, the primitive has never been a bottleneck in our system.

## 3.3 Overview of query execution

The debugger finds answers to a query by sequentially evaluating all constraints of the query for the query's domain variables. Constraint evaluation is similar to a relational database join coupled with a selection. The initial inputs are individual domains, but during the evaluation these domains are joined; consequently later evaluations consume tuples of objects. Figure 2 shows the query execution of the query

```
objectOutliner o; columnMorph m; rowMorph r.
(o morphs includes: m) && (m morphs includes: r).
```

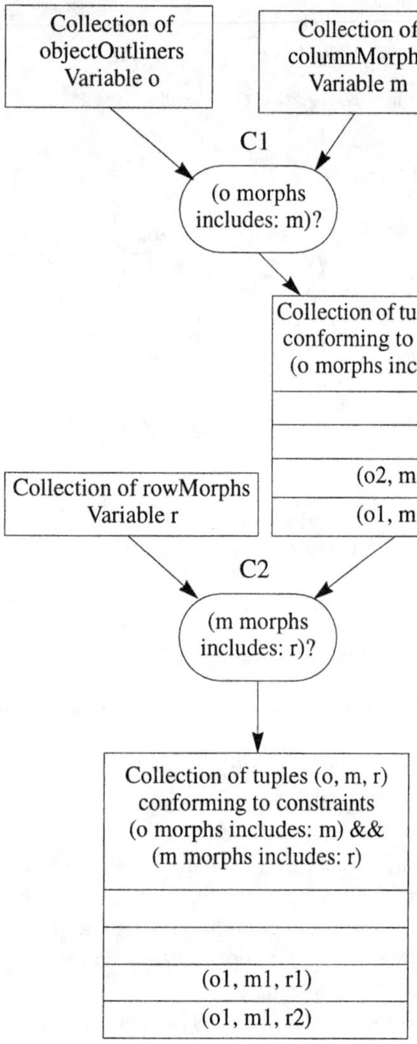


**Figure 2.** Overview of query execution

This query consists of two constraints, each involving two of the three domain variables. The first constraint, (o morphs includes: m) consumes object outliners and column morphs as input; the second constraint consumes tuples with object outliners and column morphs.

Following the evaluation procedure outlined in Figure 2, the system performs a chain of joins, and ends up with a single output collection containing tuples with all objects. Since only the tuples satisfying earlier constraints are passed along the chain, the output contains only tuples satisfying all constraints. In our example, tuples (o1, m1, r1) and (o1, m1, r2) conform to both constraints and are results of the query.

The system could form the chain of joins in an arbitrary way, but some execution orders are more efficient than others, presenting an opportunity for optimization.

### 3.4 Join ordering

The execution order of the individual joins of a query significantly influences overall performance. To see why, let us first consider the cost of a single join. The input size of a single join affects its execution time, while its selectivity affects the input sizes of subsequent joins. (The selectivity is the ratio of tuples that do not conform to the constraint to the number of input tuples in the Cartesian product.†) Both the selectivity and the input sizes of a join depend on the join ordering. In particular, evaluating joins with low selectivity at the beginning of join chain can produce large intermediate results that slow down the evaluation of subsequent joins. For example, the Cartesian product of two 10,000-element relations produces a relation with 100,000,000 tuples. Such a relation would not only be costly to store but also very time-consuming to use.

To optimize the query execution, we must minimize the intermediate results by finding an optimal join ordering. There are no general algorithms that find an optimal join ordering in polynomial time—in fact, this problem is NP-complete [IK84]. Several algorithms produce optimal or near-optimal orders for restricted cases. For example, the KBZ algorithm [KBZ86] computes optimal join orders for left-deep ordering where the join graph is acyclic (for cyclic graphs the algorithm gives approximate results), and assumes perfect knowledge of join sizes and selectivities.

Numerous heuristics try to find near-optimal orderings [IK84, KBZ86, SI93, SMK93]. One such heuristic is the *minimum-cost heuristic* that performs the lowest-cost join first. It uses the size of the input relations as the sole cost factor, with the join's cost being the product of the inputs' sizes for the nested loop join. The minimum-cost heuristic is based on the observation that performing cheap joins in the beginning should shrink the intermediate result size, making the expensive (large) joins at the end less expensive to perform.

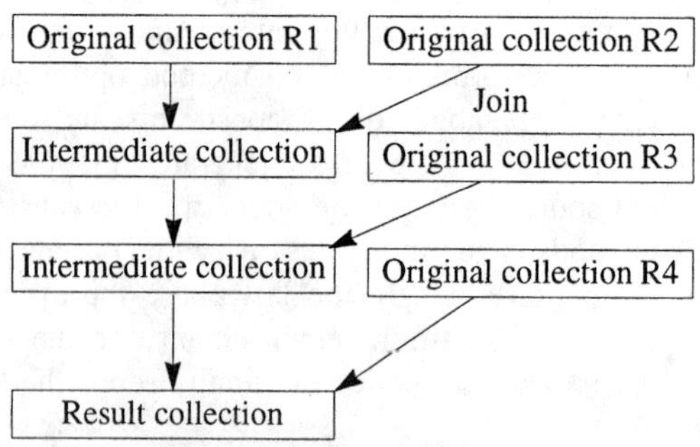


**Figure 3.** Left-deep join

† The database community uses an inverse terminology where "high selectivity" means "many tuples pass the selection". We find it more intuitive for "highly selective" to mean "only few tuples pass the selection".

In addition to using the minimum-cost heuristic, we impose a restriction on the join order by using *left-deep ordering*. Left-deep ordering [SAC+79, SMK93] requires each join to have one and only one intermediate result relation as an input (Figure 3). Left-deep ordering increases the probability of finding an efficient join order since it has a larger percentage of "good" orderings in its search space [SMK93]. It also simplifies incremental result delivery as explained further below.

### 3.5 Maximum-selectivity heuristic

Another heuristic used to order joins is the *maximum-selectivity heuristic*. It performs joins with the highest selectivity first because such joins eliminate the most tuples and consequently produce smaller input sizes for subsequent queries. Although the usefulness of selectivity has been well-documented in the database literature (e.g., see [KBZ86]), its use in the query-based debugging is different. Queries asked during debugging typically have modest output sizes of a few dozen objects, despite search domains that may encompass many thousands or even millions of tuples. This is not a coincidence—programmers want to inspect the objects in the query result, and thus are unlikely to pose queries that have large outputs. Consequently, the selectivity of a typical query is very high (e.g., 99.99% of all tuples do not pass the condition).

In our debugger we know the precise input sizes of joins because all domains are enumerated before determining the query evaluation order. However, we do not know the selectivities of the joins. To accurately estimate selectivity, the query optimizer would have to sample a large number of tuples, a process which can negate the potential speedups gained from better query ordering.

To improve query optimization our system uses *imprecise* selectivity information by randomly choosing ten objects from each domain and evaluating the constraint for all tuples formed by these objects. The number of tuples satisfying the constraint indicates the selectivity of the join. While imprecise, it still allows to distinguish highly-selective constraints (selectivities larger than 0.80) from constraints that have low selectivities (less than 0.50). We decrease the priority of the joins containing low selectivity constraints by multiplying their cost by a factor of 100.

How big should the sample be that is used to estimate selectivity? Larger samples allow more precise estimates, but small samples reduce the cost of estimating the selectivity (and thus the overhead of query optimization). We experimented with several sample sizes and found a sample size of 10 to be a good compromise between accuracy and cost. On average, a sample size of ten produces selectivity estimates with a standard deviation of 0.035, which is accurate enough for our high-low distinction. Increasing the sample size to 100 reduces the standard deviation to 0.01 but is 100 times more costly for a two-object constraint.

The debugger uses a modified minimum-cost heuristic that takes into account two-level (high-low) selectivity estimates. For example, for the query

```
cecil_method a b; cecil_formal c d.
(a formals includes: c) && (b formals includes: d) &&
(c name = d name) && (c != d) && (a != b)
```

the minimum-cost heuristic alone would choose to evaluate the constraints in the following order: (c name = d name), (b formals includes: d), (a != b), (a formals includes: c), (c != d), resulting in a query execution time of 37 seconds. By using selectivity estimates the system recognizes that the join (a != b) has a low selectivity and should be evaluated as late as possible. Consequently it chooses a different evaluation order: (c name = d name), (b formals includes: d), (a formals includes: c), (a != b), (c != d). This improved evaluation order reduces the query execution time to 5.9 seconds.

### 3.6 Hash Joins

Many query constraints have the form $\alpha = \beta$, where $\alpha$ and $\beta$ are expressions involving two different domains. In such cases the system can compute the corresponding join using the *hash-join* method instead of using less efficient nested-loop method [ME92]. Consider the following query about Cecil structures:

```
cecil_named_object n; cecil_top_context t;
cecil_object_binding o.
(n defining_context = t) &&
(t varBindings includes: o) && (o value = n)
```

In this Cecil query we can use a hash join to evaluate the (n defining_context = t) constraint. Hash joins do not affect the join semantics; they are simply a more efficient way to evaluate a join.

To evaluate a constraint using a hash join, we first construct a hash table mapping all result values of expression $\alpha$ to the domain variable(s) that produced these results. In Figure 4 that uses the above example, the hash table maps contexts (the results of applying n defining_context expression to objects n1 and n3) to cecil_named_object objects n1 and n3. Then, we evaluate the expression $\beta$ for each object of the corresponding domain and probe the hash table with each result. If the probe is successful (i.e., if the hash table contains one or more tuples that evaluated to the same value using expression $\alpha$), all of these tuples are added to the result because they satisfy the condition $\alpha = \beta$. In Figure 4, the cecil_top_context object t2 is mapped to the same slot as the cecil_named_object n3, and t2 = n3. Consequently the tuple (n3, t2) satisfies the constraint and belongs to the result. Using the hash join method, the join result can be

| Query | Input | Output |
|---|---|---|
| 1. morph a b c. (a morphs includes: b) && (c morphs includes: b) && (a != c) | 37*37*37 | 0 |
| 2. objectOutliner a; rowMorph b; columnMorph c. (a morphs includes: b) && (b morphs includes: c) | 12*146*370 | 0 |
| 3. objectOutliner a; rowMorph c; columnMorph b. (a morphs includes: b) && (b morphs includes: c) | 12*146*370 | 1 |
| 4. objectOutliner a; columnMorph b. (a morphs includes: b) | 12*370 | 11 |
| 5. objectOutliner a; rowMorph b. (a morphs includes: b) | 12*146 | 0 |
| 6. objectOutliner a. (a morphs size = 0) | 12 | 1 |
| 7. objectOutliner a; smallEditorMorph b. (a titleEditor = b) && (b owner = a) | 12*16 | 0 |
| 8. objectOutliner a; columnMorph b; labelMorph c. (a morphs includes: b) && (c owner = b) && (a moduleSummary = c) | 12*370*1006 | 0 |
| 9. cecil_named_object a; cecil_top_context b; cecil_object_binding c. (a defining_context = b) && (b varBindings includes: c) && (c value = a) | 69*4*79 | 68 |
| 10. cecil_named_type a. (a instantiations size != 0) | 198 | 0 |
| 11. cecil_named_type a. (a subtypes size != 0) | 198 | 3 |
| 12. cecil_method a. (a resultTypeSpec printString = 'int') | 167 | 2 |
| 13. point a; rectangle b. (a x = b origin y) && (a x = 6) | 11195*4579 | 6,780 |
| 14. point a. a x = 256 | 11195 | 2 |
| 15. point a; rectangle b b1. (a x = b origin y) && (b height = b1 height) && (b != b1) && (b1 height = 1000) | 11195*4579*4579 | 0 |
| 16. point a; rectangle b b1. (a x = b origin y) && (b height = b1 height) && (b != b1) && (b1 height > 1000) | 11195*4579*4579 | 12,467 |
| 17. rectangle b b1. (b height > (b1 height + 800)) && (b width < (b1 width - 900)) | 4579*4579 | 0 |
| 18. cecil_method a b; cecil_formal c d. (a formals includes: c) && (b formals includes: d) && (c name = d name) && (c != d) && (a != b) | 167*167*179*179 | 7042 |
| 19. mutableString a. (a asSlotIfFail: [ abstractMirror ]) isReflecteeSlots | 15540 | 11,281 |

**Table 1:** Sample queries with their input and output sizes

the first join does not completely fill its output buffer it would run to completion before a thread switch occurs, and the first query output would not appear before the entire first join is completed. Instead, the scheduler preempts threads after they have used up their time slice and schedules the new highest-priority thread. Thus, if the first join produced any intermediate results during its time slice, these results are pushed down the pipeline, shortening the time to produce the first result. To keep thread switching overhead low, we keep time slices reasonably long (e.g., 100 ms per slice).

## 4. Experimental results

We tested the debugger on a number of realistic and synthetic queries. For our tests we used an otherwise idle Sun Ultra 2/2200 machine (with a 200 MHz UltraSPARC processor) running Solaris 2.5.1 and a modified version of Self 4.0. Execution times reported are elapsed times. Times were measured with millisecond accuracy. We observed a variance of about 10% in the measurements due to various asynchronous events in the Self VM and user thread scheduling effects. We also measured the total CPU time to verify that no other processes disrupted the measurements. We chose the lowest time observed during three repetitions of a measurement.

### 4.1 Benchmark queries

We ran the tests using both realistic queries as well as artificial queries. Table 1 lists the queries and their sizes. We selected a number of realistic queries and tried to present a fair sample in terms of query complexity, query evaluation methods, and query input and output sizes. The realistic queries (1–12) dealt with inputs ranging from 10 to 1,000 objects per type (see Table 1). Queries 1-8 involve the Self GUI, and queries 9-12 involve the Cecil compiler.

To test the limits of the debugger's performance, we also evaluated difficult synthetic queries (queries 13-19) that are less likely to be asked in real life. These queries involved larger inputs that contain tens of thousands of objects (except query 18). Some of them were difficult to evaluate efficiently because the system could not use hash joins (query 17), or because they had an empty result set (query 15), where incremental delivery techniques did not help. Queries 18 and 19 are realistic but time-consuming, so they were grouped together with other queries that place considerable stress on the debugger's performance.

Queries can be divided into the following broad classes:

- Queries 6, 10, 11, 12, 14, and 19 are simple one-constraint selection queries. Since these queries along

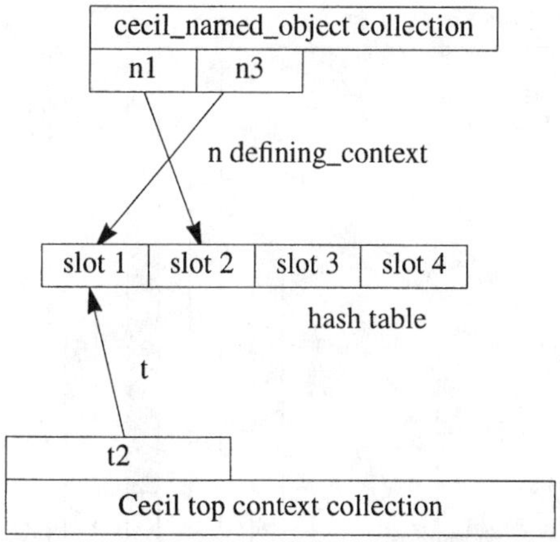


**Figure 4.** Hash join

constructed with a single scan through all tuples in β's domain.

On average hash joins are more efficient than nested loop joins because they execute in O(|α| + |β|) time if the output is small, compared to O(|α| * |β|) time required for a nested loop join regardless of the output size. If the output is close to the size of Cartesian product then the cost of a hash join will also be O(|α| * |β|). Our join ordering algorithm uses |α| + |β| to estimate the cost of a hash join. For example, if there are 4 cecil_top_context objects and 69 cecil_named_object objects, the estimated cost of the hash join (n defining_context = t) is 73.

The experiments in section 4.5 demonstrate that hash joins can dramatically improve performance for some queries.

### 3.7 Incremental delivery

Because a query-based debugger is a part of an interactive programming environment, we would like to achieve interactive performance for the widest possible class of queries. But sometimes it is impossible to compute the entire query result within a short time, for example, the input relations may be very large or the individual query expressions may involve time-consuming operations. Incremental delivery improves the response time of long-running queries by delivering the first result(s) as quickly as possible, so that the user can inspect them while the rest of the result is being computed. To achieve this goal, we developed a technique that dynamically adjusts the CPU time allocated to individual constraints to produce the first result as quickly as possible.

In our system, each join executes as a Self thread and is connected to the next join by a limited-size intermediate result buffer. Figure 5 shows buffers of size 4, and both buffers contain two tuples. This arrangement resembles a pipeline where intermediate results flow along the pipeline toward the next query. As in the classical producer-consumer problem, a thread in the pipeline blocks when its output

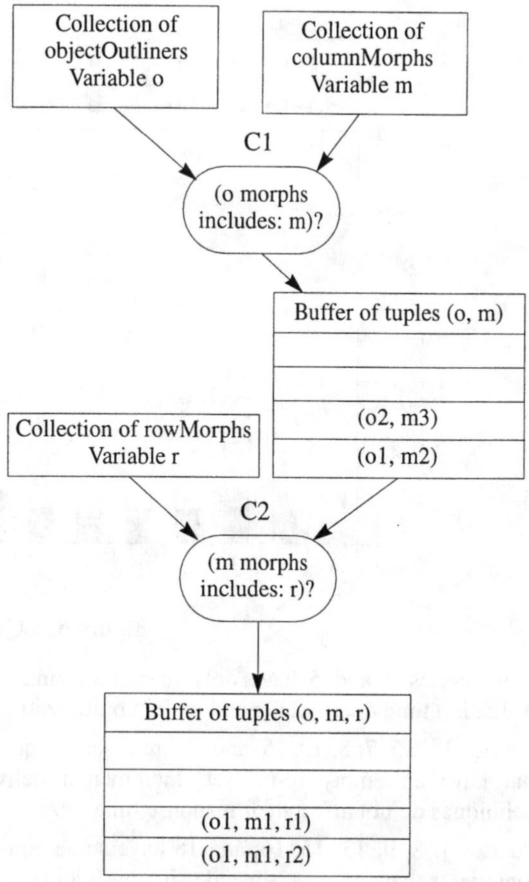


**Figure 5.** Incremental delivery pipeline

buffer is full or when its input buffer is empty. Whenever a thread blocks, the query scheduler picks the next thread to run. By keeping the size of the intermediate buffers small—on the order of 100 elements—the system can "push" intermediate results down the pipeline towards the output before early joins compute their complete results.

The join threads must be scheduled correctly to minimize the response time. We use a simple queue scheduling scheme that prefers threads closer to the end of the pipeline. As a result, intermediate results flow towards the end of the pipeline because consumers closer to the end will run before joins earlier in the pipeline will produce new intermediate results. For example, in Figure 5 the thread executing join C1 will block when it fills the remaining slots in the intermediate buffer or when it finishes scanning through input collections. Then the scheduler will select and run the thread executing join C2 because it is closer to the end of the pipeline and it has non-empty input and non-full output buffers.

Although the thread pipeline by itself increases the speed of output generation, we optimize it further by time-slicing the threads. Time-slicing prevents a slow (or highly selective) join at the beginning of the pipeline from running for a long time before filling its output buffer. Without time-slicing, if

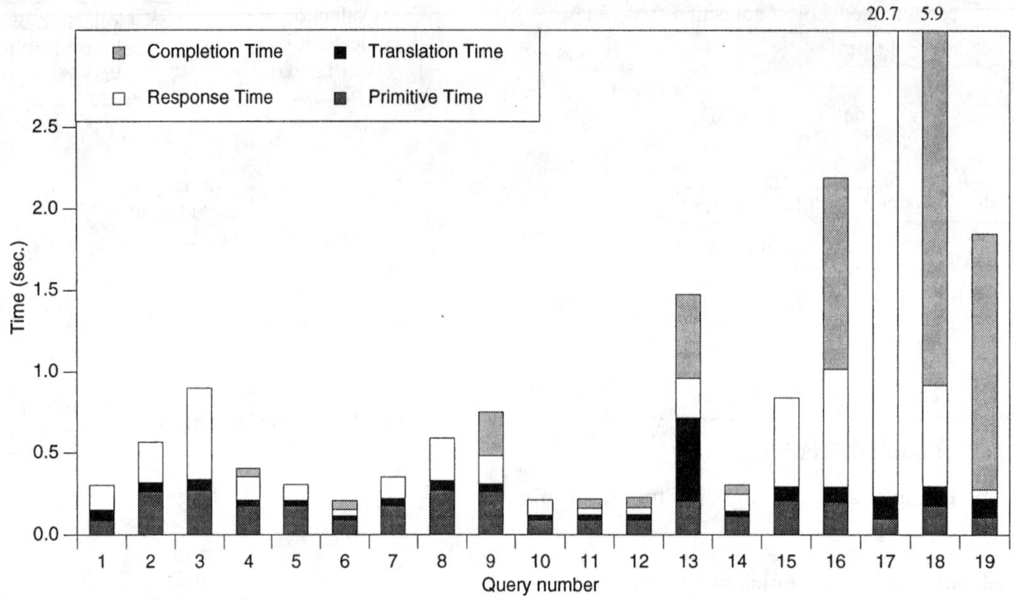


**Figure 6.** Query execution times

with queries 4 and 5 have only one constraint, their evaluation time does not depend on join optimization.

- Queries 1, 2, 5, 7, 8, 10, 15, and 17 are assertion queries that have an empty result set. Incremental delivery techniques do not affect their response time.
- Queries 7, 8, 9, 13, 15, 16, and 18 have some equality constraints that can be evaluated using hash joins, while the other queries use only nested-loop joins.

## 4.2 Execution time

Figure 6 shows the execution times of all queries, split into four components:

- *Primitive time*, the time spent computing the input domains of the query using the primitive described in section 3.2.
- *Translation time*, the time spent choosing a query evaluation order and generating the code to execute the query.
- *Response time*, the time spent producing the first result (not including the time needed to display it in the graphical user interface). For queries producing an empty answer, the response time includes the entire query evaluation because the user has to wait until the end of the query evaluation to learn the outcome.
- *Completion time*, the remaining execution time needed to complete the query and produce all results.

For example, for query 16 it took less than 0.2 seconds to collect all points and rectangles, and less than 0.1 seconds to translate the query into Self code. The first result appeared after an additional 0.7 seconds, and it took another 1.2 seconds to complete query evaluation.

Overall, the results are encouraging, with most of the realistic queries (1-12) taking less than a second to evaluate. For these queries, the median response time was 0.33 seconds, and the median completion time was 0.33 seconds. Query 18 was the only realistic query that took a long time to evaluate, but even there the first result appeared in less than a second.

Some of the artificial queries (13-16) also executed in the subsecond range. For these queries, the median response time was 0.89 seconds, and the median time to complete the query was 1.14 seconds. Query 17 took 20.7 seconds to complete. This query is difficult for the system to evaluate efficiently because it does not contain equality constraints. Consequently the system can not use hash joins. The debugger had to execute a nested-loop join for 4579×4579 rectangles, evaluating the first constraint 21 million times. Query 19 took 2 seconds to complete. This query is a simple selection query, but it performs a time-consuming operation—compilation of the Self code string—for each mutable string.

We found that many queries had such enormous outputs that our machine ran out of memory trying to produce results. Usually, such queries are asked by mistake, since the programmer probably would not want to look at millions of tuples in a result. A straightforward restriction on the result size eliminates system crashes and alerts users to this type of mistake.

## 4.3 Join ordering

To see how well the query optimizer works, we compared its performance against the best and worst join orderings. In this experiment, we executed the queries using all possible left-

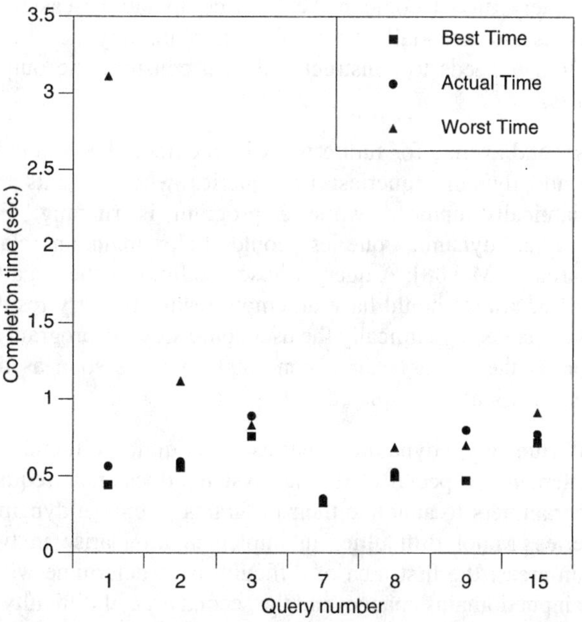


**Figure 7.** Completion time depending on join ordering (small queries)

deep orderings that perform selections first. Such orderings correspond to the search space of our join ordering algorithm. In all cases the best ordering in this search space was indeed the globally optimal ordering, so the search space limitation did not influence the results. We did not include queries with only one constraint in this experiment.

Figure 7 compares the best and the worst query completion times to the completion time using the ordering found by our system. The results show that query optimization works well for small queries†, but the join ordering does not matter very much for such queries since even in the worst case they take less than a second to execute.

However, larger and more complicated queries have much wider range of best and worst times (Table 2). Queries 16 and 18 clearly demonstrate the need for join order optimization. Our system evaluates query 16 in 2.2 seconds, but the worst-case execution time is more than 10 minutes. Our system does not perform optimally all the time; it sometimes finds fairly bad orderings but the outcome of the join ordering may be cushioned by the incremental delivery methods discussed later.

† Sometimes, though, the debugger has an execution time slightly higher than the "worst" one due to optimization overhead and random system events.

| Query number | Best | Actual | Worst |
|---|---|---|---|
| 16 | 1.1 | 2.2 | 631 |
| 17 | 17 | 20.7 | 27.2 |
| 18 | 3 | 5.9 | 130 |

**Table 2:** Completion time depending on join ordering (large queries)

## 4.4 Incremental delivery

Incremental delivery significantly reduces the response time of the system. For example, query 18 took 5.9 seconds to complete but produced the first result in less than a second. Overall, the response time ranged from 12% to 100% of the completion time with a median of 87% (recall Figure 6). Excluding queries with empty answer sets (which cannot benefit from incremental delivery) the median ratio is 73%, i.e., incremental delivery reduces the waiting time for the programmer by about 27%.

The use of incremental delivery also limits sizes of intermediate collections. For example, query 18 runs out of memory when executing in non-incremental mode because it produces enormous intermediate results. In incremental mode, it evaluates successfully because intermediate result sizes are limited by buffer sizes.

To check the influence of time-slicing on the response time of different queries, we evaluated all queries using time slices ranging between 100 ms and infinite time slice. The experiments showed that time-slicing does not have visible effect on most queries. However, time-slicing becomes important for large queries with small result sets. For example, if we take assertion query 17 that has an empty result set, and add an object to the system that violates the assertion, the query execution pattern changes. The assertion originally took 20 seconds to verify, but the object violating the assertion is found early in the execution. Consequently, the response time is 3 seconds, while the completion time remains 20 seconds. If the time-slicing is disabled, the first join in the query does not fill the intermediate buffer, so no thread switches occur almost until the end of the execution. As a result, without time-slicing the response time becomes equal to the completion time of 20 seconds.

In summary, incremental delivery can substantially shorten the response time; large queries and queries with nested loop joins benefit most from incremental delivery. Time-slicing is a useful enhancement when dealing with large queries.

## 4.5 Hash joins

Many queries can use hash joins to avoid computing the full Cartesian product. But as explained in section 3.5, some joins must be computed the hard way, using nested loops. How much slower are such joins? To answer this question we re-executed all queries that use hashed joins with hashing disabled. Table 3 shows the slowdowns of these query evaluations. In our test system, slowdowns ranged from 0.6 to 2 with a median of 0.98. Query 15 experienced a speedup because the optimizer found a better join ordering for nested loop joins than the one used for hash joins. When we increased the size of each relevant domain by five times to simulate a larger system, the slowdowns became substantial (right column of Table 3), ranging from 0.32 to 15.6 with a median of 1.97.

The results of these preliminary experiments indicate that hash joins can be more efficient than nested-loop joins, although they slow down several of our test cases. With large input domains, the performance advantage of hash joins can exceed an order of magnitude (e.g., in query 18).

| Query number | Small system | 5x larger system |
|---|---|---|
| 7 | 0.93 | 1.13 |
| 8 | 1.18 | 1.97 |
| 9 | 2 | 6.42 |
| 13 | 1.94 | 5.76 |
| 15 | 0.63 | 0.32 |
| 16 | 0.98 | 0.91 |
| 18 | 0.6 | 15.6 |

**Table 3:** Slowdown of nested queries vs. hash queries

Fortunately, even if hash joins could not be used, incremental delivery can mask much of the nested loop join overhead by producing the first result quickly. Table 4 shows the response times both with and without hashing. For these queries the first results can be produced in less than a second, and the response time varies by less than a factor of two between the two configurations.

| Query number | Nested (sec.) | Hash (sec.) | Ratio |
|---|---|---|---|
| 7 | 0.33 | 0.35 | 0.93 |
| 8 | 0.7 | 0.6 | 1.18 |
| 9 | 0.7 | 0.5 | 1.46 |
| 13 | 0.89 | 0.96 | 0.92 |
| 15 | 0.5 | 0.8 | 0.63 |
| 16 | 0.93 | 0.98 | 0.95 |
| 18 | 0.72 | 0.92 | 0.78 |

**Table 4:** Response time (time to first result)

## 5. Future work

The current query-based debugger can be extended in a number of ways. First, the query model can be extended to include projection or even arbitrary computations that involve the selected objects. For example, it would be useful to write queries that calculate the average length of certain lists. Although this is possible to do now by iterating over the tuples in the query result, integrating such functionality into the query model could make such computations easier to express and potentially more efficient. In this way the system no longer needs to construct and then consume the output tuples.

A second avenue for future work is to extend the system to provide dynamic queries; i.e., queries whose results are dynamically updated while a program is running. For example, dynamic queries could help maintain class invariants [Mey88]. A query whose condition is the negated class invariant should have an empty result. If query results were updated dynamically the user could stop the program as soon as the result became non-empty, i.e., as soon as the class invariant was violated.

Unfortunately, dynamic queries are quite difficult to implement, especially if the system does not require programmers to annotate their programs to enable dynamic queries. Major difficulties in implementation arise in two main areas: the first area of difficulty is to determine when the input domains change, and the second area of difficulty is to determine when it is safe to reevaluate an expression. Consider the query

```
p: Point, r: Rectangle.  (p = r origin).
```

Its result may change if the program creates new points or rectangles or if old objects become garbage. Furthermore, the result can also change if a rectangle's origin changes, either when a new point is assigned to the origin instance variable or when the existing origin is mutated (e.g., by assigning to the x instance variable). In addition, the system would also have to analyze the equality method to determine which objects and fields it transitively references, and then to add all of these to the set of objects that need to be monitored for changes. Efficiently keeping track of these dependencies during millions of object mutations per second will be a challenging task. This is especially true for a language as dynamic as Self which is less amenable to static analyses like slicing [Tip95, Wei81].

Even if the above problem can be solved efficiently, dynamic queries still face another challenge: how can the query evaluator know when it is safe to update the query result? Consider a query involving list operations such as the Cecil queries in section 2.3.2. If the system evaluates such a query expression at the same time that a new element is being inserted into the list, the query may lead to an error because the list at this moment in the execution is in a temporarily inconsistent state. Therefore, queries should be updated only when all abstractions involved are in a consistent state. For the system to determine consistent states automatically is probably impossible. It might be difficult even to formulate a heuristic that handles many common cases satisfactorily, especially in the presence of multiple abstractions that cooperate to maintain a higher-level invariant.

Clearly, an implementation of dynamic queries is difficult, but their many attractive features encourage us to study their feasibility more closely. We plan to identify a subset of dynamic queries that is restricted enough to be implemented efficiently yet flexible enough to be useful during debugging.

## 6. Related work

We are unaware of other work that directly corresponds to query-based debugging. Sefika et al. [Sef96, SSC96] implemented a system allowing limited, unoptimized selection queries about high-level objects in the Choices operating system. The system shows program state and run-time statistics at various levels of abstraction. Unlike our query-based debugger, the application (Choices) was specifically instrumented to allow queries.

While no one has investigated the query-based debugging specifically, various researchers have proposed a variety of enhancements to conventional debugging [And95, Cop94, DHKV93, DKV94, GH93, KRR94, Laf97, LM94, LN97, LN95a, LN95b, LN95c, ZL96]. The debuggers most closely related to query-based debugging allow the visualization of relationships—usually references—among objects. Duel [Gol93] allows users to display data structures by writing script code. HotWire [LM94], Look! [And95], Object Visualizer [DHKV93, KRR94, DKV94], and Program Explorer [LN97, LN95a, LN95b, LN95c] provide numerous graphical and statistical run-time views with class-dependent filtering but do not allow general queries. Our debugger can gather statistical data through queries ("How many lists of size greater than 500 exist in the program?") but does not display animated statistical views.

Software visualization systems such as BALSA [Bro88], Zeus [Bro91], TANGO/XTANGO [Sta90], POLKA and Pavane [RC93, Rom92] offer high-level views of algorithms and associated data structures. Software visualization systems have different uses than everyday debugging. They aim to explain or illustrate the algorithm, so their view creation process emphasizes vivid representation. Hart et al. [HKR97] use Pavane for query-based visualization of distributed programs. However, their system only displays selected attributes of different processes and does not allow more complicated queries. Consens et al. [CHM94, CMR92] uses $Hy^+$ visualization system to find errors using post-mortem event traces. This work is complementary to ours because it focuses on querying and visualizing run-time events while we query object relationships. Noble's observations regarding the use of Self for the Tarraingim program visualization system [NGB95] coincide with our own observations.

The query optimizations discussed in section 3.4 were influenced by research in the area of databases. Ullman [Ull82] discusses basic insights about efficient join evaluation. Numerous researchers [IK84, KBZ86, SI93, SMK93] have developed algorithms to find optimal or near-optimal join orderings. The characteristics of the query-based debugger are different from databases—the number of objects per domain is smaller than in databases, but all objects reside in the main memory, so input/output time is not a factor. The debugger has to deliver interactive, subsecond performance, and cannot spend much time finding the optimal join order. Dynamic queries are related to incremental join result recalculation [BC79, BLT86]. Slicing [Wei81, Tip95] and data breakpoints [WLG93] could provide a foundation for dynamic queries, although they would need to be extended and adapted for this purpose.

Pre-/postconditions and class invariants as provided in Eiffel [Mey88] can complement queries and are checked at the beginning or end of methods. Unlike queries, they cannot check multi-object constraints nor can they invoke arbitrary methods. We view the two mechanisms as complementary, with queries being more suitable for program exploration as well as specific debugging problems.

## 7. Conclusions

Understanding and debugging complex software systems is difficult. Most conventional debuggers offer only a limited low-level view of the program state and offer little support for the exploration of large data structures. Our work provides a system that allows programmers to ask queries about the program state, helping to check object relationships in large object-oriented programs. Our implementation of the query-based debugger combines several novel features:

- A new approach to debugging: Instead of exploring a single object at a time, a query-based debugger allows the programmer to quickly extract a set of interesting objects from a potentially very large number of objects, or to check a certain property for a large number of objects with a single query.
- A flexible query model: Conceptually, a query evaluates its constraint expression for all members of the query's domain variables. The present model is simple to understand and to learn, yet it allows a large range of queries to be formulated concisely.
- Good performance: Many queries are answered in one or two seconds on a midrange workstation, thanks to a combination of fast object searching primitives, query optimization, and incremental delivery of results. Even for longer queries that take tens of seconds to produce all results, the first result is often available within a few seconds.

Although the system described here is based on the Self system, the query model as well as its implementation could be adapted fairly easily to other languages. We believe that the system demonstrates the usefulness of query-based debugging, and hope that similar functionality will be integrated into future mainstream debuggers, making the daunting task of debugging easier for programmers and facilitating the development of more robust object-oriented systems.


### Acknowledgments

The authors would like to thank Karel Driesen for his comments on an early version of this paper. This work was supported in part by National Science Foundation CAREER grant CCR-9624458, an IBM Faculty Development Award, and by Sun Microsystems. Some work was performed on the SGI workstations acquired under NSF instrumentation grant CDA-9421978.


## 8. References


[AK89] Abiteboul, S.; Kanellakis, P.C., Object identity as a query language primitive. 1989 *ACM SIGMOD International Conference on Management of Data*, Portland, OR, USA, 31 May-2 June 1989). *SIGMOD Record*, vol.18, (no.2), pp. 159-73, June 1989.

[And95] Anderson E., Dynamic Visualization of Object Programs written in C++, *Objective Software Technology Ltd.*, http://www.scotnet.co.uk/ost, 1995.

[BC79] Buneman, O.P.; Clemons E.K., Efficiently Monitoring Relational Databases. *ACM Transactions on Database Systems,* 4(3), pp. 368-382, September 1979.

[BKK88] Banerjee, J.; Kim, W.; Kim, K.-C., Queries in object-oriented databases. In: Proceedings Fourth International Conference on Data Engineering, Los Angeles, CA, USA, 1-5 Feb. 1988. Washington, DC, USA: IEEE Comput. Soc. Press, pp. 31-8, 1988.

[BLT86] Blakeley, J.A.; Larson P.-A.; Tompa F. Wm.; Efficiently Updating Materialized Views. *Proceedings of the ACM SIGMOD Conference on Management of Data*, pp. 61-71, Washington, D.C., USA, May 1986. Published as SIGMOD Record 15(2), June 1986.

[Bro88] Brown, M.H., Exploring Algorithms Using Balsa-II, *IEEE Computer* 21(5), pp. 14-36, May 1988.

[Bro91] Brown, M.H., Zeus: A System for Algorithm Animation and Multi-View Editing, *Proceedings of IEEE Workshop Visual Languages*, pp. 4-9, IEEE CS Press, Los Alamitos, CA., 1991.

[CHM94] Consens, M. P., Hasan M.Z., Mendelzon A.O., Debugging Distributed Programs by Visualizing and Querying Event Traces, *Applications of Databases, First International Conference*, ADB-94, Vadstena, Sweden, June 21-23, 1994, Proceedings in Lecture Notes in Computer Science, Vol. 819, Springer, 1994.

[CMR92] Consens, M.; Mendelzon, A.; Ryman, A., Visualizing and querying software structures, *International Conference on Software Engineering*, Melbourne, Australia, May 11-15, 1992, ACM Press, IEEE Computer Science, p. 138-156, 1992.

[CUL89] Chambers, C., Ungar, D., Lee, E., An Efficient Implementation of SELF a Dynamically-Typed Object-Oriented Language Based on Prototypes, In *Proceedings of OOPSLA'89*, pp. 49-70, New Orleans, LA, October 1989. Published as SIGPLAN Notices 24(10), October 1989.

[Cha93] Chambers. C. Cecil language: specification and rationale. *UW-CS Technical Report* 93-03-05, 1993.

[Cop94] Coplien, J.O., Supporting truly object-oriented debugging of C++ programs., In: Proceedings of the 1994 USENIX C++ Conference, Cambridge, MA, USA, 11-14 April 1994. pp. 99-108, Berkley, CA, USA: USENIX Assoc, 1994.

[DHKV93] De Pauw, W.; Helm, R.; Kimelman, D.; Vlissides, J. Visualizing the behavior of object-oriented systems. In *Proceedings of the 8th Annual ACM Conference on Object-Oriented Programming Systems, Languages, and Applications, OOPSLA 1993*, Washington, DC, USA, 26 Sept.-1 Oct. 1993. SIGPLAN Notices, Oct. 1993, vol.28, (no.10):326-37.

[DKV94] De Pauw, W.; Kimelman, D.; Vlissides, J. Modeling object-oriented program execution. In: *Proceedings of the 8th European Conference on Object-Oriented Programming, ECOOP '94*, Bologna, Italy, 4-8 July 1994. pp. 163-82, Edited by: Tokoro, M.; Pareschi, R. Berlin, Germany: Springer-Verlag, 1994.

[Gol84] Goldberg, A., *Smalltalk-80: The Interactive Programming Environment*, Addison-Wesley, Reading, MA, 1984.

[GH93] Golan, M.; Hanson, D.R. Duel-a very high-level debugging language. In: USENIX Association. *Proceedings of the Winter 1993 USENIX Conference*. San Diego, CA, USA, 25-29 Jan. 1993. Berkley, CA, USA: USENIX Assoc, 1993. p. 107-17.

[GR91] Gold, E.; Rosson, M.B., Portia: an instance-centered environment for Smalltalk. *OOPSLA '91. Object-Oriented Programming Systems, Languages, and Applications*, Phoenix, AZ, USA, 6-11 Oct. 1991. Published as *SIGPLAN Notices*, vol.26, (no.11), pp. 62-74, November 1991.

[GWM89] Gamma E., Weinand A., Marty R., Integration of a Programming Environment into ET++ - a Case Study, *Proceedings ECOOP'89* (Nottingham, UK, July 10-14), pp. 283-297, S. Cook, ed. Cambridge University Press, Cambridge, 1989.

[HKR97] Hart D., Kraemer E., Roman G.-C., Interactive Visual Exploration of Distributed Computations. To appear in the *International Parallel Processing Symposium* 1997.

[HU96] Hölzle, U.; Ungar, D., Reconciling Responsiveness with Performance in Pure Object-Oriented Languages, *ACM Trans. Programming Languages and Systems* 18(4), pp. 355-400, 1996.

[IK84] Ibaraki T., Kameda T., On the Optimal Nesting for Computing *N*-Relational Joins., A*CM Transactions on Database Systems*, Vol. 9, No. 3, pp. 482-502, September 1984.

[KBZ86] Krishnamurthy, R., Boral, H., Zaniolo, C., Optimization of Nonrecursive Queries., *Proceedings of International Conference on Very Large Data Bases* (VLDB), pp. 128-137, 1986.

[KRR94] Kimelman D., Rosenburg B., Roth T., Strata-Various: Multi-Layer Visualization of Dynamics in Software System Behavior, Proceedings of Visualization'94, pp. 172-178, IEEE 1994.

[Laf97] Laffra C., *Advanced Java: Idioms, Pitfalls, Styles and Programming Tips*, pp. 229-252, Prentice Hall 1997.

[LM94] Laffra C., Malhotra A., HotWire: A Visual Debugger for C++, *Proceedings of the USENIX C++ Conference*, pp. 109-122, Usenix Association 1994.

[LN95a] Lange, D.B., Nakamura Y. Program Explorer: A Program Visualizer for C++, *Proceedings of USENIX Conference on Object-Oriented Technologies'95*, pp. 39-54, June 1995.

[LN95b] Lange, D.B., Nakamura Y. Object-Oriented Program Tracing and Visualization, *IBM Research Report*, July 1995.

[LN95c] Lange, D.B., Nakamura Y. Interactive Visualization of Design Patterns Can Help in Framework Understanding, *Proceedings of OOPSLA'95*, pp. 342-357, Austin, TX October 1995. Published as SIGPLAN Notices 30(10), October 1995.

[LN97] Lange, D.B., Nakamura Y. Object-Oriented Program Tracing and Visualization, IEEE Computer, vol. 30, no. 5, pp. 63–70, May 1997.

[Mey88] Meyer B., *Object-oriented Software Construction*, pp. 111 - 163, Prentice-Hall, 1988.

[ME92] Mishra, P., Eich, M. H., Join Processing in Relational Databases, *ACM Computing Surveys*, vol. 24, No. 1, pp. 63-113, March 1992.

[NGB95] Noble J., Groves L., Biddle R., Object Oriented Program Visualisation in Tarraingim, *Australian Computer Journal*, 27:4, November 1995.

[NOT96] Nishimura, S.; Ohori, A.; Tajima, K., An equational object-oriented data model and its data-parallel query language. In: *OOPSLA '96: Eleventh Annual Conference on Object Oriented Programming Systems Languages and Applications*, San Jose, CA, USA, 6-10 Oct. 1996). Published as *SIGPLAN Notices*, vol.31, (no.10), pp. 1-17, October 1996.

[RC93] Roman G.-C., Cox K.C., A Taxonomy of Program Visualization Systems, *IEEE Computer* 26(12), pp. 11-24, December 1993.

[Rom92] Roman, G.-C. et al., Pavane: A System for Declarative Visualization of Concurrent Computations, *Journal of Visual Languages and Computing*, Vol. 3, No. 2, pp. 161-193, June 1992.

[SAC+79] Selinger, P. G., Astrahan, M. M., Chamberlin, D. D., Lorie, R. A., Price, T. G., Access Path Selection in a Relational Database Management System, *Proceedings of the ACM SIGMOD Conference on Management of Data*, pp. 23-34, Boston, USA, June 1979.

[Sef96] Sefika M., Design Conformance Management of Software Systems: An Architecture-Oriented Approach. *Ph.D. thesis*, University of Illinois at Urbana-Champaign, July 1996.

[SMK93] Steinbrunn, M., Moerkotte, G., Kemper, A., Optimizing Join Orders, *Technical Report MIP 9307*, Universität Passau, FMI, September 1993.

[SMU95] Smith, R.B.; Maloney, J.; Ungar, D. The Self-4.0 user interface: manifesting a system-wide vision of concreteness, uniformity, and flexibility. *OOPSLA '95: Conference on Object Oriented Programming Systems Languages and Applications. Tenth Annual Conference*, Austin, TX, USA, 15-19 Oct. 1995. Published as *SIGPLAN Notices*, vol.30, (no.10), pp. 47-60, October 1995.

[SSC96] Sefika M., Sane A., Campbell R.H., Architecture-Oriented Visualization, In *Proceedings of OOPSLA'96*, pp. 389-405, San Jose, CA, October 1996. Published as SIGPLAN Notices 31(10), October 1996.

[Sta90] Stasko, J., TANGO: A Framework and System for Algorithm Animation, *IEEE Computer* 23(9), pp. 27-39.

[SI93] Swami, A., Iyer, B., A Polynomial Time Algorithm for Optimizing Join Queries, *Proceedings of the IEEE Conference on Data Engineering*, pp. 345-354, Vienna, 1993.

[SZ90] Shaw, G.M.; Zdonik, S.B., A query algebra for object-oriented databases. In: Sixth International Conference on Data Engineering, Los Angeles, CA, USA, 5-9 Feb. 1990. pp. 154-62, Los Alamitos, CA, USA: IEEE Comput. Soc, 1990.

[Tip95] Tip, F., A survey of program slicing techniques. *Journal of Programming Languages*, vol.3, (no.3) pp. 121-89, Sept. 1995.

[Ull82] Ullman, J.D., *Principles of Database Systems*, pp. 268-316, Computer Science Press 1982.

[US87] Ungar, D., Smith, R.B., Self: The Power of Simplicity, *Proceedings of OOPSLA'87*, pp. 227-243, Orlando, FL, October 1987. Published as SIGPLAN Notices 22(12), October 1987.

[Wei81] Weiser, M., Program slicing. In: *5th International Conference on Software Engineering*, San Diego, CA, USA, 9-12 March 1981. New York, NY, USA, pp. 439-49, IEEE, 1981.

[WLG93] Wahbe R., Lucco S., Graham S.L., Practical Data Breakpoints: Design and Implementation. *Proceedings of ACM SIGPLAN conference on Programming Language Design and Implementation* 1993, Albuquerque, June 1993. ACM Press 1993.

[WG94] Weinand, A.; Gamma, E. ET++-a portable, homogenous class library and application framework. In: *Computer Science Research at UBILAB, Strategy and Projects. Proceedings of the UBILAB Conference '94*, Zurich, Switzerland, 1994. pp. 66-92. Edited by: Bischofberger, W.R.; Frei, H.-P. Konstanz, Switzerland: Universitätsverlag Konstanz, 1994.

[ZL96] Zeller A., Lütkehaus D. DDD - A Free Graphical Front-End for UNIX Debuggers. *ACM SIGPLAN Notices*, Vol. 31, No. 1, pp. 22-28, January 1996.

# Back to the Future

## The Story of Squeak, A Practical Smalltalk Written in Itself

by

Dan Ingalls  Ted Kaehler  John Maloney  Scott Wallace  Alan Kay

at Apple Computer while doing this work,
now at Walt Disney Imagineering
1401 Flower Street, P.O. Box 25020, Glendale CA 91221
dani@wdi.disney.com

### Abstract

Squeak is an open, highly-portable Smalltalk implementation whose virtual machine is written entirely in Smalltalk, making it easy to debug, analyze, and change. To achieve practical performance, a translator produces an equivalent C program whose performance is comparable to commercial Smalltalks.

Other noteworthy aspects of Squeak include: a compact object format that typically requires only a single word of overhead per object; a simple yet efficient incremental garbage collector for 32-bit direct pointers; efficient bulk-mutation of objects; extensions of BitBlt to handle color of any depth and anti-aliased image rotation and scaling; and real-time sound and music synthesis written entirely in Smalltalk.

### Overview

Squeak is a modern implementation of Smalltalk-80 that is available for free via the Internet, at

```
http://www.research.apple.com/research/
        proj/learning_concepts/squeak/
```

and other sites.

It includes platform-independent support for color, sound, and image processing. Originally developed on the Macintosh, members of its user community have since ported it to numerous platforms including Windows 95 and NT, Windows CE, all common flavors of UNIX, and the Acorn.

Squeak stands alone as a practical Smalltalk in which a researcher, professor, or motivated student can examine source code for every part of the system, including graphics primitives and the virtual machine itself, and make changes immediately and without needing to see or deal with any language other than Smalltalk. It also runs bit-identical images across its wide portability base.

Three strands weave through this paper: (1) the design of the Squeak virtual machine, which differs in several interesting ways from the implementation presented in the Smalltalk "Blue Book" [Gold83] and explored in the "Green Book" [Kras83]; (2) an implementation strategy based on writing the Squeak virtual machine in Smalltalk and translating it into C, using an existing Smalltalk for bootstrapping until Squeak was able to debug and generate its own virtual machine; and (3) the incremental development process through which Squeak was created and evolved over the course of a year.


**OOPSLA '97 10/97 GA, USA**
**© 1997 ACM 0-89791-908-4/97/0010...$3.50**

### Background

In December of 1995, the authors found themselves wanting a development environment in which to build educational software that could be used—and even programmed—by non-technical people, and by children. We wanted our software to be effective in mass-access media such as PDAs and the Internet, where download times and power considerations make compactness essential, and where hardware is diverse, and operating systems may change or be completely absent. Therefore our ideal system would be a small, portable kernel of simple and uniform design that could be adapted rapidly to new delivery vehicles. We considered using Java but, despite its promise, Java was not yet mature: its libraries were in a state of flux, few commercial implementations were available, and those that were available lacked the hooks required to create the kind of dynamic change that we envisioned.

While Smalltalk met the technical desiderata, none of the available implementations gave us the kind of control we wanted over graphics, sound, and the Smalltalk engine itself, nor the freedom to port and distribute the resulting work, including its host environment, freely over the Internet. Moreover, we felt that we were not alone, that many others in the research community shared our desire for an open, portable, malleable, and yet practical object-oriented programming environment. It became clear that the best way to get what we all wanted was to build a new Smalltalk with these goals and to share it with this wider community.

### Project Plan

We did not have to start from scratch, as we had access to the existing Apple Smalltalk-80 implementation, which was a gold mine of useful software. This system consisted of an *image*, or object memory, containing the Smalltalk-80 class library, and a separate *interpreter*, or VM (virtual machine), for running on the Macintosh. However, the Apple image format was limited by its use of indirect pointers and an object table. Worse yet, the original interpreter consisted of 120 pages of sparsely commented 68020 assembly code that had passed through the hands of seven authors. Portable it was not.

We determined that implementation in C would be key to portability but none of us wanted to write in C. However, two of us had once adapted the Smalltalk formatter (pretty-printer) to convert a body of code to BCPL. Based on that experience, we determined to write and debug the virtual machine in

Smalltalk. Then, in parallel, we would write (also in Smalltalk) a translator from Smalltalk to C, and thus let Smalltalk build its own production interpreter. Out of this decision grew the following plan for building a new Smalltalk system in the shortest possible time:

Produce a new image:
- Design a new Object Memory and image file format.
- Alter the ST-80 System Tracer to write an image in the new format.
- Eliminate uses of Mac Toolbox calls to restore Smalltalk-80 portability.
- Write a new file system with a simple, portable interface.

Produce a new interpreter written in Smalltalk:
- Type in the Blue Book descriptions for the Interpreter and BitBlt.
- Write a completely new Object Memory class.
- Debug the new Object Memory, Interpreter and BitBlt.

Compile the interpreter to make it practical:
- Design a translator from a subset of Smalltalk-80 to C.
- Implement this translator.
- Translate the virtual machine to C and compile it.
- Write a small C interface to the Mac OS.
- Run the compiled interpreter with the new image.

By following this plan, facilities became available just as they were needed. For example, the interpreter and object memory were debugged using a temporary memory allocator that had no way to reclaim garbage. However, since the system only executed a few byte codes, it never got far enough to run out of memory. Likewise, while the translator was being prepared, most of the bugs in the interpreter and object memory were found and fixed by running them in Smalltalk.

It was easy to stay motivated, because the virtual machine, running inside Apple Smalltalk, was actually simulating the byte codes of the transformed image just five weeks into the project. A week later, we could type "3 + 4" on the screen, compile it, and print the result, and the week after that the entire user interface was working, albeit in slow motion. We were writing the C translator in parallel on a commercial Smalltalk, and by the eighth week, the first translated interpreter displayed a window on the screen. Ten weeks into the project, we "crossed the bridge" and were able to use Squeak to evolve itself, no longer needing to port images forward from Apple Smalltalk. About six weeks later, Squeak's performance had improved to the point that it could simulate its own interpreter and run the C translator, and Squeak became entirely self-supporting.

We attribute the speed with which this initial work was accomplished to the Squeak philosophy: do everything in Smalltalk so that each improvement makes everything smaller, faster, and better. It has been a pleasant revelation to work on such low-level system facilities as real-time garbage collection and FM music synthesis from within the comfort and convenience of the Smalltalk-80 language and environment.

Once we had a stable, usable interpreter, the focus shifted from creation to evolution. Performance improved steadily and support for color, image transforms, sound synthesis, and networking were added. These improvements were made incrementally, as the need arose, and in parallel with other projects that relied on the stability of the virtual machine. Yet despite the apparent risk of frequent changes to the VM, Squeak has proven as dependable as most commercial Smalltalks we have used. We attribute this success partly to our passion for design simplicity but mostly to the strategy of implementing the virtual machine in Smalltalk.

The remainder of the paper discusses various aspects of the Squeak implementation, its memory footprint and performance, the evolution of its user community, and plans for its future.

## The Interpreter

We knew that the published Blue Book interpreter description would suffice to get us started. Moreover, we were spared from the tedium of transcription by Mario Wolczko, who had already keyed in the code for use as an on-line reference source for a Smalltalk implementation project at the University of Manchester.

The interpreter is structured as a single class that gets translated to C along with the Object Memory and BitBlt classes. In addition, a subclass (Interpreter Simulator) runs all the same code from within a Smalltalk environment by supporting basic mouse, file, and display operations. This subclass was the basis for debugging the Squeak system into existence. All of this code is included in the Squeak release and it can run its own image, albeit at a snail's pace (every memory access, even in BitBlt, runs a Smalltalk method). Having an interpreter that runs within Smalltalk is invaluable for studying the virtual machine. Any operation can be stopped and inspected, or it can be instrumented to gather timing profiles, exact method counts, and other statistics.

Although we have constantly amended the interpreter to achieve increasing performance, we have stayed pretty close to the Blue Book message interface between the Interpreter and the Object Memory. It is a testament to the original design of that interface that completely changing the Object Memory implementation had almost no impact on the Interpreter.

## The Object Memory

The design of an object memory that is general and yet compact is not simple. We all agreed immediately on a number of parameters, though. For efficiency and scalability to large projects, we wanted a 32-bit address space with direct pointers (i.e., a system in which an object reference is just the address of that object in memory). The design had to support all object formats of our existing Smalltalk. It must be amenable to incremental garbage collection and compaction. Finally, it must be able to support the "become" operation (exchange identity of two objects) to the degree required in normal Smalltalk system operation.

While anyone would agree that objects should be stored compactly, every object in Smalltalk requires the following "overhead" information:

- Size of the object in bytes: 24 bits or more,
- Class of the object: a full 32-bit object pointer,
- Hash code for indexing objects: at least 12 bits,
- Format of the object, specifying pointer or bits, indexable or not, etc.: 4 bits at least,
- ...and, of course, a few extra bits for storage management needs.

A simple approach would be to allocate three full 32-bit words as the header to every object. However, in a system of 40k objects, this cavalier expenditure of 500k bytes of memory could make the difference between an undeployable prototype and a practical application. Therefore, we designed a variable-length header format which seldom requires more than a single 32-bit word of header information per object. The format is given in Tables 1 and 2.

| offset | contents | occurrence |
|---|---|---|
| -8 | size in words (30 bits), header type (2 bits) | 1% |
| -4 | full class pointer (30 bits), header type (2 bits) | 18% |
| 0 | base header, as follows...<br>storage management (3 bits)<br>object hash (12 bits)<br>compact class index (5 bits)<br>object format field (4 bits, see below)<br>size in words (6 bits)<br>header type (2 bits) | 100% |

**Table 1: Format of a Squeak object header**

| | |
|---|---|
| 0 | no fields |
| 1 | fixed pointer fields |
| 2 | indexable pointer fields |
| 3 | both fixed and indexable pointer fields |
| 4 | unused |
| 5 | unused |
| 6 | indexable word fields (no pointers) |
| 7 | unused |
| 8-11 | indexable byte fields (no pointers):<br>low 2 bits are low 2 bits of size in bytes |
| 12-15 | compiled methods:<br>low 2 bits are low 2 bits of size in bytes.<br>The number of literals is specified in method header, followed by the indexable bytes that store byte codes. |

**Table 2: Encoding of the object format field in a Squeak object header**

Our design is based on the fact that most objects in a typical Smalltalk image are small instances of a relatively small number of classes. The 5-bit compact class index field, if non-zero, is an index into a table of up to 31 classes that are designated as having compact instances; the programmer can change which classes these are. The 6-bit size field, if non-zero, specifies the size of the object in words, accommodating sizes up to 256 bytes (i.e., 64 words, with the additional 2 bits needed to resolve the length of byte-indexable objects encoded in the format field). With only 12 classes designated as compact in the 1.18 Squeak release, around 81% of the objects have only this single word of overhead. Most of the rest need one additional word to store a full class pointer. Only a few remaining objects (1%) are large enough to require a third header word to encode their size, and this extra word of overhead is a tiny fraction of their size.

## Storage Management

Apple Smalltalk had achieved good garbage collection behavior with a simple two-generation approach similar to [Unga84]. At startup, and after any full garbage collection (a mark and sweep of the entire image), all surviving objects were considered to be old, and all objects created subsequently (until the next full collection) to be new. All pointer stores were checked and a table maintained of "root" objects—old objects that might contain pointers to new objects. In this way, an incremental mark phase could be achieved by marking all new objects reachable from these roots and sweeping the new object area; unmarked new objects were garbage. Compaction was simple in that system, owing to its use of an object table. Full garbage collection was triggered either by an overflow of the roots table, or by failure of an incremental collection to reclaim a significant amount of space. That system was known to run acceptably with less than 500k of free space and to perform incremental reclamations in under 250 milliseconds on hardware of the 80's (16MHz 68020).

For Squeak, we determined to apply the same approach to our new system of 32-bit direct pointers. We were faced immediately with a number of challenges. First, we had to write an in-place mark phase capable of dealing with our variable-length headers, including those that did not have an actual class pointer in them. Then there was the need to produce a structure for remapping object pointers during compaction, since we did not have the convenient indirection of an object table. Finally there was the challenge of rectifying all the object pointers in memory within an acceptable time.

The remapping of object pointers was accomplished by building a number of relocation blocks down from the unused end of memory. A thousand such blocks are reserved outside the object heap, ensuring that at least one thousand objects can be moved even when there is very little free space. However, if the object heap ends with a free block, that space is also used for relocation blocks. If there is not enough room for the number of relocation blocks needed to do compaction in a single pass (almost never), then the compaction may be done in multiple passes. Each pass generates free space at the end of the object heap which can then be used to create additional relocation blocks for the next pass.

One more issue remained to be dealt with, and that was support of the **become** operation without an object table. (The Smalltalk **become** primitive atomically exchanges the identity of two objects; to Smalltalk code, each object appears to turn into, or "become," the other.) With an object table, the **become** primitive simply exchanges the contents of two object table entries. Without an object table, it requires a full scan of memory to replace every pointer to one object with a pointer to the other. Since full memory scans are relatively costly, we made two changes. First, we eliminated most uses of **become** in the Squeak image by changing certain collection classes to store their elements in separate Array objects instead of indexed fields. However, **become** operations are essential when adding an instance variable to a class with extant instances, as each instance must mutate into a larger object to accommodate the new variable. So, our second change was to restructure the primitive to one that exchanges the identity of many objects at once. This allows all the instances of a class to be mutated in a single pass through memory. The code for this operation uses the same technique and, in fact, the very same code, as that used to rectify pointers after compaction.

We originally sought to minimize compaction frequency, owing to the overhead associated with rectifying direct addresses. Our strategy was to do a fast mark and sweep, returning objects to a number of free lists, depending on size. Only when memory became overly fragmented would we do a consolidating compaction.

As we studied and optimized the Squeak garbage collector, however, we were able to simplify this approach greatly. Since an incremental reclamation only compacts the new object space, it is only necessary to rectify the surviving new objects and any old objects that point to them. The latter are exactly those objects marked as root objects. Since there are typically just a few root objects and not many survivors (most objects die young), we discovered that compaction after an incremental reclamation could be done quickly. In fact, due to the overhead of managing free lists, it turned out to be more efficient to compact after every incremental reclamation and eliminate free lists altogether. This was especially gratifying since issues of fragmentation and coalescing had been a burden in design, analysis, and coding strategy.

Two policy refinements reduced the incremental garbage collection pauses to the point where Squeak became usable for real-time applications such as music and animation. First, a counter is incremented each time an object is allocated. When this counter reaches a threshold such as 4000 objects, an incremental collection is done even if there is plenty of free space left. This reduces the number of new objects that must be scanned in the sweep phase, and also limits the number of surviving objects. By doing a little work often, each incremental collection completes quickly, typically in 5-8 milliseconds. This is within the timing tolerance of even a fairly demanding musician or animator.

The second refinement is to tenure all surviving objects when the number of survivors exceeds a threshold such as 2000 objects, a simplified version of Ungar and Jackson's feedback-mediated tenuring policy [UnJa88]. Tenuring is done as follows. After the incremental garbage collection and compaction, the boundary between the old and new object spaces is moved up to encompass all surviving new objects, as if a full garbage collection had just been done. This "clears the decks" so that future incremental compactions have fewer objects to process. Although in theory this approach could hasten the onset of the next full garbage collection, such full collections are rare in practice. In any case, Squeak's relatively lean image makes full garbage collections less daunting than they might be in a larger system; a full collection typically takes only 250 milliseconds in Squeak.

We have been using this storage manager in support of real-time graphics and music for over a year now with extremely satisfactory results. In our experience, 10 milliseconds is an important threshold for latency in interactive systems, because most of the other critical functions such as mouse polling, sound buffer output and display refresh take place at a commensurate rate.

## BitBlt

For BitBlt as well, we began with the Blue Book source code. However, the Blue Book code was written as a simulation in Smalltalk, not as virtual machine code to run on top of the Object Memory. We transformed the code into the latter form, made a few optimizations, and this sufficed to get the first Squeak running. The special cases we optimized are:

- the case when there is no source (store constant),
- the case when there is no halftone (store unmasked),
- the horizontal inner loop (no partial word stores).

Once Squeak became operational, we immediately wanted to give it command over color. We chose to support a wide range of color depths, namely: 1-, 2-, 4-, and 8-bit table-based color, as well as 16- and 32-bit direct RGB color (with 5 and 8 bits per color component respectively).

It was relatively simple to extend the internal logic of BitBlt to handle multiple pixel sizes as long as source and destination bit maps are of the same depth. To handle operations between images of different depth, we provided a default conversion, and added an optional color map parameter to BitBlt to provide more control when appropriate. The default behavior is simply to extend smaller source pixels to a larger destination size by padding with zeros, and to truncate larger source pixels to a smaller destination pixel size. This approach works very well among the table-based colors because the color set for each depth includes the next smaller depth's color set as a subset. In the case of RGB colors, BitBlt performs the zero-fill or truncation independently on each color component.

The real challenge, however, involves operations between RGB and table-based color depths. In such cases, or when wanting more control over the color conversion, the client can supply BitBlt with a color map. This map is sized so that there is one entry for each of the source colors, and each entry contains a pixel in the format expected by the destination. It is obvious how to work with this for source pixel sizes of 8 bits or less (map sizes of 256 or less). But it would seem to require a map of 65536 entries for 16 bits or 4294967296 entries for 32-bit color! However, for these cases, Squeak's BitBlt accepts color maps of 512, 4096, or 32768 entries, corresponding to 3, 4, and 5 bits per color component, and BitBlt truncates the source pixel's color components to the appropriate number of bits before looking up the pixel in the color map.

## Smalltalk to C Translation

We have alluded to the Squeak philosophy of writing everything in Smalltalk. While the Blue Book contains a Smalltalk description of the virtual machine that was actually executed at least once to verify its accuracy, this description was meant to be used only as an explanatory model, not as the source code of a working implementation. In contrast, we needed source code that could be translated into C to produce a reliable and efficient virtual machine.

Our bootstrapping strategy also depended on being able to debug the Smalltalk code for the Squeak virtual machine by running it under an existing Smalltalk implementation, and this approach was highly successful. Being able to use the powerful tools of the Smalltalk environment saved us weeks of tedious debugging with a C debugger. However, useful as it is for debugging, the Squeak virtual machine running on top of Smalltalk is orders of magnitude too slow for useful work: running in Squeak itself, the Smalltalk version of the Squeak virtual machine is roughly 450 times slower than the C version. Even running in the fastest available commercial Smalltalk, the Squeak virtual machine running in Smalltalk would still be sluggish.

The key to both practical performance and portability is to translate the Smalltalk description of the virtual machine into C. To be able to do this translation without having to emulate all of Smalltalk in the C runtime system, the virtual machine was written in a subset of Smalltalk that maps directly onto C constructs. This subset excludes blocks (except to describe a few control structures), message sending, and even objects! Methods of the interpreter classes are mapped to C functions and instance variables are mapped to global variables. For byte code and primitive dispatches, the special message **dispatchOn:in:** is mapped to a C switch statement. (When running in Smalltalk, this construct works by **perform:**-ing the message selector at the specified index in a case array; since a method invocation is much less efficient than a branch operation, this dispatch is one of the main reasons that the interpreter runs so much faster when translated to C).

The translator first translates Smalltalk into parse trees, then uses a simple table-lookup scheme to generate C code from these parse trees. There are only 42 transformation rules, as shown in Table 3. Four of these are for integer operations that more closely match those of the underlying hardware, such as unsigned shifts, and the last three are macros for operations so heavily used that they should always be inlined. All translated code accesses memory through six C macros that read and write individual bytes, 4-byte words, and 8-byte floats. In the early stages of development, every such reference was checked against the bounds of object memory.

```
& | and: or: not
+ - * // \\ min: max:
bitAnd: bitOr: bitXor: bitShift:
< <= = > >= ~= ==
isNil notNil
whileTrue: whileFalse: to:do: to:by:do:
ifTrue: ifFalse: ifTrue:ifFalse: ifFalse:ifTrue:
at: at:put:
<< >> bitInvert32 preIncrement
integerValueOf: integerObjectOf: isIntegerObject:
```

**Table 3: Operations of primitive Smalltalk**

Our first translator yielded a two orders of magnitude speedup relative to the Smalltalk simulation, producing a system that was immediately usable. However, one further refinement to the translator yielded a significant additional speedup: inlining. Inlining allows the source code of the virtual machine to be factored into many small, precisely defined methods—thus increasing code-sharing and simplifying debugging—without paying the penalty in extra procedure calls. Inlining is also used to move the byte code service routines into the interpreter byte code dispatch loop, which both reduces byte code dispatch overhead and allows the most critical VM state to be kept in fast, register-based local variables. All told, inlining increases VM performance by a factor of 3.4 while increasing the overall code size of the virtual machine by only 13%.

## Sound

Several of us were involved in early experiments with computer music editing and synthesis [Saun77], and it was a disappointment to us that the original Smalltalk-80 release failed to incorporate this vital aspect of any lively computing environment. We determined to right this wrong in the Squeak release.

Early on, we implemented access to the Macintosh sound driver. As the performance of the Squeak system improved, we were delighted to find that we could actually synthesize and mix several voices of music in real time using simple wave table and FM algorithms written entirely in Smalltalk.

Nonetheless, these algorithms are compute-intensive, and we used this application as an opportunity to experiment with using C translation to improve the performance of isolated, time-critical methods. Sound synthesis is an ideal application for this, since nearly all the work is done by small loops with simple arithmetic and array manipulation. The sound generation methods were written so that they could be run directly in Smalltalk or, without changing a line of code, translated into C and linked into the virtual machine as an optional primitive. Since the sound generation code had already been running for weeks in Smalltalk, the translated primitives worked perfectly the first time they ran. Furthermore, we observed nearly a 40-fold increase in performance: from 3 voices sampled at 8 KHz, we jumped to over 20 voices sampled at 44 KHz.

## WarpBlt

As we began doing more with general rotation and scaling of images, we found ourselves dissatisfied with the slow speed of non-integer scaling and image rotations by angles other than multiples of 90 degrees. To address this problem in a simple manner, we added a "warp drive" to BitBlt. WarpBlt takes as input a quadrilateral specifying the traversal of the source image corresponding to BitBlt's normal rectangular destination. If the quadrilateral is larger than the destination rectangle, sampling occurs and the image is reduced. If the quadrilateral is smaller than the destination, then interpolation occurs and the image is expanded. If the quadrilateral is a rotated rectangle, then the image is correspondingly rotated. If the source quadrilateral is not rectangular, then the transformation will be correspondingly distorted.

Once we started playing with arbitrarily rotated and scaled images, we began to wish that the results of this crude warp were not so jagged. This led to support for over sampling and smoothing in the warp drive, which does a reasonable job of anti-aliasing in many cases. The approach is to average a number of pixels around a given source coordinate. Averaging colors is not a simple matter with the table-based colors of 8 bits or less. The approach we used is to map from the source color space to RGB colors, average the samples in RGB space, and map the final result back to the nearest indexed color via the normal depth-reducing color map.

As with the sound synthesis work, WarpBlt is completely described in Smalltalk, then translated into C to deliver performance appropriate to interactive graphics.

## Code Size and Memory Footprint

Table 4 gives the approximate size of the main components of Squeak in lines of code, based on version 1.18 of December, 1996. Our measurement includes all comments, but excludes all blank lines. We present these statistics not as rigorous measurement, but more as an order-of-magnitude gauge. For instance, the entire virtual machine is approximately 100 pages. Of that, 6547 lines are in Smalltalk (translator not included) versus 1681 lines of OS interface in C that may need to be altered for porting.

| Smalltalk | Lines | C | Lines |
|---|---|---|---|
| Interpreter | 3951 | OS interface | 1681 |
| Object Memory | 1283 | | |
| BitBlt with Warp | 1313 | | |

**Table 4: Lines of code in Squeak VM**

The size of the 1.18 Squeak release image, with all development support, including browsers, inspectors, performance analyzers, color graphics, and music support is 968K bytes on the Macintosh. The code for the virtual machine, simulator, and Smalltalk-to-C translator, which are only needed by those engaged in virtual machine development, adds 290K to this figure. The interpreter, when running, requires 300K on a Power PC Macintosh, and the entire Smalltalk environment runs satisfactorily with as little as 200K of free space available. In monochrome, the system runs comfortably in 1.8 MB. We distribute a 650K image with the complete development environment that runs in less than 1MB on the Cassiopeia hand held computer.

## Performance and Optimization

Thanks to today's fast processors, Squeak's performance was satisfactory from the moment the translator produced its first C translation of the virtual machine. Since this debut, Squeak's performance has improved steadily, and the current version, 1.18, executes about four million byte codes or 173 thousand message sends per second on a 110 MHz Power PC Mac 8100. Table 5 shows the improvement in Squeak's performance over its first year. Two simple benchmarks from the release were used to track the approximate byte code execution rate ("10 benchmark") and the cost of full method activation and return ("26 benchFib"). Note that the latter benchmark measures the worst case; not all message sends require a full activation.

| Date | byte codes/sec | sends/sec |
|---|---|---|
| Apr. 14 | 458K | 22,928 |
| May 20 | 1,111K | 60,287 |
| May 23 | 1,522K | 69,319 |
| July 9 | 2,802K | 134,717 |
| Aug. 1 | 2,726K | 130,945 |
| Sept. 23 | 3,528K | 141,155 |
| Nov. 12 | 3,156K | 133,164 |
| Dec. 12 | 3,410K | 169,617 |
| Jan. 21 | 4,108K | 173,360 |

**Table 5: Squeak performance over time**

The rapid early leaps in performance were due partly to removal of scaffolding—such as assertion checks and range checks on memory references—and partly to improving the runtime model of the translator. For example, object references were originally represented as offsets relative to the base of the object memory rather than as true direct pointers. After May, however, the easy changes had all been made and improvements came in smaller increments, sometimes only a few percent at a time. The most significant of these optimizations include:

- recycling method contexts (this cut the allocation rate by a factor of 10)
- managing the frequency of checks for user and timer interrupts
- keeping the instruction and stack pointers (IP and SP) in registers
- making the IP and SP be direct pointers, rather than offsets into their base object
- patching the dispatch loop to eliminate an unneeded compiler-generated range check
- eliminating store-checks when storing into the active and home contexts
- comparing small integers as oops rather than converting them into integers first
- peeking for and doing a jump-if-false byte code that follows a compare

Table 6 compares Squeak's current performance over a small suite of benchmarks with that of several commercial Smalltalk implementations that cover a cross-section of implementation technologies, including a bytecode interpreter similar to the original Smalltalk-80 virtual machine (Apple Smalltalk), an aggressively optimized interpreter (ST/V Mac 1.1), and two implementations using dynamic translation to native code (ParcPlace Smalltalk 2.3 and 2.5). In order to draw meaningful comparisons between Squeak and these 68K-based virtual machines, all timings except those in the last column were taken on a Duo 230 (33Mhz 68030). Since Squeak runs significantly better on modern processors with instruction caches and a generous supply of registers, the final column of the table, SqueakPPC, shows Squeak's performance relative to C on a Power PC-based Macintosh.

| | AppleST | ST/V | PP2.3 | PP2.5 | Squeak | SqueakPPC |
|---|---|---|---|---|---|---|
| IntegerSum | 185.00 | 32.00 | 7.58 | 6.92 | 62.34 | 72.56 |
| VectorSum | 99.00 | 30.00 | 10.30 | 11.50 | 61.70 | 41.01 |
| PrimeSieve | 53.00 | 40.00 | 16.07 | 12.10 | 70.53 | 51.57 |
| BubbleSort | 88.23 | 35.29 | 21.35 | 13.98 | 80.29 | 63.12 |
| TreeSort | 43.90 | 5.00 | 20.29 | 1.98 | 16.33 | 7.31 |
| MatrixMult | 40.79 | 6.00 | 22.80 | 2.94 | 18.00 | 36.74 |
| Recurse | 28.26 | 9.47 | 3.73 | 2.08 | 50.26 | 35.19 |

**Table 6: Virtual machine performance** relative to optimized, platform-native C for various benchmarks. Smaller numbers are better. A result of 1.0 would indicate that a benchmark ran exactly as fast as optimized C.

So far in the design of Squeak, we have emphasized simplicity, portability, and small memory footprint over high performance. Much better performance is possible. The PP2.3 and PP2.5 columns of Table 6 are examples of Deutsch-Schiffman-style dynamic translation (or "JIT") virtual machines [Deut84]. Dynamic translation avoids the overhead of byte code dispatch by translating methods into native instructions kept in a size-bounded cache. The Self project [ChUn91] [Hölz94] broke new ground in high performance by investing more compilation time in heavily used methods, using inlining to eliminate expensive calls and enable further optimizations. This work, which was later extended to Smalltalk and Java [Anim96], shows that one can obtain performance approaching half the speed of optimized C without compromising the semantics of a clean language. Unfortunately both of these approaches have resulted in virtual machine implementations that are, by Squeak standards, unapproachable and difficult to port.

We believe that Squeak can enjoy the same performance as commercial Smalltalk implementations without compromising malleability and portability. In our experience the byte code basis of the Smalltalk-80 standard [Inga78] is hard to beat for compactness and simplicity, and for the programming tools that have grown around it. Therefore dynamic translation is a natural avenue to high performance. The Squeak philosophy implies that both the dynamic translator and its target code sequences should be written and debugged in Smalltalk, then automatically translated into C to build the production virtual machine. By representing translated methods as ordinary Smalltalk objects, experiments with Self-style inlining and other optimizations could be done at the Smalltalk level. This approach is currently being explored as a way to improve Squeak's performance without adversely affecting its portability.

## The Squeak Community

As exciting as the day the interpreter first ran, was the day we released Squeak to the Internet community. In the back of our minds, we all felt that we were finally doing, in September of 1996, what we had failed to do in 1980. However, the code we released ran only on the Macintosh and, although we had worked hard to make it portable, we did not know if we had succeeded.

Three weeks later, we received a message announcing Ian Piumarta's first UNIX port of Squeak. He had ported it to seven additional UNIX platforms two weeks later. At the same time, Andreas Raab announced ports of Squeak for Windows 95 and

Windows NT. Neither of these people had even contacted us before starting their porting efforts! A mere five weeks after it was released, Squeak was available on all the major computing platforms except Windows 3.1, and had an active and rapidly growing mailing list. Since that time, Squeak ports have been done for Linux, the Acorn RISC, and Windows CE, and several other ports are underway.

The Squeak release, including the source code for the virtual machine, C translator and everything else described in this paper, as well as all the ports mentioned above, is available through the following sites:

```
http://www.research.apple.com/research/
        proj/learning_concepts/squeak/
ftp://ftp.create.ucsb.edu
ftp://alix.inria.fr
ftp://ftp.cs.uni-magdeburg.de/pub/
        Smalltalk/free/squeak
```

The Squeak license agreement explicitly grants the right to use Squeak in commercial applications royalty-free. The only requirement in return is that any ports of Squeak or changes to the base class library must be made available for free on the Internet. New applications and facilities built on Squeak do not need to be shared. We believe that this licensing agreement encourages the continued development and sharing of Squeak by its user community.

## Related Work

For the Smalltalk devotee, nothing is more natural than the desire to attack all programming problems with Smalltalk. Thus, there has long been a tradition of using Smalltalk to describe and debug a low-level system before its final implementation. As mentioned earlier, the Blue Book used Smalltalk as a high-level description of a Smalltalk virtual machine, and this description was actually checked for accuracy by running it. In LOOM [Kaeh86], the kernel of a virtual object memory was written and executed in a separate, simplified Smalltalk virtual machine whenever an "object fault" occurred. For better performance, this kernel was later translated into BCPL semi-automatically, then fixed up by hand. This experience planted the seed for the approach taken in Squeak two decades later.

A number of recent systems translate complete Smalltalk programs into lower-level languages to gain speed, portability, or application packaging advantages. Smalltalk/X [Gitt95] and SPiCE [YaDo95] generate C code from programs using the full range of Smalltalk semantics, including blocks. Babel [MWH94] translates Smalltalk applications into CLOS, and includes a facility for automatically winnowing out unused classes and methods.

Producer [Cox87] translated Smalltalk programs into Objective C, but required the programmer to supply type declarations and rules for mapping dynamically allocated objects such as Points into Objective C record structures. Producer only supported a subset of Smalltalk semantics because it depended on the Objective C runtime and thus did not support blocks as first-class objects. Squeak's Smalltalk-to-C translator restricts the programmer to an even more limited subset of Smalltalk, but that subset closely mirrors the underlying processor architecture, allowing the translated code to run nearly as efficiently as if it were written in C directly. The difference arises from a difference in goals: The goal of Squeak's translation is merely to support the construction of its own virtual machine, a much simpler task than translating full-blown Smalltalk programs into C.

Squeak's translator is more in the spirit of QUICKTALK [Ball86], a system that used Smalltalk to define new primitive methods for the virtual machine. Another Smalltalk-to-primitive compiler, Hurricane [Atki86], used a combination of user-supplied declarations and simple type inference to eliminate class checks and to inline integer arithmetic. Unlike Squeak's translator, Hurricane allowed the programmer to also use polymorphic arithmetic in the Smalltalk code to be translated. Neither QUICKTALK nor Hurricane attempted to produce an entire virtual machine via translation.

Type information can help a translator produce more efficient code by eliminating run-time type tests and enabling inlining. Typed Smalltalk [JGZ88] added optional type declarations to Smalltalk and used that type information to generate faster code. The quality of its code was comparable to that of QUICKTALK but, to the best of the authors' knowledge, the project's ultimate goal of producing a complete, stand-alone Smalltalk virtual machine was never realized. A different approach is to use type information gathered during program execution to guide on-the-fly optimization, as done in the Self [ChUn91] [Hölz94] and Animorphic [Anim96] virtual machines. Note that using types for optimization is independent of whether the programming language has type declarations. The Self and Animorphic virtual machines use type information to optimize declaration-free languages whereas Strongtalk [BrGr93], which augments Smalltalk with an optional type system to support the specification and verification of interfaces, ran on a virtual machine that knew nothing about those types. The subset of Smalltalk used for the Squeak virtual machine maps so directly to the fundamental data types of the hardware that the translator would not benefit from additional type information. However, we have contemplated building a separate primitive compiler that supports polymorphic arithmetic, in which case the declaration-driven optimization techniques of Hurricane and Typed Smalltalk would be beneficial.

## Future Work

Work on Squeak continues. We are overhauling Squeak's graphics model to supplant the MVC model with a new one along the lines of Morphic [Malo95] and Fabrik [Inga88]. We also plan to complete Squeak's sound and music facilities by adding sound input and MIDI input and output.

We are collaborating with Ian Piumarta to produce a dynamic translation engine for Squeak, inspired by Eliot Miranda's BrouHaHa Smalltalk [Mira87] and his later work with portable threaded code. A top priority is to build the entire engine in Smalltalk to keep it entirely portable.

Just as we wanted Squeak to be endowed with music and sound capability, we also wanted it to be easily interconnected with the rest of the computing world. To this end, we are adding network stream and datagram support to the system. While not yet complete, the current facilities already support TCP/IP clients and servers on Macintosh and Windows 95/NT, with UNIX support to follow soon.

## Conclusions

As far as we know, Squeak is the first practical Smalltalk system written in itself that is complete and self-supporting. Squeak runs the Smalltalk code describing its own virtual machine fast enough for debugging purposes: although it requires some patience, one can actually interact with menus and windows in this mode. This is no mean feat, considering that every memory reference in the inner loop of BitBlt is running in Smalltalk.

To achieve useful levels of performance, the Smalltalk code of the virtual machine is translated into C, yielding a speedup of approximately 450. Part of this performance gain, a factor of 3.4, can be attributed to the inlining of function calls in the translation process. The translator can also be used to generate primitive methods for computationally intensive inner loops that manipulate fundamental data types of the machine such as bytes, integers, floats, and arrays of these types.

The Squeak virtual machine, since its source code is publicly available, serves as an updated reference implementation for Smalltalk-80. This is especially valuable now that the classic Blue and Green Books [Gold83] [Kras83] are out of print. A number of design choices made in the Blue Book that were appropriate for the slower speed and limited address space of the computer systems of the early 1980's have been revisited, especially those relating to object memory and storage reclamation. Squeak also updates the multimedia components of this reference system by adding color support and image transformation capabilities to BitBlt and by including sound output. While Squeak is not the first Smalltalk to use modern storage management or to support multimedia, it makes a valuable contribution by delivering these capabilities in a small one-language package that is freely available, and that runs identically on all platforms.

## Final Reflections

While we considered using Java for our project, we still feel that Smalltalk offers a better environment for research and development. At a time when the world is moving toward native host widgets, we still feel that there is power and inspiration in having all of the code for every aspect of computation and display be immediately accessible, changeable, and identical across platforms. Finally, when most development environments fill 100 megabytes of disk space or more, Squeak is a portable, malleable, full-service computing environment, including browsing, split-second recompilation, and source debugging tools, all in a 1-megabyte footprint. Though many of its strengths are rooted in the past, Squeak is suited to the intimate computing potential of PDAs and the Internet, and our work is, now more than ever, inspired by the future.

## Acknowledgments

The authors wish to acknowledge the support of Apple Computer throughout this project, especially Jim Spohrer, Don Norman, and Elizabeth Greer. We especially appreciate their wisdom in seeing that Squeak would be worth more if it were made freely available. We also wish to thank the entire Squeak community for their encouragement and support, especially those who have submitted code or donated their time and energy to maintaining Squeak ports and the Squeak mailing list and web sites.

## References

[Anim96] Animorphic Systems, Exhibit at OOPSLA '96. Animorphic Systems was a small company that included several members of the Self team and produced extremely high performance virtual machines for Smalltalk and Java. The company has since been purchased by Sun Microsystems.

[Atki86] Atkinson, R., "Hurricane: An Optimizing Compiler for Smalltalk," *Proc. of the ACM OOPSLA '86 conf.*, September 1986, pp. 151-158.

[BrGr93] Bracha, G. and Griswold, D., "Strongtalk: Typechecking Smalltalk in a Production Environment," *Proc. of the ACM OOPSLA '93 conf.*, September 1993.

[Ball86] Ballard, M., Maier, D., and Wirffs-Brock, A., "QUICKTALK: A Smalltalk-80 Dialect for Defining Primitive Methods," *Proc. of the ACM OOPSLA '86 conf.*, September 1986, pp. 140-150.

[ChUn91] Chambers, C. and Ungar, D., "Making Pure Object-Oriented Languages Practical," *Proc. of the ACM OOPSLA '91 conf.*, November 1991, pp. 1-15.

[Cox87] Cox, B. and Schmucker, K., "Producer: A Tool for Translating Smalltalk-80 to Objective-C," *Proc. of the ACM OOPSLA '87 conf.*, October 1987, pp. 423-429.

[Deut84] Deutsch, L., and Schiffman, A., "Efficient Implementation of the Smalltalk-80 System," *Proc. 11th ACM Symposium on Principles of Programming Languages*, January 1984, pp. 297-302.

[Gitt95] Gittinger, Claus, Smalltalk/X, http://www.informatik.uni-stuttgart.de/stx/stx.html, 1995.

[Gold83] Goldberg, A. and Robson, D., *Smalltalk-80: The Language and Its Implementation*, Addison-Wesley, Reading, MA,1983.

[Hölz94] Hölzle, U., *Adaptive optimization for Self: Reconciling High Performance with Exploratory Programming*, Ph.D. Thesis, Computer Science Department, Stanford University, 1994.

[Inga78] Ingalls, D., "The Smalltalk-76 Programming System, Design and Implementation" *Proc. 5th ACM Symposium on Principles of Programming Languages,* Tucson, January 1978.

[Inga88] Ingalls, D., Wallace, S., Chow, Y., Ludolph, F., and Doyle, K., "Fabrik: A Visual Programming Environment," *Proc. of the ACM OOPSLA '88 conf.*, September 1988, pp. 176-190.

[JGZ88] Johnson, R., Graver, J., and Zurawski, L.,"TS: An Optimizing Compiler for Smalltalk," *Proc. of the ACM OOPSLA '88 conf.*, September 1988, pp. 18-26.

[Kaeh86] Kaehler, Ted, "Virtual Memory on a Narrow Machine for an Object-Oriented Language," *Proc. of the ACM OOPSLA '86 conf.*, September 1986, pp. 87-106.

[Kras83] Krasner, G., ed., *Smalltalk-80, Bits of History, Words of Advice*, Addison-Wesley, Reading, MA,1983.

[Malo95] Maloney, J. and Smith, R., "Directness and Liveness in the Morphic User Interface Construction Environment," *UIST '95*, November 1995.

[Mira87] Miranda, E., "BrouHaHa—A Portable Smalltalk Interpreter," *Proc. of the ACM OOPSLA '87 conf.*, October 1987, pp. 354-365.

[MWH94] Moore, I., Wolczko, M., and Hopkins, T., "Babel—A Translator from Smalltalk into CLOS," *TOOLS USA 1994*, Prentice Hall, 1994.

[Saun77] Saunders, S., "Improved FM Audio Synthesis Methods for Real-time Digital Music Generation," in *Computer Music Journal 1:1*, February 1977. Reprinted in *Computer Music*, Roads, C. and Strawn, J., eds., MIT Press, Cambridge, MA, 1985.

[Unga84] Ungar, D.,"Generation Scavenging: A Non-Disruptive High Performance Storage Reclamation Algorithm," *Proc. ACM Symposium on Practical Software Development Environments*, April 1984, pp. 157-167. Also published as *ACM SIGPLAN Notices 19(5)*, May 1984 and *ACM Software Engineering Notes 9(3)*, May 1984.

[UnJa88] Ungar, D. and Jackson, F.,"Tenuring Policies for Generation-Based Storage Reclamation," *Proc. of the ACM OOPSLA '88 conf.*, September 1988, pp. 18-26.

[YaDo95] Yasumatsu, K. and Doi, N., "SPiCE: A System for Translating Smalltalk Programs Into a C Environment," *IEEE Transactions on Software Engineering 21(11)*, 1995, pp. 902-912.

# Constraint Diagrams: Visualizing Invariants in Object-Oriented Models

**Stuart Kent**

Division of Computing,
University of Brighton, Lewes Rd., Brighton, UK.
http://www.it.brighton.ac.uk/staff/Stuart.Kent
Stuart.Kent@brighton.ac.uk
fax: ++44 1273 642405, tel: ++44 1273 642494

**Abstract.** A new visual notation is proposed for precisely expressing constraints on object-oriented models, as an alternative to mathematical logic notation used in methods such as Syntropy and Catalysis. The notation is potentially intuitive, expressive, integrates well with existing visual notations, and has a clear and unambiguous semantics. It is reminiscent of informal diagrams used by mathematicians for illustrating relations, and borrows much from Venn diagrams. It may be viewed as a generalization of instance diagrams.

**Key words**: Analysis and design methods, language design, formal methods, software engineering practices.

## 1 Introduction

This paper proposes a new diagrammatic notation for precisely expressing invariant constraints on object-oriented (OO) models.

In essence, all OO modelling notations may be viewed as documenting constraints either on the set of allowable system states, i.e., the instance diagrams which one is allowed to draw, or on the allowable execution paths through those states.

Current graphical notations are inadequate in the constraints they are able to impose, so need to be supplemented by mathematical assertions describing the more intricate constraints, as is done in methods such as Syntropy (Cook and Daniels, 1994), Catalysis (D'Souza and Wills, 1995, 1997) and BON (Walden and Nerson, 1995). So far this has been the only way of achieving a level of detail necessary for a comprehensive behavioral description, at a level of abstraction that avoids irrelevant implementation or design detail. Unfortunately it is also unintuitive and off-putting to many working software engineers. Parnas (1996) characterizes the problem as follows:

> "Mathematical methods offered to the working software engineer are not very practical [...]. Most, but not all, are theoretically sound but much more difficult to use than the mathematics that has been developed for use in other areas of engineering. [...] We need a lot more work on notation. The notation that is purveyed by most formal methods researchers is cumbersome and hard to read. Even the best notation I know (mine of course) is inadequate."

The diagrammatic notation proposed here, called ***constraint diagrams***, replaces the need to write many assertions mathematically and is potentially more intuitive to, hence more likely to be used by, the practising software engineer. The notation has similarities with informal diagrams used by mathematicians for illustrating properties of functions and relations (e.g., Gerstein 1987) and borrows much from Venn diagrams. It may be viewed as a way of describing sets of instance diagrams, and is a natural development of instance (object) diagrams in UML (UML 1997).

Whilst we have some clear ideas of how the notation might be used to improve the lot of the software modeler/designer, it is inevitable that the focus of this first paper on the subject is on describing the notation. This is best done by relating it to something that is more familiar. Therefore a careful characterization of an object-oriented model is given in Section 2, using diagrammatic notation from UML, supplemented with invariants expressed mathematically where UML diagrams are unable to express the desired constraints. This section also serves to demonstrate the claim made above that there are some constraints that can not be expressed using diagrammatic notations currently proposed for object-oriented modelling.

Section 3 introduces the notation by using it to express the invariants identified in section 2. This demonstrates that it is indeed more expressive than current diagrammatic notations.

Section 4 is a discussion focussing on:

- use of the notation to visualize action contracts (pre/post specifications),
- relationships with other diagrammatic notations,
- limitations, possible extensions, semantic issues and usability of the notation,
- impact on automated tool support for modelling.

The latter gives a sketch of how the notation could be used as a basis for automated tool support to the construction of precise specifications of constraints from instance diagrams, and vice-versa. It is proposed that similar techniques could be used for semantic checking of models.

A summary of the notation is given in an appendix.

## 2 Library System in UML and Catalysis

This section sets the context for the constraint diagram notation introduced in this paper, by specifying a small case study - a library system - using the diagrammatic notation of UML supplemented with mathematical notation from Catalysis to express those constraints that can not be expressed using diagrams from UML (or, indeed, other OO modelling notations). UML has been chosen as it incorporates and unifies many of the notations of its predecessors, so may be viewed as representative of them, and is fast becoming the de facto standard in OO modelling.

The approach taken is to express as much as possible diagrammatically, resorting to mathematical assertions only where strictly necessary. This serves three purposes: it proves the point that there are some constraints that can not be expressed diagrammatically using


OOPSLA '97 10/97 GA, USA
© 1997 ACM 0-89791-908-4/97/0010...$3.50

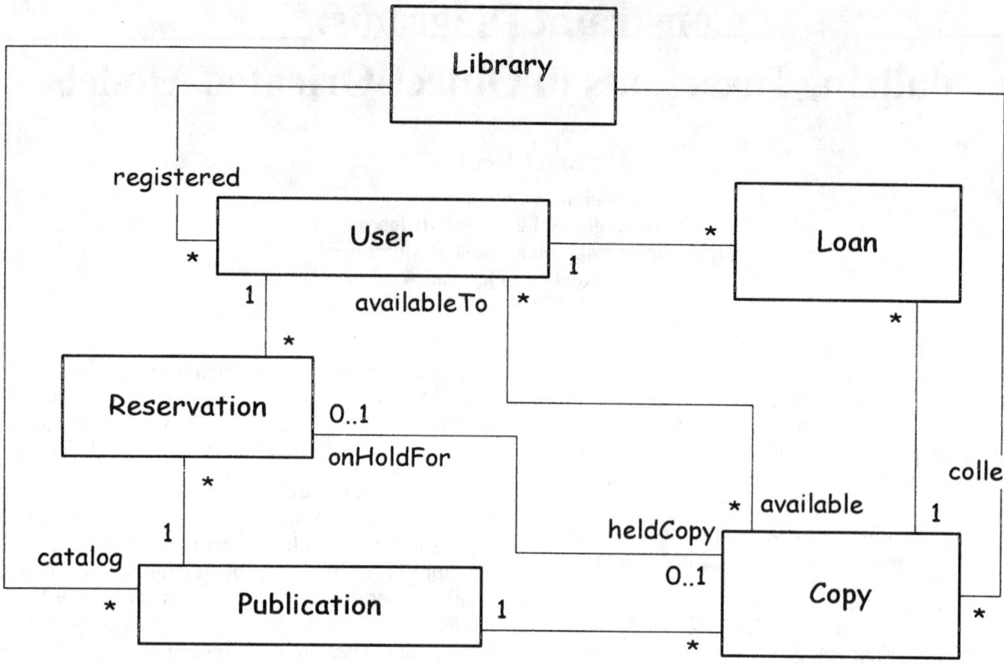


**Figure 1: Type diagram for library**

existing notations; it provides the examples (those constraints) for the section following which introduces the constraint diagram notation; it illustrates the pattern of specification required (mixing of type and state diagrams) to express as much as possible using diagrams from existing notations.

### 2.1 Informal Requirements

The general requirements are to produce a computerized system to support the management of loans in a university library. A library maintains a catalog of publications which are available for lending to users. There may be many copies of the same publication. Publications and copies may be added to and removed from the library. Copies available for lending may be borrowed by active users registered with the library. When a publication (or more specifically a particular copy) has been borrowed it is on loan, and is not available for lending to other users. However, it still belongs to the library and so is still part of its collection. Users are able to reserve publications, when none of the copies are available for loan. A user may not place more than one reservation for the same publication. When a copy is returned after it has been out on loan, it may be put back on the shelf or, alternatively, held for a user who has reserved the publication of which it is a copy. This may be done immediately on return, or delayed, and done as part of a batch of returned copies.

### 2.2 Type Diagram

The main type diagram for the library is given in Figure 1. This is UML notation. `Publication`, `User` and `Copy` are types of object we expect to find in a library. A publication is a record of all the details of a book: title, authors, ISBN, etc. A publication may have many copies (or none), which correspond to the physical books. A copy only has one set of publication details. A copy may be `availableTo` loan to many users, and a user may have many copies which are `available` for loan to her. All the publications known to the library are in the `catalog`, all the copies form the library's `collection`, and all the users known to the library must be `registered`.

`Loan` and `Reservation` characterize objects used to record loans and reservations, respectively. A loan records which copy is on loan to which user, and a reservation records which publication has been reserved by which user. A copy may be put `onHoldFor` a reservation, which means that it is waiting to be collected by the user who made the reservation. After the copy has been collected the reservation will have been fulfilled.

Some associations in the diagram have been given rolenames at one or both ends. Following Catalysis (D'Souza and Wills, 1997) we adopt a convention for constructing default rolenames where they have been omitted.

- If the association is unlabeled the name of the type at either end is used, with the first letter in lowercase and pluralized if this makes sense: for example we can refer to the `loans` of a user or the `user` associated with a loan.
- If the association is labelled at one end only, then the name used at the reverse end will be that label prefixed with ~: for example `~collection`, `~catalog`, `~registered` will always take us back to the library object(s) from an object of the corresponding types.

### 2.3 States

The type diagram on its own can not express all the constraints that we would wish to express for the library system. In particular, multiplicity restrictions do not allow relationships between associations to be expressed. For example, it should be a constraint that the publication of a copy `onHoldFor` a reservation is the one that has been reserved. Figure 2 shows an instance diagram which satisfies the type model, but which does not satisfy this constraint. It satisfies the type model because it satisfies all the multiplicity restrictions. It does not satisfy the constraint because the held copy is not associated with the same publication as the reservation it is held for.

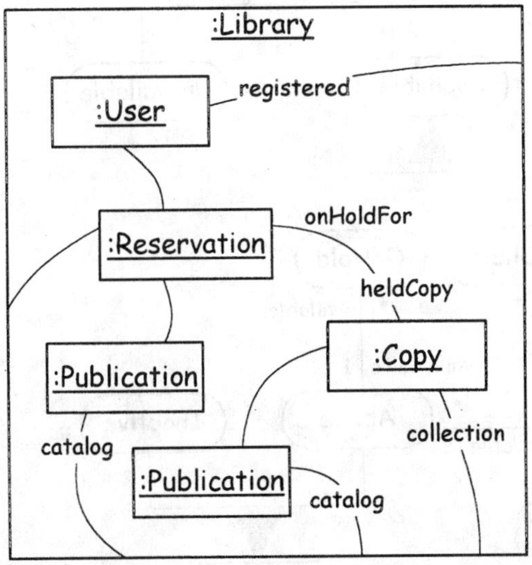


**Figure 2: Instance diagram not satisfying constraint, but satisfying type diagram**

However, we have not yet made any use of states. Often further constraints can be imposed by introducing states for particular types of object, and then adding further multiplicity conditions on associations, which will depend on the state chosen. In this section we show that for this system (and by extrapolation probably for most systems) this is still not enough. In particular the constraint above can not be expressed in this way.

Figure 3 shows four diagrams defining the states of particular types. The notation used is similar to that used in OMT (Rumbaugh et al. 1991), Syntropy and Catalysis, transformed to UML, which strangely says nothing about defining states outside state diagrams. The filled in subtype arrow indicates partitioning: the type Copy is partitioned between those objects in the state Available and those in the state Unavailable. Subtyping is used to bring states into type diagrams, based on the semantic intuition that every Available object is a Copy object, but not vice-versa.

In an attempt to unify notation, we have chosen to use a box with rounded corners to represent a state, i.e. the same shape of box that is used in state diagrams. The aforementioned methods generally use  .

In the true spirit of subtyping states can be further constrained: they can have associations that objects not in that state do not have and may further constraint multiplicities on associations obtained from the supertype/superstate.

The diagrams in Figure 4 place additional constraints on states for this example. The left hand diagram indicates that when the copy is in the OnHold state it is onHoldFor exactly one reservation in the ToBeCollected state, but is not onHoldFor any reservation when in a different state. Similarly, a reservation in the ToBeCollected state has exactly one heldCopy, but no held copies when in a different state. Clearly this diagram does place some constraint on the nature of the copy held, that it is in the state OnHold, but this is not enough; in particular it does not state that the publication associated with the held copy is the same as that reserved.

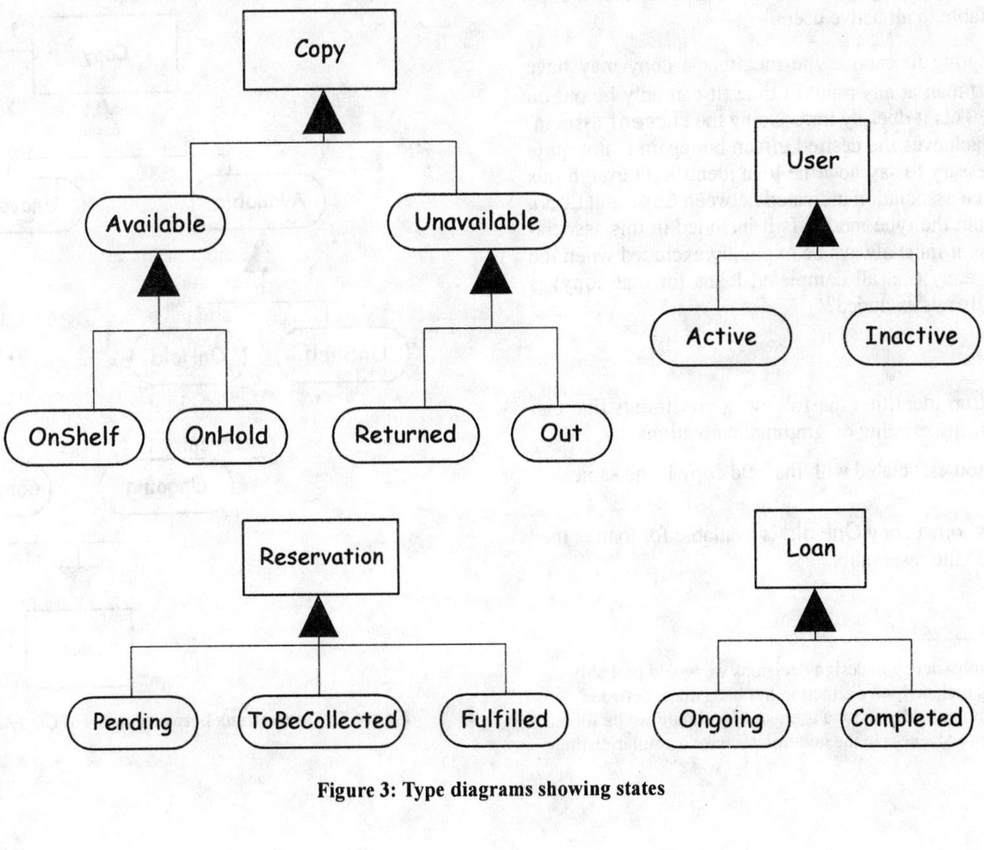


**Figure 3: Type diagrams showing states**

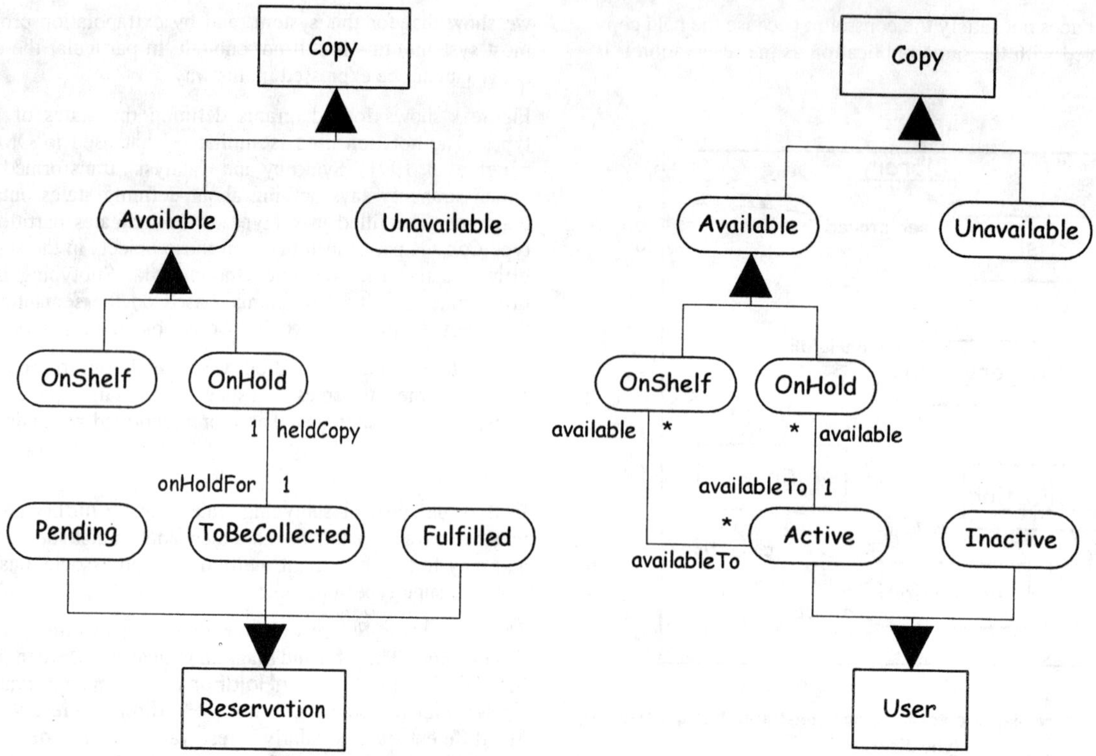


**Figure 4: Multiplicities on associations between states**

Similarly the right hand diagram places constraints on the number and state of users to which a copy is available, depending on the state of the copy. However, again it is not sufficient; specifically it does not state that the single user to whom a copy OnHold is available for loan is the one who made the reservation, or that a copy OnShelf is available to all active users.

Figure 5 is attempting to capture the idea that a copy may have only one onGoing loan at any point in time (it can only be out on loan to one user). This it does by introducing the **current** association. This nearly achieves the desired effect, but again is not quite enough. It is necessary to say how the loan identified through this link is related to the association indicated between Copy and Loan, which is taken from the type model. Is it included in this association, in which case it must always be explicitly excluded when the loan history of a copy (i.e. all completed loans for that copy) is retrieved, or is it always excluded?[1]

## 2.4 Invariants

The previous section identified the following constraints that can not be expressed using existing diagrammatic notations:

1. The publication associated with the held copy is the same as that reserved.
2. The user to whom a copy OnHold is available for loan is the one who made the reservation.

1. To maintain a consistency in design decisions we would probably wish to say it is included: no distinction has been made between ongoing and completed loans for a user, so why should we be forced by a lack of expressiveness in the notation to make a similar distinction here.

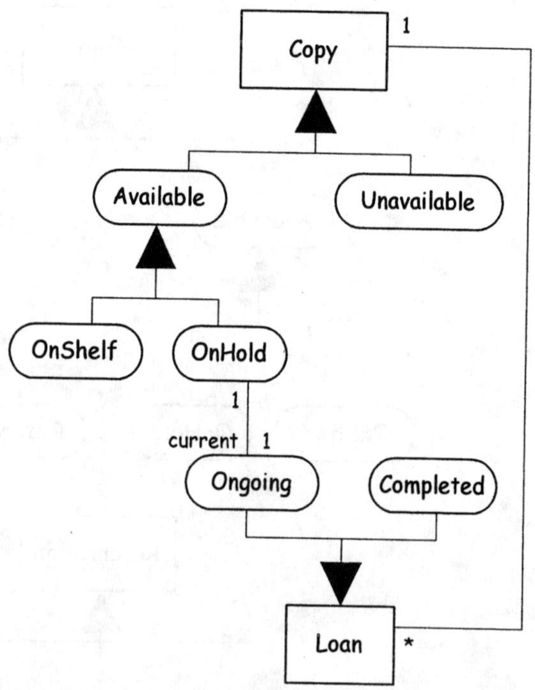


**Figure 5: Associations between states of Copy and Loan**

3. A copy OnShelf is available to all active users.
4. A copy may be associated with only one ongoing loan.

In addition there are some additional constraints which have not been touched upon:

5. The collection is equivalent to all the copies of all publications in the catalog.
6. The reservations known to the library are exactly all the reservations made by users or all the reservations there are for the publications in the catalog.
7. The loans known to the library are exactly those associated with copies in the collection and these are exactly those associated with registered users.

These seven constraints can not be expressed even if one is prepared to fully exploit the inclusion of states on type diagrams. More naive designs which e.g. use associations to model states will come up with many more constraints relating associations which can not be expressed using current diagrammatic notations. It seems that naive designs are likely to be par for the course, considering, for example, that the latest UML documentation (UML 1997) makes no mention of including states on type diagrams.

Methods such as Catalysis and Syntropy solve this problem by the use of mathematical assertions to write ***invariants***. The invariants stated are written in mathematical notation using Catalysis syntax, as follows:

1. The publication associated with a copy OnHold is the same as that which has been reserved.

   $$\forall c{:}Copy,\ (c.OnHold \wedge c \in collection) \Rightarrow c.onHoldFor.publication = c.publication$$

   $c \in collection$ has been included as really this constraint only applies to copies in the collection; it can not be guaranteed e.g. for copies passed into the library via a parameter which have yet to be placed in the collection. Of course multiplicity constraints in type diagrams don't make this distinction.
2. The user to whom a copy OnHold is available for loan is the one who made the reservation.

   $$\forall c{:}Copy,\ (c.OnHold \wedge c \in collection) \Rightarrow c.availableTo = c.onHoldFor.user$$
3. A copy OnShelf is available to all active users.

   $$\forall c{:}Copy,\ (c.OnShelf \wedge c \in collection) \Rightarrow c.availableTo = registered[Active]$$

   where registered[Active] is the set of registered users in the active state.
4. A copy may be associated with only one ongoing loan.

   $$\forall c{:}Copy,\ ((c.Out \wedge c \in collection) \Rightarrow |c.loans[Ongoing]| = 1) \wedge ((\neg c.Out \wedge c \in collection) \Rightarrow |c.loans[Ongoing]| = 0)$$

   This will work whether the current association suggested in Figure 5 on page 4 is included or not. If this association is included, then the above constraint is not necessary; instead the constraint

   $\forall c{:}Copy,\ c \in collection \Rightarrow c.current \in c.loans$ is required.
5. The collection is equivalent to all the copies of all publications in the catalog.

   $$collection = catalog.copies$$

   The meaning of navigation in this instance originated in Syntropy (Cook and Daniels 1994, p57) and is used in Catalysis. catalog is a set. catalog.copies is then the union of the sets arrived at by navigating the copies link from each publication in catalog. That is catalog.copies is equivalent to writing

   $$\{x{:}Copy \mid \exists y{:}Publication,\ y \in catalog \wedge y.copy = x\}$$

   The Syntropy/Catalysis interpretation of navigation is fully exploited in the constraint diagram notation introduced here.
6. The reservations made by users are exactly all the reservations there are for the publications in the catalog.

   $$registered.reservations = catalog.reservations$$
7. The loans associated with copies in the collection and these are exactly those associated with registered users.

   $$collection.loans = registered.loans$$

## 3 Constraint diagrams: visualizing invariants

This section introduces the constraint diagram notation, by giving a constraint diagram for the invariants written mathematically in §2.4, p.4. Thus it demonstrates how constraint diagrams can express invariants that can not be expressed diagrammatically in current notations. A summary of the notation can be found in the Appendix.

Perhaps the easiest invariants to show diagrammatically are 5, 6 and 7. The corresponding constraint diagram is given in Figure 6. The basic notation can be summarized as follows:

- Associations are depicted as relations between *sets* of objects.
- Venn diagrams can be used to express relationships between associations. In this case the relationships are simply equivalences, i.e. a number of arrows target on the same set. In general, relationships such as intersection and containment can be depicted. Examples of such relationships appear throughout this section.
- There are four ways of depicting a set depending on the number of elements in the set:
  - ● has 1 element,
  - ○ has 0..1 elements,
  -  has 0 or more elements,
  -  has n elements.
- Types are depicted as (universal) sets.
- Navigation always begins at an object or set with no incoming arrows. In this diagram the only such item is the self object. Enclosing the types within the object has no semantic relevance. It is an aid to drawing the diagram, and gives a sense of where navigation begins.

Links are directed for the following reason. Consider the top diagram in Figure 7. The association available indicates, for any user, which set of copies is available for loan to that user. If the arrow was omitted then we would not know in which direction to read the diagram. Reading the link in the other direction would mean that any set of copies are always available only to a single user which is the same for all copies in that set. This is clearly not

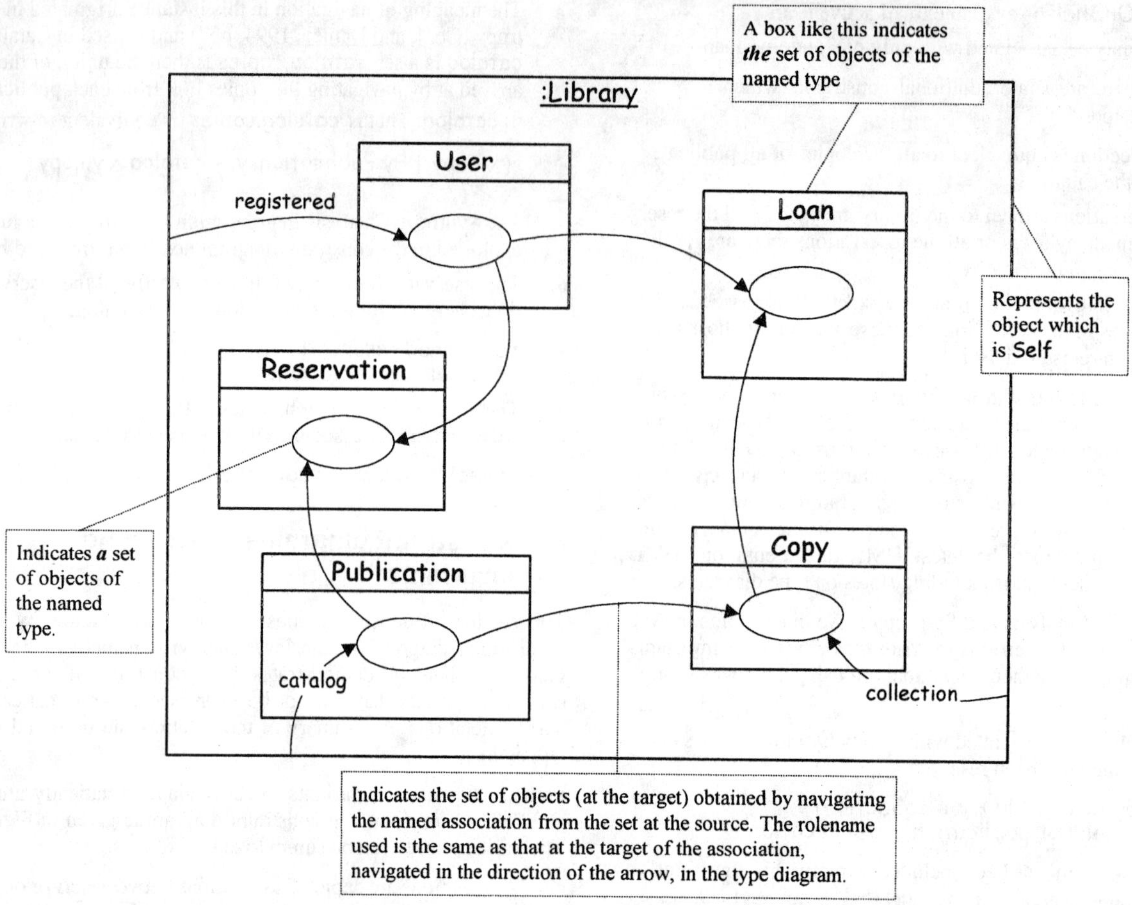


**Figure 6: Constraint diagram for invariants 5-7**

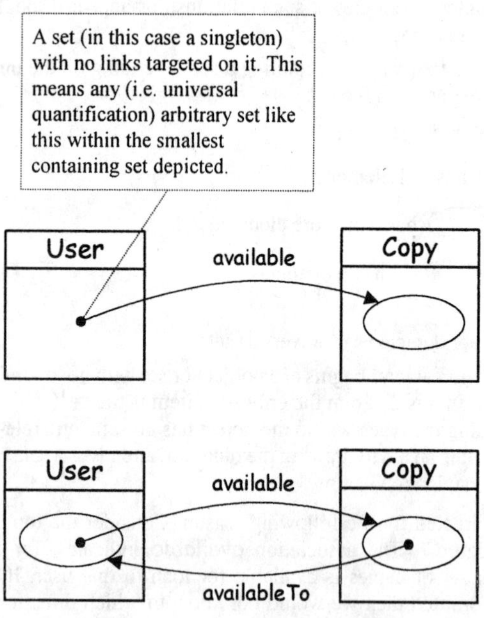


**Figure 7: The availableTo link**

the case. Instead we could draw the bottom diagram, which says that for any user there is a set of copies available to that user (possibly empty), and for any copy in that set, that user is *one of* the users to which the copy is available for loan.

The constraint diagram, Figure 8, for invariant

1. The publication associated with a copy OnHold is the same as that which has been reserved.

   $\forall$c:Copy, (c.OnHold $\wedge$ c $\in$ collection)
   $\Rightarrow$ c.onHoldFor.publication = c.publication

introduces a new piece of notation: a shorthand for representing those objects in a particular set (in this case collection), which are in a particular state (in this case OnHold). It is probably worth highlighting how a constraint can be placed on an arbitrary object chosen from a particular set: by showing a set (if a singleton then this corresponds to an object) with no arrows targeted on it. In this case, c represents any object in the state OnHold and in the collection. The label c is not strictly necessary; it has been included so to clarify the mapping from the diagram to the mathematical form of the invariant.

Equivalently one could draw Figure 9, where, as in §2.3, p.2, a box with rounded corners is used to represent the set of objects in the named state.

The short hand notation is especially useful when objects in two or more different states need to be referred to.

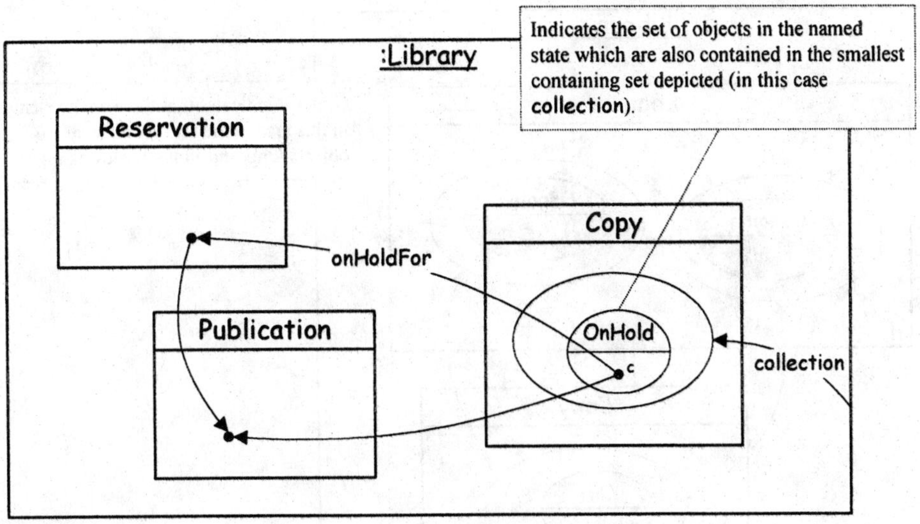


**Figure 8: Constraint diagram for invariant 1**

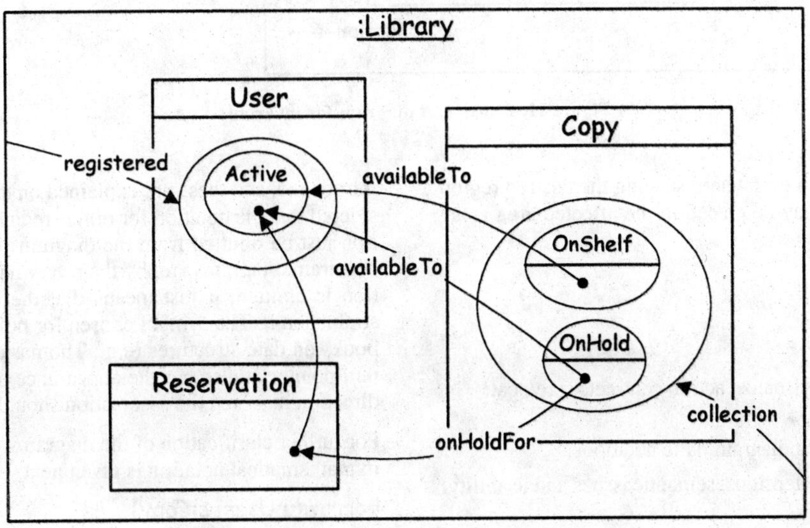


**Figure 10: Constraint diagram for invariants 2, 3**

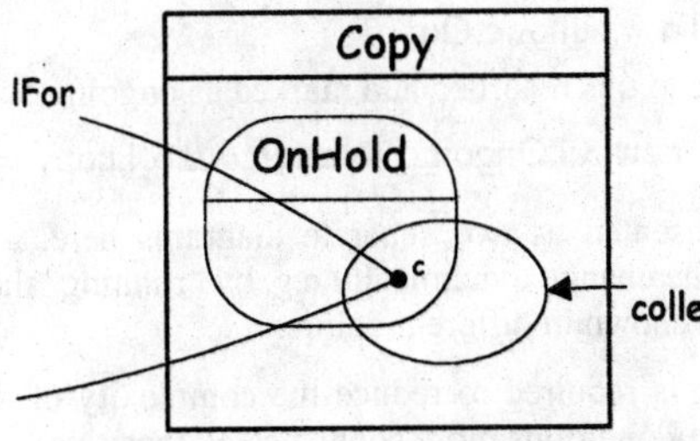


**Figure 9: States on constraint diagrams**

It is natural to combine invariants

2. The user to whom a copy OnHold is available for loan is the one who made the reservation.

   $$\forall c{:}Copy,\ (c.OnHold \wedge c \in collection) \Rightarrow c.availableTo = c.onHoldFor.user$$

3. A copy OnShelf is available to all active users.

   $$\forall c{:}Copy,\ (c.OnShelf \wedge c \in collection) \Rightarrow c.availableTo = registered[Active]$$

into the same diagram, Figure 10, as they both concern the same association. There is little that requires comment here.

Finally, Figure 11 is the diagram for the invariant

4. A copy may be associated with only one ongoing loan.

   $$\forall c{:}Copy,\ ((c.Out \wedge c \in collection) \Rightarrow |c.loans[Ongoing]| = 1) \wedge ((\neg c.Out \wedge c \in collection) \Rightarrow |c.loans[Ongoing]| = 0)$$

This diagram introduces one new piece of notation, which is explained on the diagram in one place that it is used. In the second place it is used, it indicates that, apart from the single object depicted, there are no other Ongoing loans in the set of loans for a copy that is Out, i.e. a copy which is Out is associated with exactly one Ongoing loan.

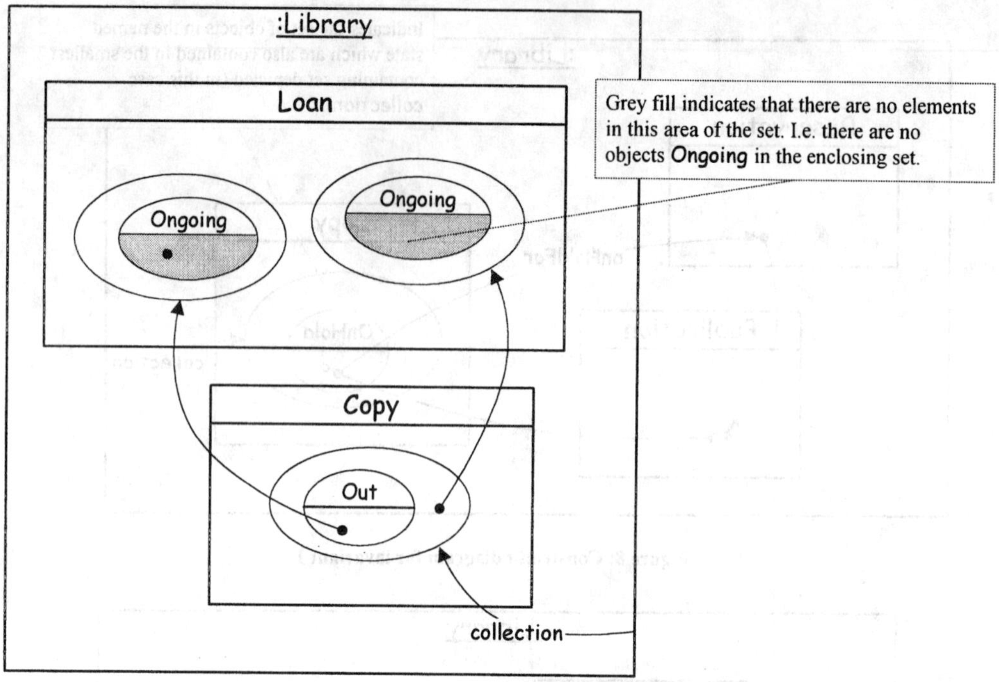


**Figure 11: Constraint diagram for invariant 4**

For drawing by hand or in a tool where shading the desired region may be difficult, a cross may be placed in the affected area as an alternative.

## 4 Discussion

This section discusses:

- use of the notation to visualize action contracts (pre/post specifications),
- relationships with other diagrammatic notations,
- limitations, possible extensions, semantic issues and usability of the notation,
- impact on automated tool support for modelling.

### 4.1 Visualizing action contracts

Some preliminary work (Kent 1997) has been done on using constraint diagrams to visualize behavioral specifications for actions, expressed in terms of pre and post conditions. A pre/post specification is sometimes called a contract. In UML and its precursors, state diagrams (based on Harel's statecharts – Harel, 1987) are used to specify dynamic behavior, and as is the case with invariants, they are limited in the constraints they are able to express. Methods such as Catalysis and Syntropy therefore supplement state diagrams with pre and post conditions which must be expressed using mathematical notation if precision is required.

Constraint diagrams can be used unchanged to express pre-conditions. However, a post-condition is predicated over two states, and this causes further complications. The idea proposed to solve this is to borrow from the Catalysis idea of a ***filmstrip*** (a sequence of instance diagrams), replacing instance with constraint diagrams. An example is given in Figure 12. This is the filmstrip characterizing the post-condition of the action borrow(u:User,c:Copy). Items appear on the first constraint diagram if they are subject to change by the action. Three new pieces of notation have been introduced, and these are explained on the diagram. It may be considered that the notation for null is redundant: couldn't the association just be omitted from the diagram? Omission doesn't work as constraint diagrams are, by their very nature, partial: if an association is omitted, it just means that the diagram imposes no constraints on it. The symbol chosen for null is used in many standard books on data structures (e.g., Thomas et al., 1988) to represent a null pointer. It also has the appearance of an arrow, suggesting the direction in which the association should be read.

For further clarification of the diagrams, the post-condition written in mathematical notation is given next.

borrow(u:User, c:Copy)
<u>pre</u>
...
<u>post</u>
c is out and no longer available for lending.

c.availableTo = null ∧ c.Out

The loan of c to u is recorded and marked as ongoing.

∃l : loan, l ∈ new ∧ l.Ongoing ∧ l.user = u ∧ l.copy = c

Although presented as two separate diagrams here, a case tool could show the change dynamically e.g. by "running" the filmstrip with changes shown in different colors.

Further work is required to reduce the complexity of these filmstrips for post-conditions more sophisticated than this.

### 4.2 Relationships with other diagrammatic notations

**States in state and type diagrams.** In constraint diagrams a state is viewed as the set of objects in that state. We have already argued for the use of the same shape of box (one with rounded corners) to represent a state wherever it appears. However, constraint

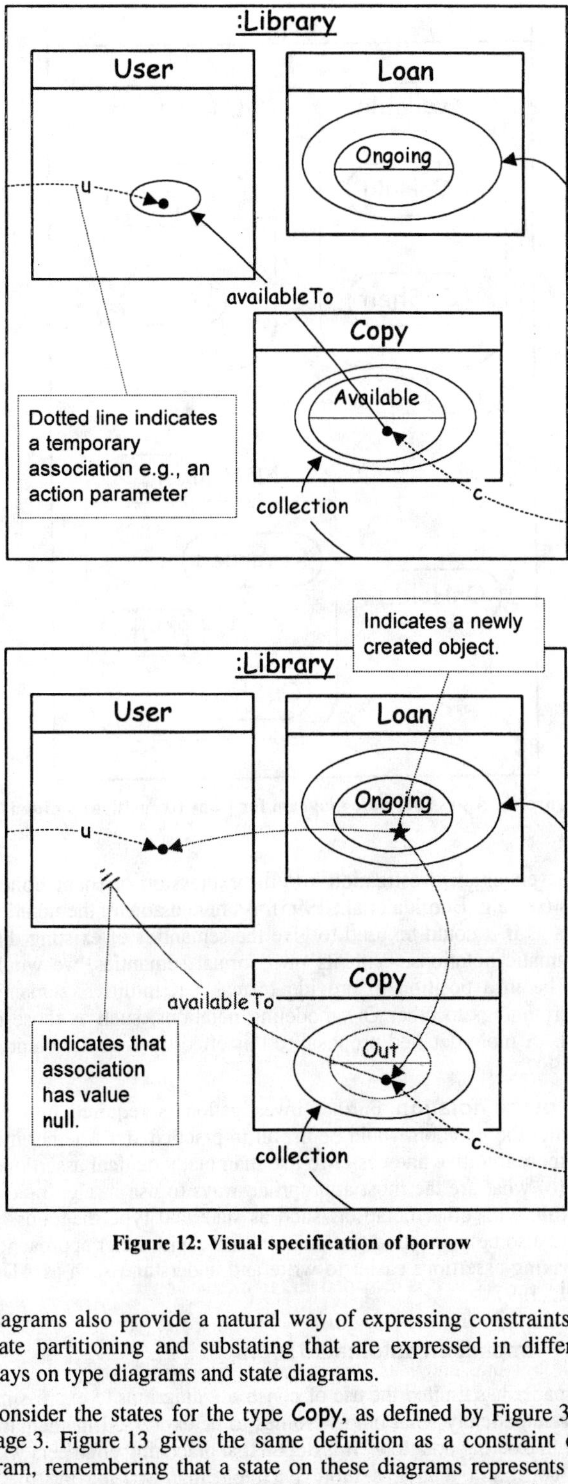


**Figure 12: Visual specification of borrow**

diagrams also provide a natural way of expressing constraints on state partitioning and substating that are expressed in different ways on type diagrams and state diagrams.

Consider the states for the type Copy, as defined by Figure 3 on page 3. Figure 13 gives the same definition as a constraint diagram, remembering that a state on these diagrams represents the set of objects in that state. This is like a state diagram with the transitions omitted. The area around the states has also been grayed out to indicate that the type is partitioned by the two top-level states. This is required because, as stated in Section 4.1, constraint diagrams are partial; without explicitly indicating that the states partition, there is the possibility that there may be other states defined on a different diagram.

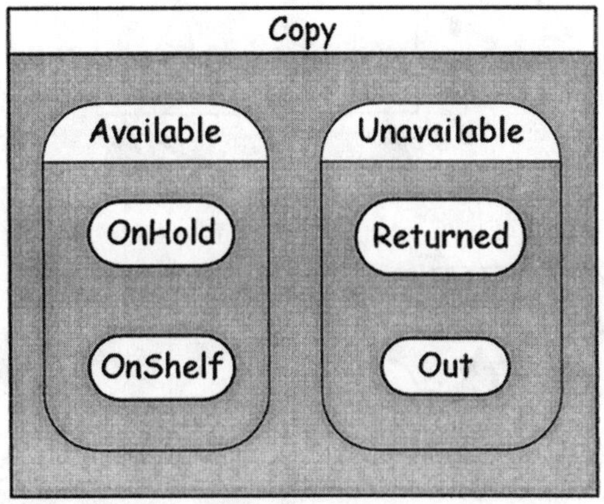


**Figure 13: A grouping of states for Copy**

A second constraint diagram (Figure 14), which is consistent with Figure 13, may be drawn. It defines a different grouping of nested

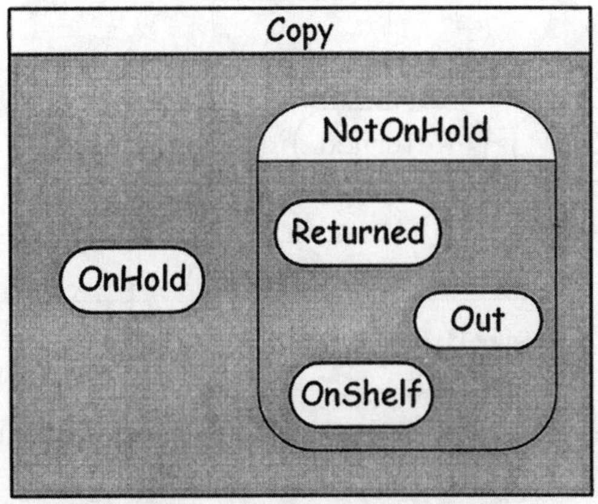


**Figure 14: Another grouping of states for Copy**

states for Copy. This can be expressed using states on one or more type diagrams, though this seems more cumbersome (Figure 15). It can not be expressed using a state diagram, as there may only be one state diagram per type, and a state diagram enforces a single grouping of nested states. The closest approximation is given by Figure 16, where transitions have been omitted as they are irrelevant to this discussion. Unfortunately, the usual interpretation of state diagrams treats, e.g., the two OnShelf states as different.

**Subtyping in type diagrams.** A similar notation could be used for showing relationships (partitions, disjointedness, etc.) between static subtypes. This accords with explanations of subtyping based on Venn diagrams, in e.g. Wirfs-Brock et al. (1990).

**Object (instance) diagrams in UML.** Object diagrams in UML already include a notation for showing sets of objects - placing a * in an object. However they do not allow sets to overlap, and they have no representation for navigation expressions (in our notation, arrows from sets targeted on other sets), which is fundamental to the expressiveness of constraint diagrams. Thus constraint diagrams could be regarded as the natural development of what has already been started in UML.

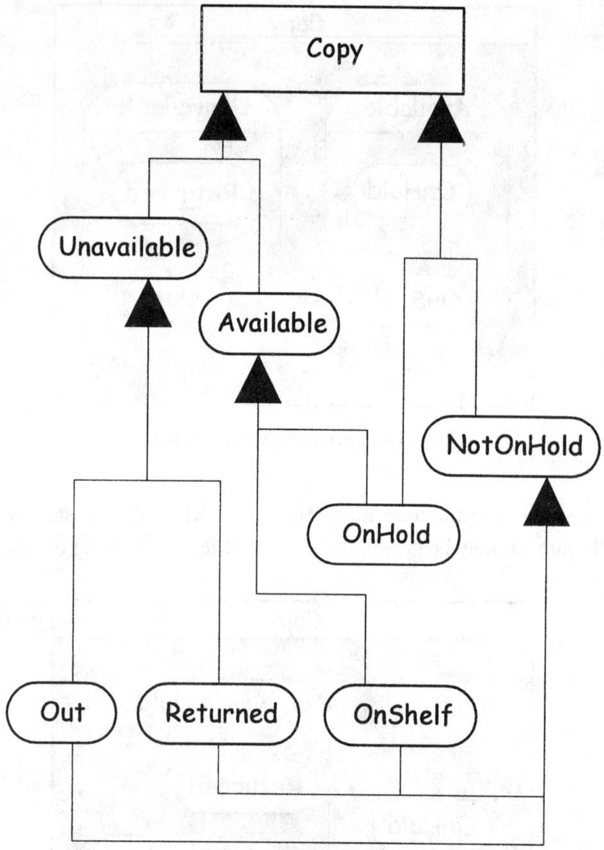


**Figure 15: Grouping states on a type diagram**

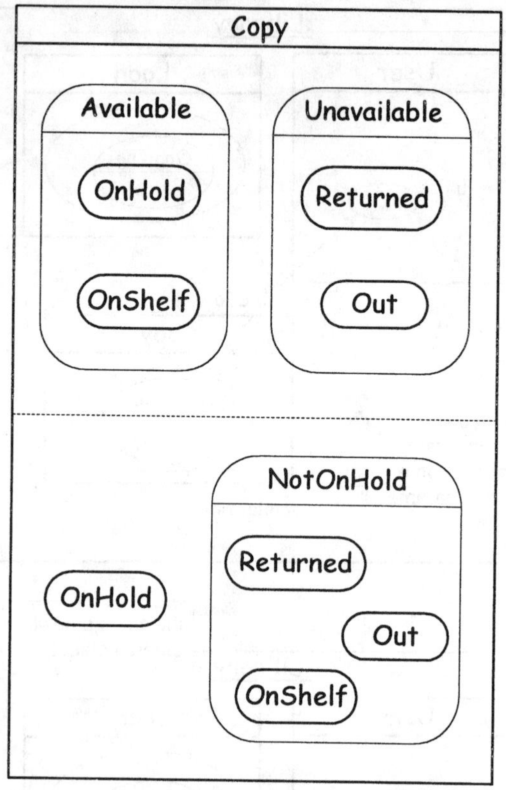


**Figure 16: A possible state diagram for Copy (transitions omitted)**

### 4.3 Limitations, Extensions, Semantics, Usability

**Limitations and extensions.** The assertions expressed using the notation in this paper have not involved all kinds of logical operators and connectives. Notable omissions are existential quantification and disjunction. Notation is given in the appendix for existential quantification over sets. With regard to disjunction, the two disjuncts could be represented as different constraint diagrams and composed disjunctively (see below).

Another limitation is the difficulty of showing constraints on attributes which hold values, e.g. of type `Integer`, rather than identify objects. It is expected that this could be cured by showing values like objects on instance diagrams, sets of values like sets of objects on constraint diagrams, and relationships between them as associations.

The notation also suffers from the same limitations as Venn diagrams - it is hard to show the intersection of more than three sets. We have a (rather cumbersome) notation that will get round this problem, but do not believe it will occur very often. There is inevitably other published research on this problem, but we have yet to find it.

**Semantics.** Work has begun on describing the semantics of the notation in terms of logical theories in Larch (Guttag and Horning, 1993). This builds upon recent work in interpreting existing modeling notations (Bourdeau and Cheng, 1995; Hamie and Howse, 1997). The aim of this work is to check the consistency and expressiveness of the notation - basically to ensure that no stone has been left unturned. A particular area of interest is to look at diagram composition, both disjunction and conjunction. This may open up new avenues of investigation into the expression of frame conditions (see e.g. Borgida et al., 1995). As hinted above, the notation looks as if it could be used to give the semantics of existing diagrammatic notations. With its own formal semantics, we would then be in a position to provide formal, yet intuitive, semantic underpinnings to other OO modeling notations, such as those in UML. A more detailed proposal to this effect is given in (Kent et al., 1997).

**Use of the notation.** Further investigation is required into (a) whether the notation would be useful in practice and whether it is any more intuitive and easier to use than mathematical assertions; and (b) what are the most appropriate ways to use it, e.g. in conjunction with other notations such as state and type diagrams. It would also be interesting to compare its use with other approaches to making assertions easier to write and understand such as ADL (ADL, 1997).

### 4.4 Impact on automated tools

The paper has limited the use of constraint diagrams to expressing diagrammatically what otherwise has to be expressed mathematically in existing notations. It is hoped that practising engineers will find constraint diagrams more palatable than writing the math though we have no evidence to support this claim. However, this is not, we believe, the only or even main contribution of the notation. More importantly, it could open the way to providing automated support for the construction of sophisticated constraints in CASE tools, as well as semantic cross checking between different views of a model (e.g. between instance diagrams and type diagrams, type diagrams and state diagrams, etc.).

First notice the correspondence between constraint diagrams and instance diagrams; constraint diagrams are essentially characterizations of sets of instance diagrams. We can imagine a tool that could assist with constructing constraint diagrams from instance diagrams and vice versa.

Suppose, for example, that a tool was presented with the instance diagrams in Figure 17, where the first should be accepted by the model but the second not. The goal is to construct the constraint

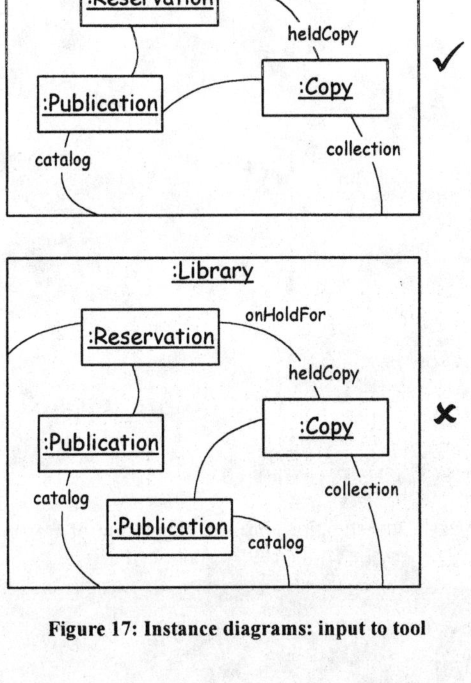


**Figure 17: Instance diagrams: input to tool**

diagram which ensures that this is the case. Assuming that a type diagram has been drawn, a constraint diagram can be derived which represents the multiplicity constraints for associations mentioned in the instance diagrams, composed with the part of Figure 6 relevant to these associations. This is given in Figure 18.

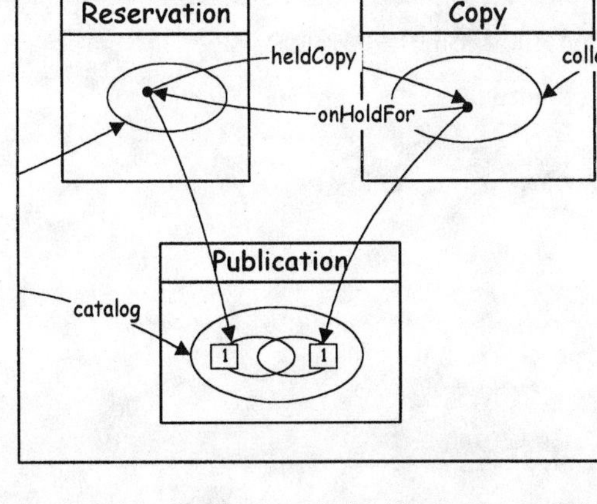


**Figure 18: Constraint diagram: derived by tool from existing diagrams**

Focussing on the Publication type, Figure 19 (a) admits two possibilities, (b) and (c). Pattern matching with the instance diagrams indicates that (b) should be accepted but (c) rejected. This gives rise to the final constraint diagram in Figure 20.

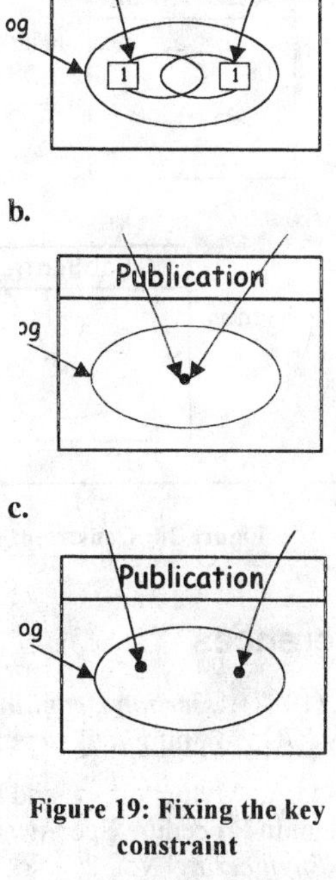


**Figure 19: Fixing the key constraint**

This is a very simple example and some details of the various steps have been omitted. However, it is hoped that the example is convincing enough to warrant that the approach is worthy of further investigation.

As this paper has illustrated, the mapping from constraint diagrams to mathematical notation is quite systematic. Once a constraint diagram had been constructed a tool could automatically generate an equivalent mathematical form, if desired.

Constraint diagrams could also assist with cross-checking between different views of a model. Constraints imposed by existing diagrammatic notations may be expressed using constraint diagrams instead (for example, an indication of how multiplicity constraints may be characterized has just been given). This suggests that a systematic hence automated conversion could be performed. Cross-checking is then a matter of "overlaying" constraint diagrams and looking for conflicts. It may be possible to automate this process, in which case any conflict could be shown visually using an appropriate constraint diagram.

By a similar process instance diagrams could be checked against constraints by converting an instance diagram into a constraint diagram[1] and overlaying as above.

Finally, as constraint diagrams characterize sets of instance diagrams, they could be used for animating models where actions have under-determined specifications: that is, given a starting instance, there may be a set a of possible instances which could be reached and that satisfy the specification. This goal will be more achievable once the extensions of the notation for visualizing action specifications have been fully worked out.

## Acknowledgments

I am grateful to the BIRO research team at Brighton, in particular Franco Civello, John Howse and Richard Mitchell for many useful comments and feedback. Thanks are also due to Alan Wills and Desmond D'Souza whose work on Catalysis has had considerable influence on my recent thinking. Finally I would like to thank the anonymous reviewers and the OOPSLA program committee, in particular Yossi Gil, for their positive and detailed comments and feedback. This research was partially funded by the UK EPSRC under grant GR/K67304.

1. A constraint diagram characterizes a set of instance diagrams, including singletons!

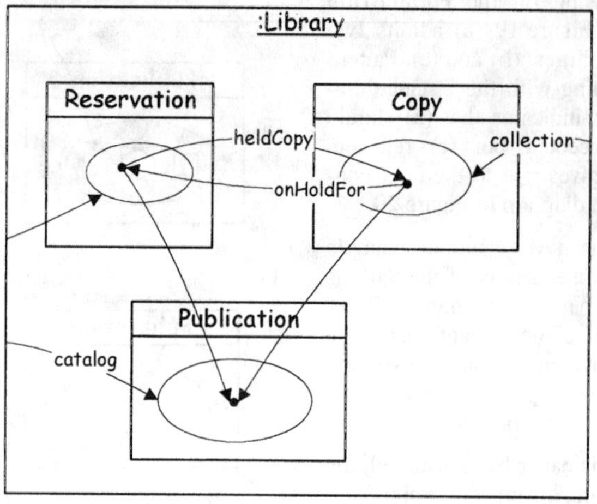


**Figure 20: Constraint diagram: output from tool**

## References

ADL (1997) *Assertion Definition Language*, The Open Group (formerly X/Open), http://adl.xopen.org.

Borgida A., Mylopoulos J. and Reiter E. (1995) "On the Frame Problem in Procedure Specifications", *IEEE Transactions in Software Engineering*, Vol. 21, No. 10.

Bourdeau H. and Cheng B. (1995) *A Formal Semantics for Object Model Diagrams*, in IEEE Transactions on Software Engineering 21, 799-821.

Cook S. and Daniels J. (1994) *Designing Object Systems*, Prentice Hall Object-Oriented Series.

D'Souza D. and Wills A. (1995) *Catalysis: Practical Rigor and Refinement*, technical report available at http://www.iconcomp.com.

D'Souza D. and Wills A. (1997) *Component-Based Development Using Catalysis*, book submitted for publication, manuscript available at http://www.iconcomp.com.

Gerstein L. J. (1987) *Discrete Mathematics and Algebraic Structures*, Freeman New-York.

Guttag J. and Horning J. (1993) *Larch: Languages and Tools for Formal Specifications*, Springer-Verlag.

Hamie A. and Howse J. (1997) *Interpreting Syntropy in Larch*, Technical Report ITCM97/C1, University of Brighton.

Harel D. (1987) "Statecharts: a visual formalism for complex systems", *Science of Computer Programming* 8:231-274.

Kent S., Hamie A., Howse J., Civello F. and Mitchell R. (1997) "Semantics Through Pictures: towards a diagrammatic semantics for object-oriented modelling notations", to appear in *Procs. of ECOOP'97 Workshop on Precise Semantics for Object-Oriented Modeling Techniques*, Jyväskylä, Finland, June 10, 1997.

Kent S. (1997) *Constraint Diagrams: Visualizing Assertions in Object-Oriented Models*, Technical Report ITCM97/C2, University of Brighton.

Parnas D. (1996) "Mathematical methods: What we need and don't need", in *An Invitation to Formal Methods*, IEEE Computer.

Rumbaugh J., Blaha M., Premerali W., Eddy F. and Lorensen W. (1991) *Object-Oriented Modelling and Design*, Prentice Hall.

Thomas P., Robinson H. and Emms J. (1988) *Abstract Data Types: Their specification, representation, and use*, Oxford Applied Mathematics and Computing Series, Oxford University Press.

UML (1997) *Unified Modeling Language v1.0*, Rational Software Corporation, available at http://www.rational.com.

Walden K. and Nerson J-M. (1995) *Seamless Object-Oriented Architecture*, Prentice Hall, Object-Oriented Series.

Wirfs-Brock R., Wilkerson B. and Wiener L. (1990) *Designing Object-Oriented Software*, Prentice Hall.

## Appendix – Summary of Notation

### Normal Sets



A set with one element.



A set with 0..1 elements.

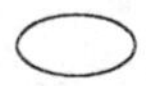

A set with 0, 1 or more elements.

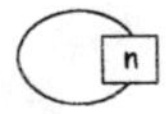


A set with n elements; n may be any numerical expression.

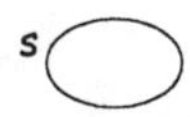


Optionally sets can be explicitly labeled. This can be useful for referring to them in accompanying explanations, or when mapping a constraint diagram to a math expression.

Venn Diagrams

Standard Venn diagram notation may be used to show relationships between sets.

### Types and States

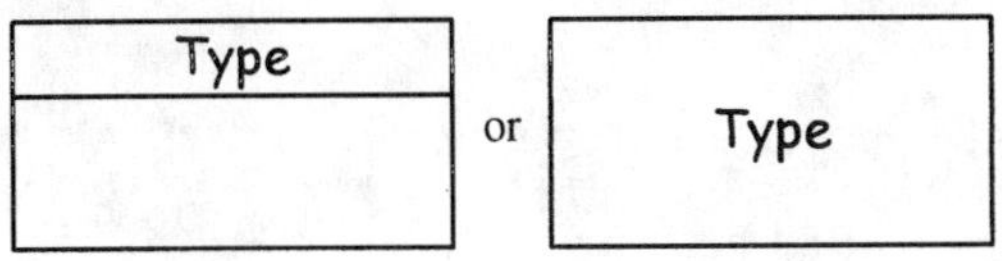


The set of objects of the named type Type.

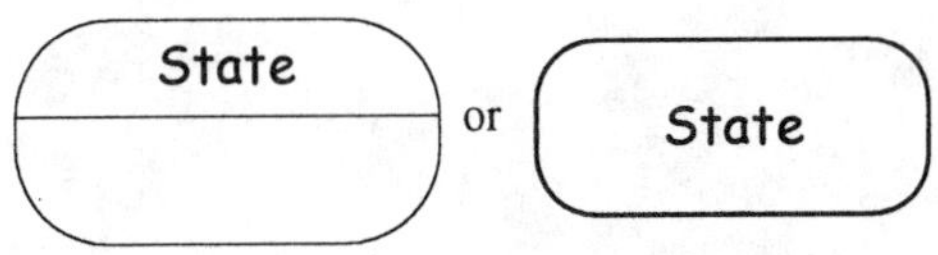


The set of objects in state State.

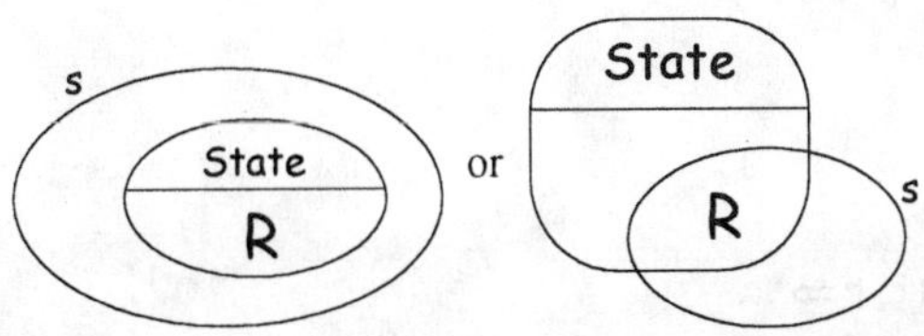


The region labeled R is the set of objects in state State, which are also in the set labeled s.

### Navigation

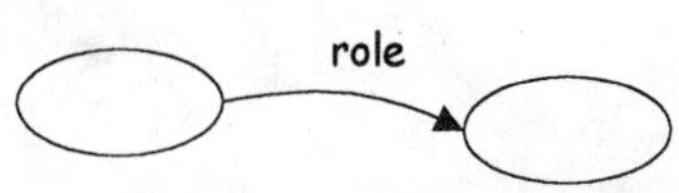


The set at the target of the arrow is the union of the sets reached by navigating the association labeled role from each element in the set at the source.

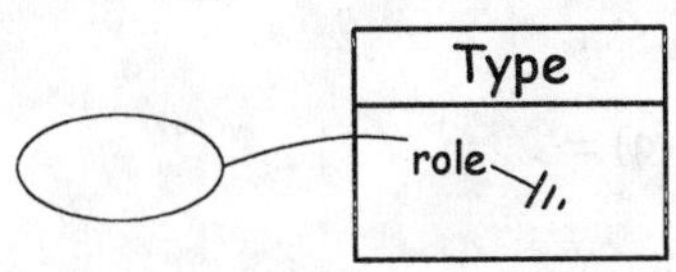


The value of the association to Type and labeled role, when navigated from the source set, is the empty set or null.

### Areas with no elements

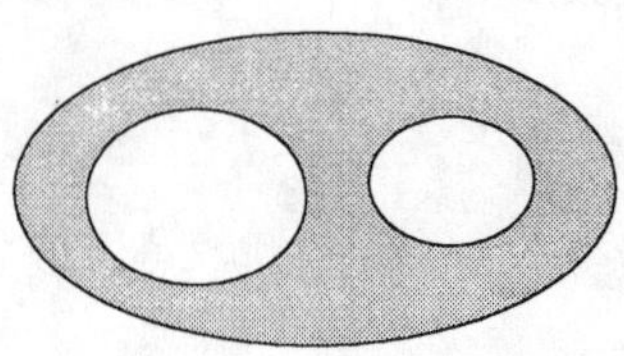

Grey fill indicates that there are no elements in that area of the set. In this case this means that the two subsets partition the containing set.

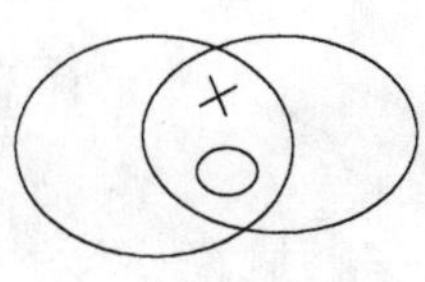

In those cases where grey fill is difficult to achieve (e.g., by hand or with some drawing tools), a simple cross in the area may be used as an alternative. In this case, the cross means that the set contained in the intersection *is* the intersection – particularly useful for sourcing/targeting arrows from/to an intersection.

**Typical (quantified) sets**

A normal set with no arrows targeted on it is assumed to be a typical subset of the set in which it is contained. When converted to a math expression this translates to universal quantification: "for any subset of the containing set, ...".

This notation is often used with singleton sets, with effect "for any object in the containing set, ...".

Existential quantification is achieved by introducing a temporary, unlabeled association.

As usual specific labels for sets are optional.

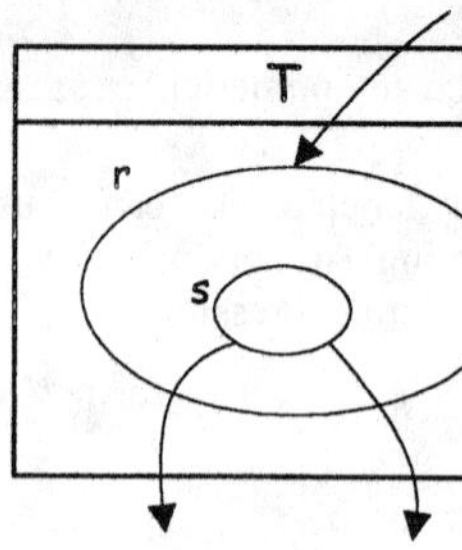


$\forall s : Set(T), s \subseteq r \Rightarrow \ldots$

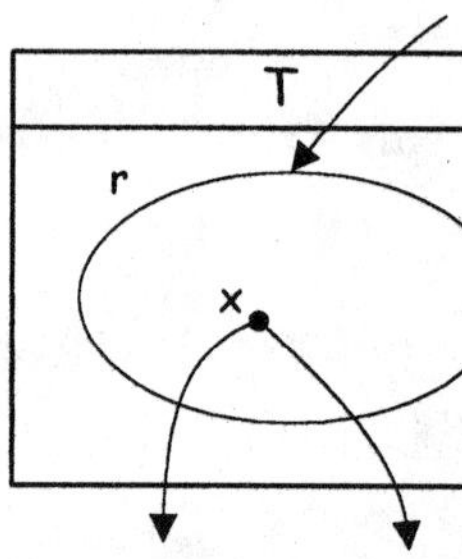


$\forall x : T, x \in r \Rightarrow \ldots$

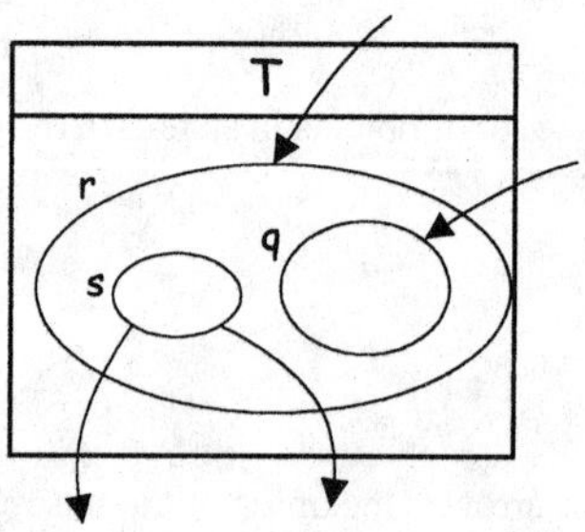


$\forall s : Set(T), s \subseteq r \Rightarrow \ldots$

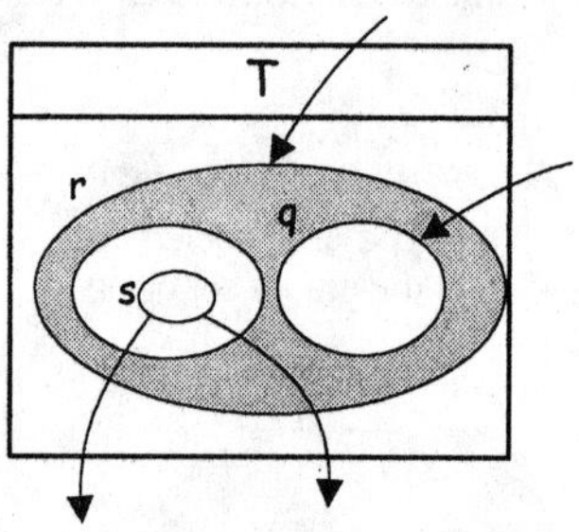


$\forall s : Set(T), s \subseteq (r - q) \Rightarrow \ldots$

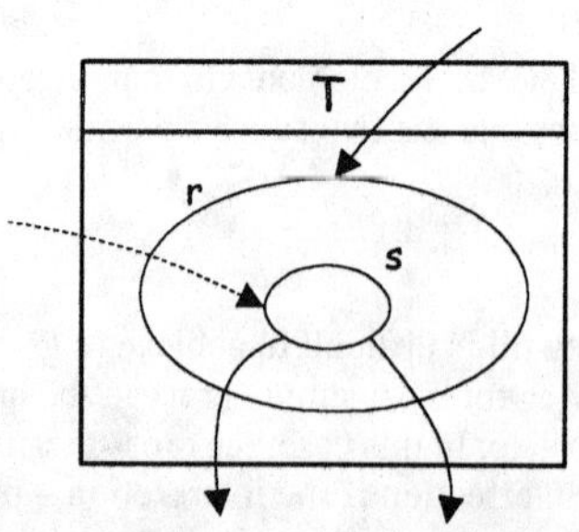


$\exists s : Set(T), s \subseteq r \wedge \ldots$

**New objects (filmstrips only)**

The following symbols only appear in the second or subsequent frame of a filmstrip. Each represents a set of objects that did not exist in the previous frame. The symbol differs, depending on the cardinality of the set.

| Symbol | Meaning |
| --- | --- |
| ★ | A set containing exactly one new object (i.e., a new object). |
| ☆ | A set containing 0..1 new objects. |
| 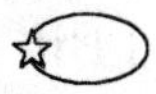 | A set containing 0, 1 or more new objects. |
|  | A set containing n new objects; n may be any numerical expression. |

# Beyond the Hype: Do Patterns and Frameworks Reduce Discovery Costs?

## Panel Session

Moderator: Steven Fraser

Panelists: Kent Beck, Grady Booch, Jim Coplien, Ralph Johnson and Bill Opdyke

**Abstract:** Patterns and frameworks are two approaches to the development of both new and evolving software systems. An implicit hypothesis is that "discovery costs" are reduced by leveraging knowledge previously collected, analyzed, organized, and packaged. "Discovery costs" (or "getting started" costs) include both the costs of understanding the problem to be solved and the cost of understanding the tools, methods, existing software, etc. For large, multi-year development projects in industries such as defense or telecommunications, discovery costs can dominate the overall cost (and risk) of software development.

This panel will share its experience and perspectives with the audience with a discussion initiated by the following questions:

- Have patterns and frameworks really delivered on their claims for reducing discovery costs? Can current best-practices be characterized as meaningful or marginal (what are the measures)?
- What are the discovery cost factors where frameworks and patterns appear to deliver the biggest bang for the buck?
- While mature pattern languages and frameworks may reduce the learning curve, they do not eliminate it. How much of a learning curve is required to develop a sufficient shared context with the authors of a set of patterns or a framework?

*Steven Fraser is manager of the Software Design Process Engineering team at Nortel's Lab in Santa Clara, California. Previous to this he spent four years at Bell-Northern Research's Computing Research Laboratory in Ottawa, Canada. In 1994 he was a Visiting Scientist at the Software Engineering Institute (SEI) collaborating with the Application of Software Models project on the development of team-based domain analysis techniques. Since joining BNR in 1987, Fraser has contributed to the ObjecTime project, an OO-based CASE-Design Tool and to the BNR BCS software development process. Fraser completed his doctoral studies at McGill University in Electrical Engineering. He holds a Master's degree from Queen's University at Kingston in applied Physics and a Bachelor's degree from McGill University in Physics and Computer Science. He is an avid operatunist and photographer.*

### Kent Beck

First let me restate the question to be explored by the panel: "Does experience help?" The answer is, of course, "Duh" (translation for those who didn't attend American schools, "Obviously, you idiot").

Whenever the answer is obvious, either everyone else is stupid or you are asking the wrong question. Let"s assume the latter. Two aspects complicate the question. First is the focus on patterns and frameworks as the media of expression for experience. Second is the focus on "discovery costs", as opposed to all the other costs of software development.

Our flippant answer to the original question would no longer hold if patterns and frameworks don't communicate experience, or communicate it in such a way that it costs more to learn a pattern or framework than to have and reflect on the experience in the first place. So, do patterns and frameworks really communicate experience? As a consumer of both patterns and frameworks my experience is that they certainly do. When I come into a new situation and I find patterns or frameworks in place, I begin making progress much more quickly than when I have to just start by asking a bunch of questions about a sea of code. As a writer, I have seen developers become productive much more quickly within the structure of existing patterns and frameworks.

The second challenge to the obvious answer comes when you limit the discussion to "discovery costs". Does experience help with discovery costs? Sure. "Hey, this looks like another good fit for Gemstone," is a statement that if correct is worth hundreds of thousands or millions of dollars. Can the kind of encoding of experience represented by patterns or frameworks help with discovery costs?

Here's an example of where I have used a framework to reduce discovery costs — I was working with a framework for payroll processing. We were interviewing the customer. She mentioned a new requirement. I asked the developers, "What more is this than just another station?" "We can't see anything," they replied. We explained the visible ramifications of the decision to the customer. She agreed. This was a kind of discussion I have seen take weeks. By casting it in terms of a framework proven to solve similar problems, it took all of ten minutes.

Here's an example of patterns reducing discovery costs. I have learned a handful of patterns, most from Prof. Johnson, regarding the design of counting systems, those concerned with managing transactions and accounts. Now when I talk to a client about a new systems, I can quickly discover the complexity of the architecture by asking which patterns apply. For instance, I know the Posting Date pattern, so I know to ask if the client needs to print reports as of a certain date.

For me and for the teams I coach, frameworks and, to a larger degree, patterns do reduce discovery costs. They also reduce costs throughout the software lifecycle. Most importantly, though, by reducing nasty surprises and stress, they make developing more fun.

*Kent Beck is a guitarist and folk singer, father of four, and programmer. He is the author of a whole bunch of articles on software development, some of which he is still proud of, and the book "The Smalltalk Best Practice Patterns". He is currently exploring the humanistic discipline of Extreme Software while employed at CSLife in Zurich, Switzerland.*

*Kent Beck has "pursued" patterns for almost 10 years and is a founder and director of the Hillside Group. In 1991, Kent founded his company First Class software which produces applications and development tools in Smalltalk and provides consulting services. From 1989 to 1992 Kent was the programming tools project manager at MasPar Computer for a massively parallel supercomputer written in C++ and Smalltalk. From 1987 to 1989, while Apple Computer, Kent worked with a group under Alan Kay designing, implementing, and testing Playground, an object language for children. Prior to this Kent worked at Tektronix TekLabs to research and develop an advanced programming environment in Smalltalk. Kent holds a BS and MS in Computer Science from the University of Oregon.*

## Grady Booch

There's considerable anecdotal evidence and some empirical evidence that points to the benefits of patterns and frameworks in reducing discovery costs. From a methodological perspective, their use has two places in the software development life cycle: as a factor in avoiding new development via the reuse of preexisting components, and as a risk mitigator in the sense of providing components that are already proven in practice. In the first case, theoretically, this should reduce discovery costs; and in the second cast, this should reduce software scrap and rework. However, software development is not a frictionless environment, so it's reasonable to ask the question: what are costs associated with patterns and frameworks? The short answer is that there are some costs, and depending upon the culture of the development organization, these costs can be prohibitive. In high ceremony organizations, the use of patterns becomes so bureaucratic that any opportunity for benefit is crushed. In low ceremony organizations, the use of patterns becomes so informal that their impact often never reaches beyond the individual developer. In the optimal case, the use of patterns are institutionalized, but in a manner that balances the need for control and the need for creativity.

*Grady Booch has been with Rational Software Corporation as chief scientist since shortly after its founding in 1980. He was instrumental in developing two major concepts: an iterative model of software development and the importance of software architecture. He developed Ada-language reusable components and the Booch C++ source-code components, which helped to popularize software reuse and make it economically feasible. Grady's methods and ideas are being used to develop complex and demanding software systems, ranging from air traffic-control systems to commercial aircraft avionics to financial trading systems to telecommunication switching networks to defense systems. Grady has served as an architectural mentor for a number of large software projects and was also one of the original developers of the Rational Environment, the company's original software-engineering environment, and its compiler technology. Grady was the original architect for the Rational Rose object-oriented analysis and design tool and has used a variety of object-oriented and object-based languages, including Ada, C++, and Smalltalk.*

*Grady is the author of five books, his fifth and latest book, "Best of Booch: Designing Strategies for Object Technology", was released in October 1996. Grady has also published more than 100 technical articles on object- oriented technology and software engineering. Grady has consulted and lectured on these topics throughout the world. Grady is a Distinguished Graduate of the United States Air Force Academy, where he received his B.S. in computer science in 1977. He received an M.S.E.E. in computer engineering from the University of California at Santa Barbara in 1979. Grady is a member of the American Association for the Advancement of Science, the Association for Computing Machinery, the Institute of Electrical and Electronic Engineers, Computer Professionals for Social Responsibility, the Association for Software Design, and the Airlie Software Council. Grady is also an ACM Fellow.*

## Jim Coplien

Too many projects look for the "home run" in reusable platforms and frameworks. Frameworks work well only if they can predict well: to predict what will change, and what will not. This is a difficult enough problem for individual objects or modules, let alone for extensible application skeletons. Small frameworks like MVC work, but few large frameworks enjoy success. The main problems are rooted in the socioeconomic systems that tie together the vendor and customers of a framework. In common practice, each customer approaches the vendor for customizations. Even internal implementation customizations, or addition of new sites of parameterization, can't be kept invisible from other customers. It's nice in theory, which lights up the eyes of the academics who are my fellow pattern members. It looks good on paper, which delights the project management and system engineers on the panel who don't write code. But practical experience with CORBA, pSOS, and dozens of supposedly standard internal frameworks have just not borne out the theoretical success of this lucrative idea. To the contrary, they have increased overhead and development costs in the names of reuse, standards, and NIH.

Frameworks work to the extent they are small, or to the extent that their sites of parameterization can all be dealt with at run time. Patterns help solve this by engaging human intellect. Coding the result of a transmogrified pattern is easy. Give me the code to start with, and it just gets in my way.

*Jim Coplien is a member of the Software Production Research Department in Bell Laboratories. He holds a BS in Electrical and Computer Engineering, and an MS in Computer Science, both from the University of Wisconsin at Madison. His early career work includes applied research in software development environments, version and configuration management models, and in object-oriented design and programming.*

*He is currently studying organization communication patterns to help guide process evolution. This research has already created a generative pattern language that has successfully been used for business process engineering in corporations worldwide. His other research areas include multi-paradigm design and architectural patterns of telecommunication software.*

*He is author of "C++ Programming Styles and Idioms," the foremost high-end C++ book in the industry, and co-editor of two volumes of "Pattern Languages of Program Design." He writes a patterns column for the C++ Report. He sits on the board of the Hillside Generative Patterns Group, a small consortium of industry leaders developing pattern languages as an adjunct to object-oriented approaches. He was program chair of ACM OOPSLA'96.*

## Ralph Johnson

Asking whether patterns and frameworks reduce discovery costs is like asking whether someone who knows something about billing is going to have an easier time making a billing system than someone who doesn't. Of course! The problem is whether we have the right patterns and frameworks to reduce discovery costs. If not, how can we get them?

Most of the current patterns are design patterns, and design patterns might help you reverse-engineer a system, but they will not help you analyze a problem and learn the application domain. I think this is what you mean by "discovery cost". The kind of patterns we'll need for that are like those in Martin Fowler's book. We don't yet have the right patterns for decreasing discovery costs.

Frameworks are similar. Most of the available frameworks are for technical problems like user interface or persistence. These won't help reduce discovery costs very much, except that they make it easier to build prototypes, which is a popular discovery technique. But domain-specific frameworks can have an enormous impact on discovery costs.

I've been working with a company that has built a telecommunications billing framework. They have developed a method for analyzing telecommunications companies' billing systems in terms of their frameworks. They then build a customized billing application. The can analyze a customer, design a billing application, implement and install it, in about three months. The first two months are analysis and design, the implementation and installation take only a month.

As you might expect, one of their problems is teaching their framework to new employees. We are uncovering the patterns that they use, documenting them, and including them in a training program so that new employees can learn them faster.

*Ralph Johnson is on the faculty at the University of Illinois. He is a co-author of "Design Patterns" and has been to every OOPSLA.*

## Bill Opdyke

For much of the past several years I have been researching, consulting and involved in product evolution activities related to frameworks. Part of my job has involved selling the benefits of frameworks to product groups.

Frankly, I feel that developers experienced in *using* frameworks are in a better position than many of us consultants, researchers and academics in assessing the real discovery cost implications. So, I asked several of them to share their experiences with me. Our discussions focused on discovery costs and frameworks, but not upon patterns. Personally, I feel that patterns are important in reducing discovery costs, but I'll leave it to my fellow panelists to discuss that connection.

Discovery costs are significant for evolving systems. For all but the first release, the system itself is a major (perhaps *the* major) constraint on the design. Discovery costs are greatest for new staff — but are still significant for other, more experienced staff.

People new to a project need to gain an understanding of the paradigm, application domain, language, library of available components and the development environment. They discover how a system works by reading documentation, dabbling, interacting with other staff and building something (preferably a simplified example). Mature frameworks help ease this discovery process.

Developers who have worked with a mature (or nearly mature) framework felt that such a framework reduced their overall development times in half, reduced their discovery costs by more than half and in some cases provides as much as 90% of the functionality that they needed. The greatest benefit of mature frameworks came in the design phases. Framework documentation helped reduce discovery costs; the paradigm, domain abstractions and other design information embodied in a mature framework provided a shared language that facilitated communication among team members. The object-oriented framework implementation technology supported rapid prototyping and iterative development, facilitating discovery through building simplified examples.

Unfortunately, *mature* frameworks seem to be the exception rather than the norm. In industry, frameworks are often viewed as the *means* while products are the (revenue generating) *ends*. Framework maturity takes time and involves churn; both can be disruptive to application/product development. Tools and process issues can also inhibit the development of a mature framework.

*Domain-specific* frameworks, to maintain their funding/survival, are often "married" to an early application/development project. These applications are motivated to make expedient specializations and other framework changes that compromise the generality of the framework. Similarly, unless there are mechanisms for sustaining *domain-independent* pieces outside of a particular application, new applications may end up re-developing these pieces. Discipline and executive commitment are need to mature a framework and to maintain framework identity in the midst of these influences.

In conclusion, mature frameworks can and have made a difference in reducing discovery costs and reducing development intervals. The path to a mature framework can be rocky and requires expert navigators. As with software reuse and software developments in general, the success of a framework is often more tied to organizational and cultural issues than to the technical concerns.

Many thanks to Don Brown, Ian Bruce, Joe Davison, Larry Mayka, Warren Montgomery, Ralph Straubs and Tom Williams for contributing their insights.

*Bill Opdyke is currently involved in advanced network services architecture and platform planning projects at Bell Labs—Lucent Technologies. He consults with platform and application development projects on topics such as reusable assets and distributed object computing. Bill previously focused on intelligent network and decision support applications of object-oriented technology. Bill's doctoral research at the University of Illinois focused on refactoring C++-based object-oriented application frameworks.*

# author index

# title index